DUE

	PRINTED IN U.S.A.

Religion in the Oval Office

RELIGION IN THE OVAL OFFICE

The Religious Lives of American Presidents

GARY SCOTT SMITH

OXFORD
UNIVERSITY PRESS

OXFORD
UNIVERSITY PRESS

Oxford University Press is a department of the University of
Oxford. It furthers the University's objective of excellence in research,
scholarship, and education by publishing worldwide.

Oxford   New York
Auckland   Cape Town   Dar es Salaam   Hong Kong   Karachi
Kuala Lumpur   Madrid   Melbourne   Mexico City   Nairobi
New Delhi   Shanghai   Taipei   Toronto

With offices in
Argentina   Austria   Brazil   Chile   Czech Republic   France   Greece
Guatemala   Hungary   Italy   Japan   Poland   Portugal   Singapore
South Korea   Switzerland   Thailand   Turkey   Ukraine   Vietnam

Oxford is a registered trademark of Oxford University Press
in the UK and certain other countries.

Published in the United States of America by
Oxford University Press
198 Madison Avenue, New York, NY 10016

Cataloging-in-Publication data is on file at the Library of Congress
ISBN 978-0-19-939139-4

A version of the John Quincy Adams chapter is included in Peter Prud' Homme, ed., Faith
and Politics in America: From Jamestown to the Civil War (New York: Peter Lang, 2011), 115-79
and is used by the permission of the publisher.

1 3 5 7 9 8 6 4 2
Printed in the United States of America
on acid-free paper

Contents

Acknowledgments

I could not have written this book without the assistance of numerous archivists, librarians, colleagues, and scholars at other institutions. Their help was invaluable in examining, analyzing, and describing the religious convictions and spiritual biographies of these eleven presidents. I want to thank the archivists at the Library of Congress and the presidential libraries of Herbert Hoover, Harry Truman, Richard Nixon, William Clinton, and George H. W. Bush for helping me locate, use, and understand various materials. The librarians at Grove City College, especially Conni Shaw and Joyce Kebert, assisted me in procuring hundreds of books and articles. Grove City College colleagues Gillis Harp, Paul Kemeny, and Paul Kengor provided thoughtful, useful critiques of chapters of my book. Daniel Dreisbach of American University, H. Larry Ingle of the University of Tennessee at Chattanooga, Corwin Smidt, formerly the director of the Henry Center at Calvin College, Daniel Williams of the University of West Georgia, and Mark David Hall of George Fox University also helped me to sharpen my analysis. In addition, several Grove City College students assisted my research: Dorothy Williams, Samuel Williams, Richard Kriebel, Corinne Gressang, Marissa Brincka, Laura Gaudio, Sarah Markley, and Claire Vetter. Copy editor Lynn Childress offered many constructive suggestions and made many helpful revisions. As with my last two books, my biggest debt of gratitude is to my wife Jane who accompanied me on numerous research trips, found obscure sources and references, and supplied beneficial stylistic suggestions.

G.S.S.

Abbreviations

AM	Atlantic Monthly
CA	Christian Advocate
CC	Christian Century
CH	Church History
CSM	Christian Science Monitor
CT	Christianity Today
JAH	Journal of American History
JCS	Journal of Church and State
LAT	Los Angeles Times
NR	New Republic
NYT	New York Times
PB	Presbyterian Banner
UP	United Presbyterian
WP	Washington Post
WSJ	Wall Street Journal
WT	Washington Times

Religion in the Oval Office

Introduction

[American presidents] engage in moral—and explicitly religious—activity. Literally they preach, reminding the American people of religious and moral principles and urging them to conduct themselves in accord with these principles. They lead prayers, quote from the Bible, and make theological statements about the Deity and His desires for the nation. . . . They are the moral leaders and high priests of American society. . . . Presidents themselves are contributing to the impression and indeed consciously cultivating it.

BARBARA HINCKLEY, *The Symbolic Presidency: How Presidents Portray Themselves* (New York: Routledge, 1990), 73

I can't imagine how a president could do his job without faith. [However,] it is impossible for us to know their hearts. It's barely possible to know your own. Faith is important, but it's also personal. When we force political figures to tell us their deepest thoughts on it, they'll be tempted to act, to pretend.

PEGGY NOONAN, "People Before Prophets," *Wall Street Journal*, November 24, 2007

DATING ALL THE way back to George Washington, faith has played a very important and often controversial role in the lives of American presidents. Nevertheless, few scholars have carefully analyzed how chief executives' religious convictions affected their lives, policies, or decisions. Substantial evidence contradicts the frequent claim that a president's faith matters little in how he governs.[1] Numerous presidents have exhibited a deep and meaningful faith that has shaped their worldviews and characters and have testified that their religious convictions influenced their political philosophy, analysis of issues, decision-making, and performance in office. Their religious commitments strongly affected John Quincy Adams's efforts to fund roads, canals, and educational institutions and promote diplomacy; William McKinley's decisions to declare war against Spain and take control of the Philippines; Herbert Hoover's quests to reform prisons and defend civil liberties; Harry Truman's approach to the Cold War and decision to recognize Israel; Bill Clinton's promotion of religious liberty; Barack Obama's policies on poverty and gay civil rights; and the crusades of several presidents to advance world peace. Many presidents have asserted that their faith in God helped them cope with immense challenges and gave them courage and equanimity in the midst of the storms that swirled around them. Several insisted that their faith grew stronger during their years in office.

While the First Amendment separates church and state, it has not divorced religion from politics. Religion is woven deeply into the fabric of political life in the United States. Although numerous factors affect how citizens vote and evaluate presidents' character, actions, and policies, their faith strongly influences many Americans. Moreover, the religiously devout have often participated in politics either to protect or advance their principles and values. Ignoring religious considerations leads to an inadequate understanding of American politics and the presidency. The proper role of religion in government and the religious convictions of presidential candidates have often provoked controversy: from false charges that Thomas Jefferson was an atheist to spurious claims that Barack Obama is a Muslim. Americans have hotly debated the role of religion in promoting morality, government funding of religious enterprises and activities, the travel and work of presidents on Sundays, prayer and the teaching of religion in public schools, and public displays of religious symbols, to name just a few issues.

When I began research on *Faith and the Presidency: From George Washington to George W. Bush* (2006), only a handful of scholars had examined the relationship between religion and the presidency. Since then, however, there has been a flood of books on the topic.[2] While this outpouring of books testifies to both scholarly and popular interest in religion and politics, it has not fully explained the faith of American presidents. As did my first volume, this book analyzes eleven of our nation's most interesting and influential chief executives: John Adams, James Madison, John Quincy Adams, Andrew Jackson, William McKinley, Herbert Hoover, Harry Truman, Richard Nixon, George H. W. Bush, Bill Clinton, and Barack Obama. This group includes one Congregationalist, one Unitarian, one Presbyterian, one Methodist, two Episcopalians, two Southern Baptists, two Quakers, and one United Church of Christ member. In terms of political affiliation, it is two Federalists, four Republicans, and five Democrats. I examine the beliefs of these presidents as expressed in their letters, interviews, and addresses; the testimonies of those who knew them well; and their actions, especially their participation in church services, prayer, and reading of the Bible and devotional and theological works. I also closely analyze their views of God, Jesus, human nature, salvation, and life after death and carefully assess their character, use of religious rhetoric, relationships with religious leaders and groups, and specific policies that were shaped in significant part by their religious commitments. While faith was important to other presidents, especially Rutherford Hayes, James Garfield, Benjamin Harrison, William Howard Taft, Calvin Coolidge, Lyndon Johnson, and Gerald Ford, the twenty-two men examined in my two volumes are arguably the half of America's presidents for whom faith (especially as it affected their policies) or religious issues (especially in the case of John F. Kennedy) was most important.

"A President's world view," insisted James David Barber, "consists of his primary, politically relevant beliefs, particularly his conceptions of social causality, human nature, and the central moral conflicts of the time." It affects how he sees the world and responds to events. His worldview shapes his "conception of reality," perception of people, understanding of "how things work in politics," and primary aims. These pivotal, unprovable assumptions, Barber averred, enable presidents to make sense of life and to devise priorities. The presuppositions of chief executives determine what they most highly value and to what they pay attention. Their religious convictions have strongly influenced their understandings of the meaning of life, the basis of morality, the nature and purpose of society, the role of government, and the dignity of humans. "If a man's faith is sincere, it is the most important thing about him," argued presidential biographer Stephen Mansfield; "it is impossible to understand who he is and how he will lead without first understanding the religious vision that informs his life." "A person's faith commitment is a key window" into his "system of values and beliefs," *Washington Post* columnist Nathan Diament avowed. "A president's religion matters" because it often affects his policy choices.[3]

Presidents, like other politicians, use religion to further their own purposes—to gain the approval of various groups, enhance their popularity, win elections, increase support for their policies, and fortify their claim to be virtuous and honest. They employ religious and moral rhetoric to defend their own policies, programs, and actions and to criticize those of their opponents. Religious and moral appeals help connect particular policies with transcendent norms, elevating them above mundane, pragmatic concerns and strengthening citizens' commitment to them.

Presidents also frequently use biblical and moral discourse because Americans, who are much more religious than citizens of other postindustrial nations, expect it. A president's testimony to his faith and use of religious and biblical language enables millions "to identify on a very basic level with the most powerful man in the world." Using religious rhetoric also helps chief executives gain support for programs and policies that parochial interest groups, political opposition, and the government's system of checks and balances make difficult to pass.[4] Presidents are especially likely to employ religious discourse to rally public support for particular causes, justify complex policies or complicated legislation, fulfill their promises to provide moral leadership, or seize the initiative from Congress on important issues. The use of moral and religious arguments helps bolster the president's authority and enables him to claim the moral high ground.[5]

Polls consistently report that most Americans want their presidents to have a strong faith in God, which further encourages chief executives to stress their religious convictions and practices.[6] Many Americans feel more comfortable when they know (or at least believe) that presidents pray about decisions they make and policies they adopt (although many still protest when they do not like these decisions or policies). Moreover, the nation's robust Judeo-Christian heritage and the absence of a national church demands that presidents serve as our civic chief priest, the person who sanctifies America's dominant institutions and values and provides comfort in times of crisis and tragedy. Custom, Congress, and current events all require presidents to play this role.

The president reinforces and promotes the nation's shared civic beliefs, strengthening core American values and helping to unify and motivate citizens.[7] The president is expected to proclaim national days of prayer, celebrate the religious holidays of various faith communities, address national prayer breakfasts, lead citizens in mourning the death of statesmen and heroes, send condolences to grieving families, and speak at some major religious gatherings. Because most Americans find religious rhetoric to be inspiring, reassuring, and soothing, they appreciate presidents' evoking divine aid, calling for prayer, and giving thanks to God as they cope with war, natural disasters, terrorist attacks, and other tragedies.

While presidents have generally played this priestly role very well, their use of prophetic civil religion to challenge the nation's norms and practices, chastise citizens for their selfishness and shortcomings, urge Americans to repent of their sins, and exhort them to practice greater justice, compassion, and generosity has been less frequent and effective. However, by trumpeting religious tenets and transcendent values, presidents have prodded Americans to build a better society and world.

Because religion can be employed to further a wide variety of purposes, many, especially academicians and journalists, are cynical about presidents' professions of piety, use of biblical and spiritual language, attendance of religious services, and relationships with religious leaders and groups. They see these actions primarily as means of advancing presidents' political aims, rather than as genuine expressions of personal faith or reliance on God. Presidential religiosity, many protest, is a sham, charade, or smokescreen. It is a device presidents employ to achieve ulterior motives—personal aggrandizement, electoral victory, or policy success. Presidents clearly do engage in religious activities and use biblical and moral rhetoric in part because of Americans' expectations and to help accomplish political ends, but this does not necessarily indicate that their faith is disingenuous.

Moreover, it is often difficult to determine the role presidents play in crafting their speeches and to what extent these discourses convey their true convictions. Although all presidents have received assistance in composing their addresses and, since Calvin Coolidge, all have employed professional speechwriters, it is reasonable to assume that presidents' addresses often express their actual beliefs on a variety of subjects, including their religious convictions and understanding of Scripture. However, as noted, chief executives employ religious rhetoric to serve numerous purposes—to promote national unity, assuage collective grief, promote particular policies, and impress devout citizens. It is very challenging, therefore, to disentangle their personal convictions from their political uses of religion. As a result, in assessing presidents' faith, it is important to appraise their religious practices over their entire lives, not just their years in office or on the campaign trail, and to examine both their private correspondence (which is often less guarded and more revealing) and their public statements. Evaluating the testimonies of colleagues, companions, and disinterested observers about presidents' faith also provides insights into their personal beliefs and commitments.

Throughout American history many citizens have viewed strong faith as an asset, if not a requirement, for politicians, especially presidents. However, many Americans have expressed concerns about how a president's faith guides his work. Almost two-thirds of the 846 historians who responded to a 1982 survey did not want presidents to allow their religious beliefs to influence their performance. Moreover, a majority of the historians who were personally interviewed for this survey maintained that the deeper an individual's faith, the greater the danger it posed to his success as president.[8] In numerous recent polls, more than two-thirds of respondents have declared that they want the president to be a person of faith.[9] However, according to a 2011 ABC News-*Washington Post* poll, Americans, by a 66 percent to 29 percent margin, say that "political leaders should not rely on their religious beliefs in making policy decisions."[10] Most Americans seem to want presidents to be pious, but not religious zealots. Americans want chief executives to pray, attend church regularly, revere the Bible, and depend on God—but not to base their decisions directly on their intuitive perception of God's will.

Most Americans also expect the president to uphold the nation's highest values and to serve as its moral leader. As the embodiment of the state, the president's character and actions should be consistent with the nation's religious heritage and most venerated principles. The president, wrote Barber, should "personify our betterness in an inspiring way," express our moral idealism, and provide "an example of principled goodness." By his words and example, George Washington set a moral tone that other presidents have sought to follow. "The foundation for national policy," he asserted in his first inaugural address, "will be laid in the sure and immutable principles of private morality." Presidents have consistently contended that conventional moral standards should guide American conduct, that politicians' private conduct and public service are closely connected, and that the nation's government should provide a model of morality for the world. Truman claimed that the United States had supplied "one of the world's greatest examples of political responsibility and moral leadership." Dwight Eisenhower asked God to give his administration "the power to discern clearly right from wrong, and allow all our words and actions to be governed thereby." "America's moral example," Obama asserted, "must always shine for all who yearn for freedom and justice and dignity."[11]

Political scientist Ruth Morgan maintains that Americans expect presidents to serve as "a moral force" in formulating policies, "set high standards of personal ethics," model "integrity in official conduct, and set the moral tone" for their administration. A chief executive's moral authority, Frank Keesler affirms, depends on his or her ability "to demonstrate integrity, high-minded propose, [and] political savvy," "retain the public trust," and provide justice and security for citizens. The immoral actions of recent presidents, especially Nixon and Clinton, and the development of an omnipresent and much more adversarial media has led the conduct and statements of presidents to be exhaustively scrutinized and often attacked on television and radio talk shows, online, and in print, making it more difficult for them to be positive role models.[12]

Many politicians, journalists, and academicians insist that Americans expect too much from their presidents. They argue that citizens assign too much responsibility to presidents (and other political officials) for the moral condition of the nation, often leading to disappointment and disillusionment. Moreover, many contend that families, schools, churches, other civic organizations, and the media have a more important role to play than presidents in inculcating individual and corporate morality.[13] "We tend to overpersonalize our political hopes," *Washington Post* columnist David Broder asserted, and thus contribute to the inevitable "letdown that comes when mortal men fall short of the godlike myths we construct around them." "Potential presidents," Nixon speechwriter Ray Price declared, "are measured against an ideal that's a combination of leading man, God, father, hero, pope, [and] king." Americans want their presidents "to be larger than life, a living legend, and yet quintessentially human." The presidency, maintained Michael Genovese and Thomas Cronin, supplies "our basic need for a visible and representative national symbol to which we can turn our hopes and our aspirations." Consequently, presidents are often considered either national heroes or scapegoats based on people's assessments of their performance and the nation's political, economic, social, and moral conditions.[14]

Most pundits and ordinary Americans agree that presidents' character—the underlying commitments and dispositions that shape people's behavior—is at least as significant as their intellect, administrative abilities, or speaking talents. David McCullough insists that "character counts in the presidency more than any other single quality." "In a president," Peggy Noonan, a Reagan speechwriter, avows, "character is everything." He or she "can employ wise and clever advisors." However, a president must bring courage, decency, and a strong moral sense with him. While a "coherent political philosophy," a strong grasp of issues, "an analytical mind," "the ability to recruit and keep talented advisers," outstanding communication skills, and the capacity to mold and mobilize public opinion are all important in a president, William Bennett asserts, character is paramount. James Pfiffner avers that good character includes "honesty, integrity, courage, loyalty, consistency," and marital fidelity. Others add that a president's personal ethics, candor, willingness to accept responsibility, and treatment of people are essential character traits.[15]

John Adams argued in 1765 that the American people had "an indisputable, unalienable, indefeasible" right to know "the characters and conduct of their rulers." John Jay wrote in Federalist 64 that he expected Americans to choose presidents "whose reputation for integrity inspires and merits confidence." Through his character, Washington "endowed the presidency with the prestige" that has enabled the office to function effectively for more than 200 years, "despite the dubious conduct of some" of his successors. During the 1992 presidential campaign, George H. W. Bush repeatedly argued that Horace Greeley's assertion that "fame is a vapor, popularity an accident, riches take wing; only character endures" was "especially true in the Presidency." Bush criticized his opponent, Bill Clinton, for claiming that "it's not the character of the President but 'the character of the Presidency'" that mattered.

"They're interlocked," Bush responded. "People judge our country to a large degree" by presidents' actions.[16]

Others contend that presidents are not like handymen we hire to fix our houses whose personal morality, apart from honesty, matters little to us. Presidents represent us, speak for us, symbolize our national values, influence our children, and make important decisions that affect our lives.[17] They set the country's domestic and foreign agendas and are "the most visible example of our values." As we seek to be "the world's exemplar of human rights, the rule of law, and moral standards," declares historian Robert Dallek, "it is embarrassing to have men seeking and/or serving in the presidency who fall short of our highest ideals." Americans "are eager to believe that presidents manage to rise above the limitations that beset the rest of us."[18]

Numerous journalists and scholars counter that presidents' personal morality and private actions have little or no effect on their policies and the performance of their duties. In judging presidents, competence, not character, counts; a president's "personal goodness and political effectiveness" are largely unrelated. *Newsweek* columnist Joe Klein maintains that presidents with "interesting sexual histories" have been better leaders. *Washington Post* columnist Richard Cohen argues that a president can be simultaneously "conventionally immoral in his personal life" and an outstanding "person in his public life." As in the case of Kennedy, his leadership can trump what he does privately. Personally virtuous leaders, Methodist pastor Philip Wogaman avers, have sometimes carried out detrimental policies, while statesmen with badly flawed characters have significantly advanced the public good. "Neither personal virtue nor sincere piety," Christian ethicist John Bennett points out, guarantees social wisdom.[19]

Clinton argued in 1996 that "what you fight for and for whom you fight" rather than a person's private life "most effectively" demonstrated his character. He asked Americans to assess his character by the policies he promoted: the Family Leave Law, the Assault Weapons ban, the v-chip, and "keeping tobacco out of the hands of kids." "We should worry more," wrote Wendy Kaminer in 1998, about Clinton's "politics and policies than his fitness as a 'role model.'" It is childish and "potentially dangerous" to expect a president "to serve as our moral exemplar." Others reject Clinton's argument that character "has nothing to do with personal behavior" and complain that his high approval ratings during and after his impeachment trial testify that many in our morally relativistic, nonjudgmental culture are not concerned about the private conduct of presidents. Mark Melcher asserts that recent polling data and anecdotal reports indicate that millions believe that a president's "personal behavior is not relevant to" his leadership.

Many Americans accept a postmodern philosophy that rejects the notion of transcendent truth and argue instead that right, wrong, truth, and character are subjective.[20]

While paying close attention to historical contexts and America's shifting social and moral values, the profiles that follow explore the lives, beliefs, character, policies, elections, use of religious rhetoric, and relationships with religious constituencies of eleven of the nation's more colorful, charismatic, and complex leaders. Although numerous factors influenced them, these presidents cannot be properly understood without taking into account their religious convictions. Their faith significantly affected how they viewed the world and particular stances they took on issues. To provide a few examples, John Adams's religious commitments helped shape his perspective on America's mission and destiny and his efforts to avoid war with France. Presuppositions derived from Scripture and history led James Madison to champion religious liberty and the separation of church and state. Influenced by antebellum frontier evangelism, Andrew Jackson believed that God providentially directed his life, the events of his presidency, and the course of the world. Herbert Hoover's Quaker background played a significant role in his campaigns to increase racial equality, reform prison conditions, and promote world peace. Harry Truman's Baptist-inspired belief in freedom and equality strongly affected his positions on civil rights, the recognition of Israel, and the Cold War. His commitment to liberal Protestant principles help guide Barack Obama's approach to social justice, especially his efforts to aid the poor and provide universal healthcare. Their faith traditions, their personal religious convictions, and the dominant religious credos and ethos of their respective eras significantly influenced the eleven presidents discussed here. A complete understanding of their lives, actions, and administrations is impossible without considering these factors. Moreover, their presidencies cannot be fully comprehended without analyzing the role religious factors and issues played in their elections to office or the relationship these chief executives had with religious leaders and constituencies.

I

John Adams

A CHURCH-GOING SAGE

The science of Theology is indeed the first Philosophy—the only Philosophy—it comprehends all Philosophy—and all science, it is the Science of the Universe and its Ruler—and what other object of knowledge can there be.

TO ANDREW NORTON, November 24, 1819

Our Constitution was made only for a moral and religious people. It is wholly inadequate to the government of any other.

"To the Officers of the First Brigade of the Third Division of the Militia of Massachusetts," October 11, 1798

I have been a church-going animal for seventy-six years, from the cradle.

TO BENJAMIN RUSH, August 28, 1811

Introduction

John Adams casts a long shadow in American history. He was a delegate to the First and Second Continental Congresses, a diplomat to France and Holland, the chief designer of the Massachusetts Constitution of 1780, a prodigious political thinker, and the first vice president and second president of the United States. During the Revolutionary War, he served on Congress' Board of War and helped procure European aid. Adams was a "radical firebrand," the American Revolution's "premier political theorist," a competent chief executive, and an influential "emeritus activist."[1] Despite being revered for his political philosophy, vital contributions to American independence, and impressive character, Adams has frequently been viewed as "somewhat of a loser."[2] He is the only president among the first five who lost his campaign for reelection, his Federalist Party never again captured the White House, and scholars have not ranked him as a great or near-great president. Historians have generally had "far greater regard for Adams the revolutionary radical than for Adams the president and peacemaker."[3] Moreover, until David McCullough's best-selling 2001 biography and the acclaimed 2008 HBO miniseries, public interest in Adams was much less than in George Washington, Thomas Jefferson, and Benjamin Franklin.

Adams's faith is difficult to decipher, not because like many other presidents, he said little about his personal convictions, but rather because he said so much and his views are so complex. Before age 12, Adams explained in 1820, he began reading polemical religious works, and for more than seventy years he continued to do so "as far as the wandering, anxious, and perplexed kind of life, which Providence has compelled me to pursue, would admit." Adams had "endeavored to obtain as much information" as possible about all of the world's religions, and he diligently studied the history of major theological disputes, including the battle over the Trinity that produced the Athanasian Creed.[4] One of the most theologically astute laypeople of his generation, Adams sought to steer a middle course between Deism (a philosophy which asserted that God created the universe but did not intervene in it; rejected scriptural revelation, divine providence, and miracles; elevated reason and natural law; emphasized morality and human goodness; and despised organized Christianity) and skepticism, on one side, and Calvinism, on the other. He leaned toward Arminianism and ultimately embraced Unitarianism, a theological perspective which asserts that the concept of the Trinity is both unbiblical and irrational and that only God the Father is divine.[5] He believed in a loving, involved Creator, people's duty to help others, patiently accepting the pitfalls of life, and an afterlife.[6] Rejecting the Deist belief that God was an uninvolved first cause and the Calvinist tenets of predestination, election, and Christ's limited substitutionary atonement, he argued that God was actively involved in the world, people had free choice, and salvation depended on behavior rather than belief.[7] Although his religious views became more liberal and less orthodox after his mid-twenties, Adams continued to affirm God's existence, goodness, justice, and benevolent direction of the world. His diary, letters, public statements, and actions all testify to his staunch religious convictions and belief that Christian principles provided the best basis for private conduct and social institutions.[8] The Christian religion, Adams asserted, expressed "the character of the eternal, self-existent . . . all powerful and all merciful creator, preserver, and father of the universe." "Neither savage nor civilized man, without a revelation," he added, "could ever have discovered or invented it."[9] Christianity was the world's "most sublime and benevolent" religious system.[10] Nevertheless, Adams admitted to his wife Abigail in 1799 that his religious convictions were "not exactly conformable to that of the greater Part of the Christian World."[11]

In their voluminous correspondence between 1813 and 1825, one of the most fertile intellectual exchanges in American history, Adams and Jefferson discussed at length the credibility of Christianity, the nature of morality and virtue, and the relationship between freedom and fate.[12] In the final analysis, the sage of Quincy had a strong, if unorthodox, faith, which enabled him to cope with personal tragedy, political defeat, and national crises and contributed to his impressive achievements. Given their importance, Richard Ryerson notes, Adams's religious convictions, "have received far less attention than they deserve."[13]

Although Adams repudiated many specific tenets of Calvinism, he was strongly influenced by Reformed ideas about humanity, politics, society, and God's direction of the world. Most New England congregations retained the covenantal theology of sixteenth-century reformer John Calvin, summarized by the acronym TULIP—total depravity, unconditional election, limited atonement, irresistible grace, and perseverance of the saints—until the American Revolution. Reformed Christians stressed that God was building His kingdom in this world and that His followers had a responsibility to direct and shape cultural life in ways that were consistent with biblical norms and glorified God. They also urged Christians to develop a deep personal relationship with God.[14] Like the Puritans who settled Massachusetts and Connecticut and dominated these colonies until 1776, Adams was skeptical about human nature, strove to restrain and regulate people through "a governmental system of checks and balances," and believed that God chose Americans to institute this system.[15] Puritanism was also a major source of Adams's contention that public and private virtue was critical to the successful functioning of a republic. Moreover, reading sixteenth- and seventeenth-century Calvinist revolutionaries convinced Adams that no aspects of the British government were sacrosanct and affected his choice of means to attain American independence.[16]

Adams also continued his Puritan forebears' practice of personal introspection. While they constantly examined their hearts to prepare for salvation, Adams scrutinized his heart primarily to prepare for his earthly vocation and assess whether he was worthy of worldly success.[17] "Adams was always looking inward—surveying, evaluating, and judging the state of his soul—raising his sights and stoking his ambition with dreams of great and heroic accomplishments."[18] He had a passionate desire to make his mark and to improve the world. "The Man who lives wholly to himself," Adams told a friend, "is of less worth than the Cattle in his Barn." Adams wanted to serve society and others through his calling,[19] but he also wanted to be remembered for his achievements. He strove to avoid the fate of the "common Herd of Mankind, who are born and eat and sleep and die" and are forgotten. He hoped instead to obtain "an Immortality in the Memories of all the Worthy, to [the] End of Time." In his early twenties, Adams wondered whether "Heaven [would] furnish the proper Means and Opportunities" to enable him to attain such acclaim.[20] However, the events of the American Revolution soon catapulted Adams from local recognition to national renown. His vital contributions to American independence and invaluable political service to the new nation enabled Adams to receive the fame he craved. Like the Puritans, Adams was convinced that an all-powerful God ruled the world, and he believed God had called him to help lead America. The North Parish in Braintree, he told his wife in 1782, was "a remarkable Spot" that had "vomited Forth more Fire than Mount Etna. It has produced three mortals, Hancock and two Adams's, who have, with the best Intentions . . . set the World in a blaze."[21]

The Faith of John Adams

Born in 1735, John Adams grew up in a religiously devout family in Braintree, Massachusetts, during the First Great Awakening. Led by theologian Jonathan Edwards and itinerant evangelist George Whitefield, the revival emphasized personal conversion and religious experience and generated substantial conflict among Congregationalists and Presbyterians over its methods. Adams's father was a farmer, a selectman, a church deacon, and a lieutenant in the town militia. "In Wisdom, Piety, Benevolence and Charity in proportion" to his "Education and Sphere of Life," Adams insisted, "I have never seen his Superiour."[22] John attended the local Congregational church twice every Sunday and undoubtedly participated in regular family devotions that included Bible reading, prayer, memorization of the Westminster Shorter Catechism, and discussion of sermons. As a result, he grew up in a family, church, and community where Puritan attitudes, theology, and piety deeply influenced thinking and behavior.[23]

However, Adams came of age at a time when many Boston ministers, influenced by their education at Harvard and reading of English theological works, were rejecting the traditional Calvinist tenets of human depravity and predestination and adopting Arminianism (which asserted that people's rational faculties, although enfeebled by the Fall, could enable them to understand God's expectations, accept God's gracious offer of salvation, and live by Christian ethical standards) or more liberal Protestant perspectives. Three events—his own education at Harvard, discussions of religious issues with liberal Christians and skeptics in Worcester, Massachusetts, where he taught school after graduation, and a controversy at Braintree over the orthodoxy of pastor Lemuel Briant—led Adams to abandon much of his Reformed heritage, decide against becoming a minister, and eventually espouse Unitarian theology. While attending Harvard from 1750 to 1754, Adams participated in morning and evening prayer services. Under its president Edward Holyoke and theologian Edward Wigglesworth, Harvard in the mid-eighteenth century was moving away from "the strict tenets of New England Calvinism" toward Arminianism and rational Christianity (Christianity's claim to have a supernatural origin must be subjected to the same canons of reason and empirical evidence that apply to other historical events). Its students studied the cosmology of Isaac Newton, the political theory of John Locke, the new biblical criticism of English theologian Samuel Clarke, and the mild Arminianism of leading Anglican theologians such as John Tillotson and Daniel Whitby.[24] The study of these works and the teaching of John Winthrop, a professor of mathematics and natural philosophy, Harvard's most distinguished faculty member, and America's leading astronomer, strongly influenced Adams's worldview and stimulated him to use reason and scientific and historical observation more than Scripture to evaluate religious and philosophical issues. Adams was also strongly influenced by his discussions of religious and philosophical questions with dissenters and freethinkers at Worcester. His diary includes many accounts of his dialogues and debates with Arminians, Deists, and atheists. He found the ideas, intellectual exchange, and camaraderie of these opponents of Calvinism invigorating and provocative and lost confidence in the defense of orthodoxy by the local Congregationalist pastor Thaddeus Maccarty whose sermons Adams regularly attended and commented on in his diary.[25] Calvinist parishioners constantly criticized Briant, who pastored the Congregational Church in Braintree from 1722 to 1754, for rejecting the Puritan tenets of original sin and divine election. His sermons and publications produced great division in the congregation, and both Adams's father and uncle Ebenezer called for his removal. However, John sided with Briant, members voted to retain him, and the congregation's theological perspective gradually shifted to Arminianism and eventually to Unitarianism.[26]

As a young man, Adams, prodded by his father, considered becoming a minister, but he soon decided that he was not temperamentally or spiritually equipped to be a clergyman. Adams observed that a pastor had substantial time to study, great opportunity to "subdue his Passions," and "fewer Temptations to intemperance and injustice." However, ministers had to combat "a Thousand Obstacles," including poverty, their parishioners' prejudices, and potential charges of heresy.[27] As he neared his twenty-first birthday, Adams confessed to a friend that "the frightful engines of ecclesiastical councils" always terrified him when he considered becoming a minister.[28] Explaining later why he had chosen to practice law instead, Adams noted that despite one young pastor's genius, "indefatigable study," noble disposition, and "strictest virtue," he was "despised by some, ridiculed by others, and detested by more, only because he is suspected of Arminianism." Most people cared only about the orthodoxy, not the piety, integrity, or learning, of young ministers.[29] Adams also feared that becoming a clergyman "would involve me in endless Altercations and make my Life miserable, without any prospect of doing any good to my fellow Men."[30] His rejection of Calvinism, doubts about aspects of Christian orthodoxy, self-perceived character flaws, and the problems of the ministry dissuaded Adams from pursuing this vocation. However, while serving as a lawyer and a statesman, he remained deeply interested in religious history and theology his entire life.

Moreover, during his time in Worcester, Adams experienced "the New England equivalent to the early Christian retreat to the desert" during which monks sought to purge their worldly ways and become God's earthly instruments. Like his Puritan ancestors, Adams confronted "his own sinfulness— his vanities, ambitions, jealousies—" and acknowledged that they could be controlled, but not completely conquered. These profane drives must be harnessed and redirected to accomplish God's designs. Throughout his life, Adams cultivated humility, self-denial, and virtue, not just as means to ends but as ends in themselves.[31]

Adams has been called a Puritan, a moderate Deist, a humanist, and a theistic rationalist, but he is best labeled a Unitarian.[32] Beginning in the 1730s, numerous clergy in the Boston area began to reject the major tenets of Calvinism, especially the doctrine of election. They stressed God's benevolence and desire that all individuals be saved, humanity's free will, and people's dignity rather than their depravity. Their education, which in many cases emphasized the truths of nature as revealed through human reason, and their response to the emotional excesses of the Great Awakening, its emphasis on a dramatic new birth experience, and the threat posed by its itinerant preachers pushed many pastors, led by Charles Chauncy, Jonathan Mayhew, and Ebenezer Gay, toward Arminianism, theological liberalism, rational Christianity, and eventually Unitarianism. By the early nineteenth century, many New England clergy were embracing Unitarian doctrines. Two pivotal events were the election of liberal Henry Ware as the Hollis Professor of Divinity at Harvard in 1805, despite vigorous objections by orthodox Christians, and a pamphlet debate during the next decade that culminated in William Ellery Channing's 1819 sermon, "Unitarian Christianity." By 1820 many Congregational churches had split between liberal and orthodox factions, and Unitarians often gained control of the church buildings and congregational funds. Although the American Unitarian Association was not created until 1825, the year before Adams's death, Unitarian doctrine made deep inroads into New England much earlier.[33]

Adams's Puritan heritage convinced him that God's laws governed the universe and helped shape his views of humanity, calling, morality, and America's destiny. However, he rejected the divinity of Jesus, the concept of the Trinity, the infallibility of the Bible, and the five points of Calvinism. His voracious reading of theology and philosophy and extensive and painstaking reflection led Adams's worldview to become more Unitarian during the last thirty years of his life. "I have never known any better people than the Calvinists," he declared in 1820. Nevertheless, "I cannot class myself under that denomination."[34] Adams long identified with the party within Congregationalism that in the 1820s officially embraced Unitarianism.[35] He believed deeply in God's just and compassionate direction of the world and the power of prayer. Adams assiduously read the Bible, was fascinated by theological questions and issues, and, except for part of the time he served as a diplomat in Europe, regularly attended church on both Sunday mornings and afternoons.[36] Unlike most Deists, Adams believed in miracles, prayer, providence, and the Bible as God's special revelation. Although his father did not believe in the Athanasian Creed or other "doctrines usually called Calvinistic," John Quincy Adams insisted, he "was a firm believer in Christianity."[37]

C. Bradley Thompson contends that scholars have overestimated the impact of the Puritan worldview and underestimated the influence of "modern philosophic rationalism" in Adams's "mental and moral universe." Disavowing much of his Puritan heritage, Thompson argues, Adams espoused a view of humanity, nature, and moral duties that depended heavily on Francis Bacon, Isaac Newton, and John Locke.[38] Some scholars have exaggerated the effect of Puritanism on Adams, but it did play a significant role in shaping his understanding of God's sovereignty, human nature, sin, and morality.[39]

In 1764 Adams married Abigail Smith, the daughter of the pastor of the First (Congregationalist) Church of Weymouth, Massachusetts. Her father was part of a sizable group of Massachusetts Congregationalist clergy who denounced the First Great Awakening because some of its adherents insisted that their direct communication with God entitled them to challenge the authority of pastors they deemed to be unconverted. Shortly before her fifteenth birthday, Abigail publicly confessed her Christian faith and joined the Weymouth church. Like her father and husband, she was a religious liberal who preferred sermons that appealed to reason rather than emotions.[40] Abigail's strong faith shaped her understanding of the world, supplied her sense of mission, and helped her raise children and cope with illnesses, deaths, and long separations from her husband. Her religious convictions directed her "values, attitudes, and behavior." The Bible provided instructions for living and taught her to contribute to the welfare of society and to believe that God would reward good and punish evil in the afterlife.[41] Like her husband, she disliked creeds, believed that God controlled history, prized prayer, and considered religious faith and practice essential to the well-being of the republic.[42] Dozens of her letters testify to her devout faith. She told her son John Quincy that "the foundation of Religion is Belief" in "the one only God" who is infinitely "wise, just and good," to whom he owed "the highest Reverence."[43] As did John, Abigail frequently testified that God was providentially directing the United States and her family's life.[44] When her husband and John Quincy barely survived a storm that carried their ship to the coast of Spain instead of France in 1780, she rejoiced that the winds and seas were "under the particular government" of God who created the universe and held "the ocean in the hollow of his hand."[45] In coping with illness, the death of loved ones, and other trials, Abigail derived comfort and consolation from her faith.[46] While living in both New York and Philadelphia, Abigail had trouble finding preaching she enjoyed. Most pastors were too Calvinist, evangelical, or unintellectual to suit her liberal Congregationalist tastes.[47] Shortly before her death, she told her son John Quincy that she had become a Unitarian in the way that William Ellery Channing employed the term. "There is not any reasoning," she wrote, "which can convince me, contrary to my senses, that three, is one, and one three." "I acknowledge myself [to be] a unitarian—Believing that the Father alone, is the supreme God, and that Jesus Christ derived his Being, and all his powers and honours from the Father."[48] John and Abigail enjoyed a long, happy, and mutually enriching marriage. Their shared faith helped them nurture their children, cope with many challenges, and support one another in trying times.

John Adams hungrily read the leading ancient philosophers and medieval theologians and the principal theologians, philosophers, and moral theorists of the eighteenth and early nineteenth centuries. He devoured the tomes of the orthodox—Joseph Butler, Jonathan Edwards, Daniel Waterland, Joseph Hopkins, and Ezra Stiles Ely—and of the heterodox—Joseph Priestley, Theopholis Lindsey, Francis Adrian Van Der Kemp, Conyers Middleton, Thomas Emlyn, and French philosophes Voltaire and Marquis de Condorcet—as well as Baptist John Leland's 1754 attack on Deists.[49] "Controversies between Calvinists and Arminians, Trinitarians and Unitarians, Deists and Christians," and atheists and all these groups, Adams explained, especially "attracted my attention."[50] Adams and Jefferson had a long, philosophical correspondence about many religious issues, especially the various works of

Priestley, a Unitarian theologian, author, and scientist, who sought to reconcile Enlightenment principles with Christian theism.[51]

Adams reduced Christianity to a few core tenets. Its general principles,
he asserted, "are as eternal and immutable as the existence and attributes of
God."[52] "The ten commandments and the sermon on the mount," Adams
told Jefferson, "contain my religion."[53] Adams valued the essential precepts of
Christianity, but like Jefferson, he argued that Christ's teachings had been distorted and that Christianity had been corrupted. When a Bible society proposed
in 1816 to disseminate the King James Bible throughout the world, Adams
asked: "Would it not be better" to use this money "to purify Christendom from
the corruptions of Christianity than to propagate those corruptions in Europe,
Asia, Africa, and America?"[54] "The substance and essence of Christianity," he
avowed, "is eternal and unchangeable" "but it has been mixed" with unreasonable "extraneous ingredients," which must be separated.[55] Unlike Jefferson
and Priestley, however, Adams did not precisely delineate what these corruptions were (except for the doctrine of the atonement).[56]

Adams revered Christianity "in its primitive purity and simplicity" as "the
religion of reason, equity, and love," as "the religion of the head and of the
heart."[57] Christianity, he contended, promoted "Wisdom, Virtue, Equity and
Humanity" more than any other religion.[58] It enabled the masses to know,
believe, and venerate "the great Principle of the Law of Nature and Nations,
'Love your Neighbour as yourself, and do to others as you would that others
should do to you.'" Neither educational institutions nor governments could
achieve this end.[59]

Adams's religion centered on "the love of God and his creation." He
affirmed that God is infinitely wise, good, and powerful.[60] God's design of the
human body and the moral and physical universe, Adams insisted, provided
ample evidence for His existence. God gave people copious blessings and
deterred them from committing improper and potentially fatal acts. God provided objects that gratified people's senses and gave them reason to discover
truth and the purpose for their existence.[61] He also made impiety, injustice,
malevolence, and intemperance "appear Shocking and deformed."[62] The fine
tuning of the universe further testified to God's existence. All matter acted in
accordance with God's "Stupendous Plan" and advanced His "great and complicated Drama."[63] It was highly improbable, Adams reasoned, that life began
on earth by chance. "Even a small variation in climate or in the velocity of the
Earth's orbit around the sun" would make human life impossible.[64] Therefore,
he concluded, "an intelligent and benevolent mind" had designed the Earth.[65]
Adams derived great "joy and comfort" from the abundant evidence that "this
stupendous & immeasurable universe" was not governed by fate, chance,

"caprice, anger, resentment," or vengeance, but rather by "intelligence, wisdom, and benevolence."[66]

Adams's belief in divine creation led him to three key religious convictions: God is sovereign, religion is the primary basis for morality, and the afterlife is real.[67] "If I had not steadfastly believed in a Government of the Universe, wise beyond my comprehension, and benevolent beyond my conception," he wrote in 1815, "I should have been constantly" dejected and despairing.[68] Like Jonathan Edwards, Adams expressed great reverence for the awesome Creator of the planets, stars, and satellites. "I feel an irresistible impulse to fall on my knees," he declared, to adore God's power, wisdom, and benevolence.[69] His belief in God's direction of the universe usually led him to accept the events of his life without repining and sometimes with rejoicing.

For Adams, "the doctrine of a supreme, intelligent," sovereign God was the foundation for "all morality, and consequently of all civilization."[70] By promoting morality, justice, virtue, and decorum, Christianity helped supply the order and civility a republic needed to flourish. It accentuated human dignity and gave life meaning.[71] While he did not accept every aspect of Christian orthodoxy, he considered belief in Christianity essential to civic virtue and righteous private conduct.[72]

Adams was much more concerned about virtue than piety. For him, piety involved cultivating three essential habits: "Contemplating the Deity and his transcendent Excellences"; achieving "Dependence upon him"; and expressing "Reverence and Gratitude" to God. For Adams, religious devotions were more a habitual practice than an intimate, personal, heart-felt relationship with God.[73] He criticized the First Great Awakening for promoting religious emotion and enthusiasm and producing controversy and division.[74] While Christianity "is the religion of the heart," Adams averred, "the heart is deceitful above all things, and unless controuled [sic] by the dominion of the head, it will lead us into Salt Ponds."[75]

Adams regarded Jesus very highly, but he did not believe that He was God incarnate. Like Jefferson, Adams denied the deity of Christ, but considered Him to be a great teacher and exemplary moral guide. To Adams, the doctrines of Jesus's incarnation and deity were an "awful blasphemy."[76] Instead, he asserted, "Jesus is benevolence personified, an example for all men."[77] Adams praised and sought to practice Jesus's key moral teachings, especially the call to love one's neighbors. However, he denounced the doctrine of the atonement. "An incarnate God!!! An eternal, self-existent, omnipotent author of this stupendous universe, suffering on a cross!!!" "It has stupified [sic] the Christian world" and "been the source of almost all the corruptions of Christianity."[78]

While Adams did not deny the Trinity publicly, he did so privately. Because of public expectations, in proclaiming days of national humiliation, prayer, and fasting in 1798 and 1799, Adams called Jesus "the Redeemer of the World" and "the Great Mediator and Redeemer" and invoked the aid of the Holy Spirit.[79] However, like Washington and many other founders, Adams was much more likely to refer to Providence than to God, Christ, or even Christianity. Writing to Jefferson in 1813, he bellowed: "Had you and I been forty days with Moses on Mount Sinai, and admitted to behold the divine Shechinah, and there told that one was three and three one, we might not have had courage to deny it, but we could not have believed it. The thunders and lightnings and earthquakes, and the transcendent splendors and glories, might have overwhelmed us with terror and amazement, but we could not have believed the doctrine." Because of this, he added, Calvinists and Athanasian divines "will say I am no Christian; I say ye are no Christians, and there the account is balanced. Yet I believe all the honest men among you are Christians, in my sense of the word."[80] Two years later he professed amazement that John Quincy believed in the Trinity.[81]

Throughout his life Adams struggled to determine the best source of authority and basis for human understanding. Deeply influenced by the Enlightenment, the sage highly valued reason. Unlike many philosophes, however, he considered philosophy, which reason created, to be God's first revelation to humans. "When this revelation is clear and certain, by intuition or necessary inductions," Adams asserted, "no subsequent revelation, supported by prophecies or miracles, can supersede it." Philosophy should be used to impartially examine "all terrestrial religions."[82] People had a duty "to read, examine and judge . . . what is right." Neither priests nor popes, Adams contended, had the authority to tell people what to believe, and he would not believe one word they said "if I think it is not founded in Reason and in Revelation."[83] "Private individual judgment" was both a "divine right" and a "sacred duty."[84] The human mind must be freed from superstition and dogmatism, he told John Quincy.[85]

The principal question confronting humanity, Adams wrote in 1814, was "whether authority is from nature and reason, or from miraculous revelation; from the revelation from God, by the human understanding, or from the revelation to Moses and to Constantine, and the Council of Nice[a]." Did authority reside in people or in offices? Were spiritual and temporal offices instituted by men or by God? "Are the original principles of authority in human nature, or in stars, garters, crosses, golden fleeces, crowns, sceptres, and thrones?" People had grappled with "these profound and important questions" for centuries. They had provoked crusades, wars, and massacres. Would "Zinzendorf,

Swedenborg, Whitefield, or Wesley prevail?" Or would Ignatius Loyola and the Inquisition triumph?[86]

For sixty-five years, Adams declared, "I have searched after truth by every means and by every opportunity in my power, and with a sincerity and impartiality, for which I can appeal to God, my adored Maker." Ultimately, Adams concluded, individuals were responsible to God and themselves to reach "an impartial verdict and judgment."[87] Influenced by the works of John Locke, Adams concluded that the Bible fortified, but was not the primary source of, moral truth and that people, despite their weaknesses, were rational beings who could derive "standards of moral obligation and virtuous behavior from [their] observation of the external world and of the operations" of their own minds.[88] The Creator, Adams asserted, gave people reason so that they could "find out the Truth."[89]

Adams agreed with the Puritans, however, that people's understanding of the universe would always be incomplete. The "eternal, self-existent being" possessing "infinite wisdom, goodness, and power" who created the universe is the only "being who can understand" it. Therefore, it was "not only vain but wicked for insects to pretend to comprehend it." It was arrogant and presumptuous for humans to think they could "penetrate far into the Designs of Heaven." Instead, they should reverently accept God's decrees, recognizing that He could bring good out of adversity. In May 1775, for example, as the British and colonists clashed in Boston, Adams told his wife that he believed that God intended the present calamity "to bind the Colonies together in more indissoluble Bands, and to animate their Exertions." He prayed that "the Furnace of Affliction may refine them." Adams insisted that people must "submit to the decisions of Heaven" even though they "are inscrutable to us."[90] "The Ends of Providence," he declared, "are too profound, too sublime, [and] too vast" for people to understand. God overthrew "empires and kingdoms," sent "plagues, earthquakes, storms, [and] sunshine," and permitted "good and evil" "in a manner we cannot comprehend."[91]

After examining all sacred scriptures as extensively as his circumstances allowed, Adams concluded that "the Bible is the best book in the world. It contains more of my little philosophy than all the libraries I have seen."[92] Adams argued that the Bible taught "the most profound philosophy, the most perfect morality, and the most refined policy"; following its commandments preserved a republic.[93] Adams's speeches, essays, and letters contained many biblical passages, allusions, and examples, including the stories of Balaam, David, Mordecai, and many others.[94] The Scriptures directly revealed "eternal and immutable" "general principles" such as "the existence and attributes of God."[95] The Bible was God's "direct and special revelation," but it was not completely reliable because it had been "conditioned by both time and place." Humans had established the biblical canon, and they must use the divine gift of reason to interpret Scripture.[96] Although revelation and reason usually complemented each other, when they conflicted, reason must be followed.[97] Adams told Jefferson, however, that the parts of the Bible "I cannot reconcile to my little philosophy, I postpone for future investigation."[98] He also revered the Bible because it was "the most republican book in the world."[99] Adams insisted that any nation that made the Bible its only law-book and whose citizens followed biblical precepts would be a utopia characterized by love, peace, goodwill, temperance, and industry and the absence of drunkenness, lust, trifling amusements, theft, and dishonesty.[100]

Adams believed in miracles. Whenever He had a sufficient reason to do so, the Almighty author of nature could suspend its laws. Jesus and His disciples had performed miracles, the sage averred, to gain people's attention, overcome their prejudices and passions, and help convince them to accept Christianity.[101] Adams believed that God had flooded the earth in the days of Noah and even raised Jesus from the dead (although denying Christ's deity).[102]

Adams treasured prayer and frequently asserted that he prayed for others. He asked God to "bless, preserve, and prosper" his family. Adams wrote to his daughter's fiancé in 1784: "I pray God to bless and prosper you both." In 1798 he told the residents of Cincinnati: "in return for your prayers for my personal happiness, I sincerely offer mine for the prosperity of the north-western territory." Adams asked God to guide Judge Oliver Ellsworth and Governor William Davie in their diplomatic mission with France in 1799. The Federalist prayed that "the citizens of Philadelphia" would "maintain the honorable character of their ancestors, and be protected from every calamity, physical, moral, and political." Speaking to Congressmen in the Capitol, the president declared, "It would be unbecoming [to] the representatives of this nation to assemble, for the first time, in this solemn temple, without looking up to the Supreme Ruler of the universe, and imploring his blessing." After receiving word that John Quincy had been selected president by the House of Representatives in 1825, Adams wrote, "May the blessing of God Almighty continue to protect you to the end of your life, as it has heretofore protected you in so remarkable a manner from your cradle!"[103]

Almost anywhere he was—Quincy, Worcester, Boston, New York, Philadelphia, Paris, London, Brussels, Amsterdam, or even on ships crossing the Atlantic—Adams faithfully attended Sunday services. He worshipped at Anglican, Presbyterian, Baptist, Methodist, Quaker, Moravian, and Catholic services, but he preferred Congregational or Unitarian ones.[104] Declining a request from prominent physician Benjamin Rush in 1811 to write an address to the American people to promote Christianity and morality, Adams explained, "If I should recommend" scrupulous observance of the Sabbath or even only regular attendance of public worship "as a means of moral instruction and social improvement," "I should be charged" with "a selfish desire to revive the remembrance of my own punctuality in this respect; for it is notorious enough that I have been a church-going animal for seventy-six years, from the cradle."[105] Adams conscientiously listened to Boston's leading ministers, including Samuel Cooper of the Brattle Street (Congregational) Church and Charles Chauncy of First (Congregational) Church, and to Presbyterians John Witherspoon in Princeton and George Duffield in Philadelphia, Unitarians Richard Price in London and Joseph Priestley in Philadelphia, and dozens of lesser known pastors.[106] Adams often attended two services on Sundays; one Sunday in October 1774 he attended three in Philadelphia—a Presbyterian church in the morning, a Baptist church in the afternoon, and a Methodist meeting in the evening.[107] Adams filled his diary and letters with comments on the substance and style of the ministers he heard. Accepting Puritan mores, Adams was reluctant to travel on the Sabbath.[108]

Adams rejected the doctrine of Christ's substitutionary atonement and rarely discussed God's grace or forgiveness. The Puritans contended that salvation depended wholly on Christ and not at all on people's merit. Adams, by contrast, labeled the concept that Christ atoned on the cross for human sins an "absurdity," disputed this doctrine with pastors and friends, and saw salvation as depending primarily on people's upright conduct and good works.[109] As a young man, Adams insisted that "our Happiness or Misery in a future life will be alloted us, according as our Characters shall be virtuous or vicious."[110] Those who contemplated God and practiced compassion and self-discipline increased their "Prospect of everlasting Felicity."[111] People who praised God for His goodness and mercy, strove to be good neighbors, and lived virtuously, Adams promised, would win His approbation and reward.[112] "My moral or religious Creed," he wrote in 1816, has for "60 years been contained in four short words, 'be just and good.'"[113] Paraphrasing Micah 6:8, he summarized his life philosophy as "Do justly. Love mercy. Walk humbly. This is enough."[114] Christianity taught that "Prudence, Justice, Temperance and Fortitude" were "the means and Conditions of future as well as present Happiness."[115] While he considered Christianity as he understood it to be the best religion, Adams thought that those who faithfully followed the precepts of almost all religions would go to heaven.[116] Everyone who strove to obey God's commands and live by the Golden Rule, he asserted, had "the sure prospect of a happy immortality."[117] "I believe with Justin Martyr, that all good men are Christians, and I believe there have been, and are, good men in all nations, sincere and conscientious."[118]

A passage in his autobiography illustrates Adams's struggle to forgive his enemies as well as his use of Scripture to bolster his arguments. Alexander Hamilton had sharply criticized Adams's work as a member of the Continental Congress, vice president, and president. "Although I have long since forgiven this Arch Ennemy [sic]," Adams wrote, "Vice, Folly and Villany are not to be forgotten, because the guilty Wretch repented, in his dying Moments [on his deathbed Hamilton had a Christian conversion experience]. Although David repented, We are no where commanded to forget the Affair of Uriah"; "though the Thief on the cross was converted, his Felony is still upon Record. The Prodigal Son repented and was forgiven, yet his Harlots and riotous living" must "not be forgotten. Nor am I," Adams asserted, "obliged by any Principle of Morality or Religion to suffer my Character to lie under infamous Calumnies" because their author "died a Penitent." However, charity required Christians to hope that Hamilton's "humiliation was sincere" and that "he was forgiven."[119]

Earlier in life, Adams lambasted Catholics as debased, Calvinists as theologically mistaken, Quakers as troublemakers, and Jeffersonians as infidels, but later in life he reconciled with Jefferson, celebrated religious diversity, praised Hinduism, and extolled "universal toleration."[120] Throughout his life, Adams often criticized church creeds as restrictive. Where, he asked, did the gospels require councils, creeds, oaths, subscriptions, "and the whole Cartloads of trumpery" that encumbered religion?[121] Adams considered Catholicism to be superstitious and irrational and its teachings to be inimical to religious and political liberty. He deplored the Catholic doctrine of transubstantiation and the church's contention that God had given it "the keys of heaven" to determine who was admitted and excluded. Adams complained that Catholic lay people were deceived by popes, bishops, and local priests. Scripture forewarned that the pope "would exalt himself above all that was called God," and for centuries, people had been "chained fast" in "cruel, shameful, deplorable Servitude" to the pontiff and his "Subordinate Tyrants."[122] Moreover, in countries where "Romish superstition" prevailed, Adams protested, lay people were kept illiterate to prevent them from detecting "the gross Impostures of the Priesthood" and shaking "off the Yoke of Bondage."[123] While worshipping at a Catholic cathedral in Brussels in 1780, Adams witnessed a scene that appalled him. Thousands of worshippers knelt and adored a tapestry that depicted "Jews stabbing the Wafer, the bon Dieu, and blood gushing in streams." Viewing "this insufferable Piece of pious Villany" led him to denounce the "Knavery of the Priesthood and the brutal Ignorance of the People."[124] Adams especially condemned the Jesuits. They had inhibited "the progress of reformation and the improvement of the human mind" "much longer and more fatally" than had the French Revolution or "Napoleon's despotism or ideology."[125] Adams denounced Pope Pius VII's restoration of the Jesuits in 1814 as a step back toward "cruelty, perfidy, despotism, [and] death."[126]

Adams also excoriated Calvinism. He repudiated the Reformed doctrines of human depravity and original sin, deprecated the concept of unconditional election as "detestable," "invidious," and "hurtful," and argued that the tenet of limited atonement inhibited ethical conduct.[127] The Calvinist dogma that "infinite benevolence, wisdom, and power created, and preserves for a time, innumerable millions, to make them miserable for ever, for his own glory" falsely depicted God as wretched, ambitious, vain, and vengeful.[128] Even Hottentots and Mohawks "would reject with horror" the contention that God "elected a precious few" to "eternal Life, without regard to any foreseen virtue, and reprobated the rest without regard to any foreseen Vice." Moreover, this doctrine discouraged "the practice of virtue."[129] Adams protested that the fatalism of Calvinists as well as of Muslims, "Materialists, Atheists, [and] Pantheists" appeared "to render all prayer futile and absurd."[130] Neither popes, councils, nor enthusiasts would ever convince him that "such arbitrary Will or inflexible fatality" governed the universe.[131] Adams also rejected the Reformed tenet that Adam's sin damned "the whole human race" without any of them committing "actual Crimes" because it made God appear arbitrary and unjust. People were guilty and needed to repent because of their own "Wickedness and Vice," not because of the actions of their first parents.[132] "I am answerable for my own sins," Adams asserted in 1815, because "they were my own fault."[133] Unless people were responsible for their own sins, eternal rewards and punishments made no sense.[134]

Although Adams applauded many aspects of the Enlightenment, especially its broadening of the human mind, he deplored the assault of many philosophes on Christianity. Deist Thomas Paine's abusive attack, stolen from Voltaire and others, Adams argued, could "never discredit Christianity," which would "last as long as the world."[135] For Adams, the worst epithet was "atheist."[136] Adams denounced Denis Diderot, Friedrich Melchior Grimm, and other French philosophes as "indubitable atheists" because they taught that the universe was eternal, the spiritual dimension did not exist, and people had no freedom. For them, every human "thought, word, passion, sentiment . . . and action was [causally] necessary." The concepts of conscience and morality were simply products of fate. The philosophes vainly strove to "perfect human nature, and convert the earth into a paradise of pleasure."[137] Judged by its consequences, Adams alleged, atheism "is worse than even Catholicism."[138]

Despite his harsh criticisms of these various Christian groups, Adams claimed in his later years that he rejected religious bigotry and called for greater religious toleration. He had attended the worship services of many denominations in numerous nations and believed that belonging to any of these religious bodies was much better than having no religion.[139] "Ask me not," Adams wrote in 1810, "whether I am a Catholic or Protestant, Calvinist or Arminian. As far as they are Christians, I wish to be a fellow-disciple with them all."[140] Adams applauded George Whitefield's statement that "He who feareth God and worketh righteousness, shall be accepted of him" (Acts 10: 35).[141] In 1818 the sage praised the "honor, probity, [and] generosity" of Jews and hoped that they would be granted full citizenship in every country.[142] Two years later he urged Massachusetts to provide "equal protection of the laws" to "all men, of all religions, demeaning themselves as good subjects."[143]

Convinced that God controlled the universe, Adams constantly thanked Him for directing his own life and the United States. Like many of his contemporaries, he insisted that the all-powerful, benevolent God, not "Blind and Unintelligent Necessity," guided history in just but inscrutable ways.[144] Adams asserted in 1756 that his youth had been "marked by divine Providence."[145] After summarizing the principal events of his life in 1809, Adams concluded, "I have every reason to acknowledge the protecting providence of God, from my birth, and especially through my public life."[146] In 1821 Adams declared, "Providence has preserved and supported me for eighty-five years" through "many dangers and difficulties." "I am not afraid, he added, "to trust in its goodness to all eternity."[147]

In 1766 Adams praised God for the repeal of the Stamp Act and agreed with pastors who preached on the texts "the Lord reigneth, let the Earth rejoice" (Ps. 97:1) and "ye thought evil against me; but god meant it unto good" (Gen. 50:20).[148] His belief that God had summoned him to serve his new country enabled Adams to cope with personal financial problems, concerns about the health of his wife and children, long separations from his family, and numerous American defeats during the Revolutionary War. "I have been called by Providence to take a larger share in active Life," he wrote in October 1775, than is agreeable to "my Health, my Fortune or my Inclination."[149]

His personal sense of divine calling was reinforced by his conviction that God was directing and blessing the American cause. The quest to gain independence, Adams avowed in 1776, was clearly "the work of the Lord."[150] The day the Continental Congress approved the Declaration of Independence, Adams argued, "ought to be commemorated, as the day of deliverance, by solemn acts of devotion to God Almighty." He wrote to his wife, "I must submit all my hopes and fears to an overruling Providence, in which . . . I firmly believe." "It is the will of Heaven," Adams added, that Britain and the United States "should be sundered forever." God might also will that Americans suffer dreadful calamities and distresses to produce many virtues and "correct many errors, follies and vices which threaten to disturb, dishonor, and destroy us. The furnace of affliction produces refinement, in States as well as individuals."[151] Adams credited his ability to procure loans from the Dutch in 1782 to "the great scheme of Providence." It proved yet again that God directed human events and used people as His instruments (although he insisted that his diplomatic skills and initiative had also contributed to the outcome).[152]

As president, Adams repeatedly affirmed that God guided the nascent republic. In his inaugural address, he thanked God for protecting the United States by His "overruling Providence." Adams beseeched the "Being who is supreme over all" to continue to bless the "nation and its Government and give it all possible success and duration consistent with the ends of His providence."[153] In various other messages and addresses, the Federalist, following a long-standing New England pattern, gave God gratitude for America's tranquility, security, affluence, civil and religious liberties, and the preservation of its moral and religious principles "against all open and secret attacks."[154] "The safety and prosperity of nations," Adams proclaimed, depended on "the protection and the blessing of Almighty God."[155]

In the midst of the United States' crisis with France, Adams proclaimed a national day of humiliation, fasting, and prayer in March 1798. He urged citizens to "acknowledge before God the manifold sins and transgressions with which we are justly chargeable as individuals and as a nation," imploring "His infinite grace, through the Redeemer of the World, freely to remit all our offenses, and to incline us by His Holy Spirit to that sincere repentance and reformation which" would enable Americans to "hope for his inestimable favor and heavenly benediction."[156] In December 1798, Adams praised God for ending "the alarming and destructive pestilence" that had afflicted several cities.[157] In proclaiming a second day of fasting and prayer in March 1799, Adams trumpeted: "No truth is more clearly taught" in the Bible or "more fully demonstrated" by history than that "a Supreme Being" governs the universe and that all people are accountable to "the searcher of hearts and righteous distributer of rewards and punishments." Acknowledging this furthered both "the happiness and rectitude of individuals" and "the well-being of communities." Adams entreated God to impress upon Americans that "righteousness exalteth a nation, but sin is a reproach to any people" (Prov. 14:34) and to "turn us from our transgressions and turn His displeasure from us."[158]

Various statements Adams made as president also testified to his belief in divine providence. As Americans mourned the death of Washington in December 1799, Adams professed that trust "in the wise and righteous dominion of Providence" required "humble resignation" to God's will.[159] Adams exhorted soldiers to firmly rely on the protection of the "God of armies."[160] Guided by God, he told Senators in 1800, "the wisdom and virtue of our citizens will deliver our national compact unimpaired to a free, prosperous, happy, and grateful posterity."[161] After leaving office, Adams declared that only the "providence of Almighty God" could have brought him safely and successfully through the many difficult and dangerous trials he faced.[162]

Adams's faith also helped him cope with personal tragedy and sorrow. Shortly after learning that he had lost the presidential race of 1800, his son Charles, who had long suffered with depression and alcoholism, died. "The affliction in my family," Adams wrote, "has been very great, and has required the consolation of religion" to endure it. "There is nothing more to be said," Adams added, "but let the Eternal will be done."[163] God's design of the physical world, the constitution of the human body, and the fleeting nature of earthly pleasures, Adams asserted, show that this world was not created to be "a lasting and happy State, but rather" to be "a State of moral discipline" to inspire individuals to pursue virtue, piety, and self-control while cheerfully accepting "all the Events of Providence."[164]

Throughout his life, especially as he aged and suffered from various physical ailments, Adams often reflected on the problem of evil and pain. He told a minister that "'sufferings become powerful means of checking the progress of folly and vice,' that 'the miseries we feel or fear are the consequences of [our] manifold abuses of Divine goodness.'"[165] When fire destroyed Josiah Quincy's house in 1759, Adams, sounding like a Puritan divine, admonished him not to mourn the loss of inconsequential material things. Adams counseled him to instead consider the fire "a punishment of your Vices and follies" that is designed to arouse "your attention" to "more permanent" things. He urged Quincy not to "grieve, but rejoice, that the great Parent of the World" had corrected him for his own good.[166] Stoics, Christians, Muslims, and Native Americans agreed "that complaint is unmanly, unlawful, and impious. To bear torment without a murmur, a sigh, a groan," Adams insisted, "is consummate virtue, heroism, and piety." People should "make the best we can of inevitable evils," he avowed. "We may fret and fume and peeve, and scold and rave, but what good does this do? It hurts ourselves," and our "weak, silly, foolish example" may "hurt our neighbors."[167] Grief, Adams told Jefferson, prompts "serious reflection, sharpens the understanding, and softens the heart." It compels people to assert their reason "over their passions, propensities and prejudices." Grief is a form of pain and, therefore, raises "the great question": "what is the origin and what [is] the final cause of evil." Since only God knows the answer, mortals must strive to bring "all the good we can out of all inevitable evils, and to avoid" all other ones. By exercising patience, resignation, and tranquility, individuals could experience much happiness in the midst of life's challenges.[168] Like the Puritans, Adams welcomed "the Furnace of Affliction" God employed to "refine" His people.[169]

While repeatedly insisting that God controlled all events, Adams rejected the widespread belief that God used earthquakes, pestilence, and famine to punish human sins and "alarm and arouse sinners" to behave virtuously.[170] However, like many of his contemporaries, Adams saw a clear relationship between people's behavior and God's blessings. For example, when the Revolutionary army confronted William Howe's much larger British forces at New York City in July 1776, Adams wrote to James Warren, "May Heaven grant Us victory, if We deserve it; if not, Patience, Humility, and Pennitence [sic] under Defeat."[171] That October, when Benjamin Rush asked Adams if America would prevail in the war, he responded, "Yes, if we fear God and repent our sins."[172] His two presidential proclamations for days of prayer also asserted that God's benediction depended on Americans' conduct. After the United States secured its independence, Adams continually worried that its citizens would not be sufficiently virtuous to sustain their new republic.

By the 1790s, Adams appeared to have rejected the contention of Massachusetts Bay Colony governor John Winthrop and others that America was the new Israel, but he did insist that God had given the United States an exceptional opportunity to prove that a properly constituted government could ensure liberty and promote morality and prosperity. In 1765 Adams declared, "I always consider the settlement of America with reverence and wonder, as the opening of a grand scene and design in Providence for the illumination of the ignorant and the emancipation of the slavish part of mankind all over the earth."[173] Although Adams once called the United States "our Israel,"[174] he did not view Americans as God's chosen people. "There is no special providence for Americans," Adams averred, "and their nature is the same" as that of other groups.[175] "We are not a chosen people that I know of," he later added.[176] However, Adams did maintain that America was exceptional because of its God-assigned mission to further liberty under law.[177] Americans, he argued in 1787, "had the best opportunity" that God had given people since the transgression of Adam and Eve. If they betrayed this trust, they deserved even greater punishment than residents of other nations had suffered from His righteous indignation.[178] More positively, he asserted, "If ever any people merited honor and happiness," it was Americans because they embodied the best qualities of the Romans in their "most prosperous and virtuous" era.[179]

In his 1765 *Dissertation on the Canon and the Feudal Law*, Adams defended the sensible New England Puritans against those who denounced them as bigoted, narrow-minded, religious enthusiasts. This caricature, he avowed, was grossly "injurious and false."[180] The Puritans were "illustrious patriots" who had established "a government of the church more consistent with the scriptures, and a government of the state more agreeable to the dignity of human nature" than had any European nation. Using the rich resources of revelation and reason, they designed a government to promote the "religious liberty with which Jesus had made them free."[181] Their society, founded on the Bible, common sense, and a proper understanding of human nature, fostered "industry, virtue, piety and learning."[182] While the Puritans strove to create a godly community built on the teaching of Scripture and the tenets of Calvinism, Adams hoped to construct a new, purified political community resting on the principles of Christianity and the radical Whigs.[183]

Adams often professed belief in life after death. John told Abigail in 1764 that he hoped to live with her until they both became "desirous of Transportation to a wiser, fairer, better world."[184] "I hope soon to meet you in another country," Adams wrote Jefferson in 1813.[185] "I believe," he declared to a friend, "in a future state of rewards and punishments."[186] Christianity, Adams assured his good friend Benjamin Rush, had conquered death and taken away its sting.[187] "What is there in life to attach us to it," Adams asked Jefferson, "but the hope of a future and a better [life]?" "The Maker of the universe" had stimulated people in all nations to expect "a future and a better state." "If it is a fraud," he reasoned, "we shall never know it; we shall never resent the imposition, be grateful for the illusion, nor grieve for the disappointment; we shall be no more."[188] After Rush died, he wrote his widow that not "a doubt [about the afterlife] can be entertained for a moment."[189] Mourning the death of his beloved Abigail, Adams declared, "Blessed are the dead who die in the Lord" (Rev. 14:13).[190] "That you and I shall meet in a better world," Adams told pastor Samuel Miller, "I have no more doubt than I have that we now exist on the same globe." "Jesus has taught us, that a future state is a social state, when he promised to prepare places in his father's house of many mansions for his disciples."[191] Adams anticipated conversing with his wife, relatives, friends, and sages in heaven.[192] He wrote to David Sewall, we "are candidates for promotion to another world, where I hope we shall be better acquainted."[193] Adams also expected to grow in knowledge while in heaven because Christianity taught that human intelligence "is capable of progressive improvement."[194]

Adams's belief in an afterlife was integrally connected with his views of God and morality. "Without the supposition of a future state," Adams asserted, the universe is "a Chaos."[195] If it were demonstrated that no future state existed, he proclaimed in 1816, my advice "would be, as our existence would be in our own power, to take opium." "Nothing in this world," he argued, is "worth living for but hope, and every hope will fail us, if the last hope, that of a future state, is extinguished."[196] "I know not how to prove, physically, that we shall meet and know each other in a future state," he wrote to Jefferson in 1818; "nor does revelation" provide "any positive assurance of such a felicity." However, he believed in heaven because he could not conceive that God would create human beings "merely to live and die on this earth. If I did not believe [in] a future state, I should believe in no God. And, if there be a future state, why should the Almighty dissolve forever all the tender ties which unite us so delightfully in this world, and forbid us to see each other in the next?"[197] Like Immanuel Kant, Adams also argued that the promise of rewards and punishments in a future life supplied the most powerful sanction for good conduct. God governed the cosmos "by proportioning Rewards to Piety and Virtue, and Punishment to Disobedience and Vice." Because virtue was not always rewarded in this world and vice was not always punished, God prepared "the Joys of heaven" and "the Horrors of Hell" to perfect "the moral Government of the Universe."[198]

Philosophy of Government

His belief that "the divine science of politics is the science of social happiness" and that "the blessings of society depend entirely" on prudently devised constitutions led Adams to devote much time and energy to trying to construct the best form of government.[199] Because God created and ruled the universe, it had a fixed structure, a comprehensible order, immutable moral laws, and a purpose. If no divine designer and lawgiver existed, a capricious ideology or fanatical creed would dominate society, anarchy would prevail, and individuals would lose their fundamental rights. People must seek to discern the order and rationality of the universe, adjust their lives to it, and strive to devise institutions and laws to fulfill God's aims. God ordained the state and expected leaders to govern in accordance with His statutes and will and advance the welfare of their constituents.[200] These presuppositions shaped Adams's understanding of human nature, individual rights, the ends of government, and the responsibility of the president to be the custodian of liberty, justice, and the public interest.

Adams clearly believed that the United States was a Christian nation. The Federalist closed his inaugural address by contending that respect for Christianity provided an excellent basis for public service.[201] His two proclamations of days of humiliation, fasting, and prayer also reinforce this claim. The foundation "on which the fathers achieved independence," Adams told Jefferson in 1813, was "the general principles of Christianity," which "I then believed, and now believe." Adams wanted the government to be explicitly Christian (but non-sectarian), to promote religion and benevolence, and to practice evenhanded justice.[202] Why then did Adams sign a treaty with Tripoli in 1797 declaring that the United States "is not in any sense founded on the Christian Religion"? This treaty was negotiated because Barbary pirates, sanctioned by Tripoli, were seizing American ships attempting to trade in the Mediterranean and selling their crewmen into slavery. Negotiators probably adopted this wording to make it easier to reach a commercial agreement with Tripoli. The fact that the treaty was passed unanimously by the Senate and aroused no public opposition indicates that neither Adams, any other founder, or ordinary devout citizens believed that the treaty meant that Christian principles had not strongly influenced the early settlement, state governments, or public life of America. Rather, the treaty simply testified that unlike European powers, with which Muslim nations had often fought, the United States had no national established church or desire to wage holy war against Tripoli or other Muslim nations in northern Africa. Taken more inclusively, the statement conflicts with state constitutions, American practices, and the way countless politicians, historians, ministers, educators, and authors have viewed the United States during its first century of existence.[203]

Adams argued that belief in a "wise, almighty sovereign of the universe" was "the great essential principle of all morality" and the basis for civilization.[204] "Right and wrong in the universe," he alleged, depended on the supposition of "an intellectual and moral governor."[205] Moral laws are as inviolable as natural ones, and they must be heeded.[206] Without a divine arbiter and judge, Adams reasoned, people had only their own whims, desires, and subjective opinions to direct them. Moreover, he cautioned, disavowing the Creator undermined human dignity. If those who believed that people are not fashioned by God, but are mere "fireflies," gained control of governments, he warned, humans would no longer be "an object of respect."[207]

Only those who understood human motivation and behavior, Adams argued, could devise a good government. Therefore, he studied human passions to determine which ones were most relevant to devising constitutions and delineating governmental powers.[208] God created individuals, Adams averred, as rational beings and free moral agents.[209] Ellis Sandoz contends that Adams's insistence that government be based on a "true map of man" is "the great secret" that "lies at the heart of the Constitution of the United States and its elaborate institutional arrangements."[210]

Adams rejected the Calvinist dogma that individuals are "totally depraved." "The most abandoned scoundrel," he asserted, still had pangs of conscience.[211] Nevertheless, Adams argued that all people were weak and prone to fits of passion and irrational prejudice.[212] Three times he quoted Jeremiah 17:9 to urge Americans to "look into their own hearts, which they will find to be deceitful above all things and desperately wicked."[213] Adams agreed with Greek historian Thucydides that "a thirst for power," rooted in "rapacious and ambitious passions," is the source of all evils and with Joseph Priestley that people's "love of domination, selfishness, and depravity" made it dangerous to elevate some individuals over others.[214] When he reflected on "the various passions and appetites to which" human nature "is subject," Adams declared, "I am ready to cry out with the Psalmist, Lord what is Man?"[215] "Avarice and ambition, servility and adulation, hopes, fears, jealousies, envy, revenge, malice, and cruelty," he proclaimed, "are continually buzzing in the world."[216] Influenced by both Puritans and radical Whigs, Adams often portrayed humans as being inescapably egotistical and predisposed to sin and constantly complained about people's greed, selfishness, and vanity. In 1779 he bemoaned, "I see so much corruption, wherever I cast my eyes. I see the virtuous few struggling against it, with so little success."[217] No one, Adams asserted, was entirely "free from weakness and imperfections in this life." The best and brightest were often "slaves to the Love of Fame." They frequently used "mean tricks and artifices" to enhance their reputation and were "envious, malicious, and revengeful."[218] "Whoever would found a state," Adams insisted, agreeing with Machiavelli, "must presume that all men are bad by nature: that they will not fail to show that natural depravity of heart whenever they have a fair opportunity."[219] Such statements challenge C. Bradley Thompson's arguments that Adams's understanding "of human nature was thoroughly secular" and consistent with the Enlightenment perspective of his era and that Adams rejected the Calvinist view that people were evil, "sinful, or even bad by nature."[220] Although Adams repudiated the doctrines of original sin and human depravity, he insisted that most people were both weak and wicked.[221]

Adams disagreed with Thomas Hobbes and John Locke that people's rational self-interest prompted them to respect the rights of others so that others would respect their rights. Most individuals, Adams countered, could not live by "the rules of reason" because they were "driven by much deeper passions."[222] People often failed to use God's gift of reason to control their appetites. Few individuals consistently consulted their reason and obeyed their consciences. Therefore, any theory of human nature that assumed people normally acted reasonably was not suitable for crafting a constitution.[223] In creating a government, Adams insisted, statesmen must remember that "although reason ought always to govern individuals," it had not done so "since the Fall, and never will till the Millennium." Human nature must be regarded "as it is, as it has been, and as it will be."[224] While some people unswervingly respected the rights of others, the vast majority did not.

Government, Adams avowed, must be based on a realistic appraisal of human nature. Because "the law of nature," the Decalogue, and civil laws could not alone control people's passions and appetites, constitutional architects and lawmakers must take advantage of people's "desire of reputation" to motivate them to be "good members of society."[225] The craving to be "esteemed, praised, beloved, and admired" by others, Adams contended, was one of people's "keenest dispositions."[226] The "passion for superiority," he claimed, predominates human nature "from cradle to grave" regardless of gender, age, race, or status.[227] The state must reinforce people's propensity to gain the "*esteem* and *admiration* of others" by acting virtuously and cooperating with others and their desire to avoid "*neglect* and *contempt*" that doing evil or being antisocial brings.[228] It must stimulate ordinary individuals to "emulation"—"the desire to shine in the eyes of one's fellows."[229] "Emulation next to self-preservation," Adams averred, "will forever be the great spring of human actions." Only "a well-ordered government" could stop "emulation from degenerating into dangerous ambition, irregular rivalries, destructive factions, wasting seditions, and bloody, civil wars."[230] Society, he added, should channel eminent people's desire to excel "toward socially useful ends."[231] Properly "gratified, encouraged, and arranged on the side of virtue," ambition could be used benefit society.[232]

To protect society against the selfish ambitions of individuals and groups, Adams asserted, competing forces and interests must be balanced and factions must be prevented from gaining too much power.[233] Therefore, governments required checks and balances to function properly. No group or class should be trusted to govern a republic.[234] A "well ordered, mixed, and counterpoised" government best ensured that people obeyed "the commandment, 'Thou shalt not steal.'"[235] Moreover, history clearly showed that separating the executive and legislative branches was necessary to protect individuals' rights and liberties.[236]

Because human "rights derived from the great Legislator of the Universe," they must not be "repealed or restrained by human Laws."[237] Everyone shared a common nature, Adams averred, and, therefore, should have "equal rights and equal duties." However, individuals were clearly not equal in talent, effort, or accomplishments and, consequently, some deserved greater rewards and status than others.[238]

As the only government official elected by all the people, Adams argued, the president alone could "act in the best interests of the entire nation rather than of a faction, section, or special interest."[239] Statesmen, he maintained, were "trustees for the people."[240] This conviction led him, as chief executive, to

strive to preserve his political independence and to arbitrate among competing groups as well as between the Senate and the House.[241] The weakest members of society needed "an independent mediator" to promote their welfare.[242]
Adams denounced the argument of the "rich and noble" that God inflicted
"poverty and misery" on individuals because of His "wrath and displeasure"
toward their actions as "shallow and execrable." The wealthy must reject this
contention and work alongside the poor "in the bands of mutual affection."[243]

Adams lamented that many tried to use politics to further their "own little
passions and mean private interests." Through politics these "baseborn sons of
fallen Adam" sought to obtain a fortune, "a gilded coach, a train of horses, and
a troop of livery servants, balls at Court, [and] splendid dinners and suppers."
Posterity would much more highly esteem the "independent statesman" who
revered nothing "but truth, virtue, and his country" "than those who worship
hounds and horses." Such a leader would advance the welfare of his nation
rather than trying to "make his own fortune."[244] He would violate his lifelong
standards for private and public conduct, Adams told Mercy Otis Warren, if
he ever permitted the "public authority entrusted to me" to be "subservient
to my private views, or those of my Family and Friends."[245] "I have invariably
acted according to my best judgment for the public good," Adams claimed in
1807; "never [have I] engaged in public affairs for my own interest, pleasure,
envy, jealousy, avarice, or ambition."[246] However, Adams's vanity, desire to be
venerated, jealousy of the accolades accorded to Washington, Franklin, and
other founders, and overreaction to some valid criticisms often kept him from
fulfilling this lofty aim.

Government, Adams argued, should further "the good of the whole community."[247] Its success depended on citizens' virtue and devotion to the common good. Public morality, in turn, rested upon private righteousness and
"pure Religion." He urged Americans "to sacrifice their private Pleasures,
Passions, and Interests" to promote the public welfare.[248] A republic could
succeed only if its citizens subordinated their desires, prejudices, and friendships to the public good and pursued justice, morality, and piety.[249] "Justice is
a great Christian, as well as [a] moral, duty and virtue," Adams averred, "which
the clergy ought to inculcate and explain."[250] Public virtue, he insisted, is even
more essential to a republic's success than good laws.[251]

Liberty, Adams repeatedly asserted, was a God-given right. God values
"liberty, peace, and good-will" and, therefore, "consenting to slavery" is as
offensive to Him "as it is derogatory" to human honor, interest, or happiness.
"Liberty must at all hazards be supported. We have a right to it, derived from
our Maker."[252] To preserve freedom, Adams declared, governments must take
into account both the dignity and flaws of human beings.[253]

Influenced by radical Whig ideology, Adams argued that religion, educa-tion, and government could restrain people's powerful passions and inspire citizens to perform their duties, act virtuously, and advance the common good.[254] He insisted that science, liberty, and religion were inseparably con-nected. Without their influence, "no society can be great, flourishing, or happy."[255] "Religion and virtue," avowed Adams, "are the only foundations, not only of republicanism and of all free government, but of social felicity" under all forms of government and types of society.[256] "Moral principles, sanctified and sanctioned by religion, are the only bond of union, the only ground of confidence of the people in one another, of the people in the government, and the government in the people."[257] Statesmen, Adams opined, "may plan and speculate for liberty," but "religion and morality alone" established "the prin-ciples upon which freedom can securely stand." If Americans did not act virtu-ously, Adams warned in 1776, "they may change their rulers and the forms of government, but they will not obtain a lasting liberty. They will only exchange tyrants and tyrannies."[258] The best possible system of government, Adams maintained, could not successfully overcome "human passions unbridled by morality and religion. Avarice, ambition, revenge, or gallantry, would break the strongest cords of our Constitution as a whale goes through a net. Our Constitution," he trumpeted, "was made only for a moral and religious people. It is wholly inadequate to the government of any other."[259]

The Election of 1800

The issues of religion and character played a prominent role in the pivotal and highly contentious election of 1800. Termed "tumultuous," "revolution-ary," and "a magnificent catastrophe" by historians, this election peacefully transferred power from the more elitist Federalist Party to the more populist Republican Party.[260] During a campaign filled with mudslinging, slander, and outrageous accusations, both Adams and Jefferson were repeatedly lambasted as morally profligate scoundrels whose election would endanger the fragile, fledgling republic. A frustrated Abigail Adams feared that this campaign would produce "abuse and scandal enough to ruin and corrupt the minds and morals of the best people in the world."[261] Many Federalists censured Jefferson as either an atheist or a Deist who lacked "conscience, religion, and charity."[262] A man who made no "*profession* of Christianity," a pamphle-teer charged, could only be "a decided . . . hardened infidel." This radical "arch priest of Jacobinism and infidelity" would destroy the nation by put-ting the interests of revolutionary France ahead of those of the United States.

France's civil chaos demonstrated the horrific consequences of rejecting Christianity. Under Jefferson's administration, "murder, robbery, rape, adultery, and incest" would "all be openly taught and practiced," the *Connecticut Courant* warned in the fall of 1800.[263] If Jefferson were elected, a "Christian Federalist" predicted, he and his Jacobin allies would repeal the laws that protected citizens from being murdered, women from being seduced, property from being plundered, and religion "from contempt and profanation." Summarizing the indictment of Jefferson by hundreds of New England ministers, a Connecticut Federalist asked, "Do you believe in the strangest of all paradoxes—that a spendthrift, a libertine, or an atheist is qualified to make your laws and govern you and your posterity?"[264] Led by Timothy Dwight, the president of Yale College and a Congregationalist pastor, many clergy urged Christians to impose their own religious test on the candidates and vote for Adams. New York minister William Linn argued that because of Jefferson's disbelief in "the Holy Scriptures" and "attempts to discredit them, he ought to be rejected for the Presidency."[265] Ministers recounted lurid stories of Jefferson holding bizarre worship services at Monticello during which he allegedly prayed to the Goddess of Reason and sacrificed dogs on an altar.[266] Abigail complained that Jefferson did not believe in "an all wise and supreme Governour of the World." She accused him of rejecting the essential tenets of Christianity and viewing religion as valuable only because of the political purposes it could serve.[267]

While Congregationalists, Episcopalians, and Presbyterians, who saw their religious tenets and practices as under assault by forces of Enlightenment Deism and secularism, on one side, and religious enthusiasm, on the other, tended to support Adams as the bulwark of conventional religion, tradition, and social and political order. Federalists heralded Adams's church attendance, invoking of God in public addresses, and declaration of days of fasting and prayer. Republicans, meanwhile, defended Jefferson's religious positions and highlighted his record of responsible citizenship and championing of religious freedom.[268] John Beckley composed and sent 4,000 copies of a pamphlet to voters in critical states titled *A Vindication of the Public Life and Character of Thomas Jefferson.* Republicans strove to win the votes of Baptists, Methodists, and members of various smaller denominations by "contrasting Jefferson's support for religious liberty in Virginia with Adams's deference to an established church in Massachusetts." They stressed that he believed in equal rights for Moravians, Mennonites, Dunkers, Catholics, and Jews. Jefferson was "a friend to real religion," one supporter argued, which permitted every person to worship God in accord with "the dictates of his conscience."[269] The leading Republican newspaper *Aurora* described voters' choice as between "an established church, a religious test [for public office], and an order of priesthood" under a Federalist administration or "religious liberty, the rights of conscience, no priesthood, truth, and Jefferson."[270]

Adams reportedly was disturbed by claims that Jefferson was irreligious. According to Fisher Ames, Adams protested that his rival was "a good patriot, citizen, and father," and he worried that Federalist attacks on Jefferson's religion were backfiring.[271] In mid-September Adams complained privately that overzealous Federalist attacks on Jefferson's faith had aided his rival's campaign.[272] However, Adams did not try to stop the Federalist press's attack on Jefferson's alleged atheism. Privately Jefferson denounced the claims of his detractors as "absolute falsehoods," but he did not respond publicly to their charges for fear that it would call more attention to their "lying pamphlets," thereby making matters worse.[273]

Adams was accused of being inept, a monarchist, and a warmonger. Alexander Hamilton urged fellow Federalists to vote for Charles Pinckney rather than Adams (Pinckney was technically the Federalist vice presidential candidate, but members of the Electoral College could vote for either or both candidates as president) because his many blunders and outbursts as president revealed "great and intrinsic defects in his character" including his "disgusting egotism," "distempered jealousy," and "horrible temper."[274] Colorful rumors circulated that Adams had schemed to marry one of his sons to a daughter of British King George III to create an American dynasty and that he had sent a navy vessel to England to bring him four mistresses.[275]

Federalist denunciations of Jefferson's religious views were ironic because little difference existed between the theological perspectives of the candidates. Both were Unitarians who held similar positions on the nature of God, Scripture, prayer, providence, human nature, and morality, as previously explained. However, Adams attended church more regularly than Jefferson and kept his heterodox views more hidden from the public.

In the final analysis, Republicans' portrayal of themselves as the defenders of national independence, individual liberty, and ordinary citizens, which Adams and his party had betrayed by favoring the social and financial elite, ratifying John Jay's unpopular, seemingly one-sided treaty with Britain, maintaining a standing army, and passing the repressive Alien and Sedition Act, helped Jefferson win a close election (the electoral vote tally was 73 to 65). Their message of small government, low taxes, reliance on state militias, and repeal of the widely despised act resonated with many voters.[276]

Church and State

As noted, Adams considered the United States to be a Christian nation. In "A Declaration of the Rights of the Inhabitants of the Commonwealth of Massachusetts" (1779), he argued that because good morals were necessary to preserve civil society and because belief in God's "providential government of the world" and "a future state of rewards and punishment" were "the only true foundation of morality," the state should financially support "public worship of God" and "teachers of religion and morals" and encourage citizens to regularly attend church. This document, which provided the basis for the 1780 Massachusetts constitution, sought to create a distinctly Christian state by mandating that the governor and all others serving in the state government be Christians. While making the Congregational Church the state's established religion, the constitution allowed members of other denominations to use their tax dollars to support their own pastors, an arrangement Adams termed "a most mild and equitable establishment of religion." However, this liberty of conscience extended only to those who worshipped God.[277] In drafting this constitution, John Witte, Jr. contends, Adams sought to balance the religious freedom of individuals with "a Publick Religion" that was essential to preserving moral order and social stability.[278]

Moreover, Adams frequently expressed his hope that "true religion" would "flourish forever" in America.[279] As discussed, functioning as national high priest, he used explicitly Christian language in proclaiming two national days of prayer. The General Assembly of the Presbyterian Church had urged Adams in 1798 to call a national fast because its leaders feared that domestic and foreign developments threatened to undermine American religion and morality.[280] Adams's proclamations, while not repeating their rhetoric, reiterated their concerns and ominous assessment of the situation.

Adams contended that his decision to issue these proclamations contributed to his losing the election of 1800. "A general suspicion prevailed," Adams explained in 1812, that the Presbyterian Church wanted to be established as a national church. "I was [falsely] represented as a Presbyterian" who headed "this political and ecclesiastical project. The secret whisper ran through all the sects, 'Let us have Jefferson, Madison, Burr, anybody, whether they be philosophers, Deists, or even atheists, rather than a Presbyterian President.'"[281] Responding to criticisms of his action, Adams wrote, "When most, if not all of the religious sects in the nation, hold such fasts among themselves, I never could see the force of the objections against making them, on great and extraordinary occasions, national." The only possible valid objection was the fear of individual states that the federal government might become too powerful.[282]

Character

Character was extremely important to Adams, and he strove to be upright in both his private and public actions. Like his Puritan forebears, he insisted that all sins were significant and offended God.[283] "I have no Confidence in any Man," Adams declared, "who is not exact in his Morals."[284] The most important theme in Adams's diary, C. Bradley Thompson argues, is self-mastery. For the sage, it was "the indispensable foundation for a worthy life and the end to which virtues like moderation, frugality, and industry" must be directed.[285] Because piety and virtue were imperative to maintaining liberty, Adams avowed, government should exhort citizens to "lead sober, religious and peaceable Lives" and to avoid blasphemy, "Contempt of the holy Scriptures and of the Lords Day," and immoral acts.[286] Mercy Otis Warren praised Adams's "unimpeachable character." His "morality, decency and religion," she insisted, provided a positive example for the younger generation.[287]

Adams was deeply concerned about achievement, reputation, and fame, but he did not seek them as ends in themselves; he believed that their pursuit must promote magnanimous goals. Although love of fame motivated him, Adams refused to contravene his rigid code of conduct to attain popularity in the present or praise after his death. The sage strove to act in ways he deemed "right and just, regardless of reward or punishment." From his legal defense of British Captain Thomas Preston against the charge that he was responsible for the Boston Massacre in 1770 to his effort to preserve peace with France as president, Adams sought to stand above his cause or party; his "code of honor" did not permit him to place personal gain above principles or the long-term interests of his nation.[288] "I have never sacrificed my judgment to kings, ministers, nor people," Adams claimed in 1790, "and I never will."[289]

Despite his strenuous effort to act virtuously, Adams, like all politicians, had many detractors, most notably Alexander Hamilton, who repeatedly denounced his fellow Federalist as "perverse," "capricious," and "vain." During the 1800 campaign, his opponents censured Adams as a monarchist and an aristocrat who had little respect for the Constitution.[290] Adams refused Rush's request in 1811 to write an exhortatory address to the American people, claiming that his enemies "will charge me with selfishness and hypocrisy" and seeking "to make my son a king." While everything Washington and Franklin did "was imputed to pure, disinterested patriotism," Adams protested, everything he did "was ascribed to sinister motives." He disputed Rush's opinion that "friends and enemies agree in believing me to be an honest man." Judging by the newspapers and pamphlets of the last twenty years, Adams argued, both the Federalists and Republicans considered "me the meanest villain in the world." At least he had not been accused of sexual immorality. "Among all the errors, follies, failings, vices, and crimes, which have been so plentifully imputed to me, I cannot recollect a single insinuation against me of any amorous intrigue, or irregular or immoral connection with [a] woman, single or married."[291]

Adams struggled his entire life with vanity and pride, and his belief in his own superiority diminished his effectiveness as president. As a young man, he sought to "achieve humility in both social behavior and in his heart of hearts." Adams strove to drive out of his mind "every mean and base affection," conquer his "natural Pride and Self Conceit," and "acquire that meekness, and humility, which are sure marks" of "a great and generous Soul."[292] "Vanity," he confessed, "is my cardinal Vice and cardinal Folly."[293] While his Puritan ancestors used their diaries for daily self-examination to soften their hearts and prepare them for salvation, Adams used his to break down his pride and equip him to attain his worldly destiny.[294] While this quest, coupled with his great intellectual gifts and prestigious work ethic, helped propel Adams to phenomenal achievements and fame, he never conquered his pride. His desire to be celebrated by future generations was too powerful. Highly introspective, Adams repeatedly professed that he had no interest in his reputation as he unsuccessfully sought to "exorcise the Devil's agent, vanity."[295] His narcissism, keen mind, and argumentative nature prompted him as president often to work alone and rarely to involve others in decision-making.[296] Adam's moodiness, obstinacy, and difficulty compromising also reduced his effectiveness. "Thanks to God," Adams declared, "that he gave me stubborness [*sic*] when I know I am right."[297] A statesman must risk the people's "Displeasure sometimes," the sage added, "or he will never do them any good in the long run."[298]

Public Policy: Restoring Peace with France

As Adams began his presidency, Americans were divided over many issues and in the midst of an economic depression. They disagreed over the provisions of the 1796 Jay Treaty with England and whether to ally themselves with England, France, or neither nation. Many of those living west of the Appalachian Mountains felt little loyalty to the national government.

Meanwhile, the American army and navy were too small to protect either its citizens or commerce against foreign encroachment.[299] Threat of war with France loomed for almost Adams's entire presidency. His four years in office, argue Stanley Elkins and Eric McKitrick, involved "to a degree unequaled in any other presidency," "a single problem, a crisis in foreign relations." Adams risked his political career to oppose prolonging an undeclared war with France and considered restoring peace with France his greatest achievement. He told a friend, "I desire no other inscription over my gravestone than: 'Here lies John Adams, who took upon himself the responsibility of the peace with France in the year 1800.' "[300] While Adams pursued actions that he deemed effective to preserve America's reputation, interests, and tranquility, he insisted that only "the Supreme Disposer of Events" could bring justice, equity, benevolent relationships, and peace among the world's nations.[301] During the controversy, Adams urged Americans to pray for peace, sought to protect America's moral and religious principles, and insisted that true peace rested upon transcendent moral norms. God, he maintained, was the ultimate source of justice, order, liberty, and peace.[302]

French leaders denounced the Jay Treaty as "a virtual declaration of war" because it accorded trade privileges to their enemies, the British. They were further upset when Americans decided to stop repaying French loans that had helped win their independence from Britain (Americans argued these loans were owed to the French crown, not to the Republic). The French retaliated by seizing the cargoes of American ships and selling them in France. Between July 1796 and June 1797 the French commandeered 316 American merchant ships, greatly reducing American products reaching Britain. French leaders also hoped this would help Republicans, who were much more favorable toward their nation, gain control of Congress in 1798. In addition, they refused to receive the new US minister Charles Cotesworth Pinckney in December 1796.

Adams's primary options in 1797 were to send an emissary to negotiate, stop all trade with France, arm American merchant ships, "license privateers to prey on French shipping," prepare for war, or declare war against France. Adams chose to send a commission to France to testify to his peaceful intentions and give the United States time to strengthen its military. He hoped that the commissioners could negotiate a treaty to give the French the same trading rights the British enjoyed. However, if they were rebuffed instead, it would help justify a decision to go to war.[303]

"Peace and harmony with all nations," Adams proclaimed in a May 1797 message to Congress, "is our sincere wish." However, his Puritan-influenced view of human nature as well as the record of history led him to conclude that "effectual measures of defense" were needed to provide that "national self-respect and confidence at *home* which is the unfailing source of respectability *abroad*, to check aggression and prevent war."[304] While hoping that the United States could negotiate a treaty that was compatible with its "safety, honor and interest[s]," nothing would contribute more to peace and justice, Adams reasoned, than a wise use of "those resources for national defense which a beneficent Providence has kindly" given the nation.[305] By continuing Washington's "prudent measures," Adams strove to preserve an "impartial neutrality with the belligerent powers of Europe." However, like his predecessor, he insisted that neutrality must not "be purchased with bribes, by the sacrifice of our sovereignty and the abandonment of our independence, by the surrender of our moral character, [or] by tarnishing our honor."[306] At stake in the conflict were the commercial rights of neutral nations during war. "If the principle of *free ships, free goods*," were truly "established and honestly observed," Adams wrote, it would end "all maritime war, and render all military navies useless." Although Christianity desired it, philosophy approved it, and it would benefit humanity, Adams was convinced that neither the British nor the French would respect this principle.[307] American commerce, which was essential to national "growth, prosperity, and happiness," would "be plundered" without naval protection.[308]

In 1797 Adams sent Pinckney, John Marshall, and Elbridge Gerry to Paris to negotiate a settlement with France. However, three French agents, referred to in the delegates' reports simply as X, Y, and Z, told them that before formal negotiations with Foreign Minister Charles Maurice de Talleyrand could begin, they must pay a sizable bribe, the United States must loan France money to fight Britain, and Adams must apologize for his anti-French statements. The delegates refused to comply with these terms. After Adams disclosed the XYZ Affair in mid-1798, protests against France erupted throughout the United States. In July Congress annulled all treaties with France and instructed the navy to destroy French warships and privateers that were interfering with American commerce. The United States had treated France with civility and friendship, Adams alleged, but the French had refused to receive its ambassadors and acted belligerently in Europe. In September Adams complained that French rulers had responded contemptuously to his patient efforts to resolve disputed issues.[309]

Adams argued that America's policy toward both France and England was based on pure motives and "Christian faith."[310] His attempt to avoid both military conflict with France and an alliance with Great Britain put him at odds with Republicans who "feared England and were uncritical of France" and with the majority of Federalists, including members of his cabinet and the party's most influential leaders, who favored Britain and detested France.[311] Effective preparation for war, Adams insisted, could "alone ensure peace." The United States, he maintained in December 1798, had "uniformly and perseveringly cultivated" peace.[312] Arch Federalists protested that the president was "soft on France" and "willing to make peace at the cost of honor." Adams sought to steer a middle course between staunch Federalists, including Alexander Hamilton and his Secretary of State Timothy Pickering who wanted to declare war against France, and Jefferson and Madison who called for accepting France's good intentions unquestioningly. Adams's resolve was continually tested by his suspicion that French leaders were offering "peace feelers only to further divide American sentiment" and make it difficult for his administration to take a firm position.[313]

Adams argued that he relied on God, the support of Congress, and "the virtue and patriotism of my fellow-citizens" to maintain a "just and impartial" policy toward other nations, preserve peace, safeguard the United States, and implement its fundamental principles.[314] In dealing with France, Adams declared that he trusted God for "protection and success."[315] During the crisis, Adams proclaimed two national days of humiliation, fasting, and prayer to exhort Americans to seek God's pardon for their sins, ask for His protection, and pray for peace. "The safety and prosperity of nations ultimately and essentially depend on the protection and blessing of Almighty God," Adams asserted in 1798. Recognizing "the just judgments of God against prevalent iniquity," people always had a duty to repent and reform their ways, but especially "in seasons of difficulty or of danger." "The unfriendly disposition, conduct, and demands of a foreign power," he insisted, had placed the United States "in a hazardous and afflictive situation." France had repeatedly refused to receive America's "messengers of reconciliation and peace," interfered with its commerce, and inflicted injuries on its merchants.[316] In his 1799 proclamation, Adams denounced France's "hostile designs and insidious acts" and its "dissemination among them of those principles, subversive of the foundations of all religious, moral, and social obligations, that have produced incalculable mischief and misery in other countries." The "public religious solemnities" of repentance and prayer could help Americans "avert the evils" they should deprecate and motivate them to perform the duties God required.[317] Nothing was "more sublime and affecting," Adams later asserted, than all citizens "on their knees" before God "acknowledging their faults and imploring his blessing and protection" when confronted with "great danger and calamity."[318]

Adams feared that peaceful relations with France would be difficult to attain for a variety of reasons. First, in the French Revolution "one of the pillars of the ancient monarchy"—the army—had crushed "the other two, the nobility and the clergy." This subverted "all the political, religious, and social institutions, which time, experience, and freedom have sanctioned."

Second, the French had violated America's sovereign rights by refusing to receive its ambassadors, publicly heaped "indignity, insult, and contempt" on the United States, and interfered with its commerce based on their faulty and "contemptuous opinion that we are a divided, defenceless, and mercenary people."[319] Although Christianity taught "as much as possible, to live peaceably with all men," Adams argued, it was "impossible to be at peace with *injustice* and *cruelty*, with *fraud* and *violence*, with *despotism, anarchy*, and *impiety*." War was "infinitely preferable" to a peace based on paying tribute.[320]

Third, Adams deplored the crusade to deChristianize France. Ending the harm Christianity had caused and ensuring the rights of conscience would greatly benefit France. However, he contended, this would not be accomplished by replacing Christianity with Greek mythology, worshipping modern heroes, or glorifying reason, virtue, or beauty. "All the abuses of Christianity, even in the darkest ages," when the pope dominated nations had not been "so bloody and cruel," destroyed the "independence of the human mind" by the use of "such terror and intolerance, or taught doctrines which required such implicit credulity to believe, as the present reign of pretended philosophy in France" was doing.[321]

Fourth, Adams insisted that France's governmental structure and political situation were very perilous. Napoleon's power was rapidly increasing, and some predicted that the monarchy would be reestablished. France sought to dominate Europe, and if France became "the model and arbiter of nations, the liberties of the world will be in danger."[322] In addition, France was suffering from its current administration's pomp, "profusion of expense," and "proud usurpation," and inequality and "prostitution of morals" were worse now than under the old monarchy.[323]

Fifth, its "sense of moral and religious obligations" had been so weakened, its "public faith and national honor" had "been so impaired," and its respect for treaties had "been so diminished" that "the law of nations" had lost "much of its force" in France. Despite these problems, Adams promised he would treat France with "candor," "integrity," and a "friendly disposition." The French might act vengefully, Adams declared, but he would not.[324]

The pressures on Adams were so powerful in 1799 that many, including French leaders, expected him to ask Congress to declare war. However, his sense of justice, conception of the national interest, and abhorrence of war, all rooted in his understanding of Scripture, led Adams instead to send another envoy to Paris.[325] Several factors prompted him to redouble his efforts to attain peace. Public support for war was diminishing because of the increased taxes enlarging the army and the navy required, and the threat of disunion was growing. Meanwhile, Republicans denounced the 1798 Alien and Sedition Acts, which raised the residency requirement for US citizenship from five to fourteen years, empowered the president to incarcerate or expel aliens considered "dangerous to the peace and safety of the United States," and restricted speech that criticized government actions as "a Federalist plot to establish despotic rule."[326] These acts were the most criticized aspect of Adams's presidency. His strong rebuttals of pro-French critics, whom he intimated were almost traitors, helped create "the climate of opinion" that enabled these acts to be passed.[327] Although Adams was not involved in devising this legislation, he "willingly signed the Sedition Act and eagerly urged its enforcement."[328]

Many Federalists complained in early 1799 that Adams's French policy was politically unpopular and would prevent his reelection. Maintaining the threat of war "with its attendant jingoism" or waging war against France, by contrast, would ensure Federalist victory in 1800.[329] In American history "a party never turned on its own president as virulently as the High Federalists" attacked Adams. They pleaded with him to change his position, demeaned his character, and castigated him in editorials. Adams even faced anonymous threats of assassination.[330]

Although he recognized that it would further irritate powerful members of his cabinet and leaders of his party and might cost him the 1800 election, Adams sent Chief Justice Oliver Ellsworth and North Carolina Governor William Davie to France in November 1799 to pursue peace, clearly putting the welfare of the nation above partisan political interests.[331] In September 1800, the commissioners finally negotiated a treaty with the French government that ended the long-standing, undeclared naval war between the two nations. Ratified by Congress on February 3, 1801, the treaty declared their friendship and granted each other most favored nation trade status. Adams was convinced that his approach, grounded in biblical and moral principles, had triumphed.

Final Assessment

John Adams played a pivotal role in the founding of the United States, especially the campaign for independence, the devising of state constitutions, and the creation of America's diplomatic tradition. The Massachusetts Constitution of 1780, which he principally authored, was "the most important American source" for the federal Constitution. The only two men who could not be removed from America between 1774 and 1787 without fundamentally changing its history, Richard Ryerson argues, were George Washington and John Adams. "Their unique combination of character, personality, talent, and education" was "required to design, initiate, and sustain the American Revolution."[332] Adams, Paul Conklin argues, surpassed "all other architects of American independence" "in the scope of his contributions, in the length of service and personal sacrifice, and in the sophistication of his political advice."[333] "Adams played so many important roles at such critical points in the movement for independence and in the formation of the national polity," C. Bradley Thompson asserts, that studying his thought and deeds is crucial to understanding the founding.[334] Benjamin Rush claimed that "every member of Congress in 1776 acknowledged" Adams "to be the first man in the House." Jefferson simply called him "our colossus on the floor."[335] "Adams was ridiculously vain, absurdly jealous, [and] embarrassingly hungry for compliments," historian Edmund Morgan contended, "but no man ever served his country more selflessly."[336] He sacrificed a promising law practice, time with his family, and his physical health and put his life at risk to travel 29,000 miles, crossing the Atlantic four times, and traversing France, Spain, England, and the Netherlands to aid his country.[337] Although not as cosmopolitan or clever as Jefferson and Franklin, Adams was "better informed, more critical and logical in his thinking, and more gifted in argument." No other American public figure of his generation "read so much, absorbed so much knowledge, or displayed so much erudition."[338]

"In many respects Adams was a fitting successor to George Washington" because his policies helped preserve America's neutrality.[339] Facing threats of war against France and England and civil strife at home, Adams maintained America's independence, improved the navy, negotiated a treaty with France, and worked to end political disputes. The nation was stronger and more prosperous in 1801 than it had been in 1797.[340] Like Washington, Adams emphasized the efficacy of education, the perils of wealth, the necessity of private and public virtue to America's success, and, in his later years, the importance of religious liberty and toleration.[341] Despite major divisions in his own party, "disloyalty and intrigue within his cabinet," and the obstructionism and attacks of his political opponents, Adams attained his principal goals.[342] As he left office in 1801, the sage rejoiced that the nation had "fair prospects of a peace" with all nations, flourishing commerce, and "uncommonly productive" agriculture.[343]

Today when many politicians seem to be guided primarily by opinion polls and concerns about reelection, Adams's approach to political leadership is refreshing. He urged citizens to choose leaders based on their character, education, experience, and principles. Statesmen, Adams argued, should carefully study issues and situations, make judicious decisions, and convince their constituents of the merit of their positions. The president pursued "a lonely and difficult search" to determine the most prudent policies and courses of action. He always sought to do what he deemed best regardless of the public response.[344] Conklin contends that Adams's honesty and openness and refusal to manipulate or deceive people limited his success as a politician.[345]

On July 4, 1826, two of the brightest stars in the American pantheon—John Adams and Thomas Jefferson—were extinguished. Renowned mathematician Nathaniel Bowditch calculated that the chance that two of its original signers would die on the 50th anniversary of the Declaration of Independence as "one in twelve hundred millions." While Americans were stunned at this coincidence, many also saw it as providential. Diplomat Richard Rush pictured Adams and Jefferson as "hand in hand ascending to heaven."[346] Given his friendship with Jefferson, their lively discussion of religious topics, and Adams's desire to spend eternity with companions and savants, he probably would have appreciated this portrait. Although his religious convictions became more liberal in his later years, the central ones remained remarkably consistent. Adams's faith played a vital role in his long and distinguished life. It significantly affected his worldview, determined his moral standards, helped shape his character, and supplied many of his goals. His belief that God governed the world and directed the course of nations and the lives of individuals gave the church-going sage the courage and confidence to fight passionately and effectively for the causes he valued and to contribute so significantly to the birth and success of the United States. John Adams died assured that "he had labored faithfully in the Master's vineyard."[347]

2

James Madison

CHAMPION OF RELIGIOUS LIBERTY

*God is "the Just and All-powerful Being who holds in His
hand the chain of events and the destiny of nations."*
"FOURTH ANNUAL MESSAGE," November 4, 1812

*If the public homage of a people can ever be worthy [of] the
favorable regard of the Holy and Omniscient Being to whom
it is addressed, it must be that in which those who join in it
are guided only by their free choice, by the impulse of their
hearts and the dictates of their consciences; and such a spectacle must be interesting to all Christian nations as proving
that religion, that gift of Heaven for the good of man . . . can
spread its benign influence everywhere.*
"Proclamation—Recommending a Day of Prayer," July 23, 1813

Introduction

Although James Madison does not appear on Mount Rushmore or have a
memorial in Washington, DC, he played a pivotal role in devising the United
States. Like John Adams, Madison made monumental contributions to the
early American republic, especially in framing the Constitution and promoting
religious liberty. One of the nation's most cerebral and celebrated founders, he
served in the Virginia legislature after the United States declared independence,
the Virginia House of Delegates, the Virginia Privy Council, the Continental
Congress, and the House of Representatives.[1] Madison penned the extremely
influential *Memorial and Remonstrance against Religious Assessments* in 1785 to
argue for ending Virginia's Episcopal establishment and providing complete
religious freedom. Historians label the *Memorial and Remonstrance* "the most
powerful defense of religious liberty ever written in America" and a manifesto

worthy of John Milton, Thomas Jefferson, or John Stuart Mill. "Religious liberty," biographer Ralph Ketcham argued, was the "one subject upon which Madison took an extreme, absolute, undeviating position throughout his life."[2] No other founder had as great an impact on the nation's conception and practice of freedom of conscience, religious liberty, and the separation of church and state. Madison urged the United States to revise the Articles of Confederation, was a Virginia delegate to the Constitutional Convention, and led the effort to create a new constitution and to procure its ratification by coauthoring the *Federalist Papers* with Alexander Hamilton and John Jay. His contributions are so significant that Madison is often called "the father of the U.S. Constitution." After serving eight years as Thomas Jefferson's secretary of state, he followed his fellow Virginian as a two-term president and directed the nation's war against Great Britain and westward expansion. After leaving the presidency, Madison wrote essays to defend federalism and participated in the Virginia Constitutional Convention in 1829–30. As a scholar, political philosopher, and statesman, political scientist Garrett Ward Sheldon argues, Madison, more than any other founder, embodied "Plato's ideal of a 'philosopher king'" who identified the best foundational principles for government and strove to put them into practice.[3]

Like both John Adams and John Quincy Adams, Madison is remembered and revered more for his ideological and other political contributions to the United States than for his presidency. Madison is typically rated an average performer in the office. Numerous biographers and editors of collections of Madison's writings devote little space to his presidency.[4] The same question can be asked about both Madison and John Adams: why did men who were such brilliant constitutionalists and shrewd politicians have such mediocre presidencies? After analyzing three explanations for Madison's lackluster presidency—the circumstances he confronted, his temperament, and errors he made as chief executive—Garry Wills concludes that Madison's life experience, personality, and character flaws were the most important reason. Unlike his three predecessors, he did not serve as a commander-in-chief, an ambassador, or a governor before becoming president. Neither charismatic nor assertive, he worked best behind the scenes or in secret. "By temperament and talent he was better equipped to be a legislator than an executive."[5]

Like John Adams, as a young man Madison briefly considered becoming a minister. Both of them also read widely in theology and philosophy. However, while Adams wrote extensively and revealingly about his religious convictions in private letters, Madison, like George Washington, divulged very little about what he believed. Apparently considering his relationship with God to be a very private matter, Madison disclosed little about his personal religious convictions after his mid-twenties.[6] Because Madison's statements about his personal faith are few, veiled, and seemed to have changed over time, it is very difficult to pigeonhole him. Madison's mature religious views, Lance Banning contends, "are a matter for conjecture"; his doctrinal beliefs are "an enduring scholarly enigma." Throughout his life, the Virginian usually worshipped in Episcopal churches and his funeral service followed the Episcopal Book of Common Prayer, but he never joined an Episcopal congregation or even identified himself as an Episcopalian. He may never have called himself an Episcopalian because of his Presbyterian education at Princeton or because of his efforts to promote religious liberty and objections to established churches.[7] In response to a rumor that he had become a *"methodist,"* Edmund Randolph wrote to Madison, it will be difficult to convince your friends "that you have fastened Yourself to any sect."[8] Madison's much greater interest in metaphysical and philosophical questions than in creeds and dogma, Irving Brant argued, also influenced his decision not to join a church.[9]

Library of Congress historian James Hutson insists that the writings of the mature Madison provide "no clue as to his personal religious convictions." After 1773 he did not mention either Jesus or any issues that concerned "a practicing Christian." Following his presidency, Madison made "a few enigmatic references to religion." Consequently, scholars peer "into a void" when trying to determine his "personal religious belief." Nevertheless, because Madison played such a significant role in the controversies of the founding era over the relationship between religion and government, scholars have labored ardently to try to discern his personal religious convictions. Because of the paucity of evidence, Madison's religious perspective has been labeled a variety of ways. However, like John Adams, his views seem to fit most closely with those of early nineteenth-century Unitarianism.

The Debate over Madison's Religious Convictions

James Madison was born in 1751 to James and Nelly Conway Madison. The oldest of twelve children, he grew up on a large plantation in central Virginia that depended on slave labor. His wealthy, prestigious father was an Anglican vestryman whose library primarily contained religious books. Madison's mother was a pious Anglican, a bulwark of her congregation and one of its "few faithful witnesses" when the parish "was downtrodden and depressed."[10] James was baptized in an Anglican church as an infant. His devout paternal grandmother, Frances Taylor Madison, provided most of his primary education. From age 12 to 16, Madison was educated at a boarding school operated by Scottish immi-grant minister Donald Robertson. A graduate of the universities of Aberdeen and Edinburgh, Robertson tutored Madison in Latin, Greek, French, English literature, mathematics, geography, and Reformed theology. Madison studied such works as Thomas à Kempis's *Imitation of Christ* and the Westminster Confession of Faith with Robertson, whom he later called "a man of extensive learning."[11] After Madison returned home, another Scottish-American pastor, Thomas Martin, a recent College of New Jersey (later Princeton) graduate, supervised his education.[12]

At age 18, after passing entrance exams in New Testament, Greek, English, and Latin, Madison matriculated at Princeton, probably because of Martin's enthusiastic recommendation and its president John Witherspoon's "reputa-tion as a friend of religious freedom." His parents may also have preferred an orthodox Christian college with strong moral standards over the more reli-giously skeptical and morally lax Anglican William and Mary.[13] Princeton's fac-ulty strove to teach all subjects from a Christian perspective, and Madison took several courses from Witherspoon, a prominent Calvinist theologian. Like his classmates, Madison was spiritually mentored by professors, met with other students and faculty twice a day for prayer, studied the Bible in numerous classes, and was continually encouraged to cultivate a personal relationship with Jesus.[14] He may also have participated in the spiritual awakening that took place at Princeton while he was there.[15] At Princeton Madison took copi-ous notes on a popular biblical commentary, and he copied a debate between an atheist and theist in which the theist used the "Fabric of the Universe" to argue for God's existence.[16] He also helped create the American Whig Society to promote Scottish Presbyterian ideas.[17] After completing his requirements in two years (1769–71), Madison did an additional year of graduate work with Witherspoon in Hebrew, theology, and other subjects.[18] Madison continued to study theology during three years he spent at home after leaving Princeton. During part of this time at home, he led family devotions.[19] Madison had sev-eral close friends at Princeton who either became or considered becoming Presbyterian ministers, and he corresponded with them for many years.[20] He told one of them that "the specious Arguments of Infidels have established the faith of Enquiring Christians."[21]

Twenty years later, Madison, at age 43, married Dolley Todd, aged 26, in an Episcopal ceremony. Dolley had been raised as a Quaker in Philadelphia, and her first husband John Todd, who died in a yellow fever epidemic in 1793, was also a Quaker. Some strict Quakers had complained that the attractive Dolley liked "the gayeties of this world too much" and wore clothing that offended their moral sensibilities.[22] After her marriage to Madison, the Quaker meeting house "read her out" of their community. Dolley is much better known for her charisma, charm, parties, wardrobe, and saving Gilbert Stuart's painting of George Washington from the White House when the British invaded Washington, DC, during the War of 1812 than for her piety. The historical record provides few hints about her faith (except that she was confirmed as an Episcopalian, which Madison never was, but continued to effusively praise Quakerism) or how her religious convictions influenced her husband. Her principal biographer devotes only one paragraph to Dolley's religion, characterizing her as "a lifelong, albeit sporadic churchgoer" and reporting that substantive reflections on "God and religion play only a small part" in her extant letters.[23] Ironically, a woman reared in a Quaker culture that prized simplicity and modesty became the United States' most famous woman in the first half of the nineteenth century.[24]

Madison's reticence to discuss his religious convictions has led to very different conclusions about what he believed. Some Christians depict Madison as a devout evangelical, while more secular historians often label him a Deist. His principal early biographer, Democratic Senator William C. Rives, a pious Episcopalian, insisted that Madison accepted the major doctrines of Christianity. Rives concluded that notes Madison copied from Scripture and biblical commentaries as a young man testify to his "orthodoxy." Moreover, Rives argued, Madison carefully researched the history "and evidences of Christianity" by analyzing the work of leading proponents and opponents of the faith from the church fathers and schoolmen to "the infidel philosophers of the eighteenth century." Few theologians engaged in "more laborious and extensive inquiries to arrive at the truth" than Madison did. Madison's extensive knowledge of theology, Rives asserted, prompted Jefferson to ask him to compile a list of ancient and modern theological works for the library at his new University of Virginia.[25]

More recently, others have also portrayed Madison as an orthodox Christian whose perspective on life and politics was strongly shaped by biblical presuppositions. Labeling Madison "a lay theologian," historian James Smylie maintains that like Witherspoon, he espoused a Christian worldview and crafted a political system that recognized people's evil tendencies without excusing their actions. Philosopher Michael Novak contends that Madison's understanding of life is "unintelligible" without his Christian faith. Garrett Ward Sheldon avers that Madison "operated from a Christian perspective." "Madison's presidency, church-state views, and public philosophy," Sheldon adds, "cannot be understood apart from his religious training and tenets, because his politics are premised in his theology." Witherspoon, who synthesized the three dominant ideologies of revolutionary America—"Lockean

liberalism, classical Republicanism, and Christian theology"—strongly influenced Madison.[26] Madison's long service to his nation, Sheldon asserts, rested
upon "his firm Christian faith and principles," especially his beliefs that God
was sovereign and directed all events, that people were innately sinful and
needed to be redeemed through Jesus Christ, and that human selfishness
and hubris required a "system of checks and balances to prevent tyranny and
oppression." Madison's vacillation "between Lockean and classical philosophical perspectives" was generally "guided by the Christian realist view" that sinful "people are prone to pride" and use political power selfishly. Madison's
political writings, Sheldon claims, are replete with direct references and allusions to his religious instruction and biblical principles. Madison crafted
"carefully reasoned, tightly constructed arguments," and he saw faith and reason as working together to promote God's glory.[27]

Sheldon also maintains that Madison's character and demeanor, especially
his conviction that secular occupations were divine "callings" (he saw his governmental service as a Christian vocation), his faithful performance of all tasks,
and his "personal humility, kindness, and self-control that reflected the fruit
of the Spirit" all testified to his Christian convictions.[28] Moreover, Madison's
Memorial and Remonstrance draws upon "the truths of Scripture and the lessons of logic and church history." Similarly, his argument that religious liberty would enhance the purity of the Christian faith echoed the Westminster
Confession's declaration that "God alone is the Lord of the conscience and has
left it free from the doctrines and commandments of men." Sheldon claims
that Madison's interactions "with family, friends communications, and his
constituents during his presidency also reveals his Christian sensibilities."
Although most of these were part of unrecorded conversations (or were deliberately destroyed, including most of his letters to his wife), Madison's surviving correspondence provides "a general sense" of his Christian worldview. In
addition, several of his Princeton classmates, most notably Presbyterian pastor George Luckey, and physician Benjamin Rush wrote to Madison as if he
shared their faith.[29]

Sheldon does admit that Madison displayed a stronger Christian commitment before age 25 and after leaving the presidency than during the intervening years when he never explicitly mentioned his personal beliefs. The
contentious debate about the proper place of religion in American society
during his years of public service may have led Madison to not disclose his
own religious convictions. The Virginian's contention that demonstrating
one's faith through deeds was more important that talking about it, Sheldon
suggests, helps explain why he was "publicly silent about his personal religious views" and "instead let his public policy initiatives" speak for him as

he fought to ensure the separation of church and state and enable members of all denominations to practice their faith freely.[30] His actions showed that Christian presuppositions guided his work as a public servant. Sheldon maintains that most contemporary scholars have either ignored the "important religious dimension of his presidency and political thought" or projected their own religious skepticism on to Madison and other founders.[31]

Mary-Elaine Swanson agrees that Madison's education led him to adopt a Reformed view of humanity and politics.[32] The notes he took in his logic course with Witherspoon showed that Madison was "a devout Christian."[33] She claims that Witherspoon strongly influenced Madison's view that people were "prone to do evil," that man's fallen nature required a civil government of checks and balances, and that people owed allegiance to the sovereign Lord of the universe. Swanson also argues that Madison held the same religious conviction as his closest friends at Princeton, including future Pennsylvania politician William Bradford, future ministers John Blair Smith and Caleb Wallace, and Madison's tutor Samuel Stanhope Smith, Witherspoon's successor as president.[34]

Similarly, John Noonan, a Catholic jurist, calls Madison "a pious Christian" and a "true follower" of Jesus. He was raised in a Christian home, baptized as an infant, educated by ministers, graduated from a Presbyterian college, studied with one of the nation's leading moral philosophers, and seriously pondered the truths of sacred Scripture. Madison spoke, Noonan avows, "as a believer in Christianity's special light" who hoped for "the evangelization of the world."[35] In his *Memorial and Remonstrance*, the Virginian refers to Christianity as a "precious gift" and a "light," echoing the metaphor John 1 employs about Jesus. The convictions Madison "expressed as a young man are muted but perceptible" in his reflections as an ex-president, especially in his letters and unpublished Detached Memoranda. Madison called the separation of church and state divinely ordained and a just and "truly Xn principle." The argument that Madison's religion was simply a matter of political pretense, "because he did not publicly display his piety," ignores his modesty.[36]

Other scholars object to characterizing Madison as a devout Christian. The case for doing so is largely inferential. It ascribes ideas and phrases to Madison that he did not use and reads Christian assumptions into his writings. The argument also attributes too much significance to the observations he made about passages he copied from John's Gospel and the Book of Acts and from William Burkitt's *Expository Notes* on the New Testament. Madison's focus was academic and moral, not theological or devotional, and he often simply presented competing positions on theological disputes without giving his personal views about them.[37] Moreover, the contention that Madison was an orthodox Christian makes the leap from Witherspoon's teaching of certain tenets—human depravity, salvation through Christ, providential history, and politics based on Christian principles—to Madison's believing these precepts, without convincingly showing that he actually did. For example, Sheldon asserts that Federalist 51 testifies to Madison's view that "sinful human nature" could be "redeemed through the saving grace of God." However, Scott Kester contends, nothing in this essay proves that Madison believed this.[38]

Taking a very different position, some have argued that Madison was either a Deist or a secularist rather than a Christian. Writing in the 1850s, Virginia Episcopal Bishop William Meade, who knew Madison personally, maintained that his religious commitment "seemed to be short-lived." Madison's interactions with political associates who espoused "infidel principles" led him to question religious orthodoxy. While he never expressed any public hostility to Christianity, Meade asserted, "his creed was not strictly regulated by the Bible."[39] In his influential biography, Irving Brant categorized Madison as a Deist. He contended that Madison rejected Witherspoon's "rigid orthodoxy and conservatism" and espoused "a quiet unorthodoxy differing more in manner than in matter from the housetop-shouted heretical deism of Jefferson." Madison's Deism was "the logical result of his own predilections and studies." In a conversation with Harvard professor George Ticknor in 1815, the president "distinctly intimated" that he accepted Unitarian doctrines. Historian Douglass Adair labeled Madison a Unitarian who repudiated "orthodox doctrines." Why "a man, who as a youth, had an ambition to preach religion and save souls, should in his later years, refuse to discuss" religion at all except in relation to public policy, Franklin Steiner asserted, "is an enigma." Many reasons could be given for why a man who had ceased to be religious refused to talk, but no plausible reasons existed for someone who was "convinced of the truth of Christianity" to do so. Historian Frank Lambert identifies Madison as a Deist and skeptic, while David Holmes contends that Madison's "religious associations and the comments of his contemporaries" indicate that he was a "moderate Deist." No definite evidence exists, political scientist Vincent Phillip Munoz avers, that Madison believed "in the precepts of Christianity." "More than any other major Founder," John West, Jr. asserts, Madison "was the forerunner of the modern secularist."[40]

Hutson contends that two pieces of evidence appear "to corroborate the claims of those who assume that the mature Madison either lost interest in religion" or became a Deist. First, unlike numerous other political luminaries, including John Adams, John Jay, John Dickinson, and many of his Princeton classmates and friends, Madison did not help finance the 1802 publication of a collection of Witherspoon's sermons. Madison may have refused to sponsor this work, Hutson hypothesizes, because of his disagreement with its theological positions. Second, in an 1824 letter to Jefferson, Madison protested that Presbyterian "Sectarian Seminaries" were "disseminating obsolete religious doctrines, by which he clearly meant Calvinism." Madison complained that creeds, "however absurd or contrary to" modern knowledge, were being propagated. He insisted that "religious truth must evolve to incorporate the discoveries of science and other branches of modern learning," a position most antebellum church leaders repudiated.[41]

Although Madison frequently used Christian vocabulary and arguments, historian Scott Kester maintains, "careful scrutiny of his correspondence" and public statements shows that Madison "rejected the Christian faith." Because of his background and education, Madison was strongly influenced by "a residual but powerful sense of Christianity" and was "haunted" by the Calvinist emphasis on human depravity. Ultimately, however, Madison accepted the Enlightenment convictions that human reason, not divine revelation, is the best source for attaining truth and solving humanity's problems, that human nature is malleable, not inherently corrupt, and that the world was increasingly improving as humans better understood its operation. Madison "was deeply influenced by both biblical teaching and Enlightenment thought, and he could speak both languages with some skill." Madison's lack of direct references to his personal faith in Christ in his correspondence, use of religious rhetoric in public statements that is absent in private letters, and belief that reason rather than revelation, tradition, or intuition was the primary source of truth indicate that he was an enlightened Deist not a Christian.[42]

Political scientist Gregg Frazer reaches a similar conclusion. Madison's religious beliefs, he argues, are "perhaps the most enigmatic" among the nation's principal founders, and the sources revealing Madison's personal views are very limited. However, the evidence indicates that he was a theistic rationalist whose worldview combined theism, rationalism, and natural religion, but gave precedence to rationalism when these three perspectives clashed. Madison "referred to God and nature more or less interchangeably."[43] He called religious and civil rights the "gift of nature" and "divine."[44] Unlike the orthodox theologians of his era, Madison insisted that there was a "road from nature up to nature's God" that did not require written revelation.[45]

Other scholars take a middle position. Joseph Loconte insists that Madison was neither a devout Christian nor "the Enlightenment skeptic of liberal imagination."[46] Biographer Ralph Ketcham argued that Madison "neither embraced fervently nor rejected utterly the Christian base of his education." He accepted many of its tenets, which helped shape his worldview. Madison was deeply attached to some "aspects of Christian belief and morality."[47] The

Virginian, Ketcham alleged, believed that the universe was orderly and benevolent, human nature was fragile, human understanding was limited, and the
world was sometimes "out of joint." Some scholars, despite no direct evidence,
wrongly assume that Madison shared Jefferson's skepticism and Deism.
However, while Jefferson blatantly rejected orthodox Christianity, Madison
was close-mouthed about his personal convictions. It is unwarranted, Ketcham
contended, to portray him "as a Voltairian skeptic" who hoped that ending
state sponsorship of religion would lead to its demise. Rather, Madison valued
religion because it promoted "the psychological health of human beings and
the moral order of society."[48]

Ketcham asserted that two sources especially informed Madison's
worldview—Enlightenment rationalism and Scottish "Common Sense" realism. Promoted by Witherspoon at Princeton, this latter perspective was in
some ways a reaction against rationalist theology, but in others it was a synthesis of Christianity and Enlightenment philosophy.[49] Witherspoon and Madison
had a very close relationship as professor/student at Princeton and as colleagues in the Confederation Congresses of 1781 and 1782, and the Calvinist
significantly influenced the statesman.[50]

Ketcham argued further that the writings of theologian Adam Clarke,
whom Witherspoon commended as a great champion of rational religion,
also strongly impacted Madison. He was especially impressed by Clarke's use
of facts and reason, rather than Scripture, to rebut atheists such as Thomas
Hobbes and Baruch Spinoza. Clarke argued that rational reflection and the
structure of the natural world, fortified by new scientific discoveries, including the laws of mechanics, the orderliness of the universe, and the circulation
of blood, proved the existence of God. That Madison still insisted in 1825 that
Clarke's argument was logically compelling, Ketcham contended, indicates
that, unlike John Adams, he read little philosophy and theology after entering public life. Madison displayed no awareness of David Hume's penetrating
assault on Clarke's type of rationalism or Immanuel Kant's argument that
God's existence could not be proven but must be assumed to bolster moral
conduct.[51]

The Faith of James Madison

Evaluating these conflicting views of Madison's faith requires examining
what he believed about key Christian doctrines and practices. Like Adams
and Jefferson, Madison had broad-ranging religious interests. While serving
as a member of the Virginia Assembly in 1778, he corresponded with his

Princeton classmate Samuel Stanhope Smith about predestination and free will. Although Madison's reply to Smith is lost, it appears from Smith's letters that the future president was very conversant with the major arguments in the dispute between Arminians and Calvinists, including the pertinent writings of Jonathan Edwards.[52] Years later in response to a request from Jefferson about which theological books should be placed in the library of the University of Virginia, Madison suggested several works of the church fathers books by scholastics Thomas Aquinas and Duns Scotus, Erasmus, Jesuit Robert Bellarmine, Jansenist Blaise Pascal, and Protestant theologians John Calvin and Samuel Clarke. While Madison's list is theologically eclectic, it included no Deists, skeptics, or infidels; all the works were written by Christians.[53]

Madison called Christianity "the best and purist religion" and referred to Christianity as a "precious gift."[54] He asserted that initially God had miraculously aided Christianity, and the miracles Jesus and His apostles performed helped to validate Christianity. However, God soon left Christianity "to its own evidence" to win converts.[55] Madison called theology "the most sublime of all Sciences."[56] On the other hand, Madison sometimes asserted that all religious systems are essentially equal. His statement that everyone worshipped "the God of all" implied that all religions revered the same God. Madison emphasized that as president, like Washington, he used "general terms" for God that included "all who believed in a supreme ruler of the Universe."[57]

Banning argues that Madison's *Memorial* was written from a distinctively Christian perspective. Madison maintained that the proposed bill to fund all "Teachers of the Christian Religion" in Virginia would adversely affect "the diffusion of the light of Christianity." The number of those who had embraced Christianity, he asserted, was much smaller than "the number still remaining under the dominion of false Religions." Moreover, Madison appeared to connect greater acceptance of Christianity with "the victorious progress of Truth."[58] While the use of these arguments "may have been a tactical consideration," Banning avows, "it was not a necessary tactic" in the debates in Virginia. Because Madison was neither a propagandist nor a dissembler, the *Memorial* demonstrates that as late as 1785 he still accepted the authority of biblical revelation.[59]

Madison contended that the idea of a self-existing, all-powerful being is more intellectually satisfying than that of the universe's random beginning. The mind found it much easier to assent to "the self-existence of an invisible cause possessing infinite power, wisdom & goodness, than to the self-existence of the universe, visibly destitute of those attributes, and which may be the effect of them."[60] However, no evidence exists that Madison ever cited the Bible as a basis for believing in God's existence or explaining His nature.[61]

Influenced by Witherspoon who taught that God worked in history to accomplish His purposes, Madison, like Washington, Adams, and many other founders, insisted that God played an active role in human affairs, although the Virginian tended to accentuate God's superintendence of large scale rather than personal affairs.[62] God is "the Just and All-powerful Being who holds in His hand the chain of events and the destiny of nations."[63] The "Great Disposer of Events," the Virginian avowed, controls "the welfare and the destiny of nations." People who acted unjustly, Madison warned, might experience "heavenly vengeance."[64]

Madison sought to prove that Providence had chosen Americans to "test man's capacity for self-government."[65] Madison saw God as guiding the Virginia Assembly's debate on religious liberty and the Constitutional Convention's framing of a new government. "It is impossible," he declared in Federalist 37, for pious individuals not to perceive in the Constitution "a finger of that Almighty hand which has been so frequently and signally extended" to aid Americans "in the critical stages of the revolution."[66] Responding to Washington's address to Congress in April 1789 on behalf of the House, Madison declared that the representatives "feel with you the strongest Obligations to adore the INVISIBLE HAND which had led the American people through so many difficulties" and joined in his "fervent supplication for the blessings of Heaven on our Country."[67]

As president, Madison repeatedly referred to God's providential direction of the United States, especially during the War of 1812. In his first inaugural address, he extolled the "guardianship and guidance of that Almighty Being whose power regulates the destiny of nations [and] whose blessings have been so conspicuously dispensed to this rising Republic." The "happy union" of the states "under Divine Providence," Madison proclaimed in March 1809, guaranteed Americans' liberties, safety, tranquility, and prosperity. In a November 1809 message to Congress, Madison announced that Americans were "indebted to that Divine Providence whose goodness has been so remarkably extended to this rising nation." Therefore, they should express "devout gratitude" and implore God to bless their efforts to increase America's well-being. Two years later, as trouble brewed with Britain, Madison invoked "the blessing of Heaven" on all means that Americans might employ to vindicate their rights and advance their welfare.[68] After a peace treaty ended the War of 1812, Madison accentuated God's numerous blessings. God had given Americans one of the best places on earth to dwell. During the Revolutionary War, Americans had experienced "multiplied tokens of His benign interposition."

"Under His fostering care," their principles, practices, and pursuits had prepared them for their later "independence and self-government." God had given them the strength and resources "to assert their national rights and to enhance their national character in another arduous conflict"—the War of 1812. The "Divine Author of Every Good and Perfect Gift" had also bestowed "privileges and advantages, religious as well as civil," which the citizens of "this favored land" "richly enjoyed."[69]

In his Annual Message to Congress in 1812, Madison thanked God for His "providential favors" including the nation's robust health, agricultural abundance, successful industries, and prosperity.[70] In an 1813 message to Congress, Madison expressed gratitude to God for America's wealth, tranquility, stable institutions, and, especially "the light of divine truth and the protection of every man's conscience in the enjoyment of it."[71] While Americans had gratefully acknowledged God's protection during their war with England, Madison proclaimed in February 1815, they must continue to obey the nation's laws and faithfully serve the republic to assure "national independence and prosperity."[72]

Although Madison seldom mentioned God in his personal correspondence, one of his few surviving letters to his wife concludes "God bless you." He used the same phrase in a 1787 letter to Eliza House Trist and a 1788 letter to Philip Mazzei.[73] He wrote to a friend that "the best human means should ever be employed" to avoid "a lazy presumptuous dependance [*sic*] on Providence."[74]

Like Washington, Madison rarely referred to Jesus. In 1773 Madison told a friend: "I have sometimes thought there could be no stronger testimony in favor of Religion or against temporal Enjoyments" than for men who "are rising in reputation and wealth, publicly to declare their unsatisfactoriness by becoming fervent Advocates in the cause of Christ." Because "such instances have seldom occurred," this action would be "striking" and would serve as a "Cloud of Witnesses."[75] He also occasionally used the terms "the Saviour," the "Author" of Christianity, and "that holy name."[76] Some scholars claim that Madison employed these phrases to help persuade Christians to support his perspective of public issues, rather than to affirm that he saw Jesus as a divine redeemer.[77]

While affirming people's intrinsic dignity, Madison accentuated the dark side of human nature—"the infirmities and depravities of the human character."[78] The "depravity in mankind" necessitated being wary about everything people do, especially in the political arena. Madison maintained that depravity affected all human aspects and actions. People's imperfections and weaknesses had caused quarrels and jealousy throughout history. The seeds of political faction, he declared, are "sown in the nature of man."[79] Madison attributed territorial conflicts among states to "envy and jealousy" and quoted the "Jeremiah Doctrine that the heart of man is deceitful above all things and desperately wicked" to explain a rumor about a traitorous act during the Revolutionary War.[80] Madison complained about people's insatiable "love of power."[81] People naturally divided into different parties; they were so prone "to fall into mutual animosities" that "the most frivolous and fanciful distinctions" had often incited "their unfriendly passions" and produced "violent conflicts." People were "much more disposed to vex and oppress each other than to co-operate for their common good."[82] The "emptiness," "allurements and vanities" of "Earthly Happiness," Madison averred, required Christians to acknowledge the "follies of mankind" and to live by "the precepts of Wisdom and Religion."[83] He argued that checks and balances in government were necessary to curb people's lust for power.

Gregg Frazer disagrees that Madison derived his view of human nature from Calvin and Witherspoon,[84] an argument based on Madison's use of the phrase "depravity in mankind" in Federalist 55 and his emphasis on the darker aspects of human nature in Federalist 10. However, Frazer asserts, Madison never stated that either Calvin or Witherspoon influenced his political views. Nor did he directly affirm the Reformed doctrine of total depravity or use the word "sinful" in any of his public papers or extant letters in describing human nature.[85] Rejecting this concept, Madison instead avowed that "a degree of depravity in mankind" required some "circumspection and distrust." He maintained that good qualities are present "in a higher degree" than bad ones and argued that some human qualities justified confidence in people. Like most other educated, upper-class Americans, Frazer concludes, Madison saw human nature as "an alloy of virtue and vice."[86]

While Madison thought that "avarice, vanity, cruelty, and depravity" normally guided life, Ralph Ketcham contended, he hoped that giving individuals the maximum amount of freedom, coupled with people's "virtue, honor, and intelligence," would enable republican government, unlike tyranny and anarchy, to succeed.[87] "Republican government presupposes the existence" of positive human qualities, Madison declared in Federalist 55, "in a higher degree than any other form." He believed that people were sufficiently virtuous for a republic to thrive. Moreover, he insisted republics helped human behavior to improve.[88] However, Madison, like John Adams, argued that people could not create an earthly utopia as Robert Owen and his followers sought to construct. People's sinful nature precluded the possibility of banishing all evil, abolishing the curse connected with work, or creating a totally egalitarian society.[89]

Although Madison referred only once to Christ's atonement, in his proclamations of national days of prayer, he urged Americans to repent of their sin and seek God's forgiveness. He exhorted citizens to acknowledge "the transgressions which might justly provoke" God's displeasure and to seek "His merciful forgiveness and His assistance in the great duties of repentance and amendment." Confessing "their sins and transgressions" and changing their behavior might prompt God to "pardon all their offenses against Him."[90]

Madison believed that the Bible was God's revelation, but he was more influenced by the principles and conclusions of reason. In 1785 he opposed a Virginia bill partly because it "discourages those who are strangers to the light of revelation" from experiencing it.[91] However, Madison wrote in Federalist 37, that when God spoke to humans, He addressed them in "their own language" and, therefore, "his meaning, luminous as it may be, is rendered dim and doubtful by the cloudy medium through which it is communicated."[92] Nothing was mysterious to God, Madison declared; "the mystery lies in the dimness of the human sight."[93] The seeming murkiness of God's message may have led Madison to value reason over revelation as a means of obtaining truth. He celebrated the "rapid progress of reason" and its triumph "over error and oppression."[94]

Madison used biblical and theological language much more sparingly than many other founders. When the Virginian quoted the Bible, he primarily cited isolated phrases, including "loaves & fishes," "bone of our bones, and flesh of our flesh," God's decree that "man earn his bread by the sweat of his brow," and "the Serpent creeping with his deadly wiles into Paradise," to illustrate points.[95] None of the *Federalist Papers* he wrote contains a direct biblical reference.

Several factors indicate that Madison valued prayer. Bishop Meade claimed that Madison led devotions for his family guided by *The Necessary Duty of Family Prayer, With Prayers for Their Use* for family devotions.[96] The future president urged William Bradford to "pray for Liberty of Conscience" so that the truth of Christianity could be freely preached in Virginia.[97] On a few occasions Madison told people he was praying for them. He ended a letter to his father in 1794 "with my sincerest prayers that perfect health and every other good may attend you," offered members of the Ursuline Catholic Convent in New Orleans his prayers for their happiness, prayed "earnestly" that the Virginia Assembly would make wise decisions, and several times stated that he was praying for his country.[98] Madison thanked the residents of Essex County, New Jersey, in 1809, for praying for him and prayed that they would "experience the choicest tokens of divine favor."[99] In 1812 Madison "fervently" affirmed the prayer of the inhabitants of Milton, Massachusetts, that God would direct the councils of government.[100] The character of the American people and their devotion to liberty, justice, and the Constitution, Madison declared in December 1816, "animate my prayers for the happiness of my beloved country."[101]

Madison never joined a church, but he often worshiped at Episcopal churches.[102] His attendance was sporadic while serving in Congress during the 1780s and 1790s. In 1791 Madison attended a Congregational Church in Bennington, Vermont, while touring New England with Thomas Jefferson. When asked how he liked the music, he admitted that he had not been to church recently enough to make a comparison.[103] However, as president, like Washington, Adams, and Jefferson, he worshipped almost every Sunday, in his case, at St. John's Episcopal Church adjacent to the White House, the Hall of the House of Representatives, or St. Thomas Episcopal Church near Montpelier. Hutson contends that Madison attended church in part to advance his political career. In the early national years no politician "wanted to be branded an infidel, as Jefferson had been, and Madison certainly knew that public expressions of piety would please the Baptist voters in his political base in Orange County."[104] On May 29, 1812, Madison and his wife heard James Brackinridge preach at a service at the Hall of the House of Representatives. In his sermon, the Presbyterian pastor censured members of Congress for not properly observing the Sabbath and warned that "your palaces will be burned to the ground." After the British torched many public buildings including the White House and Capitol on August 24, 1814, Dolley wrote to Brackinridge that she had not thought that his "denunciation would be so soon realized."[105]

Like many other founders, Madison saw religion's most important function as promoting morality and virtue. He insisted that everyone had a moral duty "to practice Christian forbearance, love, and charity."[106] Madison urged people to devise arguments to bolster Americans' belief that an "All Powerful wise & good" God is "essential to the moral order of the World & the happiness of man."[107] Madison maintained that people's practice of public virtue helped sustain the republic and that religion encouraged people to act virtuously, but he strongly disagreed with the long-standing argument that religion needed the support of government to thrive.

Madison said less about an afterlife than many other founders. He told a friend in 1772 that people must not let their desire to obtain "more than ordinary Happiness and prosperity" interfere with their "views towards a future State." "A watchful eye must be kept on ourselves lest while we are building ideal monuments of Renown and Bliss here we neglect to have our names enrolled in the annals of Heaven." He did not want to pursue, he added, "any thing that is difficult in acquiring and useless in possessing after one has exchanged Time for Eternity."[108] Although his *Memorial* rests on the assumption of an afterlife, Madison's addresses and surviving correspondence after his young adult years contain only one direct reference to eternal life. Belief in "an invisible cause" of the world and of their "future existence," he argued in 1833, seemed to be built into people's nature.[109] When a Presbyterian minister wrote Madison a few months before his death in 1836 to remind him of "the necessity of . . . Divine influence to qualify you for heaven," Madison simply replied that he had a "general rule of declining correspondence on the subject [of] my religion."[110]

That Madison said almost nothing about his religious convictions after his mid-twenties has led to rival claims: some scholars insist that the arguments of skeptical authors and politicians, including Jefferson and Thomas Paine, destroyed his youthful piety, while others assert that his strong religious convictions continued throughout his life despite his unwillingness to speak or write about them. Some also question whether Madison was truly religiously devout in his earlier years. Madison was clearly influenced by John Witherspoon and other orthodox Calvinists at Princeton, and intellectually and perhaps spiritually, he was affected by the religious awakening that swept the college while he attended. Madison's post-graduate study of theology and Hebrew, notes taken on biblical commentaries in 1772, and leading of family devotions as well as the content and tone of his letters to William Bradford following their graduation all suggest that his religious convictions were deep and genuine. However, his attention soon shifted from religion to politics, and he seemed to abandon his interest in theological questions. Thereafter, Madison neither reaffirmed nor denied his earlier professions of faith. Unlike John Adams and Jefferson, he never attacked Christianity or the clergy (except for their support of religious establishments and denial of rights to other religious bodies), and he insisted that religion helped promote upright morality and republican government. Moreover, his fervent defense of religious freedom displayed no hostility to Christianity. Rather, Madison repeatedly contended that religious liberty strengthened Christianity's vitality and increased its contributions to society. No particular events provide clues that explain why Madison stopped discussing his own religious commitments or shed decisive light on the "puzzle" of his private faith.[111]

Despite saying almost nothing about his personal faith, Madison maintained cordial relationships with most religious bodies during his many years of public service. Ketcham argued that Madison enjoyed "warm feelings of mutual respect" with a "wide variety of religious groups" in large part because of his prominent role in America's provision of religious liberty. Madison had especially close ties with Baptist pastor John Leland who ardently opposed religious establishments.[112] In a 1795 Congressional debate, Madison refuted claims that the "priesthood had done more mischief than [the] aristocracy."

Several times he denounced the ridicule of Catholics. Their religion, Madison avowed, contained "nothing inconsistent with the purest republicanism." He praised both Catholics and Jews for being "good citizens during the revolution."[113]

Promotion of Religious Liberty

Although both his father and his uncle Edmund Pendleton, a judge and politician, were staunch supporters of Virginia's established Anglican Church, Madison, Ralph Ketcham contends, held no other principle "with greater vigor and tenacity" than religious liberty.[114] Several factors contributed to Madison's position on and promotion of religious liberty—the intellectual environment at Princeton that helped broaden his religious perspective, Witherspoon's emphasis on freedom of conscience, Locke's writings on toleration, his personal observations of the persecution of Baptists in Virginia, and his knowledge of the positive impact of religious pluralism in Pennsylvania and Holland. Madison marshaled several arguments to support religious freedom: it was a divinely bestowed right, using tax revenue to support only one denomination was unjust, disestablishment benefited both individuals and society and best encouraged virtuous conduct, and history showed that religious establishments inhibited the growth and vitality of Christianity and produced persecution. Madison insisted that all people had an inalienable prerogative "to believe, or not believe, whatever their consciences dictated."[115] Religious freedom, he contended, was a God-given right that preceded the creation of society. Therefore, governments had no authority to establish a religion, favor one religion over others, or even aid all religions equally. Both his understanding of Scripture and the historical record convinced Madison that Christianity flourished when it relied on persuasion, prayer, and the Holy Spirit rather than the coercive power of a state-established church.[116] Moreover, the competition among "rival sects, with equal rights," promoted upright morality.[117]

The Anglican Church's persecution of Baptists and Presbyterians in pre-revolutionary Virginia powerfully affected Madison's views of religious liberty. Between 1768 and 1776, the colony jailed about fifty dissenters for preaching without a license or overstepping the boundaries for ministry it imposed.[118] As a youth, Madison was deeply impacted by listening to several Baptist pastors in the village of Orange, who were incarcerated because of their religious views and practices, preach through the windows of their jail cell to a small band of followers.[119] In January 1774 Madison complained to William Bradford that a "diabolical Hell conceived principle of persecution" raged near his home in Virginia. Five or six "well meaning men" were incarcerated in an adjacent county "for publishing their religious sentiments, which in the main are very orthodox." Moreover, a Baptist elder had been jailed for praying in a private home, and a Baptist pastor, Elijah Craig, had been arrested twice, once while in the pulpit.[120] The efforts of vindictive Anglican clergy and vestrymen to prevent dissenters from preaching infuriated Madison. Rectors told "incredible and extravagant stories" to discredit the "enthusiasm" of evangelical revival services—people allegedly danced, bellowed wildly, and fell down during preaching—to convince the Virginia legislature to outlaw their practices and continue the Anglican establishment in order to ensure stability, order, and decorum. These jailed Baptist preachers had done nothing more than several of Madison's Princeton classmates who were preaching in the South after graduation. They were all striving to help the unchurched and apathetic Anglicans develop a vital faith.[121] Madison hoped that the Virginia Assembly would grant "greater liberty in matters of Religion" to all groups in the colony, but he thought that this was unlikely.[122] Aided by the bishops and the king, "the numerous and powerful" Anglican clergy employed "all their art and interest to depress their rising Adversaries"—Baptist and Presbyterian ministers who endangered "their livings and security."[123]

Madison also questioned whether religion required or even benefited from governmental support. "Is an Ecclesiastical Establishment absolutely necessary to support civil society?" he asked Bradford.[124] At Princeton Madison met numerous "sincere and energetic Presbyterians" who were vastly superior to the many "dissolute and idle Anglican clergy" he observed in Virginia. These Anglican rectors, he lamented, had discredited Christianity and diminished its vitality. When the state established a religion, Madison insisted, its leaders inevitably used their power to limit religious dissent and restrict the opportunities of other religious bodies. "Religious bondage," he added, "shackles and debilitates the mind, and unfits it for every noble enterprize [sic]." State-funded religion encouraged persecution. "If the Church of England had been established" in all the colonies, Madison alleged, religious and moral "slavery and subjection" would have prevailed. The ecclesiastical establishment in Virginia, he argued, had produced "Pride, ignorance, and Knavery among the Priesthood and Vice and Wickedness among the Laity."[125]

In 1776 Madison served on a committee charged to devise a new constitution and bill of rights for Virginia. To increase religious freedom, George Mason proposed "that all men should enjoy the fullest toleration in the exercise of religion" that did not endanger the public safety. Seeking to disestablish the Anglican Church, Madison offered substitute wording that "all men are equally entitled to the full and free exercise" of their faith. He also proposed that "no man or class of men ought, on account of religion to be invested with peculiar emoluments or privileges," which would have ended Virginia's paying the salaries of Anglican rectors. Although this second provision was rejected, the first one passed easily. By affirming the concept of equal religious rights rather than mere toleration, Virginia took a major step toward the contemporary idea of religious liberty.[126] Soon thereafter, Madison served on the legislature's Committee on Religion, which enabled him to continue to aid Christians who were discriminated against in Virginia. The committee recommended eliminating the requirement that dissenters pay taxes to support the Anglican Church and that the state stop paying the salaries of Anglican rectors, which would have effectively disestablished this denomination.[127]

Madison's 1785 *Memorial and Remonstrance* articulated his position on religious liberty most completely and compellingly. Alarmed that Baptists were still being fined or imprisoned for holding unauthorized assemblies, dissenters were being taxed to support established churches, and ministers had to obtain licenses to preach in some colonies, Madison helped convince Virginians to accept his position that "all men are equally entitled to the free exercise of religion, according to the dictates of their consciences." Established religion violated people's religious freedom and was inconsistent with republican government.[128] Madison assumed that people have a responsibility to God, and that they should respond to God based on their reason and conscience, not because of the coercive force of government. "The duty we owe to our Creator and the Manner of discharging it," he averred, "can be directed only by reason and conviction, not by force or violence." Protecting citizens' varied religious beliefs and practices was "most favorable to the advancement of truth."[129] For Madison, religious liberty was a matter of fair play and was made necessary by the nature of religious belief. "Whilst we assert for ourselves a freedom to embrace, to profess and to observe the religion which we believe to be of divine origin," Madison argued, "we cannot deny an equal freedom to those whose minds have not yet yielded to the evidence which has convinced us." Moreover, he asserted, each person had an "unalienable right" to choose his own religion. Everyone had a duty "to render to the Creator" the homage "he believes to be acceptable to him."[130] People should determine their religious beliefs guided only by "reason and conviction" and "the dictates of conscience."[131]

Madison asserted that civil magistrates were not competent judges of religious truth, Christianity did not need governmental support, and "ecclesiastical establishments" violated people's liberty and corrupted and stultified true religion. Christianity, he proclaimed, did not depend on "the powers of this world." It had "flourished, not only without the support of human laws, but in spite of every opposition from them." The fifteen centuries that Christianity had been legally established, Madison insisted, had produced bad results: "more or less in all places" it had generated "pride and indolence in the Clergy; ignorance and servility in the laity; in both [groups] superstition, bigotry and persecution." Moreover, Madison argued, the American experience demonstrated that "equal and complete liberty, if it does not wholly eradicate" the disease of religious discord and violence, "sufficiently destroys its malignant influence on the health and prosperity of the state."[132] His *Memorial* helped persuade the Virginia Assembly to pass Jefferson's landmark Statute for Religious Freedom in 1786. This victory gave Madison greater pleasure and sense of accomplishment than any of his other legislative victories.[133] Thereafter, Lance Banning contends, Madison, "with unwavering consistency," "envisioned total freedom of opinion, absolute equality for various denominations, and an end" to the long-standing intermingling of church and state.[134]

After helping to disestablish the Episcopal Church in Virginia, Madison played a pivotal role in the adoption of the First Amendment. The Virginian initially opposed adding a bill of rights to the Constitution because he thought that the federal government's distinctly defined and limited powers guaranteed that it would not interfere with citizens' God-given rights, including the right of liberty of conscience. After deciding to support a Bill of Rights, Madison made religious liberty a chief priority. The two amendments on religion he proposed to the Constitution—"the civil rights of none shall be abridged on account of religious belief or worship, nor shall any national religion be established, nor shall the full and equal rights of conscience be in any manner, or on any pretext, infringed" and "no State shall violate the equal rights of conscience"—were more sweeping and less ambiguous than the wording actually adopted.[135] Madison served on the select committee of the House of Representatives that evaluated various amendments pertaining to religion. The proposals they reported to Congress were clearly based on Madison's original drafts: "no Religion shall be established by law, nor shall the equal rights of conscience be infringed" and "no state shall infringe the equal rights of conscience."[136] The House of Representatives passed two amendments. The first stated that "Congress shall make no law establishing religion, or to prevent the free exercise thereof, or to infringe the rights of conscience." The second declared "no State shall infringe . . . the rights of conscience." Because the Senate passed a slightly different version, a conference committee was appointed, and Madison headed the House delegation. This committee's compromise statement produced the actual language of the First Amendment: "Congress shall make no law respecting an establishment of religion, or prohibiting the free exercise thereof." However, the Senate rejected the second amendment the House approved, which would have applied to the states. Although Madison's language for the amendment was not chosen, he undoubtedly influenced its final wording. Had Madison disagreed with this final version, he would have very likely have written essays in protest.[137]

Madison's attempt to prevent both the federal and state governments from encroaching on individuals' religious liberty is a major example of how his faith helped shape his public policies. He firmly believed that God wanted people to have freedom of conscience, and he despised religious persecution because it harmed individuals, groups, and society. Madison rejoiced that the United States had a "multiplicity of sects," which was the "best and only security for religious liberty in any society" because it prevented one religious body from oppressing and persecuting the others.[138] "Torrents of blood have been spilt in the old world," Madison maintained, "by vain attempts" of governments "to extinguish religious discord." Thankfully, "time has revealed the true remedy" for this problem—freedom of conscience.

Madison took other actions to promote religious liberty. As a member of the House of Representatives, he proposed that "no person religiously scrupulous of bearing arms shall be compelled to render military service in person" and opposed all immigration policies that discriminated against Catholics.[139] After leaving Congress, Madison denounced the Alien and Sedition Acts, passed in 1798 to restrict the freedom of the press to criticize the federal government, as a precedent that could be used to adopt laws that limited religious freedom.

After his presidency, Madison continued to emphasize the benefits of religious liberty. "The experience of Virginia," he insisted in 1819, conspicuously disproved the previously "universal opinion" that the government "could not stand without the prop of a religious establishment" and that Christianity "would perish if not supported by a legal provision for its clergy." The separation of the church and state, he contended, had clearly increased the number, quality, industry, and morality of the clergy and the devotion of the laity.[140] The American experience, Madison wrote to a New York pastor in 1821, proved that the idea "so long rooted in the unenlightened minds of well-meaning Christians as well as in the corrupt hearts of persecuting usurpers, that without legal incorporation of religious and civil polity, neither could be supported" was erroneous. Instead, when church and state were independent, practical religion, social harmony, and political stability had most prospered.[141] Madison told Rabbi Mordecai Noah that he considered "the freedom of religious opinions and worship" to be "the best human provision for bringing all [people] either into the same way of thinking, or into that mutual charity which is the only substitute." Consequently, he rejoiced that Jews were partaking "of the blessings offered by our Government and Laws."[142]

Madison protested in 1822 that some Americans continued to believe that "without some sort of alliance or coalition between Govt. & Religion neither can be duly supported." However, experience demonstrated that the church and state had "greater purity the less they are mixed together." The example of Holland and the American colonies, now states, which had no establishments and treated all denominations equally, proved that this arrangement "was safe & even useful." When all religious bodies were placed "on a footing of equal and entire freedom," religion flourished. In Virginia, he asserted, religion was more zealous and the clergy were more exemplary than when religion was "established and patronised by Public authority."[143] Madison correctly anticipated that voluntary support of religion "would more than compensate for the loss of state revenues." Religion would remain vital and vigorous without state funding because their competition "in the spiritual marketplace would inspire each denomination's adherents to support their own cause."[144]

To many American Christians, especially Baptists, what mattered most about Madison was not his personal piety or presidential policies, but his pivotal role in securing religious freedom. In 1812 a Massachusetts legislator insisted that Madison's defense of religious liberty would stand as "an eternal monument to crown him with everlasting honors when generations yet to come shall rise up and call him blessed." When Madison was reelected later that year, pastor Elias Smith predicted that the efforts of his administration to advance civil and religious liberty would be "greater and more successful" than in any four-year period since the Revolutionary War.[145]

Philosophy of Government

While noting that he was also influenced by Lockean liberalism and classical republicanism, Sheldon argues that Madison's support for religious liberty, understanding of public justice, and frequent references to biblical tenets demonstrate that Christianity helped shape his view of government.[146] Mark Noll contends that during the colonial period, religious principles were "central to the outworking of republican theory" at Princeton, and Sheldon claims that Madison followed Witherspoon in basing his political theory on Reformed theology.[147] In his "Lectures on Moral Philosophy," Witherspoon examined philosophy, politics, law, and ethics from a biblical perspective and insisted that people's "natural" rights "are always subordinate to God's law and will."[148] People could discern and follow God's will by employing a combination of faith, reason, and education. However, for Witherspoon, revelation always trumped reason. He declared that "there is nothing certain or valuable in moral philosophy, but what is perfectly coincident with the Scriptures where the glory of God is the first principle of action."[149]

Sheldon insists that Madison's education at Princeton taught him how to integrate Christian faith with philosophy and reason. Christianity, he adds, "had a profound influence on Madison's political theory and philosophy before and during his presidency."[150] Strongly influenced by Witherspoon, Madison maintained that people are naturally self-centered and sinful and seek to dominate and control others through politics. Therefore, checks and balances are necessary in government to restrain human selfishness and advance the public good. Witherspoon stressed the doctrine of human depravity and the importance of balancing political power. A republic, he wrote, should "be complex, so that the one principle may check the other."[151] Echoing Witherspoon, Madison asserted that distributing and balancing power would effectually check and restrain the interests of people and parties. He sought to craft a government that inhibited individuals' innate tendency to use the political process to achieve their own selfish aims. Dividing authority in three branches of government (executive, legislative, and judicial) and in three levels of government (federal, state, and local) could best accomplish this and prevent anarchy, on the one extreme, and dictatorship, on the other.[152] To create a just state, Madison declared, "ambition must be made to counteract ambition."[153]

Madison agreed with John Adams that political mechanisms were needed to curb people's ambitions, passions, and desires, prevent the accumulation of power, and promote the common good. To keep people's drive for dominance from corrupting the government and causing injustice, Madison proposed distributing power, limiting terms for political officials, and holding frequent elections. The government must "divide and arrange the several offices" in such a way that they served as a check on each other and that "the private interest of every individual may be a sentinel over the public rights." Sheldon contends that as president wherever Madison "saw the greatest threat to justice, or the greatest source of injustice (democracy's tendency to oppress the minority or concentrated national power's tendency toward tyranny), he appealed to the other component to check and neutralize that evil."[154]

Madison insisted, however, that even the best constitution could not totally suppress human wickedness.[155] He argued that people were prone to self-love, "unfriendly passions," and "mutual animosities," that leaders "ambitiously contended for pre-eminence and power," and that parties were "more disposed to vex and oppress each other than to co-operate for the common good."[156] Although he rarely used the biblical term "sin," the constitutional system Madison helped craft was consistent with the Christian position that because people are sinners it is unwise and unsafe to give any of them too much power.

If people were angels, Madison maintained, government would not be needed or if angels governed humans, "neither external nor internal controls on government would be necessary." Because people were deeply flawed, Madison asserted, in devising a government, Americans must "first enable the government to control the governed" and then "oblige it to control itself."[157]

Madison argued that three motives could restrain the majority from oppressing the minority: "a prudent regard to private or partial good, as essentially involved in the general good of the whole"; respect for character; and religion. Because these three motives were insufficient to achieve this purpose, governmental checks and balances were necessary. Strikingly, Madison concluded that religion was often not a positive social force, a position that put him at odds with almost all the other founders.[158] As early as 1772 he noted that "nothing is more Subject to delusion than Piety. All manner of Errors creep and hide themselves under that Veil. Piety takes for sacred all her imaginations of what sort soever."[159] "We well know," Madison asserted in 1787, "that neither moral nor religious motives can be relied on as an adequate control" "against tyrannical majorities." Religion, "even in its coolest [non-enthusiastic] state" had more often been "a motive to oppression than a restraint from it." Fortunately, Madison argued, in larger republics the number and variety of religious groups, civic associations, and political interests helped prevent any group from dominating the others.[160]

The "sole object" of government, Madison averred, was to promote the "public good."[161] Laws should advance "the good of all."[162] "All political institutions," Madison proclaimed, must strive to ensure "the safety and happiness of society" as "the transcendent law of nature and of nature's God" instructed them to do.[163] Institutions should be designed to ascertain and promote the common good.[164]

Scott Kester disagrees that biblical presuppositions underlie Madison's political theory and contends that the Virginian placed his faith in republicanism, not Christianity. For Madison, republicanism was the primary instrument for obtaining truth. In a republic, he wrote, "light will prevail over darkness, truth over error." Madison saw the United States as "a harbinger of progress and freedom."[165] Rejecting the Christian position that people are sinners who need God's grace to reform them, Madison accepted the Enlightenment tenet that the proper political arrangements could produce "UNIVERSAL AND PERPETUAL PEACE."[166] His understanding of government, Kester contends, was based more on Locke's social contract theory than on Puritan covenantal theology. Whereas the Puritans argued that God's transcendent norms are the foundation for government, Madison insisted that "ultimate authority" resided "in the people alone."[167]

Church and State

During his presidency, Madison dealt with several issues pertaining to the separation of church and state. Despite protests by many clergy, he signed a law
in 1810 that authorized mail delivery on Sunday. The major church-state issues
Madison confronted were whether it was constitutional to issue proclamations
recommending that citizens pray, fast, and repent of their sins and seek God's
blessing for the nation during crises, to employ chaplains in Congress and
the military, and to incorporate churches. While vetoing congressional legislation to incorporate churches, Madison issued four proclamations and did
not oppose the federal government's appointment and payment of chaplains.
After his presidency, however, he sharply criticized these two practices.

As president, Madison yielded to pressure to give religion a larger role
in the public square, especially during the War of 1812. Although he had
supported proclamations of days of prayer and humiliation as a Virginia legislator and a member of the Continental Congress, by the time he became
president, Madison considered these declarations constitutionally suspect.
Nevertheless, during the conflict with Britain, he proclaimed four days
of prayer, fasting, and thanksgiving. However, in all four, he emphasized
that he was responding to requests from Congress and that he simply recommended that citizens pray. Moreover, he used these proclamations to
argue that religious freedom brought benefits to both churches and society.
America's "public homage" would be worthy of God's "favorable regard," the
president asserted, only if it were offered by people who were "guided only
by their free choice, by the impulse of their hearts and the dictates of their
consciences." He argued "that religion, that gift of Heaven for the good of
man," when "freed from all coercive edicts," and an "unhallowed connection with the powers of this world which corrupts religion into [either] an
instrument or an usurper of the policy of the state" would "spread its benign
influence everywhere." Only religious freedom permitted people to genuinely offer "humble supplication, thanksgiving, and praise which alone can
be acceptable to Him."[168]

Madison scrupulously avoided sectarian language in his proclamations.
He used generic titles for God and, unlike John Adams, made no references to
the Redeemer of the world.[169] Although some of his terminology was biblically
based, a "Bible Christian" protested that Madison's July 23, 1813 proclamation
contained nothing that would offend "a pagan, an infidel, [or] a deist" and little
that would bother an atheist. Meanwhile, the *Federal Republican* denounced
Madison for invoking God's blessing on a war that had been provoked by
American anger and been waged in such a depraved and disastrous manner.

The Baltimore *Patriot*, by contrast, lauded the proclamation's lofty piety and patriotism.[170]

After leaving the presidency, Madison confessed that some of his actions, especially declaring national days of prayer, had violated his personal convictions and the First Amendment's establishment clause. In numerous writings, especially his Detached Memoranda, penned sometime between 1817 and 1822, Madison articulated a strict stance on church-state separation.[171] Although Congressmen knew that he was "disinclined" to issue religious proclamations, he complained, they passed joint resolutions requesting them. Madison had not considered it proper to refuse to comply.[172] Moreover, the dangers the War of 1812 entailed and the precedents established by presidents and governors, he insisted, overruled his personal objections to doing so.[173] Madison also pointed out that the Continental and Confederation Congresses had issued twenty such pronouncements between 1774 and 1784. Although he felt compelled "to follow the example of [his] predecessors," Madison argued that he was "careful to make the Proclamations absolutely indiscriminate, and merely recommendatory." That is, he simply designated days "on which all who thought [it] proper might *unite* in consecrating it to religious purposes, according to their own faith & forms."[174]

While defending his actions, Madison objected in his Detached Memoranda to such proclamations on five grounds. First, because the federal government had no power to mandate that citizens fast or pray, he reasoned, it should not recommend these actions. Second, their constituents had not given government officials the prerogative to advise them in their religious practices. Third, such presidential proclamations "seemed to imply and certainly nourished the erroneous idea of a *national* religion." Fourth, the proclamations tended to reflect the views of the nation's predominant religious bodies. Fifth, Madison warned that these declarations could be used for partisan advantage, which would hurt some religious groups and increase "party animosities."[175] Madison's objections did not win the day as most of his successors continued to issue proclamations.

Madison's defense of his actions is questionable. Jefferson had already declined to issue such proclamations as president, a precedent Madison could have followed. Madison's decision was undoubtedly influenced both by America's trials during the War of 1812 and his judgment that refusing to issue proclamations would be politically unpopular.[176] Moreover, these proclamations helped "unite the divided country during the War of 1812 by focusing attention on the national covenant" with God "that superseded regional and political factionalism."[177]

In his Detached Memoranda, Madison also objected to Congress's appointment and payment of chaplains to minister to public officials and members of the military, although he had not opposed the employment of chaplains as a Virginia congressman or made any attempt as president to stop this practice. By 1809, Congress had been appointing and paying chaplains "for more than thirty years, ample time, he evidently thought," to establish a precedent for "a practice he personally deplored."[178] However, after leaving office, Madison argued that the practice was unfair. Denominations with small numbers of adherents or whose tenets were deemed "obnoxious" by larger religious bodies were very unlikely to have one of their clergy appointed as a chaplain.[179] Instead of using tax money to pay for chaplains, Madison reasoned in 1822, Congressmen could have given "better proof to their Constituents of their pious feeling" if they had paid chaplains "from their own pockets."[180]

While yielding to popular pressure on proclamations and chaplains, President Madison firmly opposed granting charters of incorporation to churches. In February 1811 he vetoed a bill Congress had passed to incorporate the Protestant Episcopal Church of Alexandria in the District of Columbia and to provide procedures to elect and remove the congregation's rectors. Madison argued that this would constitute a religious establishment by empowering the state to enforce laws governing the church's internal operations. Moreover, the bill gave the church the power to "provide support for the poor" and to educate their members' children. This could unwisely provide a precedent for giving religious bodies the legal authority to perform actions that should instead be "a public and civic duty." Arguing that the First Amendment forbad using public funds to support religious societies, Madison vetoed another congressional act a week later that provided five acres of federal land in the Mississippi Territory to build a Baptist church.[181] In a message to Congress, Madison underscored his pledge to prevent all "encroachments and compacts between religion and the state."[182]

Madison further explained his actions in his Detached Memoranda. Americans, he complained, had not paid sufficient attention to "the dangers of silent accumulations & encroachments, by Ecclesiastical Bodies." Charters of incorporation, he warned, might be the crevices through which "bigotry may introduce persecution; a monster, that feeding & thriving on its own venom, gradually swells to a size and strength overwhelming all laws divine & human." Are Americans aware, Madison asked, "of the precedents they are establishing" by making it easy for congregations to acquire and hold real and personal property? Incorporation could make the churches of Virginia as bloated with wealth as the English monasteries were before their dissolution in the sixteenth century; the enormous resources of those religious societies had fueled their gross corruptions. Incorporating religious societies opened the door for greater abuses.[183]

Madison's actions and statements have produced a variety of interpretations of his position on the separation of church and state. Given his role in shaping the First Amendment, what Madison believed about this issue is very important. James Hutson asserts that the bedeviling "uncertainty about Madison's personal religious convictions" makes it very difficult to know what motivated him to propose his policy initiatives on the relationship between religion and government, "an area in which his impact on American law and politics was extraordinary in his own lifetime and continues to be" today. Many scholars argue that Madison and Jefferson were the principal advocates and apologists for what today is labeled the "strict separationist" perspective of church-state relations—the position that "the spheres of religious activity and civil authority" must be completely separated by prohibiting all "public aid or support for religion."[184] They insist that especially after leaving the presidency, Madison took a stringent separationist stance in accordance with Jefferson's "wall of separation." Madison contended that Congress's incorporation of churches, granting public lands to churches, and giving tax-exempt status to religious entities all violated the establishment clause.[185] The government, he argued in 1833, should avoid all interaction with religion except "preserving the public order, & protecting each sect against trespasses on its legal rights by others."[186]

Vincent Phillip Munoz disagrees that Madison espoused strict separationism.[187] Rather, he worked to keep the government "from either privileging or penalizing religion." Unlike many today, Madison did not want to exclude "religion from the public square."[188] Madison's record, Ketcham avows, refutes the assertion that his vigorous advocacy of the separation of church and state meant that he was hostile to religion or thought it had a pernicious effect on society.[189] Madison later argued that he tried to keep Virginia from recognizing Christianity in 1786 because he did not want "to profane it by making it a topic of legislative discussion." Moreover, he did not want to make Christianity "the means of abridging the natural and equal rights of all men, in defiance of His [Jesus's] declaration that His Kingdom was not of this world."[190] He told a Lutheran pastor in 1819 that "a due distinction . . . between what is due to Caesar and what is due to God, best promotes the discharge of both obligations. . . . A mutual independence is found most friendly to practical religion, to social harmony, and to political prosperity."[191]

Public Policy: The War of 1812

Madison's faith is most evident in his presidency in his frequent charge to Americans to rely on God's providence. He took office at a challenging time. Americans' effort to remain neutral during European wars and to trade with all nations, including combatants, had not worked. After fifteen years of the nation's ships and crews being "seized, harassed, and humiliated," President Jefferson and Madison, his secretary of state, decided to prohibit American overseas trade in 1807 to avoid being drawn into a war with England or France, the world's preeminent powers. Except for stimulating American manufacturing, the Embargo Act that Congress passed had disastrous consequences. During the fourteen months it operated, the combination of England's plentiful harvests and increased trade with Spain and its colonies made American products less needed in Britain. Moreover, some American merchants disobeyed the law and traded with Britain. The prices of American agricultural products dropped calamitously, and unemployment was high in coastal cities. Protests by enraged New England merchants and shippers contributed to the act's repeal in 1809.[192] The United States reopened trade with Great Britain and France, but promised to embargo the other nation if either country pledged to halt its aggressive actions. After Napoleon accepted this condition, the United States discontinued trade with Britain in early 1811.

America's troubled relations with Great Britain that culminated in the War of 1812, dubbed "Mr. Madison's War" by detractors, dominated much of his presidency.[193] Madison repeatedly justified the United States' policy and actions by appealing to moral and religious considerations. Many of his contemporaries and today's scholars repudiate Madison's contention that America's reasons for declaring war against England in June 1812 were just.

After delineating the major challenges the United States faced, Madison concluded his first inaugural address by declaring his faith "in the guardianship and guidance of that Almighty Being whose power regulates the destiny of nations." The president closed another address two months later with a prayer that the United States would continue to experience "the Divine blessings, by which it has been so signally favored."[194]

Shortly after assuming office, Madison declared that the "true intent of our Country" as well as "the precepts of Religion and humanity" necessitated that political leaders "cherish peace."[195] He wanted to solve the maritime trade war through "rational and provident measure[s]" rather than resorting to "the sword stained with blood" of open warfare.[196] The president argued on June 1, 1812, that although the United States had long pursued a policy of "moderation and conciliation," Great Britain had continued its lawless assault on American vessels. Britain was, in effect, he reasoned, waging war on the United States. His administration had to decide if it was going to passively submit to Britain's "progressive usurpations" or use force to defend American rights and commit its "just cause into the hands of the Almighty disposer of events."[197]

The United States declared war on Great Britain on June 18, 1812, for three primary reasons: to stop the British policy of impressment, protect the trade rights of neutral nations, and further its desire to expand into the West, Florida, and Canada. The "War Hawks" in Congress, who protested that Britain had insulted and disrespected the United States, urged Madison to declare war. Britain, alleged Speaker of the House Henry Clay, had forced Americans "to submit to debasement, dishonor, and disgrace." Between 1790 and 1812, the British had impressed about 15,000 American citizens into their navy. If Americans continued to submit to British indignities, warned Congressman Peter Porter of New York, the British would soon seize Americans' property and trample on their civil rights.[198] Many Americans believed that the United States should drive the British out of North America. They expected a quick victory that would end Britain's provocation of Native Americans and monopoly of the fur trade. Moreover, through war the United States could expand its territory in the West and even add Florida and Canada to the new republic. "This ambitious agenda caught the public imagination and put immense pressure on the president."[199]

Although he was also motivated by practical aims, Madison principally used the rhetoric of just war theory to defend his actions.[200] He insisted that Americans had been forced to go to war, "the last resort of injured nations," to right the wrongs England had committed. Under God's direction, Americans would strive to limit the war's calamities and obtain "a speedy, a just, and an honorable peace."[201] America's conflict with Britain, Madison told Congress in November 1812, "is a war neither of ambition nor of vain glory." "It is waged," he asserted, not to violate the rights of other nations, but to maintain our own. Americans had exercised amazing patience in the face of "wrongs accumulating without end." The United States had not declared war until "every hope of averting it" had been extinguished by British declarations that they could not revoke their "hostile edicts against our commercial rights and our maritime independence" without violating their obligations to other powers and their own interests.[202]

Americans could "trust in the smiles of Heaven on so righteous a cause," Madison asserted. While "friends of liberty and of the rights of nations" deplored "the evils of war," they saw other evils as greater, including being reduced to a "degraded condition" by other countries.[203] He accused Great Britain of violating American rights and using extensive "forgery and perjury" to undermine the "principles of morality and religion which are the best foundation of national happiness." Moreover, Britain was employing deformed and depraved "modes of warfare" to try to dissolve Americans' "ties of allegiance" and "sentiments of loyalty." "The civilized and Christian world," the president predicted, would censure Britain's "demoralizing and disorganizing contrivances."[204] Americans' "love of country," pride in liberty, desire to emulate the founders' successful defense of their rights, and "sacred obligation" to transmit the benefits of freedom to future generations, which they held as a trust "from the goodness of Divine Providence," Madison maintained, also prompted them to fight.[205]

Madison claimed that the United States, unlike Britain, was using just methods to wage war. He declared in his second inaugural address that America's war effort was "stamped with that justice which invites the smiles of Heaven."[206] He asked God to help Americans stop Britain's "hostile" efforts "to degrade us on the ocean, the common inheritance of all." Britain sought to deny Americans their "rights and immunities" "as a coequal member of the great community of independent nations." Madison also entreated God to give their enemies moderation, justice, and the "spirit of reasonable accommodation which our country" had persistently manifested so that Americans could "beat our swords into plowshares" and each person could enjoy "the fruits of his honest industry and the rewards of his lawful enterprise."[207] In the midst of the United States' many setbacks during the war, most notably the British invasion of Washington, DC, and burning of many government buildings, including the White House and the Capitol, Madison continued to invoke the support of "an omnipotent and kind Providence."[208]

The religious community sharply disagreed about whether the war was just and prudent. Most Baptists and Methodists, who were loyal both to the Republican Party and to Madison personally as the champion of religious liberty, approved it, while New England Congregationalists, Quakers, and some Presbyterians, opposed it. Congregationalists and Presbyterians published many more articles in religious journals and sermons about the war than Baptists and Methodists. Therefore, antiwar rhetoric dominated the religious media during the conflict. Christians who disapproved of the war, including Unitarian pastor William Ellery Channing, typically did so because they thought the United States should be fighting not against England, but against France, whose government was "morally depraved" and whose revolutionary excesses threatened America. Some insisted that Napoleonic France was "an infidel nation, controlled by the antichrist." Britain alone "prevented this beast of Babylon from conquering the world." Nothing "good could come from warring against the enemies of God's enemies." Critics also denounced the war as an "instrument of [American] deists, slave holders, [and] Francophiles."[209] On June 26, 1812, Federalist Governor of Massachusetts Caleb Strong argued that citizens should lament fighting against "the nation from which we are descended and which for many generations has been the bulwark of the Religion we profess." He proclaimed a day of prayer in Massachusetts to beseech God to forgive Americans' sins and to protect their country "from entangling and fatal alliances with foreign powers," by which he principally meant infidel France. Numerous antiwar newspapers, religious magazines, and sermons quoted his proclamation, and several Boston clergymen denounced the war as unjust and likely to produce civil strife.[210] Republicans charged Strong with "exciting rebellion," "sneering at our own government," and "encouraging the enemy."[211]

Led by Baptists, the religious groups that backed the war "were theologically disparate, often suspicious of one another," and competed for members, but they were united by "their hatred for Britain and her American admirers."[212] Supportive ministers asserted that God saw the war "as His own cause" and that "the Lord will plead our cause."[213] Hundreds of pastors across the country traced God's assistance in American history, deplored the impiety of the British, and prayed for victory. Some warned that a British triumph might curtail religious freedom in the United States, and others served as chaplains with the American military.[214] Countless clergy applauded Madison for opposing British tyranny and cruelty and declaring war. Britain, declared a New England Baptist minister, was the principal supporter of "Babylon the great, the mother of harlots, and the abomination of the earth."[215] Like patriotic societies, some clergy and congregations celebrated America's decision to wage war. A martial sermon preached by William Parkinson, a New York City pastor, in August 1812 was widely circulated to support Madison's reelection. The bellicose Baptist exhorted his congregants to pray for God to bless their leader:

> *Our President with wisdom crown,*
> *His soul with rich graces adorn*
> *Resolve his heart, 'midst all his foes,*
> *"To launch the stream which duty shows."*[216]

During the war, Madison issued four national days of "public Humiliation and prayer" to exhort Americans to repent and seek God's blessing on their enterprise. He proclaimed the first one on July 9, 1812, to pay God the homage He was due and to beseech Him to take Americans "under His peculiar care and protection," "guide their public councils," "bestow His blessing on their arms," "inspire all nations with a love of justice and of concord and with a reverence for the unerring precept of our holy religion to do to others as they would require that others should do to them," and to turn "the hearts of our enemies" from their violent and unjust acts to restore "the blessings of peace."[217]

While many Americans applauded Madison's proclamation, others denounced it. Must the clergy curse our enemy, asked John Fiske of Braintree, Massachusetts, "because the king commands it?"[218] "Not content with forcing upon the nation a war that must destroy it," a Boston critic protested, Madison asked Americans to supplicate God for "success in a battle against your liberties and your God."[219] On the other hand, Francis Scott Key penned a poem during the British shelling of Fort McHenry in Baltimore in September 1814 that expressed the views of many Americans including Madison. It declared:

> Blest with victory and peace, may the heaven-rescued land
> Praise the Power that hath made and preserved us [as] a nation!
> Then conquer we must, when our cause it is just,
> And this be our motto: "In God is our trust!"

Parts of this poem, conveying Key's delight that the American flag still flew over the fort after the British bombardment, became the national anthem. Key, Madison, and many others were convinced that the God who had established and preserved the United States would enable Americans to prevail in their righteous crusade against Britain.

Ralph Beebe argues convincingly that this conflict did not satisfy the traditional criteria for a just war because the United States did not exhaust all possibilities of peacefully adjudicating its dispute with Britain. Britain's crop failures, skyrocketing food prices, riots, and factory closures led the House of Commons to repeal its bellicose policy toward the United States on June 16, 1812, two days before the United States declared war on Britain. Diplomats sailed past each other on the Atlantic without knowing the messages their counterparts were carrying. If the federal government had subsidized merchants hurt by the embargo or simply been more patient, Beebe avows, war could have been avoided.[220] Had the United States agreed earlier, as it finally did in the spring of 1813, to stop using British sailors on its ships and to surrender deserters without the British having to conduct searches at sea, Garry Wills adds, war might have been evaded.[221] Moreover, Beebe maintains, the American invasion of Canada in July 1812 violated the stipulation that a just war must be defensive.[222] Madison incorrectly believed that because England was preoccupied with fighting France, Canada could be quickly conquered, which would prevent Canadian products from getting to England and deeply damage its war effort. Furthermore, Madison accused the British of inciting Indian hostility in the Northwest, but the movement of American settlers into the region was the primary cause.[223] Robert Rutland insists that Madison blundered into a war that could have been avoided because of his "ignorance of military strategy," "total dependence" on his generals, and willingness to follow "public opinion rather than to shape it." His lack of a firm policy led Madison to fall into a trap constructed by "British inflexibility, pressures from public opinion, and his own gullibility." The United States' declaration of war, Beebe maintains, displayed "a shocking degree of selfishness and nationalism."[224]

In addition to violating the principles of just war theory, the United States suffered many military defeats and financial problems, but the results could have been even worse. As it had thirty-six years earlier, the United States, still a relatively weak nation with a very limited military, took on the world's wealthiest, most powerful nation with its huge navy and a well-trained army. This, coupled with misconceptions about the competence of the American militia and generals and how poorly defended Canada was, quickly led to embarrassing routs.[225] The invasion of Canada was disastrous, American morale quickly deteriorated, and contraband trade flourished. After the British and their allies defeated Napoleon in 1814, the British navy blockaded the United States' coast, raided oceanside cities, and overwhelmed Washington.

Given the outcome of the war, the peace treaty was probably the best the United States could have obtained. Originally the British had demanded that the Northwest Territory be given to Native Americans and that part of New England and New York be ceded to Canada. However, three factors led Britain to soften its demands: its people were exhausted by two decades of conflict; the British military setbacks in the fall of 1814; and the British position at the Congress of Vienna would be stronger if they could assure other powers that they would not be distracted by fighting the United States.[226] Approved by Congress on February 16, 1815, the treaty restored the situation that existed before the war began. It did not mention either impressment or neutral rights, which the United States had listed as its principal reasons for going to war.[227] The British did not surrender their right to impress American crewmen or to obstruct the commerce of neutrals during wartime. However, because the war with France had ended, the British need to continue these practices drastically declined. Although the United States lost most of the war's battles and did not achieve any of its stated goals, the announcement of the peace treaty, coupled with Andrew Jackson's sensational victory at New Orleans in early January 1815 where Americans suffered only one-seventh as many casualties as the British, led most Americans to rejoice.

Despite the course of the war and the shortcomings of the treaty, many religious and political leaders pronounced the conflict a glorious triumph. As one newspaper put it, "the war was just and necessary"; "the Lord has fought for us" and given us "signal and marvelous" victories.[228] After the peace treaty was signed with Britain, Madison recommended that Americans devoutly thank "Almighty God for His great goodness" in restoring "the blessing of peace. No people," he added, had "greater obligations to celebrate" God's goodness than Americans. He praised God for giving Americans the strength and resources to defend themselves in their "arduous conflict" with Britain, "which is now so happily terminated" by "peace and reconciliation."[229] Madison also insisted that God had brought many blessings out of the evils of the war. The nation had become more economically self-sufficient by developing its own manufacturing establishments, gained new territory in Florida and the Northwest, and strengthened its army and navy, thereby discouraging future attacks.[230] The economy quickly improved, the threat of New England seceding from the Union dissipated, and Republicans remained in political ascendency for ten more years. Because the United States was not decisively defeated, it gained greater respect, and it would never again be treated as a second-class nation.[231]

Federalists countered that God had graciously granted Americans "not a pardon but a stay of execution." They urged citizens to choose more pious politicians than the current president, warned that the United States might be destroyed if it did not repent, and exhorted Americans to renew their New England ancestors' covenant with God. America, lamented Presbyterian Elias Boudinot, had "departed from her original principles" and "left her first love." Many Americans of all parties had "forsaken the God of their fathers." If they did not return, he cautioned, God would fight against them.[232]

Final Assessment

As a Congressman, crafter of the Constitution, co-founder of the Republican Party, party leader, president, and elder statesman, James Madison contributed immensely to the United States. Garry Wills maintains that only two founders—Washington and Franklin—were more important than Madison. Moreover, "as a framer and defender of the Constitution, he had no peer."[233] Madison also had an enormous influence on the new nation's position on freedom of conscience and the separation of church and state.[234] "As a champion of religious liberty," Wills contends, Madison "is equal, perhaps superior to Jefferson—and no else is in the running."[235] Madison, argues John Noonan, was the first statesman who, although himself a believer and not the victim of religious persecution, "had enough empathy" with others who were to denounce the idea of "enforced religious conformity" and work to end it.[236]

During his tenure in office, both Federalists and disgruntled Republicans criticized Madison's performance, and writing in 1889, Henry Adams described Madison as an incompetent, indecisive chief executive. Following Adams's lead, other historians long portrayed the Virginian as a stubborn, second-rate leader who mismanaged his office, had a poor relationship with Congress, and "inspired little affection and no enthusiasm."[237] More recent scholars generally rate Madison a "mixed success as president and party leader."[238] Nevertheless, many try to explain how such a brilliant theorist could be an average or even a "less-than-successful president." Wills calls him a "hapless commander in chief." James Barber contends that he was neither innovative nor assertive.[239] Based on Madison's work as an opinion shaper, legislative leader, chief executive, diplomat, and commander-in-chief, Bryon Daynes and Mark Hopkins rate his performance as president as mediocre. Although he preserved civil liberties and applied republican principles flexibly, Madison's lack of interpersonal skills, introverted personality, and understanding of the presidency inhibited his ability to deal effectively with numerous crises, most notably the conflict with Great Britain. Madison failed to mobilize popular support for the war effort, choose good generals and cabinet members, and wage war effectually, which led to the British burning much of the capital, a tragedy with which Madison is widely associated in the popular mind. Unlike the nation's strongest, most successful presidents, Madison did not exude great energy, decisiveness, or optimism. He was unable to appeal winsomely to citizens, secure the unfaltering allegiance of members of his party or administrative team, or gain the respect of Congress. His weak leadership style, lack of charisma, poor judgment in selecting subordinates, difficulty in working with many of them, and faulty assessment of some political issues prevented him from bargaining successfully with powerful interest groups or responding well to crises.[240]

On the other hand, many of Madison's colleagues were deeply impressed by his character and contributions. Speaking for them, Edward Coles claimed that Madison was "the most virtuous, calm, and amiable, of men" and possessed "one of the purest hearts, and best tempers" of any man.[241] "I do not know," Jefferson proclaimed, "a man of purer integrity, more dispassionate, or devoted to genuine Republicanism; nor could I" in all of America and Europe "point to an abler head."[242] Everyone at the Constitutional Convention, declared Georgia delegate William Pierce, acknowledged Madison's greatness. Blending the scholar with the statesman, he was "the best informed man" on every debated issue.[243] John Quincy Adams praised the "irresistible power of his eloquence, and the inexhaustible resources of his gigantic mind."[244]

Some contemporary scholars also laud Madison. Jack Rakove calls him the new republic's "most powerful and probing political intellect." Although his place in the nation's historical memory is less prominent than that of Washington, Franklin, and Jefferson, his "achievements are arguably no less important."[245] Robert Rutland praises Madison for winning "major concessions at the peace table." His performance and popularity enabled James Monroe, his designated successor, to enjoy an "era of good feelings."[246] Under Madison, the United States became "a full-fledged member of the community of nations."[247] While arguing that Madison's administration had many "faults and blunders," John Adams graciously concluded, it had "acquired more glory and established more Union, than all three Predecessors, Washington, Adams, and Jefferson, put together."[248]

Madison saw "the American Revolution as an extraordinary event in human history, the harbinger of a new" and better experience for all humanity. He expected the United States to serve as a "workshop of liberty" where other nations "could learn about the blessings of self-government."[249] A "well-founded commonwealth," Madison predicted, "may be immortal." The last survivor of the Virginia Convention of 1776 and the Federation Convention of 1787, he died on June 28, 1836, one week before the 60th anniversary of the Declaration of Independence. Although Madison's reticence to discuss his religious convictions make it impossible to know conclusively what he believed, his education, relationships, statements, and actions suggest that his faith, while not conventionally Christian, had a significant impact on his political philosophy and policies. Motivated by his faith, Madison maintained a "lifelong zeal for religious freedom," which powerfully affected its conception and practice in America.[250] Arguably, no American did more to ensure that the new republic rested on prudent principles. For more than 225 years, the political system Madison helped design has enjoyed substantial success and has served as a model for many other countries.

3

John Quincy Adams

A REPUBLIC OF VIRTUE

I implore [God] to enable me to continue to render essential service to my country, and that I may never be governed in my public conduct by any consideration other than that of my duty [to God and men].

MEMOIRS, December 31, 1807

> *Oh! God, my only trust was thou*
> *Through all life's scenes before;*
> *Lo, at thy throne again I bow,*
> *New mercies to implore. . . .*
> *Grant active power, grant fervid zeal,*
> *And guide by thy control,*
> *And ever be my country's weal*
> *The purpose of my soul. . . .*
> *Extend, all seeing God, thy hand,*
> *In memory still decree,*
> *And make to bless my native land*
> *An instrument of me.*
> Memoirs, September 21, 1817

Introduction

Early on the morning of June 13, 1825, as was his daily custom, 57-year-old President John Quincy Adams went swimming in the Potomac. Instead of swimming near the bank as he usually did, Adams and his servant Antoine Guista decided to row a small boat across the wide river and swim back. When they were halfway across the river, a fierce wind suddenly arose, and their boat filled with water, forcing them to jump overboard. Antoine, who was naked, easily swam to the other side. Adams, however, still wearing a long-sleeved shirt and pantaloons, gasped for breath and struggled to stay afloat as the shirt sleeves filled with water and hung like heavy weights on his arms. After many moments of terror, the exhausted president finally reached the shore. Guista returned to Washington and had trouble finding a vehicle to transport Adams to the White House. Almost five hours elapsed before the president made it back to his residence, leading some newspapers spread a rumor that Adams had drowned. That night a fatigued, but grateful, president wrote in his diary, "By the mercy of God our lives were spared, and no injury befell our persons."[1]

The story of John Quincy Adams's life is in many ways the story of America during the eventful years from the Revolution to the Mexican War. Born in 1767, Adams witnessed the course and triumphant conclusion of Americans' struggle for independence. The eldest son of America's "preeminent revolutionary couple," Adams viewed the battle of Bunker Hill, followed the drafting and ratification of the Constitution, and participated as a senator in the controversy over the Louisiana Purchase. As secretary of state, president, and a congressman, he wrestled with the moral and practical dilemmas involved in the nation's treatment of its two principal minorities—Indians and blacks.[2] The only major statesman birthed by the American founders, he was the American ambassador to Holland, Portugal, Prussia, Russia, and Great Britain and helped negotiate the Jay Treaty of 1796 (which led Britain to withdraw all its troops from American soil), the Treaty of Ghent (which ended the War of 1812), and the Transcontinental Treaty of 1819 (which gave Florida to the United States). In addition, he fought legal battles before the Supreme Court and championed human rights, serving his nation for more than sixty years under ten presidents. His 14,000-page diary, "the most complete, personal, day-to-day record of events and life in the New World" during its era, provides "a sweeping panorama of American history" from the American Revolution to the late 1840s.[3] The last tie to the founders, his memorable death while serving as a congressman in 1848 marked the end of an era. As one call for public mourning put it, "A Patriarch has gone to his rest—a link between the past and the present is broken—a sage has fallen at his post."[4]

Moreover, Adams embodied and expressed the concerns of many of his countrymen about the importance of a personal relationship with God, of morality to the well-being of the nation, and of creating a virtuous republic as a model for the world. Although not an evangelical Protestant, Adams incarnated and articulated many of the emphases and goals of the Second Great Awakening that occurred during the first four decades of the nineteenth century. As Christian values were being stamped very deeply into the language, education, culture, and ethos of the United States, Adams, by personal example and verbal exhortation, accentuated the benefits of public worship, Bible reading, prayer, and righteous conduct.[5] Like his father, Adams's wide travels and personal curiosity led him to personally investigate and read about many different religious traditions. During a three-month period in 1811 he attended Sunday services, weddings, baptisms, and funerals at a Catholic church, a Russian Orthodox church, and an Anglican mission congregation in St. Petersburg. In his diary, he analyzed the theology and worship of Greek and Russian Orthodox, Anglicans, Catholics, Muslims, Hindus, and Jews.[6]

Neither Adams's political philosophy nor actions can be understood without comprehending how integral his faith was to his life. Adams, his contemporaries, and later historians all emphasized his strong religious commitment. He engaged regularly in Christian worship and Bible study and insisted that only religion was "sufficiently powerful to control the appetites of man" or to dictate his actions. His diary contains dozens of statements like the following: "I close . . . with sentiments of gratitude to God for all . . . [His] favors, preservations, and blessings." Adams implored God to bless his wife, parents, children, friends, country, and the world and especially asked "for the aid of his spirit, that my future life may be more thoroughly devoted to his honor and glory and to usefulness on earth!"[7] When government officials were discussing what design should be placed on top of the Capitol in 1825, President Adams suggested an anchor of hope to testify to Americans' reliance on the "Supreme Disposer of events" and a pedestal with the dates, July 4, 1776, and March 4, 1789, inscribed on it. This motif would declare to the world that the United States was based on the Declaration of Independence and the Constitution, "supported by Justice in the past," and depended "upon Hope in Providence for the future."[8]

Adams's faith was central to his convictions, character, and conduct.[9] Few statesmen, one of his contemporaries remarked, acted "with a more continual and obvious reference to religion as motive, as a guide, [and] as a comfort."[10] Numerous commentators insisted that Adams pursued biblically based policies in an effort to construct a Christian commonwealth.[11] It was hard to conceive, proclaimed Congregationalist pastor Richard Storrs, of a person better suited than Adams to advance God's purposes to make America "a refuge for the oppressed, an asylum for the persecuted, a bulwark for the defence of the liberties of the world," and a model of constitutional government, equitable laws, and justice. "The crowning glory" of Adams's character, declared fellow Massachusetts Congressman Charles Hudson, "was his devotion to the cause of his Redeemer."[12]

"The premises of Christianity," wrote political theorist George Lipsky, provided the foundation for Adams's "entire intellectual system." Historian

William Weeks argued that Christian conviction guided Adams's life "more than that of any other political leader of his age." Unless we appreciate how deeply Adams was motivated by his belief that God had chosen the United States to do his work on earth, "much of his life is difficult to understand." Adams was convinced that God had designated America as his redeemer nation and chosen him to play a vital role in its mission of global redemption. The New Englander saw himself as God's instrument, the leader of a new generation called to continue what the founders had begun. Adams attributed his achievements during his six decades in public service to divine inspiration and aid. God had given him "a trust, a special responsibility—indeed, a heavy burden—from which he expected neither profit nor enjoyment."[13]

Throughout his life, Adams's religious principles strongly influenced his political ideals and practices. Few American politicians more consistently connected the course of their personal lives and national and international affairs with God's providential direction of history. "I have but one formula suited to all occasions," Adams told John Calhoun when they both served in James Monroe's cabinet: "Thy will be done." The day Adams was selected president, he wrote to his father declaring that he would close the day "as it began, with supplications to the Father of Mercies that its consequences may redound to His glory and the welfare of my country."[14]

Most biographers devote relatively little space to Adams's four years as president, calling them by such titles as "The Worst of Times," "The Tragic Presidency," and "Problems of a Minority President."[15] As Samuel Flagg Bemis puts it, Adams "had two notable careers" as a "diplomatic and continentalist" and as "a crusader in the House of Representatives against the expansion of slavery," "separated by an interlude as President."[16] Given Adams's significant political contributions before and after his presidency and the extent to which some of his views evolved, especially with regard to the rights of Indians and blacks, this chapter, more than others, will focus on Adams's entire career.

Adams was one of the nation's most intelligent and erudite presidents. He spoke several languages, read widely, wrote poetry, and, like Thomas Jefferson, was very knowledgeable about the sciences. In 1820 Adams was elected president of the American Academy of Arts and Sciences, and he helped create the Smithsonian Institute in Washington.[17] Before the Civil War, Bemis averred, only Benjamin Franklin did as much to further the cause of science in America as Adams.[18] Like his father, the sixth president had a powerful sense of duty and was highly introspective.[19] His parents instilled in him a "republican culture of civic virtue," which Adams strove to embody and pass on to his own children. As a senator, secretary of state, president, and congressman, Adams frequently sought God's guidance. "To His overruling providence," the president concluded his inaugural address, "I commit, with humble but fearless confidence, my own fate, and the future destinies of my country."[20]

The Faith of John Quincy Adams

Born in Braintree, Massachusetts, in 1767, John Quincy Adams was the second child of John and Abigail Adams. Even before the United States became an independent nation, they prayed, planned, and prepared their son for leadership. Stressing diligence, industry, piety, and education, they wanted their children to excel in every area of life.[21] From his early days, John Quincy's parents had exceedingly high expectations for him, as excerpts from two letters indicate. His mother repeatedly told him that like his father he must be "a guardian of the laws, liberty, and religion of your country." His father declared in 1794: "You come into life with advantages which will disgrace you if your success is mediocre. And if you do not rise to the head not only of your Profession, but of your Country, it will be owing to your own Lasiness, Slovenliness and Obstinacy."[22] Motivated by his parents' expectations, his sense of duty to God, and the needs of his nation, Adams sacrificed the possibility of financial gain, his desire to live a tranquil life as a man of letters, and marital happiness on the altar of service to his country. Because the founders took an active interest in him beginning in his teenage years, his father (who was constantly placed before him as "the personification of virtue and wisdom") played pivotal roles in the revolution and the new republic, none of the other founders had sons who entered politics, and the alcoholism and dissipation of his two brothers, "no American bore a greater burden of history and destiny."[23] Adams was the only American leader whose parents explicitly planned his life to fulfill that role.[24]

John Quincy's parents had a substantial impact on his faith. As explained in chapter 2, John Adams rejected Calvinism as a theological system, disavowed aspects of his Puritan heritage, and instead adopted a Unitarian perspective of God, Scripture, and salvation. Adams did accept two basic Calvinist premises, which he bequeathed to his son: human sinfulness required checks on people's behavior and limits on their power and, although people were prone to folly and evil, they were called to be God's agents on earth and to promote lofty causes.[25]

Because serving his country kept John away from home so much, he entrusted the socialization of their children principally to Abigail, whose faith was more orthodox. John urged her to provide their children's moral, religious, and educational training, a charge Abigail took very seriously.[26]

When precocious 11-year-old John Quincy accompanied his father to France for his diplomatic mission, his mother wrote, "Adhere to those religious sentiments and principles instilled in your mind and remember that you are accountable to your Maker for all your words and actions." Two years later she reminded him that "the only sure and permanent foundation of virtue is religion."[27] Abigail taught her son to believe that God was "infinitely wise, just, and good" and promised eternal life to all who lived virtuously on earth. Fulfilling his parents' expectations was paramount to Adams throughout his life. From his boyhood, John Quincy clearly saw himself as a child of destiny. "We are Sent into this World for Some end," he later wrote his brother Charles. "It is our duty to discover by Close Study what this end is" and then "pursue it with unconquerable perseverence [sic]."[28] John Quincy accepted his parents' belief that the United States could be a redeemer nation only if its leaders were morally upright and well-educated. By serving the republic, he would serve both God and humanity. He thanked his mother for teaching him that God's superintendence "of the universe is indeed sufficient for the preservation and well-being of all His creatures."[29]

No other president attended public worship more faithfully or read the Bible more devotedly than Adams. Moreover in his letters, poems, political addresses, published essays, and especially his diary, Adams extensively discussed his views of the doctrines of the Trinity, the atonement, human depravity, and salvation. He thought deeply and wrote profusely about the person and nature of Christ, the importance of virtue, and life after death. Adams insisted that he detested theological debate and metaphysical argument, but he took stances on many disputed issues. In addition, some of his positions changed over time, and in several cases they seem to be inconsistent with one another. This, coupled with the fact that he worshipped at varied churches, makes it hard to classify him denominationally. The only congregation he ever joined, however, was the Unitarian church in Quincy, and he frequently worshiped at a Unitarian church in Washington. Therefore, although he did not agree with all the doctrines of Unitarianism, never explicitly denied the deity of Christ, and appreciated aspects of numerous theological perspectives, it seems fair to label him a Unitarian.

In 1797 Adams married Louisa Catherine Johnson, the daughter of an American diplomat serving in London. Like her husband, Louisa had a strong faith that was shaped by her childhood experiences and the trials of life. She was devoted to the Episcopal Book of Common Prayer. She derived consolation from her faith after their infant daughter died in 1812, and the death of two of their sons also prompted periods of intense religious reflection.

Throughout their long marriage, she urged John Quincy to focus on serving God and people rather than on self-gratification or fame.[30]

During the first half of his life Adams attended church more to fulfill social and political expectations than because of strong interest or fervent belief. While serving as a minister to Russia, he periodically went to Catholic or Orthodox services since there were no Protestant churches.[31] Like some other presidents, Adams had pivotal moments that solidified and strengthened his faith. At a New Year's Eve party in Berlin in 1800, a young, popular, army officer suddenly dropped dead, prompting Adams to reassess "the vanity and frailty of earthly enjoyments" and to reevaluate his faith.[32] This tragedy, coupled with the birth of his first child four months later, helped deepen Adams's relationship with God, which until this point had been rather perfunctory.[33] His faith also became deeper as he coped in 1812 with the death of his daughter Louisa Catherine at age one while the Adams were in Russia. It prompted the future president to study the Bible and Christian theology more diligently. "Religious sentiments," he wrote, were becoming "more constantly habitual to my mind." However, in later life, Adams lamented that he had not attended church regularly while in St. Petersburg, Holland, Berlin, or France, and thereby had lost "rich opportunities" to obtain religious, moral, political, and intellectual instruction.[34]

In 1819 Adams began attending church twice each Sunday, a pattern he continued for the rest of his life.[35] When sickness or special sessions of Congress required Adams to miss church, he lamented that he felt "deep mortification." He usually went to morning and afternoon services held in either the Hall of the House of Representatives, All Souls' Unitarian Church, St. John's Episcopal Church, or Second Presbyterian Church.[36] Although many Protestants denounced Unitarians as infidels, he helped found and often worshipped at this small Unitarian congregation in Washington.[37] Believing that Christians of various denominations were traveling by different roads to the same destination, he attended almost every congregation in Washington at least once. As a "frequent sinner," Adams wrote, he needed to be constantly admonished and "exhorted to virtue," which all Christian denominations did. Almost every Sunday, he declared, the sermon had a "pointed application to my own situation," often providing "consolation, support, encouragement," "and sometimes warning and admonition."[38]

Although his forebears had belonged to the First Parish Church in Quincy (part of the liberal wing of Congregationalism that became Unitarian) for generations, Adams had been reluctant to join this church because of often residing in other places and dissatisfaction with his spiritual condition. Soon after his father died in 1826, Adams finally joined, publicly promising to live by the precepts of Christianity.[39] He conceded that he should have taken this step thirty years earlier, instead of permitting the "tumult of the world, false shame, [and] a distrust of my own unworthiness" to keep him from doing so. During the remainder of his life Adams participated regularly in the life of this church whenever he was in Quincy, frequently serving as its delegate at the ordination of ministers of neighboring congregations.[40]

Adams argued that in corporate worship people should confess their sins, give gratitude to God, praise His perfections, and entreat Him to meet their spiritual and physical needs. Thanksgiving should spring from people's recognition of God's "innumerable blessings" and from the "wonder and veneration, mingled with love, which the displays of infinite benevolence and unbounded power" prompted in their hearts.[41] Public worship helped Adams to experience "the goodness of God," rely on "His mercy in affliction," and trust that He would bring "good out of evil." From the public reading of Scripture and the singing of hymns, he added while president, "I do gather strength and fortitude" and confidence that he could pass "unhurt through the furnace that awaits me." In 1838 Adams deplored "the neglect of public worship" in Washington as "an increasing evil," and protested that "the indifference to all religion throughout the whole country portends no good."[42] After he died, many lauded his faithful participation in worship. As a Unitarian eulogist put it, "neither age and feebleness, nor storm and darkness, detained him from his accustomed place on the Lord's day."[43]

As a former professor of oratory at Harvard, Adams had high standards for preaching, and in his diary, he regularly commented on both the delivery and content of sermons he heard.[44] Preaching had been the "most effectual weapon" of the Reformation. Although sermons had intensified battles over "speculative doctrine and ecclesiastical discipline," he asserted, they had been the "most energetic instruments" of Christianity. Because enlightening the mind was an "effectual mean of amending the heart," preachers must teach, refute error, discourage vice, and promote virtue. Pastors must help their parishioners live more righteously and defend the Christian faith against the attacks of atheists and Deists.[45] Despite such comments, Adams clearly preferred sermons on moral conduct to ones on theology.[46]

Adams tried to reserve Sundays for worship and spiritual reflection. While serving as a minister to Holland, Adams stopped attending the meetings of a society of learned men when they switch them to Sundays because he believed the Lord's Day should be devoted to religious activities. After he was chosen president of the National Sabbath Convention in 1844, its members passed a resolution praising "the testimony he has borne to the importance of the Sabbath."[47] However, because he thought the government should not force people to obey the first four of the Ten Commandments, Adams, while serving as a congressman, opposed legislation to make Sunday a mandatory day of rest.

For much of his life, every morning Adams read four or five chapters of the Bible and often commentaries on these passages, usually reading the entire Bible each year.[48] He refused to allow any other responsibilities to interfere with his "daily and systematic perusal of the Bible." As one contemporary put it, he read the Bible "daily and critically and delighted in its study."[49] Adams studied the Bible in Greek, German, French, and English, and he urged people to use "critical and explanatory notes" to better understand the Scriptures.[50] He maintained that the Bible should be understood as God's revelation, a historical record of the Jews, a system of morality, and an unequaled literary masterpiece.[51] Adams paraphrased all the Psalms and wrote commentaries on some of them. The Bible, he testified, supplied "light, strength, and comfort." Adams insisted that "Book of books," which "contains the duties, the admonitions, the promises, and the rewards of the Christian gospel," had been "a soothing consolation" to him.[52]

To help make the Bible widely available and encourage people to read it, Adams served as one of the vice presidents of the American Bible Society from 1824 until 1848.[53] "I believe that the respect and veneration of any person for the Bible," wrote Adams, "will increase in proportion to the intimacy of his acquaintance with its contents."[54] He urged people of all ages to read attentively and meditate on several chapters of the Bible each day to guide their conduct in this world and prepare them for the next.[55] Adams insisted that people needed divine assistance to understand the Scriptures.[56] He adopted Jesus's admonition to Peter in the Garden of Gethsemane, "Watch and pray, that ye enter not into temptation," as his motto, had the text inscribed on a signet ring, and composed a sonnet titled "Watch and Pray."[57]

Adams's thorough knowledge of the Bible is evident in his numerous quotations of and allusions to Scripture in his diary and public addresses. In debates with opponents, he often cited the Bible to support his positions. For example, Adams presented a petition in the House from a group of women opposing the annexation of Texas. When another congressman rebuked these women for participating in politics, Adams asked where his colleague got the idea that women could not engage in political life. Certainly, he had not found "it in sacred history." Had he never heard of Miriam the prophetess, Deborah the judge, Jael the warrior, or Esther who saved her people by petitioning a king?[58]

While serving as the American minister in St. Petersburg, Adams wrote a series of letters on the importance of studying the Bible to his son George

Washington who was residing with relatives in Massachusetts. Perusing the Bible, collections of sermons, theological works, and Greek philosophers to prepare these letters bolstered Adams's own knowledge and faith.[59] He exhorted his young son to read and reflect upon the Bible to become "wiser and more virtuous." The study of Scripture could make children "useful citizens," "respectable members of society, and a real blessing to their parents." His personal study, Adams declared, helped "strengthen my good desires and subdue my propensities to evil." He emphasized that the Bible revealed God's will and contained "a system of religion and morality" that people could "examine upon its own merits, independent of the sanction it receives from being the Word of God." Adams also lauded the Bible's "unrivalled" moral code.[60] Scripture taught that people had duties to God, others, and themselves encapsulated in the two great love commandments.[61]

Throughout his life, Adams cultivated a close relationship with God not only by attending public worship and studying the Bible but through other forms of Christian piety including praying, striving to obey all biblical commandments, reflecting in his diary, writing poems, and composing hymns. If God had created all things and people were morally obligated to obey His will, he contended, then piety was both rational and essential. Christ commanded his disciples to "aim at absolute perfection," which involved "self-subjugation and brotherly love," the "complete conquest of our own passions," and benevolence toward others, even "our most inveterate enemies."[62] His diary entry the day he was inaugurated illustrates Adams's faith: "I entered upon this day with a supplication to Heaven." "I closed the day" with "thanksgiving to God for all His mercies and favors past, and with prayers for the continuance of them to my country and to myself and mine."[63]

Adams prayed constantly about all aspects of his life and frequently asked others to pray that God would help him faithfully discharge his public duties and cope with his personal afflictions and grief.[64] When Adams refused to overrule his dismissal from the army in 1826, a disgruntled physician, George Todson, threatened to kill the president. The incident reminded Adams of the "frail tenure" of human life, and he prayed that "the Spirit of God [would] sustain me and preserve me from any weakness unworthy of my station." He wrote, "My life is in the hands of a higher power than the will of man." His pastor in Quincy, William Lunt, declared that Adams believed in the efficacy of prayer and testified that Adams's prayer for a gravely ill child had moved him deeply.[65]

Despite his personal commitment to prayer, Adams, unlike many other presidents including his father, did not declare any national days of prayer and thanksgiving. When James Laurie, pastor of the Second Presbyterian Church in Washington, asked him to do so in November 1825, he declined. He argued that his opponents would likely denounce such a declaration as a political ploy and an imposition of "New England manners."[66]

Adams also expressed his piety by composing numerous hymns, writing religious verse, and delivering addresses to defend Christianity.[67] A hymnal used in the 1840s contained twenty-two of Adams's compositions.[68] Shortly after his death, a collection of his poems was published as *Poems of Religion and Society*.[69] Concerned about increasing skepticism and infidelity, Adams gave a lecture on faith many times in the early 1840s, arguing that true Christians believed in God, biblical inspiration, Christ's divine mission, and eternal rewards and punishments.[70]

To Adams, the Bible's "three fundamental pillars" were "the unity and omnipotence of God," people's immortality and accountability to the "Creator in a future world" for all their earthly deeds, and a system of morality based on the commandments to love God with all one's heart, mind, and strength and one's neighbor as oneself.[71] "I have at all times," Adams wrote in 1843, sincerely believed "in the existence of a Supreme Creator of the world," in people's responsibility to God for their conduct, and in "the divine mission of the crucified Saviour," who proclaimed eternal life and preached "peace on earth" and "the natural equality of all mankind."[72] Adams also stressed the importance of the "Great Commission" of Matthew 28, which required Christians to teach all nations about the doctrine of everlasting life and Jesus's new commandment to love one another. To Adams, the wonders of the world and humanity provided overwhelming evidence for God's existence. In "Lord of All Worlds" he declared,

> The fool denies, the fool alone,
> Thy being, Lord, and boundless might;
> Denies the firmament, thy throne,
> Denies the sun's meridian light;
> Denies the fashion of his frame,
> The voice he hears, the breath he draws;
> O idiot atheist! To proclaim
> Effects unnumbered without cause![73]

Like his father, Adams continually asserted that God providentially directed all human affairs. In 1809 he declared that he could be content spending the remainder of his life as a Harvard rhetoric professor "if he who rules the destinies of men has so decreed." Reflecting on Napoleon's defeat in 1814, he stated that God's "interposition" in producing this event "has been so signal, so peculiar, so distinct from all human operation" that people living in an earlier era might have considered it a miracle. The pious would consider it "a judgment of Heaven." That same year Adams declared, "On the providence of God alone is my reliance. . . . [L]et his will be done." Adams pronounced the Transcontinental Treaty with Spain in 1819 "the work of an intelligent and all-embracing Cause." As Americans were voting in the election of 1824, Adams wrote that he was ready "to meet the fate to which I am destined" by God. In his inaugural address Adams promised to govern knowing that "except the Lord keep the city, the watchman waketh but in vain." In his First Annual Message to Congress, Adams asserted that Americans owed "gratitude to the Omnipotent Disposer of All Good for the continuance of the signal bless-ings of His providence."[74] After losing the 1828 presidential election, Adams declared, "My only trust is in the Divine Disposer." He asked God to "stay the hand of His wrath, to grant me fortitude to endure" and to dispose "of me as to Him shall seem wise and good." Adams admitted that he struggled to humbly accept "the will of God," and he implored God's "mercy to direct my path."[75]

Although Adams believed that God had performed miracles, he questioned many of the ones recorded in Scripture. He did not completely reject miracles, but they made it more difficult for him to trust the veracity of Scripture. "The miracles in the Bible," he maintained, "furnish the most powerful of all objec-tions against its authenticity, both historical and doctrinal." Adams preferred the Bible's "sublime morals," "unparalleled conceptions of the nature of God," and "irresistible power over the heart, with the simple narrative of the life and death of Jesus, stripped of all . . . supernatural agency."[76] At the same time, though, Adams professed belief in Genesis's description of creation and the historicity of the flood and the tower of Babel incident.[77] When Unitarian min-ister Horace Holley argued in a sermon that the biblical account of creation was no different than the fables of other ancient literature, Adams declared, "I could scarcely sit and hear him with patience."[78]

While frequently affirming his faith in God the Father, throughout his life Adams deeply pondered biblical teachings about the Trinity, never either repudiating or affirming the doctrine. He noted that many Christian apolo-gists distinguished between "things *above reason*, which, as mysteries of reli-gion," should be believed, and "things contrary to reason," which "must be false." On this basis, Protestants repudiated the Catholic doctrine of tran-substantiation. However, Adams contended that the "Trinity, the Divinity of Christ," "the atonement, all miracles, the Immaculate Conception of Jesus, and a devil maintaining war against Omnipotence" were as contrary to rea-son as "the *Real Presence* of the Eucharist." Like his father, Adams especially liked 1 Corinthians 1:27: "But God hath chosen the foolish things of the world to confound the wise, and God hath chosen the weak things of the world to confound the things that are mighty."[79] Unlike theistic rationalists, he did not make reason the final arbiter. Although reason was "a guard and check" on people's "religious appetite," it would be presumptuous to make it "the umpire of our faith."[80] Adams admitted that his own reason was as fallible as the pope's and "probably much more so than the collective reason of an ecclesiastical Council." Therefore, he refused to reject a dogma merely because his reason did not sanction it. The problem with the doctrine of transubstantiation was not its absurdity but "its pernicious tendencies" to subject the human mind "to the arbitrary dominion of the priesthood—weak, corrupt, and fallible men like ourselves." If a person believed that priests had special power to "turn a wafer into a God" and a "cup of wine into the blood of my Redeemer," then the next "natural step would be to believe" that people's "eternal weal or woe depended upon the fiat of the same priest," which encouraged individuals to propitiate the clergy instead of God.[81]

Writing to his son in 1811, Adams admitted that "so many passages, both in the Gospels and the Epistles" supported "the doctrine of the Divinity of Christ and so many" appeared to be "incompatible with it," that "it is not among the things clearly revealed." "I therefore conclude it is one of those mysteries not to be unfolded to me during this present life." Whether Jesus was "a manifestation of Almighty God in the form of a man, or whether he was but the only begotten Son of God, by whom he made the world, and by whom he will judge the world" was a "speculative question" upon which he refused to take sides.[82] However, in a letter to his father two years later, Adams insisted that one could not call Christ "a mere man," without "pronouncing him an Imposter." Jesus "sometimes positively asserted, and at other times," allowed his disciples to assert "that he was God."[83] Adams wrote in 1827 that Christ's divinity was "often obscurely intimated" and sometimes directly and other times indirectly asserted in the New Testament, but, on the whole, the Bible neither "demonstrated [n]or refuted" the doctrine. That same year Adams declared, "I believe in one God, but His nature is incomprehensible to me." In the debate between the Unitarians and Trinitarians, Adams had "no precise belief" because he had "no definite understanding."[84] He told Daniel Baker, pastor of the Second Presbyterian Church, that he was not "either a Trinitarian or a Unitarian."[85] Like many early Unitarians, Adams was reluctant to explicitly state that Christ was not divine. During the Second Great Awakening, Adams sought to steer a middle course between Unitarians and evangelicals. He deplored the argument of some Unitarians that religion is "merely a system of morals."[86] On the other hand, Adams wished that evangelicals would acknowledge, as he did, that many theological questions could not be resolved.[87]

Adams told Baker in 1828 that he believed "Jesus Christ was superhuman; but whether he was God or only the first [in rank] of created beings was not clearly revealed to me in the Scriptures."[88] Jesus came to earth to "preach repentance and remission of sins," to proclaim God's glory, and to reveal the purpose of life. Jesus, Adams asserted, lived a life of "absolute perfection," under circumstances no other human ever faced, especially the agony of the cross. "Christ repeatedly declined to use" His "miraculous powers sufficient to control all the laws of nature" to save himself from suffering.[89] Jesus performed miracles and forgave sins, Adams asserted, to validate His authority as the Son of God. Moreover, after His crucifixion, God raised Him from the dead and hundreds of disciples saw Him during a forty-day period. Adams complained that an Easter sermon he heard in 1834 had not discussed the resurrection, an event Christians should celebrate "with religious fervor." Easter was more important than Christmas because the resurrection completed Christ's earthly mission and guaranteed that life was everlasting.[90] Adams insisted that "Jesus was a *teacher* sent from God" to explain how people could obtain "eternal blessedness in Heaven."[91]

To Adams, Jesus was much more than the master teacher and the great exemplar; He was the supreme revelation of God, whom Adams repeatedly called "my savior" and "my redeemer."[92] Comparing Socrates and Jesus, as Joseph Priestley did, Adams protested, was like comparing a "farthing candle and the Sun!"[93] It is not clear, though, how Adams thought Jesus provided salvation. Reflecting on a sermon he heard on John 3:16 in 1828, Adams wondered "How could belief in the Son of God save the believer from perishing and confer upon him everlasting life?"[94] Adams argued, however, that by their transgression "the first parents of mankind" forfeited their "immortality, innocence, and happiness." As a result, humanity could only be redeemed by "the intervention of a Saviour." Christ's blood had washed away "the pollution of our original sin," and people could be assured of "eternal happiness in a future life" if they obeyed God's will. Summarizing his beliefs, Adams wrote, "I reverence God as my creator" with "holy fear. I venerate Jesus Christ as my redeemer; and as far as I can understand, the redeemer of the world. But this belief is dark and dubious."[95]

Ultimately, Adams concluded he did not need to take a definitive stance on Christ's deity because it did not affect what he considered the essence of religion—good works. He insisted that "the question of Trinity or Unity, or of the single or double personal nature of Christ," had "no bearing whatsoever" on human conduct.[96] For Adams, morality was an indispensable aspect of religion. God had not prescribed one system of morality for the clergy and another for laypeople he argued; the divine precepts were the same for everyone.[97] Shortly before leaving office, Adams reflected on his four years of frequent frustration and failure. In every situation, he wrote, people had a "line of conduct" God expected them to follow. Even in the midst of adversity, individuals must exercise virtues that displayed human dignity and promoted God's glory. Adams repeatedly argued that "a resurrection of bliss to all who have done good" and "condemnation to all who have done evil" was "a fundamental article of Christianity."[98] He declared that God gave man the Bible "to enable him, by faith in his Redeemer, and by works conformable to that faith, to secure his salvation in a future world, and to promote his well-being in the present."[99]

His conviction that conduct was more important than doctrine and varied worship experiences led Adams not to completely affirm the beliefs of any particular denomination. Moreover, like Jefferson, he despised internecine feuds between religious communions and deplored the lack of tolerance of some groups. Debates over religious doctrine, he complained, were irresolvable and divisive and impeded Christians from concentrating on morality and service.[100] He urged preachers to focus on conduct and the positive fruit of religion rather than dogma. Sadly, the church, he wrote, had always been "distracted with controversy."[101]

The doctrine of the atonement especially troubled Adams. "That the execution, as a malefactor, of one person, the Creator of all worlds, eighteen hundred years ago, should have redeemed me" "from eternal damnation" was "too shocking" to believe, "solemn nonsense," and "inconceivable absurdity."[102] To Adams, Christ's mission was "to teach all mankind the way to salvation." His death "was necessary to the universal spread of His doctrine. . . . Christ died as a man, not as God."[103]

Unable to believe that Christ had paid for his sin on the cross, Adams struggled with whether or not he was saved and ultimately found comfort, despite his emphasis on works, in his belief in God's mercy. In 1830 Adams complained that "the general character of Presbyterian preaching" was "to terrify rather than allure. This does not altogether suit my temper." His belief "in the goodness and mercy of the Creator" led him to repudiate the position that God existed "only to hurl thunder." "Exhortations to righteousness and truth, brotherly kindness and charity" motivated him more than "unceasing denunciations of vengeance and punishment." After attending the Second Presbyterian Church one Sunday in 1837, he wrote, "Whether I am or shall be saved is . . . unknown to me. I know that I have been, and am, a sinner,—perhaps, by the depravity of the human heart, an unreclaimable sinner; but I continue to believe in God's tender mercies; that, having the power to make me both will and do, however He may chastise, He will not cruelly punish."[104] Near the end of his life, Adams wrote, "I have daily and nightly warnings to be prepared for a sudden summons to meet my maker. My hope is of mercy."[105]

While struggling to understand the nature of salvation, Adams repeatedly asserted his belief in life after death. He asked God to help him prepare to appear "in thy presence to give an account of the deeds done in the body" and to grant him "the hope and fruition of a blessed immortality." "If the existence of man were limited to this life," Adams wrote, "it would be impossible for me to believe the universe made any moral sense."[106] Like German philosopher Immanuel Kant, Adams reasoned that since virtue was not always rewarded and vice was not always punished on earth, a divine reckoning would occur in the afterlife.[107] Since everlasting life could not be proven philosophically, people must "seek for proofs of our immortality" in the Bible.[108]

In addition to repudiating Calvinism's conception of election, Adams also rejected its doctrine of human depravity. However, he constantly bemoaned humanity's weaknesses and moral deficiencies. Adams told his father that he had little "confidence in the wisdom and virtue of men." He complained that the "base and dirty tricks" his political rivals had used to try to destroy his character were "sorry pictures" of the human heart. He even admitted that the doctrine of human depravity explained the motivations of his own heart quite well.[109] However, he protested that Calvinist clergy thought too "ill of human nature" and that some of them saw themselves as chaplains in "a penitentiary, discoursing to the convicts."[110] How could people who had good "reasoning faculties," he wondered, sincerely believe in the absurd doctrine of "the universal depravity of mankind"? Adams lambasted an Isaac Watts hymn for portraying people as "more base and brutish than the beasts." "If Watts had said this on a weekday to any one of his parishioners, would he not have knocked him down?" (perhaps illustrating Watts's point!). The Bible's declaration that the heart was "deceitful and desperately wicked," Adams contended, should be interpreted figuratively. People had selfish passions, but they could learn to control them. In addition to contradicting Scripture and experience, the claim that all human beings were depraved, Adams argued, degraded people and hampered their efforts to be virtuous.[111] Endowed with a basically good nature, people were capable of following the moral precepts Jesus taught. Religious and moral training, Adams maintained, enabled most individuals to lead upright lives.[112]

During his long life, Adams's faith remained strong even though he experienced much disappointment, grief, and depression. One of his children died in infancy and two in the prime of life. His presidency was a painful ordeal, and he lost his bid for reelection to Andrew Jackson whom he had come to despise. Shortly after Jackson's inauguration in 1829, James Laurie preached on the trials of Job at Second Presbyterian Church to a congregation that included both the sixth and seventh presidents. His sermon deeply moved Adams. Soon after leaving office, he prayed, "Almighty God, bestow upon me a spirit of Gratitude, of Humility, of Cheerfulness, and of Resignation." He asked God to make him grateful for the "numberless blessings" he enjoyed; humble as he recognized his "infirmities and unworthiness"; cheerful as he contemplated the favors God bestowed; and resigned "to the Dispensations of Thy Will."[113]

During the late 1820s, Adams's eldest son George amassed sizable gambling and drinking debts. Worried that their son would follow the path of drunkenness that the president's brothers had taken that led to their destruction, Adams and his wife urged George to eschew liquor, tobacco, and other vices. The president tried to persuade him to join the church, arguing that it would encourage spiritual reflection, benevolence, and virtue. Shortly after Adams left office, George died, possibly by accidental drowning, but probably by suicide. Still mourning his loss to Jackson, Adams poured out his grief in his diary. However, it did not shake his strong faith in God. Learning that his son had died, a grieving Adams wrote that only "the power of prayer" could console him. "May I not be forsaken of my ever living, almighty benefactor, nor of my confidence in him." Several months after later, Adams thanked God for His blessings. God's "chastisements have been most afflictive, but I have experienced mercy with judgment. The loss of power and of popular favor I could have endured with fortitude . . . . But my beloved son!" He concluded, "grant me fortitude, patience, perseverance, and active energy, and let thy will be done."[114]

Samuel Flagg Bemis concludes that meaningful activities and prayer helped Adams survive his trials and lift him from depression and despair. Whether it was historical or allegorical, Adams argued, the book of Job taught "the lessons of patience under affliction, of resignation under the divine chastisement, of undoubting confidence in the justice and goodness of God under every possible calamity, and of inflexible adherence to integrity under every temptation."[115] In 1834 the Adams's second son, John Adams II, died, seemingly the victim of overwork, but possibly of the alcoholism that had contributed to the death of his two uncles and his older brother. Despite his grief, the ex-president professed that "my lot has been a happy one upon earth" and offered "gratitude to Him who is the disposer of events."[116]

Although problems with alcohol plagued his family, Adams usually drank a glass of wine after dinner, sometimes served wine to guests, and was a wine connoisseur throughout his life.[117] Adams lauded the temperance movement, but he argued that wine was a gift of God when consumed in moderation. While temperate use of wine was beneficial, Adams argued, intoxication was "a heinous sin." Consequently, he never took a pledge to abstain from alcohol or joined an association to promote temperance.[118]

Philosophy of Government

Greg Russell argues that Adams's "intellectual universe" was "a compound of Christian faith and classical virtue." Building upon medieval thinkers, he insisted that nations were subject to transcendent moral standards, that rulers were responsible to their constituents, that governments were subordinate to laws, and that international relations rested on moral principles. Few American statesmen have written as extensively on the moral purposes of government, especially its obligation to promote justice and liberty. Despite his personal problems and the nation's perplexing dilemmas, Adams avowed that God was progressively improving the human condition and that He used governments to accomplish this.[119]

Adams's conviction that government was an instrument the Creator designed to glorify Himself and benefit humanity helped shape his understanding of its responsibilities. As a congressman, Adams declared that he strove to faithfully serve his constituents, his state, the whole country, people "in every quarter of the globe," and especially God "who rules the world in justice and mercy."[120] Because God was the supreme sovereign, the authority of magistrates was delegated and derivative. Political officials, therefore, could not simply do what the majority (even the vast majority) of the people wanted; they must do what was morally right.[121] Eternal standards of justice, Adams averred, must guide governments in both their domestic and foreign policies. The principles of Christianity, he asserted, applied to "the government of states as much as the conduct of individuals."[122] "The eternal and immutable laws of justice and of morality," Adams insisted, "are paramount to all human legislation."[123]

The preamble to the Constitution, Adams stressed, mandated the federal government to "establish justice," "provide for the common defense," and "promote the general welfare."[124] Fulfilling these responsibilities and dealing effectively with other nations, required a strong and active federal government. The government must undertake projects that were beyond the scope of private initiative, including subsidizing education, creating a favorable business climate, and improving transportation.[125] He repudiated Scottish philosopher

Adam Smith's argument that individuals' pursuit of their own self-interest automatically advanced the good of society. Instead, Adams urged individuals to intentionally promote the common good to help strengthen social cohesion and elevate the nation's morality.[126] Rejecting the widespread conviction that government primarily had negative functions—preserving order, protecting property, and punishing evildoers—he maintained it also had positive duties—ensuring equality and liberty and increasing opportunities and material comforts.[127] Since God had made man a "sociable being," the happiness of humans was interdependent. Thus, as both president and a congressman, Adams promoted government projects to enrich the entire country.[128] He supported a stronger federal judiciary, a national banking system, a national bankruptcy law, and a tariff rate he thought benefited all sections of the country. Without these bonds, Adams feared, the federal union, torn by dissension and discord, would unravel.

While he wanted to increase the federal government's power to promote the public good, Adams did not want the state to regulate personal morality. Jesus "came to teach, and not compel," he asserted. "His law was a LAW of LIBERTY." Christianity demanded "freedom of thought." He opposed passing laws that prohibited liquor consumption because self-government alone could ensure that people did not abuse alcohol. Adams urged reformers to teach people "more by example than by precept." The dictates of individuals' consciences and the power of their own wills, not the force of law, could develop virtues.[129]

Throughout his long political career Adams often strongly defended positions he deemed to be moral no matter what the political repercussions. Like his father, Adams believed the "magistrate is the servant not of his own desires, not even of the people, but of his God."[130] Convinced that his ultimate responsibility was to God and biblical principles, not to his party or constituents, if Adams thought an action was right, he usually did it even if it was politically unpopular.[131] After being the only senator who voted against a bill in 1806, he declared, "Everything on earth but a sense of duty dictated silence to *me* on this subject, if not acquiescence. I have acted upon inflexible principle, and am to take the consequences." "Adams never surrendered to any man or party," Bemis concludes, "only to the will of God." However, Adams insisted that loyalty to principle "is wise only" if "the principle is important" and adhering to it produced "practical good."[132]

Like George Washington, whom he revered, Adams believed the government must serve all citizens, and he repudiated parties, sectionalism, and interest groups, which were increasingly influencing American politics. Although he vigorously strove to further the common good throughout his entire political career, only as a congressman in the 1830s did Adams acquire the label of the "Man of the Whole Nation." He protested that parties often prevented political officials from making decisions based on principles. "The Prince of Darkness could not spur the most devoted of his instruments upon the earth," Adams wrote, to create "anything *more* pernicious than parties."[133] As president, he denounced the spoils system and appointed individuals on the basis of merit, not personal or party loyalty. Adams also refused to remove officials appointed by his predecessors unless they were incompetent or immoral. Adams blamed his inability to accomplish many of his objectives as president on partisan politicians who sought to benefit their faction or region rather than the nation.

To Adams, the United States was a Christian country that had a God-given mission in the world. The Puritans came to New England, he maintained, "to advance the kingdom of our Lord Jesus Christ, *and* to enjoy the liberties of the Gospel in *purity, with peace.*" Because of the United States' exaltation of the "natural equality of mankind" and "the two eternal principles" upon which it stood—"civil and religious liberty"—it "must be that kingdom of Christ against which the gates of hell shall not prevail."[134] His belief that God had selected America to help redeem the world led Adams to strongly support continental expansionism. The laws of nature decreed that the United States would occupy the entire North American continent, he argued, just as surely as "that the Mississippi should flow to the sea."[135] Adams maintained that God had chosen Americans to civilize and Christianize the entire continent, model liberty, eradicate European colonialism, and spread democracy to the world.

Adams saw democracy and Christianity as closely connected. Since democracy was "the corner-stone of the Christian religion," he averred, Americans could simultaneously promote republican government and the gospel. Because the United States had more liberty than any other country, he argued, it would become the world's "most powerful nation."[136] During the congressional debates over Oregon in 1845, a Georgia Whig asked Adams why he believed the United States had the right to control the entire Oregon territory. The Massachusetts congressman responded by asking the clerk to read Genesis 1:28, which instructs people to "be fruitful and multiply, and replenish the earth and subdue it." The United States claimed Oregon, he proclaimed, "to make the wilderness bloom as the rose, to establish laws, to increase, multiply, and subdue the earth, which we are commanded to do by the behest of God Almighty." Lord George Bentinck denounced Adams in Parliament for "impiously and blasphemously" using "the word of God as a justification for lighting up the firebrand and unleashing the hell-dogs of war."[137]

Adams envisioned and worked persistently to create a model republic, an orderly, stable community, united by its citizens' shared political, religious, and moral convictions to provide a shining example of liberty and virtue for the whole world. He warned that both internal and external forces threatened this goal. Raucous political debates over the power of the federal government, national expansion, the rights of Indians, and the morality of slavery were likely to diminish American strength. So would going abroad "in search of monsters to destroy." The nation must resort to war, Adams maintained, only if its security was directly endangered or its rights violated. Although Americans wanted all nations to gain independence, their government must not support revolution either in Europe or South America. Democracy must spread because of its intrinsic appeal, not because of the use of force.[138] Throughout most of the nineteenth century, American foreign policy followed the course Adams prescribed: while sympathizing with the quest of other nations for independence, the United States did not provide financial aid or intervene militarily to help achieve it.[139]

For both moral and economic reasons, Adams urged the United States to increase its trade with other nations. He strove to create a community of nations committed to commercial exchange, democracy, and liberty. Increased trade could help knit the world's diverse societies into a new global community and make war obsolete. Elevating trade to a moral duty, Adams protested against policies that inhibited it. As a diplomat, secretary of state, and president he strove to maintain the freedom of the seas, prevent the impressments of sailors, and protect the ships of neutral countries in wartime. As secretary of state, Adams protested when China refused to trade with Western powers. He contended that people had a duty "to contribute, as much as is in their power to one another's happiness." Through commerce they could increase one another's "comfort and well-being." The Chinese, he complained, did not "consider themselves bound by the Christian precept to love their neighbour as themselves." Instead, they espoused the "execrable principle of [Thomas] Hobbes" "that the state of Nature is a state of War." Because commerce was one of people's "natural rights and duties," China's unwillingness to trade with the West on "terms of equal reciprocity" was selfish, unchristian, and "unsocial" and inhibited international progress.[140] While all nations should be guided by the laws of nature, Adams averred, Christian nations must also follow "the laws of humanity and mutual benevolence" Christ taught. If all nations adhered to the "fundamental maxim of nature" that people should do unto others as they wanted others to do unto them, "it would solve all political, as well as individual, problems."[141]

Despite its divisions and struggles, Adams remained confident God would use the United States to further the world's material and moral progress. In 1830 Adams proclaimed, "never since the foundation of the world" had the prospects "been more encouraging" "that the religion of Jesus shall prevail throughout the earth."[142] In an 1845 article he insisted that God's plan for His chosen nation was near fruition. Fusing biblical teaching with French philosopher Marie Jean Antoine Condorcet's famous 1795 essay on progress, the former president argued that America "stood on the threshold of [creating] the best possible world."[143]

Adams maintained that transcendent principles revealed in both Scripture and nature should govern the behavior of both individuals and nations. In both private and public life, Adams doggedly sought to follow moral principles, and he repeatedly urged other political leaders to do the same.[144] In 1820 members of James Monroe's cabinet debated whether the United States, while claiming to be neutral, should clandestinely help South American rebels gain independence from Spain. The discussion prompted Adams to complain in his diary that "moral considerations seldom appear to have much weight in the minds of our statesmen, unless connected with popular feelings." Neither President Monroe nor other cabinet members thought that "the dishonorable" act "of giving secret aid to the revolutionists, while openly professing neutrality" should "stand in the way of measures otherwise expedient, especially if supported by popular prejudice." Adams countered that the more that "pure moral principle" guided "the policy and conduct of a Government, the wiser and more profound that policy will be." While virtue was not always "crowned with success," God expected people to always act righteously. Adams recognized that "the path of virtue" was "not always clear" and argued that because human affairs were complicated, "artifice and simulation" might "occasionally be practised [sic]." Even the sternest moralists allowed such actions in war, and they might sometimes be justifiable when a nation was contemplating war. It was a universal maxim, however, that "*fraud* is never justifiable where *force* would not be equally justifiable to effect the same object."[145] The light of the divine gift of reason, Adams contended, would enable people to discover and implement God's will in the world. He believed that "the human mind had a natural affinity for truth and justice."[146] However, since reason did not govern international relations, the use of force might sometimes be necessary to protect freedom.[147]

Adams's Faith and Political Policies

Four candidates split the electoral vote in the presidential election of 1824, with none of them winning a majority. The House of Representatives selected Adams to be president even though he finished second to Andrew Jackson in both the popular and electoral count. Another candidate, Henry Clay of Kentucky, supported Adams and was later named secretary of state, prompting claims of a "corrupt bargain" that plagued Adams throughout his tenure in office.[148] Bemis argues that Adams could have only been elected president at this unique period of one-party government in the Era of Good Feelings. He belonged to no political party, had no political platform, controlled no political machinery, and lacked the charisma to build one. His primary credentials were his distinguished political lineage, sterling character, vast political experience, and undisputed competence for the office.[149]

Adams's religious convictions shaped his understanding of human rights, peace, liberty, and the United States' calling as a nation.[150] The impact that his faith had on his policies as a senator, diplomat, secretary of state, president, and congressman can be seen by examining his views of internal improvements, Indian rights, slavery, and religious liberty.

As a senator, Adams introduced a bill in 1807 that called for a national plan to construct canals and roads. As secretary of state, he wrote in 1822 that a nation's "first duty" was to better "its own conditions by internal improvements."[151] Breaking with Jefferson and James Madison, who thought that Congress could only do what was "expressly delegated" by the Constitution, President Adams advocated a substantial program of internal improvements.[152] Adams celebrated the benefits of improved transportation and communication, Daniel Walker Howe declares, "and undertook to marshal the resources of the federal government to further them." His proposals were motivated in part by his belief that God gave humans a "cultural mandate" in Scripture to develop the earth.[153]

As president, Adams continued to argue that the federal government should use its resources to improve the nation's transportation system and political, social, intellectual, and moral life. In his inaugural address, he called for the construction of an infrastructure to rival ancient Rome's. In an address to Congress in 1825, Adams insisted that God had assigned to nations, as well as individuals, the responsibility of "moral, political, [and] intellectual improvement." Enriching the lives of citizens was a "sacred and indispensable" political duty.[154] In his reports to Congress, Adams urged members to establish a naval academy, a national university, and federal programs to explore the continent and the heavens; to build roads and canals; to devise a uniform system of weights and measures and a more effective patent law to encourage inventors; to protect American industry; and to craft a more just Indian policy. He pressured Congress to create a Department of the Interior and exhorted members to appropriate money to complete the Cumberland Road, construct a thoroughfare from Washington to New Orleans, and build the Chesapeake and Ohio Canal.

The Creator expected people to enhance their own condition and that of their fellow citizens. Unless Americans took "gigantic strides" in public improvement, they would "cast away the bounties of Providence" and doom their country "to perpetual inferiority."[155] His proposals, Adams asserted, would enable the nation to better utilize its natural resources, expand its industry, and increase its power. Moreover, shared roads and canals, a national university, and common moral values and political ideals would bind Americans more firmly together. Convinced that the United States had a divine destiny to occupy the entire continent, he persistently advocated building roads and canals to encourage settlement of the West. Speaking at groundbreaking ceremonies for the Chesapeake and Ohio Canal in 1828, Adams, citing Genesis, declared that God commanded people to "replenish the earth, and subdue it." Because this was the preeminent purpose of the project, the president beseeched God to bless it and "other similar work" the nation undertook.[156]

Members of his cabinet cautioned Adams against making such sweeping proposals, arguing that many would consider them unconstitutional and impractical. The president recognized that they would be unpopular and that he must "remember that 'it is not in man that walketh to direct his steps.' "[157] His father, Washington, and Jefferson had also recommended establishing a national university, which Adams argued could help elevate America's moral and social practices. However, Madison's argument that it was unconstitutional generated substantial opposition, and Congress refused to do so. The sixth president was only able gain funds for minor projects such as the Delaware breakwater and to build the national road westward from Wheeling, Virginia to Zanesville, Ohio. Such piecemeal legislation fell far short of his goal of funding major educational, scientific, cultural, and physical improvements.

Several other factors thwarted the realization of Adams's grandiose schemes. Rallying under the banner of Andrew Jackson, westerners demanded free or very cheap land, and southern politicians, led by John Calhoun, called for increased states' rights. Fears that a strong national government would sell land at too high a price to fund its ventures and limit states' rights thwarted the president's plan to provide extensive internal improvements. Adams's political capital was diminished by his alleged crooked deal with Clay, his strong principled stands that alienated many professional politicians, his lack of personal warmth, and his appointment of people to political posts on the basis of ability rather than party affiliation and personal loyalty.[158] Moreover, he failed to solicit the help of those who could have been his allies in Congress, and after 1826 both houses were dominated by his opponents. Adams lamented that the nation had failed to use "the bounties of Providence" to increase its territory or elevate its life.[159] Discouraged but not defeated, Adams continued as a congressman to fight actively for causes designed to improve American intellectual, social, political, and moral conditions.

Like his quest for internal improvements, Adams's attitude toward Indians and their relationship to the federal government was based in part on his Christian convictions, and his position contributed to his problems as president. Racial prejudices combined with the economic self-interest of southerners and westerners to make Adams's policies toward Native Americans unpopular and to increase Jackson's strength in these regions. Soon after becoming president, Adams discovered that a treaty the federal government had negotiated with the Creek Indians in Georgia was fraudulent. Bribed by federal and state officials, Creek agents had ceded all of their land to the state. Unaware of this treachery, Adams signed the treaty shortly after taking office. Although most Creeks refused to accept this agreement, the governor of Georgia planned to use it to seize their rich farmland. Until this point, Adams had not been an advocate of Indian rights, arguing that their nomadic ways, belligerent actions, and pagan practices thwarted the progress of civilization and required them to accept a permanently inferior place in American society. However, the Creeks were one of five "civilized tribes" that had become farmers, spoke English, espoused Christianity, and accepted many Anglo customs. Although he had defended Jackson's efforts to remove the Seminoles from Florida in 1818, the Creeks now seemed no different to him than the whites who craved their territory.[160] In addition to the Creeks, the other four southern "civilized tribes" of the South and most other eastern tribes had become farmers. Therefore, he no longer saw them as a major menace, threat, or obstacle to the nation's advancement.

As he meticulously studied the old treaties and relevant legislation, Adams's sympathy for the Creeks increased. He told Congress in 1826 that the United States could either forcibly evict the Creeks from their land or negotiate a new treaty to obtain the same end peacefully. However, the "nature of our institutions" and "the sentiments of justice" required the government to adopt the second solution. Adams informed Congress the next year that if Georgia continued to encroach on Indian lands that his obligation to God, which trumped "human authority," would compel him to enforce the laws.[161] Neither removal nor assimilation was a good option. Removal was blatantly unjust, while the greed of the frontiersmen made assimilation very difficult.[162] The determined resistance of Georgians and the opposition of Congress prevented Adams from devising a more equitable treaty, and the Creeks were compelled to cede all their land to Georgia and to choose between submitting to white rule in the state or moving beyond the Mississippi River.[163]

Despite these obstacles, Adams continued to advocate the long-standing American policy of assimilation, which many whites opposed because it would deprive them of hundreds of thousands of acres of land they coveted.

He rejoiced in 1828 that Anglos had been able to teach Indians "the arts of civilization and the doctrines of Christianity."[164] The president met regularly with Indians and their white representatives to discuss their grievances and concerns.[165] Although white Georgians achieved their objectives, they and other southerners denounced Adams's effort to protect Indian rights and the delay it caused.[166] His humanitarian policy angered speculators and settlers who wanted Indian lands, and his nationalism alienated southerners who prized states' rights.

Like almost all Anglos at the time, Adams never doubted the "superiority of white Christian civilization over that of pagan Indians." Adams became "increasingly pessimistic about Indians' chance for survival in the face of the land-hungry white man and the impotence of the federal government to do anything about it." Nevertheless, between 1800 and 1840, he moved from "an attitude of hostility, to one of curiosity," to a sense of outrage about the treatment of Indians.[167]

The Indian Removal Act of 1830, passed while Jackson was president, for the first time put the weight of the federal government on the side of complete separation rather than assimilation. Most whites who were sympathetic to Indian interests opposed removal on the grounds that it was unjust and Indians rejected it. Adams, who was yet serving in Congress when the bill passed, insisted that its opponents could only deplore the "perfidy and tyranny of which Indians are to be made the victims, and leave the punishment of it to Heaven."[168]

As a congressman during the 1830s, Adams became both a leading defender of the principle that Indians had rights that whites must respect and one of the most formidable critics of removal.[169] The force, fraud, bribery, and murder used to compel unwilling Indians to move infuriated Adams and many other Anglos. He denounced removal policies for violating Indian rights and damaging America's honor. To Adams, the "Trail of Tears," which took the lives of almost one-quarter of the nation's 19,000 Cherokees in 1838, was a national disgrace. As a congressman, he repeatedly condemned removal policies for exterminating Native Americans. Adams's widely reported tirades brought him public acclaim in the East and North and vituperation in the South and West and prompted leaders of the Cherokees and other tribes to solicit his help.[170] Along with other Whigs, Adams presented petitions to Congress on behalf of the Cherokees. By 1840 he considered the Second Seminole War so futile (it eventually lasted seven years, killed 1,500 soldiers and thousands of Indians, and cost $20 million) that he opposed additional funding for it.[171] In 1841 Adams warned that America's Indian policy was "among the heinous sins of this nation" God would someday punish. Speaking at a worship service at the Tuscarora reservation in New York in 1843, he stressed God's "equal care and love" for "all his children" and "the common destiny that awaits them hereafter."[172]

Like his sympathy for Indians, Adams's opposition to slavery came later in his life. Adams's public stance on slavery between 1814 and 1848 involved "shifting and continually overlapping personal, policy, and ideological priorities."[173] While condemning slavery in his diary, as secretary of state, a presidential candidate, and president, Adams made no public statements on the subject. In this case, Adams's principles did not trump political expediency. He feared that a frank declaration of his views would prevent him from being elected president.[174] Moreover, his conviction that American unity was vital to the spread of liberty around the world made Adams reluctant to do anything to fracture it. As president, he frequently met with black leaders to discuss their grievances, but he took no major steps to help them. Caught between his conscience and his desire to lead effectively and preserve national unity, Adams chose to remain silent until his election to Congress allowed him to play the role of the prophet rather than the statesman and express his moral indignation.[175] As a representative, Adams deplored slavery as a violation of basic human rights, a threat to the Union, a cause of the war with Mexico, and a divisive issue that thwarted the work of the House.

Adams's opposition to slavery first developed during congressional debates in 1820 over admitting Missouri into the Union as a slave state. Reflecting on the Missouri Compromise, Adams wrote in his diary that slavery perverted human reason, undermined "moral principle," and "polluted" national politics. What could be "more false and heartless," Adams asked, than a doctrine that made "the first and holiest rights of humanity" "depend upon the color of the skin?" He repudiated the claim of southerners that the Bible sanctioned slavery and that slaves were "contented in their condition." The Constitution, he complained, "sanctioned a dishonorable compromise with slavery."[176] Despite such convictions, Adams, as secretary of state, supported the Missouri Compromise because he thought the Constitution did not allow Congress to abolish slavery in a territory where it already existed as a condition for a state's admission into the union.[177] While concluding that the compromise was the best that could be achieved under the current Constitution, he wondered if amending it to eliminate the nation's "great and foul stain" of slavery would be a wiser course. This action would probably reduce the nation to thirteen or fourteen states, but it would then be "unpolluted with slavery." However, amending the Constitution might also stimulate some states to emancipate their slaves. If the union had to be dissolved, Adams wrote, slavery was the issue "upon which it ought to break." Slavery, he protested, was "morally and politically vicious," inconsistent with the principles of the American Revolution, and "cruel and oppressive."[178] His presidential ambitions and practical politics, however, led Adams to keep these thoughts to himself and to urge New England congressmen to support the Missouri Compromise. Although the agreement that admitted Missouri as a slave state and prohibited slavery in the remainder of the Louisiana Purchase north of latitude 36°30' was immoral, Adams argued, the Constitution's defects regarding slavery made it necessary.

As a congressman, Adams also did not support the abolitionist crusade to end slavery in the District of Columbia and to outlaw the interstate slave trade because he considered these acts politically divisive.[179] However, he did frequently protest the unjust treatment of free blacks. He objected to a South Carolina law that prohibited them from entering the state, denounced a Virginia law that permitted their imprisonment on the presumption that they were slaves, deplored their ill-treatment by Washington police, and supported their right to vote.[180]

Congressman Adams also increasingly asserted that slavery violated fundamental moral, religious, philosophical, and political principles. The Bible taught that all races descended from the same ancestors—Adam and Eve— and that all human beings were brothers and sisters because they all had immortal souls.[181] Making human rights depend on skin color was irrational and contradicted divine moral principles. Adams denounced the efforts of slave owners "to prove that the Bible sanctions slavery." They "might just as well call our extermination of the Indians an obedience to Divine commands because Jehovah commanded the children of Israel to exterminate" the Canaanites.[182]

In addition to violating biblical teaching, Adams argued, slavery contradicted American and growing international commitment to protect people's natural rights and ensure human equality.[183] Owning slaves while professing belief in the Declaration of Independence, he insisted, was a "flagrant" example of "human inconsistency." Moreover, slavery contravened the law of brotherly love.[184] Adams rejoiced that slavery was daily becoming "more and more odious," that Washington and Jefferson, although slaveholders, testified against it, and that the pope denounced it. Strikingly, a Muslim despot, a Russian czar, and an Austrian monarch, recognizing that "the laws of nature and nature's God," taught "man cannot be the property of man," had all abolished it in their nations.[185]

Slavery was not only immoral, Adams maintained, it had disastrous political effects. Slavery produced deep cleavages between Southerners who owned slaves and those who did not. Most significantly, Southerners' hypersensitivity about slavery created governmental gridlock, preventing America from solving many of its major problems.[186]

Adams insisted that the demise of slavery was "predetermined in the counsels of Omnipotence." The justice of God, Christian benevolence, and American commitment to fundamental human rights would eventually destroy it. God would use the United States, he proclaimed in 1842, to promote "the virtue, welfare and happiness" of countless millions by making natural equality and brotherhood "the foundation of all human government, and by banishing Slavery and War from the earth." "Is the lamp destined to enlighten the world," Adams asked, "to be extinguished by the blasting breath of Slavery?" Adams warned that the battle to eradicate slavery would be "terrible," but he eventually concluded that fracturing the union was preferable to maintaining this perverse institution.[187]

Two issues made Adams into arguably the nation's most effective antislavery advocate during the last decade of his life: his opposition to the "gag rule" and his legal defense of fifty-three Africans who seized the Spanish slave ship Amistad in 1839.[188] Abolitionists flooded Congress with petitions calling for the end of slavery in the District of Columbia, prompting the adoption of a "gag rule" in 1836 that automatically tabled all abolitionist appeals. Adams denounced this rule as a denial of the constitutional right of free speech and led a nine-year campaign to repeal it, which Congress did in 1845. Tricked by their Spanish hostages, the captives who took control of the *Amistad* sailed into Long Island Sound, rather than back to Africa, and were incarcerated and held for trial in New Haven, Connecticut. Realizing that their trial provided an excellent opportunity to dramatize the plight of millions of victims of the slave trade, abolitionists rallied public support for these African prisoners. They also convinced Adams to serve as their legal counsel when the Supreme Court heard their case in 1841. Adams's stirring appeal for justice, which Justice Joseph Story called "extraordinary, for its power," "bitter sarcasm," and broadranging analysis, helped the defendants win their freedom.[189] The *Amistad* case prompted the congressman to attack the nation's internal slave trade, the capture and return of fugitive slaves to the South, and masters' mistreatment of their slaves. "The world, the flesh, and all the devils in hell," Adams lamented in 1841, "are arrayed against any man who" dared to follow "the standard of Almighty God to put down the African slave trade." Adams vowed to die trying to achieve "the cause of God"—"human emancipation."[190]

Although Adams thought that whites were culturally and morally superior to other races, unlike the vast majority of his contemporaries, he asserted that all people had basic rights regardless of their skin color. Adams saw "himself as the guardian of the rights of the oppressed." Besides its exploitation of blacks, what most upset him about slavery was that it undermined America's "leadership of the cause of human freedom."[191] Undeterred by threats against his life (about a dozen a month at their peak) and a congressional trial for censure, Adams zealously labored to realize his dream that "not a slave on this earth be found."[192] While most abolitionists were disappointed that Adams did not support their full agenda, many of them deeply appreciated his efforts to end slavery.[193]

Adams's religious commitments also significant influenced his approach to diplomacy. Convinced that God had created the United States to govern the entire North American continent and that European colonization was unjust, Adams strongly influenced the writing of the Monroe Doctrine. His role was so great that some insist it should be called the "Adams Doctrine." Adams argued further that because of its greatly increasing population, wealth, territory, and power, the United States should cultivate closer relations with Latin American nations. In the mid-1820s Protestant desires to evangelize Catholic countries in Latin America reinforced the widely shared desire to promote freedom and democracy there. Many Protestants hoped that the United States would bring both true Christianity and republican government to its southern neighbors. In 1823 the American Bible Society made plans to publish a Spanish edition of the Bible and the American Board of Commissioners for Foreign Missions sent a team to investigate opportunities for mission work in South America. Inspired by these religious and political goals, Adams urged the United States to participate in the first Pan-American Congress in 1826. It might be centuries, the president asserted, before Americans had a similar opportunity "to dispense the promised blessings of the Redeemer of Mankind."[194]

His Christian convictions also prompted Adams to promote religious liberty in Latin America.[195] To him, religious liberty was a prerequisite for civil liberty. Americans would be forever indebted to the Puritans for emphasizing the "natural equality of mankind," which they derived from "the sacred foundation of the scriptures."[196] In negotiating treaties of commerce and navigation as secretary of state, Adams sought to include provisions guaranteeing liberty of conscience and religious worship. "The tendency of the spirit of the age is so strong towards religious liberty," he exulted in 1823, that it would soon banish "intolerant religious establishments" from all Latin American republics.[197]

Final Assessment

Plagued by inner tensions and anxiety, Adams engaged in constant introspection and often berated himself for not fulfilling all his religious and civic duties, accomplishing more, or achieving moral perfection. Despite his immense talents and incredible work ethic, he was deeply bothered by his shortcomings. On his forty-fifth birthday Adams confessed that "passions, indolence, weakness, and infirmity have sometimes made me swerve from my better knowledge of right and almost constantly paralyzed my efforts of good." "My whole life has been a succession of disappointments," he complained two decades later.[198] Only after his arguments helped convince the Supreme Court to free the defendants in the *Amistad* case in 1841 did Adams tell his son Charles Francis that for the "first time he felt he deserved the blood of the signer of the Magna Carta" that surged through his veins.[199] Rarely satisfied with his accomplishments, Adams regretted near the end of his life that he had not done more to eliminate humanity's two great scourges: slavery and war.[200]

Adams did have numerous character flaws. Even his "most enthusiastic eulogists" mentioned his "general irascibility."[201] Despite his high standards, extensive self-criticism, and frequent prayer that God would grant him greater humility, Adams was often self-righteous.[202] As president, he was often moody, despondent, and at times, possibly clinically depressed. Criticism deeply troubled Adams. Having gained the "respect of czars, prime ministers, and distinguished men of science and letters," he was galled by the abuse heaped on him by "unschooled and self-centered partisans."[203] Even some of his admirers admitted that Adams frequently responded too harshly and intemperately to his critics.[204]

Adams also had many positive personality traits. Friends and adversaries, at home and abroad, lauded his learning, self-discipline, industry, integrity, and vigilance.[205] Many praised his fervent pursuit of virtue, justice, and the common good, extraordinary moral courage, faithful study of the Scripture and church attendance, and heart-felt gratitude to God. Few statesmen had his broad knowledge of government, history, and public law, claimed one of Adams's contemporaries.[206] Louisa Catherine Adams's boast that her husband had more intellectual power than the rest of the politicians in Washington combined, Paul Nagel maintains, "was less exaggerated than it sounds."[207] Numerous commentators celebrated his "incorruptible integrity" and impeccable character. His character, proclaimed another admirer, was "almost unrivaled."[208] Adams was one of the hardest working individuals to ever occupy the oval office or a seat in Congress.[209]

Many have acclaimed Adams's faith. Constantly guided by principle, he was "a humble disciple of Jesus Christ" and "a diligent and daily student of the Bible," an editor declared in 1848, who greatly revered "sacred things." The chief source of the statesman's character and colossal contribution to his country was not his intellect, knowledge, or eloquence, another contemporary asserted, but his "dependence upon God." "Always devoted to righteousness," Adams insisted that "people could only prosper as their laws conformed to the laws of God."[210]

William Weeks argues that Adams sought "to remake the world in America's image" by devising policies based on reason and morality rather than on power and expediency. Statesmen must promote morality, Adams maintained, by modeling upright conduct and passing prudent laws. He complained that the "intrigue and trickery" infecting the nation's elections and legislative bodies was tarnishing America's moral image. As secretary of state, Adams entreated God that "I may not suffer my integrity to depart from me." He insisted that the same code of ethics governed nations and individuals. Adams wrote his father in 1816, "I cannot ask of Heaven success" "for my country in a cause where she should be in the wrong." "All patriotism incompatible with the principles of eternal justice," he added, is "unsound."[211]

Adams did not always adhere to his high moral standards, however. As secretary of state, he became "embroiled in an ethical quagmire" that sometimes seemed to pit patriotism against principle as he pursued policies designed to maximize American interests. Adams used persuasion, obfuscation, and intimidation to promote what he deemed the nation's welfare. He deliberately "distorted, dissembled and lied about the goals and conduct of American foreign policy to both the Congress and the public," William Weeks contends, "so that a slave labor–based society he loathed could expand into the Floridas." In a letter to Spanish leaders, Adams justified Andrew Jackson's actions in Florida, implicitly supporting "Indian removal, slavery, and the use of military force without congressional approval—all of which," as a congressman he later opposed.[212]

As a candidate for the presidency Adams typically displayed a "scrupulous above-the-fray" perspective that did not reflect his true feelings or deal effectively with the political realities of his era. He insisted that the presidency should go to those who were "the most able and most worthy," "not to those with the most friends in the Congress and the press." Adams denounced obtaining an office by making promises to political supporters as "essentially and vitally corrupt."[213] He did not actively campaign for the presidency in 1824. Adams expected to be chosen president on the basis of his abilities, achievements, and character and believed the nation must reward virtue, sacrifice, and service. Adams, "symbolically the most principled individual in the history of American politics," refused to graciously concede the presidency to Jackson, whom Jefferson labeled a "dangerous man." Adams believed that he "faced an agonizing choice between preserving his personal integrity and preserving the nation to which he had dedicated his life." His concern for

America's welfare prompted him to spend the two months preceding the House of Representatives' vote to determine the president in February 1825 visiting congressional boardinghouses and practicing the "classic art of political horsetrading."[214] Bemis argues that the "implicit but certainly not corrupt bargain" between Adams and Clay was "the least questionable of the several deals" Adams made to secure his election. His actions prompted a Jacksonian newspaper to sarcastically declare, "Expired at Washington on the ninth of February, of poison administered by the assassin hands of John Quincy Adams . . . the virtue, liberty, and independence of the United States." Ironically, Adams, who had long tried to prevent factionalism in American politics, contributed significantly to "the rise of the second American party system by his dogged determinism to become president."[215]

Although Adams's presidency itself was largely devoid of scandal, during the 1828 campaign mudslinging was rampant. His opponents lambasted the president as a "pimp, gambler, and spendthrift," all of which were patently false. Adams claimed that Jackson was "incompetent" because of "his ignorance and the fury of his passions."[216] Meanwhile, Adams's supporters circulated a story that Jackson and his wife Rachel had committed adultery before she was divorced from her first husband, which the president did nothing to stop. Jackson blamed Adams personally for this defamation, which he believed contributed to Rachel's premature death shortly after he won the election.[217]

Adams was stricken after casting a vote in the House of Representatives in February 1848. As he lay dying, the House and Senate adjourned and congressmen prayed and waited. The dramatic death of the nation's senior statesman two days later mesmerized Americans. His composure impressed his contemporaries. Very appropriately, the venerable leader died as a soldier at his post, a sentinel doing his duty. Adams's widely reported last words expressed his readiness to meet his Maker.[218]

Only Washington's death a half century earlier had evoked so much effusive praise or widespread pathos. "One of the first 'media events' in American history" thanks to the invention of the telegraph in 1844, Adams's death provided a platform for proclaiming the "moral superiority of the American political and social system," celebrating the religious and cultural superiority of Whig over Democratic party values, and lamenting America's religious decline. Northern clergy and politicians used Adams's death to reaffirm "both Puritan religion and Yankee culture," which they judged "to be under attack." He was widely revered as an aged warrior, as the remaining link with the founders, and as "Old Man Eloquent" struck down while serving his beloved country. Although Adams was not a popular president, his long career as a diplomat and chief executive, coupled with his courageous stands as a congressman, made the New Englander a heroic figure in death. Adams had been in the limelight for four decades and was closely identified with much of the United States' history as an independent nation. Thousands viewed his glass-covered coffin in the House of Representatives, and hundreds of thousands saw it at train stops in Baltimore, Philadelphia, several New Jersey towns, New York City, and Boston on its way to Quincy.[219]

During the two and one-half weeks between Adams's death and burial, hundreds of eulogies, tributes, and funeral sermons were delivered. The countless newspaper accounts and the extensive public viewing of his body etched Adams's death more deeply into American minds than even the simultaneous passing of his father and Thomas Jefferson on the 50th anniversary of the Declaration of Independence. To rebut foreign criticisms of American materialism, immorality, and lack of culture, Adams was lauded as the "intellectual equal and moral superior of the Old World's" leading statesmen.[220] Many eulogists, especially northern Congregationalist and Unitarian ministers, praised Adams's wisdom, integrity, and Christian character.[221] They commended his frequent profession of Christianity, copious use of biblical citations and stories in his speeches, faithful church attendance, and contribution to numerous religious groups. Adams's letters to his son on the study of the Bible were widely reprinted and quoted. Many ministers used their eulogies to deplore the nation's moral and spiritual declension and to call for renewal and reformation. They also insisted that the best way to combat the rising tide of religious indifference and secularism was to support the Whig Party to which Adams belonged as a congressman.[222]

Funeral sermons consistently praised Adams's character, integrity, and sense of duty. "Like Washington," insisted a Unitarian minister from Philadelphia, "his personal character was stainless, above reproach and above suspicion." A Boston Universalist clergyman praised Adams's "inflexible adherence to principle," "steadfast integrity," and "independent boldness."[223] At the First Parish Church in Quincy where the Adams family had worshipped since before 1640, pastor William Lunt preached a funeral sermon based on Revelation 2:10: "Be thou faithful unto death, and I will give thee a crown of life." Adams "had been," he argued, "what the Scripture declares a good magistrate to be, 'a minister of God for good' to his native land." Carrying moral principles into public life, he sought to base public policies on justice, absolute truth, and God's law. In moral courage, New York Whig William Seward argued, Adams excelled his model Cicero and rivaled Cato.[224]

Despite his long and varied public career, Adams has not obtained the historical rank his contemporary admirers expected. However, some diplomatic historians rate Adams as America's greatest secretary of state. His policies and treaties ensured peace, reduced future tensions, and helped the United States expand across the continent and enlarge its international trade.[225] Bemis argues that Adams played the major role in "defining, defending, and sustaining American foreign policy" in the first half-century of independence. Moreover, Adams advocated principles that directed American foreign policy for the next century after his death—freedom of commerce and navigation, non-involvement in European affairs, continental expansion, self-determination of peoples, and Pan-Americanism—and called for ending European colonization of the New World, suppressing the African slave trade, and using international arbitration to settle boundary disputes.[226]

On the other hand, many scholars rate Adams's presidency as one of the least successful in American history. Like James Truslow Adams, they see him as "a foil for the more charismatic Andrew Jackson" and attribute his failures to personal flaws and regional antagonism. Like his father, he was a one-term chief executive, whose hopes for impressive achievements were dashed by political opponents. Shortly before leaving office, Adams wrote that he had devoted his presidency "to the Union, and to the improvement, physical, moral, and intellectual, of my country."[227] However, he failed in his campaign to expand the nation's transportation network, public education system, or scientific endeavors. The circumstances of his election tarnished his claim to moral leadership and helped produce a Congress that stymied his "farsighted plans for national unity and development."[228] Harlow Giles Unger calls Adams the "most ineffective President in early American history" because many of his proposals were far ahead of their times and he did not actively solicit support for his programs, persuasively answer his critics, or winsomely explain his vision to ordinary citizens.[229] Several other factors thwarted Adams's ability to govern successfully: he lacked a political base, his political philosophy conflicted with the democratic impulses of the era, and the widening franchise made reasoned arguments less persuasive in the political arena.[230]

Other historians portray Adams's presidency more positively. Mary Hargreaves praises him for pursing the good of the whole nation over personal, local, and regional interests. Samuel Flagg Bemis maintains that Adams, not Henry Clay, was the true father of the American System. By advocating a protective tariff, a more extensive system of roads, canals, and railroads, scientific and educational advancement, wise distribution of public lands, and prudent financial policies, Adams worked to make the nation more stable, prosperous, and powerful. George Lipsky argues that Adams's fervent nationalism, emphasis on a strong, positive role for government, belief that moral laws governed international relations, and commitment to natural law was unique among the American leaders of his era.[231]

Brooks Adams argued that his grandfather repudiated Christianity and died an agnostic, "convinced that no God who had permitted Andrew Jackson to triumph, the public lands to be plundered, slavery to expand, and half of Mexico to be conquered by the United States, could be counted on to exist."[232] The evidence, however, indicates just the opposite: while Adams's confidence in the union sometimes faltered, his faith in God grew stronger in his later years.[233] As Marie Hecht contends, Adams's much quoted remarks that his grandfather's presidency was "the tragedy" of his life because it made him doubt "whether there were a God and whether this life had a purpose" is incorrect. On the contrary, "Adams seemed to rely more and more heavily on divine guidance" as the world appeared to turn against him. Bemis's conclusion rings true: Adams went through life "doubting and believing: doubtful on points of doctrine that had mystified men for centuries, convinced of the existence of God and the blessings of Divine Providence, hopeful about an after-life," and inspired by "the example of Jesus Christ and the simple Christian ethic."[234]

Although Adams never realized his ambition to contribute significantly to the worlds of literature, science, or philosophy, Paul Nagel avers, his "stubborn courage in denouncing slavery and censorship" elicited widespread "gratitude and admiration." His battle against the gag rule and defense of Africans in the Amistad case gave the aged Adams the applause he craved and the thanks he merited.[235] The titles widely applied to Adams during his congressional years—Old Man Eloquent and Man of the Whole Nation—are richly deserved. Few Americans have served their nation more devotedly for such a long time or done more to advance its welfare and virtue than John Quincy Adams.

4

Andrew Jackson

PROVIDENTIALIST PRESIDENT

Should the uncircumcised philistines send forth their Golia[t]h to destroy the liberty of the people & compel them to worship Mamon [sic], they may find a David who trusts in the God of Abraham[,] Isaac and of Jacob, for when I fight, it is the battles of my country. I am calm & composed, trusting in the Lord of hosts, I believe him Just; and therefore look forward to a time when retributive Justice will take place.

TO ROBERT YOUNG HAYNE, July 9, 1827, *Papers of Andrew Jackson* 6:357

I trust in a kind providence that he will sustain me under my labours & other troubles, & carry me through the duties assigned to me to the glory of his kingdom, & the prosperity & happiness of our country.

TO JOHN COFFEE, September 21, 1829, *Papers of Andrew Jackson* 7:444

I hope god will relieve all those who trust in him in true faith and is worthy of his favours through the atonement of our Lord Jesus Christ our savior and redemer [sic] endorsement 1833?[1]

IN THE FALL of 1829, the daughter of Andrew Donelson, Andrew Jackson's nephew who served as his personal secretary, and his wife Emily, was baptized in the East Room by the Chaplain of the House of Representatives before a congregation of congressmen, senators, military officers, diplomats, and family friends. Following the liturgy of the Episcopal Book of Common Prayer, the minister asked the godparents, Vice President Martin Van Buren and his wife Cora, "Dost thou, in the name of this child, renounce the devil and all his works, the vain pomp and glory of the world, with all the covetous desires of the same, and the sinful desires of the flesh, so that thou wilt not follow, nor be led by them?" Before the godparents could respond, the president who had helped arrange the ceremony but had no official role in it, exclaimed, "I do, sir, I renounce them all!"[2] Throughout his life, especially his teenage and young adult years, Jackson struggled mightily to vanquish the devil, defy sin, conquer his temper, and live a godly life. His childhood exposure to Presbyterianism, coupled with his frequent reading of the Bible and church attendance, helped shape "the way he thought, spoke, wrote, and saw the world."[3] During his presidential and post-presidential years, his faith grew much stronger and deeply affected his worldview, relationships, and work.

Nicknamed the Old Hero, the Old Roman, the Old Lion, and Old Hickory, Andrew Jackson was one of America's most colorful, charismatic, contro-versial, and popular presidents. Both adored and despised, Jackson achieved international fame for his military exploits, especially his numerous defeats of Indians and of the British at New Orleans during the War of 1812, and was the second of twelve generals to serve as the nation's president. With little formal education, he rose from an obscure and impoverished background to occupy the country's highest office. Jackson was born in 1767 in the backwoods of North Carolina to Scots-Irish Presbyterians who had arrived two years earlier. His father died before he was born, and his mother and brothers died dur-ing the Revolutionary War. The British captured Jackson in 1781 while he was serving a local militia as a courier. While Jackson was imprisoned, a British officer slashed his head after he refused to shine his boots, which began Old Hickory's life-long hostility to the British. While there Jackson also contracted smallpox, the first of his many health problems.

Orphaned at age 14, Jackson was employed by a saddle maker, taught school, studied law, and was admitted to the bar in 1787. After working as a solicitor in two communities in Tennessee, he served briefly as the new state's US congressman and then a senator. From 1798 to 1804, he was a judge of the Tennessee Supreme Court. In addition to his legal and political activities, Jackson acquired a plantation near Nashville and became a major slaveholder and tobacco producer. Appointed commander of the Tennessee militia in 1801, Jackson had a distinguished military career, highlighted by his stunning rout of a larger British force at the Battle of New Orleans in January 1815. Subsequent military campaigns against Indian tribes kept him in the lime-light, and in 1822 he again served as one of Tennessee's US senators. One of four candidates for president in 1824, Jackson decisively won the popular vote. However, when no candidate gained enough electoral votes to claim the presi-dency, the House of Representatives chose John Quincy Adams as the nation's chief executive. Resigning from the Senate in October 1825, Jackson spent the next three years vigorously campaigning for the presidency, which he won in 1828 by defeating Adams. Viewed as a representative of the common man, destroyer of Indian nations, temperamental statesman, wealthy planter and slave owner, and hero of New Orleans, his name is associated with his era in such terms as "Jacksonian America," "Jacksonian Democracy," and the "Age of Jackson." A 2010 Broadway musical, *Bloody, Bloody Andrew Jackson*, portrays him as a rock star who becomes president and "as a symbol of the flawed power of populism in an era dominated by vapid celebrity."[4]

Jackson served as president during the final decade of the Second Great Awakening, a massive revival campaign that both sought to save souls and reform society. Led by Methodists and Baptists, Christians created dozens of organizations to spread the gospel and fight social evils. Through these parachurch organizations and the ministries of their congregations, Christians significantly shaped antebellum economic, social, cultural, and politic life. In many ways Jackson's faith reflected the evangelicalism of the antebellum frontier. Although a Presbyterian, Jackson, like the Methodists, Disciples of Christ, and most Baptists who dominated the region, and by mid-century, the entire American religious landscape, rejected Calvinism, emphasized the virtue of the common people, and advocated personal spirituality, salvation by faith in Christ, and individual biblical interpretation.[5]

The Faith of Andrew Jackson

Like that of numerous other presidents, the nature of Jackson's faith and its impact on his life is challenging to assess. His mother Elizabeth, a very pious and strong-willed woman who wanted him to become a minister, powerfully influenced young Andrew. Every week she took him and his brothers to the Presbyterian Church in Waxhaw, a village in south central North Carolina and required Andrew to memorize the Westminster Shorter Catechism.[6] For the first fourteen years of his life, Jackson spent three to four hours almost every Sunday singing hymns and listening to scriptural readings, sermons, and prayers. He learned that good and evil were battling in the world as he heard and read stories about Israel's kings and prophets fighting against malevolent powers in God's name and strength.[7] For a few years, Jackson also attended a school operated by Presbyterian pastor James Stephenson.[8]

This religious heritage, later bolstered by the fervent faith of his wife Rachel, gave Jackson a respect for Christianity and ministers, which he never abandoned, even during the years before 1820 when he sowed some wild oats and sometimes violated biblical moral standards. Frontier evangelist Peter Cartwright declared that Jackson "was, no doubt, in the prime of life, a very wicked man, but he always showed a great respect for the Christian religion" and "ministers of the Gospel."[9] Because he was a "street brawler, duelist, gambler, and all-around ruffian," Robert Remini argued, many contend that Jackson used religion purely for political purposes and dismiss the idea that he was truly a religious person "as absurd." However, Remini maintained, Jackson "regarded himself as a practicing Christian," others testified to his Christian commitment, and his faith was genuine.[10] Although he did not regularly attend Sunday worship for many years and did not join a Presbyterian congregation until seven years before his death, Jackson was associated with the Presbyterian Church his entire life. After age 40, he read the Bible daily, attended church faithfully, and frequently expressed robust religious convictions in letters to close friends and family. Jackson's library at his house, the Hermitage, contained many books on theology, history, and biography, numerous collections of sermons (most of which belonged to Rachel), and quite a few works of English theologian and hymn writer Isaac Watts.[11]

Although Jackson's faith became stronger during his final years, it was an important part of his life for several decades. Throughout his life he depended on God's providence and accepted suffering, sorrow, and death as part of God's plan. The general frequently affirmed that to be saved people must repent of their sin and accept Christ's atoning death on the cross.[12] During the last twenty-five years of his life, Jackson was "intensely religious"; he prayed often, regularly attended worship, and accepted everything that happened as the Lord's will. Only by submitting to God's will, the general argued, could people obtain earthly peace and eternal happiness.[13] As he began his presidency, Jackson thanked God that his health enabled him to perform his duties, and he trusted that God would enable him to fulfill his responsibilities "to the satisfaction of my country."[14] One of his secretaries, Nicolas Trist, testified that the last thing the president did every night before retiring was to read from Rachel's prayer book.[15] His admonition to a friend in 1833 illustrates Jackson's religious views: "Rely on his [Christ's] promises, they are faithful and true, and He will bless you in all your" ways. "Trust in his goodness and mercies" and "always be ready to say with heartfelt resignation, 'may the Lord's will be done.' "[16] Jackson also urged his relatives and friends to raise their children "in the nurture and admonition of the Lord."[17]

After his presidency, Jackson became very devout. In 1838 John Todd Edgar, pastor of the First Presbyterian Church in Nashville, preached a sermon on the role of Providence in human affairs at the Hermitage Church on Jackson's plantation. Edgar sketched the hypothetical "career of a man, who, in addition to the ordinary dangers of human life, had encountered those of the wilderness, of war, and of keen political conflict; who had escaped the tomahawk of the savage, the attacks of his country's enemies, the privations and fatigues of border warfare, and the aim of the assassin." How could a man undergo such experiences unharmed and "not see the hand of God in his deliverance?"[18] Alone that night, Jackson seemed to have a conversion experience. After a sleepless night, in the morning, "light seemed to dawn upon his troubled soul, and a great peace fell upon him." Soon thereafter, Jackson professed his faith publicly at the Hermitage Church.[19]

For the remainder of his life, the general led family worship each evening. He read a chapter from the Bible, distributed a hymn for everyone to sing, and offered a prayer.[20] During his final days, Jackson declared, "I hope God will grant me patience to submit to his holy will. He does all things well, and blessed be his holy and merciful name." He felt grateful "to a merciful Providence, that had always sustained him through all his struggles, and in the defense of the continued independence and prosperity of his beloved country."[21] Jackson prayed that after he died "heaven would protect and prosper" "those to whom Providence has committed to his care." He thanked God for supporting him "through a long life, and for the hope of eternal salvation through the merits of our blessed Redeemer."[22]

As noted, Rachel had a strong impact on her husband's faith as evident in his correspondence and actions. "Her deep and abiding" religious commitment, "unquestioning acceptance of what she regarded as the divine will," and numerous charitable works, argued Remini, had a "profound effect on her husband."[23] Her letters, actions, and friends testified to her fervent faith. By the early 1820s, Rachel was well known for her piety, good works, and enjoyment of attending church. Nothing, Remini asserted, thrilled her "more than a good, rip-roaring, fire and brimstone sermon."[24] Rachel liked living in Washington while her husband was a senator because she could go to prayer meetings twice a week and worship services twice each Sunday.[25] Two letters she wrote in 1821 illustrate her Christian commitment. "St. Paul says 'All things shall work together for good to them who are in Christ Jesus,'" she reminded Eliza Kingsley. "I know that my Redeemer liveth, and that I am his by *covenant* promise."[26] "The Lord is my help," she told her brother John; "in him will I trust & I praise him."[27]

Like her husband, Rachel was convinced that God controlled the universe. A month after the general was elected president in 1828, she declared, "I have resolved" to "try to forget" "all the endearments of home & prepare to live where it has pleased heaven to fix our destiny."[28] Two days later Rachel wrote to another friend: "Hitherto my Saviour has been my guide & support thro' all my afflictions" and "I have no doubt" that "he will still aid and instruct me in my duties which I fear will be many and arduous."[29]

Rachel died in late December and never became first lady. Those who knew her well praised her Christian conviction, godly character, and charitable deeds. In his eulogy, a Nashville pastor lauded her steadfast faith and compassion.[30] Congressman Edward Livingston consoled the bereaved president-elect: "religion holds out the certain hope of reunion in a better world with her who so faithfully performed its precepts in this."[31] "A more exemplary . . . wife, friend, neighbor, relative, [and] mistress of slaves," proclaimed Missouri Senator Thomas Hart Benton, "never lived."[32]

Numerous ministers, editors, and politicians also testified to the sincerity, depth, and power of Andrew Jackson's faith, especially during his presidency and post-presidential years. As the general prepared to begin his presidency, Charles Coffin, a Presbyterian minister and president of East Tennessee College, applauded his "respect for the institutions and ministers of religion."[33] Later that year, Philadelphia Presbyterian pastor Ezra Stiles Ely wrote the president: "you are a different being in relations to spiritual and eternal matters, from what you was in 1819." Jackson had become a humble follower of Christ who was "more distinguished by any one Christian virtue, than by the Presidency over the happiest & most flourishing nation on the globe."[34] In *The Duty of Christian Freemen*, Ely lauded the general as a friend to Christianity.[35] Jackson's "deep-seated" piety, alleged Benton, was evident in his "reverence for divine worship, respect for ministers," and firm belief "in the goodness of a superintending Providence." Even in the "most desperate" circumstances, Benton "never saw him waver in the belief" that everything would work "out in the end."[36] Editor Francis Blair insisted that Jackson had great "faith in providence and the people." "You have never found either to fail you," he wrote the general, "through a most eventful life."[37] Jackson's physician maintained that he departed this life "with full faith in the promises of salvation through a Redeemer."[38]

Jackson's views of God, Christ, salvation, the Bible, human nature, providence, prayer, and life after death and his pattern of church attendance also confirm his Christian commitment. Jackson said little about the attributes of God. In an 1830 letter, he celebrated God's "love, charity, & justice," and he frequently emphasized God's mercy.[39] Jackson also often declared that God disciplined those whom He loved and that he had been "frequently visited by this chastening rod."[40]

On the other hand, Jackson, far more than any of his predecessors, mentioned Jesus in his private correspondence and conversations. He repeatedly referred to Jesus "our savior," "our dear Savior," "the redeemer," "the only

Savior," and "the blessed Savior."[41] Jackson also often asserted that Christ's atoning sacrifice on the cross was the basis of human salvation. He counseled people to live a godly life "to be prepared for death when it comes" and asserted that the atonement of "our blessed savior on the cross" gave people "a reasonable hope of happiness hereafter."[42] Jackson hoped to meet "friends who have gone before me in the realms of bliss thro the mediation of a dear redeemer, Jesus Christ."[43] All who believe in Christ, he insisted would someday be reunited with their deceased loved ones in "realms above" through "the merits of our Savior, who shed his blood" to atone "for the sins of the world."[44] Rejecting the Reformed concept of election, Jackson asserted that "every man has *a chance* for his own salvation."[45] "Do you mean," Jackson asked a Calvinist, "that when my Saviour said 'Come unto me all ye who labor and are heavy laden,' he didn't mean what he said?"[46]

Jackson expressed respect for varied religious traditions and maintained that people's conduct demonstrated their true beliefs. Although "I was brought up a rigid Presbeterian [sic], to which I have always adhered," he proclaimed, charity was the "basis of *all true religion*, and charity says judge the tree by its fruit." All true Christians believed "that by and through him [Christ] we must be saved." Those "whose walk corresponds with their professions," whether they were Presbyterians, Episcopalians, Baptists, Methodists, or Roman Catholics, were "all good christians" and would go to heaven.[47]

During his last days on earth, Jackson repeatedly professed his belief in Christ's substitutionary atonement and urged others to do the same. A few weeks before his death, Jackson declared: "I am in the hands of a merciful God. I have full confidence in his goodness." "The Bible is true," he asserted. "Upon that sacred volume I rest my hope for eternal salvation, through the merits and blood of our blessed Lord and Saviour, Jesus Christ."[48] A week before he died, Jackson insisted that he was "ready to go whenever his divine master thought fit to take him." "When I have suffered sufficiently," he avowed, "the Lord will then take me to himself—but what are all my sufferings compared to those of the blessed Savior, who died upon that cursed tree for me."[49] Jackson also lectured his family and slaves on God's plan of salvation and urged them to "look to Christ as their only Saviour."[50] Moments before he died on June 8, 1845, Jackson told them: "God will take care of you for me." "I belong to Him." He declared, "I want to meet you all, both white and black, in heaven."[51] In his will, Jackson stated that he hoped for "a happy immortality through the atoning merits of our Lord Jesus Christ, the Savior of the world."[52]

These statements contradict H. W. Brands's claim that Jackson was certain that Rachel was in heaven, but the general had "no such confidence that he merited heaven." However, "he worried as little about his salvation as he worried about most" other things. Jackson "knew he was as sinful as the next man. But he believed that God gave credit for trying," and he was convinced that his actions had been generally "honest and upright." Brands offers no evidence to support this questionable assertion.[53]

Jackson considered the Bible to be a "sacred Book," usually read several chapters a day, knew its contents well, perused commentaries to help him better understand Scripture, and urged others to study God's inspired Word.[54] Numerous individuals testified that Jackson read the Bible every day and derived great benefit from doing so. For example, a visitor reported in 1831 that every morning the president read one of Rachel's favorite biblical passages.[55] During the last six years of his life, the Tennessean spent much of his leisure time reading Scripture and biblical commentaries. He particularly enjoyed "Scott's Bible," a compendium of the best commentaries of the antebellum years, which he read completely twice during this period.[56] "Go read the Scriptures," he instructed an army captain; "the joyful promises it contains will be a balsome [sic] to all your troubles and create for you a kind of heaven here on earth."[57] Shortly before he died, he exhorted all his grandchildren to "read the New Testament."[58]

As Jon Meacham argues, the Bible helped shape Jackson's "habits of mind." Throughout his life when he experienced stress, the general often recalled biblical stories and passages he had learned as a child and reread as an adult that either comforted or challenged him. Moreover, many of "his let- ters and speeches echo both the scripture and the question-and-answer style" of the Westminster Shorter Catechism.[59] Jackson often quoted and alluded to the Bible. He especially cited the Golden Rule, the biblical injunction to judge a tree by its fruit, and Micah 3:9–12, which admonishes rulers to gov- ern justly.[60] In addition to other examples sprinkled throughout this chapter, after Henry Clay accepted an appointment as John Quincy Adams's secretary of state in the so-called "corrupt bargain" that gave Adams the presidency in 1824, Jackson wrote, "the Judas of the West has closed the contract and will receive thirty pieces of silver—his end will be the same."[61]

Jackson did not accept all the doctrines of Reformed theology. However, influenced by his personal experience, especially the many vicious political attacks he endured, and his study of Scripture, he did espouse the Calvinist concept of human depravity. He frequently complained about "the wickedness of the world and how prone many are to evil."[62] "I loath [sic] the corruption of human nature," he told a minister in 1833.[63]

Among American presidents, perhaps only George Washington referred to God's providence as much as Jackson. Old Hickory repeatedly insisted that God controlled military battles, illness and death, natural disasters, and political developments. "I trust in a kind providence," he asserted, "to direct me."[64] God, he added, *"orders all things well."*[65] "The will of providence," which guided the affairs of humanity, must be "cheerfully submitted to."[66] Jackson strove to accept God's will even when he did not understand it or it involved suffering for him or others he loved. He believed that God often permitted people to experience pain and anguish to get their attention, chasten them, and help them focus on spiritual matters. Jackson coped with numerous health problems throughout his adult years: bouts of dysentery, parasites, stomach and intestinal ailments, rheumatism, fevers, excruciating headaches, and lung problems caused by a bullet lodged in his chest as a result of a duel. He urged others to accept difficult circumstances as God's will and to allow adversity to strengthen their faith.

Jackson gave God credit for safety in battle and military victories. He urged Rachel during the War of 1812 to trust "that superintending Being who has protected and saved me in the midst of so many dangers."[67] The Battle of New Orleans in January 1815 made Jackson an international celebrity as almost 300 British were killed, 1,200 were wounded, and hundreds more were captured while only 13 Americans died and 39 were wounded. Reflecting on this resounding triumph, he declared, "It appears that the unerring hand of providence shielded my men from the Powers of Balls, bombs, & Rocketts [*sic*]."[68] "If ever there was an occasion on which Providence interfered, immediately, in the affairs of men," Jackson avowed, "it seems to have been this. What but such an interposition could have saved this Country?"[69] Writing to the administrator of the Catholic diocese of Louisiana shortly after the battle, the general exalted, "to have been instrumental in the deliverance" of my country "is the greatest blessing that heaven could confer."[70]

Jackson's hardest trial was the sudden death of his beloved wife Rachel shortly after he was elected president in 1828. Their marriage had long "provided Jackson an emotional security he had never previously experienced. Fatherless since birth, motherless since his early teens, with neither surviving siblings nor close cousins, Jackson made Rachel the emotional center of his universe."[71] He missed her tremendously and struggled mightily to cope with her absence. Despite his great grief and sense of loss, he yielded to God's sovereign will. "It pleased God to take her from this world," he wrote, and "to deprive me of my stay and solace whilst in it." Nevertheless, "I bow to the decree, but feel in its afflictive power." Thankfully, "divine Grace" enabled Christians to believe in the "hereafter where the good unite again, and the wicked 'disturb not.'"[72] God, he added, "knew what was best for her." Accepting "God's will," he vowed to assume his "new and arduous duties" as president without her.[73] "At the time I least . . . could least spare her, she was snatched from me, and

I was left" with "all the turmoil of public life."[74] Jackson wanted "to unite with her in the realms above—But providence has otherwise ordered & to his will I must submit."[75]

Jackson faced many other problems during his presidency, and his belief in God's providence helped him bear them with little complaint. His numerous physical ailments, he told a Virginia senator in 1830, compelled him to contemplate "the indulgence, wisdom, and mercy of Providence."[76] When Jackson learned that the Hermitage had been badly damaged by fire in October 1834, he wrote, "The Lords will be done." God "gave me the means to build it," he added, "and he has the right to destroy it, and blessed be his name."[77]

The general continually emphasized that God controlled the universe and urged people to thank Him for providing for, protecting, and preserving them. He told Emily Donelson that with the help of "a kind Providence, who holds our existence here in the hollow of His hand, I have so far recovered" from "a severe hemorrhage from the lungs." The president also thanked God for "His kindness in restoring you to health again."[78] He rejoiced that "an overruling providence" had restored the health of his friend John Coffee's wife. We should be grateful "to our savior," he added, for His "daily preservation" and the blessings He bestowed.[79]

Jackson counseled friends who had serious illnesses or had lost loved ones to submit to God's will and rejoice in the promise of heaven. In 1833 the president wrote to a friend whose mother-in-law had recently been diagnosed with cancer, "If God chooses to end her earthly existence, I trust she will be resigned to his will" and be prepared to leave "this troublesome earthly tabernacle for an eternity of bliss, for which her present suffering is designed by her heavenly father to prepare her."[80] He emphasized that Christ taught believers not to repine but to rejoice when God takes our children from "this wicked world" to a place of "peace, happiness, and glory." Let this "be a balm to your sorrow," the president exhorted a minister whose young daughter had died.[81] When the firstborn child of his nephew and niece died in 1835, the president wrote, "I am truly happy to find that you both have met this severe bereavement" with "christian meekness & submission." Their "great creator and benefactor" had given them "this charming babe." They probably had doted "upon him too much" and neglected the Giver. God had taken him to remind them "that to him your first love is due, and by this chastisement, to bring you back" to the One to Whom "we owe all things." God "giveth, and he has a right to take away, and we ought humbly to submit to his will." In the midst of their "severe bereavement," they could take comfort that their son was now with Christ "free from all the temptation, pains and evils of this world."[82]

Jackson also asserted that God directed the affairs of nations, often thanked Him for America's political stability and economic prosperity, and exhorted others to do the same. His first inaugural address affirmed the president's trust in God's "overruling Providence." God, who held "the destiny of nations" in His hands, would enable Americans "to steer, the Bark of Liberty, through every difficulty." Jackson firmly relied "on the goodness of that Power whose providence mercifully protected our national infancy, and has since upheld our liberties" and asked God to "continue to make our beloved country the object of His divine care and gracious benediction."[83] In his 1829 message to Congress, he expressed his "devout thanks to a benign Providence, that we are at peace with all mankind." The president urged citizens to seek "the guidance of Almighty God" and rely "on His merciful providence for the maintenance of our free institutions." He hoped that other nations would obtain the blessings Americans enjoyed and advance in knowledge, freedom, and happiness.[84] In a draft of this message Jackson implored "the almighty ruler of the universe" to give nations the "wisdom to discern, and united harmony to enact, all laws" that promoted "the prosperity of his Kingdom and the best interests of the union."[85] The president reiterated his faith in God's direction of history and Americans' responsibility to Him in his farewell address. "Providence has showered on this favored land blessings without number," he asserted, and had chosen Americans to preserve freedom "for the benefit of the human race. May He who holds in His hands the destinies of nations . . . enable you . . . to guard and defend" the "great charge He has committed to your keeping."[86]

Jackson also sometimes invoked God's providence to justify his own political positions and preferences. Reflecting on the death of Thomas Jefferson and John Adams on July 4, 1826, Jackson wrote, "Is this an omen that Divinity approbated the whole course of Mr. Jefferson and sent an angel down to take him from the earthly Tabernacle on this national Jubilee, at the same moment he had presented it to Congress—and is the death of Mr. Adams a confirmation of the approbation of Divinity also, or is it an omen that his political example as President and adopted by his son, shall destroy this holy fabric created by the virtuous Jefferson."[87] The general argued similarly that the sudden death of President William Henry Harrison one month after his inauguration in March 1841 was an "act of an overruling providence" "to preserve and perpetuate our happy system of republicanism and stay the corruption" of the clique Harrison represented. Harrison's death prevented him, "under the dictation of the profligate demagogue, Henry Clay," from overturning his and Van Buren's many accomplishments. "*The Lord ruleth,*" Jackson concluded, "*let our nation rejoice.*"[88]

God, Jackson averred, was actively involved in the world and answered prayer. Old Hickory insisted that prayer was beneficial and frequently promised people that he was praying for them. "I trust the god of Isaac and of Jacob will protect you and give you health," he wrote to Rachel in 1823. "He alone" can "guide us through this troublesome world, and I am sure he will hear your prayers. We are told that the prayers of the righteous prevaileth much, and I add mine for your health and preservation."[89] Jackson assured numerous friends that he would constantly offer prayers for them "at the throne of grace."[90] He also often exhorted others to pray. He urged his daughter-in-law Sarah to earnestly pray that her daughter may become "a true deciple [sic] of her blessed savior."[91] Jackson frequently wrote that he was praying for God's "choicest blessing" to be bestowed on the recipient of his letters and their families.[92] After his presidency, he used both printed and extemporaneous prayers when leading his family in daily worship.[93]

Jackson also continually affirmed his belief in heaven. He often expressed his desire to go to heaven, primarily to be reunited with his wife and other family members and friends. The general beseeched people to prepare to die and comforted numerous friends by promising that their loved ones were with God. What "exquisite & pleasing sensations we must experience on meeting with our departed friends beyond the grave," the president wrote in 1829. This "makes life *now* tolerable for me."[94] Jackson portrayed heaven as a place of incredible happiness where earth's trials, tribulations, and sorrows were no more. After Rachel died, he told his friends and neighbors: "she is now in the bliss of heaven" and she "can suffer here no more on earth. That is enough for my consolation; my loss is her gain."[95] "I would like to spend" the remainder of my life, he added, "preparing to meet her in a happier and a better world."[96] Rachel's virtues, piety, and Christian faith "ensured her that future happiness, which is promised" to Christ's followers. He hoped "to unite with her in the realms above never to be seperated [sic]."[97]

In other letters, Jackson accentuated the splendor of heaven to comfort the bereaved. The saints had gone to "mansions of bliss."[98] Trying to console a friend whose young daughter had died, the general wrote that she is "in the bosom of our savior enjoying that exquisite happiness." Only this "cheering thought" made "life supportable to me under my afflictions."[99] Jackson rejoiced that his friend John Overton "is beyond, where the wicked cease to trouble, and where the weary are at rest."[100] On his death bed, he wrote to Amos Kendall, that he hoped to meet him someday "in a blissfull [sic] immortality."[101]

In other letters, Jackson exhorted relatives and friends to be ready to meet God. Jackson urged his daughter-in-law Sarah "to be prepared to die well, and then," when death came, "we will meet it without alarm."[102] He told Emily

Donelson that illness reminds us "that we are mere tenants" on earth. People should "be prepared to die, for we know not when we may be called home."[103] When Emily, age 28, soon died, Jackson sought to console her husband: "we are commanded by our dear Saviour, not to mourn for the dead." "She has changed a world of woe, for a world of eternal happiness, and we ought to prepare, as we too, must follow."[104] Jackson admonished John Donelson to "withdraw from the busy cares of this world, & put your house in order for the next, by laying hold 'of the one thing needful'—go read the Scriptures, the Joyful promises it contains, will be a balsame [sic] to all your troubles, and create for you a kind of heaven here on earth."[105] Writing to the Coffee family to express his condolences after his son John died unexpectedly, Jackson asserted: it is "our duty to prepare" for our death. Coffee expressed regret as he lay dying that he had not joined the church and exhorted his family not to follow his example. Old Hickory urged them to heed his warning by relying on "our dear Savior" and "trusting in Christ's mercy and goodness."[106] "I am prepared to die," Jackson told a friend several months before his death. "When the angel of Death comes I shall say with pleasure—march on, I'll follow."[107] On his death bed, Jackson told his family and slaves that "Christ has no respect to color." "I hope to meet you all in Heaven."[108]

Between age 14 and his early fifties, Jackson attended church sporadically. Thereafter, he went to Sunday services very faithfully. While a member of the Senate, Jackson attended Presbyterian, Baptist, and Methodist churches, which he enjoyed if the sermon was interesting.[109] While president, he paid pew rents at both Second Presbyterian Church and St. John's Episcopal Church and alternated attendance.[110] Margaret Bayard Smith, whose family pew was in front of Jackson's at Second Presbyterian, recounted that in worship "his manner is humble and reverent and most attentive."[111] A foreign traveler reported in 1833 that his pew was not distinguished from that of other worshippers and that he freely mixed with other congregants without any air of presumption.[112] Jackson also frequently attended church when traveling during his presidential years.[113]

Jackson did not join a church until 1838, a year after he left the presidency. He attributed his failure to do so earlier to his demanding schedule and desire not to be accused of joining to gain political advantages. In 1823 he explained to his wife that if he joined the church now, "it would be said, all over the country that I had done it" for "political effect." He promised her "that when once more I am clear of politics I will join the church."[114] When Rachel's niece joined the church in 1828, Jackson wrote: "It is what we all ought to do, but men in Public business" had "too much on their mind to conform to the rules of the church, which has prevented me hitherto."[115] At a service at the Hermitage Church on July 15, 1838, Jackson declared his belief in Jesus as his savior, affirmed basic Presbyterian doctrines, promised to obey Christian precepts, and became a communicant member.[116] If he had joined the church during his political career, his opponents would have accused him of hypocrisy. Now, however, "no false imputations could be made that might be injurious to religion."[117] On Sunday mornings after he left office, he told his numerous overnight guests, "Gentlemen, do what you please in my house," but "*I* am going to church."[118]

Jackson joined the freemasons, an organization to which Washington, Alexander Hamilton, Paul Revere, and other founders belonged, much earlier than he did the church (at least by 1798). He was attracted to the principles and fellowship of the masons.[119] An 1824 masonic manual accentuated the fraternal order's ideals: masons should strive to acquire "the virtues of *patience, meekness, self-denial, and forbearance*" and to be "men of honor and honesty."[120] Freemasonry, Jackson declared, accentuated the "principles by which man in his pilgrimage below should be guided, and governed." As did Harry Truman, Jackson served as the Grand Master of a state lodge, in his case the Masonic Grand Lodge of Tennessee from 1822 until 1824. The general encouraged his fellow masons to further their "great principles of benevolence and charity" to "shine amongst men" by serving as "a lamp to their path, and a light to their understanding."[121] Although some evangelical Protestants were critical of the secrecy and religiously eclectic nature of this fraternal order, few criticized Jackson's prominent role in the organization.[122]

Jackson's Character

Evaluations of Jackson's character both by his contemporaries and later scholars are very mixed. Jackson had many character flaws and engaged in some morally dubious behavior, especially in his teenage and young adult years. As a youth, he frequently used profanity and made violent threats.[123] When Jackson resided in Salisbury, North Carolina, in the mid-1780s, one resident declared him to be "the most roaring, rollicking, game-cocking, horse-racing, card-playing, mischievous fellow" who ever lived there.[124] After moving to Tennessee, Jackson continued to gamble on horse races, cards, and cock fights and sometimes drank excessively.[125] Moreover, Jackson used violence or intimidation eight times to settle quarrels, which included fighting several duels (the only man to become president who ever did so) and killing one man.[126] These actions provided fodder for his opponents in his presidential campaigns. For example, Jess Benton's 1824 pamphlet, *An Address on the Presidential Question,* denounced Jackson's cursing, cockfighting, and gambling. Such attacks led Jackson to complain that many tried to present him as a man with "a savage disposition" who carried a "knife in one hand, and tomahawk in the other" to scalp anyone "who differed with me in opinion."[127] Despite this protestation, Jackson's verbal assaults against his political foes were ferocious, and he consistently attributed "the conduct of his opponents to the lowest [imaginable] motives."[128] Strongly opinionated and stubborn, Jackson rarely compromised or bargained; instead, he usually strove to achieve a clear victory.[129]

On the other hand, Jackson often displayed great kindness, compassion, and generosity. The general shared his bread with hungry soldiers, gave money to beggars, cared for sick slaves, and aided the oppressed.[130] He and Rachel raised nephews as their own children, provided a home for the children of a neighboring planter who died prematurely, and adopted an Indian orphan when no one else was willing to do so.[131] In 1828 Jackson cared for a complete stranger in his home until he died of tuberculosis simply because he considered this his Christian duty.[132] While president, he strongly supported the work of the Orphan Asylum in Washington and often visited its residents.[133] Jackson was very munificent and hospitable, declared Thomas Hart Benton; "love of justice and love of country" were his ruling passions.[134] Jackson strove to follow Christian principles and to exemplify integrity. "My first object is," he declared, to "possess an approving conscience."[135] "An honest man," he wrote, is "the noblest work of God" and "integrity of character" is essential.[136]

Like Washington and Jefferson, Jackson was criticized for being a slaveholder. In 1820 Old Hickory owned forty-eight field and domestic slaves. He continued to buy slaves, and by 1829 had about a hundred, far fewer than large plantations in the Carolinas and the Gulf coast, but one of largest contingents in Tennessee. The general bought and sold slaves to suit the needs of his plantation; he sought to obtain high prices when selling and the lowest possible ones when purchasing. Jackson usually refused to sell young children away from their mothers both because it reduced productivity and "offended his sympathies."[137] The planter expected his slaves to obey, and those who did not were often harshly punished. "Subordination must be obtained first," he explained, "and then good treatment."[138] Judged by contemporary standards, his slaves had decent housing and adequate food. Jackson, who was often absent from Hermitage because of his legal work, military service, and political responsibilities, frequently complained that his overseers failed to achieve "an appropriate balance" between disciplining them and treating them kindly.[139] Jackson displayed significant concern about the condition of his slaves and required his overseer Graves Steele not to abuse them.[140] "My negroes shall be treated humanely," he wrote to his son. "When I employed

Mr Steel, I charged him" to "treat them with great humanity, feed and cloath [sic] them well, and work them in moderation. If he has deviated from this rule, he must be discharged."[141] Jackson's concern for his reputation eventually led him to stop trafficking in slaves. When campaigning for president, Old Hickory understandably attempted to conceal his slave-trading past, but some publicized his profiting from this activity.[142]

Unlike Washington, Jackson did not free any of his slaves in his will. For several reasons, the general bequeathed all of them to his son Andrew, Jr. Jackson saw slavery as essential to the southern economy and feared that assaults on it would shatter the Union.[143] Like Jefferson, Jackson had a large debt when he died. Moreover, by the 1840s manumission was very difficult in Tennessee. Finally, despite his deep commitment to individual freedom, Jackson did not think it applied to blacks who he considered to be "largely ignorant," "irresponsible and untrustworthy," and ill-suited for freedom.[144] Sadly, he accepted the cultural norms of his era and locale.[145]

The Election of 1828

The question of Jackson's character also played a major role in the presidential election of 1828, one of the most vicious campaigns in American history. Both Jackson and John Quincy Adams were accused of moral transgressions; most controversially, Jackson was condemned as a bigamist and adulterer because of the complicated and allegedly immoral circumstances of his marriage to Rachel. The election contributed to the emergence of the second party system in American politics (Democrats versus Whigs) and marked the beginning of greater political participation by ordinary Americans. The increase in newspapers and pamphlets, coupled with higher literacy rates, created an unprecedented hunger for sensationalism that the campaign fed.[146] It was also the first election since 1800 in which religion played a major role.

His opponents charged Jackson with countless crimes, offenses, and improprieties; his "duels, fights and quarrels" were recounted in bloody detail and deplored as they had been in 1824.[147] His duels were "embellished to show that he took liberties with the code of honor and therefore with the lives of his antagonists."[148] Cincinnati editor Charles Hammond denounced Jackson as a profligate, "reckless, volatile adventurer" who did not deserve the public trust.[149] Jackson was also accused of slave trading, which was widely considered disreputable.[150]

The general was also depicted as "a vindictive monster," "a despot" who mistreated his soldiers. The most serious charge was that Jackson was responsible for the improper execution of six soldiers during the War of 1812. This alleged crime was popularized by a broadside titled "A Short Account of Some of the Bloody Deeds of GENERAL JACKSON," featuring "silhouettes of six coffins, representing the six soldiers executed by Jackson's order near the end of the southern campaign of the War of 1812." They were part of a group of 200 soldiers who claimed that their three-month term of service had ended and that they, therefore, had the right to leave. Their officers countered that their term was six months, and nearly all the mutineers were fined and dishonorably discharged at the end of this period. However, the six leaders of the insurgency were sentenced to death, and Jackson, who was not present, approved of the verdict.[151] Jackson maintained that these militiamen deserved the death penalty because they had led a mutiny, stolen supplies, and deserted.[152]

Most grievously, Adams loyalists indicted Jackson for stealing another man's wife. They insisted that their version of events closely followed the court's verdict that "the defendant, Rachel Robards, hath deserted the plaintiff, Lewis Robards [her first husband], and hath and doth still live in adultery with another man [Andrew Jackson]."[153] They accused the general of seducing Rachel, breaking up her first marriage, and living with her in a state of long-term adultery. Rachel was portrayed "as a loose, impetuous, and immoral woman who willingly cast off her lawful husband for an arrogant and impassioned young suitor."[154] Some anti-Jackson newspapers denounced Rachel as a whore. The *Commentator* of Frankfort, Kentucky, compared her with a "dirty, black wench!" a remark that other newspapers reprinted.[155]

The Jackson camp supplied a very different story. The Jacksons, supporters claimed, were "the innocent victims of a petty legal misunderstanding." Believing Rachel to be divorced from her first husband, Jackson had married her in Natchez, Mississippi, in 1791. They later discovered that what they had thought was a formal divorce decree simply authorized Robards to sue for divorce in a civil court, which Robards did not do until 1793. After the divorce was finalized in 1794 and the couple learned that they were not legally married, they exchanged vows before a justice of the peace in Nashville.[156]

In their conflicting narratives of the Jacksons' relationship, the two camps appealed to Americans' most deeply cherished beliefs "about manhood and womanhood, passion and restraint, and divorce and marriage." In so doing, they delineated "competing marital codes." Understandably, leaders of both parties crafted "their appeals to comport with the ethnic and religious stripes of their constituents." The pro-Adams forces emphasized that marriage was a civil contract that undergirded society and the political order. In the emerging Whig worldview, shaped by the religious activism and moral crusades of the Second Great Awakening, the state had a responsibility to determine and control marital boundaries. To convince Americans to vote for the lackluster incumbent rather than his charismatic, more popular opponent, the Adamsites sought to expose Jackson's sexual transgression and "to champion strict government control over domestic relations."[157] In newspaper articles and then a pamphlet titled *View of General Jackson's Domestic Relations*, Hammond spread the story of the Jacksons' purported bigamy and argued that as first lady Rachel would "offend" Washington society and negatively influence "public morals."[158] Adams's supporters argued further that a man's attitude toward the basic rules of marriage was "an acid test of his character," which justified their focus on the Jacksons' early relationship. By deciding to run for president, argued the *Daily National Journal*, the general "invited an investigation of his character." The nation's reputation, interest, and morals, an Adams loyalist asserted, "were all deeply involved" in this scandal, making it "a proper subject of public investigation and exposure."[159] Adamsites avowed that Jackson's immoral liaison displayed his lack of sexual restraint. He "had played the serpentlike role" and seduced, or in other accounts, abducted, a married woman. "Such a man menaced the entire civic order"; "his callous disregard for the laws of marriage" threatened "institutional efforts to uphold virtue." To vote for Jackson, Adamsites implied, was to endorse his sinful behavior.[160]

The moral code of the budding Democratic Party, by contrast, stressed the romantic and private and elevated "heartfelt sentiments over precise legal forms." Jackson supporters included Catholics and freethinkers who had less enthusiasm for Protestant moral prescriptions on the verge of the Victorian era. Their defense of Jackson was also set within "a larger framework of political secularism, cultural pluralism, laissez-faire government, and broad-based egalitarianism, at least as it pertained to white men." Marriage, they insisted, was an individual and local concern, not a public and national one. By spreading lurid stories, Adamsites were perpetuating a malicious conspiracy that could corrupt public morals. Democrats exhorted antebellum voters to recognize and repudiate these vicious tactics.[161]

Jackson's supporters counterattacked by censuring Adams's religious commitments and character. They denounced the president for being a Unitarian and accused him of Sabbath-breaking, religious bigotry, alcoholism, haughtiness, and extravagant expenditures.[162] They also charged that Adams was hostile to Catholicism as demonstrated by a July 4th oration in which he called the Catholic Church a "portentous system of despotism and superstition."[163] Adams's supporters responded that the president had appointed many

Catholics to office and contributed generously to Catholic charities.[164] They also issued a pamphlet that criticized Jackson for worshiping at a Catholic mass in New Orleans, which all good republicans and Christians could not "fail to regret."[165]

The editor of *The United States Telegraph*, the principal mouthpiece of Jackson's backers, alleged that Adams was working secretly to "unite church and state after the manner of the English monarch."[166] In addition, Democrats claimed that Adams had procured a prostitute for Czar Alexander I while serving as the American minister in Russia in the early 1810s, but this canard had little plausibility.[167] Those who had "scrutinized his private life," declared one pro-Adams newspaper, "stood ashamed and rebuked at the brightness and holiness of that which they had intended to injure."[168]

Supporters portrayed Adams as a responsible, disciplined Christian, "a man of sincere piety, impeccable purity, and prodigious intelligence" who had worked "unstintingly" to advance a "progressive national vision." Jackson loyalists, by contrast, accentuated the general's courage and heroism on the battlefield, "his chivalry as the protector of endangered women," his rugged individualism and closeness to nature as a frontier planter, and his "physical prowess and self-sufficiency," attributes which were crucial to westward expansion. They stressed that Jackson adhered to "the frontier codes of Tennessee where honor, friendship, and loyalty counted for more than legal fine print."[169]

Early in the campaign, Jackson declined an invitation from a Nashville area chapter of the American Bible Society to address its anniversary meeting. If he were to give this address, Jackson reasoned, his political enemies might charge him with using "the sacred garb of religion" to win votes. While declining the offer to speak, the general assured those who invited him that he would do all he could "to prosper the great & good cause of christianity & the true religion of Jesus christ."[170]

In 1827 Presbyterian pastor Ezra Stiles Ely called for the organization of a "Christian Party in Politics."[171] While such a party was not created, Ely argued in a sermon published in 1828, titled *The Duty of Christian Freemen to Elect Christian Rulers*, that Christians should join together to prevent pagans, Muslims, deists like Washington or Jefferson, or Unitarians like John Quincy Adams from obtaining elected offices. "Presidents," he insisted, "are just as much bound as any other person in the United States, to be orthodox in their faith, and virtuous and religious in their whole deportment." "Every ruler *should be* an avowed and a sincere friend of Christianity."[172] Ely saw Jackson as a natural leader of this Christian Party, and other ministers praised Jackson's "far-reaching faith" and benevolence. Methodist Lorenzo Dow contended that "the hand of Providence" would use Old Hickory to save the nation.[173] Jackson, meanwhile, reassured Americans of his Christian orthodoxy. In a letter that was published in part in the *Nashville Republican* in April 1828, Jackson professed that "one evidence of true religion is, when all those who believe in the atonement of our crucified Saviour are found in harmony and friendship together." "My [religious] habits," he added, "are too well fixed now to be altered."[174]

The widespread publication of the intimate and intricate details of Jackson's relationship with Rachel contained enough "ammunition to kill a regiment of presidential candidates," but Old Hickory survived, winning 56 percent of the popular vote.[175] While this sexual scandal shocked the sensibilities of some Americans and raised serious questions in the minds of many others about Jackson's character, his supporters' forceful defense of his actions, his personal popularity and policies, and his reputation as "the child of the Revolution, imbued with its spirit of virtue, committed to high moral standards, and appalled by the corruption pervading the nation's capital" enabled him to triumph.[176]

Jackson, however, paid a huge price for his victory. He had "yielded to the call of his country" in running for the presidency and had endured "torrents of abuse" and "the vilest slanders."[177] Near the end of December, Rachel died of heart failure, exacerbated by the stress and strain of her husband's campaign. The general blamed the despicable attacks of his opponents for her death, but he recognized that if he had retired to Hermitage as she wanted, she would have still been alive. Some of Jackson's foes had argued that if he truly was a gallant protector of women as he claimed, he would not have run and subjected his wife to "the ribald taunts, and dark surmises of the profligate."[178] During the campaign Rachel protested that she had been cruelly treated by her husband's enemies who had "dipt their arrows in wormwood and gall and sped them at me." Nevertheless, she echoed the words of the apostle Paul, "I C[an do all] things in Christ who strengthens me."[179] His "dear wife," Jackson lamented, was "the victim of these fiends, & demons of slander and her life [was] shortened, by the many unjust attacks upon her." At least, God had permitted her "to live to witness the triumph of virtue over the vilest slander" in his defeat of Adams.[180]

From a contemporary perspective, this scandal seems ironic, given the sexual unfaithfulness of numerous presidents before and during their tenure in office. Few presidents or other Americans loved their wives more deeply than Jackson loved Rachel or enjoyed such an intimate relationship. As Brands argues, "no one questioned his utter faithfulness and devotion to Rachel."[181]

Jackson's Relationship with Religious Constituencies

Despite the numerous attacks on his character and moral conduct during the campaign, as president, Jackson generally enjoyed good relations with the nation's religious communities. However, three issues caused some tension between Jackson and them during his tenure in office: his position on Sabbath observance, his refusal to declare a day of prayer and fasting to help stop the spread of an epidemic, and his Indian removal policy. The defeat of the campaign to stop Sunday mail service in the late 1820s strengthened the belief of many devout Americans that they must work together to save the nation from "infidelity and radicalism." Concern about the nation's failure to keep the Sabbath holy helped revive the religious community as a political interest group.[182] Speaking for many evangelicals, Jeremiah Evarts declared: "We have always viewed" delivering mail and keeping post offices open on Sundays "as a national evil of great magnitude" that demanded "national repentance and reformation."[183]

Many Christians exhorted Jackson to observe the Lord's Day conscientiously to help rescue it "from profanations which have mournfully abounded." The Bible warned, Presbyterian minister Charles Coffin declared, that "the curse of God will afflict a Sabbath-breaking nation" while "his blessing will prosper a nation that hallows the day which he has set apart for his own honour and the spiritual welfare of mankind." By refusing to receive congratulatory addresses, attend public dinners, travel, and accept political or civic honors on Sundays, Jackson could help "reform the morals and perpetuate the prosperity" of the American people.[184] One way Jackson could be the best chief magistrate in American history, Ely averred, was by not journeying "on the Lord's day, *except in a case of mercy or necessity.*" He pointed out that the press published the travels of public figures on the Sabbath without explaining why they traveled, even though some of their reasons might be "satisfactory to the strictest moralist." He also urged the president to instruct government officials not to "set an ungodly example" by violating the Sabbath.[185]

When Jackson made his "Grand Triumphal Tour" of the North in 1833, Democratic newspapers emphasized that he scheduled events to "avoid desecrating" the Sabbath, which other "distinguished men" had often done. The president honored "the institutions of heaven" by worshipping at Presbyterian, Episcopal, and Methodist church services and resting on Sundays, thereby setting "a helpful example" for millions.[186] Nevertheless, some evangelicals complained that Jackson did not scrupulously observe the Sabbath and did not support legislative efforts to stop mail service and commerce on the Lord's Day.

A few months before the 1832 election, Henry Clay asked Congress to declare a national day of prayer and fasting to beseech God to halt a cholera epidemic. Tens of thousands of Americans became sick, and several thousand eventually died.[187] The Senate approved Clay's resolution, but the House could not agree on the wording, and the bill died, prompting many religious groups to appeal directly to Jackson to issue a proclamation. Seeing the epidemic as a visitation from God occasioned by Americans' pride, lack of charity, and intemperance, ministers and editors argued it could be abated only by corporate repentance and moral reform.[188] Interpreting the First Amendment very strictly, the president refused to proclaim a fast day (which most of his predecessors had done) because he wanted to protect religion's "complete separation" from the federal government. Jackson declared that he believed in the "efficacy of prayer" and hoped that Americans would be spared from further attacks of this pestilence, but he did not think the president had a constitutional right to promote any "period or mode" of religious activity. The states and churches should "recommend the mode by which the people may best attest their reliance on the protecting arm of the almighty in times of great public distress."[189]

Jackson planned to veto Clay's proposal if Congress passed it. A draft of his veto message explained his position further. The Constitution "carefully separated sacred from civilian concerns." Signing a resolution for a national day of prayer was "incompatible" with the president's constitutional responsibilities. While Jackson urged Americans to seek God's guidance and assistance in both prosperity and calamity, as president, he must "abstain from any act" that linked church and state in a way that was "perilous" to both of them.[190]

Jackson's stance disappointed most evangelicals. New Jersey Senator Theodore Frelinghuysen, who played a prominent role in four major organizations of the Second Great Awakening and championed Protestant concerns in politics, led efforts to pass a national fast day proclamation and to prevent Indian removal. In *An Inquiry into the Moral and Religious Character of the American Government*, he traced the progress of "political irreligion" from Jefferson's unwillingness to proclaim a day of humiliation and prayer in 1807 to Jackson's in 1832. Frelinghuysen repudiated the reasoning of both presidents and strove to "establish the constitutional primacy of Christianity."[191] Others, however, denounced Clay's resolution as a blatant effort to improve his own popularity. "Could he gain votes by it," declared one critic, "he would kiss the toe of the Pope and prostrate himself before the grand lama."[192]

A third issue caused little controversy because it received scant publicity, but it sheds further light on Jackson's views. In 1831 the founders of an organization that worked to establish Sunday schools in the West requested an endorsement from Jackson who complied without carefully examining their project. When a constituent complained several weeks later that he was favoring some religious groups over others, the president responded that he thought this plan to disseminate the gospel, provide Bibles, educate the poor, and promote Sabbath observance was interdenominational. If this organization gave "preference to any sect or denomination over others," then his understanding of the Constitution would not permit him to endorse it, because "freedom and an established religion are incompatible." He was "a lover of the christian religion," not a sectarian, he explained. "I do not believe, that any" who were "received to heaven thro the atonement of our blessed Saviour," will be asked their denominational affiliation. "All true Christians, know they are such, *because they love one another.*"[193] One of the "greatest blessings" the Constitution provided, Jackson added, "is the liberty of worshipping God as our conscience dictates."[194]

Despite such statements, some evangelicals doubted whether Jackson was truly a Christian. In 1831, while visiting the White House with thirty colleagues, a Methodist pastor from Baltimore prayed so loudly that the president would be converted that he could be heard a long distance away.[195] Eventually, many evangelicals became dissatisfied with Jackson and some actively opposed him because of his failure to support strict Sabbath observance, his position on church–state separation, his Indian removal program, and his opposition to the antislavery movement.

Jackson's Political Philosophy

Jackson's faith strongly affected how he viewed the events of his own life and his nation, and his letters are peppered with religious language and scriptural quotations and allusions. The Democrat insisted that God ruled the universe, that humans should advance His purposes, and that His justice would ultimately prevail. Jackson repeatedly stressed that he sought God's guidance in devising policies and making political decisions. The president argued that South Carolina's nullification of the 1832 tariff subverted America's "sacred Union" and "happy Constitution," which "by the favor of Heaven" had brought it unparalleled prosperity and international acclaim. Jackson beseeched "the Great Ruler of Nations" to "grant that the signal blessings with which He has favored" the United States not be lost as a result of "the madness of party or personal ambition." He hoped that God's "wise providence" would enable those who had "produced this crisis" to see their folly to prevent the nation from experiencing the "misery of civil strife." God was using the Union to accomplish His purposes.[196] If people judged God's "future designs" by how

He had displayed "His past favors," Jackson declared on another occasion, "our national prosperity" depended on preserving our liberties, America's power depended on its unity, and individual happiness depended on maintaining "State rights and wise institutions."[197] God was sovereign, Jackson warned France in 1834, so if its government did not pay the debts owed to American citizens, it might experience "the retributive judgments of Heaven."[198]

While Jackson rarely connected his religious convictions directly with either his overarching political principles or with his analysis of particular policy issues, his emphasis on promoting justice, the common good, virtue, and republican ideals and eradicating corruption are consistent with biblical norms. Guided by a "relatively coherent set of ideas," Jackson sought to ensure the survival of the Union and preserve liberty in the face of the immense challenges posed by governmental corruption and sectional and elite interests. He repeatedly censured concentrated authority, aristocracy, standing armies, and established churches as inimical to freedom and commended "public and private virtue, internal unity, and social stability." While deploring "special privilege, monopoly, and excessive government power," the Democrat applauded "limited government, individual initiative, and moral constraint."[199]

During the antebellum years, many events and forces threatened to destroy the Union. The Aaron Burr conspiracy of 1805–6, the War of 1812, the Hartford Convention of 1814–15, and the nullification crisis of 1832 were all poignant reminders that domestic and foreign enemies menaced national unity.[200] His administration's primary accomplishment, Jackson claimed in 1836, was defeating "the multiplied schemes" "ambitious and factious spirits" had "devised to dissolve" *our glorious Union* and produce anarchy.[201] Experience, he proclaimed in his farewell address had proved that "the union of these States" provided "a sure foundation for the brightest hopes of freedom and for the happiness of the people." Various forces, he warned, were trying to break this great republic into "a multitude of petty states." "At every hazard, and by every sacrifice, this Union must be preserved." Only a government that rested upon the "affections of the people," secured their willing obedience to its laws, protected their life, liberty, and property, and quashed all unlawful resistance could achieve this.[202]

Jackson continually asserted that the people must govern. Republican citizens were "the sovereigns of our glorious Union."[203] The government must implement the will of the majority.[204] To accomplish this, Jackson sought to abolish the Electoral College, reduce the checks and balances established by the Constitution, and prohibit the Supreme Court from being the final interpreter of the Constitution. He also wanted to give the people control over all offices, elected and appointed, through the direct election of senators (which was not implemented until 1913) and the rotation of officeholders.[205] Despite his professed belief in human depravity, Jackson had tremendous confidence in the ability of ordinary Americans, especially farmers, mechanics, and laborers, to make wise political choices. "The great laboring and producing classes," he averred, constituted "the bone and sinew of our confederacy."[206] Given the proper opportunity, they would "decide well" and ensure the safety "of our happy republican system."[207] The virtue of common citizens was the only sound basis for republican government.[208] For Jackson, individual morality was the glue that held society together.[209] "As long as the government heeds the popular will," he declared, "the republic is safe" because the majority of Americans supported "its main pillars—virtue, religion and morality."[210]

Jackson frequently professed his commitment to promoting the public good. "The rich and powerful," he lamented often bent "the acts of government to their selfish purposes." Because individuals had different amounts of talent, education, and wealth, social distinctions would occur under all forms of government. Nevertheless, the government must provide equal protection and opportunity for all citizens and not increase the advantages and privileges of the upper classes. As God did with the rain, the government must "shower its favors alike on the high and the low."[211] "As long as our Government is administered for the good of the people," he declared in his first inaugural address, as long as it guaranteed "the rights of person and of property, liberty of conscience and of the press, it will be worth defending."[212] "It is my steady object," he declared, to "advance the good of the country." "Should Providence enable me to succeed," "I shall be amply rewarded for the cares and labours [my position] imposes upon me."[213] To accomplish this end, Jackson strove to prevent the "money power," aided by corrupt and covetous politicians, from furthering their own interests at the expense of the masses.[214] The moneyed aristocracy, he protested, was "daily gaining strength" and perverting elections and legislation.[215] To counter this, Congress must make advancing the "public good" its "sole end & aim."[216]

These guiding principles led Jackson to oppose all measures he thought would weaken the Union, including burdensome taxes, large government expenditures, monopolies, paper-money banking, speculation, and nullification. Some of them concentrated money into a few hands, and all of them eroded virtue, undermined republican institutions, and threatened liberty. High tariffs encroached on states' rights, benefited special interests, and hurt consumers.[217] Although some of his policies facilitated speculation in stocks and land, Jackson protested that this practice damaged "our virtuous Government." Speculation provided "a thousand ways of robbing honest labour of its earnings to make knaves rich, powerful and dangerous—whatever demoralises the people" tended "to destroy Institutions founded solely upon their virtue."[218]

His foundational political commitments also prompted Jackson to oppose a national bank and some internal improvement projects, denounce nullification and abolitionism, and promote Indian removal. The bank of the United States "was a morally suspect institution" and the "embodiment of unfair privilege."[219] It was, he declared, one of the "fruits of a system" that distrusted "the popular will as a safe regulator of political power." The bank's "ultimate object" was to consolidate all power in the central government.[220] Because he wanted to keep federal spending at a low level and regarded a national debt as a danger to liberty, Jackson vetoed the Maysville Road and opposed the funding of some other projects.[221] Moreover, he argued that internal improvement projects—canals, roads, and railroads—were a major source of corruption because "individual states and private companies resorted to congressional logrolling and pork-barrel tactics to win federal grants."[222] The president condemned nullification as a conspiracy of "unprincipled men" who sought to "destroy the union, and form a southern confederacy."[223] The "wickedness, madness and folly of its leaders," he protested, was unparalleled in world history.[224] Jackson censured abolitionists as malcontents who sought to discredit democracy and demolish the Union. To him and like-minded Democrats, abolitionism violated the law, threatened property rights, and assaulted liberty.[225]

Indian Removal

Given both the strong opposition of some religious groups and its horrific results, Jackson's Indian removal policy may seem to be a strange choice to illustrate how his faith affected his policies as president. However, this issue was very important to Jackson and he based his argument for removal largely on humanitarian and moral grounds. Old Hickory expended substantial time, energy, and political capital in devising and implementing this policy, and he retained as much personal control as possible over removal by asking friends, especially William Carroll and John Coffee, to negotiate with Indians and sometimes even directly talking with them himself.[226]

Jackson had more encounters with Indians than any president before or after him. His view of Indians was shaped by his frontier and military experiences, paternalism, ethnocentrism, humanitarianism, position on states' rights, concern for national security, expansionist dreams, and religious convictions.[227] Jackson saw removal as imperative both to protecting "the liberty and security of the American people" and ensuring the survival of Indians.[228]

In 1817 Jackson wrote to President James Monroe that if the federal government limited Indians' lands, gave them "the utensils of husbandry," protected them, and forced them to obey "laws provided for their benefit, they would soon "be civilized." Doing this would ensure justice for American citizens, the nation's "interest and security," and "the peace and happiness of the Indians."[229]

As president, Jackson asserted that the US government had as much right to legislate for Native Americans as it did for settlers in the territories. Fourteen years before the Supreme Court ruled in *Cherokee Nation v. Georgia* (1831) that the Cherokees had no right to sue in the Supreme Court because they were not a "foreign state" but a "domestic dependent nation," Jackson argued that Indians were not independent nations that enjoyed the right of sovereignty. The land they occupied had been given to them by the benevolence of the United States.[230]

While most historians strongly criticize Jackson's Indian policy, they generally agree that the Democrat was convinced that it was "just and humane."[231] Because of the greed of whites, cultural misunderstanding, and the inability of the two groups to live together, Jackson argued, Indians who remained in the East were likely to be degraded and destroyed. "Humanity and national honor," he declared in an 1829 address to Congress, demand that every effort "be made to avert so great a calamity." He sought to devise a policy consistent "with the rights of the States, to preserve this much-injured race."[232]

The Indian Removal Act, signed into law in May 1830, authorized the president to negotiate with the southeastern tribes to arrange their relocation to land west of the Mississippi River. When he learned that fall that the Choctaws had agreed to move beyond the Mississippi, Jackson rejoiced that "Providence appears to smile" on his administration's effort "to preserve these people from *annihilation as tribes*" and "to thwart the machinations of ours and their worst enemies."[233] Defending his policy, Jackson asserted in an address to Congress in December that "a speedy removal" was "important to the United States, individual states, and Indians." It would end conflict between the federal government and the states over Indians rights. Indian removal would enable "a dense and civilized population" to control "large tracts of country now occupied by a few savage hunters." By "incalculably strengthen[ing] the southwestern frontier," it would help the United States "to repel future invasions." The policy would enable Mississippi and Alabama "to advance rapidly in population, wealth, and power," separate Indians from close contact with white settlements, "free them from the power of the States," and permit "them to pursue happiness in their own way and under their own rude institutions." With government protection and wise counsel, they could hopefully "cast off their savage habits and become an interesting, civilized, and Christian community." No one, Jackson claimed, had a friendlier attitude toward "the aborigines of the country" than he did or was willing to do more to "reclaim them from their wandering habits and make them a happy, prosperous people." "What good man," the president asked, "would prefer a country covered with forests and ranged by a few thousand savages to our extensive republic, studded with cities, towns, and prosperous farms, embellished with all the improvements which art can devise or industry execute, occupied by more than 12,000,000 happy people, and filled with all the blessings of liberty, civilization, and religion?"[234]

Despite the difficulties and tragic results of removal, Jackson continued to defend his policy as prudent, just, and beneficial. In an 1835 message to Congress, the president argued that history demonstrated that Indians could not "live in contact with a civilized community and prosper." The government was fulfilling its "moral duty" to protect, preserve, and perpetuate "the scattered remnants of this race."[235] In his Farewell Address, Jackson proclaimed that his removal policy would enable "this unhappy race" to "share in the blessings of civilization and be saved from that degradation and destruction" they were experiencing in the East. Philanthropists should rejoice that Indians had been "placed beyond the reach of injury or oppression" under "the paternal care" of the federal government.[236]

Jackson's Indian Removal Act evoked substantial opposition primarily from religious groups. The American Board of Commissioners for Foreign Missions, comprised chiefly of Presbyterians and Congregationalists, led the fight of evangelicals to defeat its passage. Committed to helping convert and civilize Indians, this organization employed many legal, moral, religious, and humanitarian arguments against removal and had significant support in the North. Its corresponding secretary Jeremiah Evarts, the William Lloyd Garrison of the Indian rights movement, led its efforts. He had numerous Indian friends, had visited many Indian communities, and had carefully studied their legal claims and history. In numerous essays widely printed in newspapers, Evarts denounced removal as a great sin that would bring God's judgment on the nation and sought to provoke moral outrage in the religious community.[237] He also led a campaign to submit petitions to Congress opposing the Indian Removal Bill. Isolated on western reservations, thousands of innocent Indians, Evarts argued, would no longer benefit from the East's civilizing influences. Moreover, interactions with unscrupulous whites and savage western Indians would further degrade them. The core issue, he insisted, was moral: would the United States honor its treaties, recognize the land claims of the Cherokees and other groups, and protect them against the illegal acts of Georgia and other states.[238] Many missionaries and political opponents of

Jackson agreed that southern Indians had a moral right to own and govern the land they occupied because of treaties they had made with the United States. They argued that the tribes could legally and practically maintain their independence while being surrounded by whites.[239] Opponents also denounced Indian removal as coercive and censured the mercenary motives of whites who coveted Indian land. Moreover, incipient Whigs complained, this policy was designed to strengthen Jackson's support in the South and West.[240]

Frelinghuysen led the fight against the bill in the Senate. Their racial prejudice and greed, the New Jersey senator argued, led Georgians to refuse to give Cherokees their civil rights.[241] The pleas of political expediency, he declared, must not trump "unchangeable principles of eternal justice." The desire of whites for more land could not negate "the political maxim, that, where the Indian always *has been*, he enjoys an absolute right still *to be*" and to freely practice "his own modes of thought, government, and conduct." "Do the obligations of justice change with the color of the skin?" Whites did not have the prerogatives to "disregard the dictates of moral principles" when interacting with Indians, Frelinghuysen thundered.[242]

In the debate in the House over removal in April 1830, Representative Wilson Lumpkin of Georgia castigated the churches for creating a "religious party in politics" and harshly condemning Georgian whites. "These canting fanatics," he bellowed, had unfairly denounced Georgians as "atheists, deists, infidels, and Sabbath-breakers laboring under the curse of slavery." He and many other southerners also feared that their support for Indians' rights would prompt northern evangelicals to adopt a more fervent abolitionist stance.[243]

Proponents of removal also used the cultural mandate of Genesis to justify dispossessing the Indians. "The Creator," insisted Michigan Governor Lewis Cass, intended that the earth "be reclaimed from a state of nature and cultivated," which Indians failed to do.[244] "Whites had a superior claim to the land," avowed Missouri Senator Thomas Hart Benton, because they "used it according to the intentions of the CREATOR."[245] Georgia Governor George Gilmer argued that "treaties were expedients by which ignorant, intractable, and savage people were induced without bloodshed to yield up what civilized people had a right to possess by virtue of that command of the Creator" to "be fruitful, multiply, and replenish the earth, and subdue it."[246]

Jackson instructed Thomas McKenney, head of the Bureau of Indian Affairs, to try to persuade the nation's religious leaders that his removal policy was virtuous and to support it. McKenney solicited the help of Episcopalians and Dutch Reformed ministers and laypeople to establish the New York Board for the Emigration, Preservation, and Improvement of the Aborigines of America. His arguments and the board's activities helped counter protests against removal. The board petitioned Congress in 1829 to pass the Indian Removal Act. Southern and southwestern Baptists, led by pastor Isaac McCoy, also strongly supported Jackson's removal policy.[247]

Advocates of removal also argued that it would require a large number of troops to protect Native Americans from white aggression and whites from Indian attacks. Moreover, allowing Indian enclaves to remain would hinder economic development, increase federal–state conflict, and threaten the nation's security and unity. Many authors, educators, and politicians insisted that both Providence and progress required the removal of Indians who were inhibiting the nation's advancement. Ethnographers reinforced the widely held assumption that Indians were an "inferior race." Although some, including Frelinghuysen, Garrison, and Lydia Maria Child, denounced removal as a racist policy, many leading historians, scientists, and literary figures justified removal as the best policy for preventing conflict and guaranteeing Indians' survival.[248]

After the passage of the removal bill, for a while the protest against this policy grew even stronger. Evarts published a collection of key congressional speeches opposing the bill, wrote essays condemning removal, and organized another petition campaign. Although Quakers, Methodists, and Congregationalists also submitted their own memorials, after Evarts died in May 1831, the religious crusade against removal substantially declined.[249] Ultimately, the desire of both southern and northern whites to obtain more territory triumphed over the moral arguments of humanitarians and missionaries that Native Americans had intrinsic rights to continue to occupy the land where they had long resided.[250]

However, Jackson did arouse the ire of the religious community by refusing to intercede to release two missionaries—Samuel Worcester and Elizur Butler—from jail who had been arrested in Georgia for disobeying a law that prohibited whites from living in Cherokee Territory without obtaining a state license. Worchester and Butler appealed their conviction, and the case went all the way to the Supreme Court. In *Worcester v. Georgia* (1832), the justices ruled that the federal government had jurisdiction in Cherokee territory and the laws of Georgia had "no force." Chief Justice John Marshall ordered the Georgia court to reverse its decision. However, Georgia refused to do so, Jackson declined to intervene, and the missionaries remained in prison for more than a year. Over thirty years later, *New York Tribune* editor Horace Greeley recalled hearing that Jackson had proclaimed "John Marshall has made his decision; now let him enforce it." It is very unlikely that the president actually said this, but it did convey his attitude and reinforced the image of a conceited, defiant Jackson.

Vice President Van Buren worked quietly to get the missionaries released, which occurred in January 1833.[251]

The results of Indian removal were catastrophic. Beginning with the Choctaws in the winter of 1831–32, Jackson's administration oversaw the removal of almost 46,000 Native Americans to Oklahoma territory. The president was wrong that even "religious enthusiasts" would "not find fault" with the liberal and just treaties his administration was negotiating with Indians.[252] Many Indians were forced to comply with treaties they never approved and coerced or bribed to leave their ancestral homes; the Creeks and Seminoles fought federal troops to try to prevent their removal. Fraud, intimidation, and speculation were all employed to expropriate Indian land, usually at prices well below market value. The army strove to treat Indians humanely while transporting them, but its leaders lacked the resources to deal with the scope of the operation. Although whites' acquisition of 100 million acres significantly increased America's cotton crop, the cost of removal contributed substantially to federal government expenditures more than doubling between 1828 and 1836.[253] The greatest tragedy occurred in 1838 after Jackson left office. In the Trial of Tears, 4,000 of the 18,000 Cherokees who were forcibly expelled from Georgia died as a result of illness or harsh treatment during their capture, detention in stockades, or the westward trek. The former president was deeply distressed by the suffering the Cherokees endured.[254]

Because of its racist assumptions, exploitative methods, and disastrous consequences, Indian removal, for many historians, is "the great moral stain on the Jacksonian legacy, much as it was to Christian humanitarian reformers" during the 1830s. However, Jackson was more paternalistic and benevolent than some of his major political rivals, most notably Henry Clay who argued that Indians' annihilation would be "no great loss to the world." Although "Jackson's removal policy was not overly malevolent," argued Sean Wilentz, "it was insidious—and for Indians, it was ruinous."[255] Jackson, protested Donald Cole, allowed "the white majority to exploit a nonwhite minority." His administration "used bribery and intimidation," "took advantage of tribal divisions to divide and conquer," and "withheld military protection." The president allowed white speculators to use "fraud and deceit" to acquire Indian allotments.[256] Jackson's rhetoric emphasized "philanthropic ideals," Richard Latner averred, but his program involved considerable manipulation and coercion. In Michael Rogin's judgment, Jackson was primarily responsible for the destruction of Indians in antebellum America. "He won battles, signed treaties, and forced removal not simply over Indian resistance, but often over the recalcitrance of his own troops and the timidity of settlers and civilian politicians." Jackson gave Indians two choices to avoid extinction: they could adopt Christianity, civilization, and agriculture and intermarry with whites and merge into white society or they could move west of the Mississippi; both options required Indians to give up their traditional communal ways of life and enabled whites to expropriate Indian lands. "There was nothing redemptive about Jackson's Indian policy," asserted Jon Meacham; at no time did he do "the right and brave thing."[257]

To assuage their consciences and justify their actions, proponents of Indian removal employed religious and paternalistic rhetoric, Meacham insists. Jackson frequently called himself the Indians' "Great Father," and he truly believed that he knew what was best for them and that his policy would benefit both them and whites.[258] On the other hand, Ronald Satz, Robert Remini, Francis Prucha, and H. W. Brands defend Jackson's policy. Jackson, Satz argues, was not a "merciless Indian-hater" as many historians portray him. As governor of Florida, he treated Native Americans paternalistically, approved of Indian–white marriages, adopted an Indian as a son, and considered numerous Indians to be friends; his major goal was to ensure the nation's development, harmony, and safety. The general repeatedly declared that he sought to further "the interest and security of the United States, and the peace and happiness of the Indians." Remini maintains that Jackson should not be blamed for the "monstrous deed" of Indian removal. His objective was to save Indians from extinction, not destroy their life and culture. "He struggled to prevent fraud and corruption," and he promised not to force Indians to accept his removal plan. However, Jackson did warn tribal leaders that "he would abandon them to the mercy of the states if they did not agree to migrate west," and much coercion did occur. Prucha argues that Jackson was "genuinely concerned for the well-being of the Indians" and their way of life and that the missionaries who opposed removal had political motivations. Jackson's only other alternatives were to let Indians be annihilated or to defend them in enclaves in the East, neither of which was feasible. "Given the racist realities of the time," Brands avows, Jackson correctly contended that if the Cherokees remained in Georgia, they risked extinction. While Jackson cared about the welfare of Indians, his primary concern was to guarantee America's security and safety. To be militarily prepared to defend its territory against the British, French, and Spanish, who had often threatened, preyed on, or attacked the United States, whites must reside in these southern states.[259] For Jackson, preserving the union trumped all other issues, including the moral rights of Indians, which made him reluctant to oppose the claims of states.[260]

Although they criticize Jackson's approach to this complex moral and political issue, many historians maintain that given the racist attitudes of the era, whites' demand for land and lack of understanding for or appreciation of Indian culture, the nation's security concerns, and the cost of protecting Indians if they remained in the East, removal, while deplorable and disastrous, was probably inevitable. Others counter that Jackson had other more humane choices and could have handled matters more justly and compassionately. Old Hickory, they contend, contributed to the problems in Georgia by not strongly opposing the state's actions. Had he endorsed the Cherokees' position in 1829 and 1830, the outcome might have been different. Instead, his attitude and actions stiffened Georgia's resolve to expropriate their land. Moreover, Jackson could have supported Indians who wanted to remain in small settlements like the 5,000 Iroquois who continued to reside in upstate New York. Most importantly, he should have guaranteed that Indians were relocated in a more just and humane way.[261]

Final Assessment

The United States experienced immense changes and substantial turmoil during Jackson's eight years in office. Industrial, market, and transportation revolutions were transforming the nation. Jackson came to Washington in 1829 in a carriage and left on a train in 1837. Manufacturing, westward migration, political participation, and hostility over slavery (as evident in the response to the Nat Turner insurrection, anti-abolitionist riots in the North, and the Gag Rule Controversy in Congress) all increased significantly. During Jackson's presidency the standard of living improved substantially for many Americans. However, "poverty, urban crime and violence, blatant and vulgar materialism," the disparity in wealth and privilege, and racial and religious bigotry also increased.[262] At least 100 riots occurred between 1834 and 1837, the greatest wave of violence since the American Revolution. Low wages, poor working conditions, and ethnic animosities sparked labor riots; nativist riots erupted against the Irish in Boston, New York City, and Philadelphia; and blacks were attacked in the North. Jackson received threatening notes, heard rumors of insurrection, and survived an assassination attempt (the first one in American history) by an unemployed house painter in January 1835 whose two pistols misfired from eight feet away. Inspired by the Second Great Awakening, Americans created numerous organizations that sought to improve working conditions and education, end slavery, reform prisons and mental institutions, and curb intemperance to combat these ills.[263]

Jackson was an immensely popular president. Today's young children, predicted the Chicago *Democrat*, would someday proudly proclaim that they had been "born in the Age of Jackson."[264] Numerous admirers asked Old Hickory for a lock of his hair, and he sometimes complied. Many others, including Princess Victoria of England, requested his autograph. Virginia Senator Richard Parker commended Jackson for preserving the Union, fairly adjusting the tariff, making beneficial internal improvements, and settling the Indian issue "upon just and liberal principles."[265]

Many eulogists praised Jackson profusely. In a memorial oration in Washington, DC, prominent historian George Bancroft hailed Jackson as "the servant of the people." "In a just resolution inflexible, he was full of the gentlest affections, ever ready to solace the distressed, and to relieve the needy, faithful to his friends, [and] fervid for his country."[266] To Massachusetts Senator Daniel Webster, Jackson possessed "dauntless courage, vigor, and perseverance."[267] Linking the general with Washington and Jefferson, a pastor in Wilkes-Barre, Pennsylvania, predicted that his tomb would become a "modern Mecca" many would visit.[268]

Jackson's impact was tremendous. He increased the power of the presidency and created a new presidential style, which his supporters argued, "embodied the popular will." Jackson made the president the "head of state and leader of the nation." He strengthened the United States by preventing nullification, paying off the national debt, reorganizing the bureaucracy, reducing political corruption, expanding democracy, improving its status, and preserving peace. "More than any other single individual," by "his charisma, popularity, and accomplishments," the general helped the United States become a modern democracy.[269] In his farewell address, Jackson argued that the nation had a "rich and flourishing commerce" and was growing in numbers, wealth, and knowledge. No other people, he claimed, had ever "enjoyed so much freedom and happiness" as did Americans.[270]

Convinced that he "represented the people against aristocracy and privilege," Jackson labored to end corruption in Washington. The Democrat saw himself as Hercules who had come to clean out "the Augean Stable." He strove to halt the federal government's "long period of sustained official corruption," especially to stop federal bureaucrats from using public funds to influence others and enhance their political power.[271] The president expected all his appointees to "conform to a strict moral code" "to help restore virtue" to the federal government. Their fidelity and honesty would "elevate the character of the government and purify the morals of the country."[272]

While many praised Jackson's accomplishments, others criticized his character and policies. Whigs derided Jackson as "King Andrew I," "a dangerous military chieftain who usurped military and presidential power." His foes lampooned his meager education and poor spelling. In his eulogy, Bancroft called Jackson "the unlettered man of the West" who was "little versed in books" and "unconnected by science with the traditions of the past."[273] During the 1828 campaign, an anonymous pamphleteer asked what would the English periodicals that had "defamed even the best writings of our countrymen, say of a people who want a man to govern them who cannot spell *more than about one word in four*?"[274] John Quincy Adams was even more brutal. When Harvard decided to award Jackson an honorary degree in 1833, Adams complained: "I *could not* be present to see my darling Harvard disgrace herself by conferring a degree upon a barbarian and savage who could scarcely spell his own name."[275]

Numerous contemporaries and later scholars complained that Jackson's political philosophy was deeply flawed and that his policies produced poor results. To his enemies, Jackson was a "cult leader" who deceived the "lost and vulnerable." "Jacksonian democracy," they argued, "was a misnomer" because the general "was a tyrant."[276] William Seward accused Jackson of creating a spoils system that furthered corruption and dishonesty rather than patriotism and public service.[277] A Whig newspaper exulted that Jackson's farewell address was "the last humbug" which "this illiterate, violent, vain, and iron-willed soldier can impose upon a confiding and credulous people."[278] Unlike his father and Jefferson, who had also been bitter political rivals, John Quincy Adams and Jackson never reconciled in their later years, undoubtedly in part because Adams continued to serve in Congress and did not respect Jackson as his intellectual equal. Adams denounced Jackson's administration as "the reign of subaltern knaves, fattening upon land jobs and money jobs."[279] If Adams was not insane, Jackson wrote in 1838, he was "the most reckless and depraved man living."[280] This "vindictive" man, Jackson declared in 1844, was "reckless with the truth."[281] After Jackson died, Adams labeled him a "murderer" and an "adulterer."[282]

Contemporary historians also claim that Jackson had major character flaws and adopted misguided policies that had detrimental consequences. Remini maintains that Jackson made many bad appointments, sometimes did not effectively guide Congress, and ruthlessly expelled southeastern Indians from their ancestral lands.[283] Jackson, Sean Wilentz argues, "often acted on the basis of fierce personal loyalties (and hatred), and took positions that seemed at odds with his stated principles."[284] Rather than basing his understanding of justice on transcendent principles, Andrew Burstein asserts, Jackson's view of justice reaffirmed "his own impulses" and validated "his own life experience." Moreover, Jackson defended American manifest destiny as divinely mandated.[285] His argument that western expansion was God's providential plan helped justify the acquisitiveness of many of his contemporaries.[286]

It is ironic, avows Lynn Hudson Parsons, that a "slaveholder with an autocratic personality" who owned a large plantation that depended on the labor of scores of slaves was considered "the icon of American democracy for much of the nineteenth century." The personal lifestyle of Jackson's political nemesis John Quincy Adams "was far more republican."[287] In addition, Jackson did little to help blacks, Native Americans, or white women because he did not recognize them as equals or see their potential to contribute to American life. The general wanted to "preserve an idealized world of white yeomen gentrification," thereby "replicating his own path to respectability."[288] Numerous incongruities are evident in Jackson's character and life. As Wilentz claims, it is challenging to "make sense of his paradoxes and contradictions without slighting either his defects or his achievements."[289] As his first biographer wrote, he was "a democratic autocrat," "an urbane savage," and "an atrocious saint."[290]

Although his faith grew stronger and more meaningful during the last twenty-five years of his life, Jackson continued to espouse attitudes and engage in actions that clashed with Christian norms. The general's "extraordinary rage," strong desire for revenge, and great difficulty in forgiving his political and personal enemies violated his professed faith.[291] Jackson's "complexity of character," Bertram Wyatt-Brown insisted, was "truly astonishing," and he was "deeply committed to white Southern customs, convictions, and prejudices" about race, gender, and honor.[292] Jackson argued that "the principles and statutes" of the Bible "have been the rule of my life."[293] However, powerfully influenced by the spirit and values of his locale and era, like most other statesmen and ordinary Americans, he used his understanding of biblical teaching and God's will to justify his own personal preferences and defend policies he thought benefited the public good without carefully analyzing whether his preferences and policies accorded with sound biblical interpretation, political prudence, and the lessons of history. His personality, life experiences, and limited education all contributed to this. Nevertheless, Jackson strove valiantly to base his life and work as president on Christian principles, and in some ways, he succeeded admirably.

5

William McKinley

AMERICA AS GOD'S INSTRUMENT

*[We] should reverently bow before the throne of divine grace
and give devout praise to God, who holds the nations in the
hollow of his hands and worketh upon them the marvels of his
high will, and who has . . . led our brave soldiers and seamen
to victory.*

"Address to the People for Thanksgiving and Prayer," July
6, 1898

*Piety and patriotism go well together. Love of flag, love of
country, are not inconsistent with our religious faith.*

Speeches and Addresses of William McKinley (1900), 210

*The faith of a Christian nation recognizes the hand of
Almighty God in the ordeal through which we have passed.
Divine favor seemed manifest everywhere. In fighting for
humanity's sake, we have been signally blessed.*

Speeches and Addresses of William McKinley (1900), 105

Introduction

William McKinley, Jr. had a deep and devout evangelical faith that powerfully
influenced his life. After a conversion experience as a youth, he participated
regularly in the worship and ministry of the Methodist church, prayed and
read the Bible daily, often testified to his faith in private and public, and consistently followed Christian moral norms. As a high school student, he participated in the local YMCA. During the Civil War, McKinley faithfully attended
camp revivals and prayer meetings. As president, he habitually sought God's
guidance in making decisions and devising policies. His decisions to declare
war against Spain in 1898 and to take control of the Philippines were strongly

influenced by his faith and his assessment of the religious factors involved. While most American religious leaders strongly supported McKinley's policies toward Spain, Cuba, and the Philippines, critics fault him for not properly distinguishing between piety and patriotism and for arguing that America's actions served God's purposes. McKinley's policies helped make him popular, but they also helped inspire future American imperialist ventures. After he was mortally wounded by an assassin's bullet in 1901, his concern for his wife and the public interest, forgiveness of his shooter, and demeanor while dying deeply impressed Americans. His response to being shot and his character led some to compare him with Christ, and his death prompted an outpouring of grief and spiritual reassessment. A man of principle, an effective party leader, and an astute politician, McKinley increased the prestige and expanded the powers of the presidency.

The Faith of William McKinley

McKinley, born in 1843, was one of America's most intensely religious presidents. This is evident in his childhood religious training, conversion experience, deep faith in God, service to Christian organizations, regular church attendance and reading of the Bible, commitment to prayer, frequent public and private testimony to his Christian convictions, enthusiastic support of missions, compassion for others (most notably his semi-invalid wife), belief that God directed history and his own life, attempt to base his policies on biblical principles, and personal habits. Both of his parents faithfully attended Sunday morning church services and Methodist class meetings and brought their children to worship and Sunday school. His mother's example and instruction strongly shaped McKinley's view of the world and goals for life.[1] She taught the future president how to pray and often took him to mid-week prayer meetings.[2]

In 1856 McKinley had a conversion experience. At a youth meeting at the Methodist Church in Poland, Ohio, the 12-year-old confessed, "I have sinned. I want to be a Christian." "I give myself to the Savior who has done so much for me." "I have found the pearl of great price," he proclaimed several nights later. "I love God."[3] In 1860 McKinley joined the Methodist Church in Poland. As a teenager he diligently studied the Scriptures and frequently discussed its teachings with his pastor, Sunday school teachers, and other laymen.[4] McKinley stated in 1899, "I am a Methodist and nothing but a Methodist—a Christian and nothing but a Christian." As a child his mother took him "to the Methodist prayer meeting and class meeting." As a teenager, he "joined the Methodist Church and Sunday School and then became a Sunday School teacher, and afterward a Sunday School Superintendent and a member of the Epworth League," a youth group. "By the blessings of heaven," he concluded, "I mean to live and die, please God, in the faith of my mother."[5] McKinley could have added that he had also served as president of the Canton YMCA, a trustee of the First Methodist Church of Canton, and, while the nation's chief executive, on the board of the East Ohio Methodist Conference's Home for the Aged.

McKinley's commitment to Jesus Christ as his Lord and Savior was central to his life. While fighting for the Union during the Civil War, the future president strictly adhered to Methodist values. He did not drink, swear, or smoke and regularly participated in prayer meetings, which provided both fellowship and spiritual comfort. Our semi-weekly prayer meetings, he reassured people at home, "are exerting a salutary influence, not only among our own company, but upon adjourning companies."[6] Reflecting on the possibility of dying, McKinley wrote in his diary before his first battle, "This record I want to leave behind, [is] that I fell not only as a soldier of my Country, but also as a Soldier of Jesus Christ." He added, "if we never meet again on earth, we will meet around God's throne in Heaven."[7] Dedicating a YMCA building in Youngstown in 1892, McKinley, then governor of Ohio, called the organization a "recognition of the Master who rules over all, a worthy tribute to Him who came to earth to save fallen man." As president, McKinley declared, "He who serves the Master best serves man best." He affirmed "the Divinity of Christ" and argued that Christianity was "the mightiest factor in the world's civilization."[8] The Methodist often testified about how faith and prayer had helped him deal with challenges.[9] During the 1896 presidential campaign, he refused to meet with a large contingent of prominent men on Sunday and instead invited them to attend church with him.[10] Many agreed that the Ohioan believed "humbly, truly, devotedly" in Christianity.[11] A Methodist periodical argued in 1901 that McKinley's faith was as firm as the Rock of Gibraltar. One of the leading pastors of the era, T. DeWitt Talmage, called McKinley the most "genial and lovable" Christian man he knew. After meeting with the president in 1900 to discuss how the Boxer Rebellion was affecting missions work in China, veteran newspaper correspondent Guy Morrison Walker concluded, "I had never been so impressed with the real spirituality of any man." McKinley clearly "held fast to the hand of the Almighty."[12]

Throughout his life McKinley faithfully attended church. As president he worshipped at the Metropolitan Methodist Church in Washington. According to eyewitnesses, he sang hymns enthusiastically and listened intently to sermons.[13] McKinley wanted to worship like any other parishioner. The president "hated having people staring at him while he read Psalms, sang hymns, put money in the collection plate or took communion." McKinley promised he would leave a service if a pastor gushed over him. "I like to hear the minister preach the plain, simple gospel—Christ and Him crucified."[14] Whenever he was in Canton, Ohio, McKinley attended his home church, First Methodist. While president, he continued to support this congregation financially, serve as a trustee, and maintain a close relationship with its pastor Charles Manchester.[15] McKinley rarely traveled on Sundays.[16] As a congressman, he was well known for humming Methodist hymns, and as president he frequently held hymn sings at the White House on Sunday evenings.[17] McKinley gave generously to the Methodist churches in which he worshipped in Washington and Canton and supported other religious causes including the YMCA.[18]

While running for governor of Ohio, McKinley declared, "I pray to God every day to give me strength to do this work."[19] A friend who accompanied McKinley on most of his congressional and gubernatorial campaigns claimed that even after very grueling days the future president always read his Bible and knelt in prayer before going to bed. This practice, a journalist concluded, demonstrated that McKinley's faith "was woven into the very fiber of his being."[20]

Many testified that McKinley read the Bible regularly and knew its teachings well.[21] "The greatest discovery a man or a nation can make," he declared, "is to find the truth of God's Word." It was more valuable than the discovery of continents, gold mines, or scientific laboratories. The Bible was "God's great love story to man." "The more profoundly we study this wonderful book, and the more clearly we observe its divine precepts," he added, "the better citizens we will become and the higher will be our destiny as a nation."[22]

Because McKinley wrote few letters, it is difficult to determine all the factors that influenced his thinking. Nevertheless, his evangelical faith clearly helped shape his worldview and political philosophy. His theological commitments and regular fellowship with Methodists helped direct his actions. As demonstrated by his inaugural address, biographer Margaret Leech claimed, McKinley came to the capitol with Micah 6:8 foremost in his mind: "What does the Lord require of thee, but to do justly, and to love mercy, and to walk humbly with thy God?"[23] Testifying to his desire for God's guidance as president, McKinley had his Bible opened at his first inaugural to the prayer of Solomon in 2 Chronicles 1:10: "Give me now wisdom and knowledge . . . for who can judge this thy people, that is so great." At his second inaugural, his Bible was opened to: "The wise in heart shall be called prudent. . . . Understanding is a wellspring of life unto him that hath it" (Proverbs 16:21–22).

No president, argued journalist Frederick Barton, "ever regarded himself more directly under Providential destiny as ruler of the nation than William McKinley." Newspaper correspondent Charles Pepper, who spent considerable time with the Methodist, alleged that his "serene faith" in God's wisdom was evident "throughout his public career." McKinley told his closest friends he considered the presidency to be "a God-entrusted responsibility." In his first inaugural address, the Republican proclaimed, "there is no safer reliance than upon the God of our fathers, who has so singularly favored the American people in every national trial, and who will not forsake us so long as we obey his commandments and walk humbly in his footsteps." His obligation to faithfully execute his office as president was "reverently taken before the Lord Most High. To keep it will be my single purpose, my constant prayer." "May that divine Providence who has guided us in all our undertakings from the beginning of the government," McKinley stated in 1899, "continue to us his gracious and assuring favor."[24] In his Thanksgiving Proclamation that year the president urged Americans to pray that God would continue His "guidance without which man's efforts are vain."[25] McKinley declared, "Man plans, but God Almighty executes."[26] The Methodist frequently asserted that God had specially blessed America because of the faith of its founders and the principles upon which the nation was established. The founders sublimely trusted in God and sought His counsel in every step they took. Subsequent "American history abounds in instances" of "this sincere reliance" on God.[27] America, McKinley declared, was built "upon the principles of virtue, morality, education, freedom, and human rights." No matter what challenges the United States faced, he promised, it would stand firm because it was built on God as its rock.[28]

"No man gets on so well in this world," McKinley declared in 1892, "as he whose daily walk and conversation are clean and consistent, whose heart is pure, and whose life is honorable." "Nothing in this world," the president added in a speech in 1901, "counts for so much as godly living." McKinley counseled a nephew to eat properly and avoid intoxicants and immoral practices. "Keep your life and speech both clean."[29] He practiced what he preached; his language was wholesome, his conduct was exemplary, and he rarely drank alcohol.[30] McKinley did have one vice. Although never photographed with a cigar, he often smoked as many as fifteen a day.

Throughout his life, McKinley was deeply interested in missions and insisted that the United States had an important role to play in evangelizing the world. In April 1900 he spoke to the delegates of the Ecumenical Foreign Missionary Conference meeting in New York City, the largest gathering and broadest representation of missionaries to that date. Christian missions, the

president declared, had produced "marvelous results. The service and sacrifices of missionaries" constituted "one of the most glorious pages in the
world's history." Missionaries served both the Master and their fellow men,
"carrying the torch of truth and enlightenment." They deserved gratitude, support, and homage. McKinley rejoiced that the labors of missionaries, while
still "difficult and trying," had become less perilous. In some places "indifference and opposition" had given way "to aid and cooperation." "Their contribution to the onward and upward march of humanity," he argued, was "beyond
all calculation." McKinley hoped that the conference would "rekindle the spirit
of missionary ardor" "to go teach all nations" and to proclaim Christ's gospel
"to the end of time!"[31]

Many testified to McKinley's compassion, concern for the downtrodden,
commendable Christian character, and loving care of his semi-invalid wife
Ida.[32] According to Pepper, McKinley was always moved by human suffering whether it was that of the Cuban *reconcentrados*, famine-stricken people
in India, or the politically oppressed in China. The Methodist often urged
Americans to let their "charity abound toward the sick, the needy, and the
poor." David J. Hill, an assistant secretary of state, claimed he had never met
anyone "more gracious and amiable" than McKinley. The president loved his
wife deeply and cared for her affectionately.[33] McKinley often excused himself
from conferences, cabinet meetings, and callers to attend to her needs.[34] In
1901 Ida declared that few could understand "what it is like to have a wife sick,
complaining," who had been "an invalid for twenty-five years." "Never a word
of unkindness has ever passed his lips. He is just the same tender, thoughtful, kind gentleman I knew when first he came and sought my hand."[35] After
McKinley's assassination, many praised his love for his wife. "Nothing in
the President's life had done more to endear him to the American people,"
declared the *Epworth Herald* "than his ardent devotion to his invalid wife and
the rare charm of his domestic life."[36] "He was a paragon of conjugal virtue
and fidelity," asserted an Episcopal rector, who provided "a lesson of inestimable value" in a day of increasing divorce and the desecration of marriage.[37]
Wherever Christian civilization existed, contended the governor of Iowa,
wives would recount McKinley's devotion as a husband.[38]

The Elections of 1896 and 1900

Religion was a significant issue in both of McKinley's presidential contests.
Occurring at a time of economic recession and social discord, the hotly disputed election of 1896 pitted McKinley against William Jennings Bryan,
a two-term congressman from Nebraska. Republicans considered him a

formidable challenger because he had strong support in both the traditionally Democratic South and the West. Also nominated by the Populists, the
youthful, vigorous, articulate Nebraskan was an attractive candidate. Like
McKinley, Bryan had staunch Christian convictions and high moral standards.
Unlike his Republican opponent, he had a charismatic speaking style and a
magnetic personality. Their campaign styles contrasted sharply. While Bryan
crisscrossed the country, speaking to hundreds of thousands of citizens in
twenty-seven states, McKinley conducted his entire campaign from his front
porch in Canton. Recognizing that he did not have Bryan's oratorical skills and
arguing that traversing the nation "in pursuit of the presidency demeaned the
office," he stayed home and gave more than 300 speeches and "well-rehearsed
responses" to prearranged questions to an estimated 750,000 visitors.[39]

Despite Bryan's energetic campaigning, winsome personality, and enthusiastic support among certain groups, he faced major obstacles in the election.
Many Americans blamed the Democratic Party for their economic woes and
social tribulations because of events that occurred during Grover Cleveland's
second term (1893–97). The stock market had plummeted, production had
slowed, and unemployment had increased alarmingly. The march of thousands
of unemployed men in Washington, bloody confrontations at the Homestead
steel works near Pittsburgh and at the Pullman Palace Car Company outside
Chicago, and the economic recession had created a climate of fear and despair.

Religious groups and factors played a major role in the election. Shortly
before the Republican Convention, the American Protective Association,
a nativist, anti-Catholic organization, accused McKinley of having
pro-Catholic sympathies. The APA spread rumors that the Catholic bishop
of Columbus had controlled McKinley's political appointments while he
was governor of Ohio. It also claimed his children attended a Catholic pre-
paratory school (however, both McKinley children died before age 5) and
that his father was buried in a Catholic cemetery.[40] Convinced that the
APA attack would do more good than harm in some areas by helping him
win Catholic votes, McKinley decided to maintain a "dignified silence,"
rather than refute the APA's false charges. But even if these accusations
had a negative impact, the Republican declared, we cannot "countenance
any abridgement of the constitutional guarantees of religious freedom."[41]
Recognizing the strategic importance of Catholic voters in the nation's cities, Republicans worked hard throughout the campaign to gain their support. Their campaign received a boost when Archbishop John Ireland of St.
Paul, Minnesota, denounced Bryan's policies as "socialist" and endorsed
McKinley.[42] Echoing Ireland's criticism, the Catholic bishops of the diocese of Indiana and of Omaha, Nebraska, urged Americans to vote for

candidates (implying McKinley) who would uphold the nation's obligations and sound financial policies.[43]

Republicans won votes by portraying Bryan "as a wild-eyed radical, even a revolutionary and a dangerous free trader" who opposed a protective tariff. "At no time since 1860," declared the New York Times, "have the issues of a Presidential campaign been so distinctively moral." The editors urged religious periodicals to support the side "of honesty and right," which to them meant McKinley and the gold standard.[44] In his famous "Cross of Gold" speech, Bryan protested that the nation's gold standard enabled eastern financiers and businessmen to exploit southern and western debtors, primarily farmers. Bryan's policies, the Times argued, encouraged "envy and uncharitableness" and threatened to "imperil law and order."[45] Convinced that Bryan was dangerous and that his campaign slogans—a "crown of thorns" and a "cross of gold"—were sacrilegious, some Protestant ministers endorsed McKinley. A Baptist pastor in New York City charged that the Democratic platform jeopardized "the stability of the American republic" and promised to "revive the Jacobins and Robespierre."[46] Prominent Protestant ministers helped heighten the nation's hysteria. In New York City, Charles Parkhurst, the pastor of Madison Square Presbyterian Church, and Southern Baptist Thomas Dixon, Jr., preaching at the city's Academy of Music, urged listeners to vote for McKinley. McKinley stood for "patriotism and honor," Dixon declared, and Bryan for "anarchy, repudiation, and national dishonor."[47] McKinley carried only one more state than his Democratic rival, but he received 51 percent of the vote to Bryan's 46 percent and 271 electoral votes to his challenger's 176.

The election of 1900 featured the same candidates. McKinley preferred not to run again, but he capitulated to "the imperative call of duty."[48] America's foreign policy and monetary standard were the most significant issues in the campaign. The election was "the apogee of the debate over imperialism."[49] The Democratic platform condemned McKinley's policies on Cuba, Puerto Rico, and the Philippines. Bryan denounced America's use of force to subjugate Filipinos who wanted to be politically independent. "Imperialism," the Great Commoner argued in speech after speech, "finds no warrant in the Bible." "The commandment, 'Go ye into all the world and preach the gospel to every creature,' has no gatling gun attachment. Love, not force, was the weapon of the Nazarene"; sacrifice, not exploitation, "was His method of reaching the human heart."[50] If elected, Bryan promised to push Congress to grant independence to the Philippines as it had to Cuba. Endorsing his position, the Baptist Watchman challenged Republicans to show why treating the Philippines the same way as Cuba "was not wise or just."[51] McKinley countered that the United States must retain control of the Philippines to advance civilization and Christianity.[52] Upset that no Catholics had been named to either of the commissions the president appointed to investigate conditions in the Philippines and that McKinley had stopped consulting archbishop Ireland on religious and political matters, most Catholic journals strongly opposed the Republican's reelection.[53]

Although McKinley traveled many miles in 1899 to support various Republicans candidates and accentuate the accomplishments of his administration, he did not actively campaign in 1900. However, his campaign manager, Cleveland industrialist Mark Hanna, argued in speeches throughout the Midwest and West that McKinley deserved credit for the nation's prosperity. Meanwhile, vice-presidential candidate Theodore Roosevelt preached a "four-square gospel of duty, responsibility, republicanism, and Americanism" in several hundred addresses. For strategic, commercial, and humanitarian reasons, Roosevelt argued, American control of the Philippines was necessary. It was a sacred trust resulting from "the most righteous foreign war" in the last three generations; it was an obligation Providence had assigned to America.[54] Bryan again campaigned tirelessly and gained votes in the East by condemning imperialism. Although Bryan was no longer considered a threat to social stability, McKinley's margin of victory in the electoral college was the largest in thirty years—292 to 155.

Relations with Religious Groups

Throughout his presidency, McKinley enjoyed cordial relations with most Protestant communions, especially members of his own denomination. As he prepared to assume office, he received letters and resolutions of congratulation and commendation from numerous associations of Methodist pastors. A typical one extolled McKinley as "a worthy follower of Jesus Christ" whose administration would be "thoroughly in harmony with Christian precepts." In 1899 members of the General Missionary Committee of the Methodist Episcopal Church praised the president as "a Christian gentleman," "a devoted husband, and a God-fearing American statesman." McKinley occasionally met with leaders of Protestant communions. When the General Convention of the Episcopal Church held its triennial session in Washington in October 1898, McKinley received delegates at the White House and later spoke briefly at a ceremony to mark the site where the National Cathedral would be built. The next September McKinley held a reception for delegates to the Alliance of Reformed Churches who were meeting in Washington.[55] McKinley also commended the work of the Christian Endeavor Society and the Salvation Army and the revival campaigns of Dwight Moody.[56]

McKinley's stance on temperance strained his relations with many Protestants, including Methodists. In 1899 Congress passed the Anti-Canteen Bill, which prohibited the army from selling liquor on its bases. Attorney General John Griggs decided, however, that the law did not forbid civilians from doing so. When McKinley refused to overrule his interpretation, the White House was deluged with letters of protest from ministers, college presidents, professors, and many other irate citizens.[57] Resolutions passed by numerous Protestant denominations, Woman's Christian Temperance Union (WCTU) chapters, Christian Endeavor Societies, groups of churches in dozens of communities, and individual congregations as well as scores of editorials in religious papers beseeched the president to enforce the Anti-Canteen Law.[58] While affirming their high regard for McKinley's Christian faith, character, and performance as chief executive, these groups and individuals were angered by his failure to overturn Griggs's "farcical interpretation" of the law. Thousands of McKinley's "most loyal and devoted supporters," declared a Methodist bishop, challenged the president's position as "a matter of conscience."[59] Many agreed with the complaint of a Baptist pastor that widespread drinking among soldiers was producing debauchery, lost souls, and wrecked families.[60] The president of the Florida WCTU alleged that canteens "were responsible for the greater part of the sickness in the camps of the state and for a large part of the immorality and insubordination."[61] Another Methodist lamented that the "abomination of abominations, the army canteen" had brought agony to countless mothers and wives.[62] The Methodist Church of Santa Cruz, California, claimed that the canteen had caused the "death of more of our boys in blue" than had "bullets or disease."[63] Angry Protestants denounced drinking on army bases as "gross wickedness," a "criminal wrong," and "a dreadful curse."[64] The president of the University of Maine warned that if McKinley did not reverse the attorney general's interpretation of the law, his administration might become "infamous for the spread of vice and the establishment of evil precedents."[65] Despite these many strong pleas, McKinley, who had supported temperance in the mid-1870s and personally did not drink, refused to prohibit the sale of alcohol at army posts.[66]

As noted, various stories about McKinley's attitude toward, relationship with, and support of Catholicism circulated in the 1890s. McKinley rarely wrote letters, but he penned a passionate response in 1895 to a Bostonian who had informed him about rumors making the rounds in that city. "One day I am charged in Boston with being a Catholic," McKinley complained, "and another day with being a member of the A.P.A. I am neither." He emphasized that the United States guaranteed religious freedom to every citizen and added that "every man has the right to worship God according to the dictates of his own conscience." He vowed to preserve "the blessed opportunities of a free school system and the priceless privilege of political and religious freedom." "The stories about me to which you refer," he concluded, "are without truth or reason."[67]

As president, McKinley had cordial relations with two of the nation's leading Catholics—Cardinal James Gibbons and John Ireland.[68] Both of them praised the president's patience and restraint in dealing with Spain, especially after the explosion of the *Maine*.[69] Ireland defended most of McKinley's actions during the Cuban crisis and was frequently invited to the White House so that the president could solicit his support or he could provide advice on religious issues.[70] In his eulogy of the slain president, Ireland declared, "I knew him closely; I esteemed him; I loved him." He was "honest, pure of morals, generous, conscientious, [and] religious."[71] McKinley appointed Joseph McKenna, an Irish Catholic Republican, as attorney general, much to Ireland's delight.[72] Less than a year later, the president named McKenna a Supreme Court justice. Some Protestant extremists complained that McKinley was too cordial toward Catholics and condemned his friendship with Ireland.[73]

Many Catholics protested the way their co-religionists were treated in countries the United States annexed as part of the Spanish-American War. Catholics were very pleased that McKinley appointed their co-religionist Brigadier General George Davis as military governor of Puerto Rico, where nearly all the residents were Catholic, but they were very disappointed with American policies in the Philippines. About six and a half million of the archipelago's eight million inhabitants were Catholic. American Catholics complained that the Philippine Commission, which McKinley appointed to investigate conditions on the islands, contained no Catholics. They were further angered when no Catholics were named to a second commission chaired by William Howard Taft. The religious issues in the Philippines were complicated. The approximately 1,000 Spanish friars living in the archipelago owned much of the best agricultural land and commercial property. Blaming the friars for many of the Philippines' civil, economic, and moral problems, insurgents, led by Emilio Aguinaldo, wanted to expel all Catholic friars and confiscate their estates. Many of the wealthier Filipinos who supported the American occupational government advocated the same course of action. While pleased that McKinley was unwilling to do this, American Catholics were upset by the inability of his administration to stop the widespread desecrating and looting of Catholic churches or the swarming of Protestant missionaries all over the islands. They also resented attempts to convert people who, even most American officials in the Philippines agreed, "were happy and satisfied in the practice of Catholicism." Moreover, Catholics opposed plans to establish a free secular public school system to replace the islands' parochial schools. Catholics feared that this new education system would undermine their religious work on the islands and protested that many of the teachers were disguised missionaries who were distributing Protestant Bibles and tracts to students.[74]

Public Policy: The Spanish-American War

Prior to becoming president, McKinley had almost no experience in foreign affairs, but they dominated his years in office. Although he delegated many matters, McKinley took ultimate responsibility for foreign affairs.[75] For both of these reasons, analyzing why McKinley led the nation into the Spanish-American War of 1898 and how he dealt with its consequences provides the best case study for assessing how his faith influenced his policies. "Because of its expansionist consequences," writes Lewis Gould, this war has been extensively studied and highly criticized. McKinley stands at the center of the controversy, and his policies toward Spain and Cuba have been closely scrutinized and often condemned. For a long time the standard historical interpretation was that McKinley caved in to a jingoist press and public pressure and blundered into a war that could have been avoided. During the 1960s a new group of historians offered an alternative hypothesis: McKinley was "a Machiavellian and cunning executive, bent on expansion and heedless of the interests of Cubans and Filipinos," who went to war to promote "an economic imperialism that relied on overseas markets." Neither of these interpretations recognizes the complex diplomatic problems facing Spain and the United States or properly explains how McKinley worked to resolve their differences, end the fighting in Cuba, and improve life for the Cuban people. The essence of the problem was that no Spanish government that publicly accepted the loss of Cuba could remain in power, while no American administration that was perceived as pro-Spanish would enjoy popular support.[76]

Many interwoven factors contributed to the United States' declaration of war on Spain in April 1898. Anxiety abounded in the 1890s. Large-scale immigration of Jews, Eastern Orthodox, and Catholics from southern and eastern Europe was making America much more ethnically and religiously heterogeneous. Industrialization and urbanization transformed the nation's appearance, the nature of work, and people's standard of living. Rapidly growing cities were plagued with crime, political corruption, sanitation problems, and inadequate housing. At the same time, the frontier disappeared as a safety value for excess population and an economic depression rocked the country. Angry that they were not receiving their fair share of the nation's wealth, many workers looked to labor unions and farmers turned to Populism to improve their circumstances. Fears of social disorder and even revolution intensified. Some businessmen and politicians thought America could best solve its economic ills by procuring new markets overseas, especially in Latin America and East Asia. Belief in social Darwinism, Anglo-Saxon superiority, and American destiny reinforced these economic aims prompting many political leaders and journalists to implore the nation to expand its power and influence. To thrive, they argued, the United States must aggressively compete for wealth, territory, and glory. Americans were obligated "to spread their superior language, political institutions, and culture around the world and thereby uplift the darker, backward peoples." Admiral Alfred Mahan urged the nation to build a strong navy and an isthmian canal, acquire bases in the Caribbean, annex Hawaii, and expand its markets in Latin America and Asia. Meanwhile, by emphasizing Christians' calling to redeem the world, Protestant leaders helped convince many Americans to accept a larger mission for their nation in the world.[77] Numerous scholars emphasize the important role that religion played in motivating the United States to wage war against Spain to liberate Cuba. Ian Tyrell, Andrew Preston, and Susan Harris all argue that religious factors were central in American imperialism during the 1890s and early 1900s. Tyrell describes how American Protestants created an international "moral empire." Preston explains the pivotal contribution religion made to diplomacy, war, and justifying the United States' control over the Philippines. Harris contends that American leaders saw themselves as "God's arbiters" appointed to determine the destiny of the archipelago.[78]

After the Civil War, Americans frequently denounced Spain's oppressive rule of Cuba. Humanitarian concern joined with recognition of Cuba's economic potential and strategic location to fuel American interest in the island. A ten-year revolution, which erupted in 1868, ended with promises by Spanish administrators to improve conditions in Cuba. From 1877 until 1895 US companies continued to heavily invest in and trade with Cuba and gained control of its sugar industry. The Spanish government failed to provide the reforms it promised, and in 1895 rebels launched another insurrection. Both sides committed atrocities. Engaging in scorched earth policies, the insurgents sought to destroy all Spanish sources of revenue on the island. The Spanish herded Cuban peasants into "reconcentration" camps to prevent them from helping the rebels. Cuba's economy collapsed, and one-eighth of the population died of disease and starvation in two years. The widespread devastation and death prompted the US government to use diplomatic and moral pressure to try to end the fighting. When Congress pushed for Cuban independence, President Grover Cleveland called for patience and restraint. Although the Democrat preserved American neutrality and peace, by assuming that the United States had certain rights in Cuba, he set the nation "on an increasingly escalating interventionist course."[79]

The day before McKinley's inauguration, Cleveland invited him to dinner at the White House. In the course of their conversation about Cuba and the threat of war with Spain, the Republican told his Democratic predecessor, "if I can" leave office knowing "I have done what lay in my power to avert this terrible calamity," "I shall be the happiest man in the world."[80] The next day, McKinley declared in his inaugural address, "We want no wars of conquest; we must avoid the temptations of territorial aggression." War, he added, must be avoided "until every agency of peace has failed; peace is preferable to war" in almost every situation.[81] Despite such statements, a little more than a year later, McKinley signed a congressional resolution authorizing the United States to intervene to end the fighting in Cuba, and by April 25, 1898, America and Spain were at war.

McKinley had many reasons for eventually agreeing with a bellicose Congress, the jingoist press, and much of the American public that war was necessary. The 1896 Republican platform had called for Cuban independence. McKinley had long supported American trade and territorial expansion. After becoming president, he worked to annex Hawaii, gain the rights to build an isthmian canal, and increase the nation's trade.[82] Deeply moved by Cuban suffering, McKinley pursued a policy toward Cuba that incongruously blended "forbearance and impatience, pacific encouragement and hostile threats toward Spain, and good will and distrust toward the Cuban patriots."[83] He condemned Spain's use of cruel and uncivilized methods of warfare and was reluctant to accept a solution to the Cuban problem that the rebels rejected. However, the two sides were at loggerheads. The insurrectionists demanded complete independence, while the Spanish were not willing to relinquish all control of the island.

In his message to Congress in December 1897, McKinley asserted that the United States had a right to intervene in Cuba if a "righteous peace" were not soon attained.[84] During the next four months, fighting continued in Cuba and "a series of diplomatic crises and disasters" "rocked the nation and intensified the war fervor among large portions of the American public, press, and Congress."[85] On February 9, 1898, the New York Journal published a letter from Spanish ambassador Dupuy de Lome that had fallen into the hands of Cuban revolutionaries. De Lome's characterization of McKinley as "weak and a bidder for the admiration of the crowd" angered many Americans. To intimidate Spain and protect American life and property, McKinley had sent the battleship *Maine* to Cuba in late January. On February 15, it exploded in Havana harbor, killing 266 American sailors. While much later investigations concluded that the explosion was caused by heat from one of the ship's furnaces setting off the gunpowder in an adjacent magazine, the immediate American response was to blame Spain. Dozens of communities hanged Spaniards in effigy, and newspapers demanded that the Spanish withdraw from Cuba to atone for this atrocious act. Speaking for many, Methodist Bishop Charles McCabe declared that war with Spain might put the United States "in a position to demand civil and religious liberty for the oppressed of every nation."[86] A sensationalist press, led by William Randolph Hearst's *New York Journal* and Joseph Pulitzer's *New York World*, supplied vivid accounts of Spanish atrocities, some fabricated, but most true.

"As the most serious national crisis since the Civil War deepened," wrote Lewis Gould, "McKinley became the object of intense and simultaneous feelings of confidence, hope, mistrust, and disgust." Some feared that he might be "too reluctant or timid" to act decisively. While refusing to give in to the yellow press that demanded vengeance or to a Congress that called for war, McKinley did not repudiate the jingoists publicly and increased diplomatic pressure on Spain.[87] Several factors pushed McKinley toward presenting Spain an ultimatum: Madrid seemed unable to govern the island effectively; an investigation had determined that a submarine mine had caused the *Maine* to explode; many Republicans demanded that he deal more forcibly with Spain; and leading businessmen supported war. Moreover, numerous clergy were calling for "a righteous crusade against Spain on behalf of humanity, 'democracy and Christian progress'" in Cuba.[88] In several messages to Spain in late March, McKinley issued what amounted to an ultimatum: Spain must end reconcentration, halt the fighting, and agree to give Cuba independence if he decided it was necessary. The Spanish agreed to revoke reconcentration, arbitrate the *Maine* disaster, and declare an armistice if the rebels requested one. They refused, however, to promise independence to Cuba.

Accentuating Spanish atrocities and American humanitarianism and paternalism, McKinley asked Congress for a declaration of war. "I have exhausted," he asserted, "every effort to relieve the intolerable condition of affairs" in Cuba. The United States must intervene, the president argued, to end "the barbarities, bloodshed, starvation, and horrible miseries" on the island; to protect the property and life of Americans who lived in Cuba; to halt the "serious injury" to American trade and business; and to remove "a constant menace" to peace.[89] Americans had "the right and duty to speak and act" to promote the cause of humanity and civilization and defend their endangered interests. McKinley hoped that the threat of American military intervention would stop the fighting in Cuba and achieve "our aspirations as a Christian, peace-loving people." Believing the rebels had not yet demonstrated their ability to govern successfully, McKinley asked Congress not to recognize Cuban independence. If the United States did so, it "would be required to submit" to the Cuban government's direction and treat the country as "a friendly ally." The United States should instead intervene in Cuba as "an impartial neutral" that could impose "a rational compromise between contestants."[90] In asking for this declaration of war, McKinley had the strong support of many key American leaders and much of the religious community. Secretary of State Elihu Root, Alfred Mahan, Theodore Roosevelt, and William Jennings Bryan all backed the war for religious and humanitarian reasons. So did Washington Gladden, Walter Rauschenbusch, and hundreds of other Protestant ministers and Catholic priests.[91]

On April 19, Congress passed a joint resolution empowering the president to use military force in Cuba, and in the Teller Amendment, renounced any intention to annex the island. According to Augustus Cerillo, Jr., McKinley's war message "revealed how little concerned the United States was with the desires of Cuba's fighters, ostensibly on whose behalf the nation was going to war." Nevertheless, McKinley argued that because the United States was fighting to free oppressed people, its actions comported with international law and were "sanctioned by just war theory."[92]

McKinley's Christian convictions played a major role in his decision to declare war. Biblical imagery converged with belief in manifest destiny and Anglo-Saxon superiority to convince him (and millions of his fellow countrymen) that the United States had a special role to play in bringing Christianity, democracy, and civilization to the world.[93] McKinley had heard numerous preachers argue that as a chosen nation the United States was morally obligated to spread the gospel and uplift people around the world. The president also agreed with missionaries who insisted that "the time was ripe for a great, worldwide Christian advance."[94] While American Christians preferred to promote freedom, morality, and faith by peaceful means, oppressive regimes sometimes made this impossible. As public pressure for a war to liberate the Cuban people mounted in the early months of 1898, McKinley listened to Hugh Johnson proclaim in the pulpit of the Metropolitan Methodist Church that "the calm and firm attitude of the Chief Executive" assured Americans that neither "prejudice, passion, popular clamor, hysteria," nor ambition would cause the nation to rush to war. America's great power was "controlled by intelligence, patriotism, and Christian principle." Only "duty to humanity and civilization," "desire for just relations" with other countries, and national honor would compel the United States "to let loose the dogs of war. Desiring and praying for peace, let us hope that the extent and vigor of these war preparations will avert the conflict and assist the cause of peace." On April 6, the New York Methodists sent a resolution to the president deploring "the sufferings of the Cuban people" and the methods Spain had used "to keep them in subjection." They praised McKinley for negotiating calmly and patiently with Spain while preparing for all contingencies. This resolution expressed the mixed objectives of American Protestants: they fervently prayed that negotiations would preserve peace, maintain national honor, and liberate the Cuban people from Spanish oppression. McKinley constantly prayed that "we may be able to keep peace." He confided to his personal physician Leonard Wood, "I shall never get into a war until I am sure that God and man approve. I have been through one war" "and I do not want to see another."

Even after the *Maine* exploded, many ministers called for restraint while also warning that war might be necessary. A. J. F. Behrends, pastor of the Central Congregational Church of Brooklyn, argued that if Spain were responsible, it was the "most satanic crime of the century," but he urged Americans not to indict Spain until its involvement had been "proved beyond all reasonable doubt." Citizens should support the president rather than the "hotheads," he proclaimed, but if nations engaged in "policies of slow starvation and merciless extermination" and did not respond to rational arguments to desist, then it was "somebody's solemn duty" to stop "the instruments of torture and inhuman cruelty." Fellow Congregationalist Lyman Abbott, editor of the *Outlook*, also prayed that war would be avoided, but he agreed that the United States must end "Spanish inhumanity in Cuba."[95]

Shortly after McKinley's April 11 message to Congress, Robert MacArthur, the pastor of the Calvary Baptist Church of New York City, urged citizens "to stand by our patriotic, brave, sagacious President." Although war was "a relic of barbarism" whose burdens were borne chiefly by the poor and working classes, sometimes it was "a grim necessity." God, he maintained, might use Americans "as His instrument" to drive the Spanish butchers from the Western Hemisphere. Meanwhile, the *Christian and Missionary Alliance* editorialized: "We should pray not only that Cuba be free, but that these fair Eastern isles shall become scenes of gospel triumphs and the salvation of countless souls."[96]

Although the clergy had been divided over whether the United States should intervene in Cuba, after war was declared against Spain on April 25, many ministers defended it as a holy crusade. Hundreds of sermons supported the conflict by appealing to "higher principles, self-sacrifice, divine mandate, and altruism."[97] To David Gregg, pastor of the Lafayette Avenue Presbyterian Church in Brooklyn, the war involved no revenge or mercenary elements. Renowned pulpiteer T. DeWitt Talmage called it "the most unselfish war of the ages," which was "inspired by mercy." A Philadelphia Baptist minister declared that no nation had ever fought a war that was "more righteous" or better fulfilled the law that "we bear one another's burdens."[98] Because our war is waged to advance "genuine civilization and the equal rights of men," avowed John Peters of New York's St. Michael's Episcopal Church, "we can feel assured that God is on our side." Theologically liberal pastors also defended the war as necessary on moral and humanitarian grounds. Henry Van Dyke, who served Brick Presbyterian Church in New York City, argued that America had a duty to protect the weak. "We have prayed for peace. The prayer has been denied. Now we must pray for victory." Leading Social Gospeler Washington Gladden assured the president that the American people respected his "wisdom and firmness in this crisis."[99]

On July 6, 1898, McKinley urged Americans to "reverently bow before the throne of Divine Grace and give devout praise to God, who holdeth the nations in the hollow of His hands" and has "led our brave soldiers and seamen to victory." In "His inscrutable ways," God was leading American forces to "the attainment of just and honorable peace." McKinley beseeched "the Dispenser of all good" to restore peace and tranquility in war-ravaged areas. Numerous sermons preached the next Sunday praised the president's proclamation of thanksgiving. A Lutheran pastor in Brooklyn asserted that it showed he possessed "the true Christian spirit." With McKinley in attendance, Frank Bristol, pastor of the Metropolitan Methodist Church in Washington, used Psalm 98:1 as his text: "O sing unto the Lord a new song; for he has done marvelous things." "Were the guns of Dewey and Sampson less providential," he asked, "than the ram's horns of Joshua, the lamps and pitchers of Gideon, or the rod of Moses?" The Americans who fought against Spain "were the heirs of the Civil War, the American Revolution, the Pilgrims, the Reformers, the martyrs, and the apostles." "If God ever had a peculiar people," Bristol reasoned, "He has them now."[100] Celebrating the war's conclusion, the *Christian Advocate* proclaimed in August 1898: "That the yoke of Spain from the neck of Cuba has been broken with the loss of less than one thousand American soldiers" should produce wonder, admiration, and "unalloyed pleasure." Echoing these themes in his 1898 Thanksgiving Proclamation, McKinley claimed that the United States had been "compelled to take up the sword in the cause of humanity" and rejoiced that the conflict had been brief and the losses had been few considering "the great results accomplished." This should fill Americans "with gratitude and praise to the Lord of Hosts."[101]

In the final analysis, evaluations of McKinley's interactions with Spain depend on assessing what his motives and aims were, whether he exhausted all other reasonable alternatives before pursuing war, how he directed the war effort, and what impact the war and occupation had on the Cuban people. Many historians have depicted McKinley as a spineless, bumbling political opportunist who capitulated to Congress and public opinion and blundered into an unnecessary and destructive war. Supported by Theodore Roosevelt's alleged barb that the Ohio native had "no more backbone than a chocolate éclair," this interpretation dominated historical scholarship during the first half of the twentieth century. Although McKinley had great political acumen and behind the scenes could persuade individuals to do what he wanted, Joseph Fry maintained, he was "not a dynamic, forceful public leader." This, combined with his fundamental conservatism and limited view of presidential power, "precluded dramatic or concerted attempts to alter public opinion and prevent war."[102]

Some more recent appraisals are also highly critical of American imperialism during the late nineteenth century and McKinley's push to declare war against Spain. In its efforts to expand overseas trade and investment, the United States, Augustus Cerillo, Jr. argues, was not guided by "the biblical norms of equity, justice, and preference for the poor." By seeking to maximize its own economic gain, "often at the expense of impoverished indigenous workers or small entrepreneurs," the nation "sowed the seeds of future anti-American violence and revolution among underdeveloped countries." The United States' economic imperialism abroad stemmed from the same sinful attitudes of superiority that guided policies at home toward Native Americans, blacks, Asians, and immigrants from southern and eastern Europe. In both locales Anglo-Americans were motivated by "economic cupidity, territorial aggrandizement, national selfishness, and idolatrous self-worship." At the same time, Protestant evangelicals, while working to convert people around the globe, encased the "gospel too rigidly in Western cultural, technological, and economic terms" and unwittingly became "advance agents for Western penetration" into the world's least industrialized nations. Speaking for many of them, missionary Sidney Gulick argued in 1897 that God intended Anglo-Saxons' religious and social practices to mold "the civilizations of the world." Cerillo faults evangelical leaders for fusing "the gospel, racism, and nationalism," viewing the war between Catholic Spain and "Christian America" as a righteous conflict, and failing to use "God's requirements for justice, righteousness, mercy, [and] peace" to evaluate the motives of expansionists.[103]

Cerillo also accuses McKinley of seeking to remake Cuba in America's "political and economic image." This thwarted earnest, "long-range diplomatic give-and-take with Spain" and led the president to arbitrarily demand that he have the power to decide Cuba's ultimate political fate.[104] Since Spain was not willing to give up a territory it had ruled for centuries and Cuban rebels refused to accept anything less than independence, McKinley could achieve his goal—increased American influence in Cuba—only by defeating Spain militarily. Moreover, the president's belief that Cuban insurgents were incapable of effectively governing the island prompted him to refuse to recognize them as the legitimate authority and to authorize an American occupation that governed Cuba from 1898 to 1902. European nations had protested, the *Watchman* noted in March 1900, that the war was inspired by Americans' "desire to acquire Cuba and that the humanitarian aspect of the war was simply a cloak to cover our selfish designs." If the United States, which had argued it waged war purely on moral and humanitarian grounds and pledged not to control Cuba, annexed the island, its action "would be both wicked and despicable."[105] Positively, the American military government prevented further bloodshed and destruction and supplied food to thousands of hungry and impoverished Cubans. It established a free public school system, reformed the judiciary, improved municipal government, and constructed and repaired roads, hospitals, and other public facilities. American and Cuban physicians worked together to stop the spread of tropical diseases, especially yellow fever. Negatively, the occupational government used capricious methods, displayed little sensitivity for Cuban cultural mores and practices, and enabled the United States to strengthen its political and economic control of Cuba. Moreover, the military regime restricted suffrage to those who were literate and owned property in order to increase the political power of the island's conservative, primarily white, upper class who had the most positive attitudes toward the United States. Before withdrawing its military in 1902, the United States required the newly created Cuban Republic to accept the Platt Amendment, which gave America "the right to intervene" to preserve "Cuban independence" and maintain "a government adequate" to protect "life, property, and individual liberty."[106] American economic investment in the island doubled between 1898 and 1902, and in subsequent years American multinationals dominated all sectors of the Cuban economy. Michael Walzer labels America's actions in Cuba an "example of benevolent imperialism," but not of "humanitarian intervention." He maintains that the United States interceded on behalf of the Cuban people, but "against their ends." Intervention is moral only if the liberators do not "claim any political prerogative" and respect "local autonomy."[107]

Other recent evaluations conclude that McKinley "was more courageous and capable than previously portrayed" and contend that "his decision for war followed logically from his own policies rather than public or congressional pressure."[108] His foreign policy, Lewis Gould argues, was based on the premise that the more power and influence America had, the more other nations benefited. Rejecting the views that McKinley was "a weak, indecisive executive" who finally yielded to "war hysteria" or that he "was a wily expansionist" who chose war to help construct an American commercial empire, Gould insists that McKinley worked diligently for five months to maintain peace in the face of Spanish obstinacy. His diplomacy was "tenacious, coherent, and courageous."[109] Behind the scenes, the president explored various alternatives to war, including buying Cuba from Spain and allowing Spain to maintain token sovereignty over Cuba, but Madrid rejected both schemes. He also offered to mediate between Spain and the Cuban revolutionaries and proposed asking Pope Leo XIII to arbitrate the dispute between Spain and the United States.[110] Lacking the military resources to effectively fight the United States and refusing to give Cuba independence, Madrid resorted to delay, obfuscation, and denial and sought to mobilize European support against the United States. Given Spain's strategy, H. Wayne Morgan maintains, the president displayed "extraordinary patience," flexibility, and "regard for Spanish sensibilities." Only when it became obvious that diplomacy had failed and that the intolerable situation in Cuba could be ended no other way did McKinley support war. Gould maintains that his conduct "up to that point" reveals his courage and fortitude. Because of their "historic traditions, humanitarian impulses, and economic calculations," most Americans cared deeply about what happened in Cuba. Only a revolution in the attitudes of Americans could have produced a different outcome in Cuba. Gould concludes that the United States' other options would not likely have resulted in success. If the United States had not intervened in Cuba, governed the island for four years, and maintained a military presence, other nations, most notably Germany, might have tried to control Cuba.[111] McKinley concluded that ending the bloodshed and atrocities on the island was more important than recognizing the rebels as the legitimate government. Moreover, recognition might put the United States in the embarrassing position of supporting a government that was unfit to rule and repressive. When the revolutionaries appeared "capable of performing the duties and discharging the functions of a separate nation," McKinley asserted, the United States could publicly endorse them.[112]

Other scholars insist that McKinley's desire to stop the suffering of the Cuban people drove his diplomacy.[113] The Republican called the horrors and inhumanity occurring in Cuba "unprecedented in the modern history of civilized peoples." He initiated humanitarian efforts that raised several hundred thousand dollars to help Cuban victims of war.[114] McKinley eventually called for war, Robert Beisner asserts, because he wanted "what only war could bring—an end to the Cuban rebellion, which outraged his humanitarian impulses," damaged "American investments and trade with Cuba," suggested that the United States could not control events in the Caribbean, and "threatened to arouse uncontrollable outbursts of jingoism."[115]

Judged by contemporary standards that mandate respect for all cultural traditions and practices, America's military intervention and occupation of Cuba for four years seems ethnocentric, paternalistic, and unjust. Moreover, these actions negatively affected the United States' relationship with Cuba and other Latin American nations throughout much of the twentieth century. Numerous American exploits in Cuba violated the United States' professed commitment to self-determinism, democracy, and individual rights. Nevertheless, given the situation he confronted and the dominant cultural and political assumptions of his era, McKinley's actions are understandable. While he did not explore every conceivable option before requesting a declaration of war against Spain, the Republican tried most reasonable alternatives. Spain had made it clear it would not grant independence to Cuba, and nothing else seemed likely to end the horrible suffering of Cubans. While economic and political factors clearly played a major role in his decision, McKinley was strongly motivated by the plight of the Cuban people. Had he endorsed the Cuban insurgents and allowed them to control the country after Spain was defeated, many negative consequences may have been avoided. However, the prevailing cultural attitudes, fears that the rebels were not capable of governing justly or wisely, and prudential considerations made that very difficult to do.

During the war Commodore George Dewey decisively defeated the Spanish fleet at Manila Bay on May 1, 1898. As a result, when the war ended in August, the United States also had to decide what to do with the Philippine islands that Spain ruled. Believing that American control of the Philippines would provide new opportunities for missions and that God had given their nation victory over Spain, many Protestant ministers and editors strongly supported acquiring the archipelago. "Hitching the cross to the flag," they "saw foreign colonization and foreign missions as practically synonymous."[116] Presbyterians rejoiced that God had opened the Philippines to mission work. Therefore, American Christians must "go up and possess the land."[117] An American Bible Society pamphlet published in 1899 acknowledged that some Americans saw no reason for Protestants to send missionaries to the Philippines where the Catholic Church had ministered for more than three hundred years. However, its author countered, Filipinos only knew "the outward form" of Christianity, not its "inward and spiritual grace." Even "pious and devout Catholics" admitted that they were "fit subjects for the missions of their own Church." Society spokesmen also exulted that Protestants could now sell Bibles throughout the islands. W. Henry Grant told McKinley in 1900 that Christian missions stood "for everything that a Christian government desires to foster—education, local self government, commerce and industry." Moreover, missionaries demonstrated "that the Asiatic, African, Islander, or Indian, has under the regenerative power of the Gospel infinite possibilities."[118]

Meanwhile, McKinley pondered his options. The president initially rejected the idea of acquiring a large, unfamiliar territory half way around the world. When he first learned that Dewey had defeated the Spanish, McKinley admitted he had to look up the location of the Philippines on a map. "I could not have told where those darn islands were within 2,000 miles," he confessed. He recognized that acquiring former Spanish possessions involved "political risks, administration headaches," significant financial costs, and potential problems in international relations. Furthermore, the president had "denounced forced annexation as 'criminal aggression,' had disavowed 'greed of conquest,'" and had repeatedly claimed that the United States fought Spain only to end injustice and inhumanity.[119] Several factors, however, contributed to McKinley's decision to acquire the whole archipelago. First, public opinion favored doing so.[120] "The president's ear was so close to the ground," complained Congressman Joe Cannon, that "it was full of grasshoppers."[121] Missionaries wanted to be able to openly evangelize there. Businessmen coveted the archipelago as a source of raw materials, a market for products, and a stepping-stone to the lucrative Asian trade.[122] Military leaders craved the Philippines as a base for naval operations. Second, McKinley was apprehensive about the Filipino insurgents, especially their leader Emilio Aguinaldo, whom he did not trust.[123] The reports of military leaders and civilian commissioners led him to conclude that these rebels did not represent the interests of most of the 1,400 islands' inhabitants, could not govern effectively, and could not prevent a foreign power from interfering in the affairs or taking control of the Philippines.[124] Rule by an inexperienced, arbitrary faction was likely to be both unjust and dangerous to inhabitants.[125] Theodore Roosevelt later explained, "[I]t would have been both absurd and wicked to abandon the Philippine Archipelago and let the scores of different tribes—Christian, Mahometan and pagan, in every stage of semi-civilization and Asiatic barbarism—turn the islands into a welter of bloody savagery."[126] Third, McKinley feared that the European nations or Japan, which were already carving up Southeast Asia, would also seize the Philippines. Both Germany and Japan were actively trying to build a Pacific empire. The Japanese had officially offered to administer the islands if the United States declined to do so. Fourth, returning the Philippines to its Spanish oppressors made no sense. Spain had demonstrated it could not govern the archipelago. The Spanish colonial government had collapsed, rebels had gained control of several islands, and Madrid could not afford to administer the country. Its control would prolong the rebellion. Finally, McKinley briefly considered, but rejected, the idea of making the Philippines a self-governing republic under an American protectorate. This was the worst option because the United States would be responsible for the archipelago without having authority over it.[127]

For two weeks in October 1898 McKinley toured six states, speaking fifty-seven times to help shape public sentiment.[128] In his addresses, McKinley stressed God's providential direction of history and America's duty. "The faith of a Christian nation," he told a crowd at Omaha, Nebraska, "recognizes the hand of Almighty God in the ordeal through which we have passed. Divine favor seemed manifest everywhere. In fighting for humanity's sake, we have been signally blessed." "Our constant prayer" was to avoid war, if we could preserve the "honor and justice" "of our neighbors and ourselves." Because of its wisdom, courage, and sense of justice, America, guided by God, would choose the right course of action. At Glenwood, Iowa, McKinley proclaimed that God had "singularly guided" Americans "down through every crisis to the present hour." Speaking in Chicago, the president avowed, "we must accept all the obligations which the war" has "imposed on us." The United States must use its victory over Spain as a springboard to create a "higher and nobler civilization" where war was no longer necessary.[129]

In subsequent speeches, McKinley continued to justify his policies by appealing to America's destiny and duty. The territory the United States stood to gain, McKinley declared in December 1898, came not "as the result of a crusade or conquest, but as the reward" of Americans' "response to the call of conscience," which as "a liberty-loving and Christian people" they must answer. We went to the Philippines to destroy the Spanish fleet and end the war, McKinley explained in October 1899, "but in the providence of God, who works in mysterious ways, this great archipelago" fell "into our lap, and the American people never shirk duty." "The Philippines, like Cuba and Porto [sic] Rico, were intrusted to our hands by the war," the chief executive told a large audience in Boston in February 1899, and "we are committed" to fulfilling God's "great trust" to increase human progress and advance civilization. "Congress can declare war, but a higher Power decrees its bounds and fixes its relations and responsibilities."[130] Everyone agreed, McKinley claimed, that the Philippines could not be given back to Spain. Leaving them on their own would result in anarchy and chaos or their being seized by a powerful nation. Countering anti-imperialist arguments, McKinley contended, "Our concern was not for territory or trade or empire, but for the people whose interest and destiny, without us willing it, had been put into our hands." "Imperialist designs," he added, were "alien to American sentiment, thought, and purpose."[131] McKinley also refuted the charge that Americans needed the consent of the Filipino people to govern the islands. The United States was "obeying a higher moral obligation," which "did not require anybody's consent." Americans were doing their duty, which God helped them see, "with the consent of our own consciences and with the approval of civilization."[132] McKinley insisted further that American control would help Filipinos to become "self-respecting and self-governing." America's benevolent guidance would enable the archipelago to soon become: "a land of plenty and of increasing possibilities." "Redeemed from savage indolence and habits," Filipinos would enjoy the blessings of education, trade, civil and religious liberty, and comfortable homes.[133] McKinley promised that the United States would govern these new possessions not as "serfs or slaves." Americans would introduce equitable taxation, universal education, and freedom of worship, enabling their inhabitants to advance materially, intellectually, and spiritually.[134] McKinley asserted that Americans must fulfill their responsibilities to their island possessions "with manly courage" and do "what in the sight of God and man is just and right." The great majority of Filipinos, he insisted, were glad to have the protection of the United States.[135]

McKinley's faith played a major role in his decision to retain the Philippines. On November 21, 1899, five members of the Methodist General Missionary Committee met with McKinley at the White House. "I have been criticised [*sic*] a good deal about the Philippines," the president told them, "but don't deserve it. The truth is I didn't want them," and initially "I did not know what to do with them." He had "sought counsel from all sides" but received "little help." "I walked the floor of the White House night after night until midnight." Many nights he "prayed to Almighty God for light and guidance. And one night late it [the answer] came to me." McKinley then described his options. Giving the archipelago back to Spain would be "cowardly and dishonorable"; turning the islands over to France or Germany, America's commercial rivals in Asia, would be "bad business and discreditable"; the Filipinos were "unfit for self-government." That left only one alternative: the United States must acquire the islands in order to "educate the Filipinos, and uplift and civilize and Christianize them, and by God's grace do the very best we could by them, as our fellow-men for whom Christ also died."[136] McKinley's frequently quoted statement has evoked much ridicule and criticism. Some are alarmed that a president made such an important policy decision largely on the basis of an alleged revelation from God or at least his intuitive impression of God's designs. Detractors depict him "as either a hypocrite" who sanctified his own desires by arguing they were God's will or as "a bemused instrument of the Almighty."[137] Others denounce his faith-inspired decision as incongruous, frivolous, and insincere. Ignoring McKinley's strong Christian commitment, they see his religiously based explanation as cloaking economic and political motives.[138]

Gould berates McKinley's biographers for "accepting the accuracy of this remarkable revelation without making much of an effort to verify its authenticity." General James Rusling published the Republican's statement more than three years after he made it. Gould questions whether Rusling could correctly have remembered the president's exact words. Moreover, this account closely resembles a conversation Rusling reported having with Abraham Lincoln in his Civil War memoir, which was published in 1899. These similarities lead Gould to conclude that Rusling probably embellished McKinley's statement. Although the alternatives McKinley outlined in Rusling's report accurately describe the president's reflections in the fall of 1898, Gould labels "their famed religious context" "very questionable."[139] Robert Linder and Richard Pierard counter that Rusling's account "has the ring of truth" because McKinley's comments were made after the Filipino revolt had begun and he had time to "reflect on the implications of his decision." Moreover, none of the other Methodists present that day ever contradicted Rusling's version. Although "McKinley's decision to seek guidance through prayer is incomprehensible" to many secularly minded scholars, Andrew Preston argues, it "was perfectly consistent with his religious faith." It would have been very strange for the Methodist not to ask God to direct his decision.[140]

In order for the United States to annex the Philippines, the Senate had to ratify the treaty negotiated with Spain, and a diverse and incongruous group of anti-expansionists worked to defeat it. They included Mugwump Carl Schurz, industrialist and philanthropist Andrew Carnegie, Republican Senator George Hoar of Massachusetts, former president Grover Cleveland, a few Democratic senators, prominent businessmen, representatives of labor who feared Asian competition, Mark Twain and other writers, and religious leaders.[141] Anti-expansionists at times denounced McKinley as weak and a mere "weathervane for public sentiment," while at others they "pilloried him as a tyrant grasping for power." Anti-imperialists put forth a variety of arguments. They condemned imperialism as unjust, undesirable, illegal, and contrary to American values and traditions. Many protested that the United States had been pushed into war "by hysteria and unreasoning jingoism" and should not have gained control of these territories. Some insisted that America would "abandon its age-old promises of freedom and liberty if it ruled distant and alien people."[142] Others objected that governing foreign lands violated the

Constitution, imposed great financial burdens, and entailed potentially explosive racial, religious, and political problems. Asians' racial and cultural traits would prevent them from adopting American institutions and practices.[143] Imperialist ventures would also "divert attention, energy, and funds" from solving pressing problems at home.[144] Moreover, imperialism contradicted America's most important documents: the Declaration of Independence, George Washington's Farewell Address, and the Monroe Doctrine.[145] It was antithetical to America's commitment to liberty, equality, and self-government and inevitably led to cruelty, militarism, and despotism. Turning a war that had been fought to liberate oppressed peoples into one "of conquest and aggrandizement" was hypocritical and dishonorable.[146] Henry Van Dyke urged the nation's leaders not to "sell the American birthright for a mess of pottage in the Philippines." Acquiring colonies, he warned, might push America into future wars.[147]

McKinley and other supporters of annexation rebutted these arguments by stressing America's destiny and duty. America was compelled to spread its ideals and to assume "the white man's burden" to bring civilization and morality to the less fortunate. Many ministers contended that acquiring an empire would facilitate the spread of the gospel. "I believe in imperialism," declared Wallace Radcliffe, the moderator of the PCUSA General Assembly, "because I believe in foreign missions." "We have a right to civilize" the Filipinos, argued Washington Gladden. Proponents of annexation also insisted that the Philippines could serve as an effective base for the navy and for trade, American institutions could be exported, and an overseas empire would not undermine freedom or prosperity at home.[148]

Aided by Republican Senators Henry Cabot Lodge of Massachusetts, Nelson Aldrich of Rhode Island, and Mark Hanna of Ohio, McKinley skillfully guided the ratification process. They convinced fifty-seven senators to vote for the treaty, one more than necessary to ratify it, even though reports reached Washington the day before the vote on February 6, 1899, that Filipino rebels had attacked American troops. The outbreak of insurrection prompted some wavering senators to rally behind the flag and William Jennings Bryan's support and public opinion helped the treaty to pass. However, McKinley's effective use of the powers of his office and persuasion of Senators was the crucial factor.[149]

For the next three years the United States practiced what McKinley termed "benevolent assimilation." American administrators worked to establish a fair legal and judicial system, free public schools, hospitals, smoothly functioning municipal and local governments, and a sanitation system. McKinley assumed that if "the United States ruled equitably and firmly, the conservative element in Filipino society would be won over." The president, however, "underestimated the genuine support" that Aguinaldo's independence movement enjoyed.[150] This, coupled with American paternalism, cultural coercion, misunderstanding of Filipino thought and customs, widespread dislike of foreign intervention, some brutal methods the army used against the insurgents, and the fierce determination of the rebels, caused the fighting to drag on until 1902.

The anti-expansionists, led by the Anti-Imperial League, continued to criticize American actions in the Philippines after the treaty was ratified. They worked to rally public opinion to oppose "an aggressive, unjustifiable, cruel war."[151] Carl Schurz complained that the United States sought "to cover a war of conquest and subjugation with a cloak of humanity and religion." McKinley ordered military leaders to conduct the war against the insurgents in a humane way, but some atrocities occurred. Provoked by the terrorist acts of the Filipino rebels, soldiers sometimes tortured prisoners, slaughtered animals, and destroyed farm land, buildings, and church property. In addition, thousands of Filipinos died as a result of battle, disease, or starvation. Ironically, the United States used many of the same methods to put down the Filipino revolt that the Spanish had employed in Cuba. Even if American soldiers in the Philippines had scrupulously observed all the rules of war and civilian administrators had governed in a truly benevolent fashion, Gould concludes, the United States would still have been guilty of violating its promise to rule by the consent of the governed. America's governing of the Philippine "was flawed and doomed, not because bad men carried out harsh and callous policies, but because good men," such as McKinley, tried "to do the impossible." Although by contemporary standards, McKinley was misguided, paternalistic, and culturally insensitive, in his own way, Gould argues, he "was a sincere friend of the people of the Philippines." Others who ruled the islands after Spain might have done much worse.[152]

Many historians have criticized McKinley for annexing the Philippines. The views of H. Wayne Morgan, E. Berkeley Tompkins, and Augustus Cerillo are illustrative. According to Morgan, "mixed motives produced the demand for the islands: duty to the Filipinos, fear of foreign control, the glittering prospects of trade . . . in the lucrative Eastern markets, and strong feelings of destiny combined to made acquisition . . . inevitable." He faults McKinley and other expansionists for failing to realize that revolt was likely to occur in the Philippines, that ruling the islands would involve enormous costs, and that the Asian trade would bring few financial benefits. Tompkins condemns American suppression of Filipino freedom. "Whether viewed from a contemporary or historical vantage point, whether considered pragmatically, philosophically, or morally," America's takeover of the Philippines, he concludes, "was a grave mistake." Cerillo accuses McKinley of ignoring the desires of the eight million inhabitants of the archipelago and choosing annexation on political, economic, and strategic grounds. Regardless of its "specific motives—duty, destiny, evangelism, economics, strategy—the United States seized" a foreign land and controlled it "against the wishes of a fairly well-organized indigenous independence movement." While McKinley and his supporters saw the United States as an "instrument of God or Anglo-Saxon civilization chosen to bring order, justice, and peace to the Philippines," the insurgents considered America to be "a Great Babylon or Beast, a source of persecution and injustice." Simply because other great powers engaged in similar activities and some of them welcomed America's annexation of the Philippines did not justify the United States violating "its own democratic traditions of self-government and the requirement of biblical morality for governments to do good." In short, American policy was shaped by a "quest for national power, wealth, and security," Cerillo concludes, rather than "by biblical standards of justice, righteousness, and peace."[153]

Was McKinley's decision to annex the Philippines as bad as most historians maintain? Many of the long-term consequences certainly were not good. In putting down the revolt and administering the islands, America did contradict many of its most cherished traditions and values. These actions helped the United States acquire a reputation for imperialism that has negatively affected its relations with many nations in Latin America, Africa, and Asia ever since. Nevertheless, given McKinley's inadequate sources of information, the political pressure he confronted, and the lack of good alternatives, his choice should not be quickly dismissed or strongly condemned. McKinley was a product of the Victorian generation who believed in Anglo-Saxon superiority, honor, and the duty to uplift the downtrodden and to civilize and Christianize "inferior peoples." Lacking modern sensibilities about multiculturalism and appreciation of different cultural traditions, McKinley and his advisers genuinely believed that by administering the archipelago they were helping the Filipino people. Many prominent politicians and influential religious leaders agreed that America had a divine mandate, and unavoidable duty, to annex the Philippines. Connecticut Senator Orville Platt (author of the Platt Amendment), Alfred Mahan, Indiana Senator Albert Beveridge, Social Gospelers Washington Gladden, Walter Rauschenbusch, and Lyman Abbott, and mission advocates John Mott and Josiah Strong all insisted that God expected his specially chosen people to bring Christianity and social and economic progress to the Philippines.[154] McKinley also hoped that the United States would reap economic, military, and political benefits by ruling the Philippines, but they were far from certain and, in fact, few resulted.

Given McKinley's assumptions that God had chosen the United States to carry out His purposes, especially to spread the gospel and assist the poor and afflicted, his fears of what would happen to the Philippines if the United States did not control the islands, and his desire to create opportunities for American commerce, his actions are understandable and even defensible, not malicious or malevolent. Like countless religious leaders and ordinary Americans, the president believed God had uniquely blessed and used America in the past and would continue to do so in the future.[155] He did not fight to annex the archipelago primarily for crass economic gain or self-serving political benefits, but rather because he believed God willed it, duty demanded it, and constructive results would occur. Prominent educator Henry Pritchett claimed that McKinley told him in May 1899 that two factors had strongly influenced his decision to annex the Philippines: belief that it was the desire of the American people and that annexation would be a "national missionary effort" that would greatly benefit Filipinos. While McKinley's assumptions are debatable, they indicate that he believed his policies involving Spain, Cuba, and the Philippines were required by Christian moral teaching. "As distasteful as it now seems," argues Andrew Preston, McKinley saw no "conflict between benevolence and empire." Annexing the Philippines was consistent with his volunteer work with the YMCA, military service, and promotion of missions because he thought it would better the lives of Filipinos, including those who revolted against American control.[156] American policies in both Cuba and the Philippines were certainly better than the often blatantly self-serving exploits of European nations. Moreover, given the record of other nations that gained independence in the twentieth century, Cerillo's judgment that "the most incompetent independent Philippine government" could not have done as much damage as American administrators did is questionable.[157]

McKinley's Assassination and Death

McKinley's response to being fatally wounded vividly illustrated his faith, and his death evoked an outpouring of theological reflection, spiritual anguish, and praise for his Christian character and conviction. On Friday, September 6, 1901, McKinley spoke at the Pan-American Exposition in Buffalo, New York. According to the *Presbyterian Banner*, he came to the exposition "at the height of his splendid fame. The strength and purity of his character and the solidity and success of his administration" had "won him the confidence and admiration of all parties and classes." He was "personally loved as few presidents" had been loved. While greeting people after his speech, McKinley was shot twice at point-blank range by anarchist Leon Czolgosz. Worried about his wife who had recently suffered a life-threatening illness, the president urged his personal secretary George Cortelyou not to tell her what had happened. He then turned to the assassin who had been subdued by guards. Fearing that the crowd might beat him to death, McKinley raised his blood-stained hand and entreated, "Let no one hurt him; may God forgive him." The assassin, McKinley reasoned, was "some poor misguided fellow." Next the president apologized for having "been the cause of trouble to the exposition." Recounting these events, a religious periodical declared that, after being shot, McKinley's "thoughts went out in tenderness to his wife, in forgiveness to his enemy, and in unselfish regard for the public interest."[158] Many Americans were struck by the similarity of McKinley's words and Christ's on the cross. Like Jesus during his crucifixion and Stephen while being stoned, an Episcopal rector avowed, the president prayed for his murderer.[159]

One of the two bullets that struck McKinley penetrated his stomach walls, shredding his kidneys. Surgeons quickly operated, but could not locate the bullet. From all quarters, the president's friends and associates flocked to Buffalo. As Americans prayed and waited, the initial news was hopeful. Writing to Cortelyou, a businessman stated, "I would gladly give my life to save his, and everyone feels the same way." McKinley's serenity and cheerfulness impressed the nation. By Thursday, the president seemed to be getting better. However, his condition changed dramatically the next morning. Realizing the end was near, the president prayed the Lord's Prayer and murmured some of the words of his favorite hymn "Nearer, My God, to Thee." His last words, as reported by the newspapers around the nation were, "Good-bye all, good-bye. It is God's way. His will, not ours, be done." "Having regarded his whole life as under God's direction," Frederick Barton proclaimed, "he even declared his dying at the hands of an assassin to be 'God's way.'" It was as though he bravely answered "the Master's call, which others could not hear," reported the *Washington Post*. The *Baltimore Sun* expressed thanks that McKinley lived long enough to experience "the outpouring of national love," the esteem of all sections of the country, and the solace of prayers offered for his recuperation. Although "the Divine Healer did not answer . . . our prayers for his recovery," God gave him eternal life. Both fervent prayer and the best efforts of modern science were impotent, declared the Charleston *News and Courier*, and McKinley "surrendered to the inscrutable will of the Ruler of life and death."[160]

One hundred thousand sermons, contended Philadelphia Presbyterian pastor Henry McCook, "could not have taught as much as McKinley's last words." All the sermons on Christian courage, patience, and hope in heaven for the last ten years, T. DeWitt Talmage argued, paled compared with "the magnificent demeanor of this dying chief magistrate." "No Christian virgin seeking the martyr's crown in Rome's empurpled amphi-theater," declared the *Rocky Mountain News*, "faced death with courage more superb than William McKinley." During his last hours, McKinley's radiant faith in God and eternal life, maintained the *New York Herald*, eloquently reminded Americans of both Christ's death and resurrection. "Christian faith and trust," proclaimed William Jennings Bryan, was "never better exemplified than in his death." McKinley died "wonderfully as the Master died," asserted journalist Murat Halstead, providing a marvelous Christian example. Congressman Charles Grosvenor predicted that McKinley's death would be remembered as the most Christ-like the world had known since Calvary.[161]

Numerous commentators struggled to find meaning in McKinley's assas-sination. The Presbyterian *Interior* hoped that this affliction would prompt Americans to reject the "jaunty pride of prosperity" and engage in sober introspection. Through this tragedy God was summoning America to repent of its disrespect for law and toleration of corruption, oppression, and iniquity. His death challenged Americans to assess whether they had been worship-ping wealth and pleasure instead of God, declared the *Presbyterian Banner*. If the death of "our noble and beloved president" made Americans "more faithful to God, then indeed has he not died in vain." The way he died, argued Episcopal rector W. B. Huntingdon, strengthened Christianity in America. Many southerners hoped that McKinley's death would further his efforts to restore national unity. As one of them put it, "where he found strife he left peace; where he found bitterness, he left love; where he found an open wound he poured his dissolving life as a precious ointment to soothe and heal."[162] Some predicted that God would use McKinley's life and death to convert many Americans.[163] Ministers emphasized that McKinley was with God in paradise because he trusted in Jesus Christ as his redeemer and urged Americans to follow his example so they would someday experience heav-enly life. Preaching at Metropolitan Methodist Church in Washington the Sunday after McKinley's death, W. H. Chapman urged worshippers to "imi-tate his virtues" so that they would "be counted worthy of a place with him in the Kingdom of Heaven."[164] Many took comfort in their belief that although McKinley was dead, God still ruled the world, and the republic continued to flourish. Numerous editors quoted the words of James Garfield who com-forted Americans after Lincoln's assassination by declaring, "God reigns and the Government at Washington still lives."[165]

Not surprisingly, McKinley's death led to extensive discussion of how to prevent presidents from being assassinated. Many other mourners urged the government to admit no more anarchists, smash their organizations, suppress their "incendiary publications," and silence their lecturers. Some argued that the best weapons to combat anarchists were insane asylums, prisons, and scaffolds. Striking a different note, Frank Gunsaulus insisted that "more than jails or scaffold, more than national armaments or strict legislation," McKinley's "gentle, pure, just, and loving spirit," as exemplified in his life and death, would eventually "annihilate anarchy."[166] Many complained that three presidents—Lincoln, Garfield, and McKinley—had been assassinated in less than forty years, a worse record than that of despotic Russia.[167]

McKinley's Funeral

As a special train took the slain president's body from Buffalo to Washington, large crowds lined the tracks in many towns, tears flowed, flags were lowered, bells tolled, and children sang McKinley's favorite hymns. Thousands of mourners viewed his coffin at the Capitol. Two public funeral services were held: one at the Capitol and the other at the First Methodist Church in Canton. Everywhere along the route from Washington to Canton people stood silently in homage. An estimated 250,000 people gathered in Pittsburgh to pay tribute to the fallen chief executive.[168] "The outburst of tears and heartfelt grief throughout the land," an Episcopal priest concluded, was "almost unparalleled."[169] Thousands of stores, offices, homes, and saloons displayed portraits of McKinley emblazoned with his last words: "It is God's way. His will, not ours, be done."[170] In his eulogy at Canton, Charles Manchester proclaimed that McKinley "had gained in early life a personal knowledge of Jesus, which guided him in the performance of greater duties." McKinley's faith in God enabled him to serve effectively as president. At 3:30 p.m. on the day of his funeral, Americans observed five minutes of silence as vehicles, factory machinery, and conversation stopped. President Roosevelt proclaimed the day one of "mourning and prayer" and implored Americans to submit "to the will of Almighty God." McKinley, he declared, had "crowned a life of largest love for his fellowmen [and] most earnest endeavor for their welfare, by a death of Christian fortitude."[171]

McKinley's death as a widely admired, highly respected, and dearly loved chief executive who had helped heal the nation's wounds, restore national prosperity, and elevate the presidency evoked thousands of effusive eulogies. Many tributes focused on his virtues. McKinley was "beloved on every hand," declared the *Washington Post*. "No American statesman," opined the *Indianapolis Journal*, had "ever grown more steadily or rapidly in public estimation at home and abroad" than had McKinley. Many defended McKinley's leading of the United States into war. As the *Buffalo Courier* put it, "Providence willed that as President he should direct a successful war, but it was a war of humanity, waged on just principle. He abhorred its necessity, and was grateful to his Maker for its cessation."[172] Hundreds praised the deceased president's honesty, unselfishness, kindness, and affability. Ministers, politicians, editors, and friends lauded his character, wisdom, fortitude, and generosity.[173] "Honesty and courage, fraternity and justice," declared *Century Magazine*, were his "watchwords." Roosevelt praised his strength, courage, sense of justice, and concern for others. Others labeled his life "stainless," "unsullied," and "spotless."[174] His "sublime faith in Him who died to save mankind" and "his fortitude in his final hour," declared the Cincinnati *Times-Star*, were "the evidences of a life without flaw." McKinley, insisted the *Philadelphia North-American*, was "a warm-hearted, cordial, Christian gentleman." His pastor in Washington, Frank Bristol, asserted that McKinley regarded duty as the most sublime word in the English language. Few could match his "singleness of purpose," moral purity, or commitment to public duty, argued the *Buffalo Express*. Cardinal James Gibbons praised McKinley's civic virtues and the high moral standards of his administration. Secretary of the Navy John Long insisted that McKinley never tried to accomplish "a good result by improper means."[175]

Numerous eulogies compared McKinley with two of his most illustrious and revered predecessors. An Episcopal priest in Providence, Rhode Island, for example, avowed that the fallen chief executive completed a trio that would "ever shine with undiminished luster among our presidents": "Washington, the liberator of the colonies; Lincoln the emancipator of the slaves; McKinley, the deliverer of oppressed and dying Cuba." The *Ohio State Journal* predicted that history would place McKinley beside "Lincoln and Washington in high ability," "lofty character," and "far-sighted statesmanship." Neither Washington nor Lincoln, the *Springfield Union* claimed, surpassed McKinley's commitment to duty.[176]

Dozens of eulogies and editorials celebrated McKinley's faith. All of McKinley's other virtues, the *Presbyterian Banner* asserted, rested upon the foundation of his Christian faith. Neither parading nor concealing his faith, "he walked as an humble and faithful follower of the Lord Jesus."[177] An Episcopal rector described the deceased president as a "servant of God and of the Lord Jesus Christ" who was "not ashamed of the Gospel." The Civil War major was a faithful and fervent soldier of the cross who fought to help

God establish His kingdom on earth.[178] The rector of St. Patrick's (Catholic) Cathedral in New York lauded his deep faith in God and lack of religious bigotry.[179]

To many, McKinley was a martyr. He sacrificed his life for the American people, stated the Cincinnati *Times-Star*, "on the altar of his country." His death could help complete the unification of the nation to which he had devoted "his best thought and energy." He had done much, declared the Atlanta *Constitution*, to bind domestic wounds and heal sectional estrangement. His death, predicted the *Baltimore Sun*, would strengthen the republic "by bringing closer together all who love free institutions." McKinley had surrendered "personal considerations," the *Chicago Tribune* declared, "to promote the welfare of the Republic."[180]

Final Assessment

His contemporaries showered McKinley with praise. He was a "shining example," asserted the *Milwaukee Sentinel*, of the success those "born in humble circumstances" could achieve if they worked earnestly and industriously. By treating the South justly, the Birmingham *Age-Herald* argued, he had helped restore national unity. Because of how he had handled relations with the Philippines and China, the *Philadelphia Inquirer* predicted, McKinley would go down in history as one of the nation's greatest presidents. Charles Olcott insisted that "McKinley's private life was so pure, his personal integrity so well known, and his political conduct" so exemplary that he was not criticized in any of these areas.[181]

The evaluations of later historians have not been so laudatory. Despite the effusive outpouring of genuine affection expressed for McKinley after his assassination, the memory of his character and contributions faded quickly, and by the 1920s his administration was dismissed as "a mediocre prelude to the energy and vigor" of Theodore Roosevelt's presidency. Moreover, critics depicted McKinley as a puppet dancing at the end of strings pulled by Mark Hanna.[182] Gould argues that McKinley promoted his own advancement, had no charisma, and rarely inspired the American people. Lacking speechwriters and dramatic flair, McKinley, H. Wayne Morgan contends, never explained his political philosophy in a compelling way.[183]

Despite such criticisms, Gould, Morgan, and other recent biographers offer a generally positive assessment of McKinley. Claims that McKinley was a "hidebound Republican conservative," "the spokesman for untamed business in the Gilded Age, the compliant agent" of Hanna, and an irresolute executive who could not prevent a needless war with Spain, Gould maintains, are "erroneous stereotypes." In reality, the Republican effectively directed the military during the Spanish-American War as well as the diplomatic process that brought peace and territorial acquisitions.[184]

In numerous ways, scholars argue, McKinley was a transitional president. The last chief executive to fight in the Civil War, he used his power as commander-in-chief "broadly and creatively" and increased the prestige of the presidency and expanded its powers, paving the way for his more activist successors in the twentieth century. He brought experts and academicians into the government by appointing commissions. McKinley developed good relations with Congress by making it an equal partner in government and regularly consulting with leaders of both parties in crafting programs. His speaking tours and shrewd use of the press enhanced his personal popularity, giving "him a powerful lever in public controversies."[185] Although McKinley sought to discern the will of the people, he opposed their desires when his principles or circumstances dictated.[186] His political skills and experience, temperament, and tact enabled McKinley to achieve many of his domestic and foreign policy goals. These same traits helped him heal a nation torn asunder by fratricide and continued hostile feelings.[187] By strengthening the Republican Party, expanding the scope of the presidency, and directing "important departures in foreign policy," Gould concludes, McKinley had a significant legacy.[188]

McKinley's mother frequently said she was sorry her son "had only become president when he could have had such a useful and brilliant career in the church."[189] Although he never became a Methodist bishop as his mother hoped, Barton argued, McKinley was a priest whose "services were performed at the head of a nation." He advanced God's Kingdom by ending oppression and giving religious freedom to millions. "McKinley's life and work," Pierard and Linder conclude, epitomize the powerful Protestant civil religion consensus of last decade of the nineteenth century, "which provided the spiritual underpinning" that enabled the United States to become a world power. McKinley told fellow Methodists in August 1899 that "piety and patriotism go well together." "Love of flag, love of country," he added, "are not inconsistent with our religious faith."[190] Sometimes failing to properly distinguish between love of God and love of the United States, between biblical teachings and American aims, McKinley frequently defended his policies as fulfilling God's will and accomplishing His purposes. Like most other presidents, he used civil religion much more to commend rather than criticize America's actions. While endearing him to many of his contemporaries, this led him to adopt questionable policies that set some dangerous precedents in foreign relations. Nevertheless, McKinley safely piloted the ship of state through many perilous waters. Dignified, devout, duty-bound, and diplomatic, in life and death, he provided an impressive role model. "All a man can hope for during his lifetime," McKinley declared, was "to set an example, and when he is dead, to be an inspiration for history."[191] Judged by his own standard, McKinley succeeded admirably in many ways.

6

Herbert Hoover

INDIVIDUAL FAITHFULNESS AND
COOPERATIVE ASSOCIATION

I come of Quaker stock.
Speech accepting the Republican nomination, August 11, 1928

The Presidency . . . must be the instrument by which the national conscience is livened and it must under the guidance of the Almighty interpret and follow that conscience.
Speech accepting the Republican nomination, August 11, 1928

I appeal to you . . . to unite with lovers of good will and followers of the Prince of Peace for the making of human brotherhood in which the Peace of God shall prevail in the lives of men.
Address to the Ecumenical Methodist Conference in Atlanta,
October 24, 1931

Introduction

Herbert Hoover was the nation's first Quaker chief executive. Through his childhood socialization and adult involvement, the Society of Friends significantly affected Hoover's temperament and character, especially his sense of duty, work ethic, self-reliance, and abhorrence of display, and his worldview, most notably his emphasis on good works, private charity, and the passionate pursuit of peace.[1] Quaker convictions helped supply his "purpose and faith" and direct "his thoughts and actions."[2] As president, Hoover's approach to politics and policies, especially his response to the Great Depression, were guided by Quaker concepts of "ordered liberty" and "corporate individualism" and his belief, drawn from his Quaker and wartime experience, that Americans would respond generously to appeals to help those in need.[3] Hoover often affirmed his faith in God and used religious rhetoric to promote his policies. In his first statement to the press after winning the 1928 election, the Republican declared his "complete dependence on Divine guidance" in accepting the duties of the office.[4] Hoover chose not to attend a Quaker college (instead going to Stanford), rejected pacifism, and violated strict Quaker norms by smoking, drinking alcohol, dancing, attending the theater, and working on the Sabbath.[5] Nevertheless, few presidents have displayed such a consistent moral and religious philosophy throughout their lives and tenure in office or such exemplary character as the Quaker born in 1874 in West Branch, Iowa.[6] Numerous friends and scholars testified to the influence his Quaker faith had upon him.[7]

The Faith of Herbert Hoover

Hoover had strong Quaker roots on both sides of his family. The paternal side had been Quakers for six generations, and his great uncle John Y. Hoover was an influential pastor and author in West Branch, Iowa.[8] His maternal side had comparable Quaker credentials, and his mother Hulda Minthorn, like three of her siblings, was a recorded Quaker minister. As a youth, Hoover learned the tenets and practices of Quakerism from his parents, his neighbors, and religious services on Sundays and Thursdays. His parents emphasized prayer, daily reading of the Bible, and simple living and prohibited the reading of most other literature, playing cards or musical instruments, and drinking alcohol. By the age of 10, Hoover had already read the entire Bible. When reminiscing about his youth in Iowa, he sometimes complained about the austerity of Quaker practices and having to sit through long periods of silence at the Sunday meetings.[9] Hoover's parents both died before he was 10, and he soon moved to Oregon. He lived in Newberg with his uncle John Minthorn, a devout Quaker, and then at Friends Pacific Academy. Before leaving to attend Stanford, Hoover worked in Salem, Oregon, where he made a public profession of faith and helped found the Salem Monthly Meeting, remaining on the rolls of this congregation until he became president.[10] Hoover's religious training taught him the importance of self-respect, self-reliance, and moral obligation and convinced him that his conscience should guide all his activities.[11]

Scholars have explained Hoover's approach to the presidency in terms of many factors: his personality, business experience, engineering mindset, commitment to capitalism, belief in individualism, and Quaker faith.[12] While all these were important, this chapter will examine how his Quaker background and convictions affected his performance as president.

With about 110,000 members in 1926, the Quakers were one of America's smaller denominations. Founded by Englishman George Fox in the 1640s, Friends, like a number of other sects, sought to restore the primitive Christianity of the early church. While emphasizing personal piety and inward reflection, Quakers energetically worked to improve social conditions, eradicate social ills, and help the needy. Unlike most Anabaptist groups, with whom they shared a common commitment to pacifism, Quakers refused to withdraw from the world into their own sheltered communities, but instead were interspersed throughout society where they compassionately aided the victims of war, tragedy, and discrimination. Quaker William Penn founded Pennsylvania in 1682, and Friends played a major role in the colony's politics until the American Revolution. After independence, few Quakers actively participated in political life except to urge legislative bodies to eradicate slavery, reduce military spending, and pursue peace.[13]

The most thorough analysis of the origins and influence of Hoover's Quaker faith is David Hinshaw's *Herbert Hoover: American Quaker*.[14] Hinshaw labels Hoover "a Quaker by birth, environment and training." By "precept, example, and osmosis," Quaker principles permeated his inner life. Quakers' "manners and methods," Hinshaw asserts, were evident in Hoover's reticence, modesty, sympathy for the oppressed, gentleness, "undiluted spirituality," "high moral purpose," "record of selfless service," and "astounding audacity." Like other Quakers, Hoover prized simplicity in both dress and demeanor. He wore "plain, almost drab suits," had little interest in art, music, or fiction, spoke plainly, and relied on "logic and reason to support his arguments." In accordance with the best of Quaker tradition, he always strove to do what he believed was right, regardless of public opinion and the political consequences. Violating Quaker norms, Hoover drank liquor, occasionally smoked, and sometimes used profanity to underscore a point.[15]

Unlike most other denominations, Quakerism is not based on a doctrinal creed. Its most distinguishing characteristic is its emphasis on the "Inner Light" (also called the Seed, the In-speaking Voice, and the Christ within), the direct connection of each individual with the Creator. This internal mechanism guided the decisions and behavior of devout Quakers.[16] Hinshaw argues that this inner light and the Quaker "Queries" directed Hoover's thought and actions. Since the days of Fox, Quakers had been asked at their meetings if they opposed war, capital punishment, oaths, gambling, and discrimination and if they supported education, temperance, prison reform, equality of the sexes, simplicity, religious tolerance, civil liberty, and just treatment of racial minorities. These Queries expressed what Quakers thought Jesus would do if He lived in contemporary society and provided "brotherly advice." While stressing individuals' personal communion with God, Quakers pressured each other to conform to a common set of convictions.[17] These questions encouraged Friends to seek divine guidance in all areas of life including social and economic relationships and civic responsibilities. They prompted American Quakers to treat Indians fairly, strive to abolish slavery, and value men and women equally.

While living abroad during the first two decades of the twentieth century working as an engineer and directing humanitarian relief efforts, Hoover apparently did not attend Quaker services. He had little contact with Friends, did not give his sons any religious instruction, and did not supply a distinctively religious rationale for his relief work.[18] While serving as secretary of commerce in the 1920s, however, Hoover attended the Quaker Meetinghouse on I Street. After being elected president, he began worshipping at Friends Meeting House at Thirteenth and Irving Streets. He soon persuaded fellow Quakers to construct a "plain and dignified" building on Florida Avenue where he and his wife regularly worshipped during the remainder of his tenure.[19] Hoover convinced a long-time friend, Augustus Murray, the chair of the Greek Department at Stanford University, to pastor the congregation.[20] Hoover was not very interested in the devotional aspects of Quakerism (prayer, Bible reading, and mediation), but he was deeply affected by its way of conceptualizing the world—its principles for shaping both public life and private conduct.[21] Hinshaw contends that the heart of the Quaker message is to be tolerant, honest, and kind and to unselfishly serve all people in the belief that divine law and human law may someday "be made one." Judging Hoover's "words and works" "by this standard," he was a "good Quaker."[22]

In addition to his childhood training in Quakerism and regular participation in Quaker worship as president, Hoover also belonged to the International Society of Christian Endeavor. Founded by Francis Clark in 1881 and led by Hoover's friend Daniel Poling, this organization emphasized prayer, Bible study, Christian service, faithful church attendance, good citizenship, tithing, interdenominational fellowship, and peace. In a 1931 address Hoover praised Christian Endeavor for promoting "international good will and world peace" and called it a "mighty force for sobriety, righteousness, and respect for law, patriotism, and spiritual development."[23]

Throughout his long life, Hoover repeatedly maintained that national success depended on a spiritual foundation. In accepting the Republican nomination in August 1928, Hoover told 60,000 supporters at Stanford's football stadium, "Our purpose is to build in this Nation a human society,

not an economic system. . . . We shall succeed through the faith, the loyalty, the self-sacrifice, the devotion to eternal ideals which live today in every
American."[24] As this statement indicates, Hoover viewed human nature and
potential very optimistically. He shared with other Quakers "an unshak-
able faith" in humanity's "moral and spiritual purpose."[25] By recognizing
and responding to the divine spark within, Hoover insisted, individuals
became more committed to higher ideals, compassion, and self-sacrifice. The
American social and economic system, he wrote in 1922, could "march toward
better days" only if it were "inspired by things of the spirit."[26] The individual rather than nations, classes, or groups was the key to "permanent spiritual and social progress."[27] Hoover contended that the "stability, service, and
progress" of nations and individuals rested upon "spiritual advancement."[28]
The solution to "all social, economic, governmental, and international problems" was "an idealism which finds its firm foundation in religious faith."[29]
Satisfying people's material needs, he maintained, was a means to a higher
end: enabling them to respond more fully to the "promptings of the spirit."[30]
During the Depression, Hoover continually declared that the nation's problems were moral and spiritual as well as economic. He rejoiced that there had
been a remarkable sense of community cooperation, little public disorder or
industrial conflict, and greater "social and spiritual responsibility."[31] Human
happiness depended not on material goods, but on "the spiritual application
of moral ideals."[32] "The most potent force in society," he trumpeted, "is its
ideals."[33]

By the time Hoover became president, secularization had deeply affected
American education, media, morality, politics, and economics. Nevertheless,
he considered the United States a Christian nation that must be governed
and guided by biblical principles.[34] Humans, Hoover asserted, would prosper
only as they played "in tune with the purpose of Almighty Providence."[35] The
ideas and ideals of Christ, which had long "dominated the course of civilization," were still "the foundations of economic and social life."[36] Human dignity and personal freedom came from the Creator, not from governments.[37]
The nation's political principles and ideals, Hoover declared, "grew largely out
of the religious origins and spiritual aspirations of our people."[38] The United
States derived its existence and strength "not only from great political and
social truths, but from spiritual convictions," from "a deep and abiding faith in
Almighty God."[39] "As a nation," Hoover added, "we are indebted to the Book of
Books for our national ideals and representative institutions. Their preserva-
tion rests in adhering to its principles."[40]

In his inaugural address, Hoover quoted Proverbs 29:18: "Where there
is no vision, the people cast off restraint; but he that keepeth the law, happy

is he." He explained later that Christ offered humanity a new way of life based on mercy and compassion.[41] As a Quaker and a traditional moralist, Hoover strove to promote civic righteousness, which he considered crucial to American vitality. In a democracy, he asserted, the "organized conscience of the community" was the source of law and the only firm basis for its enforcement.[42] A successful democracy, he declared, "rests wholly upon the moral and spiritual quality of its people."[43] "Nothing is more true," Hoover proclaimed, "than George Washington's statement: 'National morality cannot exist in the absence of religious principle.'"[44] Hoover insisted that religious groups had "a vital part in shaping the vision of the Nation."[45] The Ten Commandments and the Sermon on the Mount should guide public life.[46] Governments depended "largely upon churches and schools to create, preserve, and increase the spiritual and moral basis essential" to their life.[47] Only religious faith could sustain freedom of worship, conscience, and speech. Without the support of transcendent moral standards, liberty degenerated into license.[48] Like other Quakers, Hoover frequently stressed that conduct was more important than doctrine.[49]

Henry Cadbury, a professor at Bryn Mawr, asked President Hoover what aspect of the Quaker tradition he regarded as most significant. "Without hesitation he answered, 'Individual faithfulness.'" To Cadbury, this phrase well described Hoover's personal life and the social approach of Quakers. Throughout Friends' history their progressive social concern had begun with individuals.[50]

Few presidents have so clearly distilled and succinctly presented their essential philosophy as Hoover did in *American Individualism* (1922). He sought to identify the "political, economic, and spiritual principles" that had enabled the United States to steadily grow in "usefulness and greatness" and to defend them against false philosophies so that they could guide the nation on "the road to progress." "Seven years of contending with economic degeneration," "social disintegration," "incessant political dislocation," and "individual and class conflict" during and following World War I had made Hoover "an unashamed individualist." The American System, as he called it, by contrast, rested on the ideal of cooperative association. It was initially tested in his relief work in Belgium, refined through his efforts to feed starving Europeans, and applied at home by thousands of community organizations like the Red Cross and YMCA.[51] Hoover argued that cooperative association was superior to the other competing social philosophies of the 1920s—communism, socialism, capitalism, and autocracy.[52] In the 1930s and 1940s Hoover often described the battle between communism and the American system as a "struggle between the philosophy of Christ and that of Hegel and Marx."[53]

Hoover avowed that the conception of individualism had reached its highest development in the United States. American society rested upon belief in equality of opportunity. During its history the United States had added this ideal to the two others the founding fathers expounded: all people are created equal and all individuals are equal before the law.[54] Hoover labeled this "demand for a fair chance" the nation's "most precious" social ideal.[55] By providing free and universal education, Hoover contended, the United States sought to give all citizens an equal start in the race of life, with the government serving as "the umpire of fairness."[56] Strong homes, brotherly love, hard work, and frugality helped individuals live ethically.[57] Americans, he claimed, could advance as far as their "intelligence, character, ability and ambition" enabled them. As Benjamin Franklin did, Hoover insisted that his own life wonderfully demonstrated the possibilities of equal opportunity. Like his eighteenth-century forebear, he had risen from humble circumstances to wealth, prestige, and leadership, providing a model for others.[58] While strongly emphasizing self-reliance, Hoover also urged people to compassionately aid others, especially the disadvantaged. Echoing Ralph Waldo Emerson and Walt Whitman, Hoover contended that individualism stimulated productivity and protected liberty. It alone celebrated "the universal divine inspiration of every human soul."[59] Despite his positive view of human nature and potential, the Quaker asserted that people's "instincts of self-preservation," acquisitiveness, fear, and desire for power and praise often prevented them from expressing more noble impulses. He maintained, however, that "with the growth of ideals through education, [and] with the higher realization" of freedom, justice, humanity, and service, "selfish impulses become less and less dominant."[60]

America's shift from an agrarian to an industrial and commercial society, Hoover acknowledged, made it much more difficult to preserve individualism. The United States' partnership between business and government during World War I posed an additional threat to individual initiative, rights, and liberties. The growing size and complexity of commerce and industry, Hoover avowed, required government regulation to prevent oligopolies and unfair business practices. The laissez-faire approach of Thomas Jefferson and Andrew Jackson had to give way to the progressivism of Theodore Roosevelt and Woodrow Wilson.[61] The Quaker insisted, however, that government regulations must always safeguard equality of opportunity and permit individual ingenuity. Consequently, Hoover is best labeled an "associational progressive" or a "corporate liberal," and the best title for his philosophy is "cooperative capitalism."[62] He believed that trade associations, labor unions, farm cooperatives, professional societies, chambers of commerce, and marketing organizations could best synthesize "individual entrepreneurship and corporate enterprise" and promote economic prosperity, social justice, and equality of opportunity.[63] The role of the federal government was to assist in research and development, mediate between conflicting groups, and sometimes regulate their activities.[64] But beyond that, government should be involved only when individuals and other institutions could not solve their problems. If the government assumed too many responsibilities, he warned, it would stifle individual initiative and make people dependent on its services.[65] As a Quaker, Hoover was confident that in the long run the right ideas would prevail. Because the events of the early twentieth century had shown that the false ideas and philosophies had a powerful appeal, he insisted, the correct ideas must be clearly delineated and forcefully defended. Throughout his life Hoover continually asserted that the United States must demonstrate how the philosophy of individualism guaranteed human dignity, freedom, and opportunity.

Hoover argued that voluntary organizations should play the leading role in alleviating suffering, aiding the poor, and promoting economic development. The parable of the Good Samaritan, he frequently argued, was the proper model for helping the indigent and disadvantaged. The Samaritan did not expect the government to assist the wounded traveler, but instead took care of him personally. Individuals must be their brother's keeper.[66] The nation's tens of thousands of voluntary associations provided all kinds of services much better than government ever could. The government's efforts to help the needy were usually "formal, statistical, and mechanical" rather than personal.[67] Hoover repeatedly lauded volunteerism and private efforts to help those in need, especially praising the work of the Salvation Army, the Mennonite Committee, the Federal Council of Churches, and the YMCA.[68]

The Election of 1928

The election of 1928 was the first time that either a Quaker or a Catholic received the nomination of a major political party. Immensely popular as a result of his leadership of humanitarian efforts in the 1910s, Hoover cruised to the Republican nomination. His Republican competitors protested that he was a Quaker pacifist, a desegregationist, and an Anglophile, and some denounced his economic policies as unorthodox.[69] In accepting the nomination, Hoover reiterated the major policies he had supported since 1921: helping farmers through cooperative marketing, strengthening the partnership between government and business through self-governing associations, using government regulation only to provide equal opportunity, conserving natural resources, enforcing Prohibition, aiding children, supporting international cooperation, reducing armaments to maintain peace, and guaranteeing religious freedom. Since the end of the Great War, Hoover argued, the United States had made great progress in reducing poverty, and continuing "the policies of the last eight years," he promised, "we shall soon with the help of God be in sight of the day when poverty will be banished from this Nation."[70] After the stock market crash of October 1929, detractors used these words against him the rest of his life.

Strongly disliking the ballyhoo of politics and giving speeches, Hoover ran a lackluster campaign that sought to educate Americans about the benefits of cooperative individualism. However, he did not need to inspire citizens because most of them regarded him as a "super expert" who could "solve any problem with his facts and figures." Democratic candidate Al Smith, the governor of New York, and Hoover shared many similarities: both were self-made men who had a strong work ethic and a solid record as efficient, progressive administrators. Both relied on the advice of experts in economic and social affairs, opposed the postwar Red Scare hysteria and the Ku Klux Klan, and lauded the nation's prosperity.[71] Their differences centered on three key factors: having never run for public office, Hoover had a reputation for being apolitical, while Smith, who had lost only one election in twenty-five years, was considered the consummate professional politician. Second, Hoover opposed, and Smith supported, the repeal of Prohibition. Third, Hoover was a Quaker, while Smith was a Catholic.

Although Smith had no decisive issues to use against his Republican rival and Hoover's popularity made him a very formidable foe, Smith's Catholicism hurt his candidacy.[72] Concerns about Smith's faith were first raised in 1927 when he appeared to be the frontrunner for the Democratic nomination. The editors of the *New Republic* questioned whether a Catholic president could remain independent of clerical authority on the issues of federal aid to schools and American relations with Mexico.[73] Similarly, attorney Charles Marshall, an expert on canon law, questioned in the *Atlantic Monthly* whether Smith, as a "loyal and conscientious Roman Catholic," held positions that could not be reconciled with the Constitution and the nation's civil and religious liberty.[74] Like John F. Kennedy in 1960, Smith responded that in his long public career he had never experienced any conflict between his Catholic faith and "patriotic loyalty to the United States" and had consistently supported "complete separation of Church from State."[75] Such attacks prompted a Catholic judge to urge Smith to stop seeking the Democratic nomination because he feared the governor's candidacy would do "incalculable harm" to the Catholic Church.[76]

Writing in *The Nation* in February 1928, Heywood Broun argued that citizens should inquire how Smith's Catholicism and Hoover's Quakerism might influence their actions as president. "Instead of saying, 'Let's keep religion out of politics,'" Americans should have "the freest and frankest possible discussion" about how the candidates' religious convictions affected their positions on issues. Given the pacifism of Quakers, would Hoover maintain a military strong enough to defend America? How would Smith's religious commitments influence his attitude toward Catholic Mexico? However, Broun dismissed popular fears that Smith would take directions from the pope or seek to abolish the public school system as "palpably silly." There was no evidence that as governor of New York Smith relied on counsel from cardinals. Nor was it sensible to attribute Smith's desire to repeal Prohibition to his Catholicism, Broun contended. Moreover, the Catholic Church did sometimes interfere in politics, especially on the local level, but Baptists and Methodists were ten times as likely to meddle in political affairs.[77]

Surprisingly, although Smith's Catholicism became a significant campaign issue, few discussed how Hoover's Quakerism might affect his role as commander-in-chief, probably because Hoover did not accept his denomination's commitment to pacifism.[78] A devout Quaker president, John Gummere contended in the *Atlanta Monthly*, could be as dangerous to the nation's safety as a Catholic one. Hoover belonged to a pacifist sect whose members had suffered persecution and imprisonment rather than serve in the military. Would Hoover, as America's military leader, repudiate his religious tradition or apply its principles to national policy? Would he use armed forces to stop an invasion of the United States or deploy the army to ensure domestic order? These questions were as vital to the nation's welfare as any questions about Smith's allegiance to the pope. Gummere acknowledged that Hoover might be a "fighting Quaker" who supported the use of arms, but he insisted that his record during the Spanish-American War and the Great War was ambiguous. He challenged Hoover to clarify his position before the election, but the Republican never did.[79]

The editors of *The Nation*, by contrast, accused Hoover in October of being unfaithful to Quaker principles on war and the use of violence. They noted that the Constitution of the American Yearly Meetings declared, "The Friends believe war to be incompatible with Christianity and seek to persuade [people to use] peaceful methods" to settle national and interpersonal disputes. They contended that Hoover had supported American involvement in the Great War to prevent German militarists from dominating the world. Although Hoover regularly attended Quaker meetings, he was quite willing to "take the oath of office," "and *as a believing Quaker*, to become Commander-in-Chief of the American army and navy." In his speech accepting the Republican nomination, Hoover had "completely abandoned the Quaker doctrine that love and not force shall rule the world." Hoover proclaimed that while he had a deep passion for peace, he strongly supported a sizable army and navy because in an armed world the "only certain guarantee of freedom" was military preparation. While recognizing that thousands of Quakers fought in the Great War and that Quakers believed in freedom of conscience, the editors labeled Hoover a "renegade Quaker." The willingness of a Friend to assume command of an army and navy was "a dreadful and an inexcusable lapse from the faith." Hoover was guilty of "insincerity and treason to the faith he professes."[80]

In his acceptance speech, Hoover accentuated that his Quaker ancestors had been persecuted for their beliefs and declared, "By blood and conviction I stand for religious toleration in both act and in spirit." In America every man had the right "to worship God according to the dictates of his own conscience." He instructed his associates to eschew negative campaigning and not to mention religion or Prohibition to avoid fanning "the flames of bigotry."[81] Nevertheless, some of his supporters attacked Smith's Catholicism and opposition to Prohibition, prompting Hoover to later call the religious issue "the worst plague in the campaign."[82] Southern fundamentalist Bob Jones, Sr. delivered hundreds of speeches arguing that no Catholic was qualified to be president, and Hoover supporters labeled New York City's Lincoln Tunnel, Smith's "direct conduit to the Vatican."[83] Assistant Attorney General Mabel Walker Willebrandt exhorted 4,000 Methodist ministers at a meeting in Springfield, Ohio, to use their pulpits to denounce Smith's position on Prohibition to help defeat him.[84] Senator George Moses, the head of Hoover's campaign in the East, sent anti-Catholic materials to North Carolina newspapers and urged a campaign worker in Kentucky to utilize an anti-Catholic strategy. Oliver Street, a national Republican committeeman from Alabama, mailed 200,000 letters throughout the South assailing Smith's religious affiliation. In late September Hoover denounced these circulars and insisted that "religious questions have no part in this campaign. I have repeatedly stated that neither I nor the Republican Party want support on that basis." Hoover also wrote Smith to convey his regret that some had used his Catholicism against him.[85] The Quaker publicly censured a letter sent by a national Republican committeewomen from Virginia that implored women to work to prevent a "Romanized and rum-ridden" republic. This attitude, Hoover wrote, "is entirely opposed to every principle of the Republican party."[86] Despite Hoover's statement, the Democratic New York *World* concluded that the Republican Party's effort to gain "partisan sectarian support" for its presidential candidate "is one of the most sinister and dangerous precedents ever established in this country." When "a political party officially allies itself with organized church bodies," it deepened "political divisions along the lines of religious differences."[87] Moreover, Catholic editors chastised Hoover for condemning religious bigotry in general terms but rarely denouncing specific attacks on Smith.[88]

Meanwhile, Lutheran editors passed a resolution expressing their opposition to a Catholic candidate, whose primary allegiance was to the pope, not the American people. They acknowledged that they had "much more in common with a believing Catholic than with Unitarians [like William Howard Taft], Quakers, and other rationalists." A faithful Catholic, however, owed "absolute allegiance" to a "foreign sovereign" who claimed to have authority over secular affairs and often attempted to put this claim into practice. The editors cited examples of the Catholic Church's current political interference and influence in Europe and quoted a number of edicts that asserted the pope's temporal power. Although religious journals should not endorse presidential candidates, they must "correct [the] false and misleading inuendos [*sic*], statements and impressions" of Catholic clergy and authors who aggressively promoted Smith's candidacy.[89]

Religious leaders and bodies played an active role in the campaign. Religious groups, particularly in the South, produced scores of pamphlets and posters depicting the dangers of "Romanism." An Oklahoma pastor reportedly pontificated, "If you vote for Al Smith, you're voting against Christ." Four Southern Methodist bishops urged members of their denomination to help prevent the election of an "enemy of national Prohibition." Northern Methodist leader John Mott urged Americans to vote for Hoover because of "his sensitive and strong social conscience," vast experience, and constructive policies.[90] Hugh Walker, the moderator of the General Assembly of the PCUSA, declared that every church member was obligated "to work and pray and vote for the election of Herbert Hoover," not because Smith was a Catholic, but because he was an "implacable foe" of Prohibition.[91] Both Henry Sloan Coffin, the president of Union Theological Seminary in New York City, and Henry van Dyke, a former moderator, strongly censured Walker for "overstepping his authority." Nicholas Murray Butler, the president of Columbia University, industrialist Owen Young, former Democratic presidential candidate John Davis, and New York gubernatorial candidate Franklin D. Roosevelt all deplored the intrusion of religion into the campaign.[92] Other religious spokesmen, while not endorsing either candidate, strongly defended the right of citizens to vote for or against candidates because of their religious affiliations and convictions.[93]

In a speech on September 20, Smith responded to the attacks on his religious faith for the first time during the campaign. What would people say, he asked, if his campaign team pressured a convention of Catholic priests to urge their parishioners to vote for him? Smith added that he did not want Catholics to vote for him because of his religious faith. "If any Catholic" believes that "the welfare, the well-being, the prosperity, the growth and expansion of the United States is . . . best promoted by the election of Mr. Hoover I want him to vote for Hoover and not for me." However, the Democrat reasoned, anyone who agreed with his policies but did not vote for him because of his religion was "not a real, pure, genuine American."[94]

Despite Smith's ardent efforts to focus the campaign on national issues, the editors of the Catholic periodical *America* lamented on the eve of the election, people would vote for or against him chiefly on "religious grounds."[95] A month after Hoover defeated Smith 58 to 41 percent in the popular vote, John Ryan, the director of the Department of Social Action of the National Catholic Welfare Conference, argued that Smith had lost primarily because of his religious affiliation. Ryan admitted that Prohibition, prosperity, party loyalty, and social and cultural prejudice had all played a role in Smith's defeat. Some had voted against the New York governor because he wanted to repeal Prohibition, the economy was thriving, they were loyal Republicans, Smith was not a college graduate, or they disliked his connection with Tammany Hall. Nevertheless, Ryan, maintained, "substantially all" the journalists who had covered the campaign concluded that Smith's religious affiliation was the principal reason he had lost.[96] Their religious intolerance prompted many, especially southerners and midwesterners, to vote against Smith. Ryan asserted that the religious factor had been injected into the campaign in three major ways. "The crudest and coarsest form" was pamphlets, cards, and newspapers with titles such as "Three Keys to Hell," "Rum, Romanism, and Ruin," and "Thirty Reasons Why a Protestant Should Not Vote for Alcohol Smith." A second way Republicans exploited the religious animosity against Smith was illustrated by an article by Methodist bishop James Cannon, Jr. titled "Is Southern Protestantism More Intolerant than Romanism?" Cannon alleged that Catholics taught that Protestants could not be saved, that the US government was morally obligated to "profess and promote" Catholicism, and that all non-Catholic marriages were adulterous and the children of such marriages were illegitimate. Moreover, the pope had reportedly branded public schools " 'a damnable heresy.' "[97] The *Christian Century*, Ryan argued, illustrated the third method of inserting religion into the campaign. In October its editors defended the right of Protestants to vote against Smith on the grounds that his election would place "an alien culture," "an undemocratic hierarchy," and "a foreign potentate" in the Oval Office.[98] If a theologically "liberal" journal thought that a Catholic president would ignore the separation of church and state, Ryan contended, then thousands of other educated Protestants probably did as well. Its editors also claimed that the Catholic Church would "go to the polls almost as one man and vote for Mr. Smith." Ryan countered that he knew of no bishop or priest who had advocated Smith's election either from the pulpit or in any other public or official manner. Moreover, many "very prominent Catholics" had endorsed Hoover and a substantial number of Catholics had voted for him. Ryan alleged that while thousands of Protestants voted against Smith, "not one [Catholic] voted against Mr. Hoover." Instead, Catholics had supported Smith because of his party affiliation or his policies or because they wanted "to vote for a fellow Catholic, or because they resented the effort to defeat him on account of his religion, or because they wished to disprove and destroy the unwritten tradition that no Catholic is fit to be or can be elected President."[99]

Hoover's perspective of the election's results was very different. He argued that the issues that defeated Smith were prosperity, Prohibition, the Republican Party's agricultural policies, and the Democrat's defense of Tammany Hall. "Had he been a Protestant, he would certainly have [still] lost and might have even had a smaller vote." The religious issue may have helped Republicans win four or five southern states, but even in them, Hoover contended, Prohibition and Smith's relationship with Tammany Hall were more important.[100] In fact, because party loyalty trumped religious animosity, Smith won more states in the South—the nation's most anti-Catholic region—than in any other section.[101]

Although Smith's Catholicism cost him votes, Hoover's victory was probably due more to his personal popularity, "Republican prosperity," his stance on Prohibition, and Smith's ineffective campaigning. Hoover was not a charismatic person or an effective speaker, but he was greatly admired and phenomenally popular. He also benefited substantially from the general affluence of the 1920s, which was associated with his Republican predecessors. During the campaign, "wets" and "drys" waged fierce battles at the state and local levels that helped Hoover more than Smith. The governor's New York City background and thick East Side accent made him unappealing to many rural Americans. Although he inspired more affection than Hoover, they differed on few substantive issues.[102] Given Hoover's reputation, the nation's prosperity, and the strength of the Republican Party, "probably no Democrat could have beaten the postwar Superman" in 1928.[103] Ironically, many evangelicals voted for Hoover, whose theological views were similar to liberal Protestants, rather than Smith who probably could have affirmed the five points of Fundamentalism.[104]

Relations with Religious Groups

Hoover's stance on Prohibition, contacts with the executives of the Federal Council of Churches of Christ, and personal friendships with key religious leaders (most notably inspirational lay speaker Fred Smith; Daniel Poling, the editor of the *Christian Herald*; Methodist missions proponent John Mott; and social worker Raymond Robins) helped him maintain cordial relations with many Protestant bodies.[105] Poling, Smith, and Robins all campaigned extensively for Hoover's reelection.[106] Before becoming president, Hoover served as a vice-president of the Federal Council. As secretary of commerce, he worked with Council executives to pressure the steel industry to reduce its workday and defended the Council against attacks that its leaders' pacifism threatened the nation's security. While president, he met and corresponded regularly with Council officers. Their relationship became strained when the Council criticized American capitalism and some of Hoover's policies to combat the Depression.[107]

Numerous Protestant journalists and pastors lauded Hoover's character and many of his policies. Expressing the high regard some ministers had for Hoover, in December 1929, S. Parkes Cadman, the pastor of the prominent Central Congregationalist Church of Brooklyn, called the president the noblest politician since Lincoln. He extolled Hoover's moral ideals, integrity, and vast knowledge of world affairs.[108] In May 1931, the newly elected PCUSA moderator, Lewis Mudge, and retiring moderator, Hugh Thompson Kerr, lauded Hoover's "personal religious convictions" and his steadfast "observance of the law."[109] The General Conference of the Methodist Episcopal Church assured the president of their confidence in and prayers for him.[110] *The Christian Century* predicted that Hoover's administration would help destroy the political, economic, and social conventions that sustained "crass, unregenerate paganism" and enable the mind of Christ to "become the mind of the state."[111] Countless Protestant publications and dozens of denominations, local and regional religious bodies, women's groups, and ministerial associations commended his efforts to reduce armaments, promote peace, and enforce Prohibition.[112]

Like other twentieth-century presidents, Hoover was deluged with requests from religious constituencies asking for special messages and greetings, meetings, statements expressing his support for their fund-raising projects, and even personal donations. The Quaker sent statements to hundreds of individual congregations, pastors, priests, and rabbis, congratulating them on significant anniversaries, new buildings, or twenty to fifty years of ministry.[113] He also met periodically with delegations from religious bodies. Hoover's secretary George Akerson stated that the president refused to endorse any effort to solicit money "no matter how worthy the object may be except in purely national emergencies."[114]

One of Hoover's messages—sent to the Lutheran Churches of America in 1930 to commemorate the 400th anniversary of the Augsburg Confession of Faith, the principal doctrinal statement of Lutheran denominations—created substantial controversy. His proclamation credited Lutherans with helping develop new conceptions of religion and government that contributed to the separation of church and state.[115] Catholic periodicals denounced the president's declaration as both inappropriate and inaccurate, prompting counterattacks in Protestant publications. Hundreds of letters poured into the White House both condemning and supporting the proclamation. John Burke, the executive director of the National Catholic Welfare Conference, alleged that Hoover had violated "the spirit, if not the letter, of his oath of office as President." Hoover should "respect the religious rights of all," instead of congratulating one particular religious body. Moreover, Burke claimed, "Luther was not a champion of the separation of Church and State, but a most arbitrary defender of state absolutism."[116] The editors of *The Lutheran Witness* defended Hoover's right to congratulate church bodies and criticized the efforts of the National Catholic Welfare Council to disseminate "propaganda," mold public opinion, and influence legislation. Reiterating the rhetoric of the 1928 election, they argued that the Catholic Church was "ceaselessly laboring to become a worldly power" and that Catholics considered the pope to be "the supreme temporal ruler."[117] Others insisted that presidents had the right to "express personal opinions on religious subjects."[118] Some newspapers complained that Hoover's remarks were "insulting," "ill-considered," and unfortunate, especially in light of the religious controversy the 1928 election had evoked.[119]

Both the animosity of the 1928 election and controversy over Hoover's greeting to American Lutherans made his relationship with Catholics less than cordial. Many Catholics chastised the Republican for not condemning religious bigotry during the campaign.[120] Catholics were insulted when Hoover met with his friend J. C. Penney after the election. The millionaire was the president of the Christian Herald Association, which had given James Cannon, who had misrepresented and vilified them during the campaign, its 1928 award for the most significant contribution to religious progress.[121]

Hoover could have improved his relationship with Catholics by appointing some of them to prominent political posts, but he failed to do so, an omission frequently deplored by the Catholic press. In 1929 rumors circulated that Catholic Colonel William Donovan had not been named attorney general because of pressure from the Ku Klux Klan and prohibitionists. The next year the National Catholic Welfare Conference protested that although Hoover had declared during the campaign that "religion has nothing to do with politics," he had appointed almost no Catholics to executive positions.[122] The New York *World* sarcastically noted that even though there were twenty million Catholics in the United States, Hoover could not find any who were qualified to serve in his administration.[123]

His efforts to enforce Prohibition and tactics to alleviate the Depression also caused tension between Hoover and Catholics. Their European backgrounds and attitudes toward liquor led most Catholics to oppose Prohibition. Many of them viewed it as a puritanical restriction of a morally acceptable and enjoyable behavior. Therefore, they had trouble understanding and respecting America's dry culture. In 1929 John Ryan attacked the "tyrannical provisions of the Volstead Law," suggesting that if the civil law contradicted the moral law, citizens were not compelled to obey it. Many Protestant publications fired back bellicose rejoinders.[124] Because they were more likely to be recent immigrants and to work in mills and factories in large cities, Catholics had higher levels of unemployment and suffered more from the Depression than Protestants. As conditions worsened, Catholic criticism of Hoover's policies intensified, most notably in the diatribes of radio preacher Father Charles Coughlin and Ryan's more reasoned attacks.[125] Ryan called for increased federal action to fight the Depression, an approach Hoover resisted. Ryan advocated many programs that the New Deal later adopted but Hoover rejected as interfering with individual initiative and voluntary government–business cooperation.[126]

Although Hoover sent greetings to Jewish organizations, publicly recognized their holy days, and acknowledged their desire to obtain Palestine as a homeland, he never established cordial relationships with Jews or won many Jewish votes. Many Jews were political liberals who were repulsed by his economic and social conservatism.[127]

Public Policies

Hoover was not only the first Quaker but also the first man born west of the Mississippi River, the first engineer, and the first businessman to serve as the nation's chief executive. He brought more administrative experience and expertise to the office than any of his predecessors. Only Thomas Jefferson had interests as diverse as his. A member of a religious tradition that exalted humility, simplicity, and pacifism, Hoover was a highly honored multimillionaire, an activist, and the commander-in-chief of one of the world's most powerful militaries. The Republican was also one of America's most analytical, thoughtful presidents. He read extensively about the economics, morality, and culture of many nations.[128] Moreover, as an engineer, a mining company executive, and the head of two major relief programs, he spent time in Australia, Asia, Africa, Europe, and North America and learned firsthand about Chinese, Mongolian, Burmese, Russian, Arabic, and European customs and cultures.

In his inaugural address, Hoover announced the priorities of his administration—to increase equality of opportunity, stimulate individual initiative, ensure "absolute integrity in public affairs," encourage the "growth of religious spirit," strengthen the home, and advance peace. Hoover argued in 1932 that improving the health of children, increasing homeownership, and encouraging social and recreational agencies were "visible evidences of spiritual leadership in the Government."[129] In another address Hoover applied Christ's parable of the judgment of the sheep and goats in Matthew 25, usually interpreted as pertaining to individuals, to countries. No thoughtful politician could "forget the dramatic picture, drawn by the Great Teacher, of nations being sent away into torment because they had neglected the sick, naked, hungry, and unfortunate." In trying to provide for human welfare, governments, Hoover insisted, welcomed the assistance of religious groups, which upheld the "ideals of courage and charity, sympathy, honor, gentleness, goodness, and faith" (all of which were Quaker principles). The "life of the world cannot be saved," he contended, if its soul "is allowed to be lost." He urged churches to emphasize that "life does not consist in the abundance of things." They must also help the government "establish and maintain plain, simple righteousness" because history taught that "righteousness exalts nations and evil breaks them down."[130] The nation's problems, Hoover declared, were to "a much greater degree" moral and spiritual than they were economic. Many government policies, he added, had an impact on the moral and spiritual welfare of its citizens.[131] His administration organized more than thirty conferences and commissions, which made recommendations on diverse issues ranging from conserving timber to eradicating illiteracy and from increasing home ownership to improving the government of Haiti.[132] His efforts to aid children, blacks, and Native Americans, reform prisons, protect civil liberties, and promote world peace illustrate how Hoover's faith helped shape his policies.

In accepting the Republican nomination in 1928, Hoover, deeply affected by being orphaned at age 9, stressed that the "greatness of any nation, its freedom from poverty and crime, its aspirations and ideals" directly depended on how it cared for its children.[133] In the October 1928 issue of the *Woman's Home Companion* "thirty-seven leading women" explained why they were voting for Hoover. A major reason was his work with the Better Homes Movement to raise the national standard of living and his creation of the American Child Health Association that had saved the lives of tens of thousands of children.[134]

"The importance of the family as the unit for spiritual and social progress, and the spiritual values of family life," Hoover proclaimed, "cannot be over-estimated."[135] One of the most notable gatherings Hoover arranged was the White House Conference on Child Health and Protection, whose 2,500 delegates from federal, state, and municipal agencies and voluntary organizations met in November 1930. Its 35-volume report served for several decades as a handbook for social workers, helped inspire numerous state and city conferences and legislative action, and increased public awareness of the problems of children. The conference adopted a "Children's Charter." The first of its nineteen rights was for every child to have "spiritual and moral training." The conference focused on improving education for children, upgrading health services and recreational facilities, abolishing child labor, and reducing delinquency.[136] Hoover argued that producing a "generation of properly born, trained, educated, healthy children" would eradicate "a thousand other problems of government."[137] While parents had the primary responsibility for raising children, he maintained, government must help them, especially by providing a first-rate public education system. Even during the dark days of the Depression, he insisted that education must remain the country's principal priority.[138]

Quaker Queries demanded that Friends work "to insure equal opportunities in social and economic life for those who suffer discrimination because of race, creed or social class."[139] Quakers had done much to improve the treatment and conditions of both Indians and blacks. Faithful to his tradition, Hoover took numerous steps to aid these groups. Hoover's desire to help Indians sprang in part from his playing with Indian children when he lived with his uncle who was the United States Indian agent on the Osage Reservation in Arkansas.[140] Hoover deplored the poverty, illiteracy, alcoholism, and unemployment that plagued most reservations. The president appointed two Quakers, Charles Rhoads and J. Henry Scattergood, both Philadelphia bankers and philanthropists, as Commissioner and Assistant Commissioner of Indian Affairs. Although most historians argue that federal government policy toward Native Americans changed dramatically during the New Deal years under the leadership of John Collier, Collier insisted that the shift in recognizing Indian rights began during Hoover's presidency. Hoover's policy strove to transform Indians from wards of the government to independent, contributing citizens while allowing them to preserve their traditional culture. His administration helped Indians become better educated, fed, and clothed, healthier, and more self-sufficient. Despite the difficulties of the Depression, funding for the Bureau of Indian Affairs nearly doubled from 1928 to 1933. Rhoads sought to incorporate Native Americans more fully in the public educational system and to help them acquire vocational skills. Many reservation hospitals were modernized and better health services were provided for Indian children.[141]

As secretary of commerce, Hoover urged the Red Cross to employ more black staff in its efforts to aid victims of floods that ravaged the Mississippi delta in 1927. This disaster made Hoover much more aware of the plight of African-American sharecroppers in the South. He sought to persuade Chicago philanthropist Julius Rosenwald to finance a large-scale project to help the rural poor, especially blacks, buy the land they farmed, and after he became president he tried to convince foundations to support this plan.[142] Hoover applauded the efforts of the National Urban League to find jobs and provide training for southern migrants. He appointed an advisor on black economic development to the Commerce Department and desegregated the department (the only federal department to be desegregated in the 1920s), prompting a deluge of southern criticism. Unlike the majority of Americans in similar situations, when they lived in Washington, the Hoovers refused to sign a covenant restricting blacks and Jews from living in their neighborhood.

As president, Hoover took numerous steps to promote racial justice. Like nineteenth-century Quaker abolitionists, he repudiated discrimination based on race. Hoover denounced denying people employment on the "grounds of race, color or creed" as "abhorrent." He significantly enlarged the number of black federal government employees, strove to increase minority employment on public work projects, and created a federal program to increase literacy among blacks.[143] While recognizing that blacks deserved some government aid because of the effects of slavery and discrimination, consistent with his general economy philosophy, Hoover stressed self-help, equality of opportunity, and private philanthropy to uplift blacks. The Quaker publicly condemned lynching but proposed no legislation to abolish it.[144] He pardoned a black man convicted of murdering a white woman whose confession he thought had been coerced. Emulating the action of Theodore Roosevelt, Hoover invited Robert Moton, Booker T. Washington's successor as president of Tuskegee Institute in Alabama, to meet with him at the White House in May 1929. Hoover's wife caused considerable controversy in June by inviting Jessie DePriest, the wife of a black representative from Chicago, to tea for congressional wives at the White House. This incident, as well as Hoover's favorable treatment of blacks, was harshly condemned in the South. Leading newspapers censured her action; one headline declared: "Mrs. Hoover Defiles the White House."[145] The president praised the work of Tuskegee, Fisk University in Nashville, and Atlanta University and gave federal aid to Howard University in Washington to help it hire more faculty and gain accreditation for its law school.[146]

Although he strove to reduce discrimination and enhance opportunities for blacks, Hoover opposed full racial integration. Like most of his white contemporaries, Hoover espoused notions of racial inferiority. He considered Anglo-Saxons superior to all other groups. Moreover, the president was caught in the crossfire between the Tuskegee camp, which favored self-help, accommodation, and education, and the NAACP, which called for protest and political activism. Injustices in the military, discrimination against black workers on federal projects, and Hoover's efforts to end corruption in the Republican Party in the South, which led to the ouster of many black officials, irritated W. E. B. DuBois and other black leaders.[147] They complained that he was not moving quickly enough to help their race.

Hoover shared the passion of many Quakers for reforming America's prison system. During the nineteenth century, Quakers labored harder than any other group to improve the nation's treatment of prisoners. Hoover advocated rehabilitating rather than punishing offenders, providing job training, reducing overcrowding, and increasing supervised parole. Working with Sanford Bates, the head of the Bureau of Prisons established in 1930, Hoover pushed a five billion dollar penal reform program through Congress. Various bills created a National Board of Parole and a probation system for federal courts; placed medical services in prisons (which previously had been woefully inadequate) under the Public Health Service; separated prisoners by offense, character, sex, and likelihood of reform, most notably by creating separate prisons for violent offenders and reformatories for male juveniles and female offenders; and upgraded education and vocational training for prisoners. His administration built two new prisons, constructed two farms for drug addicts, founded a federal school for prison guards, and formed a new full-time prison board. The new facility at Lewisburg, Pennsylvania, which included a chapel and library, embodied his emphasis on humane treatment and rehabilitation. Moreover, the percentage of prisoners granted probation and parole increased substantially during his tenure.[148]

Hoover's defense of civil liberties is yet another aspect of his presidency that compels us "to look beyond the engineer to the Quaker" and his tradition's humane, reformist culture that respected human privacy and intellectual independence. Hoover refused to support attempts to ferret out suspected communists, arranged the release of communists who had peacefully picketed in front of the White House and radicals who had been imprisoned during the Red Scare, demanded an investigation of third-degree methods used by the police in the District of Columbia, and dismissed an assistant attorney general for sending spies to investigate prisons and houses of prostitution.[149]

Because of his work overseas as an engineer, his circling of the globe four times before 1914, direction of relief to war-ravaged Europeans (which led him to visit every nation in Europe), participation in the negotiation of the Versailles Treaty, and involvement in various aspects of foreign policy while secretary of commerce, Hoover came to the presidency with more experience in foreign affairs than any of his predecessors except John Quincy Adams. Moreover, he had visited numerous parts of every inhabited continent and had read widely about world history and geography and local customs.[150] Like other presidents, Hoover exercised his greatest power in foreign affairs.[151] The global depression, the political instability of China, Japan's invasion of Manchuria in 1931, the growing strength of the Soviet Union, the dramatic decline in world trade, the problems of reparations and war debts, high tariff barriers, and revolutions in Latin America confronted Hoover's administration with unparalleled foreign policy problems.[152] His foreign policy was guided by his belief that he was accountable to Congress, the American people, world opinion, and God.[153]

Strongly influenced by his personal experiences and the tenets of Quakerism, Hoover made achieving world peace one of his highest priorities. "I have witnessed as much of the horror and suffering of war as any other American," he told the Republican National Convention in 1928. "From it I have derived a deep passion for peace. Our foreign policy has one primary object, and that is peace." He argued that two factors helped maintain peace: "the building of good will by wise and sympathetic handling of international relations" and "adequate preparedness for defense. We must not only be just; we must be respected."[154] He explained in his *Memoirs* that he strove to "lead the United States in full cooperation with world moral forces to promote peace."[155] The Quaker appealed to all "followers of the Prince of Peace" to work for human brotherhood so that "the peace of God shall prevail in the lives of men."[156] His Quaker abhorrence of war, coupled with the horrors of World War I he witnessed, led him to urge nations to "wage peace continuously, with the same energy as they waged war."[157] Convinced that disarmament could only be achieved when peaceful relations existed among nations, he worked tirelessly to develop them. He called for resolving national disputes through arbitration, treaties, and international organizations, promoted international trade, arranged conferences among countries, defended the sanctity of treaties, and called for the use of moral suasion rather than military intervention.[158] He campaigned to reduce offensive weapons and to increase the power of defensive ones to "insure greater protection from aggression."[159] Hoover announced that the United States was ready to reduce its naval armaments whenever other nations did the same.[160] Numerous denominations, the Federal Council of Churches, the *Christian Herald*, and Christian Endeavor passed resolutions or issued statements applauding the president's activities and accomplishments in promoting peace and decreasing arms.[161]

In accepting his party's nomination in 1932, Hoover stressed three major foreign policy achievements of his administration: the organization of the 1930 London Naval Treaty at which the United States, Great Britain, France, Italy, India, and Japan agreed to reduce naval armaments; the proposals made at the World Conference on Disarmament at Geneva to cut the world's armaments by one-third; and the transformation of the Kellogg-Briand Pact into an instrument to peacefully settle disputes "backed by definite mobilized world public opinion against aggression."[162] Hoover hoped that the naval treaty would help further reduce armaments and achieve a stable peace resting on defensive weapons. Unfortunately, both foreign leaders and his own military experts rejected Hoover's proposal at Geneva for arms reductions. Contradicting the facts, Hoover claimed in a 1932 radio address that because of the work of his administration, the impact of the Kellogg-Briand Pact had been greater than was "contemplated at the time of its inauguration."[163] In his *Memoirs* Hoover insisted that his administration had also established more friendly relations with Latin America, promoted "pacific methods of settling controversies between nations," emphasized arbitration and conciliation, employed peaceful means to restrain Japanese aggression in China, worked to limit naval vessels and armies, and fostered international cooperation to ameliorate the Depression through declaring a moratorium on war debts and hosting a conference that stabilized currencies and reduced trade barriers.[164]

Hoover sought to increase international understanding, goodwill, and collaboration to ensure stability, security, and peace and to prevent nations from resorting to threats or coercion. He claimed in 1929 that the world had its best opportunity in the past half century to attain peace.[165] At least in the Western hemisphere, Hoover argued, public opinion could "check violence," and he refused to use military force to promote "abstract ideals."[166] Real peace, he contended, required more than signing documents promising not to wage war. It demanded well-conceived, "unremitting, courageous campaigns," fought on "a hundred fronts."[167] If the Kellogg-Briand Pact was to be more than "another pious gesture," it must be supported "by practical and sincere measures," especially the reduction of weapons.[168]

Although his Secretary of State Henry Stimson and others called him a "pacifist President," Hoover maintained that military strength was necessary to deter aggression and that force at times might be necessary, especially to defend the United States against attack. Pacifism, he warned, courted danger "by promoting weakness."[169] Rejecting a "peace-at-any price" mentality, Hoover insisted that both peace and justice were important.[170] "We, as a nation whose independence, liberties, and securities were born of war, cannot contend that there never is or never will be righteous cause for war."[171] Only those nations that were "adequately prepared to defend themselves," he averred, could enjoy peace.[172] To guarantee peace, he argued, the United States must build a "defense that is impregnable yet contains no threat of aggression." Such statements prompted *The Nation* to deprecate him as a "sham Quaker."[173]

While accentuating military preparedness, Hoover's approach to foreign relations was guided by his Quaker convictions and commitment to use moral persuasion rather than force to deter aggression. When Japan invaded Manchuria in 1931, he urged other nations to refuse to recognize territory seized by force to pressure Japanese leaders to acknowledge the immorality of their action. Stimson helped convince the League of Nations to condemn Japanese aggression, prompting Japan to withdraw its membership. Nevertheless, many scholars argue that if Hoover had opposed Japan's takeover of Manchuria more strongly, the United States might have been able to avoid war with Japan in the 1940s.[174]

In Latin America, Hoover refused to resort to the gunboat diplomacy the United States had practiced intermittingly since 1898. While touring the region between his election and inauguration, Hoover repeatedly promised that his administration would not interfere in Latin American affairs. Instead of trying to police its sister republics, the United States would promote their welfare. Hoover did not forcibly intervene in any Latin American countries, withdrew marines from Nicaragua ending twenty years of occupation, and significantly improved relations with countries in the region.[175]

In retrospect, Hoover's approach to attaining peace appears naïve and misguided. German and Japanese aggression in the 1930s and 1940s thwarted efforts to achieve a world where stability and security rested on moral suasion and spiritual conviction rather than the threat of force. Yet, given the widely shared assumptions of the late 1920s—that the build-up of arms had contributed significantly to World War I, that national resources were desperately needed to fight the problems of the Depression, and that reason would prevail over demagogues—Hoover's policies made sense. Had Adolf Hitler, Benito Mussolini, and warlords not seized control of Germany, Italy, and Japan, the world Hoover envisioned might have been created.

Hoover's approach to foreign policy, however, contained contradictions. On the one hand, he advocated free trade and supported the United States' participation in the League of Nations and the World Court, thus talking and behaving as an internationalist. On the other hand, he called for high tariffs, distrusted Europeans, believed Anglo-Saxons were superior to all other groups, and supported immigration restrictions, thereby functioning as an elitist and isolationist. Yet, Alexander DeConde concludes, he "probably acted with no greater inconsistency in foreign policy than did most presidents." To his credit, Hoover "adhered to a strict constitutional interpretation of his office" and did not seek to expand his powers in foreign relations to achieve "national security, international stability, peace, or any other ambiguous ideal." His opposition to imperialism, unwillingness to enlarge his own power under the guise of protecting American interests, and refusal to intervene militarily in the affairs of other nations was principled, judicious, and in many ways beneficial. He did not undertake "any belligerent, ideological foreign crusade" or forcefully interfere in any country. Despite tremendous temptations, he did not use "his power in foreign relations to offset his domestic troubles."[176]

While his Quaker heritage and convictions strongly influenced Hoover's efforts to improve the lives of children, blacks, and Native Americans, reform prisons, safeguard civil liberties, and advance world peace, all of these goals were also promoted by liberal Protestants, especially advocates of the Social Gospel. Led by Walter Rauschenbusch and Washington Gladden, this move-ment flourished between 1890 and 1920 as its proponents combated a wide variety of industrial, social, and political problems. Although the movement declined in strength after 1925, many liberal Protestants continue to work vig-orously to improve social conditions, help the impoverished, end racial dis-crimination, reduce armaments, and further global peace. As noted, Hoover, as both secretary of commerce and president, enjoyed cordial relations with many liberal Protestant leaders, including the executives of the Federal Council of Churches, and he served as a council vice president prior to being elected the nation's chief executive. Hoover shared Protestant liberals' opti-mism about social progress and human nature and the ability of education and social reform to create a better world. Like them, Hoover believed that Christianity must be adapted to the progressive spirit of the twentieth cen-tury. Moreover, Hoover agreed with Protestant liberals that reason and experi-ence provided the best basis for knowledge, that Christianity was primarily an ethical way of living, and that Christianity needed to be made "credible and socially relevant to contemporary people."[177]

The 1920s was the heyday of Protestant liberalism as its theology and empha-ses became dominant in the Federal Council, *Christian Century*, many main-line denominations (especially Congregationalists, Methodists, Episcopalians, and Presbyterians), and among the faculties of the nation's most prestigious seminaries, especially Union, Chicago, Harvard, Yale, Princeton, and Boston University. In the 1920s Social Gospelers created a variety of social justice orga-nizations and peace fellowships to promote their principal aims.[178] Illustrative of the times, in the early 1930s, an interdenominational conference of ministers in

Ohio lambasted "the whole war system" and advocated an egalitarian economic system based on "cooperative industry, government regulation or government ownership." "The social conception of Christianity commands the sympathy, if not the adherence, of practically the entire Protestant ministry," Charles Clayton Morrison, the editor of *Christian Century*, claimed in 1933. In every northern Methodist, Baptist, and Presbyterian seminary and in all Congregational and Disciples of Christ seminaries, the Social Gospel was "taken for granted."[179] While Protestant laypeople had not accepted the tenets and priorities of social Christianity and theological liberalism to the extent the clergy had, numerous Protestant liberals held prominent positions in all branches of the federal government, many state governments, the business community, and the country's foremost educational and cultural institutions. By the mid-1930s, liberalism was under attack by Reinhold Niebuhr and other proponents of neo-Orthodoxy, and its leaders, including Harry Emerson Fosdick, were admitting that liberalism had gone too far in trying to accommodate the gospel message to contemporary society.[180] Nevertheless, in its period of ascendancy, it had a powerful impact on American society and government, including on Hoover and his successor Franklin Roosevelt.

The Election of 1932

Many factors contributed to Hoover's defeat by Franklin Roosevelt in the 1932 election—his poor relationship with Catholics, ineffective campaigning, lackluster speeches, and, most significantly, the Depression. He did little in his four years in office to improve his relationship with Catholics, which the 1928 election had substantially damaged. As noted, he appointed few Catholics to administrative posts and pursued several key policies Catholics disliked.[181] To improve Catholic perceptions of him, Hoover spoke at the unveiling of a statue of James Cardinal Gibbons in Washington in July 1932. He lauded Gibbons as "a great leader in his faith" and an "unfailing friend" of movements for social betterment.[182] This token gesture did little to appease Catholics, still smarting from the tactics used against Smith in 1928, and many worked to defeat Hoover in 1932.[183] A government official complained in October that in Maryland and Washington, DC, Catholic priests were exhorting parishioners to do everything possible "as a duty to the Pope to kick the rascals out."[184] The Louisville *Courier-Journal* accused the Hoover campaign of reviving the "bigotry crusade" it had used "so shamelessly" against Smith four years earlier. The editors denounced a publication of the Ku Klux Klan for effusively praising Hoover, harshly denouncing Roosevelt "as a tool of the Pope," and appealing "to dry Protestants to save the country from the curse of 'Rum and Romanism'" by reelecting the president.[185] Some prominent Catholics complained that Hoover's individualism conflicted with recent papal encyclicals on social issues.[186] Moreover, as governor of New York, Roosevelt had developed cordial relationships with numerous Catholics.

As they had in 1928, many Protestants supported Hoover because his opponent, Roosevelt in this case, favored the repeal of Prohibition.[187] Some preferred Hoover for other reasons. The *Christian Century* endorsed the president, praising his character and arguing that he was better equipped than Roosevelt to guide the nation out of the Depression. The editors extolled his promotion of peace and insisted that his policies would likely produce good results in his second term.[188] Hoover had ended American imperialism in Latin America, devised a plan to cooperate with the League of Nations if a crisis threatened, and had pledged not to recognize any territory seized by force.[189] Roosevelt offered no substantive criticisms of Hoover or compelling alternative policies and did not seem dedicated to pursuing world peace.[190] In all American history, the editors claimed, "no candidate spoke so much and committed himself to so little as did Mr. Roosevelt."[191] The *Jewish Leader* also endorsed Hoover. The president was not responsible for the Depression, and he had taken wise steps to fight it, which were beginning to bear fruit. Roosevelt had not dealt effectively with New York's economic problems, used vague rhetoric, and proposed no new ideas. Nothing pointed to his being a "great economist, statesman, [or] leader."[192]

Some religious leaders insisted that both Hoover and Roosevelt were "men of Christian faith" who publicly confessed "their reliance upon God." The *Presbyterian* lauded the outstanding character of both candidates.[193] However, numerous editors and clergy found it difficult to enthusiastically support either Hoover or Roosevelt. They argued that both party conventions made promises the candidates could not keep and displayed little moral passion or understanding "of the true principles that shape a nation's life."[194] Hoover pointed out that Roosevelt had not explained how he would create jobs, reduce tariffs, balance the budget, or stabilize the international system.[195] However, the president's speeches, which were full of "platitudes, homilies, and endless statistics," did little to inspire voters.[196] Writing in *The Nation*, Oswald Garrison Villard denounced both Hoover and Roosevelt as militarists who wanted to build a bigger navy and urged those who wanted peace to vote for socialist candidate Norman Thomas.[197]

The most significant reason Hoover lost in 1932 was that many Americans blamed him for the Depression or thought he had done too little to combat it. Exaggerating only slightly, Fred Smith, chair of the World Alliance for

International Friendship Through the Churches, wrote Hoover: "If you had been the chiefest angel from Heaven and you had had the certified keys of Heaven, the result would have not been very different than it was."[198]

Final Assessment

Throughout his long life, even during his darkest days as president, Hoover remained an optimist. In his inaugural address he declared, "I have an abiding faith" in the "capacity, integrity, and high purpose" of the American people. Almost everything he wrote or said expressed his belief "in the progress and perfectibility of America." Neither the carnage of war, the impact of the Great Depression, nor his own political struggles could destroy his sanguine perspective of life. His Quakerism "enabled him to blend the practical and the ideal."[199] Hoover was a highly respected engineer, an exceptional humanitarian, an astute social manager, a devoted public servant, and a prominent proponent of peace. His solid administrative skills, intellectual vigor, boundless energy, and strong sense of calling enabled him to achieve success in both business and government. He exemplified persistence and moral principles, especially integrity. Glen Jeansonne reports that in seven years of research, he found no "deliberate, self-serving" lies that Hoover told as president. Hoover was modest, kind, sincere, and unselfish—"traits common in his fellow Quakers but almost extinct in politicians." Compassion and desire to help others, not craving of power, motivated Hoover's public service.[200] Addicted to hard work, rigidly self-disciplined, and motivated by spiritual idealism, Hoover was often gruff, usually very serious and stubborn, and rarely seemed to be enjoying himself.[201] Historians have labeled the Republican "unusually intelligent," "perceptive," and "a dedicated defender of free enterprise and local initiative."[202] To Eugene Lyons, Hoover espoused "a peculiarly American brand" of individualism and uncompromisingly defended personal freedom.[203]

Although Hoover had warm humanitarian impulses, his scientific background led him to be motivated primarily by hard data.[204] His effort to weigh all the costs and benefits often produced solidly constructed programs, but it also led to caution and delay, which caused problems when the Depression engulfed America. Some complained that he was "overly sensitive to criticism, humorless, insecure, inflexible, unforgiving, doctrinaire, and self-righteous."[205] To his detractors, Hoover was "a dour, complacent, and reactionary figure" who could not "grasp the problems of his age" and willfully sacrificed "human welfare on the altar of an outmoded antistatism."[206] He had "no sense of social justice, no tenderness or sympathy," and far worse, no sense of reality. Either "ignorant or woefully behind the times," he espoused a "hollow and shallow" political philosophy.[207] Kinder critics saw Hoover as a "deep social thinker," but "a failed statesman."[208] While Hoover's earlier labors had made him renowned as a great humanitarian, when he left the White House many considered him to be cold and indifferent to the plight of suffering Americans. His stoicism, lack of outward emotion, and inability to effectively communicate his compassion all contributed to this view.[209]

Several personal traits hampered Hoover's performance as a president. Because of his personality and experience, he saw the president as more of an administrator than a leader.[210] Hoover was unable to winsomely convey the principles and policies he championed. He was a poor speaker, who, unlike Franklin Roosevelt, did not help suffering Americans overcome their despondency and despair. As the *Christian Century* put it in 1931, while the nation needed "leadership with a ringing voice," Hoover spoke as though "he were addressing a director's meeting."[211] His Quaker belief in hard work and perseverance, strengthened by his experiences as an engineer and a relief administrator, led him to conclude that he would succeed if he just worked hard enough, which was both "his greatest strength as a professional and his greatest liability as a human being."[212] By temperament and training, he disliked the negotiation, trading, and bargaining often crucial to political success.[213] His personality, high regard for principles, and belief that rational analysis provided the best solutions inhibited Hoover's willingness to compromise on issues and hampered his effectiveness as president.[214]

"Why did an American president who entered office with such high qualifications" and great accomplishments, asks Martin Fausold, "leave with such a reversed image?" Why was this negative image "so overwhelming and long-lasting?" Hoover was long remembered as a stoic, aloof political reactionary who, if he did not cause the Great Depression, did little to abate it. For the next fifty years, Democratic presidential candidates seemed to run against Hoover. Fausold concludes that many Americans disliked Hoover so intensely because he refused to "make the kinds of accommodation with the statist spirit" that they, Hoover's political opponents, and even some of his own associates made. Hoover's strong opposition to the New Deal rested largely on his belief in "ordered freedom," which was rooted principally in his Quakerism. His commitment to this philosophy increased as he moved from one phase of his life to the next. It provided a foundation for his career in business and engineering, helped him synthesize "New Nationalist and New Freedom thought" during his relief work in the 1910s, supplied the primary theme of *American Individualism*, guided his work as secretary of commerce, and served as "the essence of his presidency."[215] To revitalize the American economy, Hoover advocated three key Quaker virtues—greater thrift, simplicity of desire, and neighborly charity.[216] His Quaker convictions led him to emphasize self-help, community involvement, and private relief.[217] His calls for friendly coopera- tion and self-sacrifice, however, fell largely on deaf ears. While Hoover sought to craft a self-governing community, many Americans implored the govern- ment to save them. The Depression destroyed his plan to create a "socially responsible corporatism based on voluntarism and associationalism among countervailing business, labor, and farm groups." However, most citizens refused to abandon materialism or embrace cooperative individualism.[218] The editors of *Christian Century* denounced Hoover's "exaggerated individualism." While demanding that everyone receive a "fair start," he failed to recognize that the race still belonged "to the swift and the battle to the strong." The chief executive needed to move beyond his "purely individualistic point of view" and acknowledge that individual enterprise was not the "source from which all blessings flow for society." Giving everyone a fair chance to obtain society's prizes was insufficient; they must be distributed more equitably.[219]

On the eve of his inauguration, Hoover confided to the editor of the *Christian Science Monitor* that he was troubled by the public perception that he was "a sort of superman" for whom "no problem" was beyond his capacity. "If some unprecedented calamity should come upon the nation," he declared, "I would be sacrificed to the unreasoning disappointment of people who expected too much."[220] The "unprecedented calamity" Hoover feared came in the form of the nation's worst economic downturn. Three major arguments have been advanced to defend his administration's response to the Depression: it was extensive and without precedent; American capitalism contributed as much to the failure to revive the economy as did Hoover's leadership; and probably no president elected in 1928 could have successfully dealt with the Depression. Nevertheless, Hoover's closest political associates, the majority of Americans during the fifty years following his presidency, and most contemporary his- torians all contend that the Quaker's presidency was a failure because of his flawed response to the Depression.[221] The Federal Council of Churches claimed that capitalism had failed, and *Time* magazine labeled the Republican "President Reject." Americans coined new terms: "Hoovervilles"—the tin and cardboard shacks of the destitute; "Hoover hogs"—armadillos fit for eating; "Hoover flags"—empty pockets turned inside out; and "Hoover blankets"— newspapers that covered homeless people sleeping in alleys. The president was booed lustily at the 1931 World Series and made the butt of dozens of jokes. The man who saved more Europeans from starvation than Hitler and Stalin murdered, drove to his last speech in the 1932 campaign as crowds of angry New Yorkers chanted, "We want bread." When the president went to vote in San Francisco, the crowd spitefully set off stink bombs as his entourage moved up Market Street. A vindictive Republican congressman introduced an impeachment resolution after Hoover had already lost his bid for reelection, which the House defeated.[222]

Others evaluate Hoover's presidency much more favorably. Vaughn Davis Bornet and Edgar Eugene Robinson praise him as an enemy of war and armaments, a "friend of constitutional government," a supporter of voluntarism, and a "preserver of a partially regulated capitalist system" that held its own against such rival ideologies as fascism, socialism, and communism. Above all else, Hoover was "a determined spokesman for the traditional American virtues, hopes, and ideals of individual opportunity, personal freedom, and love of country."[223] Bornet argues that his "intelligence, energy, fidelity to duty," and "determination to serve the best interests" of Americans made Hoover an "uncommon President."[224]

Hoover was "a quintessential problem solver," but he rejected the idea that federal government could solve all the nation's problems as "hopelessly utopian" and strongly opposed the expansion of government power.[225] The Republican argued that government-owned economic enterprises would be less efficient than those of private groups and feared that a powerful federal government would restrict human freedom. A centralized bureaucracy was likely to be increasingly irresponsive, irresponsible, and manipulative.[226] In addition, once created, new government programs would be very hard to eliminate because they would create constituencies that benefited from their services. During the Depression, however, most Americans were much more concerned about their immediate woes than potential long-term problems. Hoover tried to pilot the ship of the nation between the rocks of "unrestricted laissez faire on the one hand and socialism on the other," but it crashed on the shoals of the Depression. Had devastating economic conditions not intervened, the result might have been quite different. As James Olson argues, "During a period of relative prosperity, Herbert Hoover would likely have been one of America's greatest presidents, for his sophisticated understanding of corporate, industrial, and bureaucratic realities would have permitted him to regulate the economy and restrain the federal government at the same time."[227] Despite his copious criticisms of the New Deal, some historians maintain that it was erected largely on the foundation the Quaker constructed.[228] Richard Norton Smith faults scholars for not recognizing the "intellectual and moral power of Hoover's position" and his commitment to defending the values he believed were best for the nation in the long run.[229]

Elected president in a landslide and revered as a national hero, the symbol of classical liberalism, and the fulfillment of the American dream, Hoover left office four years later as discredited and despised, but not disillusioned.[230] Inspired by Quaker principles and his own life experience, during his tenure he pursued progressive policies in child welfare, the treatment of blacks and Indians, penology, civil liberties, conservation of forests and petroleum, and public power (the Boulder Canyon Project, which produced the Hoover Dam, and the Grand Coulee Dam project on the Columbia River). He negotiated agreements between business and labor to preserve wages and prevent strikes, discouraged hoarding, arranged credit for farms and home mortgages, and created the Reconstruction Finance Corporation to aid banks and businesses. Historians have increasingly given Hoover high marks for his foreign policy, especially his quest to reduce naval armaments, ensure the economic stability of European governments, and improve relations with Latin American nations.[231] A prolific author, who devised and explained a coherent public philosophy, Hoover was arguably the greatest humanitarian in American history and an ardent defender of American ideals. It would be inaccurate to say that Hoover had a carefully constructed, clearly perceived Quaker theology that directed all his actions as a public servant. Yet, his childhood training in and adult practice of Quakerism, coupled with his words and deeds, suggest that this religious ideology had a significant influence upon his thought and policies. As Glen Jeansonne argues, "in the final analysis, his reputation rests more on his character than on his achievements, less on what he did than who he was."[232]

It is ironic that a man who was his era's most renowned humanitarian, who spent much of his public career effectively leading enormous relief projects in Europe, Russia, and the Mississippi delta, became so widely associated with the pain and privation of the Great Depression. However, Hoover lived thirty-one years after leaving office (longer than any other president other than Jimmy Carter), contributing to American life in many ways and resuscitating his reputation. He wrote scores of articles and numerous books (ten between the ages of 75 and 90 alone). Hoover directed efforts to provide food for thirty-eight nations during the world famine after World War II. He helped created Care, Inc. in 1945, which today works in more than seventy nations to end poverty. The ex-president chaired two bipartisan commissions to reorganize the executive branch of the federal government. Hoover helped establish the Food Research Institute at Stanford University to conduct scientific studies in this field and helped found the Graduate School of Business at Stanford to train leaders for business and industry. He also created the Hoover Institution on War, Revolution and Peace. The Quaker organized the White House Conference on Child Health, chaired the Boys' Clubs of America, was awarded ninety honorary degrees, and by his death in 1964 once again had become a living embodiment of American compassion and generosity.[233]

7

Harry S. Truman

THE GOLDEN RULE PRESIDENT

*As I have assumed my heavy duties, I humbly pray Almighty
God, in the words of King Solomon: "Give therefore thy servant an understanding heart to judge thy people, that I may
discern between good and bad; for who is able to judge this thy
so great a people?" I ask only to be a good and faithful servant
of my Lord and my people.*

"ADDRESS TO CONGRESS," April 16, 1945

*Though we may meet setbacks from time to time, we shall
not relent in our efforts to bring the Golden Rule into . . .
international affairs.*

"ADDRESS ON FOREIGN POLICY," October 27, 1945

*The good-neighbor policy, which guides the course of our
inter-American relations . . . is the application of the Golden
Rule.*

"ADDRESS IN MEXICO CITY," March 3, 1947

Introduction

Harry S. Truman's early life provided few hints that he would become the leader
of the free world. Born in 1884 to a farm family of modest means in Missouri,
he did not attend college (he was the only twentieth-century president who
did not graduate from college), failed to save his family's heavy-mortgaged
farm, and lost money in mining and oil investments. Prior to World War I,
his life was characterized by "drift and immaturity." After serving as a captain with the field artillery in France, he went bankrupt as a haberdasher, and
the Pendergast machine of Kansas City helped him procure a job as a county
judge.[1] Nevertheless, circumstances, combined with his character and work

ethic, led Truman to serve ten years as a US Senator, briefly as vice president, and as president for nearly eight years. As president, the Missouri native was often criticized as incompetent ("to err is Truman") and corrupt (because of his earlier Pendergast relationship and various scandals that rocked his second term), and he had very low public approval ratings. Nevertheless, Truman astonished pundits by winning the 1948 election, and since the 1970s, presidential scholars have ranked the Democrat highly.

Truman occupied the Oval Office during some of the most momentous years in American history. During his tenure, Germany and Japan surrendered, ending World War II. The Soviet Union extended its hegemony over Eastern Europe, and the Cold War began. Led by Mao Zedong, Communists seized control of China. Both the United Nations and NATO were created. Truman, David McCullough argues, "made more difficult and far-reaching decisions than any other president."[2] He decided to use the atomic bomb to defeat Japan, confronted the Soviets in Iran, proclaimed the Truman Doctrine (containment of Soviet expansion) that shaped American foreign policy until 1991, implemented the Marshall Plan to aid war-ravaged Europe, expanded government programs begun under the New Deal, desegregated the armed forces, recognized Israel, conducted the Berlin Airlift, and sent troops to fight in Korea.

Truman is rarely considered one of America's most religious presidents. This may be because most biographers have paid minimal attention to his faith and because of his well-known use of vulgar language. Ample evidence indicates, however, that the faith of America's second Baptist president was genuine and very meaningful and influenced him substantially. Simultaneously pious and profane, Truman had an unsophisticated understanding of Christianity and attended church irregularly as an adult, but he prayed daily for God's guidance and knew the Bible well. Jesus's example and teaching, especially His Sermon on the Mount, served as a basis for Truman's personal and professional life, guided his political philosophy, and helped shape his domestic and foreign policies. Arguably no American president used more biblical and religious rhetoric to justify his policies and promote American aims.[3] "Though not trained in theology," Truman held a "basic set of theological beliefs about God, morality, peace, freedom, and America's purpose in the world" that powerfully affected his actions.[4] Truman's "deep religious faith," as expressed in his private correspondence, addresses (to which he substantially contributed), proclamations, and news conferences, Elizabeth Edwards Spalding contends, helped inspire him "to confront communism and lead America into the Cold War." For Truman, winning this war ultimately depended more on religious values, communities, and organizations than on political alliances because he saw it as "fundamentally between the atheism of communist totalitarianism and the theism" of the free world.[5] William Inboden maintains that understanding Truman's faith "helps to explain why he opposed communism so relentlessly" and "sought to undermine the appeal and authority of communism so tenaciously."[6] As did many intellectuals during his presidency, scholars, when they have noticed Truman's religious rhetoric and biblically influenced approach to public policy, have pronounced it crude, misguided, and simplistic. His imprudent, Manichean approach to the Cold War, they maintain, hindered negotiations with the Soviets.[7]

The Faith of Harry Truman

Three of Truman's grandparents were Baptists, and the fourth, his mother's father, attended varied Protestant congregations in western Missouri. Truman emphasized that his family deplored religious hypocrites and "excessive" displays of spirituality. Truman's father John professed deep faith in God, and although neither he nor his wife was "active in the church," many of their family guidelines were based directly on Scripture.[8] His parents regularly took him to Sunday school at the First Presbyterian Church in Independence, Missouri, after moving there in 1890. There the 6-year-old Harry met the 5-year-old Virginia Elizabeth Wallace whom he would marry in 1919 and "learned all the good stories of the Old and New Testaments."[9] In high school compositions, Truman declared that the ideal man "should fear his God" and "love both his God and those around him."[10] At age 18, Truman was baptized in the Little Blue River by the pastor of a Baptist church in Kansas City to signify his acceptance of Christ as his savior. Both before and after joining this church, Truman worshipped most Sundays for many years.[11]

Numerous factors indicate that Truman had a strong faith: the testimony of pastors and friends, his own statements, his views of God, Christ, the Bible, prayer, human nature, and the afterlife, and his commendable character. Although his view of salvation stressed works more than faith, he shared most of the religious convictions of other mid-twentieth-century Southern Baptists. However, many of them, as well as other religious conservatives, complained about Truman's drinking habits, gambling, and coarse language.

Several individuals praised Truman's strong faith. "I have a very profound respect for the President's personal faith," declared Edward Pruden, the pastor of First Baptist Church in Washington, DC, which Truman attended occasionally while president.[12] Welbern Bowman, the minister of the First Baptist Church of Grandview, Missouri, to which Truman belonged for many years,

---

called him "a good Christian" who strongly affirmed Southern Baptist doctrine. H. L. Hunt, pastor of the First Baptist Church in Independence, labeled Truman "a staunch believer" who was "well versed in the Bible" and the denomination's theology.[13] Although Truman was not as outspoken about his faith as Dwight Eisenhower, Thomas Murray, a member of the Atomic Energy Commission, argued, he was "truly a religious man."[14]

As president, Truman repeatedly stressed that he "put his trust in Almighty God."[15] Responding to hundreds of letters Truman received about religious matters, his staff repeatedly stated that the president was "an earnest Christian" or "a religious, church going man."[16] For example, correspondence secretary William Hassett assured a prominent Methodist that Truman's "faithful attendance at public worship" testified to his reliance on "Divine Guidance."[17] Those who inquired about Truman's faith were often sent his addresses that discussed the importance of religion and spirituality.[18] Many ordinary Americans echoed the assessment of a couple from Mankato, Minnesota: "we firmly believe that you are a God-fearing and God-loving leader."[19]

God, Truman proclaimed, "is all seeing, all hearing and all knowing. Nothing, not even the sparrow or the smallest bug, escapes His notice." He insisted that God "will reward the righteous and punish the wrongdoers." In a statement that undoubtedly made his fellow Southern Baptists cringe, Truman avowed, "Jews, Mohammedans, Buddhists and Confucians worship the same God as the Christians."[20]

True to his Southern Baptist roots, Truman expressed an orthodox view of Christ, especially in his public statements about Good Friday and Christmas. He often referred to Jesus as "the savior of the world" and "our Lord."[21] Jesus, the president proclaimed, denounced religious display, accentuated the Ten Commandments, and reinforced the message of Amos, Isaiah, and Jeremiah.[22] Truman called Jesus the Redeemer and "the Way, the Truth, and the Life."[23] Christ's sacrifice on Calvary, he declared, demonstrated His immense love for humanity and provided a way "through which the whole human race can be saved." Christ was crucified to reconcile "countless millions" throughout the world "to the One Ever Living and True God."[24] In his 1952 Christmas message, Truman quoted John 3:16: "God so loved the world, that He gave His only begotten Son, that whosoever believeth in Him should not perish, but have everlasting life."[25] If Jesus returned to earth, Truman wrote privately that year, he would side with "the lowly and downtrodden." He would probably stand on a street corner and preach "tolerance, brother love and truth." For doing so, He would be stoned, "hanged or sent to a slave labor camp behind the iron curtain."[26]

However, Truman never explicitly explained whether he considered salvation to depend solely on people's acceptance of Christ as their savior and Lord. What Truman told his future wife in 1911 remained one of his core convictions: "I believe in people living what they believe and talking afterwards."[27] Religion, he insisted, should be practiced "on Wednesday and Thursday as well as Sunday."[28] When God weighed him on the scales of eternal justice, he told Bess in 1918, he hoped his good deeds would outweigh his bad ones.[29] "We must not only proclaim the Christian ideal," he wrote in 1948, "we must live it."[30] Given his respect for other religions and his emphasis on works, it seems unlikely that he thought that people must believe that Christ atoned for their sins on the cross to be saved.

"I'm a Baptist," Truman declared, because it provided "the shortest and most direct approach to God. I've never thought the Almighty is greatly interested in pomp and circumstance."[31] The president told the members of the Northern Baptist Convention in 1946 that he was "proud to be counted a Baptist by reason of personal conviction."[32] However, Truman highly valued other Christian traditions and argued that disagreements about how to interpret the Gospels and "controversies between sects and creeds" had caused many of the world's problems.[33]

Although his staff claimed that he "regularly attends services," Truman went to church only about once a month as president.[34] The Baptist offered several reasons why he did not go more frequently: the tremendous demands of his office; his feeling that he was on display; his presence brought many journalists and "curiosity seekers," which distracted other worshippers; and criticism that he attended church only to gain public approval. The main reason Truman worshipped sporadically was that his presidential responsibilities often interfered. "Reports and State papers pile up on me to such an extent that sometimes it is impossible for me to leave the house," the president explained, "but I go whenever I can."[35] In May 1948 he told Edward Pruden that he had wanted to attend First Baptist Church, "but I had to stay by the phone all day, hoping the rail strike would be settled before I had to take drastic measures."[36] He also complained that he could not attend church without feeling like being "on exhibit. So I do not go as often as I . . . want to. People ought to go to church to worship God—not to see some mortal."[37] A staffer declared that the president's "reluctance to turn" services "into a circus" sometimes deterred him from attending.[38] "I don't go to Church for show," Truman professed, or "to attract a crowd."[39] It was as difficult for him to be an ordinary, unobtrusive worshipper as it was for "a rich man to get into Heaven."[40] He also feared that many Americans thought he had "an ulterior motive" for attending church.[41] Truman's belief that churches did not accurately communicate the teachings of Jesus probably also limited his attendance. If Jesus returned, he wrote in 1952, "he'd be on the side of the persecuted around the world." He would not recognize his teachings "in Riverside or Trinity Churches in New York or First Baptist or Foundry Methodist Churches in Washington."[42]

Numerous Washington congregations invited Truman to worship with them. Clinton Howard urged Truman to attend church to help fulfill his prayer to "be a good and faithful servant of the Lord and my people," to "set a wholesome example" for other Americans, and to please "his venerable Baptist mother."[43] The pastor of the Metropolitan Baptist Church in Washington told Truman that his faithful church attendance would "mean much to all of us" and promised that he would "find refreshment and strength in public worship."[44] Truman chose to attend First Baptist Church, a church where he had worshipped frequently as a member of the House and Senate.[45] When in Washington, his wife and daughter attended St. Thomas Episcopal Church, and, as president, Truman went with them a few times.

Pruden argued that Truman's presence encouraged and fortified other worshippers at First Baptist and helped inspire all American Baptists as well as "the Christian forces of the world."[46] Despite his own sporadic attendance, Truman exhorted Americans to go to church. Promoting the Federal Council of Churches' Church Attendance Crusade in 1947, he argued that if people went to church for eight consecutive weeks, "the habit would become fixed."[47] In 1950 the president endorsed the theme of the Religion in American Life movement—"Take Your Problems to Church This Week—Millions Leave Them There."[48] In 1952 Truman applauded a series of television programs designed to motivate the 65 million Americans who did not attend church to do so.[49] By Truman's second term, various groups complained that Truman's irregular worship set a bad example.[50]

A journalist reported that "the President isn't perfunctory about his worship." Truman listened intensely, participated in responsive readings, and enjoyed the children's sermon.[51] Truman insisted that he went to church to "improve my familiarity with the Bible."[52] He told Pruden, "I get a lot of pleasure out of coming to church" and "I want to be treated like any other citizen." Truman hoped that his presence would not inhibit Pruden from freely expressing his convictions.[53] Although he disliked special attention, when the service ended, congregants remain seated until Truman, accompanied by secret service agents, left the church.[54] While in Germany to meet with Joseph Stalin and Winston Churchill at the Potsdam Conference in July 1945, Truman attended two services on Sunday—one led by a Protestant chaplain and the other led by a Catholic chaplain—prompting him to write to his wife, "I guess

I should stand in good with the Almighty for the coming week—and my how I'll need it."[55]

Truman claimed that he read the entire Bible "at least a dozen times" before age 15. He liked the Bible's stories; they were "about real people," some of whom he knew better than his actual acquaintances. Only by repeatedly reading the Scriptures could individuals understand their "full meaning."[56] Truman's mother claimed that he was a "thorough" student of the Bible.[57] After meeting with Truman in May 1949, Isaac Herzog, the chief rabbi of Israel, declared that the president "knows his Bible." Truman's thinking was "permeated with prophetic ideas," and the Bible provided "the fabric of his thought."[58] During their conversation, Time magazine reported, Truman, "who loves to trade Bible learning," and the rabbi swapped Old Testament passages for several minutes.[59]

His staff claimed that the Bible had long been a "source of strength and inspiration" for Truman.[60] The president declared that he formed most of his ideas about how the world operated very early in life from the Bible.[61] In numerous statements various Christian organizations issued, Truman urged Americans to read the Bible daily and to deeply ponder God's character, commands, and actions.[62] He believed that the Bible was historically accurate, displayed great reverence for its teachings, and cited it frequently to underscore political arguments. The Baptist consistently listed Exodus 20 (the Ten Commandments) and Matthew 5–7 (Christ's Sermon on the Mount) as his favorite passages. They provided, he insisted, the "best system of philosophy" and the "only fundamentally sound" moral code for public servants.[63] He often declared that the Bible supplied the answers "to all the questions" that baffled people.[64] "Every problem in the world today," Truman proclaimed in 1949, "could be solved" if individuals lived "by the principles of the ancient prophets and the Sermon on the Mount."[65] Practicing love, the essential "message of the Prince of Peace," would solve all the world's ills.[66] Truman also repeatedly cited Deuteronomy 5, which summarized the Decalogue and often quoted the first great commandment "thou shalt love the Lord thy God with all thine heart, and with all thy soul, and with all thy might."[67] In a 1948 statement for the American Bible Society, Truman asserted that the present age's "perplexing problems" could be remedied only by following the admonition of Micah 6:8 to act justly, love mercy, and walk humbly with God.[68] Only those raised to obey "the rules of the 20th chapter of Exodus, and the Sermon on the Mount," Truman maintained, would act ethically in private or public.[69]

Truman often declared that he greatly valued prayer and deeply appreciated people's prayers for him. He prayed every day that God would give him "strength and wisdom" to make critical decisions.[70] The day after he assumed office, he told the press corps: "Boys, if you ever pray, pray for me now."[71] In his 1949 inaugural address, Truman declared, "I need the help and prayers" of all Americans. The man from Missouri thanked citizens for their petitions on his behalf and professed to have an "abiding faith in the efficacy of prayer."[72] He told hundreds of groups and thousands of individuals "it means a lot to me to know that you" are "continually remembering me in your prayers."[73] "Never in the history of the country," Truman avowed in 1950, has a president needed people's support and prayers as much as "does the present occupant of the White House."[74] The only explanation for why things were going so well, the president wrote in his diary on May 27, 1945, was because of God. As he contemplated running for another term in 1952, Truman stated, "I'll know [what to do] when the time comes" because "God Almighty will guide me."[75]

Truman contended that he did not need an intermediary to approach God.[76] Moreover, he declared, "the Maker of Heaven and Earth" did not care about what words people used or where they prayed. God was not impressed by "forms and ceremonies" but by people's hearts and souls. Ordinary people could receive just as much help from God as the "panoplied occupants of any pulpit."[77]

His staff claimed that Truman's favorite prayer was the Lord's Prayer.[78] The president reported in 1950 that he had regularly said a particular prayer since his youth, and two years later it became public knowledge when it was included in a collection of his writings:

Oh, Almighty and Everlasting God, Creator of heaven, earth and the universe.

Help me to be, to think, to act what is right, because it is right; make me truthful, honest and honorable in all things; make me intellectually honest for the sake of right and honor and without thought of reward to me. Give me the ability to be charitable, forgiving and patient with my fellowmen—help me to understand their motives and their shortcomings—even as Thou understandest mine.[79]

As president, Truman proclaimed several national days of prayer. In declaring August 19, 1945, a day of thanksgiving for the end of World War II, Truman stated that God "has now brought us to this glorious day of triumph. Let us give thanks to Him" and dedicate "ourselves to follow in His ways to [achieve] a lasting and just peace and to [create] a better world."[80] In announcing July 4, 1952, as a national day of prayer, Truman maintained that Americans needed God's aid "to strengthen the foundations of peace and security." He urged

citizens to "beseech God to grant us wisdom to know" which course to follow "and strength and patience to pursue that course steadfastly." Americans
should also thank God "for His constant watchfulness" over them.[81]

Truman had a mixed view of human motives and actions. In private, he
frequently expressed a negative view of human nature. Sadly, he wrote, only
a small minority believes that "honor, ethics and right living" are "its own
reward."[82] After surveying the carnage in Germany in 1945, he wrote in his
diary that the Soviets had "looted every house left standing." "But Hitler did
the same thing to them. It is the Golden Rule in reverse." Unfortunately, "the
human animal is not able to put his moral thinking into practice!"[83] He complained the next year about Americans' "selfishness, greed, [and] jealousy."
Workers were grabbing all they could "by fair means or foul"; farmers were
"blackmarketing food," and "industry hoarded inventories."[84] Upset that he
had to lift price controls on meat, Truman wailed, "you deserted your president
for a mess of pottage." The president could not singlehandedly stop Americans
from "following Mammon instead of Almighty God."[85] On the other hand, he
called the human race an "excellent outfit" and insisted that most Americans
were "good," "honest," and "hardworking."[86] Shortly after Germany surrendered, he averred that "the combined thought and action" of "any race, creed
or nationality will always point in the Right Direction."[87] Truman's knowledge
of history also made him optimistic about human nature.[88] The Democrat,
Elizabeth Edwards Spalding argues, expected those who affirmed transcendent norms to develop good character and act morally.[89]

Truman frequently expressed his belief in heaven. While stationed in
France during World War I, he wrote to Bess that all churches "can do a
man a lot of good. I had a Presbyterian bringing up, a Baptist education, and
Episcopal leanings, so I reckon I ought to get to heaven somehow."[90] In eulogies and addresses, he rejoiced that various individuals had gone to heaven.[91]
He asserted that in order to gain "entrance into Heaven," Alfred Nobel established awards to honor those who did the most to promote peace. When people
reach "the gates of Heaven," the Baptist wrote in his diary in 1955, the "rank
and riches [they] enjoyed on this planet won't be of any value." While Truman
left no written description of his view of heaven, his daughter Margaret concluded that in heaven he expected to have "a good comfortable chair, a good
reading lamp, and lots of books around."[92]

Numerous people praised Truman's character. Many of his World War
I comrades applauded his moral standards and behavior.[93] Faithful to his
Baptist and Masonic commitments, Truman was never devious or disloyal.
The Missourian, Robert Ferrell contended, was an anomaly: "a modest, honest,
thrifty man" who held "the most powerful office in the world."[94] Scholars agree

that Truman was devoted to his wife and to their daughter.[95] His hundreds of letters to Bess testify to his love of his wife.[96] David McCullough contends that Truman's staff greatly admired "his courage, decisiveness, and fundamental honesty" and considered him an "uncommonly kind-hearted person."[97]

Truman is well known for asserting that "the buck stops here." He argued that the president should do what he thought was right rather than what was popular. "A man whose heart is in the right place" and was well informed, he reasoned, would generally make wise decisions, which would usually be viewed positively in the long run.[98] Would Moses have led the Israelites out of Egypt, would Jesus have preached the message he did, would Martin Luther have led the Reformation, if they had taken polls in Egypt, Israel, and Germany, Truman asked. To improve the world, audacious leaders must often ignore public opinion.[99]

While Truman served in the House and Senate, his political adversaries and critics attacked his earlier close association with the Pendergast machine in Kansas City. Truman claimed that Tom Pendergast never asked him to do anything dishonest,[100] and the FBI, his Republican opponents, and scholars have never found any conclusive evidence that he committed fraudulent acts.[101] William Pemberton argues that the incongruity of a rural, southern Baptist promoting "progressive government and remaining personally honest" while serving as part of a "corrupt big city machine" helped give Truman near folk hero status by the 1970s.[102]

While millions of Americans admired Truman's character, integrity, and religious convictions, many conservative Christians were upset by repeated reports of Truman's drinking, gambling, and swearing.[103] In August 1945 *Time* pictured the president playing poker and drinking whiskey with cronies while vacationing in Louisiana. Letters poured into the White House censuring Truman's behavior. A Tucson resident argued that the president's actions undercut efforts to fight gambling and "booze," the latter of which had huge financial costs, "blighted womanhood," and destroyed children. A college junior protested that by drinking and gambling and then praying for divine guidance, Truman mocked God. Others charged that gambling had led more Americans down the road to hell than any other activity. A Tennessean lamented that Truman's bad example thwarted his effort to convince a fellow businessman to quit drinking excessively; the man claimed that he was "no worse than the president."[104]

In October 1945 *Life* quoted Truman as saying that "his antidotes for trouble" included "a drink of bourbon."[105] This produced another flurry of condemnatory letters, many of which included clippings of articles about Truman's transgressions or pamphlets deploring the ills of liquor. "Do you think," asked a disgruntled Texan, that "DRINK and POKER PLAYING is" Christ's prescription for "a world seeking peace?" South Dakota Baptists accused Truman of "openly, proudly, and even flippantly" endorsing drinking. While praising Truman's "oft admitted faith in God," the California Southern Baptist Convention protested that his drinking of bourbon and poker playing clashed with Christian morality and spirituality. The Texas Baptist General Convention censured Truman's "attitude toward gambling and drinking."[106] Other Americans defended the president. The treasurer of Norfolk, Virginia, wished he could join Truman "in such harmless sociability," while another Norfolk resident invited the president to worship with Episcopalians who left matters of personal behavior to individual discretion.[107] "Don't let a little, ill-timed resolution, passed by the Texas Convention," wrote a pastor, affect "the conduct of your office." Florida Baptists "believe in you 100 percent."[108]

Books, newspaper columns, and magazine articles continued to publicize Truman's drinking, gambling, and coarse language, producing many more irate letters to the White House. After reading about Truman's "liquor-drinking, poker-playing, and profanity," a Methodist minister in North Carolina, who previously "had great hopes for a good Baptist brother in the White House," warned that God would not answer Americans' prayers for solving world problems if they did not "live above reproach" in their daily conduct. A woman chastised the president: "Prayer & Poker, God and mammon, the Lord's Word says you cannot serve both. From which are you retiring?" Residents of Alhambra, California, exhorted Truman to display the "courage of your lovely wife" and "turn down your glass when the liquor is flowing." A Methodist Sunday school class in Pembroke, Virginia, urged Truman to stop gambling and swearing "to set a worthy example as the leader of our country." A prominent Methodist accused Truman of hypocrisy for playing high stakes poker while criticizing the nation's gambling problems.[109]

After newspapers reported that Truman drank beer in a chili parlor in Kansas City in December 1950 and *Life* featured a picture of the incident a couple weeks later, the White House was again deluged with letters. Correspondents contended that Truman's actions encouraged others to use habit-forming drugs.[110] Shortly thereafter rumors circulated that the president began drinking at noon and by the evening could no longer make responsible decisions.[111] Many urged Truman to quit drinking. His staff refuted rumors that the president did "his work while under the influence of liquor." They reiterated that Truman was "a very devout man" who often beseeched Americans "to seek divine guidance."[112] Although some Baptists castigated the president for his "alleged poker playing and occasional drinks of bourbon," George Ray, pastor of the First Baptist Church in Key West, Florida, where Truman vacationed, argued, "he is at heart a better Christian than most of his critics."[113]

Truman's use of profanity is legendary. During his whistle-stop campaign in 1948, audiences often urged the president to "give 'em hell, Harry." Truman later claimed unconvincingly, "I never gave anybody hell. I just told the truth and they thought it was hell."[114] Truman occasionally used swear words in public and peppered his private speech, diary, and correspondence with profanity, especially "damn," "hell," "asinine," "SOB," and "bastards." For example, his diary entry of November 1, 1949, reads: "I have another hell of a day." Trying to motivate Congress to act had required him to kiss more butts of "S.O.B. so-called Democrats and left wing Republicans than all the Presidents put together."[115]

Truman found poker to be relaxing, enjoyed a glass of bourbon, and felt pushed to use coarse language by trying circumstances. While he frequently engaged in behaviors that conservative Baptists proscribed, Truman insisted that sound character and good deeds, not personal habits, were what counted. However, it is surprising that as president Truman did not act more circumspectly to strengthen his public image as a faithful Baptist and moral leader.

Some theologically conservative Christians were also troubled by Truman's active participation in Freemasonry, but they did not criticize him publicly. Although George Washington, Andrew Jackson, Theodore Roosevelt, and other earlier presidents had also been Freemasons, some fundamentalists and evangelicals denounced the secrecy and quasi-religious nature of this organization. Truman helped organize a lodge in Grandview in 1911 and served as its first president. Over the years, he held several other roles and even served as the Grand Master of the Grand Lodge of Missouri while a Senator. Truman received numerous masonic honors, including being awarded the 33rd degree of the Scottish Rite Masonry while he was president. He paid considerably more attention to lodge matters as president than to the activities of his home church in Grandview. Truman met with numerous masonic leaders and groups at the White House and congratulated many lodges celebrating milestones.[116] He relished the history, fellowship, rituals, and spiritual emphasis of the brotherhood and saw his deep devotion to the masons as consistent with his Christian faith.[117] "The foundation of your organization," Truman told masons in 1952, is the "first five books of Moses." He also repudiated the common charge that Freemasonry was based on "deep dark secrets."[118]

Religious Rhetoric

Truman used biblical and religious language, principles, and stories in hundreds of addresses and letters to defend assertions and bolster arguments. He continually called for a religious revival, insisted that as a Christian nation the United States had an obligation to serve God, emphasized God's providential direction of America, and invoked Scripture to challenge citizens to help the needy.

Truman frequently appealed for spiritual revitalization. The world's greatest need, he asserted in 1947, "is a renewal of faith."[119] "A moral and spiritual awakening" was necessary, Truman averred, to counter the "forces of selfishness and greed and intolerance" at home and abroad. No earthly problem could "withstand the flame of a genuine renewal of religious faith."[120] In 1948 he confided in his diary, "We need an Isaiah, John the Baptist, [or] Martin Luther" to bring a spiritual awakening—"may he come soon."[121] Truman's staff repeatedly emphasized that he passionately believed that a "revival of religion" was essential to the nation's well-being.[122] Nevertheless, hundreds of Americans exhorted him to do even more to achieve this end.[123] "If our President would come out boldly for God," wrote a Seattle woman, "wonderful" results would occur.[124] The editors of a Catholic newspaper urged readers to pressure Truman to speak out "for God and His cause" to prevent another war, stop the spread of communism, and get "God on our side."[125]

In a statement that would be hotly contested today, but caused little controversy at the time, Truman asserted that the United States "is a Christian Nation," as the Supreme Court stated in *Holy Trinity v. the United States* (1891). The Europeans who settled America "declared their faith in the Christian religion and made ample provision for its practice." "Our Founding Fathers," he proclaimed, "believed that God created this Nation." That Americans won their independence from Britain, Truman argued, was miraculous. The "faith and trust in God embodied in the Declaration of Independence and the Constitution," he added, "show that religion is deeply embedded in the American way of life." "In God We Trust," Truman trumpeted, proclaimed the nation's "civic and religious faith."[126]

This religious heritage, Truman maintained, imposed great responsibilities on Americans. It required them to "constantly strive for social justice" and to end "discrimination based upon race, creed, or national origin." It also demanded that Americans guarantee civil liberties, avoid self-righteousness, assist the needy, and "make the world a better place." Like many other American leaders, Truman thought the United States had "a special, privileged relationship" with God that involved both opportunities and obligations.

God held the United States to higher standards than other nations, Truman maintained, and like biblical Israel, its inhabitants would be more severely judged than other peoples because they had "less excuse for doing" wrong.[127]

Americans, Truman proclaimed, enjoyed numerous benefits, including prosperity and freedom, "because of the bounty of God." The nation's strength, unity, and resourcefulness were "intimately linked to the religious and moral character" of its citizens. Their many blessings should prompt Americans to ask if they were fulfilling their "moral obligations" including using their wealth and power to aid others. Truman urged citizens "to thank God for our heritage and our strength, and to ask Him for the grace and power to carry out His will in this troubled world."[128]

"Democracy," Truman contended, "is first and foremost a spiritual force." It rested on belief in God and moral principles. The structure of the American government, Truman added, owed "much to the democratic forms" and "experience of the Presbyterian church."[129] The American creed, which accentuates human dignity and freedom, Truman asserted, "is derived from the word of God." Because people are created in His image, they could effectively govern themselves.[130]

God created America and gave it "power and strength," Truman declared, to advance world peace. The United States must defend spiritual and moral values "against the vast forces of evil that seek to destroy them." If Americans fulfilled their calling, they could, like the Jews of Ezra's time, glorify God "for the victory of freedom and justice and peace."[131] God had sustained the Allies "in the dark days of grave danger" and enabled them to defeat the "forces of tyranny that sought to destroy His civilization." Truman thanked God that the Germans had failed to build an atomic bomb and that hundreds of thousands of Americans had been spared from harm by Japan's surrender before a land invasion was necessary. "God's help," Truman declared on September 1, 1945, had brought victory. His continued assistance would empower Americans to attain "peace and prosperity" for themselves and the world.[132] Like many other presidents, Truman was convinced that his focus on religion and spiritual values did not transgress "the time honored American tradition" of "the separation of church and state."[133]

Truman asserted in hundreds of speeches and letters that the church had a major responsibility for remedying social ills.[134] He challenged Americans to emulate the Old Testament prophets' passion for social justice.[135] Truman frequently cited the story of the Good Samaritan, the Golden Rule, and the parable of the sheep and goats to exhort citizens to aid others. "God forbid," the Baptist avowed, that Americans, blessed with "abundance unequaled by any other nation, should play the part of the Levite" who "passed by on the other side."[136] Truman rejoiced that many in every nation were living by "the principles of the good neighbor: the Golden Rule," which Jesus, Confucius, Buddha, and Muhammad all preached.[137] Science and religion, he asserted, both affirmed that Jesus's command to "do good to them that hate you" provided the platform for "democratic realism."[138] Christ's parable of the Last Judgment in Matthew 25, Truman declared, mandated that Americans help millions around the world who were still suffering "the miseries of war, destruction, and tyranny."[139] Christ's command to help "the least of these my brethren" required Christians to aid the starving throngs in Europe, Asia, and Africa.[140] "Let us resolve," he announced in his 1951 Christmas message, "to carry the gospel to the poor; heal the brokenhearted; preach deliverance to the captive; [and] give freedom to the slave."[141]

Truman also urged Americans to increase their charitable giving. The United States had achieved "unprecedented" prosperity following World War II, but the percentage of their income its citizens gave to charity had declined from 5.3 percent in 1932 to 1.6 percent in 1947. While tax revenues, personal savings, and spending on luxuries had risen substantially, charitable contributions had not. If Americans' prosperity only enhanced their "own personal satisfaction" and they did not significantly increase their support of "religious, educational and character building agencies," Truman argued, they would not deserve "the continued blessing of Providence."[142] The Missourian struggled financially for much of his life, but he donated as his means permitted "to an ever widening list of religious charitable and philanthropic undertakings."[143]

Truman also attacked racism and discrimination and urged people around the world to foster understanding, concord, and a global community of caring. Following "the teachings of our Savior," Truman asserted, the government must prohibit discrimination and seek to end the clash of class against class and nation against nation.[144] Belief in the fatherhood of God, he asserted, was the "only sure bed-rock of human brotherhood." Only those who accepted the "ideal of brotherhood" would work to eliminate prejudice, practice tolerance, and enhance harmony. Brotherhood, Truman insisted, was "not only a generous impulse, but also a divine command." The Baptist proposed legislation to "protect the rights of all citizens, to assure their equal participation in national life, and to reduce discrimination." Despite the United Nations' efforts to promote human rights, in some places people's fundamental rights were being denied and they were "being systematically persecuted for their religious beliefs." Thankfully, Truman argued, those who believed in God and human brotherhood refused "to worship the power of the state" or to consider their own nation or group above criticism. With God's help, he maintained, people could construct a world where everyone enjoyed "peace, freedom and justice."¹⁴⁵ "The atomic bomb," Truman announced in 1946, had "destroyed selfish nationalism" and isolationism "more completely than it razed an enemy city." In the atomic age, survival required acknowledging that God had "made of one blood all nations."¹⁴⁶

Truman also used scriptural principles to support his domestic policies. He denounced quotas for immigration ("there is neither Jew nor Greek, there is neither bond nor free . . . for ye are all one in Christ").¹⁴⁷ All the problems pertaining to wages and working conditions that caused strikes could be remedied, Truman argued, if people practiced the Golden Rule. If Americans genuinely believed in human brotherhood, Congress would not need "to pass a fair Employment Practices Act." "A truly religious fervor among our people," Truman asserted, would help establish national health, housing, and education programs and expand and improve the social security program.¹⁴⁸

Relations with Religious Groups

Although Truman considered the Baptist faith to be the best form of Christianity, his lack of religious dogmatism, interactions during World War I with individuals espousing various faiths, and friendships with a diverse group of people made him very ecumenically minded and religiously tolerant. Truman appointed numerous Catholics to his staff including William Hassett and several Jews including David Niles, Samuel Rosenman, and Max Lowenthal. He issued an executive order ending religious (and racial) discrimination in the Armed Forces and sought diplomatic recognition of the Vatican. While Truman's closest relationships were with Protestant leaders, he also strove to develop friendly associations with Catholics and Jews to strengthen their commitment to the Democratic Party and to gain their support for various policies, especially his moral crusade against communism.

Despite the controversies over Truman's personal behavior, many Americans were convinced that he could positively affect church attendance, religious practice, and spiritual vitality by his proclamations, endorsements, and actions. The president issued hundreds of statements to promote religious organizations, campaigns, and causes. Dozens of parachurch ministries and denominations invited Truman to speak at their meetings, and he addressed several religious bodies, most notably the Federal Council of Churches, the National Conference of Christians and Jews, and the Washington Pilgrimage of American Churchmen.

Truman met with numerous Protestant leaders and communicated frequently with the executives of the Federal Council of Churches (FCC). He applauded the FCC's sending of a delegation to meet with Japanese Christians in 1945.[149] He authorized a trip of FCC leaders to Germany in fall 1945 and heard a report from delegates in January 1946.[150] Truman also endorsed the FCC's proposal to appoint Protestant, Catholic, and Jewish clergy to serve as liaisons between the military government and the leaders of these faith communities in Germany.[151] More than 700 religious leaders signed the FCC's March 1948 petition to Congress urging passage of the Marshall Plan.[152] The next month several FCC executives met with Truman to discuss their "Positive Program for Peace."[153] In December 1950 the leaders of the National Council of Churches (NCC), formed by the merger of the FCC and several other national bodies, urged Truman to resist using atomic bombs in Korea "without regard for the larger moral and political considerations." They cautioned the United States "to guard against false pride and hatred" that could evoke "a holy or a preventive war."[154] Truman applauded the NCC's efforts to resettle 60,000 "victims of political tyranny" in the United States.[155] An administrative assistant argued in 1951 that the president "has had long and happy relations with the National Council."[156] Some theological conservatives chastised Truman for maintaining such close connections with the "modernist" leaders of the FCC who rejected the deity of Christ and the infallibility of the Bible.[157] A pastor in St. Petersburg, Florida, warned Truman that FCC executives were "religious apostates" who repudiated "all the great fundamentals of the Protestant faith that you as a Baptist profess to believe." How could the president "bless" an organization whose leaders were clearly "pro-Communist" and "dangerous to the welfare of our country"?[158]

Not surprisingly, Truman's closest spiritual confidants were Baptists. He and Edward Pruden exchanged numerous letters about church services, family matters, and political issues.[159] Pruden prayed at his inauguration, and the president occasionally praised his pastor's sermons.[160] Truman and Pruden met several times, although the president sometimes declined the pastor's requests to spend time together.[161] As the 1948 election approached, Pruden told Truman that he wanted "to make a few fighting campaign speeches," but he promised to limit his actions to "a good deal of praying."[162] The Missourian appreciated the lectures Pruden gave as he traveled the country as president of the American Baptist Convention in 1950 refuting claims that numerous members of the Truman administration were Communists.[163] Truman told Pruden that his prayers had helped sustain him when he explained America's Far East policy in 1951.[164]

Pruden's opposition to Truman's appointment of General Mark Clark as his personal representative to the Vatican in 1950 caused some friction in their relationship.[165] After an assassination attempt on November 1, 1950, the president did not again attend First Baptist Church. Pruden never knew whether this occurred because of their disagreement over Clark's appointment or the secret service's counsel that Truman avoid public places such as church sanctuaries. Pruden reported that when someone asked Truman one Sunday morning if he was going to church, the president replied, "No, my preacher and I have had a fight." Complaining later about the great "commotion some preachers had made about this Vatican appointment," Truman declared, "My preacher is the worst one of all."[166]

Truman enjoyed a warm relationship with Daniel Poling, who was editor of the *Christian Herald*, president of the World's Christian Endeavor Union (a youth organization), and pastor of Grace Baptist Church in Philadelphia. Truman called him "the ablest Baptist preacher I know," appointed him to his President's Committee on Religion and Welfare in the Armed Forces, and discussed numerous matters in letters and in person.[167]

Unlike most of his successors, Truman did not have a cordial relationship with Billy Graham, who by the early 1950s had become a national figure. They first met in July 1950 at the Oval Office. Graham, accompanied by three of his associates, urged Truman to call a national day of prayer for the war in Korea and prayed with the president before leaving. Truman assumed that their conversation was off the record, but Graham discussed its contents with reporters as soon as he left the White House. Graham and his colleagues knelt on the lawn to again pray for Truman, and journalists took photographs.[168] Offended and outraged, the president rejected requests from Graham to call a national day of prayer and pleas to make brief remarks at the evangelist's Washington crusade in early 1952. An internal memorandum reported that the president "did not wish to endorse" Graham's "Washington revival" or "receive him at the White House."[169] Graham criticized Truman's direction of the war in Korea and his handling of political corruption and alleged communist sedition in the United States. Ignoring Truman's many calls for moral and spiritual renewal, Graham declared in August 1952 that Americans needed "a Moses or David to lead them" in a spiritual crusade.[170]

Like Franklin Roosevelt, Truman had a positive relationship with Catholic leaders. He sent hundreds of letters to congratulate newly appointed bishops or cardinals, express condolences after prominent church officials died, help congregations celebrate milestone anniversaries, and convey greetings to Catholic conventions.[171] No other president, claimed a Catholic layman in June 1948, had so consistently heralded the importance of the church and of "dependence on and responsibility to God." He advised Democrats to publicize Myron Taylor's service as Truman's representative to the Vatican to remind America's 25 million Catholics how indebted they were to the president.[172]

Many Protestants, however, objected to Truman's appointment of a personal representative to Pope Pius XII—first Taylor, who had served Franklin Roosevelt in a similar capacity from 1939 to 1945, and then Clark.[173] Taylor's continuation in this role, Truman insisted, was critical to his campaign to achieve world peace, alleviate human suffering, and advance "Christian civilization."[174] Concern that Catholics might view terminating Taylor's appointment as an insult to the pope and that communist leaders might exploit it "in their struggle with the Catholic Church in Eastern Europe" also induced Truman to reappoint him as his personal representative.[175] *Christian Century* denounced this "ambiguous, disingenuous, and unconstitutional recognition" of the Catholic Church, which constituted an "illicit intrigue between our state department and the Vatican." The arrangement violated "the fundamental American principle of avoiding" governmental entanglement "with ecclesiastical politics and refusing to play favorites among the churches." These protests prompted Truman to promise that this appointment would be temporary.[176] When Taylor's work continued in 1947 (necessitated, Truman argued, by ongoing international turmoil), *Christian Century* demanded that Truman immediately "end the seven-year farce."[177]

Taylor resigned from his post in January 1950, and in October 1951 Truman nominated Clark, a Protestant war hero, to serve as an ambassador to the Vatican.[178] "Direct diplomatic relations" with the Vatican would strengthen American efforts "to combat the Communist menace."[179] Thousands of Protestants, including National Council of Churches executives, protested that this action violated the separation of church and state. The Senate Committee on Foreign Relations received 50,000 letters, almost all opposing the appointment. The president acknowledged that "an avalanche of correspondence replete with anger, hatred and ill will" had buried the White House.[180] *Christian Century* accused Truman of capitulating to papal pressure and of trying to win Catholic votes in the next election. The NCC and Protestants and Others United for the Separation of Church and State worked to defeat Clark's confirmation.[181] Appalled by these vehement remonstrations, Clark withdrew his name in January 1952. Although a few Protestants joined Catholics, led by Francis Cardinal Spellman, in supporting Truman's plan, public opinion and many Senators opposed appointing an ambassador to the Vatican, and formal diplomatic relations with the Holy See were not established until 1984.[182]

During much of his life, especially his earlier years, Truman expressed negative views of Jews and other ethnic and racial groups. Highly opinionated, influenced by the attitudes of rural Missouri, and lacking the broadening influences of higher education, Truman embraced America's historic nativism. Although his "views evolved over time as he experienced a wider world," even as president, he sometimes voiced prejudiced views in private.[183] For example, his July 21, 1947 diary entry reads: The Jews "are very, very self-ish. They care not how many Estonians, Latvians, Finns, Poles, Yugoslavs or Greeks get murdered or mistreated" as displaced persons as long as they receive "special treatment." "When they have power," "neither Hitler nor Stalin has anything on them for cruelty or mistreatment to the under dog."[184] Exasperated by the response of Jewish leaders to his administration's policy on emigration to Palestine, Truman complained in a cabinet meeting: "Jesus Christ couldn't please them when he was here on earth, so how could anyone expect that I would have any luck."[185]

Despite his prejudice, Truman maintained cordial relations with the Jewish community, lauded Jewish accomplishments, and helped rabbis, synagogues, and Jewish organizations celebrate achievements and special occasions. In a 1945 radio address commemorating the Passover, Truman praised Jews' outstanding "moral code" and leadership in "the fight to aid other oppressed minorities."[186] Jewish belief in "one ever living and true God" had enhanced human efforts to attain "spiritual heights."[187] Jews, Truman added, had played an "important role in the growth and development" of the United States.[188] The president lauded rabbi Stephen Wise of New York City's Free Synagogue as a "faithful servant" who had led numerous campaigns for "social betterment."[189]

Philosophy of Government

Truman claimed that his understanding of how the world operated came from Scripture and argued that political decisions should be based on transcendent moral standards.[190] The Bible, he contended, supplied "moral standards" for America's conduct "at home and abroad. We should judge our" national actions on "the scales of right and wrong." The success of the United States, he insisted, depended on its citizens obeying the biblical moral code in both private and public life.[191] The commandments Moses received on Mount Sinai, Truman asserted, provided "the fundamental basis" of the American "respect for the rights and welfare of others." The Bill of Rights also rested on scriptural principles.[192]

On several occasions, Truman stated that his administration's philosophy was based on the Sermon on the Mount.[193] The United States was the leader of the world's moral forces, of those "who believe that the Sermon on the Mount means what it says."[194] "We must always" strive, Truman avowed, to improve the world "in accordance with the divine commandments."[195] He urged citizens of all nations to "live by the principles of righteousness and justice." Jesus taught and praised efforts to apply "Christ's teaching to our everyday affairs."[196]

Truman claimed that the Good Neighbor Policy of the United States "originated in the tenth chapter of St. Luke" (the story of the Good Samaritan), which explained "what a good neighbor means." People must treat others regardless of their race or creed as they want to be treated.[197] This policy "applies to international relations the same standards of conduct that prevail among self-respecting individuals within a democratic community. It is based upon mutual respect among nations" without "distinction of size, wealth, or power." All nations must be permitted to develop as they wished.[198] The president urged national leaders to supply the justice and freedom their citizens needed to live peacefully "as Good Neighbors."[199] Some, Truman acknowledged, thought that the Golden Rule "has no place in politics and government." However, governments that followed this principle "are built on a rock, and will not fail."[200]

In "the Christian conception of society," Truman added, "the state is the servant of the individual, never the master."[201] Therefore, statesmen should serve their constituents.[202] Moreover, political policies should generally provide "the greatest good for the greatest number" of a country's citizens.[203] However, because God had established moral principles to govern human conduct, a political policy or decision, Truman insisted, should not be based on whether it is popular, "but whether it's right, and if it's right, in the long run it will come out all right."[204]

Public Policy: Quest for World Peace

Truman's faith played a significant role in many of his domestic policies.[205] It also strongly affected his foreign policy, especially his approach to the Cold War, efforts to achieve peace, and recognition of Israel. Truman strove to occupy "the moral high ground" by mobilizing both the mass media and the world's major religions to stop the spread of "godless" communism and improve international relations.[206]

The Baptist believed that God had called him to lead a crusade for world peace. His "preeminent political goal" was to halt the expansion of communism and end conflict around the world.[207] Richard Kirkendall contends that Truman's understanding of the Bible and personal experiences with war drove him to prevent World War III.[208] "God intended" America, Truman argued, "to preserve peace and restore prosperity throughout the world."[209] The United Nations and the world's religious communities, he maintained, also had a vital role to play in accomplishing this end. Religious groups could help undermine belief in the Soviet system and bring about its demise. Peace could be attained only if nations followed a biblically based moral code, provided freedom and justice for all their citizens, and practiced the Golden Rule in international relations. While human efforts were important to achieve these ends, Truman proclaimed, God alone could bring the peace millions craved.[210]

During World War II, Truman declared, the Allies had defeated the "forces of evil" that sought to destroy religion and democracy, which were both based on "the worth and dignity of the individual." Like Nazis and Fascists, Communists opposed people's right to worship God as they saw fit.[211] Communists denied God's existence, "the rule of law," and "the value of the individual." They used both military might and "deceit and subversion" to achieve their destructive aims.[212] Communism, Truman asserted, repudiated America's "basic values"—belief in God, human dignity, justice, and freedom.[213] Christianity, he averred, provided a blueprint for creating a God-based society that ensured people's greatest happiness. "Surely, we can follow that faith with the same devotion and determination the Communists give to their godless creed."[214] Christian teachings, he added, "are a sure defense against the godlessness and the brutality of ideologies which deny the value of the individual."[215] "The greatest bulwark" for thwarting the advance of communism, Truman insisted, "is our belief in a moral code, expressed in the 20th Chapter of Exodus and the Sermon on the Mount." Their faith in God empowered citizens of the free nations in Europe, including millions who faced "poverty, destitution, and misery" after World War II, to reject communism.[216]

Communism, Truman contended, "is a godless" "system of slavery." Its suppression of freedom, secret police, and constant purges demonstrated its "rulers' fear of their own people." Free societies, built on biblical principles, would eventually "prevail over a system that has respect for neither God nor man."[217] "By the grace of God and through our own determination, hard work and cooperation with other free peoples," Truman trumpeted, "we can convince the Kremlin that we cannot be conquered."[218]

Truman also expected the United Nations to lead efforts to promote world peace. He argued in 1945 that its international police force could intervene to stop "aggression at its source." Its Social and Economic Council could help distribute "the fruits of the earth" more widely. As more conflicts were settled peacefully, Truman reasoned, using war to achieve national aims would increasingly be deplored as "barbarism and savagery."[219] Unfortunately, his hopes were dampened by the beginning of the Cold War in 1947 and the inability of the Soviet Union and the West to work together effectively in the United Nations. Nevertheless, Truman announced in 1947 that the United

Nations "is man's hope of putting out, and keeping out, the fires of war for all time." Its member states, he proclaimed in 1950, had "a solemn obligation" to increase their military strength to deter aggression and to solve "the major problems and issues" that divided them. "If real disarmament were achieved," much more material aid could be dispensed. Replacing armaments with "foods, medicine, [and] tools for use in underdeveloped areas" would fulfill the biblical "promise that swords shall be beaten into plowshares, and that nations shall not learn war any more."[220]

Truman argued that the United States also had a pivotal role in bringing world peace. The sacrifices of millions of Americans during World War II revealed "a Divine purpose" to produce "an era of peace" with higher standards of living, greater social justice, and phenomenal advances in the arts and sciences. Truman constantly underscored America's actions to preserve and promote peace. By 1947, his administration had supplied more than 15 billion dollars in loans and grants to "prevent starvation, disease, and suffering," and by 1951 the Marshall Plan, which was created "to bind up the wounds of war, to feed the hungry, and to give shelter to the homeless," had provided an additional 13 billion dollars to assist nations devastated by World War II to rebuild. For the first time in world history, the Democrat claimed, a victor had helped "restore the vanquished."[221] Americans, he promised, would "not relent in our efforts" to base international relations on the Golden Rule and "prevent a third world war" that would end civilization.[222] "Mindful of its Christian heritage," Truman proclaimed in 1949, the United States would redouble its efforts to create a peaceful and prosperous world.[223] By so doing, he hoped that Americans would earn "the benediction of the Master: 'Blessed are the peacemakers, for they shall be called the children of God.' "[224]

To attain peace, Truman contended, Americans "must work constantly to wipe out injustice and inequality" and "to create a world order" that is "consistent with [their] faith." Guided by the United Nations Universal Declaration of Human Rights, Americans must "defend human rights abroad as vigorously as we work for them at home." They must construct a world order that enabled people to righteously and fearlessly "do the work of God."[225] Truman argued that the United States was working to settle disputes among nations peacefully, ensure effective international control of nuclear weapons, and build a stronger foundation for global order and justice.[226] All nations that affirmed "the brotherhood of man, under God" could "live together peacefully" and promote the common good. However, many citizens must first be liberated from disease, poverty, and God-denying tyrants who believed that "only force makes right."[227]

While denouncing Communists as immoral atheists and calling for a strong American military, Truman also pled for disarmament. In a 1950 address to the United Nations, he appealed for "a truly dependable and effective system" to reduce and control armaments based on the principles of universality, unanimity, and inspection. *Christian Century* praised Truman's "epochal" speech, exhorted churches to support disarmament, and called for an East–West competition to feed, clothe, and house the world's people.[228]

Truman constantly asserted that its religious strength was "the heart of America's greatness" and that religious institutions and teachings had an essential role to play in creating a better, more peaceful world.[229] He maintained that "an enduring peace" could "be built only upon Christian principles," and he frequently quoted scriptural injunctions to pursue peace. We must remember "that except the Lord build the house, they labor in vain who build it." As citizens of "a Christian Nation," he added, Americans strove "to banish war" because the Creator wants all people to "live together in peace, good will and mutual trust."[230] Americans' renewed religious commitment could help prevent an apocalypse.[231] Christians, Truman avowed, must use "every instrument and resource at our command" to attain "lasting peace and universal justice" and to bring nearer "a new heaven and a new earth."[232]

Truman sought to devise "a common religious and moral front" to defeat communism and advance peace. In 1946, he called for a "moral and spiritual awakening" to prevent new conflicts.[233] The next year he sent Myron Taylor to discuss this project with Pope Pius XII. Taylor also met with the leaders of the World Council of Churches, the Archbishop of Canterbury, prominent Jewish and Muslim leaders, and the Dalai Lama of Tibet.[234] "If I can mobilize the people who believe in a moral world against the Bolshevik materialists," Truman wrote to Bess, "we can win this fight." Because treaties, agreements, and moral codes meant nothing to Communists, he added, "we've got to organize the people who believe" in the "Golden Rule to win the world back to peace and Christianity."[235] Truman challenged Anglican bishops to help "mobilize the moral forces of the world for a real awakening" based on the Sermon on the Mount.[236] In 1948 Truman wrote to Pius XII: "This nation holds out the hand of fellowship to all who seek world unity under God."[237] In 1950 the president declared, "I have been trying to mobilize the moral forces of the world—Catholics, Protestants, Jews, the Eastern Church, the Grand Lama of Tibet," and Hindus—to understand that their welfare "depends on our working together."[238] Because Pope Pius XII and two leading American clerics—Cardinal Francis Spellman and Bishop Fulton Sheen—were staunch anti-Communists who like him saw the Cold War as essentially a spiritual and moral conflict, Truman considered Catholics to be especially strong allies in his moral crusade.[239]

Truman sought to convince the world's "great religious leaders" to make "a common affirmation of faith" based on Exodus 20 and Matthew 5–7. All those who believed in God must "unite in asking [for] His help and His guidance." Religious "differences seemed so petty" in the face of current perils. Communism threatened all churches and creeds. This affirmation, Truman insisted, would testify to "our confidence" in God's "ultimate victory over the forces of Satan." By collectively proclaiming God's power and mercy "against those who deny Him," he argued, the world's religions could achieve "peace in our time."[240]

Many challenged Truman's claim that the Sermon on the Mount provided a proper basis for international relations. The editors of *Christian Century* rejected his contention that if other countries followed the American example of living by Christ's discourse "the world will be all right." Numerous theologians did not think that Matthew 5–7 was "a guide for nations." Truman's crusade "to mobilize the moral forces of the world" to implement the teachings of the Sermon on the Mount was ill-advised because the "perfectionism" Christ taught in this passage was not a proper "norm for international relations."[241]

In another editorial *Christian Century* strongly denounced Truman's argument that the United States and its allies sought to follow the Sermon on the Mount while the Soviets championed atheism and immorality. His contention that "we are totally right and Russia is totally depraved" greatly oversimplified the situation and justified a campaign "to wipe Russia off the face of the earth as a service to God." The editors wondered how recently the president had carefully read the "three austere and humbling chapters" from Matthew's gospel and urged him to "invite a competent Christian to explain to him what the words of the Sermon on the Mount" actually meant. Unless Truman and many other Americans were delivered from the besetting "sins of spiritual blindness, pride and self-righteousness," tragic results might occur.[242]

For these and other reasons, the world's religious communities did not rally beneath Truman's banner. The president lamented in 1951 that Christian churches had not devised "a common statement of their faith that Christ was their Master and Redeemer and the source of their strength against the hosts of irreligion."[243] His crusade failed, Truman insisted, because of the jealousy among the world's religions and the opposition of many American Protestants.[244] Unfortunately, religious leaders had missed "an important opportunity" to promote peace and combat social ills.[245]

God's aid, Truman continually argued, was essential to achieving peace. The president concluded his 1946 speech to the United Nations: "may

Almighty God, in His infinite mercy, guide us and sustain us as we seek to bring peace everlasting to the world. With His help, we shall succeed!" "Those words," Cardinal Spellman, told Truman, struck a responsive chord "in the hearts of millions of your fellow citizens."[246] "With God's help," the president declared in his 1949 inaugural address people could produce "a world of justice, harmony, and peace."[247] "If we really have faith," Truman trumpeted, "God will give us what we are not able to attain by our own efforts."[248] Someday "the Kingdoms of this world shall become indeed the Kingdom of God and He will reign forever and ever" as "Lord of Lords and King of Kings."[249]

Truman and Israel

Truman's faith also strongly influenced his policy toward Israel and his decision to recognize the new nation minutes after it was founded on May 14, 1948. Like all other presidents since Woodrow Wilson, Truman hoped the Jews would regain Palestine as a homeland. In 1941 he joined the American Palestine Committee, a pro-Zionist organization. That year, he joined sixty-seven other Senators in calling for "the restoration of the Jews in Palestine," an action that accorded "with the spirit of Biblical prophecy."[250] Truman protested in a 1943 speech at a massive rally in Chicago that Jews were "being herded like animals" into ghettoes, concentration camps, and "the wastelands of Europe" and were being murdered by "fiendish Huns and Fascists." He urged Americans to "do all that is humanly possible to provide" a safe haven "for all those who can be grasped from the hands of the Nazi butchers." This was an "American problem," not "a Jewish problem," which must be faced "squarely and honorably."[251]

The quest to provide a homeland for Jews in Palestine confronted Truman "with a bewildering series of conflicts involving morality, politics, and the national interest." From the end of World War II to May 1948, he felt trapped in a no-win political situation, caught between a crucial constituency, American Jews, many of whom were irrevocably committed to obtaining a Jewish homeland in Palestine, and the State Department, led by Secretary of State George Marshall, which focused on American self-interest rather than moral or humanitarian considerations.[252] Both groups sought to determine Truman's position on the issue, prompting the frustrated Baptist to lament: "I surely wish God Almighty would give the Children of Israel an Isaiah, the Christians a St. Paul and the Sons of Ishmael a peep at the Golden Rule."[253] Truman, who abhorred special interests, resented the "constant barrage" of pressure Zionists put on him to aid Israel. The Democrat wanted to provide a home for millions of Jews (20 percent of all displaced persons following World War II), thwart Soviet efforts to gain influence in the Middle East, and create a functioning democracy in the region. However, he recognized that the 600,000 Jews living in Palestine were greatly outnumbered by Arabs and was not willing to send American troops there (he believed at least 100,000 would be necessary) to help a Jewish state survive.[254]

Truman condemned the Holocaust, demanded that its perpetrators be punished, and wanted to assist Jewish refugees.[255] A combination of "conviction, compassion, and political expediency" led him to support Jewish immigration to Palestine.[256] Truman denounced persecuting people because of "their race, color, or religion" and pronounced the Nazis' "organized brutality" against the Jews "one of the most shocking crimes of all times."[257] In 1946 Truman proposed that Palestine immediately accept 100,000 Jewish immigrants and urged other countries to take as many Jews as "humanly possible."[258] However, the next June, Truman counseled Americans to refrain "from engaging in, or facilitating, any activities" that might further "inflame the passions" of Palestinians, "undermine law and order in Palestine," or "promote violence in that country."[259]

In October 1947, Truman asked Texas fundamentalist pastor J. Frank Norris for his advice about the situation in Palestine. Norris asserted that the key question was: who had title to the land. He concluded, based on God's promises to Isaac (Genesis 17:19 and 26:3), Jacob (Genesis 28:13), and Moses (Deuteronomy 30:3–5) and the testimony of David (Psalm 105:9–12), that the region belonged to the Jews. Therefore, the Arabs were usurpers. Moreover, Great Britain had been given a mandate to control Palestine and to enable Jews to migrate there and create a national homeland, which both the United States and the League of Nations had supported. The Jews had already spent $650 million to construct cities and public works in Palestine. Any group that violated the Jews' divine directive, Norris claimed, would be subject to "the curse of God Almighty." The United States, he concluded, must help the Jews survive in the "land that has given the world its Bible and Saviour." Truman replied that he had "given long and extensive study to the Jewish Palestinian question" and that he deeply appreciated Norris's analysis.[260]

While encouraging extensive Jewish migration to Palestine, Truman favored partitioning it into Jewish and Arab states. Jews around the world supported partition, but Arab states fervently opposed it, and the British argued that this proposal would not work. At a secret meeting arranged by the president's former business partner Eddie Jacobson in mid-March 1948, Truman promised Chaim Weizmann, soon to become Israel's first president, that his administration would continue to support partition.[261] However, the next day the American ambassador to the United Nations, without Truman's authorization, urged the United Nations to assume a temporary "trusteeship" over Palestine. This apparent change in American policy brought a flood of criticism. Jewish spokespersons denounced this plan as "thoroughly dishonorable" and a "sellout" and promised that most Jews would desert Truman in the 1948 election. Many accused the Democrat of gross "ineptitude and caving in to base material concerns."[262] "Oh, how could you stoop so low!" Samuel Sloan, a professor at Carnegie Institute of Technology, and his wife bemoaned. While pretending to care about the plight of the Jews, they griped, "you act for the colonial interests of England, gangster Arabs, and oil."[263] The president's approval rating sank to 36 percent, and the *New Republic* proclaimed "Truman Should Quit."[264] The Jewish declaration of independence on May 14, 1948, soon, however, led the Democrat to repudiate both the partition and trusteeship options.

Despite the opposition of most of his senior foreign policy advisors, including Marshall, whom he deeply admired, Truman granted diplomatic recognition to Israel eleven minutes after its establishment. State Department officials argued that recognizing Israel was inimical to America's national security interests. It would hurt the United States' relationship with Arab nations, give the Soviet Union entrée into the Middle East, and decrease oil imports. Moreover, because of historic antagonism between Jews and Arabs and Arabs' overwhelming numerical superiority, they feared Israel could not survive.[265]

Special Counsel Clark Clifford explained that several factors informed Truman's position: his hatred of discrimination; the horrors of the Holocaust; his concern that among "the millions of homeless of World War II," only the "Jews had no homeland" "to which they could return"; his belief that the 1917 Balfour Declaration committed both Great Britain and the United States to create a Jewish state in Palestine; and his understanding of the Bible. Truman, Clark emphasized, had been a student of and "believer in the Bible since his youth." He insisted that the Jews had "a legitimate historical right to Palestine" as taught in "such biblical passages as Deuteronomy 1:8: 'Behold, I have given up the land before you; go in and take possession of the land which the Lord hath sworn unto your fathers, to Abraham, to Isaac, and to Jacob.'"[266] Truman and Clark discussed Old Testament prophesies about the return of the Jews to Palestine. Deuteronomy's declaration that the Lord showed Moses, standing atop Mt. Nebo "all the land from Gilead unto Dan" confirmed others from Genesis, Truman argued, that God intended Palestine to be the Jews' "everlasting possession."[267] Truman, State Department member Albert Lilienthal complained, "was a Biblical fundamentalist who constantly pointed" to Deuteronomy 1:8 to justify his actions.[268] Eliahu Elath, who served as the first Israeli ambassador to the United States, claimed that the Bible was Truman's "main source of knowledge of the history of Palestine in ancient times" and stressed that the president declared in his farewell address that "Israel can be made into the country of milk and honey as it was in the time of Joshua."[269] Truman often asserted that the Jews and Arabs "were cousins, all descendants of Father Abraham" who "should try and live peaceably together."[270] Palestine, he explained, "has always interested me, partly because of its Biblical background."[271]

While many scholars contend that Truman recognized Israel primarily to gain Jewish financial support and votes in the 1948 election, Michael Benson argues convincingly that Truman also sought to correct a "historic wrong" and fulfill a promise every president since Wilson had made to support the establishment of a Jewish state in Palestine. Truman recognized Israel, Benson concludes, primarily because of his "fundamental commitment to do what was right, for the right reason, and at the right time."[272] Truman hoped that the region's potential could be developed to benefit both Jews and Arabs and to accommodate 30 million inhabitants. This would "redeem the pledges" made to Jews during World War I.[273] When his Secretary of Defense James Forrestal stressed how important Saudi Arabian oil was, Truman responded that justice, not oil, would determine his response to the Palestinian question.[274] For David McCullough, Truman's diplomatic recognition of Israel, organization of the Berlin airlift, and the desegregation of the armed forces were his most impressive actions.[275]

A president's understanding of biblical injunctions and prophecy, numerous analysts argue, should not affect his policy decisions. Decisions should instead be based on prudential considerations and the national interest. Alonzo Hamby maintains that the Palestinian issue illustrates "the frequent conflict between morality and self-interest" in the fields of diplomacy and international relations. Moreover, it underscores the fact that morality is often ambiguous given the clashing perspectives and desires of nations and peoples. Hamby concludes that Truman "wanted to do the right thing and was persuaded that he had."[276] Other historians contend that Truman was so blinded by the myth of Arab backwardness that he did not consider Arabs to be fully human. His failure to realize that the principle of self-determination also had implications for Arabs, the majority group in Palestine, William Pemberton charges, led Truman to undertake actions that had "disastrous consequences for millions of people."[277]

Refusing to take the politically expedient route, Truman, guided by his Christian faith and humanitarian instincts and willing to make tough decisions, granted diplomatic recognition to Israel.[278] Administrative assistant

David Niles, who also worked for Franklin Roosevelt, insisted that Israel probably would not have survived if Roosevelt had still been president in 1948.
Trygve Lie, the UN General Secretary from 1946 to 1952, concurred: "if there
had been no Harry S. Truman, there would be no Israel today."[279] Truman was
deeply moved by Isaac Herzog's profession: "God put you in your mother's
womb so you could be the instrument to bring the rebirth of Israel after two
thousand years."[280]

Final Assessment

During his last year as president, Harry Truman had a 23 percent approval
rating, which was lower than Richard Nixon's the day he resigned. His reputation remained poor during the first two decades after he left office. Critics
castigated the man from Missouri as a weak, ineffective president who allowed
the Soviets to dominate Eastern Europe and failed to prevent, and then to
win, the Korean War. The revisionist historians of the 1960s and early 1970s
accused him of inconsistency, "indecisiveness," "poor judgment," and "lack of
leadership." A "tool of the political bosses, the Wall Street financiers, and the
military-industrial complex," the blundering president made countless mistakes. Truman's policies helped begin the Cold War, and he "missed many
opportunities" to negotiate "detente with the Soviet Union."[281]

Biographers highlight additional flaws. The Truman Doctrine and his
approach to the Cold War were based, Pemberton complains, on his conception of history as a moral drama with distinct "divisions of good and evil."
"His rural Missouri background" and his limited education, McCullough
contends, led Truman to see issues "as right or wrong, wise or foolish." His
answers, even to complicated questions, were usually "direct and assured."
To McCullough, Truman's argument that the world's nations could get along
by simply applying the Golden Rule was naïve. Pemberton contends that
Truman lacked the skills or will to pass reforms such as national health
insurance or civil rights. The Democrat refused to acknowledge that some
of his staff and friends "had betrayed his trust by engaging in unwise, if
not illegal, actions." Instead, he blamed journalists or investigators, making
matters worse.[282]

However, soon after his death in 1972, Truman became a national hero, and
in recent years prominent political scientists and historians have consistently
ranked him as either a great or near great president.[283] His personal attributes
and policies and the challenges Truman confronted as president all contribute
to this assessment. Pundits especially praise his character, which was shaped
in significant part by his faith. Journalist Robert Donovan argues that no other

president "tried harder to do what was right." Embodying the "values of common American people," McCullough contends, Truman espoused the traditional guidelines to "work hard, do your best, speak the truth" and "trust in God." Truman was "a great president," he adds, who "put character first."[284] Robert Ferrell maintains that Truman was a "folk hero: a plain-speaking, straight-talking, ordinary" man who did his duty without seeking personal gain. Mary McGrory insisted that the Baptist "lived by the Bible and history" and "proved that the ordinary American is capable of grandeur." "Courageous and personally incorruptible," Truman, Harold Gosnell declared, rose from humble origins to "a place among the presidential near greats."[285]

For many scholars, Truman's greatest accomplishment was shifting American foreign policy from isolationism to fostering order, freedom, and justice around the globe. Abba Eban, Israel's Ambassador to the United States from 1950 to 1959, argued that Truman established the central themes of America's approach to international affairs—"activism, responsibility," and an attempt to serve as "the exemplar and protector of democracy." Many scholars view Truman as a "strong and effective leader, who laid the foundations" for the United States' policies in the Cold War. However, despite his voluminous references to Scripture, spiritual weapons, and the vital role of the church, few argue that Truman's religious convictions helped shape his political perspective.[286] A major exception is William Inboden who contends that Truman crafted a political theology that guided America's course in the Cold War. It drew critical spiritual distinctions between the United States and communist countries, helped garner popular support for the nation's foreign policy, and convinced prominent American and foreign religious leaders and millions of laypeople around the world to back containment of the Soviets. While expressing lofty hopes for a just world and a lasting peace, Truman insisted that achieving this goal required political realism, military strength, and the willingness to become entangled "in a fallen world."[287]

"The essential mission of the church," Truman avowed in 1951, is to inculcate "those moral ideals which are the basis of our free institutions." Religion was "not simply a comfort to those in trouble." It was "a positive force" that impelled people to act. "We are under divine orders—not only to refrain from doing evil, but also to do good and to make this world a better place" to live. Therefore, galvanized by God's strength and wisdom, all Americans should live by the Judeo-Christian moral code. "The test of our religious principles," Truman declared, is "not just in what we say," "our prayers," and "even in living blameless personal lives—but in what we do for others."[288] Truman's own faith inspired him to help millions during his three decades of public service.

In a speech near the end of his presidency, Truman accentuated "moral principles and ethical ideals" and quoted several biblical passages, prompting Edward Pruden to declare, "It's a pity you weren't a preacher." The Baptist replied, "As a young man, I gave serious consideration to being one, but I decided I wasn't good enough."[289] It is difficult to imagine that Truman could have done more to benefit the United States or the world in any other occupation than politics. As president, Truman employed hundreds of biblical quotations and allusions, persistently preached morality, denounced communist atheism, and exuded postmillennial optimism that humans, empowered by God, could create a better world.[290]

8

Richard Nixon

A PRIVATE AND ENIGMATIC FAITH

One of the foremost aims of my Administration has been the
strengthening of those moral principles and ideals which have
made our nation great.

RICHARD NIXON TO RABBI BEREK ROTTENBERG, Jan. 23,
1973, RM Box 19, 3-2, Jewish, 1/1/73

As a life-long Quaker and church-going Christian . . .
I am determined to prove that we have . . . the God-given
resources . . . to take charge of our destiny again.

NIXON IN EARLY 1969, as quoted by Charles Henderson,
Jr., *The Nixon Theology*, 179–80

Introduction

Richard Nixon was one of the United States' most influential twentieth-century leaders. The California native served as a congressman, senator, and vice president for eight years. He was one of only three Republicans to be elected president twice during the twentieth century. Arguably, no American in the second half of the twentieth century had a better grasp of foreign affairs. Highly regarded for his foreign policy successes, most notably fashioning détente with the Soviet Union and restoring diplomatic relations with China, he resigned in disgrace in August 1974 to avoid being impeached for his cover-up of the Watergate break-in. During the twenty years between his resignation and death, Nixon's reputation was significantly rehabilitated. He wrote several best-selling books, many considered him America's senior statesman, and numerous politicians and pundits valued his opinions on varied issues, especially foreign policy.

Nixon was raised in a devout Quaker home, claimed to have a conversion experience as a teenager, attended church fairly frequently for much of his life, had close relationships with Billy Graham and Norman Vincent Peale, held worship services in the White House, often presented himself as man of faith, and repeatedly stressed the importance of spirituality and morality. He taught Sunday school in his twenties, read the Bible every day while serving in the navy during World War II, and professed that he prayed habitually. In 1971 the Religious Heritage of America named Nixon as its Churchman of the Year, commending him for "carrying his deep religious commitment into the Presidency."[1] Nevertheless, while numerous scholars have discussed Nixon's Quaker upbringing and its influence on his personality, few have paid much attention to the role of religion in Nixon's political life.[2]

His very private, complicated, perplexing personality makes Nixon's faith hard to decipher. In describing Nixon, his principal speechwriter Ray Price employed Winston Churchill's famous assessment of the Soviet Union: he was "a riddle wrapped in a mystery inside an enigma,"[3] an appraisal that also applies to Nixon's faith. His duplicity (lying to the American people about numerous matters and spying on and harassing political opponents), deceitfulness (tax evasion, use of government monies to improve his homes, and channeling of funds to campaign supporters), and vulgarity (especially as revealed by the White House tapes) raise major questions about the nature of his faith and his commitment to Judeo-Christian ethics. Nixon's calculating, conniving, often ruthless conduct has understandably prompted extensive skepticism that his religious profession was genuine. His personality and actions as president lead many to view his use of pious and moral language not as an authentic expression of his beliefs but simply as a ploy to appeal to religiously committed citizens, promote his policies, and win votes.

Although he retained his membership in the East Whittier Friends Church all his life, Nixon, unlike the nation's first Quaker president, Herbert Hoover, did not attend Friends Meeting House in Washington, DC. While some questioned Hoover's ability to serve as commander-in-chief of the armed forces because of Quakers' historic pacifism, no one objected to Nixon's fitness for this role because he had fought in World War II and belonged to a branch of Friends who did not strongly denounce the evils of war (Hoover ironically belonged to this same branch). Hoover did not send American troops anywhere abroad, but Nixon continued the United States' military involvement in Vietnam and caused great controversy by secretly bombing Cambodia and Laos.[4]

For his major speeches, Nixon selected the message, devised a basic outline, and furnished key phrases, and he wrote some important addresses himself.[5] Given Nixon's duplicity, vulgarity, and self-serving agenda, it is tempting to regard his use of religious rhetoric, biblical references, and spiritual allusions as pious cant designed only to satisfy civic expectations and accomplish political ends. Certainly, such statements were employed in part to further these purposes. On some level, however, his religious rhetoric may have been genuine; through it he sought to express the better side of his nature, convey how he generally perceived himself, and highlight the character and spiritual qualities he valued for himself and other Americans.

Responding to widespread alarm about race riots, sexual licentiousness, the rising divorce rate, campus protests, and illicit drug use, Nixon accentuated law and order, championed public morality, and promised to help restore the nation's "religious faith, strong families, and public decency."[6] Although he was not personally devout, many viewed Nixon as a moral traditionalist who could save America from imminent moral breakdown. Numerous pastors quoted his religious statements approvingly in their sermons and church newsletters. By frequently using religious and moral rhetoric, Nixon contributed to the creation of a coalition of evangelicals and conservative Catholics committed to stopping the secular drift of American society, which became the Religious Right in the late 1970s.[7] In his 1970 State of the Union Address, the president proclaimed that America's elected leaders needed to provide "spiritual and moral leadership." The hard-working, patriotic Quaker, wrote Nixon staff assistant David Gergen, "sincerely wanted to be a model president." Ironically, on October 23, 1972, after the Watergate cover-up had already begun, Nixon wrote in a personal note: "I have decided my major role is moral leadership."[8] His conduct as president fell woefully short of his stated moral standards and prevented him from achieving this goal. Nixon's actions damaged his own reputation, the office of the presidency, and the welfare of the nation.[9] Instead of leading Americans out of their ethical morass, he produced one of the nation's worst moral scandals.

The Faith of Richard Nixon

Examining Nixon's Quaker background, views of God, Jesus, the Bible, the church, Christianity, prayer, human nature, and life after death provides insights into his enigmatic faith. So does analysis of Nixon's and others' statements about his faith, church attendance, drinking, gambling, and sexual mores.

Billy Graham argues that Nixon cannot be understood without comprehending his Quaker background.[10] The maternal side of Nixon's family has a long history as Quakers. His great grandmother, Elizabeth Milhous, was a respected minister who delivered moving sermons at meeting houses across the country. His deeply committed Quaker grandmother Almira instructed her thirty-two grandchildren in her biblically based faith. She and her husband moved their family from Indiana to California when Nixon's mother Hannah was 12.[11] Hannah completed two years at Whittier College, a Quaker institution. His mother "had a very deep religious faith," Nixon declared, which "she communicated to us in her quiet, Quaker way." Her faith sustained her through the death of two sons, the Great Depression, and other tragedies.[12] His mother, Nixon explained, was "intensely private in her feelings," a trait he emulated. On the eve of her son's inauguration as vice president in 1953, Hannah handed him a note (which he kept in his wallet for years) declaring: "I know that you will keep your relationship with your maker as it should be" because it "is the most important thing in life." Her promises to pray for him whenever he had a "difficult decision to make," "a speech to prepare," or "was under attack by the media" meant very much to Nixon. Many friends and acquaintances referred to Hannah as "a Quaker saint."[13] In her eulogy, Billy Graham claimed that "Christ was always first in her life."[14]

The paternal side of Nixon's family had long been Methodists who revered the Bible and valued revivals, but his father Frank became a Quaker after marrying Hannah in 1908 in part because East Whittier Friends Church to which she belonged had embraced most of the theology and practices of evangelical Protestantism. For many years he taught Sunday school there, inspiring dozens of teenage pupils. One of them extolled his enthusiasm and ability to relate Scripture to politics.[15]

Richard, born in 1913, and his four brothers grew up in Yorba Linda, California, a community built and dominated by Friends that had no liquor stores, bars, theaters, or dance halls.[16] The boys took turns reading the Bible aloud at breakfast each morning. The family faithfully attended East Whittier Friends Church three times each Sunday—for Sunday school and worship in the morning, Christian Endeavor in the afternoon, and an evening service. "Some of my fondest recollections of my boyhood," Nixon wrote, "are related to my weekly attendance at Sunday School, where I . . . learned some of the fundamental concepts" of "the Judeo-Christian code of ethics."[17] The Nixons also regularly went to Wednesday evening prayer meetings.

The Nixons belonged to a branch of Friends that had ministers, choirs, and most other features of mainstream Protestant denominations. These Friends listened to sermons, sang hymns, and held revivals but did not practice the sacraments of baptism or communion. As a high school and college student, Nixon sometimes played the piano for worship services, led his church's Easter sunrise services, and taught Sunday school. "Our little community church," Nixon explained, "was the center of our lives." Craving even more spiritual nourishment, Nixon's parents listened to the radio sermons of Billy Sunday and two of Los Angeles's most prominent preachers—Aimee Semple McPherson, the founder of the Foursquare Gospel, and "Fighting Bob" Shuler, the pastor of Trinity Methodist Church—and drove to the city to hear McPherson and Shuler speak.[18] The future president publicly professed faith in Christ at a 1926 revival meeting in response to an altar call by pioneering radio preacher Paul Rader. Nixon later recounted that he had "joined hundreds of others that night in making our personal commitments to Christ and Christian service."[19] Fellow Friend Tom Bewley testified that Nixon had "experienced the acknowledged Quaker states of grace such as 'standing squarely in the light' " and "peace at the center."[20] Nixon continued to attend church regularly as a college student, and many Sundays while at Duke Law School he went to worship services at the University Chapel where Quaker and Methodist ministers alternately preached.[21]

The death of 7-year-old Arthur in 1925 profoundly affected the Nixon family. Hannah reacted stoically, quietly accepting the loss of her son as God's will. Frank, by contrast, saw Arthur's death as a divine punishment, which made him angry but drove him to deeper religious involvement. He attended many revival services and closed his gas station and store on Sundays. Richard was both bewildered by his brother's death and determined to succeed to help his parents cope with their loss.[22] The loss of a second brother, Harold, who died in 1933, after a long battle with tuberculosis, made Richard, then a junior at Whittier, the eldest son, and he became even more resolute, competitive, and hard-working. As Hannah later explained, he seemed to be "trying to be *three* sons in one."[23] For a while, Hannah hoped that Richard might become a Friends' minister or missionary.[24] During his college years, Nixon read widely in philosophy, history, and literature, devouring the works of Thomas Hobbes, John Locke, David Hume, Immanuel Kant, Jean Jacques Rousseau, and many others. He was especially moved by the novels and philosophical treatises of Leo Tolstoy and deeply affected by the Russian's "passion for peace."[25]

After returning to Whittier in 1937 to practice law, Nixon taught a college-age Sunday school class at his home church. One church member reported that he prepared his classes carefully and "was a provocative teacher" who elicited "hot and heavy" discussion.[26] When the United States entered World War II in December 1941, Nixon, as a life-long Quaker, could have applied for conscientious objector status or volunteered for noncombatant duty as many other Friends did. But the evangelical wing of Quakers to which he belonged practiced a selective pacifism, and Nixon maintained that "the idea of being a conscientious objector never crossed my mind."[27] Quaker pacifism, Nixon later explained, "could only work if one were fighting a civilized, compassionate enemy. In the face of Hitler and Tojo, pacifism not only failed to stop violence—it actually played into the hands of a barbarous foe and weakened home-front morale."[28] Although his mother and grandmother disagreed with Nixon's decision, they respected it and did not argue with him about it.[29]

In 1940 Nixon married Pat Ryan, a Methodist, in a Quaker ceremony, who agreed to embrace the Quaker faith.[30] However, after he was elected to Congress in 1946, the Nixons worshipped primarily at the Westmoreland Congregational Church and the Metropolitan Memorial Methodist Church in Washington, DC. While living in Manhattan from 1963 to 1967, Nixon usually attended services at Norman Vincent Peale's Marble Collegiate Church, a Reformed Church of America congregation. Nixon listened attentively and sometimes took notes during Peale's sermons, which expressed the sunny optimism of his best-selling *The Power of Positive Thinking* (1952). While at his summer home in Florida, Nixon worshipped at the Key Biscayne Presbyterian Church. As president, he held nonsectarian services at the White House and occasionally attended various Protestant churches in the capital, California, and other locales during his frequent travels around the country and world. However, he continued to consider himself as a Quaker. His mother described him as "an intensely religious man" who nevertheless shunned "the restrained rituals of the faith."[31]

In his senior year at Whittier (1933–34), Nixon took J. Hershel Coffin's "The Philosophy of Christian Reconstruction" course for which he wrote twelve essays to answer the question, "What Can I Believe?" Theological liberals led by Coffin had triumphed over fundamentalists at Whittier, and although the college was still connected to the California Yearly Meeting, it had abandoned much of its historic Quaker commitment. This course challenged Nixon's traditional Quaker faith and significantly altered his belief system.[32] Nixon later claimed that these essays provided an in-depth picture of his "beliefs, questions, and uncertainties as a college student."[33] Although he was "no longer a fundamentalist," Nixon maintained, his religious beliefs were "surprisingly strong for a college student." He quoted parts of his essays in his 1978 *Memoirs* without stating whether or not he still held these views about God, Jesus, the Bible, life after death, and Christianity.[34]

Nixon vacillated between describing God as personal and as "the creative force" behind the development of the universe. At times, he sounded like a late twentieth-century process theologian: God "is the perfection toward which we work"; "God epitomized the Good"; "God is the first cause, the greater mover." God, he wrote, personified "the highest values of human life carried to the nth degree." This conception of God did not reduce His divinity, majesty, or grandeur. Instead of sitting on "a throne in the heavens and arbitrarily governing" the universe, God actively "fills all of life."[35] Nixon insisted that belief in God

had been "a tremendous aid to mankind" because it prompted people to emulate the virtues God embodied; religion had inspired millions to strive to "realize the higher values of life." Moreover, if more people accepted "the highest
possible concept of God, it could hasten the coming of the Kingdom of God on
earth."[36] As president, Nixon often referred to God's providence and direction
of events. When Dwight Eisenhower died in 1969, Nixon urged Americans
to submit to God's will.[37] The Californian concluded his second inaugural
address by exhorting listeners to endeavor "always to serve His purpose."[38]

Nixon believed that Jesus was a great moral teacher and role model, but
as an adult he never asserted that Jesus was divine or the savior of humanity.
Sounding very much like Protestant liberals of the 1930s, he wrote in "What
I Believe" that "by closely identifying himself with God," Jesus, through His
life and teachings, gave the world its highest value system. He came so close
to God's perfection that He "seemed to be from God himself." While not
directly denying that Christ performed miracles, Nixon argued that they were
not important. "Jesus was the son of God, but not in the physical sense of the
term." Rather, He attained the world's "highest conception of God" and "lived
a life that radiated" God's values. Jesus and God, Nixon argued, "are one" in
the sense that "Jesus set the great example" that continually pulled people
toward "the ideal life. His life was so perfect that he 'mingled' his soul with
God's." By following the religion of Jesus, people could become more like God
and practice "the higher values." His ideas and life, "with all the miraculous
events shaved off," offered humanity "a tremendous opportunity" to establish
the "kingdom of God on earth." While not directly repudiating Christ's resurrection, Nixon contended that "the important fact is that Jesus lived and taught
a life so perfect" that after his death "he continued to live" "in the hearts of
men."[39] Nixon wrote little the rest of his life that contradicted this understanding of Christ. While many other presidents regularly mentioned Jesus in their
Christmas messages, in his six messages Nixon referred only once to Jesus.
His messages primarily emphasized the importance of working for peace, dispensing charity, and helping others.[40] In fact, in all his addresses as president,
Nixon refers to Jesus twice—once as the Prince of Peace and once as feeding
the multitudes.

From childhood, Nixon wrote in his college essays, he had been taught that
"the Bible was the only true book," the "perfect book" that explained everything
people needed to know. His college education had convinced Nixon that the
Bible was not inerrant, but his faith in its "fundamental teachings" "remained
intact." The Bible was "man's finest record of religious writings" and had
inspired millions to strive for "the highest values."[41] As a politician, Nixon
publicly praised Scripture. In a 1962 article in Decision magazine, he insisted

that Americans needed "more preaching from the Bible" and to know "what the Bible says to our time."[42] As president, he testified to the "ever-present influence" of the Bible in his life. It motivated millions to serve others, helped them cope with "trying times," and supplied "courage, compassion, charity, and peace."[43] The "word of God" also provided solace for despairing people. Many statesmen, he avowed, had "drawn inspiration" from "Holy Writ." He urged Americans to let "the timeless wisdom of the Book of Books" guide their daily lives.[44]

Nixon protested in his college essays that "the orthodox church" misrepresented Christianity. Sadly, most clergy supported the economic and social status quo Jesus denounced. "Instead of leading the fight" to bring "the Kingdom of God on earth," the church was "a reactionary force." Religious leaders preached about "insignificant trifles" and quibbled about dogma, while "Jesus taught that there were just two great commandments—love God, and thy neighbor." Nixon criticized "orthodox churchmen" for ignoring "the salvation of society." Influenced by Sherwood Eddy's *Religion and Social Justice* (1927), he protested that the American economic system was not based on Christ's teachings about wealth, love, and cooperation.[45]

His college education strengthened one aspect of Nixon's Quaker upbringing: his belief in pacifism. Ignoring Jesus's "message of peace," many church leaders, Nixon complained, justified war, praised patriotism, cursed enemies, and denounced conscientious objectors. War, he contended, was "the most insane of man's many vices." It killed combatants, destroyed property, harmed women and children, and thwarted "moral and social evolution." Jesus's plan for improving international relations was to repeal the war guilt and reparation clauses of the Treaty of Versailles, disarm all nations, include all countries in the League of Nations, and create a World Court to settle economic disputes. To achieve the abundant life Jesus strove to bring, all nations must practice the social, political, and economic democracy he promoted in the Sermon on the Mount.[46]

The nature of Nixon's faith is a conundrum as his own statements and comments by those who knew him indicate. In a 1971 interview on *ABC News*, Nixon asserted that the ideal president would be intelligent, courageous, and a good leader. However, "the most important single factor" is that he must have "perspective and poise, what the Quakers call peace at the center." This trait kept him from being "knocked off balance" by the "crises of the moment" and enabled him "to make decisions that were in the best interests of the country."[47] The next year, Nixon professed: "I have found my spiritual faith to be a reservoir of strength and guidance in meeting each day's challenges."[48]

In a letter that appears to be particularly heartfelt, Nixon responded in 1969 to a seminarian's question: "what role can a priest play in solving social problems?" In his twenty-three years of political life, he had been blessed to know many priests from around the world. Nixon was especially moved by their stories of those they had helped, which all had a common theme: the love of priests "for the downtrodden, the forgotten, the abused, the lonely," and God. Nixon challenged the seminarian to embody "the love and mercy and willingness to serve others that is the unique gift of those who have dedicated their lives to the service of God."[49]

In another revealing letter, Nixon responded in 1973 to David Stewart, the son of Supreme Court Justice Potter Stewart. Stewart wrote Nixon that he had "asked Jesus Christ to come into my life" about a year and a half earlier after realizing that drugs were not the answer to his problems. He asked Nixon: "Do you know Jesus Christ as your personnel [sic] Savior?" Nixon replied that when people felt disheartened and lonely, there was "no greater consolation than the certainty of God's love for us." He agreed with Stewart that "we must always ask" whether "we are living the kind of life that brings not only ourselves, but others, closer to God." While not answering Potter's question, Nixon added, Jesus "is the best friend you can have in life, and I pray He will always keep you close to Him."[50]

Thousands of Americans wrote Nixon to tell him that they were praying for him, to thank God that he was president, to encourage him, to send him copies of prayers or articles, to say they supported him, or to praise or criticize various policies. Many expressed confidence that he was a godly man who sought God's guidance. In 1970 a group of Pennsylvania Mennonites thanked God for making such a "God fearing and dedicated man" president. "We rejoice," asserted a Hawaiian woman, "to know your faith in our Lord Jesus Christ." "You are a president," another woman added, "who seeks God's will in leading this nation."[51]

In August 1972, the clerk of the Whittier Monthly Meeting wrote that many members of the First Friends Church of Whittier were "grateful to have a birthright Friend" of his "stature and Christian background in the White House." They rejoiced that he was "a man of God" who sought "to do the will of God in all circumstances" and lauded his endeavor to "be a reconciling instrument in the hand of God." These Friends were convinced that Nixon believed every problem could be solved if people earnestly sought "God's guidance."[52] Others praised Nixon's "fine example of prayer and trust in God."[53] Nixon's secretary Rose Mary Woods declared that he was "a committed Christian" whose faith was pivotal in both his personal life and work as president. He sought to be a Christian example primarily through his actions, including holding services in the White House.[54] Cabinet member Maurice Stans called Nixon "a warm and religious person under a cold-appearing shell." On the other hand, presidential advisor John Ehrlichman, a devout Christian Scientist, claimed that "Nixon was not a motivated Christian" and noted that Nixon turned down requests from several journalists and Congressmen to discuss his beliefs.[55] After Nixon died in 1994, Graham characterized him as "a man of genuine faith, rooted simply in the teachings and prayers of his devout Quaker mother."[56]

Nixon's staff assured thousands who inquired that he "is a Christian" who is "grateful for the Christian training he received in his home and Church. As a member of the Quaker Church, he has a deep religious faith."[57] Those who asked about Nixon's faith were often sent copies of speeches he gave at prayer breakfasts and statements for the Pocket Testament League, the National Day of Prayer, and National Bible Week.[58] Nevertheless, others challenged Nixon to declare his faith more openly. If the president "would just say publicly acknowledge Jesus" as "the Son of the living God," a woman wrote, crime would subside, law and order would prevail, and racial animosity would end.[59] Similarly, in May 1972, a Californian urged Nixon to use the phrase "God bless you" in his speeches and correspondence to acknowledge God "in your life and ours."[60] Interestingly, no president until Ronald Reagan regularly used this phrase, but since then it has become a standard closing for presidential addresses.

Nixon often stated that he valued prayer, deeply appreciated people's prayers for him, and prayed for individuals, and his staff echoed this point.[61] He had attended congressional prayer groups only occasionally when he was in the House and Senate, but he had found them "particularly helpful" and "inspiring."[62] When Nixon was 8, he asked his "grandmother why Quakers believed in silent prayer." She responded, "the purpose of prayer is to listen to God, not to talk to God." Nixon recounted this conversation to those assembled for the National Prayer Breakfast in 1974 to challenge them "to listen more to what God wants rather than to tell God what we want." After determining "what God wants America to be," citizens could serve Him better.[63] Nixon told aides John Ehrlichman and Charles Colson that he prayed for divine guidance every night before going to bed.[64] Billy Graham prayed with him many times, but Nixon prayed aloud only when he said grace before meals.[65]

Thousands of groups and individuals wrote Nixon to tell him that they were praying for him, and he repeatedly responded that he was "sustained by your prayers."[66] In a typical letter, the members of the Jackson, Ohio, Lions Club stated that they prayed for Nixon to continue to display his Christian convictions and be remembered as a "president who led our nation in the ways of righteousness."[67] At Graham's Knoxville crusade in May 1970, Nixon declared that he appreciated the thousands of letters reporting that people prayed for his work. He needed "spiritual guidance" and "assistance" to make "the long-range future of America" secure.[68] People's prayers gave him strength as he made decisions that affected all Americans.[69] Nixon told Senator Harold Hughes, a leading evangelical politician, that he deeply valued his prayers. "I know," he added, "the extraordinary comfort and strength that prayer offers."[70]

On numerous occasions, Nixon exhorted Americans to ask God for His aid or thank Him for His blessings. In July 1969 the president urged citizens to "pray for the successful conclusion of Apollo 11's mission to the moon and the safe return of its crew."[71] The next year Apollo 13's scheduled landing on the moon had to be aborted because an oxygen tank exploded crippling the service module and endangering the crew. Nixon called for a national day of prayer and thanksgiving on the Sunday following their return and attended a special service in Honolulu "to give his personal thanks." At that service, Nixon credited the astronaut's safety to God's assistance.[72] Nixon proclaimed a national moment of prayer on January 27, 1973, to thank God that the United States had "achieved its goal of peace with honor in Vietnam." "As a people with a deep and abiding faith," he declared, "we know that no great work can be accomplished without the aid and inspiration of Almighty God."[73]

Although Nixon was invited to attend the Friends Meeting of Washington, he opted to hold his own religious services at the White House.[74] Nixon did occasionally attend churches in Washington, at San Clemente, Key Biscayne, and Camp David, or when he was traveling abroad. Before Nixon attended services, his staff carefully checked the background and convictions of pastors who were scheduled to preach to ensure that they would not chastise the president or criticize the Vietnam War.[75] Some Christians chided Nixon for not attending church every Sunday.[76] Nixon gave little money to churches while president. From 1969 to 1972 the Republican gave only $13,445 to benevolent organizations out of a total income of over $1 million.[77]

Nixon's staff constantly assessed the potential political consequences of his involvement in religious activities. In 1970 Nixon's team suggested changing the name of the Presidential Prayer Breakfast because it placed "undue pressure on the President to attend" and sometimes put the president in "untenable and embarrassing" positions.[78] The next year Nixon's aides considered having the prayer breakfasts televised, but concluded that in their present form they were too dull and unattractive to appeal to the three major networks.[79] After weighing the potential advantages of accepting Oregon Senator Mark Hatfield's invitation to participate in an international network of prayer breakfasts, Nixon's staff concluded that doing so could help advance the president's foreign policy.[80]

What Nixon thought about human nature is hard to decipher. Charles Henderson argued that Nixon believed people "are born with an infinite capacity for good." Embracing the "liberal belief in progress," he usually ignored "the tragic flaws in the American character, the American political system, and his own policies."[81] Richard Reeves, by contrast, contended that Nixon "assumed the worst in people" and "trusted almost no one."[82] The Quaker rejected the "infinite perfectibility of man."[83] America's founders, he added, sought to devise a government that enabled "imperfect people" who lived in "an imperfect world" to have a secure and stable life.[84]

Nixon occasionally affirmed belief in an afterlife. In a college essay he declared that the grave of his brother Arthur contained only his "bodily image."[85] In offering his condolences to the bereaved, Nixon typically acknowledged their "great loss" and promised to pray for them, but said nothing about an afterlife.[86] Despite calling Eisenhower a "man of deep faith who believed in God and trusted in His will," Nixon made no reference in his 1969 eulogy to the general being in heaven. Instead, Nixon usually praised deceased individuals' tremendous contributions and urged others to carry on their work.[87] In his eulogy for J. Edgar Hoover in 1972, Nixon did declare that the former FBI director had "richly earned peace through all eternity."[88] In a 1990 book Nixon stated that he still agreed with his statement for his philosophy course at Whittier: "The resurrection symbolically teaches the great lesson that men who achieve the highest values in their lives may gain immorality."[89] Billy Graham confidently declared in his 1994 eulogy that Nixon had been reunited in heaven with Pat who had died ten months earlier. We can have "hope beyond the grave" as Nixon did, Graham proclaimed, "because Jesus Christ has opened the door to heaven for us by his death and resurrection."[90]

Stephen Ambrose claims that "Nixon was head of a warm, loving, happy family" and had a very close relationship with his daughters Julie and Trisha, but other biographers contend that Richard and Pat fought frequently during his years of public service.[91] Commerce Secretary Maurice Stans asserts that Nixon, who was "highly disciplined in his personal life," did not smoke or gamble, drank sparingly, exercised regularly, and "displayed no interest in extramarital sex."[92] Some maintain that while in the navy Nixon won a considerable amount of money playing poker and cursed "a blue streak." "The pressures of wartime" and "the oppressive monotony," Nixon explained, made poker "an irresistible diversion," which he found "entertaining and profitable."[93] Others argue that he sometimes drank to excess. As is now well known, Nixon swore profusely in certain private settings; he frequently took

God's and Jesus' names in vain, often used "hell," "damn," and "asshole," and sometimes called people "little shits."[94] However, his vulgarity only came to public light near the end of, and especially after, his presidency, and, therefore, his private behavior caused little controversy unlike that of Harry Truman and Bill Clinton.

Religious Rhetoric

Although religion and prayer were central to his family's life, Nixon explained, "they were essentially personal and private." This led him, Nixon explained, to rarely quote the Bible in his political speeches. Eisenhower had urged Nixon when he was vice president, "to refer to God from time to time in my speeches, but I did not feel comfortable doing so."[95] Consequently, Nixon did not mention God nearly as much as did many other occupants of the Oval Office. Moreover, the religious language he employed was usually generic and vague; he typically used such phrases as "a deep religious faith," "moral values," "idealism," "great spiritual sources," and "a positive spiritual and moral climate."[96] During the 1968 presidential campaign, Carl Henry, the editor of *Christianity Today*, interviewed Nixon and found him "remarkably imprecise about spiritual realities and enduring ethical concerns."[97] Unlike Franklin Roosevelt, Truman, and Eisenhower, Nixon rarely emphasized America's need for religious revival. He did insist that "the problems facing the United States and the world are so serious" that "Divine Guidance" was needed to solve them.[98]

Countless Americans were troubled by secular and hedonistic societal trends including the removal of the words "In the Beginning God" from a postal stamp commemorating the astronauts' flight around the moon and back and efforts to ban Bibles from space capsules and Bible reading and prayer in outer space. During Nixon's five and half years in office, the White House was frequently inundated with letters and petitions on these issues as well as by ones asking that prayer and Bible reading be reinstated in the schools. A South Carolinian warned Nixon that the United States was emulating "Sodom and Gomorrah and [that] God might destroy this nation" if Americans did not repent.[99]

Nixon declared that Governor John Winthrop's "presumptuous" claim in 1630 that the settlers of Massachusetts Bay Colony were "a city set upon a hill [that] cannot be hidden" expressed the spirit that made America great. Nixon challenged Americans "to awaken the moral power" of the Puritan heritage and "be the light of the world."[100] His 1972 Thanksgiving proclamation stated: "From Moses at the Red Sea to Jesus preparing to feed the multitudes, the Scriptures summon us to words and deeds of gratitude." "From Washington kneeling at Valley Forge," he added, "to the prayer of an astronaut circling the moon, our own history repeats that summons" and demonstrates its benefits. "Truly our cup runs over with the bounty of God," he proclaimed, as is evident in "our lives, our liberties," "worldly goods," and religious legacy.[101] America's mission was to provide "spiritual leadership and idealism."[102] Every president, Nixon alleged, had "recognized the spiritual heritage of this Nation" and asked God to bless its domestic and foreign affairs, and every chief executive had left office with "a very deep religious faith." When facing difficult decisions, all the presidents had turned to God.[103]

White House Worship Services

Nixon's decision to hold Sunday worship services in the White House was very controversial. During his first term, Nixon held thirty-six services (twenty-six during the first two years), a substantial number considering that he visited more than twenty foreign nations during these four years.[104] Nixon sponsored these services to remind members of his administration that "we feel God's presence here, and that we seek his guidance here." They also encouraged Americans to attend church and accentuated the nation's "faith in a Supreme Being." Moreover, these services enabled members of the administration and their families to worship with the president. The services were the most popular aspect of Nixon's administration, one staffer argued, because millions of Americans "could relate to a president at prayer."[105]

Nixon also chose to hold services in the White House because he intensely disliked "going to church for a show." Unfortunately, he could not attend church without being accompanied by the news media and "batteries of still and television cameras."[106] Citing reasons Truman and some of Nixon's successors also employed, his staff insisted that Nixon's attendance at Washington churches required them to take many precautions to ensure the safety of worshippers and caused them "grave inconvenience."[107] Nixon later explained that he deplored "descending on a church with hordes of pistol-packing Secret Service men and pencil-packing reporters." He also feared being lectured to about the war in Vietnam, as Lyndon Johnson had been, by "publicity-hungry ministers," and he wanted to avoid "the spectacle of draft dodgers defiling" a church service by demonstrating outside while he was worshipping there.[108]

These nonsectarian White House services, which typically lasted about thirty minutes, included a doxology, a prayer, two hymns, a musical selection by a choir or a soloist, and a short sermon.[109] Preachers included a cross-section of the nation's most distinguished religious leaders: Catholic priests (Terence Cardinal Cooke, John Cardinal Krol, and Archbishop Humberto S. Medeiros), the chancellor of the Jewish Theological Seminary in New York City (Louis Finkelstein), the pastor of a large black Baptist Church in Harlem, former New York Yankee Bobby Richardson, the chaplain of the House of Representatives, former Congressman Walter Judd, the General Secretary of the National Council of Churches, educators Charles Malik and Quaker D. Elton Trueblood, and prominent Protestant ministers (Presbyterians Richard Halverson and Louis Evans, Jr., Baptist Allan Watson, and Lutheran Paul Noren).[110] Billy Graham and Norman Vincent Peale both preached four times. Other clergy and politicians offered prayers, varied choirs provided special music, and the president always introduced the participants. The East Room's 250 worshippers typically consisted of a mix of government officials (cabinet members, congressmen, Supreme Court justices, and Diplomatic Corp members) and their families, White House staff and their spouses and children, and special guests.[111]

Nixon helped plan and lead these services. Nixon's Chief of Staff H. R. Haldeman reported that he gave "a great deal of time and attention" to the services and considered them "extremely important." Because of their "high degree of visibility" and potential positive or negative impact, his staff carefully arranged them.[112] Nixon made the final decision about speakers and the structure of the services and evaluated how the services could reach a larger audience.[113]

Hundreds of citizens, including politicians, religious leaders, and educators, recommended speakers or requested to preach themselves. A White House staffer noted in February 1970 that Nixon had been "besieged by Congressmen and Senators and many others urging that he select a minister of their choice for the White House services."[114] Many choirs or soloists volunteered to sing, and thousands of people asked to attend the services or inquired about their nature.[115] Correspondents also suggested ways to improve the services including taking an offering to help various charities.[116] Hatfield and other attendees told Nixon how much they benefitted from the services.[117]

Thousands praised these services, and many asserted that they testified to Nixon's faith. Anglican Orthodox Christians in Bellevue, Washington, argued that the services were "in the best tradition of the Old Testament kings" who invited the prophets to preach to them.[118] Critics of these services, a Baptist pastor in Huntington Beach, California, contended, did not understand the First Amendment. It prohibited a state church; it did not prevent people from worshipping as they wished in their own homes.[119] An army chaplain expected these services to strengthen Nixon's administration and

America's moral and political fiber.[120] A Youngstown, Ohio, rabbi applauded Nixon's attempt to gain divine guidance.[121] Senator Robert Dole wrote Nixon: "the good people of Kansas are most impressed with the Sunday morning worship services."[122] Whenever a president attended a church service in Washington, D. Elton Trueblood opined, it created a "circus atmosphere" that was not "conducive to sincere and humble worship of Almighty God."[123] The leaders of the Truth Crusaders prayed that "the contaminating influences of pro-communist, Un-American ideologies and modernistic apostate philosophies" would never infiltrate "the most vital religious services on this planet."[124]

The number of White House services was substantially reduced in 1972 allegedly to avoid all appearances that Nixon "was using religion for political purposes."[125] However, they clearly did serve numerous political aims. The president thought the services "should be used for political opportunities," and his staff continually analyzed their potential political benefits and liabilities. They carefully considered who to invite to preach and attend to obtain the optimum political results.[126] Staffers took into account the political views, ethnicity, and potential impact of prospective speakers.[127] Nixon argued that "it would be very useful" to invite publishers and editors to attend the services and instructed staff to investigate having the services broadcast on the radio. The first 24 sermons were published in 1972 as *White House Sermons*. Max Fisher, Nixon's liaison to Jews, claimed that having rabbi Louis Finkelstein preach had been "very well received throughout the Jewish community."[128] Nixon's staff sometimes even identified the positions members of Congress who attended particular services held on issues of importance to the White House.[129] As the 1972 election approached, his staff sought to schedule a prominent black minister who backed the president to preach to show Nixon's "interest in the black community" and increase support for the incumbent "in influential black religious circles."[130] In addition, many key political supporters and donors received invitations to attend. Nixon requested that "rich people with strong religious interest" be invited, including the CEOs of major corporations.[131]

Nixon's services were criticized on various grounds. Some feared that the speakers would endorse and help sanctify his policies on civil rights and Vietnam.[132] Others warned that preachers would abandon their prophetic role because of "the tact and courtesy" expected of guests in someone's home.[133] The White House countered that the pastor of any church Nixon attended would also be influenced by his presence. Nixon's staff argued unconvincingly that "holding services in the White House in no way inhibits" ministers from making comments that they would not make in their own churches.[134]

Some religious leaders complained that the services constituted an informal "establishment of religion."[135] "By a curious combination of innocence and guile," renowned theologian Reinhold Niebuhr claimed in August 1969, Nixon had circumvented the First Amendment and threatened the "wall of separation of church and state." The close relationship between the nation's chief executive and its most respected Christian leader, which Niebuhr termed the "Nixon-Graham doctrine," contravened the Bible's subjecting of "all historical reality (including economic, social and radical injustice)" to God's "absolute standards of justice." Instead, it helped consecrate some contemporary public policies that were "morally inferior or outrageously unjust." Moreover, this doctrine wrongly assumed that an individual conversion experience cured individuals of sin, which ignored both the institutional nature of sin and the actual practices of people. Graham, Niebuhr argued, had abandoned his responsibility to promote justice in order to gain the president's favor. America, Niebuhr declared, did not need an Amaziah, who colluded "with the king to maintain the status quo," but rather an Amos who prophetically criticized the "defective and unjust social order."[136] After reporting on Niebuhr's article, the New York Times was deluged with letters discussing "the proper relationship between preachers and politicians" and both lauding and castigating Niebuhr.[137] Meanwhile, Nixon instructed the FBI to investigate Niebuhr's "patriotism."[138]

In 1969 Madalyn Murray O'Hair chided Nixon for inviting only Protestants, Catholics, and Jews to preach at his White House services and forgetting about the nation's "fourth faith: faith in man." She claimed to speak for millions of American atheists and offered to deliver a "sermon" on that faith.[139] Her request was denied, and in 1973 O'Hair filed a suit in federal court to stop these services, prompting thousands of concerned citizens to urge Nixon to continue them.[140]

Were these services the consummate civil religion spectacle or were they a legitimate way for the president and other government officials to worship God and strengthen their faith? Were they a crass attempt to curry divine favor and gain positive publicity and political advantage or a testimony of American political leaders' commitment to pray to and worship the "Judge of us all," as Louis Finkelstein argued?[141] Although the services served all these purposes, the clergy ignored their prophetic calling. Most of their sermons discussed the moral implications of Christianity; few of them focused on social ills and their remedies. Many guest preachers lauded the achievements of Nixon and other government leaders. No one surpassed the adulation of Peale and Finkelstein. Speaking on Father's Day in 1969, Peale heralded Nixon as "the first father of the nation." Finkelstein prayed that future historians would be able to write that God gave Nixon "the vision and the wisdom to save the world."[142] No sermon directly challenged Nixon to change any policy or right any wrong.

Relations with Religious Groups

Nixon maintained cordial relations with numerous Protestant and Catholic leaders, most notably Peale and Graham. Nixon called Peale "one of my closest friends" and claimed he influenced him more during the mid-1960s than Graham did.[143] Peale performed the wedding ceremony of Nixon's daughter Julie and David Eisenhower in 1968. The best-selling author argued that Nixon was one of America's greatest presidents who God was using to advance "the well-being of humanity."[144]

Much has been written about the long-time friendship of Nixon and Graham, both by them and their numerous biographers.[145] Graham and Nixon first met in 1950, and in subsequent years they played golf together dozens of times. While Nixon was vice president, he spoke at three of Graham's meetings in a single day in 1956 in South Carolina and to the 100,000 attendees of Graham's 1957 crusade in Yankee Stadium.[146]

In December 1967 Nixon and Graham read and analyzed Scripture, prayed, and discussed his possible candidacy. Graham told Nixon he was "the best prepared man in the United States to be President" and that if he did not run he would always wonder whether he should have.[147] Although Graham did not publicly endorse Nixon, after his victory was confirmed on election night in 1968, Graham prayed with the Nixon family that the president and his staff would dedicate themselves to serving God.[148]

Writing to Graham as he began his second term, Nixon declared, "I shall be eternally grateful for your friendship and your support and your prayers over the years."[149] Graham explained that "the essential bond" between them was "personal and spiritual" rather than "political or intellectual."[150] Graham and Nixon had "a genuine friendship," and the evangelist was convinced that Nixon had a substantial "spiritual side."[151] Despite what Nixon wrote about Jesus and the Bible in college, Graham believed that the president accepted the evangelical position on biblical authority and the divinity of Christ. Nixon assured Graham that he believed "the Bible from cover to cover."[152]

During his presidency, Nixon and Graham discussed numerous issues in letters, on the phone, and in person. The evangelist, one Graham biographer claims, was almost a member of Nixon's cabinet.[153] They especially talked about civil rights, protest movements, and the evangelist's campaigns around the world.[154] Graham also urged Nixon to take action on draft exemptions for

Campus Crusade workers, postal rates for religious publications, and other matters.[155] When the *Christian Herald* criticized Nixon's policy in Vietnam in the summer of 1969, the White House solicited Graham's opinion. He assured Nixon that the *Herald's* circulation and influence were substantially less than those of *Christianity Today*, which had consistently supported the president.[156] The evangelist praised many of Nixon's addresses, especially his second inaugural address which "touched a deep cord in America."[157] Nixon commended Graham's "excellent political judgment" and lauded his "unwavering support of my policy of peace with honor in Vietnam" and his leading role in the White House worship services.[158]

On April 30, 1970, Nixon announced the US invasion of Cambodia, and four days later the National Guard killed four student demonstrators at Kent State University. A massive student strike shut down colleges across the nation. Despite the presence of hundreds of protestors, the president spoke at Graham's crusade in Knoxville, Tennessee, on May 28, 1970. If youth turned "to those great spiritual sources that have made America the great country that it is," Nixon argued, their principal concerns could be remedied.[159]

In January 1973, Graham promised Nixon that "you [will] always have my confidence [and] friendship" in every circumstance.[160] As the Watergate crisis unfolded, Graham kept his word. Two weeks later, Graham told Nixon that he was "appalled" by the media's attack on him. He reminded Nixon that King David had sometimes become "terribly discouraged and despondent" because others had distorted everything he did to promote "their own selfish interest." Graham assured Nixon that he was praying for him "almost night and day." He urged the president "to put your total trust in the same Christ that your dear Mother so firmly believed in."[161] In May, Graham declared that he did not think Nixon knew about either the bugging incident or the cover-up.[162] The day after Christmas, Graham reaffirmed his "personal affection" for Nixon and his "complete confidence" in the president's "personal integrity."[163]

Although his involvement in the Watergate cover-up shattered Graham's image of Nixon, and his loyal support of the president caused him considerable embarrassment and brought him much negative publicity, their friendship continued. Eight days after Nixon resigned, Graham told him: "For nearly a quarter of a century I have loved you as a friend and brother—and I have not changed!"[164] When Nixon was hospitalized in the fall of 1974, Ruth Graham arranged for a plane to fly by his window pulling a banner that proclaimed: "We love you and God loves you."[165] Ever the evangelist, Graham told Nixon that he hoped "that this entire tragic affair" had made him reassess his "own relationship to Christ. A Richard Nixon touched by the power of Christ could help lead this nation in a spiritual awakening that it desperately needs."

He reassured the ex-president, as he had publicly stated, that released tapes did "not tell the story of the real Nixon."[166] Nixon acknowledged that Watergate was "very difficult" for Graham and that he "was very troubled" by the profanity of the tapes. Despite great pressure from many quarters, Graham "did not waver in his personal friendship." Nixon rarely saw him during the last year of his presidency because "I did not want to drag him down with me."[167]

Graham insisted in 1976 that he could not believe that Nixon "took advantage of me." Nixon's behavior was "still a mystery to me."[168] Graham frequently called Watergate a "nightmare," and in his 1997 autobiography he lamented that "when the worst came out, it was nearly unbearable to me." Although Nixon was clearly culpable, Graham avowed that Watergate was a brief, incomprehensible parenthesis in "a good man's lengthy political career," a man who held "noble standards of ethics" and treated the presidency "as a public trust."[169] David Aikman argues that Graham's "desire to see the good and spiritual in everyone" prevented him from recognizing "the true complexity" of Nixon's character, "especially its deep, dark streaks."[170]

Nixon's staff carefully evaluated the responses of various religious leaders, publications, and organizations to the president's addresses, actions, and policies and assessed the political advantages of meeting with different individuals and groups. Nixon periodically hosted clergy to promote his policies and solicit their support. His staff arranged a meeting in March 1971 with seventy religious leaders to educate them "on all aspects of the drug problem," motivate them to help stem "the tide of drug abuse," and convince them to support the president's policy.[171] Nixon briefly discussed "the theological implications of drug abuse and the relation of youth and religion today" with these leaders.[172]

Some mainline Protestants complained that Nixon was ignoring their organizations. In 1972 Eugene Carson Blake, the president of the World Council of Churches, contended that Nixon consulted too much with "anti-ecumenical" Protestant leaders and Catholic officials and too little with his group. Jesuit aide John McLaughlin countered that Nixon had hosted many "distinguished churchmen" including R. H. Edwin Espe, the General Secretary of the National Council of Churches, Trueblood, Graham, and Peale who were at least "open to ecumenical contact" or "prime movers in ecumenical program." Moreover, Nixon had met with about five Protestant ministers for every one Catholic priest, even though Catholics were about a quarter of the US population.[173]

Protestant denominations criticized various Nixon policies. The General Assembly of the Presbyterian Church (USA) exhorted the Republican to reestablish diplomatic relations with Cuba and end trade embargoes against Fidel Castro's regime. Both the House of Bishops of the Episcopal Church and the American Baptist Convention petitioned the president to withdraw all American troops from Vietnam by the end of 1971. The House of Bishops and the Disciples of Christ called on Nixon to grant amnesty to draft resisters whose actions were motivated by their Christian commitment. The United Church of Christ called for a revision of the Selective Service Law to safeguard individual freedom.[174]

Although Nixon met with many more Protestants than Catholics, his administration reached out to Catholics in a variety of ways. During his first trip abroad, the president met with Pope Paul VI. In February 1970 he invited prominent Catholic educators to the White House to discuss how the federal government could help parochial schools, and throughout his presidency he worked to aid Catholic private schools. Following Truman's example, in June 1970, Nixon appointed Henry Cabot Lodge Jr. as his personal emissary to the Vatican. The Californian chose Notre Dame's president Theodore Hesburgh to head his Civil Rights Commission. He sent dozens of letters to Catholic organizations, congregations, and leaders commending them for their "work for social justice" and praising the policy proposals of Catholic officials. He also wrote an article highlighting the administration's policies benefiting Catholics for Catholic magazines and newspapers and met with numerous Catholic leaders, including Cardinal Cooke, to confer about a variety of issues.[175]

As a Republican, Nixon had a great challenge in maintaining positive relations with and gaining the votes of Jewish Americans. Nixon's tapes display his strong anti-Semitic views. These tapes and his correspondence contain hundreds of complaints about Jewish liberal attitudes, control of the media, hostility toward him, and conspiracies to undermine the government and society. Upset by the comments of a Jewish labor commissioner in 1971, Nixon went on one of his numerous tirades about Jews: "Washington is full of Jews" most of whom "are disloyal." "You can't trust the bastards," he added. "They turn on you."[176]

Nevertheless, several Jews were among his closest advisors: Secretary of State Henry Kissinger, Federal Reserve Chairman Arthur Burns, speechwriter William Safire, Chairman of the Council of Economic Advisors Herbert Stein, campaign manager and adviser Murray Chotiner, special counsel Leonard Garment, and deputy assistants Eugene Cowen and Bruce Rabb. Moreover, many Jews appreciated the Nixon administration's strong support of Israel during very traumatic years that included the 1973 Yom Kipper War. Nixon hosted Israeli Prime Minister Golda Meir in 1969, met with numerous American Jewish leaders, routinely sent greetings to Jewish conferences, and spoke to a few of them.[177] Staff who served as liaisons to the Jewish community answered letters from Jewish citizens, spoke to various Jewish groups, and advised the president on Jewish issues. Nixon commended Jewish organizations for promoting "human dignity and social justice" and uplifting "the moral and spiritual climate."[178]

The Election of 1972

Religion played a less significant role in the elections of 1968 and 1972 than it had in 1960.[179] Nevertheless, religious and moral factors were still important, especially in 1972. Nixon "shrewdly positioned himself as an ecumenical defender of the nation's" traditional morality, which led many Protestants and Catholics to view him favorably. Although George McGovern, the Democratic nominee, was the son of a Methodist minister, the Nixon campaign portrayed him as a secular candidate "who would legalize abortion and surrender in Vietnam."[180]

Throughout his first term, Nixon's staff, led by Charles Colson and speechwriter Pat Buchanan, worked to establish advantageous contacts with Catholics and publicize the president's policies that Catholics supported. Nixon defended the "sanctity of life" and opposed liberalizing abortion laws. His team reached out to the Catholic press and targeted states and congressional districts "where a hard-sell Catholic approach" could lead to victory.[181] They also conducted surveys to assess Catholic priorities and interests and evaluated the benefits and liabilities of taking pro-Catholic stands on various issues.[182]

Nixon's staff also discussed how best to win Jewish votes, especially in the crucial states of California, New York, New Jersey, Texas, and Illinois. They accentuated Nixon's strong support of Israel and efforts to help Soviet Jews emigrate and spoke to various Jewish groups to help counteract the numerous appearances of Democratic candidates at Jewish events.[183] Despite these efforts, Robert Roth of the *Washington Post* argued in February 1972 that only Truman rivaled Nixon for the title of "Israel's best friend," but Nixon had not used this fact to woo the nation's estimated three million Jewish voters.[184] Some Jewish leaders such as rabbis Herschel Schacter and Ronald Greenwald actively supported the Californian, and Nixon improved his percentage of the Jewish vote from 20 in 1968 to 35 in 1972 (although he won only 43.4 percent of the popular vote in 1968 compared with 60.7 percent in 1972).[185]

Nixon realized that like urban Catholics and Jews, various Protestant groups, including some traditionally Democratic constituencies, might vote for him if he accentuated social issues such as school prayer and family values. Recognizing the importance of the evangelical vote, he made Graham an unofficial consultant in his reelection campaign and solicited the help of other Protestant leaders. Graham provided advice and worked privately to promote Nixon's reelection. The evangelist announced that he would vote for the president but did not publicly campaign for him.[186] Nixon's campaign staff held several briefings with religious leaders, and in September 1972 Nixon met with prominent clergy, including Trueblood, televangelist Rex Humbard, Bob Harrington, the "chaplain of Bourbon Street," and Bishop William Smith of the African Methodist Episcopal Church, about how to mobilize pro-Nixon clergy and appeal to religious voters.[187]

Meanwhile, concerns about Nixon's perspectives and policies led to the formation of "Evangelicals for McGovern/Shriver" led by black evangelist Tom Skinner. In the fall, the Grand Rapids Priests' Association endorsed McGovern, declaring that his political philosophy and actions "most consistently embrace the Christian principles of peace, justice and the sacredness of human life." In a mid-October address at evangelical Wheaton College, McGovern explained how his Christian convictions helped shape his political approach and policies. A group of evangelicals, including some Calvin College professors, sponsored a newspaper ad explaining why they supported McGovern.[188] In late October, James Schaal, the president of Reformed Bible College in Grand Rapids, urged the president to emphasize his strong Christian commitment to reassure fellow believers who were "deeply concerned about his reelection."[189]

Nixon's campaign strategy worked as he won 84 percent of the evangelical vote and 52 percent of the Catholic vote (in 1968 Nixon won 69 percent of the evangelical vote and 33 percent of the Catholic vote).[190] Many evangelicals rejoiced when the president was reelected, convinced that his second term would stop the onslaught of secularism and moral permissiveness and restore the nation's Judeo-Christian moral basis. *Eternity* magazine hoped that Nixon would by "precept and example" lead "the nation out of its ethical morass."[191]

Philosophy of Government

Nixon said little about his worldview or philosophy of government. The Republican hoped that religion would have a profound impact on American politics, but he insisted that its influence was best when it indirectly affected "the morals, habits, and souls of individual Americans." Religion should help shape "the political climate and the principles" that underlay public policies rather than specific policies.[192]

Nixon occasionally accentuated moral rectitude. Americans, he asserted, believed that "God is on the side of right," not "the side with the biggest battalions." "Therefore, they prayed for wisdom to see the right and be on God's side."[193] In discussing civil rights, Nixon repeatedly declared that "we have to do what is right."[194] The Quaker claimed that he rejected "woolly-headed" utopianism and empty-minded pragmatism and instead espoused "practical idealism."[195] However, Nixon appeared to lack "a fixed ideological base," to be "the consummate pragmatist," and put his own political ambition before the nation's interests.[196] As an "opportunist" who had no overarching political philosophy, "master plan," or definitive objectives, he continually tried to keep his options open and improvised to accomplish particular policy aims.[197] Nixon's absence of "guiding principles" and "lust for power," argued Congressman John Anderson, led him to commit the Watergate cover-up.[198]

Public Policy: Campaigning for World Peace

Discerning direct connections between Nixon's faith and public policy issues is difficult, even with his policies that sought to help the poor and promote family values such as his Family Assistance Plan (which Congress never passed), or his pioneering environmental protection legislation.[199] However, Nixon's religious values did play an important role in his quest for peace. In an interview in the *New York Times*, Nixon labeled himself "a deeply committed pacifist, perhaps because of the Quaker heritage of my mother."[200] Like Truman, Nixon made the pursuit of peace a major priority of his administration and worked to create a new international framework to attain it.

Although the United States continued to wage a cold war against the Soviets and fight to stop the spread of communism (now in Vietnam instead of Korea), Nixon constantly proclaimed his desire to achieve peace. In 1969 he swore his oath of office on a Bible open to Isaiah 2:4: "He will judge between the nations and will settle disputes for many peoples. They will beat their swords into plowshares and their spears into pruning hooks. Nation will not take up sword against nation, nor will they train for war anymore." America, Nixon announced in his first inaugural address, could "help lead the world" to the "high ground of peace." "The peace we seek," he proclaimed, " 'comes with healing in its wings'; with compassion for those who have suffered; with understanding for those who have opposed us; [and] with opportunity for all the peoples of the earth."[201] Nixon journeyed to the Soviet Union and China to help improve relations with these nations.

By engaging "in patient and prolonged diplomacy in every corner of the world," Nixon sought to erect "a structure of peace" that rested "on common interests and mutual agreements."[202] He worked to construct a world where everyone could fulfill "their dreams for peace, justice, and prosperity."[203]

Creating a peaceful world required establishing networks of alliances, respecting commitments, negotiating patiently, balancing military forces and expanding economic interdependence, and giving all nations a stake in preserving peace.[204]

In February 1970, Nixon issued a report to Congress on US foreign policy for the 1970s titled "A New Strategy for Peace." He maintained that "peace must be far more than the absence of war." It depended on "a durable structure of international relationships which inhibits or removes the causes of war." This structure must be built on three pillars: partnerships with other nations, military strength, and negotiation. Without partnerships, Nixon warned, America would exhaust its physical and moral resources "in a futile effort to dominate our friends and [would] forever isolate our enemies." "Peace requires strength. It cannot be based on good will alone." True peace, he avowed, rested on recognizing "the divinely inspired dignity of man" and the brotherhood of humanity and benefited all nations. Vigilant efforts by many countries, the reduction of arms, and "the ascendancy of reason" were all crucial to attaining peace.[205]

While seeking to achieve these objectives, as a "realist," Nixon envisioned a "relative peace," ensured by a strong American military.[206] In June 1971, the president asserted that his Quaker background strongly influenced his policy on Vietnam and promised that ending the war there would help produce "a more lasting peace" in the world.[207]

In discussing peace, Nixon continually emphasized biblical and spiritual themes. Toasting the acting president of India in 1969, Nixon praised Mahatma Gandhi's teachings on peace. Peace, the president asserted, "is a spiritual condition. All religions pray for it."[208] Beginning with the ancient prophets, Nixon wrote, God had worked through people of faith to extend His truth, love, and peace to others.[209] He exhorted attendees of a 1971 Armed Forces Prayer Breakfast to pray that "our cause is just." As Americans worked diligently to procure peace, they must remember that "except the Lord keep the city, the watchman waketh but in vain."[210] Although the United States must remain dominant militarily and economically, Nixon avowed, its strong moral values and "trust in God" was its "ultimate defense."[211]

At the 1972 National Prayer Breakfast, Nixon asserted that the United States, as a "Christian nation," had "a charge and a destiny" "to play the role of peacemaker" to enable the world's peoples to discuss their "great differences" and live together harmoniously.[212] "With faith in God," ourselves, and our country, Nixon declared in 1972, "let us" "lead the way to a lasting peace in the world."[213] The United States, he declared, sought to construct "a world of open borders, open hearts, and open minds," where people could "devote their energies to the works of peace rather than to the weapons of war."[214]

Nixon frequently urged Americans to pray for peace.[215] He thanked millions for praying for his trip to China in February 1972, which he hoped would be "a significant step forward" in America's quest for world peace.[216] After returning, he maintained that his discussions with China's leaders had strengthened "the structure for an enduring world peace."[217] In early 1973, after a ceasefire was negotiated in Vietnam, Nixon thanked the congregations and individuals who had prayed for this outcome.[218]

Various groups and individuals applauded Nixon's pursuit of peace. Every Wednesday evening the 1,500 attendees of the Founder's Church in Los Angeles prayed that Nixon would continue to challenge people to work for peace and practice goodwill. They rejoiced that Nixon's "Quaker background and heritage of following the Inner Light and Inner Wisdom and Inner Presence" motivated him to pursue peace.[219] D. Elton Trueblood asserted that, like his mother, Nixon stood "in the mainstream of the Quaker tradition" in his "positive peace-making."[220]

Abandoning his earlier depictions of the USSR as the embodiment of evil, Nixon sought to improve Soviet–American relations. The central issue, the president argued, "is whether our two countries can transcend the past and work together to build a lasting peace."[221] "In the nuclear age," Nixon insisted, conscientious leaders, "whatever their philosophies," must collaborate to halt the arms race.[222] "Never before," he added, had "the needs for peace been so strong and the potential consequences of war been so catastrophic."[223] Nixon argued that the only time in world history "that we have had extended periods [of peace] is when there was a balance of power." Therefore, it was essential for "a strong, healthy United States, Europe, Soviet Union, China, [and] Japan" to balance each other. Nixon insisted that the Soviet leaders were no longer committed to world dominance because they had learned that Marxist ideology was unappealing and could not solve the problems of industrial society.[224]

Nixon emphasized that during his first term he had traveled to twenty-two countries and visited four world capitals where none of his predecessors had set foot—Peking, Moscow, Warsaw, and Bucharest—to promote peace. At the 1973 National Prayer Breakfast Nixon claimed that his trip to the Soviet Union "had enormous significance" because it was the first time the superpowers recognized "areas where they could work together" and agreed to collaborate on "certain peaceful enterprises and to limit armaments." He also rejoiced that a ceasefire had been signed in Vietnam and asked all Americans to pray with him: "Let there be peace on Earth and let it begin with me."[225] In August 1974, Nixon asserted that he had accomplished much: he had ended the Vietnam War, established diplomatic relations with China, built friendships with Middle Eastern countries, improved relations with the Soviet Union, and made "crucial breakthroughs" that helped limit nuclear arms.[226] By ending the Vietnam War, Henry Kissinger argued, Nixon "advanced the vision of peace of his Quaker youth."[227]

Critics objected that Nixon's actions, especially continuing the war in Vietnam for four years and expanding it into Laos and Cambodia, were motivated by an amoral realpolitik perspective designed to preserve his own power and enhance his legacy. Instead of promoting peace, his actions had isolated America from its friends and allies and undermined its prestige and influence in Africa, Asia, Latin America, and Europe.[228] Others pointed to the irony of allying with "the tyrannical and unpopular Thieu regime" and the increased bombing attacks in waging war in Vietnam "in the name of peacemaking," which were motivated by belief that America must not evade its divine mandate to stop communist aggression around the world.[229] Still others warned that Nixon's belief in America's righteousness and his global mission to stop the spread of communism might produce nuclear catastrophe.[230]

Watergate

Although Nixon engaged in numerous other illegal and unethical actions as president, his complicity in the Watergate cover-up is generally seen as his worst abuse and proof that he lacked fixed moral principles, good character, and genuine Christian commitment. In the final report of the Senate Watergate Committee, Sam Ervin contended that "the scope and intensity" of Watergate's "unethical and illegal actions" was without "precedent in the political annals of America."[231]

Jonathan Aitken argues that not a "single piece of evidence has emerged to suggest that the President gave any direct or indirect instructions" for the Watergate break-in. Both Nixon's initial reactions to the burglary and the fact that others had their "own motives for ordering" it support the contention that he was not directly responsible. However, the president orchestrated the cover-up, which made him "guilty of many 'crimes,'" including deceit, mendacity, and concealment.[232] David Gergen maintains that whether or not Nixon directed or knew in advance about the break-in is a moot point: he is ultimately responsible for it "because he created an atmosphere in which his subordinates" logically assumed that "this was what he expected from them."[233]

Religious groups responded in a variety of ways to the Watergate crisis, the gradual revelation of Nixon's responsibility for the cover-up, and his resignation. Some religious bodies, including the United Pentecostal Church International, stressed the importance of praying for the president and other government officials during this national crisis.[234] Others participated in a three-day fast on the Capitol steps during the latter days of the calamity. The president thanked them for their "great sacrifice" and expressed appreciation for their numerous signs stating that "God Loves Nixon."[235] Many evangelicals defended Nixon during the crisis, arguing, based on Romans 13, that citizens must be subject to the ruling powers because God had ordained them. Evangelist Billy James Hargis exhorted Christians to send stones to Congressmen who supported impeachment.[236] *Christianity Today* strongly supported the president throughout the scandal. While labeling Watergate a "debacle" and a "sordid" and "squalid affair," the editors accepted Nixon's declaration that "he was not personally involved."[237] After Nixon resigned, the editors admitted that Nixon's guilt had been "established beyond reasonable doubt" and argued that his claim that the cover-up was done for national security reasons "revealed his commitment to situation ethics."[238] Others used Watergate to illustrate and accentuate human depravity. Journalist Wesley Pippert asserted that Watergate "reminded a generation of humanists and relativists about the reality of evil in the world."[239]

In October 1973, Milton Mayer, a Quaker educator and opponent of the Vietnam War, exhorted the East Whittier Friends Church to disown or ex-communicate the president. He noted that some Friends had begun to call for disowning Nixon shortly after he was elected to Congress in 1946. Their campaign had been intensified by the Vietnam War, especially the Christmas 1972 bombing of Hanoi, and grown even stronger during the Watergate crisis. The church should disbar Nixon for four offenses specified in the Book of Discipline. He had "spoken evil," "published lies," accepted an office in civil government whose duties were inconsistent with Quaker principles, and defrauded the public revenue. Nixon should stand before his home church and declare that "he had found his birthright principles inoperative" as a statesman, that "he had been carried away from the faith" by "the arm of the flesh," or that he was unworthy to be part of their fellowship. Being rejected by his home congregation, Mayer proclaimed, would smash "the religious prop which holds up the President's crumbling image in Middle America." Disownment might be more "cataclysmic" than congressional or judicial action that did not prove Nixon's criminal guilt. Mayer expected East Whittier Friends Church to refuse to take this action, however, because almost all its members endorsed everything the government did, including the war in Vietnam, stood "in awe of the presidency," and were "proud of their great Friend's eminence."[240] Nixon's home church was soon inundated with requests from the media for interviews, prompting its pastor, T. Eugene Coffin, to respond in *Christian Century*. Coffin reported that during the bombing of Cambodia the church's ministry committee considered the issue of Nixon's membership and "concluded that it would be an unchristian act" to disown him. Instead, they pledged to prayerfully support and counsel him, which did not mean that they condoned all his actions; Christians should create a spiritual climate that enabled "wayward" members to confess their sin and "start life anew." They prayed that Nixon's judgment would be "informed by his Quaker heritage and Christian experience" and strove to "keep the lines of communication open" to influence the decisions he made.[241]

Other religious leaders, most notably Graham, expressed their disappointment and disapproval of the president's conduct, but were ambivalent about whether he should resign or be impeached. However, many clergy advocated these courses of action. Some pastors urged their parishioners to sign petitions demanding Nixon's impeachment, and several denominations exhorted Congress to impeach him. By January 1974, 200 Quaker Meetings had urged the East Whittier Friends Church to disown Nixon for "conduct unbecoming a Friend" in waging war in Southeast Asia and covering up Watergate. Citing Nixon's abuse of power, many Quakers called for his impeachment six months before he finally resigned in August 1974. Numerous evangelicals expressed great "disappointment and shock at the profane and vindictive side of Nixon" the White House tapes revealed. Televangelist Pat Robertson demanded that the Republican apologize to Christians who had been "the victims of a cruel hoax." Like others, he complained that "the private Nixon" contradicted "his public image as a man of probity and piety." Robertson also deplored Nixon's use of Graham "for political image-building."[242]

Retired rabbi Baruch Korff founded the National Citizens Committee for Fairness to the President, which defended Nixon's actions during the Watergate crisis, and he counseled Nixon during his last months in office. Nixon told him that "the peace at the center" his mother had helped instill in him enabled him to cope with the vilification and savage treatment he experienced. Moreover, as his father did when Nixon's brother Arthur died, Nixon believed that God was punishing him for his misdeeds.[243]

Final Assessment

Few presidents' legacies surpass Nixon's. His policies safeguarded the environment and blazed a path for major welfare reform. Nixon achieved détente with the Soviet Union and normalized relations with China. He desegregated southern schools and helped create a broader based Republican Party. His "scores of accomplishments at home and abroad," writes Melvin Small, make those of John F. Kennedy and Jimmy Carter "pale by comparison."[244] Aitken argues that Nixon achieved his four main foreign policy objectives: revitalizing NATO, negotiating a suitable peace agreement in Vietnam, restoring relations with China, and devising a "formula for peaceful coexistence with the Soviet Union."[245] Kissinger credits Nixon with establishing a "permanent dialogue with China," easing tensions with the Soviet Union, weakening the Soviet hold on Eastern Europe, creating "a peace process in the Middle East," and making human rights an international issue.[246] Many scholars maintain that Nixon's restructuring of American foreign policy helped "end the Cold War peacefully" and strengthen the United States.[247] Several biographers consider Nixon's reestablishment of diplomatic relations with China to be his greatest achievement. Aitken calls it "America's most outstanding foreign policy initiative in the postwar period."[248]

Despite his numerous accomplishments, Nixon's crimes, misdemeanors, and disgraceful acts have led scholars "to rank him below such abject presidential failures" as Ulysses Grant and Warren Harding.[249] For many of them, Nixon's copious misdeeds and deception trump his achievements. "No modern president," argues David Gergen, "has been more reviled by his enemies while in office, and none has been more rebuked by historians after leaving."[250] Scholars maintain that Nixon's guile and self-serving behavior deeply damaged the reputation of the presidency and hurt the United States. William Bundy labels Nixon's administration the most dishonest one in American history; "Tricky Dicky" deceived his staff, Congress, the American people, and leaders of other nations.[251] "So many layers of lies were needed to protect the layers of secrecy," declares Richard Reeves, "that no one inside the White House knew whom or what to believe."[252] Moreover, Nixon's "obsession with secrecy" and frequent duplicity prevented many government officials "from participating in policy formation." By using "dirty tricks against his opponents, allowing rogue investigations," "and unleashing the Plumbers," Nixon guaranteed that his staff would violate laws and practices he publicly praised.[253] The Republican "was a crude, bigoted, and mean-spirited fellow" who strove to destroy "real and imagined enemies."[254] Jonathan Rausch maintains that Nixon "left behind an embittered, polarized country, a nation disillusioned with its government, unsure of its place in the world."[255] In Latin America, the Middle East, and Far East, asserts Small, Nixon committed blunders, promoted neocolonialism, and performed "irrational" acts.[256] Nixon's quest for "peace with honor" in Vietnam, Larry Berman avers, achieved neither; Nixon and Kissinger were guilty of "diplomatic deception and public betrayal."[257] Others lament that Nixon's "might-makes-right" policies killed hundreds of thousands of Vietnamese and Cambodians and escalated the arms race.[258]

The incongruity between Nixon's profession (some would say pretense) of piety and his unsavory acts has prompted extensive analysis of his personality and conduct. In *Nixon vs. Nixon and Emotional Tragedy* (1977), David Abrahamsen depicts Nixon as insecure, arrogant, narcissistic, power-hungry, malicious, and antisocial. For speechwriter Ray Price, Nixon's personality consisted of three conflicting components: an "exceptionally caring, sentimental," generous aspect; a "coldly calculating, devious," manipulative part; and an "angry, vindictive, ill-tempered, mean-spirited facet." Nixon labeled pride the "most deadly" sin, but unfortunately for himself and his nation, hubris sometimes consumed him. Many accused Nixon of employing a double standard: he denounced "individual misdemeanors" and promoted "law and order" but refused to admit that deceiving the public about bombing Cambodia and other controversial actions was wrong. While presenting himself as a moral exemplar, Nixon methodically flouted "the law for partisan advantage." Tragically, Ralph Moellering argued, Nixon used his moral authority as president to achieve ends that were "amoral if not immoral."[259]

Various explanations have been offered for Nixon's reprehensible conduct. Some fault Hannah's aloof and distant mothering. Others stress Nixon's lack of a close personal friend to "whom he could confide his deepest thoughts."[260] Many accentuate Nixon's personal insecurities and obsession with control. Aitken argues that while Hannah lived, the dark side of Nixon was rarely ascendant, but after her death in 1967, this facet of his personality often took over.[261] Some blame the extraordinary political, economic, social, and diplomatic problems Nixon confronted, which were comparable only to those faced by George Washington in 1789, Andrew Johnson in 1865, and Truman in 1945.[262] Aitken maintains that the profane, hateful, unscrupulous Nixon surfaced primarily during his presidency, which can be attributed to three elements: the pressures of his office, the war in Vietnam, and Lord Acton's maxim that "absolute power corrupts absolutely."[263]

Nixon justified his numerous misdeeds as necessary to preserve his power and defend the United States during a traumatic era of violence, riots, assassinations, campus unrest, protest movements, and burning cities at home and communist insurgency and racial and ethnic conflict abroad. "If the president does it," he asserted, "that means it's not illegal."[264] Nixon never took responsibility for the Watergate cover-up or his numerous other transgressions. He did not fully apologize to the American people or admit, as Clinton did, that he had sinned. Through these actions Nixon violated one of the cardinal principles of the Quaker faith he often claimed to value: speaking the truth or integrity.

Historians, biographers, ethicists, and theologians have assessed Nixon's use of religious rhetoric and the nature of his faith. Charles Henderson accused Nixon of ignoring both "the transcendent element in the divine" and "the tragic elements in human nature." Rejecting belief in a sovereign God, Nixon made "the American dream his deity" and "patriotism his religion." He applied the "vocabulary of the church—faith, trust, hope, belief, [and] spirit"—to America, and this informed "his personal vision of what" it should be. Henderson pointed out that Nixon "never systematically expressed his own theology" or clarified what he meant by the nation's spiritual heritage. Nixon had no coherent worldview; his policies and addresses, while influenced by his religious background and principles, rested on an eclectic combination of elements. Although Nixon read widely about history, politics, and current events, Henderson maintained, before leaving the presidency, he read little about ethics or theology, which was a "remarkable" omission for someone who repeatedly argued that his religious convictions influenced his decision-making. He knew little about just war theory or Christian social ethics. Instead, Nixon relied on the views of Graham and other popularizers of the Christian message. Ignoring its prophetic function, Nixon used religion primarily "to sanctify the status quo" and justify his policies.[265] Liberal theologian Harvey Cox claimed similarly that the Nixon administration incarnated a "perverted American Christianity" that trivialized moral values.[266]

Although agreeing with Nixon that countless national problems involved spiritual issues, Reinhold Niebuhr questioned whether the president's generic, bland references to religion, morality, and spirituality could help solve any of them. Even problems with a spiritual foundation, Niebuhr reasoned, must be addressed through specific political policies. Nixon seemed impervious to the "radical distinction between conventional religion" that sanctified contemporary public policy, even if it was "morally inferior or outrageously unjust," and prophetic religion that censured all government policies that violated transcendent biblical standards. [267]

The "highly pietistic" form of civil religion Nixon and many members of the "silent majority" espoused, critics contended, identified American and biblical values. Unfortunately, most church-going Americans supported his synthesis of personal piety and "belief in the sacred character" of American traditions.[268] At the 1973 National Prayer Breakfast, Mark Hatfield denounced this type of civil religion, deplored Americans' widespread acceptance of social injustice, and exhorted them to repent of "the sin that has scarred the national soul." Many, he lamented, failed "to distinguish between the god of an American civil religion and the God who reveals himself in the Holy Scriptures and in Jesus Christ."[269]

Nixon's religious rhetoric, White House services, and relationships with religious leaders, especially Graham and Peale, in some ways did express his genuine desire, strongly influenced by his religious upbringing, to affirm the nation's Judeo-Christian heritage, advance spiritual and moral values, and help remedy the nation's ills. However, as Niebuhr and Hatfield argued, these actions also fulfilled the expectations of American civil religion and served Nixon's political purposes. The Quaker did not have the training, aptitude, or desire to systematically examine public policy from a distinctively Christian perspective, and neither Graham nor any of his other spiritual advisors helped him to do this. As a result, his use of religion, while resonating with many Americans, was not sophisticated, insightful, or inspiring. Although he frequently used pious and moralistic language to defend his policies, it is difficult to see any specific connections between his faith and policies except in his pursuit of peace, which was tarnished by some of his tactics in Vietnam.[270]

A sign in an exhibit at Nixon's Presidential Museum in Yorba Linda, California, states: "It was clear at the end of his life that Nixon had found what his Quaker grandmother would have called 'peace at the center.'" Perhaps he did, but in a 1992 interview, Nixon described this term in a way few Quakers accept. He said that stoicism, serenity, and destiny were all parts of this concept, but "deep down I am basically a fatalist," which helped "me weather the storms of the past." Many Friends, by contrast, explain "peace at the center" as deriving comfort, tranquility, and assurance from having a deep relationship with God and trusting that He controls the universe.[271]

Throughout his life Nixon repeatedly professed to be a Christian, frequently attended worship services, and often prayed.[272] Nevertheless, his immoral actions cause many to consider Nixon's claim to be a Christian disingenuous. Nixon's displays of piety and use of religious rhetoric appear to have been carefully contrived to project the godly persona many Americans wanted to see rather than a major impetus for his behavior, decision-making, and policies. H. Larry Ingle argues that although Nixon never repudiated Quakerism, he created his own religion, which enabled him "to seek a place of inner security, safety, and guidance" to provide meaning for his life and serve his own purposes. On the other hand, some of Nixon's statements and deeds hint that a spark of genuine Christian faith may have resided deep within.[273]

Nixon told Haldeman that how to feed people's "spiritual hunger" was "the great mystery of life."[274] Throughout his long, varied, and complicated life, Nixon's quest to develop a meaningful personal faith and satisfy his own spiritual appetite appeared to be largely unsuccessful. Nixon's gravestone contains words from his first inaugural address: "The greatest honor history can bestow is the title of peacemaker." Some of Nixon's actions, motivated in part by his enigmatic, Quaker-influenced faith, did further peace, but others thwarted his goal.

9

George H. W. Bush

"ONE NATION UNDER GOD"

*As I assume the office of President, I am humbled before God
and seek his counsel and favor on our land.*

"NATIONAL DAY OF PRAYER AND THANKSGIVING,"
January 20, 1989

*Heavenly Father . . . make us strong to do Your work, willing to
heed and hear Your will. . . . There is but one just use of power,
and it is to serve people. Help us remember, Lord. Amen.*

"INAUGURAL ADDRESS," January 20, 1989

*We recite the Pledge and promise our allegiance to this "one
Nation, under God. . . . We Americans believe in Almighty
God, the Source of all life and liberty.*

"FLAG DAY AND NATIONAL FLAG WEEK," June 10, 1992

*America is special because of [its] fidelity to God. We have not
forgotten that we are one Nation under God.*

"REMARKS AT AN INDEPENDENCE DAY CELEBRATION,"
July 4, 1992

Introduction

George H. W. Bush occupied the Oval Office during four momentous years
that saw the collapse of communism in Eastern Europe and the Soviet Union,
the reunification of Germany, a successful military campaign to drive Iraqi
invaders out of Kuwait, and major domestic financial problems, including
huge federal deficits and the Savings and Loan debacle. Bush used his bully
pulpit as president to attack self-indulgence, emphasis on immediate gratifi-
cation, junk bonds, and insider trading on Wall Street and to accentuate faith,

morality, service, and family values.[1] Bush was raised in a devout Episcopalian family and remained affiliated with this denomination almost all his life. Bush is a low-church (less ritualistic, more Protestant-oriented) Episcopalian, an ecumenically minded, religious moderate. In the late 1980s, Episcopalians ranked third in family income, occupational prestige, and education, behind only Unitarian-Universalists and Jews. The Episcopal Church, with 2.8 million members, was one of America's most liberal denominations on such issues as support for minority and women's rights and civil liberties and tolerance of the new sexual attitudes that began in the 1960s.[2] During his presidency, Bush clashed repeatedly with Episcopal bishops and clergy and the leaders of other mainline denominations over abortion, homosexuality, school prayer, and other issues. While continuing to worship at Episcopal churches in Houston, Washington, and Kennebunkport, Maine, Bush's theology and social policies had more in common with evangelicals than with more liberal Protestants. Although Bush did not embrace "every precept of evangelical theology," as president, he affirmed many evangelical doctrines and political positions.[3]

During Bush's presidency, religious and moral trends that had begun earlier intensified. Mainline Protestant denominations—Episcopalians, Presbyterians, Methodists, the United Church of Christ, the Disciples of Christ, and various Baptist groups—continued to lose members and influence while more conservative religious bodies gained adherents and clout. A culture war erupted that cut across traditional moral and religious communities, pitting liberal Protestants and Catholics, Reform Jews, and secularists against evangelicals, conservative Catholics, and Orthodox Jews. Espousing different positions on the family, education, law, politics, and art, these groups disagreed about many issues including abortion, homosexual civil rights, the teaching of evolution and sex education in public schools, the use of "humanist" textbooks, the disallowing of voluntary school prayer, gun control, censorship, privacy rights, and the separation of church and state. The breakdown of the religio-cultural consensus of earlier decades produced greater moral and cultural pluralism, weakened the nation's civil religion, and made religion more private, helping produce a "culture of narcissism" that stressed the pursuit of self-fulfillment more than civic engagement and the public good. As people's understanding of religious reality became more diverse and personal, religion became less of an integrative force in American life. As Alasdair MacIntyre argued in *After Virtue*, people used "different languages rooted in different notions of morality," which made moral discourse very difficult. By the late 1980s, the nation's social and religious fabric had become deeply fragmented and both ideological and moral consensus became very difficult to achieve. All of these trends strongly affected Bush's tenure in office.[4]

Bush's faith was very important to him, and it helped shape a number of his presidential policies.[5] The Republican's version of civil religious discourse was clearly Judeo-Christian; he repeatedly referred to an active, all-powerful, personal God and a divinely inspired, authoritative Bible. "One cannot be America's President," Bush repeatedly stated, "without a belief in God" and "the strength that your faith gives to you."[6] He continually exhorted Americans to seek God's aid in dealing with the nation's challenges and problems. No other chief executive argued as often as Bush that the United States was "one nation under God" and was accountable to Him.[7] Only those who understood this "fundamental conviction," the Texan insisted, could properly serve as president.[8] Americans, he averred, "are one nation under God" who were placed on Earth "to do His work."[9] "Prayer," Bush declared, "has a place not only in the life of every American but also in the life of our Nation, for we are truly one Nation under God."[10] "As one Nation under God, we Americans are deeply mindful of both our dependence on the Almighty and our obligations as a people He has richly blessed."[11] Liberals "don't like it when I say, yes, we're one Nation under God," Bush trumpeted. But "we are, and we'd better never forget it."[12]

When Bush ran for the Senate in 1964, pastor Thomas Bagley of St. Martin's Episcopal Church in Houston, which the Bushes had joined two years earlier, declared that he "is a dedicated Christian" who "would not ever do anything he thought to be contrary to our Lord and Master."[13] After meeting with the president in 1989, four Methodist bishops applauded his "strong Christian faith" and "devotion to the church."[14] Another St. Martin's rector insisted that Bush's faith "is an integral part" of his life. In naming Bush and his wife Barbara "Episcopalians of the Year" in 1991, *The Anglican Digest* praised the president's "strong spiritual leadership" and "commitment to Christ and His Church."[15] Despite such testimonies, most scholars have paid scant attention to how Bush's faith guided him personally or influenced his presidency, especially as he organized, implemented, and justified Operation Desert Storm.

Bush brought an impressive resume to the presidency: he had been a Navy pilot in World War II who flew fifty-eight combat missions and won the Distinguished Flying Cross, a US Congressman, a United Nations ambassador, the chair of the Republican National Committee, the chief of the US Liaison Office in Peking (Beijing), and the director of the CIA, and had served eight years as vice president during which he visited sixty-eight foreign countries.

The Faith of George H. W. Bush

Bush's maternal grandfather, George Herbert Walker was an investment banker and the president of the United States Golf Association. Raised as a Catholic, he embraced the Presbyterian faith of his devout wife Lucretia Wear after they married.[16] The future president's paternal great-grandfather, James Bush, was an Episcopal rector who served parishes in Orange, New Jersey, San Francisco, and New York City. Bush's father Prescott attended St. George's, an Episcopal prep school in Newport, Rhode Island, and considered becoming a minister. After graduating from Yale, however, he instead became a partner in a prominent Wall Street investment firm and served from 1952 to 1962 as a Republican senator from Connecticut. Prescott and his wife Dorothy led family worship every morning, using readings from the Episcopal Book of Common Prayer and A Diary of Private Prayer by Scottish Presbyterian theologian John Baillie.[17] They strove to teach their children how the Scriptures applied to daily life.[18] George argued that his mother's goodness, kindness, and love sprang from her "following the Bible" and "faith in God."[19] Bush's daughter Dorothy reported that her grandmother "knew her Bible" and "was lifted by her faith."[20] The Bush family regularly worshipped at either Christ Episcopal Church in Greenwich, Connecticut, or St. Ann's by the Sea in Kennebunkport, Maine.

The future president attended Phillips Andover Academy in Massachusetts where he excelled more in athletics than academics. Bush chaired the academy's chapel board of deacons and the Society of Inquiry, a religious organization that represented all of its students. Bush later testified that the academy had taught him valuable lessons about "honesty, selflessness, [and] faith in God." He had also learned at Phillips that "with God's help there is nothing we cannot do" to improve the world.[21] While serving as a Navy pilot, Bush's plane was severely damaged on a bombing mission in September 1944, forcing him to parachute into the Pacific Ocean south of Japan. Both the radioman and the gunner who accompanied Bush died, and he was wounded when his head hit the tail of the plane. The Japanese hunted him, but a US submarine soon picked him up. Bush thanked God for saving his life.[22] He later observed that in disasters people often asked why they had to suffer. Bush had instead inquired, "Why had I been spared and what did God have for me?"[23]

After graduating from Yale in 1950, George and his wife Barbara Pierce, whom he married in 1945, moved to Midland, Texas, where he worked in the oil industry. Barbara had been raised as a Presbyterian, and the Bushes joined First Presbyterian Church; George was elected an elder and both of them taught Sunday school.[24] The trial the Bushes underwent as their 3-year-old daughter Robin battled and eventually died of leukemia both tested and deepened George's faith. Bush declared that "prayer had always been part of our lives," but never as much as during this ordeal. "Our faith," he testified, "truly sustained us." After Robin died, Bush derived consolation from his belief that "she is in God's loving arms."[25] Bush later declared that because of this affliction "I really learned to pray."[26]

Attesting that his faith was important to him, Bush began his 1989 inaugural address with a prayer. "Heavenly Father," he declared, "we . . . thank You for Your love." Strengthen us "to do Your work." Make us "willing to heed and hear Your will, and write on our hearts these words: 'Use power to help people.' For we are given power not to advance our own purposes, nor to make a great show in the world, nor a name." The only "just use of power," he concluded, "is to serve people."[27]

Bush espoused orthodox Christian views of the Trinity, humanity, the Bible, faith, prayer, and life after death, and he attended church regularly. Moreover, his speeches contain dozens of scriptural quotations, stories, and examples. "I am guided by certain traditions," the Texan declared. "One is that there is a God and He is good, and his love" requires us to "be good to one another."[28] "I cannot imagine a world" without "the presence of the One through whom all things are possible."[29] Human "flaws are endless," Bush asserted, but "God's love is truly boundless."[30] Christmas, he asserted, proclaims "God's love for us" through "the gift of Christ's birth."[31] This all-powerful, compassionate, merciful God created humans, gave them free will, answered their prayers, and directed and blessed His children.[32] "Like a faithful and loving parent," Bush avowed, God "always stands ready to comfort, guide, and forgive."[33] God provides faith, hope, and love "in abundance."[34]

Bush argued that God's aid was indispensable to both individuals and nations. "Without God's help," he declared, "we can do nothing," but "with it, we can do great things."[35] From its inception, the United States, Bush claimed, "has enjoyed the mercy and protection of Almighty God."[36] "America will always occupy a special place in God's heart," the Republican insisted, if "we keep Him in a special place in our hearts."[37] This country, he added, is both "divinely blessed" and "divinely accountable."[38] By faithfully fulfilling its "divine commission," Bush trumpeted, the United States had "become a model of freedom and justice" for the world, "a shining 'city upon a hill.' "[39] "We are grateful," the president proclaimed, for the many blessings God "has bestowed on us as individuals and as a Nation."[40] God was America's rock, shelter, and salvation.[41] "By God's providence," he averred in 1992, "the cold war is over, and freedom finished first." "Bayonets have been no match for the righteousness of God."[42]

Bush repeatedly celebrated America's Judeo-Christian heritage. Its worship of the Creator, he insisted, had made America the world's greatest nation.[43] "Family and faith," Bush argued, are the nation's "moral compass."[44] America had a rich legacy of faith in God, liberty, human dignity, and the Golden Rule.[45] Bush rejoiced in 1992 that surveys showed that "no society is more religious than the United States." "Seven in ten Americans believe in life after death; 8 in 10, that God works miracles. Nine in ten Americans pray. And more than 90 percent believe in God." This, he exulted, is truly "good news for modern man."[46]

"The Bible," Bush attested, "has always been a great source of comfort to me."[47] It had helped shape America's values and institutions and enriched the lives of millions who "looked to it for comfort, hope, and guidance." "The Bible," he avowed, gives "courage and direction to those who seek truth and righteousness." As the prophet Isaiah declared, "the word of our God shall stand forever."[48] As the revelation of "God's intervention in human history," the Bible heralded "His love for mankind." Its value, Bush declared, "is time-less." "Thoughtful reading of the Bible," he contended, supplied "great inspiration and knowledge."[49]

Bush testified that several "life-changing experiences" had given him "a profound sense of faith in God," especially being rescued from a rubber raft in the middle of the Pacific Ocean during World War II and coping with the death of his 3-year-old daughter Robin. Bush filmed a video in 1986 that highlighted the experiences that had transformed his life. In 1988 Bush told *Christianity Today* that Jesus Christ is "my Savior and Lord." In 1990 Billy Graham reported that Bush states "straight out that he has received Christ as his savior, that he is a born again believer and that he reads the Bible daily."[50] For Bush, faith is a solace, shield, and shelter.[51] As president, he wrote dozens of letters to assure Americans that God would help them cope with the challenges of life. For example, in February 1992, he promised Brian Wilson of the Beach Boys that "faith will sustain us through these tough times."[52]

Numerous individuals extolled Bush's faith. His wife asserted that "we could not have survived the difficult times without our faith and the support of our religious family." Whether worshipping in large churches like St. Martin's in Houston or tiny ones like St. Ann's or the chapel at Camp David, "we always have felt we were part of a very special community."[53] The president of the Fellowship of Christian Athletes wrote Bush in 1991: "your faithfulness as a prayer warrior became so evident during Desert Storm as you led our nation to trust in God."[54] The director of Christian Aid Ministries praised the president's "courageous stand on family and moral issues and Biblical principles."[55] A black pastor in Richmond thanked Bush for upholding "Godly standards for the family" and the unborn, promoting freedom around the world, and boldly calling on God's help.[56]

"For me," Bush divulged, "prayer has always been important, but quite personal." "It has sustained me at every point in my life," including as a young boy, a teenager, and after being shot down in World War II.[57] "As President," he promised, "I will continue to pray for His grace and wisdom as I face the challenges and opportunities before me."[58] Prayer gave him great peace, Bush told a National Prayer Breakfast audience.[59] "I understand," he explained half way through his term, why Abraham Lincoln said that as president "many times he went to his knees." "As the Psalmist wrote, 'God is our refuge and strength, a very present help in trouble.' "[60] Bush's cabinet meetings began with prayer, sometimes silent and other times led by members.[61] The Bushes prayed together every night before going to sleep. "My husband," Barbara declared, "prays and believes enormously."[62] In hundreds of letters Bush thanked citizens for praying for him and testified that he drew "great strength" from their prayers.[63] A Catholic thanked Bush in March 1991 for urging Americans to pray for God's assistance in the Gulf crisis. Bush's plea aided his efforts "to instill Christian values" in his six children, and prayer was indispensable to "the speedy victory our wonderful troops accomplished."[64] Many other Americans rejoiced that their president was "a man of prayer."[65]

In proclaiming January 22, 1989, a National Day of Prayer and Thanksgiving, Bush urged all Americans to seek God's "counsel and ask Him to give guidance and wisdom to America's leaders."[66] "Belief in prayer," Bush asserted, "sustains America."[67] Its history and the experiences of millions of people, Bush avowed, "provide compelling evidence of the power of faith and the efficacy of prayer."[68] He affirmed Saint Ignatius's statement that people should "work as though all depended upon" themselves "and pray as though all depended on God."[69]

During his presidency Bush referred to prayer in 220 different speeches, proclamations, and remarks. He exhorted Americans to pray for the hostages taken in Lebanon in 1989, victory in the nation's battle against drugs, and the success of Operation Desert Storm.[70] "We asked for God's help" to win the Cold War, Bush asserted. And "we should thank God" for "this magnificent triumph of good over evil."[71] Prayer, Bush proclaimed, could help the nation solve its "tough problems" and seize its "great opportunities." People should seek "the heart of God" both for themselves and their country. Bush declared that he needed "to hear and to heed the voice of Almighty God."[72]

At the 1992 National Prayer Breakfast Bush alleged that prayer had played a "powerful role" "in the unprecedented events of the past year." Americans had "prayed for God's protection" as they fought to liberate Kuwait. During the conflict, Americans beseeched "our greatest power to bring us" peace "which passeth all understanding." After victory was achieved, they thanked God during several national days of prayer.[73]

Bush affirmed the orthodox view of Jesus as God's divine Son, frequently referring to Christ as "our Savior."[74] By giving "us His only Son," God showed His love and mercy.[75] "Through His words and example," Jesus demonstrated "the redemptive value of giving" "oneself for others, and His life proved that love and sacrifice can make a profound difference in the world."[76] Christ's incarnation fulfilled Old Testament prophecies, Bush argued, and "radically altered the course of human history by challenging men and women to live according to the will of our just and merciful Father in Heaven." Jesus healed the sick, fed the hungry, and illuminated "the path to eternal salvation."[77] His resurrection, Bush declared, brought "hope and redemption."[78]

Bush stressed both God's creation of individuals "in His own image," which gave every human "inestimable dignity and worth,"[79] and people's innate sinfulness. All individuals are "made in the image of the Creator."[80] Their "biblically inspired view of man" led the founders, Bush declared, to assert "that all men are created equal" and possess the God-given rights of "Life, Liberty and the pursuit of Happiness."[81] God placed people "on Earth to do His work."[82] While celebrating people's value, Bush also deplored their "darker side" and repeatedly referred to the battle of good and evil being waged in the world.[83]

Bush also frequently affirmed his belief in an afterlife. This conviction, Bush explained, affected how he viewed the world.[84] At a memorial service for forty-seven crewmembers of the U.S.S. Iowa in 1989, the president proclaimed that "God has called them home."[85] "May the Lord welcome all who have fallen" in the Persian Gulf Crisis, he declared in 1991, "into the glory of Heaven."[86] Bush's condolence letters to families who had lost loved ones typically assured them that he was praying for them and that God would comfort and strengthen them.[87] However, he sometimes asserted that the deceased was "now in the hands of his Creator" or that "God has welcomed" individuals "into His loving arms."[88]

Bush attended church habitually as a boy in Connecticut, at prep school, at Yale, and in Midland, Texas, Houston, China, and Washington, DC. "Worship," he insisted, "is basic to my own life."[89] While serving as the American envoy to China in 1974 and 1975, Bush worshipped regularly at the Chongmenwen Christian Church in Beijing with a handful of other ex-patriots and Chinese. Moreover, their 15-year-old daughter Dorothy was baptized at this church in 1975, the first American to be baptized in China since the nation became communist in 1949.[90]

While president, Bush continued to belong to St. Martin's in Houston. When at his residence in Kennebunkport, Maine, he attended St. Ann's Episcopal Church (where Bush's grandmother had worshipped, his parents were married, and Bush and his siblings were baptized) and the nearby First Congregationalist Church when St. Ann's closed in the winter.[91] The morning he was sworn in as president, Bush attended a private service at St. John's Episcopal Church on Lafayette Square, and two days later he participated in a nationally televised worship service at the Washington Cathedral.[92] In "An Open Letter to the Clergy," Bush invited ministers to use elements of this national service to praise God for His blessings and to ask Him to help his administration wisely lead the nation.[93]

Bush claimed in 1990 that he was "trying hard as President to go to Church every Sunday."[94] By attending church he gained guidance and peace and experienced "being in the spirit of Jesus Christ."[95] The church, Bush declared in 1991, gave him immeasurable "strength and inspiration."[96] Moreover, by faithfully attending church, Bush sought to set a good example and help show that Americans were "one nation under God."[97] As president, Bush worshipped most often at St. John's, the Washington Cathedral, and the interdenominational Evergreen Chapel, which he had constructed at Camp David.[98] St. John's rector, John Harper, called George and Barbara "religious people who take worship very seriously."[99] Bush frequently brought cabinet members to church with him and hosted several prayer meetings at the White House.[100]

Bush peppered his speeches with biblical quotations, precepts, and stories to underscore his points, including "beating swords into plowshares," "blessed are the peacemakers," "we reap what we sow," "where your treasure is, there your heart will be also," "greater love hath no man than this, that a man lay down his life for his friends," "righteousness exalteth a nation, but sin is a reproach to any people," and especially the Golden Rule and the parable of the Good Samaritan. "Do unto others as you would have them do unto you," Bush insisted, is "the most ennobling rule" for the world.[101] Bush's addresses also included inspirational stories about people of faith and quotations of famous authors on religious subjects, including Fyodor Dostoyevsky's claim that "if God is dead, then everything is permitted."[102]

The Election of 1988

Religious factors played a substantial role in Bush's two presidential campaigns. Both of them focused much more on his reputation "as a leader of experience and charisma" than on issues and ideology. In 1986 Bush hired Doug Wead to help him develop a better relationship with evangelicals, which he saw as a key to victory in 1988. Wead encouraged Bush to accentuate his close ties to Billy Graham and taught him how to use language that appealed to evangelicals. Meanwhile, Bush strove to develop a close relationship with the leaders of the Religious Right, especially Jerry Falwell, Pat Robertson, and James Dobson.[103] Wead and Bush's son George helped the vice president improve his image among religious conservatives, which became even more important because of Robertson's candidacy and second place finish in Iowa in January 1988 (Robert Dole was first and Bush was third). During the Republican primaries, many conservative Christians were wary about Bush because of his life-long Episcopalian affiliation and his pro-choice stance on abortion before 1980. However, Wead and Bush collaborated on a book published during the campaign titled *Man of Integrity*, which emphasized his friendship with Graham, Falwell, and other evangelical leaders and highlighted his positions on issues that religious conservatives supported. Wead also arranged many meetings for Bush with evangelicals at which he affirmed he had "accepted Jesus Christ as his Lord and Savior." This assurance, coupled with Falwell's endorsement and Bush's focus on issues conservatives valued, undercut Robertson's campaign and helped Bush win the Republican nomination over Dole.[104] So did Bush's emphasis on his love of fishing, hunting, speed boating, and country music, which helped him overcome both what *Newsweek* labeled "the Wimp Factor" and his elitist, Eastern background.[105]

To increase the support of religious conservatives in the fall election, Bush selected Indiana Senator Dan Quayle, a devout Christian who worshipped at a Presbyterian Church of America congregation in the Washington area, as his vice presidential candidate. Many evangelicals viewed Quayle very positively because of his faith and strong pro-life commitment.[106]

During the campaign Bush frequently declared that he valued "people of every race, creed, and walk of life,"[107] but when Roger Sherman of American Atheists asked Bush at a campaign stop in Chicago what he would do to win the votes of atheists, Bush replied that he would do little because "faith in God is important to me." Sherman countered, "surely you recognize the equal citizenship and patriotism of Americans who are atheists." "I don't know that Atheists should be considered as citizens," Bush declared, "nor should they be considered patriots. This is one nation under God." While affirming that he believed in the separation of church and state, Bush asserted, "I'm just not very high on Atheists."[108] This negative comment about atheists evoked many angry responses from atheist individuals and groups.

After the election, Jon Murray, the president of American Atheists, asked Bush to apologize to atheist citizens for these remarks and to swear his oath of office with his hand on a copy of the Constitution instead of on the Bible.

Responding to Murray, Bush's assistant C. Boyden Gray, wrote that the president "is a religious man" who did not believe that "atheism should be unnecessarily encouraged or supported by the government." However, Gray promised, Bush would respect "the legal rights of atheists."[109] Murray denounced Gray's "weasel reply" and implored Bush to repudiate his earlier "outrageous statement." Murray also asked Bush to meet with leading atheists and to appoint a liaison to the atheist community as he had to Protestant, Catholic, and Jewish groups. Despite irate letters from dozens of other atheists, the only response from Bush's staff was that he strongly believed that religious values "are a vital part of the ethical fabric of our nation."[110] Murray sent a letter to Congressmen in February 1990 urging them to pass a resolution condemning discrimination against atheists by any elected or appointed official. If Bush had made similar derogatory remarks about either blacks or Jews, Murray argued, he would not have won the Republican nomination. Congress took no action.[111]

Democrats selected Massachusetts governor Michael Dukakis as their presidential candidate. A lifelong member of the Annunciation Greek Orthodox Cathedral in Boston, he worshipped frequently and valued his faith. Some Greek Orthodox strongly supported Dukakis, hosting campaign events and raising funds to support his candidacy, and Archbishop Iakovos prayed at the Democratic National Convention. However, other Greek Orthodox priests deplored Dukakis's pro-choice stance and pointed out that he could not receive the sacraments because his wife Kitty was Jewish and that he had never had his children baptized.[112] Despite his Greek Orthodox heritage, Garry Wills labeled Dukakis "the first truly modernist" political candidate whose trust of secular values and technology had alienated many voters.[113]

Although well-known for his character and integrity and professing to live by the Eleventh Commandment, "not attacking your opponents," Bush permitted his staff to conduct a nasty, negative, and deceptive campaign.[114] He castigated Dukakis as "a card-carrying member of the A-C-L-U" and for being much more liberal than most Americans. Bush also criticized Dukakis for vetoing a measure that required students in Massachusetts to recite the Pledge of Allegiance. Moreover, Bush repeatedly lambasted Dukakis for paroling Willie Horton, a convicted black felon serving a life sentence for murder. While on parole, Horton had committed armed robbery, assault, and rape.

JustLife, an alliance of Catholics and mainline and evangelical Protestants who sought to combat nuclear arms proliferation, economic injustice, and abortion, expressed "deep disappointment" with both candidates. While praising Bush's pro-life position, its spokespersons deplored his lack of passion for aiding the hungry in American cities, Appalachia, and abroad. They commended Dukakis's commitment to reduce hunger and "restrained nuclear policy" but criticized his stance on abortion.[115]

During the 1988 campaign, Bush emphasized his character and competence and his television commercials primarily portrayed him as a statesman and a committed family man. Bush often implied that he deserved to be elected simply because of his superior qualifications and experience.[116] With two rather uninspiring candidates and few substantive issues at stake, the election of 1988 had the lowest percentage turnout of any presidential election since 1924. Bush garnered 81 percent of the evangelical vote, which helped compensate for losing 52 percent of the Catholic and 65 percent of the Jewish vote.[117] The day after the election, Bush held a special service at St. Martin's to thank God for his victory and seek His guidance.[118]

Relations with Religious Groups

Bush's closest clergy confidant and friend was Billy Graham whom he first met in 1961. Graham and Bush frequently fished and rode bicycles together. The evangelist functioned as an informal pastor to Bush's family, often discussing spiritual matters with Barbara, George, and their children. Graham gave both the invocation and the benediction at Bush's inauguration. He visited the Bushes numerous times at Kennebunkport and stayed with them occasionally at the White House. Graham told a fellow evangelist that Bush was his best friend "outside his own immediate staff."[119] Bush declared, "I love Billy Graham," and lauded the evangelist as "one of the Lord's great ambassadors."[120]

Bush also had a close relationship with Senate chaplain Richard Halverson. Halverson regularly sent Bush "a word from the Word," scriptural passages designed to encourage and strengthen him, which Bush deeply appreciated. "We are so grateful for your warm words and prayers," Bush wrote to Halverson in March 1989. "The passages you quoted in your weekly notes always seem to fill the bill of the moment."[121]

Bush managed to maintain generally cordial relations with many evangelicals by meeting periodically with key leaders and supporting items on their political agenda, especially the sanctity of life, voluntary school prayer, religiously based child care, and parental control of education.[122] The Republican spoke at Liberty University, evangelical prayer breakfasts in Washington, DC, and Houston, to the Southern Baptist Convention, the National Association of Evangelicals (NAE), and the Christian Coalition, and three times to the National Religious Broadcasters.[123] However, because he was an Episcopalian who did not always describe his faith in terms with which evangelicals reso-nated, Bush's relationship with them was not as close as Reagan's. Bush's staff sought to carefully craft speeches to appeal to evangelicals but not antago-nize other groups. In a memorandum, one staffer lamented that Bush's use of imprecise spiritual language when speaking to evangelicals had produced "some of the most difficult moments" in his political career.[124]

Moreover, evangelicals sometimes groused that Bush was ignoring them. In August 1989, James Dobson of Focus on the Family, Ed McAteer of Religious Roundtable, and Donald Wildmon of the American Family Association pro-tested that Bush's administration was taking them for granted. They were especially upset that their candidate for chair of the Federal Communications Commission had been rejected. Doug Wead countered that Bush had accepted their vice presidential choice—Dan Quayle—and retained or appointed Elizabeth Dole, Jack Kemp, Richard Thornburgh, Frank Young, and Kay James to major posts at their behest.[125] Nevertheless, many of the 180 evan-gelical leaders at a November 1989 meeting with Bush staff complained that the president had named few of their group to prominent positions. Chase Untemeyer, director of presidential personnel, argued that appointing peo-ple based on their religious beliefs violated the law. "Isn't it interesting," Pat Robertson retorted, "that you have no difficulty identifying evangelicals and their allies during the campaign, but you cannot find them after the election," causing the room to explode with laughter and cheering.[126]

While Bush opposed same-sex marriages and homosexuals serving in the military, some of his actions pertaining to homosexuality also hurt his rela-tionship with religious conservatives. They were irritated by Bush's inviting of representatives of the National Gay and Lesbian Task Force to the White House in May 1990 to witness his signing of a bill on hate crimes against minorities, his refusal to block the District of Columbia's domestic partnership law, and his statement on ABC News' "20/20" program in June 1992 that he had no litmus test that prohibited homosexuals from serving in his cabinet. The del-uge of calls by conservatives protesting the invitation of gays and lesbians to the signing ceremony forced the White House switchboard to shut down.[127] Evangelicals accused Bush of sending "mixed signals" on gays and not taking a consistent pro-family position and urged him to clearly state that he opposed the homosexual agenda. Religious conservatives argued that unlike their race and religion, people's sexual orientation should not be "a protected lifestyle."[128] Some conservatives even concluded that they must work to replace Bush with a president who would more fervently promote Christian moral stan-dards.[129] Angry letters poured into the White House after Bush's appearance on "20/20." Southern Baptist executive Morris Chapman argued that viewing homosexuality as an acceptable life clashed both with biblical principles and Bush's staunch support of conventional family values. Richard Land, another Southern Baptist leader, called Bush's "no litmus test" policy a "betrayal of his commitment" to "the traditional family values agenda." Richard Cizik of the NAE declared that evangelicals were "angered and confused" by the Bush administration's courting of gay rights activists. Appointing homosexuals to administrative posts sent the message that people's character did not matter.[130] While not wanting to offend religious conservatives, Bush countered that he was required to enforce the 1990 hate-crime law and that he sought to be compassionate and inclusive.[131] He believed that "the inherent dignity of each individual must be recognized in law and respected in practice." Guaranteeing the civil rights of various groups did not imply an endorsement of their "conduct or policy objectives."[132] Despite these explanations, Bush's stance on gay rights made it harder to energize evangelicals to work for his reelection.[133]

Bush had a better relationship with leaders of mainline Protestant denominations, especially with the executives of the National Council of Churches, than Reagan did.[134] However, his veto of the Civil Rights Act of 1990 was censured by the National Council and the Commission for Racial Justice of the United Church of Christ, as well as the American Jewish Congress and the United States Catholic Conference. Bush argued that the bill mandated extensive use of minority quotas in hiring and promotion. Critics disputed this claim and denounced his veto as "a cruel slap in the face of thousands of Afro-Americans, women, Hispanics and Jews who are the victims of employment discrimination."[135] Although many Episcopal clergy opposed Operation Desert Storm, numerous theologically conservative Episcopalians such as Maurice Benitez, the Bishop of Texas, strongly supported Bush. He also sent Bush a stream of articles descrying the leftward perspective of most staff at the National Council of Churches and the headquarters of mainline denominations.[136] Many liberal Protestants, including Episcopal bishops, disagreed with Bush's view of America's Christian heritage and his positions on school prayer, abortion, and homosexuality. A 1987 Gallup survey reported that 44 percent of Episcopalians were Republicans, 26 percent were Democrats, and 29 percent were independents. However, most Episcopal clergy supported equal rights for homosexuals, environmental protection, and direct government action to solve social problems. Encouraged by Edmond Browning, who was elected presiding bishop in 1985 and stressed the Episcopal Church's diversity and tolerance, gays and lesbians pushed the denomination to ordain homosexuals and allow clergy to bless committed, monogamous same-sex couples. Most Episcopal ministers also clashed with Bush on voluntary school prayer, increased military spending, and tax cuts.[137]

Bush actively courted Catholics by meeting frequently with American cardinals, corresponding with prominent leaders, speaking at Catholic University of America, Notre Dame, the Knights of Columbus in New York City, and other Catholic venues, supporting issues Catholics valued such as abortion, educational choice, and voluntary school prayer, and naming numerous Catholics to administrative posts. Bush appointed five Catholics to his cabinet and met twice with Pope John Paul II.[138] James Cardinal Hickey (the Archbishop of Washington), John Cardinal Krol (the former Archbishop of Philadelphia), John Cardinal O'Connor (the Archbishop of New York), and Bernard Law (the Archbishop of Boston) were Bush's staunchest Catholic supporters.[139] Doug Wead, Bush's principal liaison with Catholics, claimed that he "had been more sensitive and more accessible to the needs of the Catholic church" than any of his predecessors.[140] Thomas Patrick Melady, the US Ambassador to Vatican City, reported that Bush's administration was "receiving very high grades" among Catholic leaders, especially for his education program and dedication to family values.[141] However, maintaining good relations with Catholics was challenging because thirty different Catholic interest groups operated in Washington and advocated a variety of public policy positions.[142] His staff established a "Catholic key contact list" to enhance the president's visibility and credibility in the Catholic community and to help retain "Reagan Democrats" in the 1992 election.[143] By October 1992, the administration's Catholic media mailing list included more than 300 organizations.[144]

Many Catholics praised various actions and policies of Bush. The Dominican nuns of Buffalo thanked him for proclaiming three days of thanksgiving to God for the swift victory in the Persian Gulf. Bush's 1992 statement on National Catholic Schools Week, Hickey argued, greatly encouraged supporters of Catholic schools in the Washington area.[145] Scores of Catholic leaders and organizations applauded Bush's devotion to traditional values.[146] Meanwhile, Bush extolled the efforts of Catholics to overcome "the tragedy of abortion" by working to save the lives of unborn children and by providing new mothers "with support, opportunity, and hope."[147]

The Election of 1992

Religion played a major role in the 1992 election. God has seemed more involved in this campaign, declared a *Chicago Tribune* columnist, than at any time since 1900 as Bush and his Democratic opponent, Bill Clinton, attended services, made pleas to religious groups, quoted Scripture, and linked their policies to religious principles.[148]

Soon after the Moral Majority disbanded in 1989, Pat Robertson created a new religious coalition to promote conservative political causes, counteract the anti-Christian bias of the media, and "defend the legal rights of Christians." Led by Ralph Reed, the group gained the support of megachurch pastors Charles Stanley and D. James Kennedy, Beverly LaHaye of Concerned Women for America, and Father Michael Scanlan, president of Franciscan University in Steubenville, Ohio.[149] Bush conferred with Robertson three times to discuss the Persian Gulf crisis, the Religious Right's political agenda, his reelection campaign, and religious conservatives' complaints that they had not received sufficient representation in his administration. Despite this criticism, Robertson strategized with Bush staffers in early 1992 about "how my people can rally significant support for your campaign."[150]

During the campaign Bush worked to strengthen his relationship with evangelicals. In March 1992 he addressed the NAE in Chicago. As he typically did when speaking to religious conservatives, the president accentuated the importance of prayer and faith and discussed his policies that evangelicals endorsed—creating stronger families, restricting abortion, providing school choice and voluntary school prayer, and maintaining peace through strength. Bush celebrated the end of the Cold War, which he labeled a "magnificent triumph of good over evil," achieved by God's aid and the efforts of evangelicals who bravely brought Bibles and theological education behind the Iron Curtain. Bush argued that he had reduced the "disturbing trend" of "legislating from the bench" by appointing more than 160 judges "who understand the limits of government and the rights of parents." He also denounced the "aggressive campaign against religious belief" and the false assumption that "freedom of religion requires government to keep our lives free from religion."[151] These positions also appealed to millions of conservative Catholics whom Bush courted during the campaign.[152] Robertson invited Bush to speak at a Christian Coalition conference in Virginia Beach in September attended by 1,000 activists and hosted a reception for prominent conservatives to promote Bush's reelection campaign.[153]

Democrats nominated Southern Baptists Bill Clinton and Al Gore for president and vice president and competed vigorously for the votes of religious Americans. During their national convention in New York City, Democrats held an interfaith prayer meeting at Marble Collegiate Church.[154] Much more than Walter Mondale in 1984 and Dukakis in 1988, Clinton employed religious rhetoric and symbols in his campaign, although some evangelicals accused him of misquoting the Bible and misrepresenting its teachings.[155]

During the campaign Bush deplored "the coarseness of our culture," "outrageous television shows," "the scourge of drugs and violence," a welfare system that encouraged "dependency, not personal responsibility," and "Uncle Sam's voracious appetite."[156] The Texan also repeatedly stressed the importance of character, frequently quoting Horace Greeley's statement that "fame is a vapor, popularity an accident, riches take wing, and only character endures."[157] Bush criticized Clinton's character and patriotism by questioning his avoidance of the draft, protest against the Vietnam War, and unfaithfulness to his wife (Gennifer Flowers claimed to have had a long-standing sexual relationship with Clinton). However, evidence emerged that Bush might have had a deeper involvement with the 1986 Iran Contra affair than he admitted, enabling Clinton to counterattack on the character issue.

While Republicans celebrated "our country's Judeo-Christian heritage," Bush declared, Democrats left God out of their platform.[158] These and other Republican claims prompted both the National Council of Churches and People for the American Way to complain that the campaign's political discourse was promoting religious bigotry. Council leaders contended that asserting the moral superiority of "one political party over another" was "blasphemy," while American Way spokespersons insisted that no campaign could properly "claim to have God on its side."[159] Even conservative columnist Cal Thomas defended Clinton's rebuttal to Republican suggestions "that Democrats are somehow godless."[160] In October the pro-life organization Operation Rescue added fuel to the fire by issuing a pamphlet that argued "to vote for Bill Clinton is to sin against God." A group of Protestant, Catholic, and Jewish leaders denounced this argument and other anti-Clinton mailings asserting that various conservative stances had direct biblical support.[161] That same month, the Christian Coalition sent copies of its "Family Values Voter Guide" to 100,000 congregations, with the hope of having it distributed to 40 million potential voters. While the guide, consistent with IRS regulations, did not endorse either candidate, the issues it chose to contrast their positions, including a balanced budget amendment, abortion on demand, parental choice in education (vouchers), a voluntary school prayer amendment, increasing income taxes, homosexual rights, spending for the Strategic Defense Initiative, tax-funded abortion, and condom distribution in schools, seemed designed to portray Bush more favorably than Clinton.[162]

How did an incumbent president who enjoyed a nearly 90 percent approval rating in the spring of 1991 lose to a man eighteen months later that the RNC chair ridiculed as "the failed governor of a small state"?[163] Despite Bush's sky-high ratings after the success of Operation Desert Storm and the tremendous political capital the war gave him, Clinton won the election. A variety of factors contributed: the economy, especially the high unemployment rate; the Republican Party's close identification with its right wing and the Religious

Right; Bush's failure to fulfill many expectations of evangelicals or to motivate them to campaign energetically; his failure to start campaigning earnestly
enough, soon enough; the incoherence of Republicans' foreign policy after the
fall of communism; the fact that few Americans had a strong personal connection with or commitment to Bush; Clinton's youthfulness, charisma, and progressivism; and Ross Perot's third party candidacy.[164] With the end of the Cold
War and the demise of the Soviet Union, few Americans were interested in
foreign policy, depriving Republicans of an issue they had effectively exploited
for many years. Moreover, Bush made numerous tactical errors, especially
offering no plan to improve the economy and using "right-wing rhetoric" that
turned off many prospective voters.[165]

Despite all these impediments, many scholars argue that Bush might
still have won reelection if Perot had not run as an independent.[166] Clinton
won 43 percent of the popular vote to Bush's 37.5 percent. Nineteen percent
of Americans, including many who had supported Bush in 1988, cast ballots
for Perot. While evangelicals still constituted the crux of his vote, Bush's share
of the white evangelical vote declined from 81 percent in 1988 to 72 percent
in 1992.[167] Fewer evangelicals supported Bush for several reasons: America's
weak economy, his reneging on his 1988 pledge not to raise taxes led to questions about his integrity, his willingness to appoint homosexuals to administrative posts, and concerns that the Episcopalian was not truly one of them.[168]
Moreover, many evangelicals were disappointed by Bush's lack of progress in
limiting abortions or disillusioned by his appointment of few of their com-
patriots to high-ranking positions. What hurt Bush much more, however,
was the sizable shift in voting among mainline Protestants—he received only
38.8 percent of their votes in 1992 compared with 60.6 percent in 1988 (Perot
garnered 22.8 percent).[169]

Bush also received far fewer Catholic and Jewish votes than in 1988. The
Wall Street Journal reported in September 1992 that many Catholic "Reagan
Democrats" supported Clinton because of their frustration with the economy.
Clinton emphasized his Catholic education at Georgetown and won 47 percent
of the Catholic vote to Bush's 35 percent and Perot's 18 percent.[170] Meanwhile,
strains in US–Israel relations caused problems for Bush with Jews. Diplomat
Morris Abrams urged Bush to accentuate his strong commitment to Israel's
security and to meet with key American Jewish leaders to discuss the "remarkable advances" that he and Secretary of State James Baker had achieved.[171] Bush
had aided Ethiopian and Soviet Jewish refugees and had begun a peace process in the Middle East, but many Jewish leaders disliked his policy on Jewish
settlements in the occupied territories.[172] Clinton met with many prominent
Jews and received sizable campaign contributions from wealthy Jews.[173] Bush

procured only 11 percent of the Jewish vote (compared with 35 percent in 1988), while Clinton won 80 percent, and Perot captured 9 percent.[174]

Philosophy of Government

Bush repeatedly insisted that both individuals and nations should adhere to transcendent moral norms, America was founded upon Judeo-Christian principles, and government had a limited, but important, role to play in promoting the common good and remedying social ills. God, Bush averred, had established "fundamental moral standards." He deplored the recent "rise of legal theories and practices that reject our Judeo-Christian tradition."[175] "It is very important," the president declared, "to follow the teachings of our Heavenly Father in carrying out the responsibilities of government."[176] "Political principles" that do not rest on "moral values and faith in God," he repeatedly contended, "cannot sustain a people."[177] The president, Bush maintained, "should set the moral tone for this Nation."[178] "The same ethic" governed both people and nations. America, he asserted, "must act as a moral agent," "a force for good," and a catalyst for peace. The United States, as Paul instructed the Romans, must seek "the things which make for peace."[179] Thankfully, America, "as Christ ordained," had been "a light unto the world."[180]

Government is not people's savior, Bush avowed, but it must be their servant.[181] "As powerful and resourceful as [the federal] government is," he insisted, by itself it could not remedy America's many social ills. Alleviating them also required the active efforts of local governments, parents, teachers, businesses, and churches.[182] Government, Bush argued, must not usurp the role of parents or "attempt to replace religious institutions." However, it should "create a safe, healthy environment" and enable "citizens to lead more meaningful lives" by improving education, reducing drug usage, and retaking "neighborhoods from criminals." Through his Thousand Points of Light program, the president strove to stimulate Americans to care for and aid the needy.[183]

Like many other chief executives, Bush argued that the founders' religious convictions helped shape the government they crafted. The American republic "was built on their faith in Almighty God" and "spiritual principles."[184] Convinced that all people "are equal in the sight of their Creator," the founders devised a system of government that protected "the God-given rights of every individual."[185] Like them, Bush believed "in separation of church and state, but not in the separation" of "moral values and state."[186] The First Amendment, he argued, protected "people against religious intrusions by the state," not "the state from [people's] voluntary religious activities."[187] Bush censured the "aggressive campaign" some waged "against religious belief itself." Children should have the right to pray voluntarily at school, and parents should have the right to choose which school, including religiously based ones, their children attended.[188] "Faith in God—unencumbered by legal restrictions" and "government interference"—Bush averred, had been crucial to "maintaining high standards of morality and justice in society."[189]

Freedom of worship, Bush contended, had enabled religion to play an essential role in American society.[190] The liberty Americans enjoyed, he proclaimed, "is clearly rooted in our Nation's Judeo-Christian moral heritage and in the timeless values that have united Americans of all religions," especially "love of God and family, personal responsibility and virtue, respect for the law, and concern for others."[191]

Bush rejoiced that religious liberty was increasing around the world. Despite persecuting believers, destroying churches, and razing cemeteries, he observed, neither China nor the USSR had been able to stamp out religious faith or worship.[192] Attending Leonid Brezhnev's funeral in Moscow in 1982, Bush was amazed when his widow made the sign of the cross after taking her last look at her deceased husband. He thought: "*All the barbed wire and indoctrination classes in the world can't keep Him out.*" Prayer and worship services, Bush insisted, had helped topple communism in the Soviet Union.[193] The president was pleased that Soviet officials allowed a Christmas sermon of Robert Schuller, pastor of the famed Crystal Cathedral in California, to air on primetime television in December 1989 and that President Mikhail Gorbachev met with a group of North American evangelicals to discuss the role of religion and democracy in his nation in November 1991.[194] Gorbachev's acknowledgment that religious practice and values could help revitalize his country was a major breakthrough.[195] The victory of freedom, Bush insisted, was evident in Russia, where once oppressed citizens crowded into reopened churches and synagogues and in Eastern Europe where millions sang Christmas carols.[196] He rejoiced in 1992 that "the gigantic picture of Lenin" in Red Square had been replaced by "a massive icon of the Risen Lord, a powerful symbol of the new birth of freedom for believers all around the world."[197] Religious, political, and economic freedom in Eastern Europe, Bush proclaimed, had come by "the hand of God."[198]

Public Policies

While Bush's faith influenced many of his policies, including his intervention in Panama in 1989 and support of prayer in public schools, a voucher system to promote educational choice, family values, the war on drugs, and the

Americans with Disabilities Act, my analysis will focus on his environmental policy, Thousand Points of Light Initiative, and Operation Desert Storm.[199]

As a lover of outdoor activities, Bush cared deeply about the environment and pledged in his 1988 campaign to work actively to protect it. Keeping his promise, he appointed some staunch environmentalists to administrative posts, underscored humanity's moral obligation to safeguard the natural world, and endorsed the 1990 Clean Air Amendments and the 1992 United Nation's Framework Convention on Climate Change that strove to reduce greenhouse gas emissions. Bush argued that his administration had improved air quality by enforcing the Clean Air Act, phasing out leaded gasoline, and mandating "more stringent fuel efficiency standards for automobiles." Moreover, the United States had helped lead efforts to "address global climate change."[200] Bush's administration also established ninety-three new wildlife refuges, doubled funding for parks and wilderness and recreation areas, better protected America's lakes, rivers, and streams, and cleaned up toxic waste sites. "No president since Teddy Roosevelt," claimed the president of the Conservation Fund, "has done more to protect the wild heritage of American than George Bush."[201] The landmark Clean Air Act Amendments of 1990, which forced all cities to comply with National Air Quality Standards for ozone, carbon dioxide, and other pollutants, was Bush's "most significant victory in the domestic sphere."[202]

Bush's environmental policy rested on his belief that God expected humans to preserve nature and develop its rich resources. The world's "breathtaking beauty and order," he proclaimed, express "the magnificent designs of our Creator." People must "cherish and protect these wonderful gifts."[203] "We've hardly scratched the surface of what God put on Earth" to develop and conserve, he argued.[204] Bush challenged all nations to work together to develop natural resources justly and construct a more prosperous, peaceful world.[205]

By creating his Thousand Points of Light Initiative and his Youth Engaged in Service to America program in June 1989, Bush strove to increase volunteerism, transform the "me generation" into a global "we generation," and remedy social ills.[206] He hoped to aid millions who were illiterate, high school dropouts, drug abusers, pregnant teens, delinquents, AIDS victims, hungry, or homeless. Bush urged individuals and institutions to make service central in their daily life and work. The president challenged businesses and professional firms to consider people's community service when making decisions about hiring, compensation, and promotions. He exhorted the media to announce service opportunities, publicize effective service programs, and profile outstanding community leaders. Bush implored educational boards and college presidents to encourage faculty, staff, and students to serve others. The president appealed to nonprofit organizations to provide meaningful service opportunities for more volunteers. Bush hoped that Americans would assist the needy "on a one-to-one basis" and see service as a lifelong commitment. He sought to stimulate citizens to start literacy programs; supply tutoring, computers, and financial aid to destitute students; expand decent, affordable housing; and increase efforts to feed the hungry. His initiative also aimed to provide examples of successful programs and offer training and technical assistance to help other groups devise similar initiatives. Moreover, it strove to connect those who wanted to serve with those who needed assistance in their own communities.[207]

Bush wanted to create a society "where service to others" is "part of everyone's everyday thinking."[208] "To be a Point of Light," the president argued, is to measure "success by what you do for someone else."[209] To encourage community service, every day his administration honored one individual or institution for effectively combating a social ill.[210] By September 28, 1991, 575 individuals age 7 to 103 from a wide variety of faiths and backgrounds had been recognized.[211] On January 14, 1993, Bush awarded the 1,014th Daily Point of Light to Baltimore eighth graders who were serving as tutors and role models for special education students.[212]

In promoting this initiative, Bush frequently quoted Scripture, referred to Christ's example, and praised the work of church and parachurch organizations. "God requires us, as He says in Micah 6, 'to act justly and to love mercy.'"[213] God's love and justice, Bush trumpeted, should inspire Americans to treat the weak and oppressed with compassion and to oppose injustice.[214] "Time and again," Bush averred, "Scripture describes our Creator's special love for the poor." Because "much will be asked of those to whom much has been given," Americans had "a special obligation to care for the ill and the destitute." "In serving others," the president avowed, "we serve Him as well."[215] Every day, Bush told Southern Methodist University graduates in 1992, "we face the question posed in the New Testament: 'If anyone has the world's goods and sees his brother in need, yet closes his heart against him, how does God's love abide in him?'"[216] Because "he that gives to the poor lends to the Lord," Bush argued, "let us reach out with generosity to persons in need—strangers who are hungry and homeless, [and] neighbors who are sick or lonely."[217]

Bush used the story of the Good Samaritan to encourage executives to make community service central to their agenda. Based on Martin Luther King, Jr.'s interpretation of this account, Bush argued that the two men who passed by the wounded traveler on the road to Jericho did so "because they were too busy, had more important work waiting in Jerusalem," and were afraid. The Samaritan, by contrast, stopped to help because he focused on what would happen to the injured man if he did nothing. It required courage to confront the frightening and daunting tasks of contemporary society—helping the homeless, drug addicts, troubled youth, and residents of dangerous neighborhoods. However, unlike the Good Samaritan, Americans could pool their resources and combine their talents.[218] By becoming points of light, volunteers could show that this story was "part of the American character."[219]

In more than 500 speeches and public statements, Bush urged Americans to increase their personal efforts and financial contributions to aid the less fortunate. Service to others, Bush asserted, furthered "Christ's special mission to mankind."[220] He beseeched Americans to emulate "the selfless spirit of giving that Jesus embodied" by aiding others.[221] In September 1989, the *Christian Herald* published a plea by Bush to Christians to let their light shine by participating in his Thousand Points of Light Initiative.[222] In April 1991, Bush sent a letter to about 400,000 religious congregations exhorting their members to express their "faith in our Father above" by serving "His children in need here below."[223] Bush rejoiced that Americans were working through their places of worship and community programs as well as individually to help the hungry and homeless, teach the unskilled, and bring "the Word of God" to the illiterate.[224] "Somewhere in America," Bush alleged, "every serious social problem is being solved through voluntary service," which is "the greatest national resource of all."[225]

Critics assailed Bush's initiative as unlikely to substantially reduce the nation's "deep-rooted social problems." Middle-class volunteers could not rescue neighborhoods from "gun-toting drug gangs" or provide poor children with better healthcare, decent schools, funds for college, or job training. Only the federal government, they argued, could achieve these ends.[226] Bush, however, deplored the "social engineering of liberal Democratic presidents" and strove to decrease rather than enlarge the government's reach. Because government had limits on what it could do, voluntary community service was essential to eradicating social ills as well as to providing personal fulfillment. Moreover, Bush increased funds to fight crime by 59 percent, doubled the money spent on enforcing drug laws, and created a "Weed and Seed" initiative to decrease violent crime in communities and provide job training, drug treatment, educational opportunities, and enterprise zones.[227]

Operation Desert Storm

Bush's faith, especially his desire to discern and follow God's will, his commitment to prayer, and his attempt to morally justify American actions, substantially influenced his policy in the Persian Gulf between August 1990 and

March 1991. On August 2, 1990, the troops of Iraqi dictator Saddam Hussein invaded Kuwait. The next day the UN Security Council passed a resolution demanding that Iraq unconditionally withdraw all its military forces from Kuwait. Democratic nations took various political and diplomatic actions and imposed economic sanctions to try to compel Hussein to comply with this resolution.

Although Billy Graham rejected the claim of some fundamentalist pastors that Hussein was the Antichrist, in a sermon he preached at St. Ann's in Kennebunkport with the president in attendance later that month, he warned that the turmoil in the Persian Gulf might have "major spiritual implications." Meanwhile, evangelist Greg Laurie, speaking to an audience of 25,000 in Orange, California, claimed that Hussein was fulfilling biblical prophecies about a man who would unite many nations to wage war against Israel.[228]

Bush announced that "this aggression against Kuwait" "will not stand" and quickly sent additional troops to the Middle East (500,000 soldiers were dispatched to the region in a four-month period, the largest deployment of American troops since the Vietnam War), an action many religious bodies and leaders criticized. For example, T. J. Jemison, the head of the nation's largest black denomination, the National Baptist Convention U.S.A., argued in September that the military buildup was about oil.[229] Despite these protests, Bush declared in October that he was encouraged by Americans' widespread support for enforcing the United Nations' sanctions against Iraq and by the number of countries that had "joined the international effort to defend Saudi Arabia against [Iraqi] aggression."[230]

In early November, Roger Mahony, the Catholic Archbishop of Los Angeles, urged James Baker to continue to exert "persistent, peaceful and determined pressure against Iraq." Resorting to military action without satisfying the criteria of just war theory, he warned, would "jeopardize many lives, raise serious moral questions," and undermine international solidarity against Iraq. "The moral and ethical considerations you raise," the secretary of state replied, "weigh heavily upon all of us as we seek to redress Iraq's unwarranted invasion and brutal occupation of Kuwait." "We will," he promised "use every means at our disposal to reach a peaceful outcome." However, Baker added, "in an imperfect world" force may be required to remove an aggressor. He argued that the Vatican II document *Gaudium et Spes*, which declared that governments had "the right to legitimate defense once every means of peaceful settlement had been exhausted," described "the course we are pursuing in the present conflict."[231] Many other religious leaders, including Archbishop Daniel Pilarczyk, president of the National Conference of Catholic Bishops, feared that offensive military action would violate just war criteria. The *Christian*

Century featured a debate on how just war tradition applied to a potential war in the Gulf, and the American Society of Christian Ethics adopted a resolution opposing using military force in the Gulf based on just war reasoning.[232]

In mid-November a National Council of Churches resolution called for "the immediate withdrawal of most United States forces from the region." It accused the Bush administration of using "reckless rhetoric" and denounced the American military buildup as precipitous and imprudent.[233] Meanwhile, the National Conference of Catholic Bishops beseeched the Bush administration to "avoid war in the Persian Gulf, except as a last resort."[234] Other Christians protested that the massive deployment of troops to the region diverted "public resources and attention from the present domestic crises of unemployment, homelessness, hunger, education, and healthcare."[235] An American Muslim editor warned that the shedding of Muslim blood would inflame the anger of Muslims worldwide and damage the West's relationship with Islamic nations. Muslims would regard a defeat of Iraq by American-led forces as humiliating, which would cause a pan-Islamic backlash.[236] Others Christian leaders, by contrast, expressed their support for Bush's approach. "We know that God" made you president "for such a time as this," declared Roger Story of the American Christian Trust, "and we trust you."[237]

As Bush's staff plotted how best to counter opposition to his administration's policy and prepared to defend the use of military force if it became necessary, the Office of Public Liaison sent a memorandum to researchers and speechwriters stating, we can ignore the protests of "left-of-center religious institutions such as Pax Christ USA and the National Council of Churches, but we really do need an ongoing and friendly dialogue with conservative and mainstream churches." Therefore, the president's rhetoric should emphasize "moral objectives and goals."[238] Consequently, Bush continually took the moral high road, claiming that America's cause was just, denouncing Hussein as "the rapist of Kuwait," and accentuating Iraqi atrocities. Bush compared the Iraqi dictator with Adolf Hitler and condemned his flouting of international law.[239] Some mainline Protestants denounced Bush's use of "unfortunate and unnecessary" "rhetorical overkill" designed to help justify dispatching US troops to Saudi Arabia. *Christian Century* editor James Wall protested that "it deeply offended Arabs" who saw Hussein as a heroic leader opposing foreign interference. While Iraq must not be allowed to violate another nation's sovereignty, the president must not enable Hussein to promote "pan-Arab sentiment by handing him easy propaganda victories that play so well in the emotional cauldron" of the Middle East.[240] Baker, in contrast to Bush, often stressed the potential negative effect of Iraqi's actions on jobs and the cost of gasoline in the United States.[241] Not surprisingly, opponents of the war pounced on this argument. Meanwhile, Bush's staff sent mass mailings to various constituencies, including Arab Americans, veterans, business leaders, and evangelical leaders, to explain and defend the administration's policy, and they held meetings with many groups.[242]

In his Thanksgiving message on November 21, 1990, Bush urged Americans to express their "appreciation for God's power to protect us and His wisdom to guide us." The next day at a Thanksgiving service on the USS *Nassau* in the Persian Gulf, Bush recalled a similar service on the USS *San Jacinto* off the coast of the Philippines during World War II. The war had taught him that the Lord provided the blessings of "faith and friendship, strength and determination, [and] courage and camaraderie" to people "who face adversity in the name of a noble purpose." Bush argued that both the Bible and the Qur'an emphasize "the love of liberty" and the "cause of peace." He concluded by asking God to "show us your way, the way of liberty and love. Soften the hearts of those who would do us harm. Strengthen the hearts of those who protect and defend us. We rely upon your guidance and trust in your judgment." "Amidst this threat of war, help us," Bush declared, "to search for peace." "Blessed are the peacemakers," he added, "for they shall be called the children of God."[243]

The UN Security Council passed a resolution on November 29 giving Iraq until January 15, 1991 to withdraw from Kuwait and authorizing its members to use "all necessary means" to force Iraqis to leave Kuwait after this deadline. Speaking for many mainline church leaders, the presiding bishop of the Episcopal Church, Edmond Browning, presented his case against war to Bush on December 20 at the White House. Bush asked Browning whether it was moral to do nothing to stop the Iraqi carnage in Kuwait detailed in an Amnesty International report. The president promised to read Browning's letter opposing war, while the bishop pledged to read the account of atrocities.[244]

As the January 15 deadline for Iraq to withdraw for Kuwait approached, Billy Graham asserted that "no sane person wants war." He added, however, that "sometimes it becomes necessary to fight the strong in order to protect the weak."[245] Many evangelicals, most notably Southern Baptist, Assemblies of God, and Missouri Synod Lutheran leaders, backed America's policy in the Middle East. SBC president Morris Chapman told Bush that Southern Baptists joined him in "praying for world peace and for God's supernatural intervention in the Persian Gulf Crisis."[246] Some mainline Protestant officials, including the Episcopal Bishop of Fort Worth, wrote Bush to convey their support. "I am grateful to Almighty God," the bishop declared, "for the sound judgment you have exhibited."[247] Author and activist Tim LaHaye urged Bush to proclaim a National Day of Prayer on January 13 for the Middle East to "invoke the blessing of God" and possibly cause the "Butcher of Baghdad to withdraw peacefully."[248] Some congregations held prayer vigils to pray for the president, military leaders, and the troops already deployed in the Persian Gulf.[249] Intercessors for America sponsored forty days of worldwide prayer and fasting for the Middle East beginning on January 1, 1991.[250]

Other religious groups and leaders continued to beseech Bush not go to war. The National Council of Churches led the assault on Bush's policy. Abandoning the Christian realism of Reinhold Niebuhr and Paul Ramsey, the Council, George Weigel argued, pursued a blame America first approach and contributed little to "serious moral debate about the ends and means of U.S. policy in the Persian Gulf."[251] In a message to the American people on December 21, 1990, the leaders of eighteen mainline and Greek Orthodox organizations declared that American use of armed force "would be politically and morally indefensible" and produce "certain catastrophe."[252] Browning traveled to the Middle East in early January to promote a peaceful solution to the crisis and organized a peace vigil outside the White House on January 14.[253] Numerous Episcopal bishops wrote Bush to support Browning's position. A United Methodist executive urged him "to work with the United Nations to develop political and diplomatic solutions to the crisis" instead of using military force. Military action, the Presbytery of the Pacific protested, would produce hundreds of thousands of casualties and "incalculable material loss," shatter the international consensus, and seriously damage America's "interests and reputation" in the Middle East.[254] On January 15, the heads of thirty-two mainline denominations and ecumenical organizations urged Bush to "not lead our nation into this abyss," because this war would not be able to be "contained in either scope, intensity, or time."[255] Other Christian organizations also urged Bush to avoid war, including Network (a National Catholic Social Justice Lobby), the Interfaith Center on Corporate Responsibility, PAX Christi USA, and the Mennonite Board of Education. The National Conference of Catholic Bishops insisted that war was likely to violate Catholic principles, but Catholic leaders were generally ambivalent about the possibility of war.[256]

In early January, as he confronted what he termed "the most momentous decision facing a President in modern times," Bush talked with many Christian leaders. The pope wired Bush, and Cardinal Law, Browning, Graham, Robert Schuller, Campus Crusade president Bill Bright, and other evangelicals phoned him to offer their prayers. "I hope to God," Bush wrote in his diary, that the people holding a prayer vigil outside the White House "know we are praying" too.[257]

Bush prayed with Graham before speaking on January 16 to one of the largest television audiences in American history to inform citizens that, authorized by a UN resolution and with the consent of the US Congress, allied forces from twenty-eight countries had begun to liberate Kuwait. Graham spent that evening at the White House with the Bushes watching planes drop bombs on Iraqi troops. When Secretary of Defense Dick Cheney reported that things were going very well, Bush felt a sense of gratitude to God and "the need to pray."[258] The next day Bush prayed with American military personnel and listened to Graham preach at a service at Arlington, Virginia.[259]

Bush wrote Cardinal Law on January 22 to explain his actions. "Before ordering our troops into battle," Bush declared, "I thought long and hard about casualties." But, he added, "I also thought of unchecked aggression" and what "would happen if the butcher of Baghdad" emerged as a hero. I kept asking, Bush observed, "How many lives would have been saved" "if Hitler's aggression had been checked earlier on?" The Republican disagreed with Law that "all war is wrong—morally." "After exhausting all diplomatic initiatives," doing nothing would have been immoral because "it would have convinced our coalition that standing up to evil does not work." "War is hell," Bush admitted, but "Iraq's brutal dictator" had arrogantly thumbed "his nose at the rest of the world." Bush disliked opposing Bishop Browning and "many others I respect." However, he declared, "I too have prayed over this matter. I pray that God will spare" the innocent, "this war will end soon," "Kuwait will no longer have to suffer" "brutal torture," and "out of this turmoil" peace will "eventually come to the entire Middle East." "The bottom line," Bush concluded, is that in certain situations "using force is not immoral" or "against God's will."[260]

Speaking to the National Religious Broadcasters on January 28, 1991, Bush argued that the conflict in the Gulf "is not a Christian war, a Jewish war, or a Moslem war." It had "nothing to do with religion per se," but it had "everything to do with what religion embodies: good versus evil" and "human dignity and freedom versus tyranny and oppression." Moreover, he claimed, it met all the criteria for a just war established by theologians Ambrose, Augustine, and Thomas Aquinas. First, Operation Desert Storm advanced "a just cause." Coalition troops sought to force Iraqis to withdraw from Kuwait completely, immediately, and unconditionally; to stop the rape, pillage, and plunder of its people and restore its legitimate government; to preserve "the security and sta-bility of the Gulf"; and to ensure that "naked aggression will not be rewarded." Americans sought nothing for themselves. Second, Bush explained, the war was just because it was "declared by [a] legitimate authority." It was "supported by unprecedented United Nations solidarity," endorsed by twelve Security Council resolutions, and waged by twenty-eight nations from six continents.[261]

Third, Bush asserted, "a just war must be a last resort." His administration had tried for 166 days to resolve this conflict. Baker held more than 200 meet-ings with foreign dignitaries, went on ten diplomatic missions, and traveled more than 100,000 miles to talk with members of the United Nations, the Arab League, and the European Community. Hussein had flatly rejected every overture the United States and other countries made "to resolve the matter peacefully," which justified "the use of force." Fourth, Bush contended, to be just, a war must employ just means. Coalition forces were acting humanely and striving to keep casualties to a minimum and "to avoid hurting the innocent."[262]

Bush alluded to a fifth criterion of just war theory—reasonable prospects of victory—by stating that war should never be "undertaken without total commitment to a successful outcome." "God willing," he added, "this is a war we will win." Military action would do more than simply liberate Kuwait and punish aggression. Victory would restore America's credibility and give it "a key leadership role" in bringing a just and durable peace to the entire Middle East. This, Bush contended, could help "create a new world order."[263] The United States was committed to promoting a new political structure based on "the rule of law and the guarantee of real economic," political, and religious freedom.[264] This new political arrangement, he maintained, would enable dozens of countries with disparate cultures and significant ideological differences to work together through the United Nations to prevent aggression.[265] In an October 1990 address to the United Nations, Bush explained that he sought to create "a new partnership of nations that transcends the Cold War" based "on consultation, cooperation, and collective action, especially through international and regional organizations." By agreeing on common principles and the rule of law, nations could increase democracy and peace and reduce arms.[266]

Numerous religious groups and leaders supported Operation Desert Storm, including the National Religious Broadcasters, the Southern Baptist Convention, the National Catholic Evangelization Association, the Lutheran Church Missouri Synod (LCMS), the Synagogue Council of America and the Union of American Hebrew Congregations, many Mormons, and several Catholic archbishops and Episcopal bishops.[267] The president of the LCMS urged members to support the war against Iraq. Anthony Bevilacque, the Archbishop of Philadelphia, reported that thousands of families were filling local churches to pray for American troops.[268] Although he had earlier expressed reservations about turning Hussein into a martyr and fears that using lethal force to liberate Kuwait would be condemned as immoral, Cardinal Bernard Law argued a week after it was launched that Operation Desert Storm, though regrettable, was morally justified.[269] Texas evangelist James Robison commended Bush for handing the crisis "with God-given wisdom."[270]

On January 28, the National Religious Broadcasters (NRB) adopted a resolution pledging to support Bush who had "conscientiously and persistently tried to make peace." Lloyd John Ogilvie, pastor of the First Presbyterian Church of Hollywood, California, sent the president a prayer he had composed for the NRB meeting, but was unable to deliver because his flight to Washington was grounded in Denver. "Lord," he began, "we lift before You our brother in Christ," the "spiritual, moral and visionary leader of the free world. He has sought Your guidance." "Lord," Ogilvie continued, protect "those gallant women and men deployed in the Persian Gulf" in "the battle for a just peace." He concluded, "for Your glory and the peace of the world, may Desert Storm quickly" become "Desert Victory."

The president of the Southern Baptist Convention declared that Southern Baptists pledged "unwavering support" for the troops serving in Operation Desert Storm and urged its 15 million members to uphold Bush in prayer. Leading evangelical social ethicist Carl F. H. Henry and Moral Majority founder Jerry Falwell strongly endorsed Bush's policy. The president of Agudath Israel of America wrote Bush: "How reassuring it is to know that our Commander-in-Chief is a man of faith who understands that victory is ultimately in the hands of the Al-mighty."[271] The Episcopal Bishop of San Joaquin promised Bush his "prayers and full support" for his decisions. Not acting now would require the United States to wage "war at even greater cost to lives and property at a later date."[272]

Numerous Christian leaders found Bush's just war argument convincing. Glenn Smith of Share the Word Television, the world's largest Catholic television program, offered his complete support for Bush's efforts to win "this 'Just War.'"[273] In a newsletter to its members, NAE executive Robert Dugan, Jr. contended that Bush had made a "clear and compelling case that the war against Iraq does meet the just-war criteria." After a month of hostilities, Richard Land insisted that "the criteria laid down for conduct of a just war have been met."[274] Christian ethicist James Turner Johnson argued that the just war criteria "were amply satisfied" in deciding to use military force against Iraq. The failure of negotiations, Hussein's unrelenting obstinacy, "the ongoing process of military buildup by Iraqi forces, the continuing systematic rape of Kuwait," Iraq's treatment of its dissident citizens, and its threats to use violence against neighboring nations all indicated that non-military means were highly unlikely to be successful. The coalition's use of force was proportionate to the wrong that needed to be righted, and the operation had reasonable hope of success and was based on a desire to establish peace in the region.[275]

Bush proclaimed February 3 a National Day of Prayer for peace, the safety of allied troops and innocent civilians, and God's continued blessing of America, and millions responded.[276] Functioning as the national high priest, Bush asserted that "as one Nation under God," "Americans are deeply mindful" of "our dependence on the Almighty." Throughout their history, Americans had "relied upon God's strength and guidance in war and peace." They had "a responsibility to serve as a beacon to the world" and use their "resources to help those suffering" from "tyranny and repression." He asked God to "watch over and support the courageous" troops who were fighting to "liberate Kuwait and to deter further Iraqi aggression." Bush exhorted citizens "to unite in humble and contrite prayer to Almighty God," especially for the families of the "selfless military personnel who have earned their final rest in the arms of God."[277]

While opposition decreased after airstrikes began, some Christians continued to vehemently denounce Operation Desert Storm. Jean Bethke Elshtain complained that Bush had clothed himself "in the moral mantle of purity" and warned against "presumptions of moral triumphalism." By labeling the conflict "good versus evil, right versus wrong, [and] human dignity and freedom versus tyranny and oppression," Bush had employed the "moralistic trumpeting" that just war theory cautioned against.[278] The *Christian Century* accused the US government of hypocrisy: it had tolerated all sorts of Middle East tyrants as long as oil flowed. Now, however, the United States had "overreacted against one isolated tyrant" primarily because he threatened the oil supply.[279] The executive director of the Buffalo Council of Churches beseeched Bush to stop killing innocent victims in his "personal war with Saddam Hussein."[280] In mid-February, the leaders of more than twenty Protestant and Orthodox denominations and fifteen Roman Catholic bishops called for a ceasefire. The teaching of the Gospel, they asserted, "cannot be reconciled" with the war in the Gulf. The violence it unleashed would "multiply and reverberate" for decades. Representatives of the National Council of Churches, the United Methodist Church, the Evangelical Lutheran Church in America, the Presbyterian Church (U.S.A.), the Episcopal Church, the Greek Orthodox Church, the Orthodox Church in America, the United Church of Christ, the Disciples of Christ, the American Baptist Churches, and the Reformed Church in America as well as five largely black denominations signed this statement.[281] Protesting that the war was "wrong, unnecessary, [and] unprincipled," other black Christians demanded an immediate ceasefire. Because nations possessed massive weapons that could destroy the entire planet, no war could be just. Although they deplored Hussein's invasion of Kuwait, unprovoked attack on Israel, and use of chemical and biological weapons, these black pastors objected to the "Christian West" trying to "define reality," "dictate economic terms" to, and exploit the resources of the "Muslim East." Moreover, war was "an immoral and unspiritual diversion" from "our domestic responsibilities."[282]

Bush continued to call for prayer for divine intervention. The president announced that allied military ground action would begin in the Persian Gulf on February 23 and exhorted all Americans to pray for coalition forces.[283] The next day Bush and many cabinet members and White House staff attended a communion service at St. John's to pray for the success of this venture.[284] A week after victory was achieved on February 28, Bush told Congress that throughout the course of Operation Desert Storm Americans had prayed faithfully for their troops. "We went halfway around the world to do what is moral and just and right," he asserted, "and we ask nothing in return."[285] He thanked God for the success of the operation and urged Americans to pray that a just peace would prevail in Iraq.[286]

Bush designated April 5–7 National Days of Thanksgiving to recognize God's "guidance in the liberation of Kuwait."[287] "It is fitting," he averred that Americans thank "our Heavenly Father" for "His mercy and protection." In his proclamation Bush quoted Psalm 118:1 ("O give thanks to the Lord for He is gracious, for His mercy endures for ever"); Psalm 46:9 (The Lord "makes wars to cease to the end of the earth"); and Zechariah 4:6 (God gives victory "not by might, nor by power" but by His spirit). Bush thanked God for answering Americans' prayers "for a swift and decisive victory" and for the "low number of allied casualties," which the commanding general labeled "miraculous." Americans rejoiced at the prospect "of a safer, more peaceful world" and prayed for "reconciliation with all peoples."[288]

The campaign to expel Iraqi forces lasted forty-two days and included only four days of ground operations. In waging war, Bush explained, coalition forces had tried to be sensitive to Muslim culture and religious principles. The major reason "the Arab world hasn't exploded," Bush argued, is that Islam did not condone the brutality Hussein had employed.[289] A week later, Bush told journalists, "I don't find anything" in "the principal teachings of Islam" that contradicts the actions of Operation Desert Storm. Islam, like Judaism and Christianity, exalts love, kindness, helping neighbors, and taking care of children. Therefore, he insisted, American actions had not been "anti-Islam."[290] The "coalition victory in the Persian Gulf," Bush avowed, reinforced the biblical teaching that "the cruel hand of tyranny" could never crush liberty.[291]

Bush declared in April that he had benefited from hearing various views on the Gulf conflict, including those of Bishop Browning and Catholic bishops who disagreed with him.[292] He testified that "my faith in God guided and sustained me during this difficult time."[293] "During the Gulf crisis, Barbara and I," along with most other Americans "found guidance and comfort in prayer. And throughout the struggle," he told Southern Baptists in June 1991, "prayers sustained us." After "months of asking for God's guidance," Bush added, Americans had spent three days in April thanking God "for sustaining our nation through this crisis."[294]

Despite the quick victory of coalition forces, critics remained unconvinced that allied actions were justified. Pronouncing Operation Desert Storm "Another Failure in a Bankrupt Foreign Policy," the *Christian Century* opined that the war, which "bombed Iraq back into a preindustrial state" and caused as many as 200,000 deaths, taught that American worshipped "the twin gods of financial power and military security." Others protested that the United States acted to further its "influence and power in the Gulf" and control "the flow of oil."[295] Others contended that American actions were morally justified. The Gulf War, argued Catholic author and social activist George Weigel, "satisfied the eight classic criteria of the just war tradition," even though Hussein was not deposed and, after the ceasefire, inflicted great suffering on the Kurds in northern Iraq and the Shiites in southern Iraq. Elshtain protested that Bush abandoned just war theory in refusing to intervene in Iraq to help the Kurds and instead resorted to the "language of strategy, diplomacy," and pragmatic considerations.[296]

Final Assessment

George Bush argued that his principal accomplishments as president were the Clean Air Act that improved air quality, the Americans with Disabilities Act that expanded opportunities for 37 million people, the fall of communism that ended political and religious oppression, and the victory in the Gulf War that increased "respect for America around the world." When he left office, "our nation was at peace, our economy was strong, our environment was cleaner, and our future was brighter." "If I could leave but one legacy to this country," the Republican declared at the end of his presidency, it would be to have America again adopt "the moral compass" that produces strong families and "millions of Points of Light." "When I assumed this great office," Bush proclaimed, "I pledged" to "honor, encourage, and increase volunteer efforts" to light "every dark corner of our country." We adopted "a national strategy" to increase volunteerism and alleviate social ills, he explained. First, we sought to motivate Americans to "define a successful life as one that includes serving others"; second, to enlarge efforts that were already working; third, to encourage "leaders to help others become Points of Light"; and finally, to connect people to community organizations through which they could assist others. "Everything I've done as President," Bush argued, supported this strategy.[297] His Points of Light initiative did boost voluntary activity. Volunteers logged millions of hours helping needy individuals during Bush's four years in office, and these activities continued after his presidency. In 2011, for example, 4.3 million Americans and 77,052 partners in twenty different countries provided 32 million hours of service through 260,000 volunteer projects connected with Bush's Points of Light Foundation.[298]

Many scholars commend *Time* magazine's decision to name Bush its "men of the year" in January 1991 to symbolize the "president's contradictory track record: steadfast and determined on foreign policy issues, halting and lackluster on the domestic front."[299] Bush greatly preferred foreign over domestic affairs, and his greatest achievements were in diplomacy.[300] Although the Texan had limited charisma and rhetorical skills, his administration "impressed adversaries and reassured allies in a period of rapid and dramatic international change." Timothy Naftali lauds Bush's prudent response to the challenges the United States faced as the Cold War ended.[301] Many scholars praise Bush for ending a blatant injustice in the Middle East, promoting his New World Order, and improving the United States' relationship with the Soviet Union. Another president, Michael Beschloss argues, may have concluded the Cold War on "terms less favorable to the West." Bush used his "gift for building relationships with other leaders" to help Mikhail Gorbachev end communism in the USSR and his diplomatic skills to help swiftly unify Germany. Beschloss and Strobe Talbott maintain that by "refraining from pushing the Soviet government too hard," Bush "made an indispensable contribution" to the Cold War's culmination. John Greene lauds Bush for embodying integrity, crafting a judicious foreign policy, and making America more stable.[302]

Thomas Friedman labels Bush "one of our most underrated presidents" and applauds the "balanced conservatism" of his economic, environmental, and foreign policies. "When the deficit started spiraling to dangerous levels," Bush repudiated his promise not to implement new taxes and compromised with Democrats "to raise several taxes" and increase spending cuts "as part of a budget deal that helped to pave the way for the prosperity" of the 1990s. After driving Iraqi forces out of Kuwait, Bush wisely chose not to depose Saddam Hussein.[303]

Many other historians and political scientists, however, contend that Bush lacked political vision and did not lead effectively either at home or abroad.[304] The Republican, they claim, never forthrightly explained his fundamental goals for the nation. He did not "articulate a clear vision or grand strategy" to direct the United States' response to post–Cold War international relations. Bush did not seize the opportunity this new situation provided "to redefine the objectives of American diplomacy."[305] He was "far more adept," David Gergen maintains, "at cleaning up the debris of an old world than building the framework of the new."[306] "Mired in a Cold War past," Bush failed to "dream grand dreams, set new standards, [or] pursue bold changes," thereby missing a golden opportunity to "refashion how the international system operated."[307]

While recognizing that Bush faced major obstacles, most notably a Democratic Congress, an oppositional Supreme Court, and a congressional mandate to eliminate the huge federal deficit by 1991, numerous scholars and journalists fault him for not working more actively to overcome these impediments. Some deride him as a "do-nothing president" who frequently failed to act decisively.[308] Cartoonists, impersonator Dana Carvey, and pundits lampooned Bush as an overly circumspect chief executive whose closest advisors were "patience and prudence." To numerous political analysts, the Republican was "a passive, guardian president" whose only major goal was to be reelected in 1992.[309] They claim that Bush was "more of a manager than a visionary, more a cautious pragmatist than a bold leader." As a reactor instead of an initiator, he was often "buffeted by circumstances." Bush was the "Revlon president" whose solutions for problems were merely cosmetic.[310] Unlike Reagan, Bush advisor Charles Kolb asserts, the Texan had no "driving vision." Bush had "the self-assurance, honesty, and integrity" to be an effective president, but he never defined "what he wanted to achieve and where he wanted to lead the country." Consequently, his administration lacked "intellectual coherence and consistency" and his failure to act aggressively or promptly caused "the Reagan coalition to fray and ultimately collapse" and led Bush to cave in to his adversaries on taxes, spending, and regulatory policy. The Republican's public remarks inspired few because "he had little of substance to communicate."[311] Journalist Hugh Sidey counters that Bush's intelligent approach to governing, support of traditional virtues, and role in helping the United States remain the world's leader in the post–Cold War era was a sufficient mission.[312] Some scholars argue that the highly partisan Democratic Congress "made it almost impossible" for Bush to be "a successful, activist, domestic policy president."[313]

Others disparage Bush's character and actions. Kevin Phillips lambasts the Bush family as "great in power, not morality." Its members practiced "crony capitalism with a moral arrogance." "Deceit and disinformation," he alleges, were George H. W. Bush's "political hallmarks." To journalists Michael Duffy and Dan Goodgame, the Texan was a "ruthless campaigner" and "remorselessly deceitful when it served his purpose." Tom Wicker contends that Bush resorted to "the most deplored and denounced campaign tactics of modern times to win" the 1988 election. Historian Stephen Graubard denounced Operation Desert Storm as an act of "naked aggression."[314]

Speaking for Bush admirers, Robert Charles argues that Bush's "personal traits, policy priorities, recorded achievements, and use of the bully pulpit" demonstrate that he was "an exceptional and underrated moral leader" who "altered the course of history" by "tapping his own life's moral lessons and by trusting his moral compass." The Republican devised "a strong foreign policy" and "a sound long-term budget," tackled environmental threats, expanded the war against drugs, and aided less fortunate Americans by his homeownership program, emphasis on volunteerism, and expansion of civil rights. Bush's greatest legacy is his example of "strength and compassion, decisiveness, patience and humility under fire, congeniality, and honesty."[315]

The day after losing the 1992 presidential election, Bush wrote words in his diary that summarized his philosophy of life: "be strong, be kind, [and] be generous." "Ask God for understanding and strength." In late November he confided to his brother John, "I want people to know I stood" for "Duty, Honor, Country," and "service." "What really matters," Bush declared in 1997, are a person's faith, family, and friends.[316] Numerous political associates praise Bush's "decency, integrity, and commitment to community, country and family."[317] Motivated by his faith, Bush has been an exemplary Point of Light who energetically and effectively served God and millions around the world through his presidency and other political roles for five decades.

Bill Clinton

SIN, ATONEMENT, AND REPAIRING THE BREACH

Our ministry is to do the work of God here on Earth.

"REMARKS AT THE FULL GOSPEL A.M.E. ZION CHURCH
IN TEMPLE HILLS, Maryland," August 14, 1994

*I always felt that protecting religious liberty and making the
White House accessible to all religious faiths was an important part of my job.*

MY LIFE, 558

*I placed my hand [on Isaiah 58:12]—"Thou shalt raise up the
foundations of many generations, and thou shalt be called the
repairer of the breach, the restorer of paths to dwell in"—when
I took the oath of office, on behalf of all Americans, for no
matter what our differences in our faiths, our backgrounds,
our politics, we must all be repairers of the breach.*

"ADDRESS BEFORE A JOINT SESSION OF THE CONGRESS
ON THE STATE OF THE UNION," February 4, 1997

*Pursuing peace in the Middle East "was a part of my job as
President, my mission as a Christian, and my personal journey of atonement."*

"REMARKS CELEBRATING THE 160TH ANNIVERSARY OF
THE METROPOLITAN AFRICAN METHODIST EPISCOPAL
CHURCH," October 23, 1998

Introduction

Like Richard Nixon's faith, Bill Clinton's is hard to decipher. Unlike many
other presidents, including Nixon, and despite his disclaimer that a "person's spiritual journey should be intensely private and shared only with

God," Clinton was very open about his faith.[1] Like Nixon, he professed to have had a "born again" experience as a youth. He frequently testified that his faith was important to him, attended church regularly as president, had an impressive knowledge of the Bible, and quoted scriptural passages and cited biblical principles as much as any other chief executive. Clinton argued that personal religious convictions had an important role to play in the public square, and his beliefs influenced his policies on numerous matters including religious liberty, racial reconciliation, welfare reform, and international peacemaking. While Clinton took an inclusive and pluralistic approach, affirming the merit and contributions of all world religions, he especially lauded the virtues of Christianity and asserted that implementing its principles was essential to enriching individuals' lives and alleviating America's social ills.[2] Clinton, wrote Kenneth Woodward in Newsweek, "cannot be fully understood without grasping the nuances of his Baptist upbringing," and I would add, his adult Christian convictions.[3] The clash between his religious principles, personal ambition, and sexual desires produced tremendous tension for Clinton. Despite his frequent discussion of his own faith, emphasis on the civic benefits of Christianity, and public quest for redemption in the aftermath of the Monica Lewinsky scandal, no religious biography of Clinton has been written.

This is understandable in light of the perplexing nature of Clinton's faith. His seemingly sincere testimony to his Christian commitment and his public displays of religiosity were combined with tawdry actions that violated biblical moral standards. Like Nixon's, Clinton's "candor, integrity, and fidelity to [his] ideals" have been widely criticized.[4] While Democrats denounced Nixon as "Tricky Dicky," Republicans lambasted Clinton as "Slick Willie." Despite their comebacks, rebirths, and apologies, critics contended, both were incorrigible scoundrels and pathological liars. Clinton's presidency was marred by the Whitewater investigation; the firing of the nation's chief prosecutors; a ransacking of Vince Foster's files; the state trooper flap; the Paula Jones case; Filegate; the Lewinsky scandal; impeachment; and several other moral controversies. In a 2000 C-SPAN poll, historians and political pundits rated Clinton last in moral authority among all presidents.[5]

Clinton's personal behavior, especially his sexual affairs and lying, contravened traditional moral norms, leading many to question the genuineness of his Christian profession. How could someone who was so narcissistic, who served as "the poster boy for defective character in the 1990s," truly be a Christian? While not denying Clinton's profession to be a Christian, many others label him a hypocrite because of his sexual improprieties and mendacity.[6] The jarring incongruity between Clinton's words and actions led to much debate about the authenticity of his faith and how important it was in his public and private life.[7]

Unlike the biographers of most other presidents, many of Clinton's have discussed his faith because of his extensive use of religious rhetoric, religious conservatives' vehement protests about his views of homosexuality and abortion, and the clash between his avowed Christian convictions and his sexual transgressions. Clinton's religious background and interests are eclectic. Raised as a Southern Baptist, Clinton was the nation's first president to graduate from a Catholic college. Its professors helped shape his worldview, especially his perspective on economic and social justice.[8] His wife Hillary is a lifelong Methodist. While Clinton worshipped primarily in Baptist and Methodist churches, he attended a Pentecostal camp for many summers and greatly enjoyed the more emotional, fervent style of Pentecostal and black churches.[9] When the president spoke at Notre Dame, argued *Washington Post* columnist E. J. Dionne, he sounded Catholic; when Clinton spoke at African-American churches, he sounded like a black preacher.[10] Friends attributed Clinton's optimism and efforts to promote camaraderie among American politicians and reconciliation between nations to his religious background and convictions.[11] Clinton's perplexing faith, coupled with his decision to seek public redemption for his affair with White House intern Monica Lewinsky make religion a crucial element in assessing both him and his presidency. His actions "broadened a national argument that had been about sexual behavior and allegations of perjury and obstruction of justice to the vexing question of how a political leader uses—or in the eyes of critics, misuses—religion."[12]

"The biggest moral challenge," Clinton told reporters in 1992, "is trying to live by what you believe in every day." As he aged, he had sought "to consider the moral implications" of his actions.[13] As president, Clinton strove to strengthen his faith and apply it to his work as he grappled with personal moral failures and taxing domestic and international problems. Two of his principal speechwriters—Michael Waldman and Taylor Branch—testified that Clinton played an active role in composing his addresses. Therefore, it is reasonable to assume that they reflect his personal commitments and faith.[14] Considerable evidence indicates that his faith, as shaped by Southern Baptist, mainline Protestant, black evangelical, Pentecostal, and Catholic influences, affected many of his domestic and foreign policies.

Elected in 1992 at the age of 46, Bill Clinton was the nation's first baby boomer president and third youngest, following Theodore Roosevelt and John F. Kennedy. Reelected in 1996, he joined Woodrow Wilson and Franklin Roosevelt as the only Democrats to win a second term since Andrew Jackson. Despite impressive accomplishments at home—NAFTA, welfare reform, economic prosperity, and a booming stock market (the Dow Jones average almost tripled in value from 1993 to 2001)—and abroad—he helped broker peace treaties in Northern Ireland and Bosnia and between the Israelis and the Palestinians—Clinton became the second president to be impeached when the House of Representatives voted in December 1998 to charge him with lying to a grand jury about his affair with Lewinsky and obstructing justice in the Paula Jones sexual harassment lawsuit. Although the Senate voted to acquit Clinton in February 1999, his impeachment tarnished his reputation, raised questions about the genuineness of his faith, cast a cloud over his last two years in office, and diverted scholarly and public attention from his many significant achievements.

The Faith of Bill Clinton

Bill Clinton's father died in an automobile accident before he was born in 1946, and his mother Virginia Kelley remarried Roger Clinton in 1950. Bill regularly attended a preschool program at First Baptist Church in Hope, Arkansas, where he learned about Jesus. He also went to its Sunday school and summer Bible school program.[15] His stepfather, who never completed high school, frequently got drunk and often beat his wife. Eager to escape the turmoil at home, at age 6, Bill began walking a mile alone to attend Park Place Baptist Church after his family relocated to Hot Springs, Arkansas. None of his friends attended this church, but Clinton "felt the need" to go.[16] By age 9, Clinton wrote, "I had absorbed enough of my church's teachings to know that I was a sinner and to want Jesus to save me. So I came down the aisle at the end of Sunday service, professed my faith in Christ, and asked to be baptized." The pastor, James Fitzgerald, "convinced me that I needed to acknowledge that I was a sinner" and "to accept Christ in my heart, and I did." Attending church as a child, Clinton later explained, was very important to him. The church provided important moral instruction and helped him understand "what life was all about."[17] Cora Walters, who served as his family's housekeeper and nanny for eleven years, had the most spiritual influence on young Clinton. She was an "upright, conscientious, deeply Christian" grandmother, who, according to Clinton's mother, "lived her Christianity."[18] In 1959 Clinton attended Billy Graham's crusade in Little Rock. He was so impressed with Graham's message and refusal to segregate his audience, especially in the aftermath of the controversy over the integration of Central High School and pressure from the White Citizens Council and Little Rock businessmen, that he began sending part of his allowance to the evangelist.[19]

Clinton's struggles at home produced what he described as a "major spiritual crisis" at age 13. He experienced religious doubts because he could not prove God's existence or understand why God created "a world in which so many bad things happened."[20] Nevertheless, by numerous accounts, Clinton displayed a strong Christian commitment in high school, and some of his teachers thought he might someday become an evangelist. His music teacher and mentor Virgil Spurlin declared that Clinton's "Christian character and beliefs" always took "priority in his dealings with others."[21] Because of his academic achievement and sterling reputation, Clinton was invited to give the closing prayer at his high school graduation, which expressed his "deep religious convictions." Clinton beseeched God to "sicken us at the sight of apathy, ignorance, and rejection so that our generation will remove complacency, poverty, and prejudice." He prayed that "we will never know the misery and muddle of life without purpose." Clinton claimed in his 2004 autobiography that "I still believe every word I prayed."[22]

While at Georgetown University from 1964 to 1968, studying philosophy, politics, and economics as a Rhodes Scholar at Oxford from 1968 to 1970, and at Yale Law School from 1970 to 1973, Clinton's faith had less influence on his life and he attended church sporadically.[23] The Arkansas native's assessment of Nixon's 1969 inaugural address provides a window into his spiritual struggles during this period. Nixon's "preaching of our good old middle-class religion and virtues," he wrote, "left me pretty cold." These values could not "solve our problems" with Asians, who did not share the Judeo-Christian tradition; "Communists, who do not even believe in God"; "blacks who have been shafted so often by God-fearing white men that there is hardly any common ground left between them"; and youth, who "prefer dope to the audacious self-delusion of their elders." "I believed in Christianity and middle-class virtues, too," Clinton added, but "I thought living out our true religious and political principles would require us to reach deeper and go further than Mr. Nixon was prepared to go."[24]

In 1975 Clinton married Hillary Rodham, who he had met at Yale Law School, and in 1978 Arkansas residents made him the nation's youngest governor. The shock of losing his reelection bid in 1980 to a fundamentalist Baptist left him confused, despondent, and adrift. Bill and Hillary had marital problems, and rumors spread that he was having extramarital affairs. These experiences, coupled with the birth of his daughter Chelsea in 1980, brought Clinton back to the church. He joined Immanuel Baptist Church, a 4,000-member Southern Baptist congregation in Little Rock and began singing in the choir and studying the Bible seriously. While critics accused Clinton of attending church to impress Arkansas voters, Betsey Wright, his longtime chief of staff, explained that having "a church family" helped Clinton deal with his traumatic defeat and overcome "what he regarded as his own personal failure."[25] Clinton benefited greatly from the biblically based sermons and the nonjudgmental spiritual guidance of the church's pastor W. O. Vaught.[26]

Clinton's 1981 tour of Israel with Vaught gave him a "deeper appreciation for my own faith, a profound admiration for Israel," and "some understanding of Palestinian aspirations and grievances." It produced his "obsession to see all the children of Abraham reconciled on the holy ground" where Christianity, Judaism, and Islam began.[27] After 1980 Hillary's faith also became very important to her. She read the Bible regularly, filled a notebook with biblical citations, gave numerous lay sermons at Methodist churches in Arkansas, and participated in a women's prayer group.[28] David Maraniss explains that the Clintons' faith "eased the burden of their high-profile lives, sometimes offering solace and escape from the contentious world of politics, at other times providing theological support for their political choices." Their religious pattern reflected that of many other baby boomers: they went to church consistently as adolescents and infrequently during their late teens and twenties. Their faith and church involvement became more important again as they became middle-aged parents. "The intensity of their faith seemed to increase in proportion to their growing ambitions and responsibilities in careers where the rewards of adulation and accomplishment were counterbalanced by the strains of compromise and criticism."[29]

As Clinton began his presidency, his Christian convictions were on display. The morning of his inauguration, he participated in a stirring worship service at the Metropolitan African Methodist Church.[30] The third week of his presidency Clinton exhorted National Prayer Breakfast guests "to seek the help and guidance of our Lord." "I have always been touched," Clinton declared, by the "example of Jesus Christ." He challenged the audience to "live out the admonition of President Kennedy, that here on Earth God's work must truly be our own."[31]

Clinton believed that an all-powerful God had crafted the universe, directed history, aided individuals, and someday would judge everyone. "The world," Clinton asserted, "was created by, is looked over by, and ultimately will be accountable to one great God."[32] Clinton accentuated God's love, righteousness, protection, and providence. By sending His Son Jesus, God demonstrated His "infinite love." God's love for every person was "enduring and unconditional."[33] God's direction of history was often inscrutable, Clinton told families who had lost loved ones in the bombing of the Federal Building in Oklahoma City in 1995, but, in the words of an old hymn, "Further along we'll understand why." "The God of comfort," the president proclaimed, "is also the God of righteousness." His justice will prevail, Clinton promised. God's "amazing grace" enabled people to get "through and beyond our individual and collective sins and trials."[34]

Clinton frequently referred to Jesus as "our Saviour" and affirmed his belief in Jesus's miracles and resurrection, "the central event" in the Christian history of salvation. Easter, he proclaimed, demonstrated that "good conquered evil, hope overcame despair, and life triumphed over death." "God's only Son," Clinton declared, brought "the assurance of God's love and presence in our lives and the promise of salvation." Jesus is " 'the true Light' that illumines all humankind." Those who fed the hungry, cared for the sick, nurtured children, and promoted peace and justice reflected Christ's light.[35] Jesus's "suffering, death, and rising from the dead" and "victory over sin and death" empowered those who believe in Him to overcome sin. Although Jesus was "born in poverty," was never elected to any position, and "never had a nickel to his name," He had "more followers than any politician who ever lived." Christ's resurrection demonstrated that love could "triumph over the forces of misunderstanding, fear, and hatred." Christians, Clinton declared, "celebrate God's redemptive love as revealed" in Jesus's life, teachings, sacrificial death, and resurrection.[36]

Clinton contended that God created people of different races in His image as equal and gave them "the right to life, liberty and the pursuit of happiness." As a result, everyone "had a hunger to find" a meaning in life that transcended "temporal things." All individuals had "an equal right" to "rise as far as they can go." "All of us are sinners," Clinton asserted; everyone has "fallen short of the glory of God." "Because of flaws in human nature," he declared, "we'll have problems until the end of time." "Evil is a darkness within us all" that "metastasizes and explodes in a few." "Do not be overcome by evil," Clinton admonished, "but overcome evil with good."[37]

Although Clinton believed in "the constancy of sin," he also affirmed the "possibility of forgiveness, the reality of redemption and the promise of a future life." As a Baptist, he argued "that salvation is primarily personal and private, that my relationship is directly with God and not through any intermediary." As a forgiven sinner, he needed "the power of God."[38] By reflecting "God's love and forgiveness," Clinton reasoned, Christians could help end hostilities around the world. They should let their light shine and "give glory to the Father in heaven."[39]

Clinton testified that worship was important to him. The church, he declared, was "a place not for saints but for sinners."[40] When in Washington, Clinton regularly attended Foundry Methodist Church with Hillary. He also often attended services at Camp David's Evergreen Chapel with about fifty people and sang in the small choir.[41] As his presidency ended, Clinton thanked the members of Foundry for their prayers and support during the "storm and sunshine of these last 8 years." He especially appreciated Foundry's social ministry and its welcoming of Christians of various races, nations, and sexual orientations. Disputing claims that he attended church for political purposes, Clinton insisted that he went because it helped him spiritually and emotionally. His "church home" gave him peace, comfort, and strength. Sunday morning worship was "one of the best hours of the week." He could take his "Bible, read, listen, sing," and forget about everything else.[42]

As a child and an adult, Clinton read the Bible from cover to cover numerous times. His childhood friend Patty Criner reported that Clinton owned fifteen Bibles, many of which contained copious handwritten notes. Members of his presidential staff also testified that his Bibles were filled with hundreds of marginal comments. Arkansas political advisor Carol Willis claimed that Clinton often quoted biblical verses, while political strategist Paul Begala insisted that the Democrat had "a deep facility for Scripture" and discussed specific passages in many of their conversations.[43] Clinton avowed that as president he had many "opportunities to be alone and to pray." He asserted that he read the Bible regularly and the books of numerous Christian authors, including Tony Campolo's Wake Up America![44] The Bible, Clinton averred, provided the "answer to all of life's problems."[45]

Clinton explained that he read more modern versions of the Bible, but they were "not nearly as eloquent" as the King James Version, his favorite.[46] Clinton displayed substantial knowledge of the Bible, often making extemporaneous remarks about passages.[47] The Baptist argued that faith is "real and tangible." "When you believe" in God's redemption and power, he added, "there's nothing you can't do."[48] Clinton peppered his addresses with biblical citations (almost always the KJV) and allusions and positive examples of congregations and parachurch organizations, especially ones that aided the poor.[49] Clinton especially liked the book of Psalms. In many Psalms, he asserted, David prayed for the strength to deal with adversity and "his own failures."[50] Clinton declared that psalms that focused on trusting in God, following the right path, the importance of wisdom, and God's unfailing love, faithfulness, forgiveness, salvation, help, and protection of people from their enemies were particularly meaningful to him.[51]

Numerous individuals labeled Clinton's faith authentic. In 1994, evangelical author Philip Yancey reported, "I have not met a single Christian leader who, after meeting with Clinton, comes away questioning his sincerity." A Christian college president professed to be "absolutely convinced of his deep and sincere faith" and impressed by Clinton's knowledge of the Bible.[52] The executive director of the Arkansas State Baptist Convention called Clinton a "genuine born-again believer." Philip Wogaman, pastor of the Foundry Methodist Church, concluded that Clinton's faith was "genuine." Another Clinton confidante, Tony Campolo, a sociology professor at Eastern College in Philadelphia, insisted that Clinton affirmed the Apostles' Creed and considered "the Bible to be an infallible message from God." Bill Hybels, pastor of the Willow Creek Community Church near Chicago, declared that in their monthly private meetings he had seen Clinton grow spiritually. Despite such testimonies, many denounced Clinton's faith as disingenuous because they considered his stances on political issues to be unbiblical.[53]

Clinton argued that all Christians had a calling to serve God.[54] As Martin Luther King, Jr. asserted, a street sweeper should clean the streets as if he "were Michelangelo painting the Sistine Chapel."[55] By seeking to know and live by God's will, learning "to forgive ourselves and one another," and focusing on others, Christians glorified God and provided a positive witness.[56]

In 1992 Clinton stated, "I pray virtually every day."[57] He asked Americans to pray that political leaders would remember Micah's admonition to "act justly and love mercy and walk humbly with our God."[58] Clinton exhorted Americans to ask God for wisdom in raising their children, protecting the environment, and promoting freedom, peace, and human dignity around the globe.[59] He solicited the prayers of Muslims, Jews, and Christians for his "mission of peace in the Middle East." Clinton also beseeched people to pray for peace in Bosnia, Kosovo, and Northern Ireland. When people did not know how to pray, the Holy Spirit "intercedes for us."[60] The president often thanked Americans for their prayers and for the encouraging letters and scriptural exhortations many sent him.[61]

Clinton often expressed belief in life after death. When his stepfather was dying of throat cancer in 1967, Clinton assured him that "death doesn't end a man's life." The Baptist explained that he believed in heaven because "I need a second chance." When Secretary of Commerce Ronald Brown died in 1996, Clinton promised his loved ones that he "was reaping his reward" "in a place where every good quality he ever had has been rendered perfect." Giving a eulogy for a navy admiral a month later, Clinton declared, he had been "welcomed on the pier by God's loving, eternal embrace." At a memorial service for firefighters in Worcester, Massachusetts, Clinton stated, "we commend their souls to God's eternal loving care." Those who died in the Oklahoma City bombing, Clinton alleged, "now belong to God. Some day we will be with them."[62]

While often praising Christianity, Clinton, like other recent presidents, also highlighted the contributions of other religions. "Let us," he declared in 1994, "rededicate ourselves to the spirit of Easter, of Passover, of Ramadan" "and to the common values" that "make America a land of limitless hope and opportunity for all." He had "been immeasurably enriched by the power of the Torah, the beauty of the Koran, the piercing insights of the religions of East and South Asia and of our own Native Americans, [and] the joyful energy that I have felt in black and Pentecostal churches."[63]

As president, Clinton had a close relationship with five ministers—Rex Horne, Jr., who served as his pastor at the Immanuel Baptist Church in Little Rock from 1990 to 2006; Bill Hybels; and a trio of ministers who counseled him after his affair with Monica Lewinsky—J. Philip Wogaman, Tony Campolo, and Gordon MacDonald, pastor of Grace Chapel near Boston.[64] Horne discussed a variety of matters with Clinton in weekly phone calls, in frequent letters, and sometimes in person.[65] As president, Clinton occasionally worshipped at and regularly gave money to Immanuel Baptist Church, and Horne sometimes sent him video tapes of his sermons and other religious materials.[66] The minister asserted in 1994 that he sought to aid Clinton in his spiritual journey.[67] Horne insisted that "I have never been an apologist for the president. I have just tried to be his pastor."[68] He did complain, however, that many Christians had unfairly judged Clinton's faith and policies. Rather than focusing on criticizing Clinton's views of abortion and gay civil rights, with which Horne also publicly disagreed, Christians should support the president's efforts to fight racial injustice and aid the poor.[69] Clinton looked to Horne for spiritual guidance and thanked him for being "such a good friend, counselor, and source of inspiration."[70] Shortly before leaving office in January 2001, Clinton told Horne that "your friendship, prayers, and support over the years" has "meant a lot to me."[71]

In an October 1997 letter to Horne, Paige Patterson, the president of the Southeastern Baptist Theological Seminary in Wake Forest, North Carolina, denounced Clinton's appointment of Virginia Apuzzo, a "lesbian activist," to direct the White House management shop, as a "breach of Christian conduct." He argued that 1 Corinthians 5 mandated that if a parishioner's sin was "widely known in the church and beyond," it must discipline and even exclude him. Patterson recognized that this action was "thoroughly unthinkable" and had "political overtones," but he argued that Clinton was unlikely to "make any substantive changes in his lifestyle if he is not confronted" in such a way.[72] Immanuel Baptist did not discipline Clinton, but in 1999 Horne wrote the president to protest his proclamation of Gay and Lesbian Pride Month.

Clinton responded that he respected Horne's views on homosexuality and stressed that his proclamation had not taken "a position on homosexuality as a religious matter." Instead, it recognized the nation's diversity and highlighted "initiatives aimed at ending discrimination, violence, and intolerance based on sexual orientation."[73]

Hybels met with the president in the White House almost monthly and asked Clinton "point blank" questions about his spiritual life. They also discussed political issues and prayed together.[74] As Clinton's pastor in Washington and spiritual counselor, Wogaman conversed frequently with the president. Clinton thanked Wogaman for being his minister, advisor, and friend.[75] Campolo, a strong advocate of social justice, evangelism, and missions, met with Clinton about once a month to pray about personal and policy matters.[76] Clinton also met periodically with MacDonald the last two years of his presidency. MacDonald had resigned from Grace Chapel in 1987 after publicly admitting to having an affair. Following a two-year "restoration process," MacDonald published *Rebuilding Your Broken World* about his experience, which Clinton read.[77]

All of these ministers said that their conversations with Clinton focused on prayer, the Bible, and personal spiritual growth. Clinton claimed that these relationships helped him "stay centered" and remain "humble and optimistic."[78] The demands of the presidency, Clinton insisted, could crowd out everything that kept its occupants "growing and whole." His spiritual counselors helped him immeasurably because they did not seek to please him, tell him what he wanted to hear, or try to get something from him.[79]

During his presidency Clinton had numerous exchanges with Billy Graham. In March 1995 Clinton congratulated Graham on his "Global Mission," which was designed to reach more than one billion people in 185 nations. In November 1995 Clinton told Graham that he felt strengthened by his prayers and hoped that God would use him as "a special agent" to help millions around the world. Asking Graham to participate in his second inaugural ceremony, Clinton wrote, "your counsel, friendship, and prayers have long been a source of strength and joy to me."[80] Graham assured Clinton everyone who was present was deeply impressed by his tenderness and love in comforting mourners after the bombing of the Federal Building in Oklahoma City in April 1995.[81] Soon after accounts of Clinton's alleged affair with Lewinsky began to surface in March 1998, Graham declared that he would forgive Clinton, "a remarkable man" who had faced "a lot of temptations," if he were indeed guilty. While the Clintons were comforted by Graham's statement, other theological conservatives criticized his promise of blanket forgiveness.[82]

Relations with Religious Groups

Clinton used a variety of means to maintain good relationships with religious leaders and communities and had moderate success. As he prepared to take office, National Council of Churches executives, representing 45 million Americans, expressed their agreement with his agenda, and pundits noted that he had not made commitments to any particular religious communities as Reagan and Bush had done with evangelicals.[83] During his years in office, Council leaders were again invited to White House conferences and had an entrée to the president. Like other post–World War II presidents, Clinton assigned White House staff to serve as a "bridge to the religious communities." He spoke at all eight National Prayer Breakfasts held during his tenure in office. The president also hosted six ecumenical prayer breakfasts to discuss various issues with religious leaders and to explore ways to work together to "alleviate social problems at home and humanitarian problems around the world."[84]

Clinton's closest relationships were with black Christians, while his most contentious ones were with theological conservatives, especially fellow Southern Baptists. Clinton worked diligently to develop cordial associations with black pastors and congregations. He often consulted with African-American clergy and emphasized his efforts to reform welfare, reduce crime, improve education, stop church burnings in the South and punish the perpetrators, and appoint blacks to his administration.[85] He named five African Americans to his cabinet, two and a half times as many as had ever served in the nation's history, and nominated forty-two blacks for the federal bench.[86] The Democrat strongly advocated affirmative action and urged Americans "to love your neighbor as yourself" in order to end racial prejudice and discrimination.[87]

Clinton had an especially combative relationship with the leaders of his own denomination. During the 1990s moderates and conservatives battled for control of the Southern Baptist Convention (SBC). As a moderate who supported abortion and gay civil rights, Clinton faced extensive, often very hostile, opposition from Southern Baptist conservatives who denounced abortion and homosexuality as moral travesties.[88] Southern Baptists designated the first forty days of 1994 as a special period to pray "diligently and consistently" for Clinton, guided by a booklet titled *Pray for the President*, and Clinton met periodically with Southern Baptist leaders.[89] Throughout Southern Baptist history, its leaders had generally remained aloof from politics, with the exception of their firm support of Prohibition. Not since they passed resolutions opposing Franklin Roosevelt's efforts to repeal Prohibition in 1933 had the SBC so strongly clashed with a chief executive. In 1993 the SBC passed a resolution opposing Clinton's positions on abortion and gay rights, which beseeched the president to "affirm biblical morality in exercising [his] public office." Resolutions were also introduced but defeated at every annual meeting of the SBC during Clinton's presidency urging Immanuel Baptist Church to publicly rebuke or discipline him because of his support of abortion and gay rights, including his appointment of pro-choice individuals, his healthcare plan that covered abortions and paid for the distribution of contraceptives, and his efforts to legalize a pill that induced early abortions.[90] Some of these failed resolutions demanded that the SBC withdraw from fellowship with Immanuel if the church refused to oust Clinton as a member, but Immanuel's leaders never seriously considered disciplining the president or dismissing him as a member. Rather, its pastors and members strongly supported him. Many Sundays, demonstrators picketed outside during Immanuel's services, carrying signs condemning Clinton, Horne, and parishioners.[91]

While some evangelicals adopted a wait and see approach after Clinton's election in 1992, others berated those who had voted for the Democrat and predicted that his election would swell the ranks of Religious Right organizations. Adrian Rodgers, the pastor of the 23,000-member Bellevue Baptist Church in Memphis, called voting for Clinton a "sin against God."[92] Five days after Clinton was elected, Moral Majority founder Jerry Falwell claimed that he possessed a tape of Clinton and former Arkansas cabaret singer Gennifer Flowers discussing oral sex. D. James Kennedy, a televangelist and the pastor of the huge Coral Ridge Presbyterian Church in Fort Lauderdale, argued that Clinton's affair with Flowers testified to the president's moral dereliction. It was difficult to believe a man who had broken wedding vows, Kennedy avowed, "would keep his vows" to the American people.[93]

Clinton's stances on abortion and homosexuality and his sexual practices hurt his relationship with many evangelicals. The Democrat argued that a culturally and morally pluralist society should grant women the right to have abortions in almost all circumstances and give civil rights to gays and lesbians. Theologically conservative Christians countered that the Bible condemned abortion as murder and homosexual acts as sin. Clinton angered many evangelicals early in his presidency by reducing governmental restrictions on abortion, expanding gay rights, and appointing staff who seemed either unresponsive or antagonistic to religious conservatives. These actions prompted many evangelicals to question whether Clinton's faith was sincere. For millions of evangelicals and conservative Catholics, Clinton's support of abortion made him "a mass murderer." No claims he made about his personal faith could "counteract the devastating effect of that one policy."

Clinton lamented that their making "abortion and homosexuality the litmus test of whether you're a true Christian" led many evangelicals to dislike and distrust him.[94] Trying to overcome these difficulties, Clinton hosted various meetings to which prominent evangelicals were invited. Nevertheless, some evangelicals complained that they had increasingly less access to and influence upon him.[95]

Clinton argued that "abortion should be safe, legal, and rare." He asserted that the Bible never clearly explained, theologians disagreed over, and no one knew for sure when the spirit entered the body and personhood began. W. O. Vaught, who maintained that the Bible did not prohibit abortion in all circumstances, strongly influenced Clinton's position.[96] According to Clinton, Vaught believed that personhood began at birth when God breathed life into infants. This did not mean that abortion "was right all the time or that it wasn't immoral," but it was not murder.[97] Moreover, in a democracy, government positions on issues should depend on popular opinion. A majority of Americans, Clinton argued, were both "pro-choice and anti-abortion. That is, they don't believe that the decision should be criminalized" because in most cases whether to terminate a pregnancy "should be left to the people who are involved." Although most Americans thought that "abortion is wrong" in most circumstances, he concluded it should remain legal in most situations.[98]

Numerous theological conservatives, including Horne, Hybels, and Lee Strobel, an author and minister at Willow Creek, strove to persuade Clinton to oppose late-term abortions. Strobel sent the president a six-page letter providing moral and legal reasons for banning this procedure. Conservatives were deeply disappointed when Clinton refused to do so. Some theological moderates also urged Clinton to ban partial birth abortions. Yale Law School professor Stephen Carter emphasized that "this gruesome procedure" was not medically necessary and that the American Medical Association had endorsed the ban. He censured the pro-choice response—that this abortion procedure was "a private matter between a woman and her doctor"—as "incoherent." As soon as the fetus placed a foot outside the womb, Carter argued, he "is a human child, and thus inviolable." Clinton explained to Carter that he vetoed the bill because Congress refused to exempt "those few but tragic cases in which the procedure is necessary to save the life of a woman or prevent serious harm to her health." He opposed using this procedure in cases where a woman's health was not at risk. Clinton regretted that Congress had not crafted a law that banned partial birth abortion except in situations where women faced "serious adverse health consequences."[99]

Ed Dobson expressed the confusion Clinton caused many evangelicals. The president knew the Scriptures well, valued prayer, attended church every week, and repeatedly testified that he had been born again.[100] Moreover, like religious conservatives, Clinton emphasized family values and personal responsibility. He called for "spiritual renewal," "hard work, self-discipline, and commitment to family."[101] However, many evangelicals could not reconcile Clinton's faith with his policies and after August 1998 his personal behavior.

While some evangelicals appreciated Clinton's seemingly sincere efforts to reach out to them, other religious conservatives and journalists denounced his actions as a political ploy "to confuse and divide an important Republican constituency." Family Research Council president Gary Bauer advised evangelicals to judge the president "by what he does, not what he says." Focus on the Family president James Dobson protested that the demise of the family was "being orchestrated at the highest levels of government." As did Southern Baptists, Dobson and others complained that Clinton had appointed few evangelicals to important positions. Beverly LaHaye, president of Concerned Women for America, denounced the "massive government intrusion into every aspect of our lives: dramatic tax increases, socialized medicine, government price controls, federal regulation of businesses," attempts "to redefine the American family, the use of federal tax dollars for abortion, and mandatory 'valueless' sex education and pro-promiscuity programs in our public schools."[102] Falwell distributed a videotape titled *The Clinton Chronicles* that accused Clinton of conspiracy to murder his enemies, drug-dealing, and sexual harassment of Paula Jones, which Campolo and numerous other evangelicals denounced.[103] "It wouldn't surprise me," Philip Yancey declared, to hear someone call Clinton the Antichrist. "Not since John Kennedy has a president caused such alarm in evangelical churches."[104]

Clinton also sought to build cordial relationships with Catholics aided by his educational background and concern for social justice. Clinton's education and experiences at Georgetown, a Jesuit institution, helped him relate effectively to many Catholic constituents in Arkansas.[105] Thomas Reese argued that Catholic social teaching strongly influenced Clinton, especially in his concern for human rights, civil rights, and the indigent. The Catholic bishops agreed with Clinton's efforts to convert foreign military aid to development assistance, reform welfare to include job training and child care, pressure China to stop human rights violations, and strengthen labor unions. Moreover, many middle-income, baby boomer Catholics who favored individual conscience over the authoritative church stances backed the president's policies. However, numerous conservative Catholics disliked Clinton's support for abortion, gay rights, the death penalty, and condom distribution in public schools and his opposition to federal aid to parochial schools.[106] Clinton did not establish a particularly close connection with any Catholic leader. The president praised the Catholic Church for helping the poor, the elderly, the afflicted, and families through its thousands of charitable activities, network of hospitals, 9,000 elementary and high schools, and more than 200 colleges.[107]

Many religious groups responded enthusiastically to Clinton's challenge to increase their endeavors to reduce violence. In 1993 Clinton called for a partnership between government, businesses, and churches to combat the crime, drugs, and brutality afflicting American society. Christian efforts to create a more peaceful and safer society, he asserted, fulfilled the biblical injunction to be "the salt of the Earth and the light of the world" and "give glory to the Father in heaven."[108] A coalition of organizations, including the US Catholic Bishops Conference, the National Council of Churches, the Baptist Joint Committee, the Congress of National Black Churches, and the Synagogue Council of America, commended Clinton for "using the moral power of the Presidency" to stop the "swelling tide of violence sweeping America." These organizations strove to halt gun proliferation in our streets, schools, and homes, "counter the 'culture of violence' that pervades" the media, and protect children from the nation's "epidemic of violence."[109]

Clinton also sought to develop positive relationships with Jewish Americans. He appointed several Jews to prominent positions in his administration: Lawrence Summers was Secretary of the Treasury; Rahm Emmanuel was a Senior Advisor for Policy and Strategy; and Richard Holbrooke served in several foreign policy positions.[110] Clinton affirmed America's support of Israel, celebrated Jewish holidays, applied lessons from Jewish history and theology to contemporary life, and lauded Jewish contributions to American life. Clinton told the Israeli Knesset in October 1994 that he was working with "Congress to maintain the current levels of military and economic assistance" to give Israel "the safety and security" it deserves.[111] The Day of Atonement, Clinton asserted in 1999, offered "a powerful lesson" about "the true spirit of reconciliation and the unconditional love of God." "From neighborhood stores to the corridors of Congress," "from the Armed Forces to the Supreme Court," our nation, Clinton announced in 2000, "has benefited immeasurably from the character, values, and achievements of our Jewish citizens." American Jews had promoted "tolerance, justice, human rights, and the rule of law." They had greatly assisted "health and human services programs, civil rights groups, [and] educational institutions."[112]

In 1996 Clinton won large majorities of Catholic, Jewish, and black Protestant voters as well as of people with no religious faith, but he lost the majority of the white Protestant vote, in large part because of his stances on abortion and homosexuality.[113] Clinton did not fulfill his 1992 campaign pledge to end the ban against gay men and women serving openly in the military. He did, however, order the armed forces to stop asking recruits about their sexuality and not to investigate the sexual orientation of military personnel unless they engaged in misconduct. Labeled "don't ask, don't tell," this policy was adopted by the armed forces in 1993.

More than any of his predecessors, Clinton strove to develop good relationships with American Muslims, as their numbers (six million adherents and 1,200 mosques and Islamic centers) and prominence increased at home and around the world (one-quarter of the world's people were Muslims). Clinton's statements on Ramadan highlighted values that Islam, Judaism, and Christianity shared and promoted his commitment to peace and, ironically, given Islam's historical record, religious liberty. Because of its emphasis on sacrifice, discipline, generosity, and human dignity, Islam was "one of the world's great religions." Muslims had contributed enormously to American life. "The core values of Islam—commitment to family, compassion for the disadvantaged, and respect for difference"—helped strengthen America.[114] Clinton's claim that God revealed "the Koran to Muhammad," unlike similar statements by Barack Obama, caused no controversy.[115]

Muslims, Clinton insisted, enriched America's political and cultural life and provided "leadership in every field of human endeavor." Unfortunately, however, they continued to face discrimination, intolerance, and occasional violence because of ignorance and faulty stereotypes about Islam. "To be a force for peace and reconciliation across religious and ethnic" divisions in the Middle East, Northern Ireland, the Balkans, Africa, and Asia, Americans must reject religious bigotry and practice tolerance at home.[116]

Philosophy of Government

Clinton sought to develop "a public philosophy rooted in [his] personal religious values." Politics, the Democrat proclaimed, "should be guided by what our Lord" called the two greatest commandments—"to love the Lord, our God, with all our heart" and "to love thy neighbor as thyself."[117] Clinton insisted that Stephen Carter's *The Culture of Disbelief* (1993) significantly influenced his approach to governing and his understanding of the role of religion in public life.[118] Clinton argued that the First Amendment did not require citizens to refrain from expressing their religious convictions in the public square. James Madison and Thomas Jefferson, he insisted, "did not intend to drive" religion out of public life. Instead, they sought to set up a system that allowed people's religious convictions to play a vital role in private and public life without anyone telling others what to do.[119] While the Republicans' agenda focused on opposition to abortion and gay rights and promoted the concentration of wealth and power, Democrats strove to advance the common good, help the poor, the vulnerable, and middle-class families, and preserve "our God-given environment."[120]

Clinton labeled his approach to politics the New Covenant, a phrase with strong biblical connotations. Rejecting the political Right's "every-man-for himself" and the Left's "something-for-nothing," Clinton argued that government should expand people's opportunities to fully and fruitfully use their gifts. It must work to improve the economy, reform welfare, reduce crime, improve parenting, and increase civic responsibility.[121] Both "the American dream of opportunity" and the nation's "tradition of responsibility" needed to be restored. The New Covenant, Clinton asserted, was based on the idea that all Americans had "a solemn responsibility to rise as far as their God-given talents and determination can take them and to give something back to their communities and their country." Opportunity and responsibility, he proclaimed, went "hand in hand" and were both essential to America's success.[122]

Clinton repudiated the Republican "view that the Federal Government is the cause of every problem" and the Democratic position that "big Government can fix every problem." He sought to create "a Government that is limited but effective," "not a savior," but "a partner in the fight" to create a better future.[123] Washington's "old way of governing" "protected organized interests" rather than promoting the welfare of "ordinary people." It divided Americans "by interest, constituency, or class," while the New Covenant sought to unite them by supplying "a common vision of what's best for our country." The old system "dispensed services through large, top-down, inflexible bureaucracies," while the New Covenant strove to shift resources and decision-making to citizens by emphasizing choice, competition, and individual responsibility.[124]

"Ideological purity," Clinton insisted, "is for partisan extremists." What the nation needed instead was "practical solution[s], based on real experience, hard evidence, and common sense." "My whole political philosophy is basically rooted in what I think works." Both weak government and insensitive, bureaucratic, "special-interest-dominated" government were ineffective. The government is "neither the Satan nor the savior of America but a catalyst" to "create the conditions and give people the tools to make the most of their own lives."[125]

Clinton rejected the common argument that because the Bible taught that humanity would confront problems "until the end of time," it was fruitless to work to remedy particular ills. Clinton countered that people must strive "to move forward" "in the right direction."[126] Although the government should promote traditional moral values and alleviate social ills, Clinton maintained, it could never supplant the job of families, churches, and community organizations.[127] By carrying "their faith into action" and aiding children and people in distress, clergy and congregations helped advance the New Covenant. Clinton strove to inspire "people of faith to work together" to remedy social problems by improving interpersonal relationships and meeting spiritual needs.[128]

Clinton insisted that he never claimed that his policy embodied the biblical stance on a particular issue or that God had directly told him to take specific actions.[129] Instead, he repeatedly proclaimed that, in the words of the Apostle Paul, "we see through a glass darkly" and never know "the full truth." "Every one of us is subject to error in judgment." Remembering Paul's admonition to the Romans—"take thought for what is noble in the sight of all; do not be overcome by evil, but overcome evil by good"—people should practice civility in politics. Clinton wanted "the wisdom to change" when he was wrong and "the courage to stay the course" when he was right.[130]

Clinton's pragmatic approach led critics to complain that he had "no authentic center" and, therefore, "no real core of ideals" to direct his presidency. The Democrat, they insisted, often refused to make the hard choices the presidency required.[131] Some accused him of "expediency," "well-intended equivocation," "dissembling," "moral relativism," and making contradictory promises to different groups.[132] Many scholars and policy analysts concluded that he seemed to have "few core beliefs" and did not hold to any ultimate truths. In fact, some postmodernists praised Clinton for his ideological flexibility and refusal to be captive to any ideology or perspective.[133] Three issues will be discussed to examine Clinton's philosophy of government and the influence his faith had on his policies: his advocacy of religious liberty, welfare reform, and reconciliation between religious groups and nations.

Public Policy: Religious Liberty

Clinton strongly promoted religious freedom at home and abroad, most notably through the passage of the Religious Freedom Restoration Act of 1993 and the American Indian Religious Freedom Act Amendments of 1994, his guidelines for Religious Expression in Public Schools issued in 1995, his Guidelines on Religious Exercise and Religious Expression in the Federal Workplace distributed in 1997, and his June 1998 visit to China. For Clinton, religious liberty was the first and "most precious of all American liberties," which undergirded other American freedoms. The First Amendment created "twin pillars of religious liberty" by ensuring that individuals could freely practice their religion and banning the federal government from establishing a religion.[134]

Clinton considered the passage of the Religious Freedom Restoration Act of 1993 to be one of his major achievements. Sponsored by 60 Senators and 170 Congressmen, strongly supported by numerous religious groups, and decisively passed by both Houses, the act permitted the federal government to restrict individuals' religious freedom only if it had a compelling interest for doing so and only by employing the "least restrictive means" of furthering its interests. This act reversed a 1990 Supreme Court decision and reestablished a standard, Clinton claimed, that better protected "Americans of all faiths in the exercise of their religion" and was "far more consistent" with the founders' intentions than the court's ruling. This act, Clinton maintained, honored "the principle that our laws and institutions should not impede or hinder but rather should protect and preserve fundamental religious liberties."[135] Clinton rejoiced that Jewish, Catholic, evangelical, and Muslims leaders, who rarely worked together, had stood "arm in arm" to help pass this act.[136]

Speaking to Native Americans in 1994, Clinton declared that "traditional religions and ceremonies are the essence of your culture and your very existence." Therefore, "no agenda for religious freedom will be complete until traditional Native American religious practices" received the protection they deserved. He promised them that the federal government would respect their religions, values, identity, and sovereignty.[137] Soon thereafter Congress passed the American Indian Religious Freedom Act Amendments to ensure that the management of federal lands did not interfere with traditional Native American religious practices and to permit the use of peyote in their religious ceremonies.

Clinton also strove to increase the role of religion in public schools. Religion, he insisted, was too important to America's history and heritage and to promoting traditional values to be kept out of its schools. Teachers should discuss the basic teachings of various religions and their contributions to history, values, and the arts throughout the world.[138] Schools, Clinton argued, helped nurture children's "souls by reinforcing the values they learn at home and in their communities." Schools could not advocate specific religious beliefs, but "they should teach mainstream values and virtues," some of which were distinctively religious. Schools should devise and teach a widely endorsed "set of civic values" that included good citizenship, respect, honesty, and nonviolence.[139]

Clinton protested that many public school students had been prohibited from reading the Bible in study hall and saying grace before eating their lunch and that numerous student religious groups had been forbidden to publicize their meetings.[140] Some public school officials, teachers and parents had incorrectly assumed that any type of religious expression "is either inappropriate" or "forbidden altogether." However, he asserted, the First Amendment did "not require students to leave their religion at the schoolhouse door." Students could advertise their religious gatherings, meet in school facilities, and pray out loud at their meetings. They could also distribute religious flyers and pamphlets and wear T-shirts that promoted religion. Students could express their religious beliefs in homework, art work, and class presentations, as long as they were relevant to the assignment. "If certain subjects or activities are objectionable to their students or their parents because of their religious beliefs," Clinton argued, "then schools may, and sometimes they must, excuse the students from those activities." Finally, he argued, people should "be able to freely pray and to acknowledge God" at school sports events and graduation exercises.[141]

These convictions led Clinton to issue comprehensive guidelines for religious expression in public schools in July 1995. Its signers included individuals who held very different ideological positions: Presidents Gerald Ford and Jimmy Carter; Reagan's Secretary of Education William Bennett and Lane Kirkland, the president of the AFL-CIO; Norman Lear and Phyllis Schlafly; and Coretta Scott King and James Dobson. The directive, Clinton noted, also borrowed heavily from a document titled "Religion in Public Schools: A Joint Statement of Current Law," issued in April 1995 by "a broad coalition of religious and legal groups." The guidelines specified that students had the right to pray privately at school, say grace at lunchtime, hold religious meetings on school property, and "use school facilities, just like any other club." Students could also read "any religious text during study hall or free class time." Moreover, schools could actively teach "civic values and virtue."[142]

During his second term, Clinton took additional steps to expand religious liberty. The most significant one was the guidelines his administration issued in 1997 to strengthen the right of religious expression in the federal workplace. They mandated that federal employees could participate "in personal religious expression" to "the greatest extent possible, consistent with workplace efficiency and the requirements of law." They prohibited federal employers from discriminating in hiring on the basis of religion and ordered agencies to "reasonably accommodate employees' religious practices."[143]

Defending these actions, Clinton contended that religious liberty was deeply rooted in American history. By making "their settlements havens for freedom of conscience," William Penn, Roger Williams, and numerous others had laid "the foundation for the great tradition of religious liberty" expressed in the First Amendment. The founders cared deeply about religion, Clinton maintained, because they thought it promoted the character and conduct necessary for their republic to succeed. The framers of the Constitution, Clinton argued, "recognized the awesome power of religious liberty" to unite citizens to promote the common good. For more than two centuries, he avowed, America's religious institutions and practices had fostered faith, morality, character, community, and responsibility.[144]

Clinton, like many other presidents, argued that religious freedom was crucial to America's success. For more than 200 years, he asserted, the First Amendment had enabled "many faiths to flourish" in the nation's homes, workplaces, and schools. If every American child attended a religious institution weekly, he insisted, their character would improve greatly and drug usage, crime, and violence would decline dramatically. Clinton maintained that the nation's religious freedom had helped Americans live together in unprecedented peace and create "the world's strongest democracy and its most truly multi-ethnic society." This "precious liberty" encouraged individuals holding various beliefs to "respect and celebrate" their differences while uniting around shared ideals, which strengthened the country.[145]

Religious liberty, Clinton contended, had produced other wonderful results. "Because we are free to worship or not, according to our own conscience," he declared, "Americans worship deeply and in very great numbers." "In this highly secular age," the United States was "clearly the most conventionally religious country" in the postindustrial world. It had higher weekly levels of attendance at churches, synagogues, and mosques than in any other highly developed country. In addition, more Americans believed that religion was "directly important to their lives" than in any other postindustrial nation. Our various places of worship, Clinton asserted, "bring us together, support our families, nourish our hearts and minds, and sustain our deepest values." These houses of worship also served as centers of community service and civic life and stimulated Americans "to build a civil society based on mutual respect, compassion, and generosity."[146]

Clinton repeatedly defended the right of all Americans to practice their religious convictions. He urged citizens to "respect one another's faiths." The United States could meet its economic and social challenges only if its citizens "honestly and openly" debated their differences and reached common ground. Respecting religious diversity, Clinton maintained, promoted community and harmony. Religious hatred and discrimination, by contrast, fueled violence. "The freedom to follow one's personal beliefs, to worship as one chooses," Clinton stressed, was a core American principle. Every year people who espoused "every conceivable faith" still came from every place in the world to attain this freedom.[147]

Clinton also sought to promote religious liberty abroad. In 1996 he proclaimed that the United States must be "an international advocate" "for the basic rights that sustain human dignity and personal freedom." It must assist "all who struggle against religious oppression." In 1997 Clinton called "our commitment to religious liberty" "a key part of America's human rights policy." The United States had pressed "for religious freedom at the United Nations" and in its "relations with other countries across the globe." People had "the fundamental right," he stated in January 1998, "to believe and worship according to their own conscience, to affirm their beliefs openly and freely, and to practice their faith without fear or intimidation." Clinton extensively discussed religious freedom with Russian President Boris Yeltsin and other world leaders. Clinton established a high-level advisory committee on religious liberty in 1996, and in June 1998 he named Robert Seiple, the former president of World Vision, Ambassador at Large for International Religious Freedom, to ensure that religious liberty received "close attention in our foreign policy."[148]

That same month Clinton praised China for releasing from prison two influential religious leaders, Gao Feng and Bishop Zeng Jingmu, and for announcing that it would sign the International Covenant on Civil and Political Rights that guaranteed freedom of thought and religion. However, he protested, numerous Chinese Christians, Muslims, and Buddhists remained imprisoned for their religious activities and the government harassed many other believers. Therefore, Clinton promised that when he visited China later in the month, he would emphasize human rights and religious freedom and urge China to release all prisoners of conscience. Clinton had previously told President Jiang Zemin both privately and publicly that China would become more stable, stronger, and more influential "in direct proportion to the extent to which" it permitted "liberties of all kinds and especially religious liberty."[149] Before Clinton left for China, the International Fellowship of Christians and Jews presented him with an *Appeal for Religious Liberty in China* signed by hundreds of Jewish, Christian, Muslim, and Buddhist leaders and urged him to make religious freedom a primary topic of discussion with Chinese officials.[150]

Fulfilling his pledge, during his visit to China in late June and early July 1998, Clinton raised the issue of religious liberty. At a news conference with Jiang, Clinton declared that Americans firmly believed "that individual rights, including the freedom of speech, association, and religion, are very important." He applauded "China's decision to sign the International Covenant on Civil and Political Rights, the recent release of several prominent political dissidents, the hospitality China graciously accorded to American religious leaders, and the resumption of a human rights dialog between China and the United States." On the other hand, Clinton criticized China's use of force to stop protests at Tiananmen Square in 1989 and "the tragic loss of life" that occurred there. Nations that restricted freedom, Clinton warned, would pay a great price in a world where economic growth depended on ideas, information, exchange, and debate. Jiang insisted that China's constitution protected freedom of religious belief. Clinton also protested privately that 2,000 dissidents were reportedly still imprisoned in China.[151]

At a speech at Beijing University, Clinton argued that "the darkest moments" in American history included denying freedom to people either because of their race, religion, or espousal of disfavored views. By contrast, America's "best moments" had been when it "protected the freedom of people who held unpopular opinions." Certain rights, he proclaimed were universal, "now enshrined in the United Nations Declaration on Human Rights: the right to be treated with dignity," to express one's opinions, to select one's leaders, "to associate freely with others, and to worship or not, freely, however one chooses." Clinton rejoiced that during his visit he had witnessed many manifestations of freedom, including a village choose its own leaders. The president had seen cell phones, video players, and fax machines bringing "ideas, information, and images from all over the world." He had "heard people speak their minds" and had "joined people in prayer" in his own freely chosen faith. "The freest possible flow of information, ideas, and opinions and a greater respect for divergent political and religious convictions," Clinton insisted, would make China stronger and more stable.[152] Surprisingly, despite worshipping at Chongwenmen Church in Beijing with 2,000 people, Clinton did not directly denounce China's policies that restricted the activities of churches and limited its citizens' ability to worship as they pleased.[153] Chinese Christians had hoped that Clinton's visit to their country would increase religious freedom and help the gospel advance, but the state-controlled media paid little attention to his trip.

In November 1998 Clinton issued a "Statement on the International Day of Prayer for the Persecuted Church." It declared: "we pray for those who suffer for their beliefs—a suffering forewarned by Scripture." But God promised, "I will give you . . . wisdom, which none of your adversaries will be able to deny or resist" (Luke 21:12). In observing this occasion the next year, Clinton argued that every government must guarantee the "fundamental human right" of religious freedom. The United States must aid millions around the world who were "harassed, imprisoned, tortured, and executed simply for seeking to live by their own beliefs." In 1998 the United States passed the International Religious Freedom Act, which directed the president "to take diplomatic and other appropriate action with respect to any country that engages in or tolerates violations of religious freedom." The act prompted the State Department to publish an annual report, beginning in

1999, on the status of religious freedom worldwide that identified "the most severe international violators."[154]

Welfare Reform

Clinton considered welfare reform to be a crucial component of his New Covenant.[155] He wanted to "restore faith" in "basic principles that our fore-bears took for granted: the bond of family, the virtue of community, [and] the dignity of work." Nowhere was the gap greater between good intentions and misguided consequences than in the welfare system, which rewarded irresponsibility. Welfare, he repeatedly declared, should provide "a second chance, not a way of life." The government must work to ensure that children were born to married couples. Clinton sought to end the "something-for-nothing mentality" by restoring the values of responsibility, work, family, and community.[156]

In February 1995 Clinton claimed that welfare benefits were 40 percent lower than they had been twenty years earlier. People went on welfare not for the money but rather for the child care, food stamps, and the medical care for their children it provided. He wanted to give the states more control over welfare and allow them to use churches or community organizations to "repair" families. Americans, he insisted, did not "object to spending tax money on poor people." However, they did oppose financing a system that perpetuated destructive and irresponsible conduct. "We must demand more responsibility, tougher child support enforcement, [and] responsible parenting" and mandate that to receive benefits, people must be attending school or preparing for work.[157] The welfare system must be reformed, Clinton contended, because recipients hated it and it encouraged dependency.[158]

"Both the Republican contract and my New Covenant," Clinton stressed in 1995, "have focused heavily on welfare reform." They agreed that welfare should have time limits, states should have flexibility in implementing programs, child support laws should be rigorously enforced, and recipients must take more responsibility for themselves and their children. Clinton insisted that children must not be taken off the welfare rolls "simply because their parents are under 18 and unmarried." Doing so would cut spending on welfare, but it would not "promote work and responsible parenting." Many Catholics argued persuasively, Clinton emphasized, that this action would lead to more abortions. Moreover, Republicans and Democrats agreed that all welfare recipients who could work must do so and the government should pay for child care to enable single mothers on welfare to work.[159] The bill, which Clinton signed in August 1996 ended the federal government's sixty-one-year practice of aiding all families with dependent children. It stipulated that adult welfare recipients had to obtain a job within two years and could receive welfare for only a total of five years.

Clinton argued that churches had a significant role to play in improving the welfare system and alleviating poverty, especially after the Charitable Choice Act of 1996 encouraged states "to involve community and faith-based organizations in providing federally funded welfare services to the poor and needy."[160] State and local governments could now partner with congregations to provide various programs and services such as developing supervised accommodations for young mothers and their children so they would not have to live in their parents' dysfunctional homes.[161] Clinton asked religious leaders in January 1997 for their guidance, prayers, and suggestions to make welfare reform work. He argued that if every church hired one welfare recipient, the welfare rolls would be greatly reduced, and if every church member who employed more than twenty-five workers hired another recipient, the welfare problem "would go away."[162] Numerous clergy praised Clinton's plea.[163]

In 1998 Clinton rejoiced that many Americans agreed that faith-based organizations and the government could work together at the national, state, and local levels to reinforce universally held values and increase the impact "of the good things that the government is funding." Thousands of young volunteers had worked with various faith-based organizations under the auspices of AmeriCorps. This did not violate the Constitution's establishment clause, Clinton contended, and it benefited countless people. The president also argued that through its counseling and outreach programs the faith community could help protect children from violence, support "commonsense gun legislation," stop youth violence, and form "community partnerships to identify and intervene in the lives" of troubled individuals.[164]

Clinton also often underscored the biblical mandate for the government, congregations, and individuals to help the poor. The "only thing the Bible tells us hundreds and hundreds of times" about politics "is to care for the poor, the weak, the needy." As Americans celebrated the birth of Jesus, Clinton reminded them that "one day we will be asked whether we lived out His love" by treating "all of our brothers and sisters," "even the least of them," as "we would have treated Him."[165] Christ taught that everyone would be judged by whether they aided the hungry, thirsty, naked, strangers, and imprisoned.[166] In four speeches Clinton urged people to act as Good Samaritans,[167] to live by the motto, "Whatever is mine is yours if you need it."[168] Paul reminded us in Galatians 6, Clinton proclaimed, to bear "one another's burdens and so fulfill the law of Christ."[169]

Clinton cited the Old Testament concept of gleaning to encourage Americans to use food banks, houses of worship, and community groups to feed their neighbors. His administration took numerous steps to help the indigent. Hundreds of AmeriCorps employees joined with private volunteers to increase food for the poor by working with farmers, the Atlanta Community Food Bank, and the Congressional Hunger Center. In 1996 Clinton signed an act that encouraged "private businesses, local governments, and ordinary citizens to donate food by protecting them from lawsuits." Clinton directed every administrative department and agency to distribute surplus food from their cafeterias and public events to the poor. His administration released *The Citizen's Guide to Food Recovery* to explain how to start this endeavor, provide the names of charities that recouped food, and highlight lessons learned in communities across America.[170]

The nation's new welfare program, coupled with increased private sector assistance, initially appeared to be a colossal success. The number of Americans receiving welfare declined from 14.1 million in January 1993 to 6.3 million in December 1999.[171] By the end of Clinton's tenure, the number of welfare recipients had fallen nearly 60 percent, resulting in the smallest welfare rolls in thirty-two years.[172] Critics contended that welfare rolls had decreased primarily because economic growth had provided many new jobs and warned that if the economy contracted, the number of poor would again expand.

The United States, aided by its faith communities, Clinton insisted, also had a responsibility to help other nations by providing debt relief for poor countries, reducing AIDS, and halting drug wars. "The most fortunate country in the world" must not "confine its compassion and concern" within its own borders.[173]

The Repairer of the Breach

The aftermath of the Cold War brought a new global situation where ethnic, religious, and separatist conflict abounded, America's interests were complicated, its enemies were not clearly defined, and the public was "ambivalent about most overseas ventures."[174] As the United States sailed into these uncharted foreign policy waters, Clinton, inspired in significant part by his faith, sought to be a "repairer of the breach" (Isaiah 58:12) and to promote reconciliation.[175] In Haiti, Northern Ireland, Bosnia, and the Middle East, he strove to end strife, broker agreements, and establish more stable governments. Often disregarding public opinion, Clinton took risks and devoted a significant amount of time and political capital to achieve these ends. His mediation helped produce the Oslo Accords of 1993 affirmed by Israel and Palestine; the Washington Declaration of 1994 involving Israel and Jordan; the Dayton Accords of 1995 ending fighting between Bosnian Muslims, Croatian Catholics, and Serbian Orthodox Christians in Bosnia; the Wye Plantation Memorandum in 1998 signed by the Israelis and Palestinians; and the Good Friday Accords of 1998 agreed to by Protestants and Catholics in Northern Ireland.

Clinton rejoiced that the Cold War had ended and "a system of atheistic controlling, communism" had been rejected. However, although all the world's major religions called for peace, compassion, tolerance, and understanding, he lamented, millions of people espousing different religious faiths were fighting each other. The Hebrew Torah "warns people never to turn aside the stranger, for it is like turning aside the most high God." The Bible instructs people to "love their neighbor as themselves." The Qur'an declares that "Allah created nations and tribes that we might know one another."[176] While trying to help end the long-standing animosity between Catholics and Protestants in Northern Ireland, Clinton spoke at the lighting of a Christmas tree in Belfast in 1995. He concluded, "We celebrate the world in a new way because of the birth of Emmanuel: God with us. And when God was with us, he said no words more important than these, 'Blessed are the peacemakers, for they shall inherit the Earth.' "[177]

Clinton told members of the Israeli Knesset in 1994 that his pastor W. O Vaught had warned him: "If you abandon Israel, God will never forgive you." "It is God's will," he added, "that Israel, the biblical home of the people of Israel, continue forever." Inspired by this belief, Clinton worked to achieve a wide-ranging peace in the Middle East. The president promised Knesset members that "you are now far closer to the day when the clash of arms is heard no more" and all Abraham's children "will live side by side in peace." The prophet Muhammad, Clinton asserted, told "peoples of other faiths" that "there is no argument between us and you. God will bring us together." Before the Jews entered the Promised Land, Moses declared, "I have set before you life and death, blessings and curses. Choose life so that you and your descendants may live." Both Israel and the United States, Clinton proclaimed, must "choose life" by devising a "comprehensive peace in the Middle East," which rested on "a qualitative change in the relations between Israel and its neighbors" that included full diplomatic ties, free trade, and joint economic projects.[178]

More than any of his predecessors, Clinton reached out to Muslims around the globe, underscoring their humanity and contributions. His statements on Ramadan highlighted the Muslim commitment to cooperation and compassion and called for increased efforts to promote peace in the Middle East.[179] Rejecting the argument that insurmountable religious and cultural obstacles prevented the United States and Middle Eastern nations from working together, Clinton told Jordanian Parliament members in 1994 that Islam's traditional values, especially "devotion to faith and good works, to family and society, are in harmony" with American ideals. The Qur'an, the Bible, and the Torah, he added, all commanded believers to love their neighbors and welcome strangers. "The Qur'an tells us," Clinton declared, "that we are all People of the Book" who "share a common humanity and dignity," and it exhorts people to live in peace.[180]

The conflict in the Middle East, Clinton asserted, was "a contest between tyranny and freedom, terror and security, bigotry and tolerance," and "fear and hope." He applauded Jordanians for approving "a treaty based on a fundamental law of humanity"—"that what we have in common is more important than our differences." The prophet Muhammad told peoples of other faiths: "There is no argument between us and you. God shall bring us together." Because the Jordanians and Israelites had "reached across the Jordan River" and "chosen life," "we say, thanks be to God."[181]

Because many Muslims had suffered "the terrible consequences of war, poverty, and unrest," Clinton proclaimed in January 1998, "we must renew our efforts" to "remove the causes of strife." The United States, he added, is determined to "bring a just, lasting, and comprehensive peace to the Middle East" by enabling Palestinians "to live as a free people" and Israelis "to live in security." He also expressed sympathy for the people of Algeria and Afghanistan who had endured great suffering and pledged to help afflicted Iraqis receive food and medicine. Clinton told Iranians that Americans regretted "the estrangement of our two nations and hoped to create more exchanges and better relations."[182]

While trying to get the Israelis and Palestinians to agree on a peace plan during eight demanding days of negotiation in the fall of 1998, Clinton kept thinking of Scripture verses such as "let us not grow weary in doing good, for in due season, we shall reap if we do not lose heart" and "they who wait upon the Lord" will "run and not grow weary." Clinton persuaded Israeli Prime Minister Benjamin Netanyahu and Palestinian leader Yasir Arafat to adopt an agreement that neither thought was totally fair and that many in their nations opposed. Numerous scholars conclude that Clinton negotiated the best possible agreement available at this time.[183]

Speaking in Gaza City in December 1998, Clinton urged the Palestinians to work with the Israelis to attain peace in the Middle East. He appealed to values Muslims, Christians, and Jews shared and to the teachings of Jesus.

"It is profoundly wrong," Clinton warned, "to equate Palestinians, in partic-ular, and Islam, in general, with terrorism or to see a fundamental conflict between Islam and the West." "For the vast majority of the more than one billion Muslims in the world, tolerance is an article of faith and terrorism a travesty of faith."[184]

Peace in the region, Clinton insisted, must include "legitimate rights for Palestinians" and "real security for Israel." It depended on each group rec-ognizing the humanity of the other. "During the Golden Age of Spain," he declared, "Jews, Muslims, and Christians" enjoyed "remarkable tolerance and learning." Moreover, numerous twentieth-century disputes many considered to be permanent had been or were being resolved, including the Cold War between Americans and Soviets, and the animosity between Catholics and Protestants in Northern Ireland, between the Chinese and Japanese, between black and white South Africans, and between Serbs, Croats, and Muslims in Bosnia. "In this small place," Clinton continued, "the home of Islam, Judaism, and Christianity, the embodiment of my faith was born a Jew and is still rec-ognized by Muslims as a prophet." Jesus is "known as the Prince of Peace" because He knew how "to make peace. And one of the wisest things He ever said was" "mercy triumphs over judgment." Clinton urged Palestinians and Israelis "to judge each other in the way you would like to be judged" and to "feel each other's pain."[185]

Discussing his role in the Middle East peace talks in 1998, Clinton declared: "I felt so blessed" to "engage in these labors" for the United States and the land that is "the home of Christianity, Judaism, and Islam." "It was a part of my job as President, my mission as a Christian, and my personal jour-ney of atonement. And I am grateful that God gave me the chance to do this." His work, Clinton argued, helped fulfill Exodus' promise that "If thou shalt do as God command thee, the people shall go to their place in peace" and the Qur'an's prophecy that "They shall not hear therein any vain discourse, but only peace." It was what Isaiah 58:12 called repairing the breach.[186]

In December 1998 Clinton explained why the United States had bombed sites in Iraq that produced nuclear, chemical, and biological weapons— Saddam Hussein had terrorized his own people, gassed Kurdish civilians in northern Iraq, caused at least half a million deaths during the war with Iran in the 1980s, and in 1990 "invaded Kuwait, executing those who resisted, looting the country, spilling tens of millions of gallons of oil into the Gulf, [and] fir-ing missiles at Saudi Arabia, Bahrain, Israel, and Qatar." He had "massacred thousands of his own people" and failed to abide by a condition for the Gulf War ceasefire—disclosing and destroying Iraq's weapons of mass destruction. Speaking to Arab nations, Clinton claimed that Americans "have the most profound admiration for Islam." The United States' dispute, he declared, was with a leader who threatened both Muslims and non-Muslims.[187] Continuing his efforts to promote peace, in 2000 Clinton addressed the Pakistani people on television from Islamabad and held a summit with Egyptian President Hosni Mubarak.[188]

Character

In recent years the marital infidelities of numerous politicians and sports stars, including governors Eliot Spitzer and Mark Sanford, Congressmen Newt Gingrich and Anthony Weiner, athletes Kobe Bryant and Tiger Woods, Senator John Edwards, and Republican presidential nominee Herbert Cain, have placed them in the limelight. Nevertheless, Bill Clinton's sexual liaisons garnered more attention and caused much more controversy than those of any other politician or celebrity. Gennifer Flowers, Paula Jones, Kathleen Willey, Juanita Broaddrick, and Monica Lewinsky all claimed to have had a sexual relationship with Clinton, and he eventually admitted to having intercourse with Flowers (although he denied her claim that they had a long-term sexual relationship) and to engaging in inappropriate sexual acts (but not intercourse) with Lewinsky. During the 1992 presidential campaign, the tabloid the *Star* publicized Flowers's claim that she and Clinton had had a twelve-year affair. In an interview in July, Clinton admitted that he and Hillary had "worked hard on our marriage; we'd had difficulties, and we'd saved it." However, he repeatedly denied that he had had a sexual relationship with Flowers.[189]

In May 1994 Jones filed a lawsuit against Clinton, claiming that he had exposed himself and propositioned her while he was governor of Arkansas. Because she was a state employee at this time, her suit charged that Clinton's actions constituted sexual harassment. Her case preoccupied both the Clinton administration and the press during much of 1998. Although Clinton denied her accusations and never apologized to her, he settled with Jones for $850,000.[190]

In his deposition in the Jones case and in an address to the nation on January 26, 1998, Clinton denied having a sexual relationship with Lewinsky. On August 17, 1998, after Lewinsky agreed to cooperate with Independent Counsel Kenneth Starr's investigation of the president, Clinton admitted that they had engaged in sexual acts, but not intercourse. Lewinsky claimed that they had ten sexual encounters most of which involved oral sex between November 1995 and March 1997.[191]

At a breakfast with religious leaders on September 11, Clinton confessed that he had sinned and stated that he had asked his family, friends, staff, cabinet, Lewinsky and her family, and the American people for their forgiveness. Simply expressing sorrow for his actions, he added, was insufficient. Forgiveness required "genuine repentance, a determination to change," and recognition that he needed God's help to become the person he wanted to be. While instructing his "lawyers to mount a vigorous defense," the president insisted that it "must not obscure the fact that I have done wrong." He promised to seek pastoral support to help him "continue on the path of repentance." Arguing that God could bring good out of people's sin, Clinton pledged to intensify his "efforts to lead our country and the world toward peace and freedom, prosperity and harmony." If his "repentance" was "genuine and sustained," God could use him to accomplish "greater good." Clinton asked these religious leaders for their prayers and assistance in healing the nation. My prayer, he concluded, is that "God will search me" and "give me a clean heart." Clinton later called his statement "a full and adequate apology" that was "brutally frank" and "personally painful." Wogaman admitted that Clinton's sexual activities, which involved "large discrepancies in age, power, and position," "set a bad example for the nation." However, when critics complained that Clinton still had not truly apologized, Wogaman countered that he had expressed "deep repentance and contrition."[192]

The Starr Report, issued on September 11, 1998, contained lurid details of masturbation, phone sex, and Clinton inserting a cigar in Lewinsky's vagina, and perhaps as shocking, evidence of the immaturity of their relationship, which included "petulant fights," furtive encounters, "cheesy gifts," and "desultory and banal chats." White House spokespersons denounced the report's "pornographic specificity," "biased recounting, and unconscionable overreaching." Some Democrats and several prominent newspapers exhorted Clinton to resign, arguing that "his repeated, reckless deceits" had "dishonored his presidency beyond repair." Many religious conservatives also called for Clinton's resignation on the grounds that his actions disqualified him for the nation's highest post and that his continuation in office would negatively affect America's youth.[193] However, in various polls more than 60 percent of Americans rated Clinton's job performance favorably and opposed his impeachment or resignation, in part because of the nation's economic prosperity. Moreover, some pundits, politicians, media personalities, and religious leaders continued to support the president.[194]

On Sunday, September 13, Rex Horne told his congregation that the president was "reaping the wages of sin and should be a lesson to fellow Baptists." He encouraged Clinton to "make things right with God."[195] In an ABC News interview, Horne called Clinton's actions "indefensible but not unforgiv-able."[196] Clinton met weekly with Wogaman, Campolo, and MacDonald for prayer and Bible study to help him, in Campolo's words, understand what "led to the tragic sins" that "so marred his life and the office of the presidency."[197]

Wogaman and Campolo remained loyal political supporters of Clinton despite protests that they helped legitimate "an unscrupulous president" and his policies. These pastoral counselors, journalist Cal Thomas charged, were cloaking Clinton with "the mantle of respectability even while he lives and lies as he pleases." Campolo and MacDonald both promised that Clinton would not receive "cheap, swift grace." Wogaman compared Clinton's rehabilitation to a process used in early American revivals in which Christians surrounded a miscreant and forced him to understand that his actions were "really harmful, sinful, [and] evil."[198]

In October Clinton sent a letter to Immanuel Baptist Church expressing "sadness for the consequences of his sin on his family, friends and church family" and asking members for forgiveness.[199] In November, Arkansas Southern Baptists overwhelmingly passed a resolution to pray for, rather than chastise, Clinton.[200] On the other hand, 140 Catholic and Protestant leaders signed a declaration protesting that through his inappropriate relationships with women, especially Lewinsky, Clinton had exploited "serious misunder-standings of repentance and forgiveness" to gain "political advantage." The moral confusion his "confessions" produced threatened both "the integrity of American religion" and "the foundations of a civil society." Clinton had asked Americans to forgive him even though he had not demonstrated true repentance. The signers also feared that the president's highly publicized rela-tionship with his spiritual counselors might mislead people to conclude that religious institutions approved of his immoral conduct.[201] Only his resignation from office, they contended, would show that he had truly repented.[202]

Some journalists and many ordinary Americans were more upset with Clinton's opponents than with him. Historian Harold Perkin wrote, "Clinton has publicly and tearfully" "confessed his sins, and most Americans, according to the polls, have forgiven him." The 1998 midterm elections demonstrated that voters "were more incensed by the shameless attempt by cynical politi-cians to bring government to a halt and prevent it from tackling" substantive issues such as "welfare and the economy than by the backroom fumblings of consenting, if ill-matched, adults in the White House."[203]

Because he had apologized and suffered the consequences of his actions, Clinton insisted in March 1999, he should be able to finish his presidency; after all, "every person makes mistakes." The Bible included stories about the failures of its "great figures" to teach that everyone sins but "has a chance to go on." In September, Clinton declared that he had been "profoundly moved" by the "unmerited forgiveness" he had experienced from his wife and daughter, other politicians, the American people, and God. In a 2000 interview, Clinton claimed that his faith had deepened while he served as president and that he was working hard to avoid resentments, disappointment, and anger and "to understand that in seeking forgiveness I had to learn to forgive." Discussions with his pastoral counselors and South African President Nelson Mandela about how he was able to pardon his oppressors had helped him better understand forgiveness.[204]

In another interview that year, Clinton asserted that he was trying "to totally rebuild my life from a terrible mistake I made." He strove to understand "the fundamental importance of character and integrity." Integrity meant "doing what you believe is right" and "consistent with the will of God." His counselors forced him to search his soul and rely on "the power of God's love." During the year between his deposition in the Paula Jones case and his acquittal in the Senate, many evenings Clinton spent a couple hours reading the Bible and books on faith and forgiveness.[205] Although Clinton frequently accentuated forgiveness in his addresses after his public apology, he still wrote in his autobiography: "my personal flaws, no matter how deep, were far less threatening to our democratic government than the power lust of my accusers." Moreover, throughout his presidency Clinton often demonized those who opposed his policies—the press, lobbyists, special interests, "profiteering" drug companies, "greedy" physicians, and Republicans.[206]

Clinton's indiscretion with Lewinsky had numerous consequences. Republicans voted for his impeachment and conviction on the grounds that he had committed perjury and obstructed justice in trying to hide his sexual relationship with her. As had the AIDS epidemic a decade earlier, his actions provoked public discussion of subjects (especially oral sex) that most people preferred to avoid. For many, this episode confirmed that the other sexual allegations women had brought against Clinton were true, further tarnishing his reputation and reducing his political clout.

Final Assessment

Many scholars consider Clinton to be an effective president. He promoted public education, reformed a dysfunctional welfare system, helped reduce racism, and worked to resolve international conflicts.[207] During his presidency, the income of the bottom 20 percent of Americans rose substantially and the poverty rate declined to its lowest level in thirty years. Births out of wedlock, divorces, teenage pregnancies, crime, teenage violence, and drug usage among youth, all of which had been steadily climbing, began to decrease. Many scholars argue that his policies contributed to these developments. His legislative achievements include balanced federal budgets, NAFTA, family leave, the Brady Bill, and national service. In foreign affairs, he promoted European unification and NATO expansion, advanced the Middle East peace process, and helped halt genocide in the former Yugoslavia and diminish poverty in Africa.[208] For some, Clinton was "a good centralist president" whose sexual dalliances and deception were a private matter.[209]

Critics counter that Clinton failed to achieve many other major initiatives, most notably comprehensive healthcare, campaign finance reform, Social Security reform, the Comprehensive Test Ban Treaty, and the Kyoto environmental accords.[210] Moreover, he was a scoundrel, the consummate combination of dissolute policies and immoral character.[211] Clinton's sexual indiscretions clashed with his New Covenant emphasis on values, faith, and the family, provoking moral indignation and charges of hypocrisy. Conservative columnist George Will accused Clinton of launching cruise missiles against Afghanistan, Sudan, and Iraq "to distract attention from problems arising from the glandular dimension of his general indiscipline," committing and suborning perjury, tampering with witnesses, and otherwise obstructing justice. Clinton, Will declared, was "the worst person" ever to serve as president. William Bennett censured Clinton's "reckless and irresponsible private behavior," "habitual lying," "abuse of power," and assault on traditional moral norms. Many objected that Clinton blamed "everyone but himself for his sins," especially his family background and "conservative conspirators."[212]

How can we explain the blatant inconsistencies between Clinton's profession to be a Christian who sought to follow biblical ethical standards and his immoral actions? Scholars suggest several explanations, and Clinton's background and statements offer helpful hints. Presidential character and conduct can be evaluated by two competing standards. Stephen Carter argues that moral people integrate all the aspects of their lives; they establish basic values and consistently adhere to them in both private and public. Theologian Reinhold Niebuhr, by contrast, insisted that moral virtues differ in the private and public realms. While love and self-sacrifice are the highest virtues in private life, prudence and justice are the paramount virtues in the public realm where statesmen operate. To be successful, politicians must adapt their ideological commitments to political issues and historical circumstances. Judged by this second standard, Betty Glad contends, Clinton deserves high marks.

He truthfully explained and constantly strove to implement his political convictions and aims, including his promises to balance the budget, reduce the national deficit, supply universal healthcare, create a new welfare system that did not foster dependency, and promote free trade. Evaluated in light of his political goals, impediments (a harshly negative press and a recalcitrant Congress), and personal skills (his intelligence, energy, work ethic, and empathy), Clinton was "a good president."[213] Others insist that Clinton often pursued the policies he believed to be best for the nation in the face of significant political opposition and potential negative political repercussions, including NAFTA, gun control, and intervention in Haiti, Bosnia, and Kosovo.[214] Despite his "glaring foibles," wrote journalist John Brummett, Clinton is "a special politician, the best of his generation." Although he is an undisciplined, "self-justifying rogue," *New Times* reporter Todd Purdum declared, Clinton is one of the nation's "most talented, articulate, intelligent," and "colorful" presidents. Clinton, asserted psychologist Stanley Renshon, is "a man of puzzling contradictions," whose "substantial personal and political talents" are "overshadowed and undercut by his character."[215]

For some, the sexual conduct of presidents is irrelevant to their work. They argue that the affairs of several twentieth-century presidents—Warren Harding, Franklin Roosevelt, John F. Kennedy, and Lyndon B. Johnson—had little effect on their performance. Others counter that a president's sexual infidelity is pertinent because it is a betrayal of trust, which is crucial to political life. Moreover, Clinton's actions with Lewinsky were "reckless and irresponsible," distracted him from more important tasks, and "put at great risk his political agenda and legacy." Additionally, Clinton's lying under oath violated the principles of the judicial system.[216]

Psychologist John Gartner contends that Clinton's hypomanic temperament explains his incongruous actions. These addictive personalities "have a large libido," frequently exercise "poor judgment in their sexual behavior," and constantly "seek stimulation and excitement." These individuals are often charismatic leaders because of their "immense energy, drive, confidence, visionary creativity, [and] infectious enthusiasm," but they have difficulty controlling their impulses. Such individuals are persuasive, charming, and gregarious, but they are also "risk takers, who seem oblivious to obvious dangers." Gartner maintains that Clinton's family background deeply affected his personality development. At home, no one had moral authority over him or established limits for him. Consequently, Clinton concluded that he could determine his own rules of conduct. As an adult, his conduct with regard to the big issues—promoting justice, aiding the poor, and resolving international disputes—was exemplary, but he did not like to be held accountable for his

private morality. Similarly, historian David Holmes attributes Clinton's enigmatic behavior to his dysfunctional family, "need to please," excessive desire
for praise, immense political ambition, compulsion to distort the truth, "cava-
lier attitude toward martial fidelity," and seeming inability to admit his own
mistakes.[217]

Clinton advisor David Gergen insists that the Democrat's basic problem
was that he lacked an inner compass. He was David Reisman's archetypical
other-directed person who had no interior gyroscope to direct his moral behavior and based his self-definition on how others viewed him. Because of his
family background, constant campaigning, and demanding administrative
responsibilities, Clinton engaged in little self-reflection and had "an underdeveloped sense of self." Because his mission was righteous, Clinton reasoned,
he had special privileges. He saw life as a golf game where he could take a
"mulligan" if things went wrong.[218]

Clinton's 1996 campaign manager Dick Morris offers a simpler explanation for his moral schizophrenia: two Bill Clintons existed—"Saturday night
Bill," who, while avoiding his mother's gambling and abuse of alcohol and
drugs, emulated her practice of illicit sex, and "Sunday morning Bill" who
read the Bible and attended church regularly and proclaimed that Christian
virtues were vital to public life. Clinton never fully integrated these two per-
sonas "into one consistent identity." Biographer David Maraniss argues similarly that "the pious Clinton" should not be simply dismissed as "a poseur"
who sought "to cover up less righteous aspects of his life." Clinton was "a
man of contrasts and contradictions" who moved easily through "many different worlds" but frequently failed to reconcile them. Clinton's faith sometimes supplied "solace and escape from the contentious world of politics,"
while other times it provided theological support for his "personal actions
and political choices."[219]

Clinton explained his incongruities in an autobiographical essay for his
junior English class: "I am a living paradox—deeply religious, yet not as
convinced of my exact beliefs as I ought to be; wanting responsibility yet
shirking it; loving the truth but often times giving way to falsity." "Some
of whom are very dear to me," he added, "have never learned how to live.
I desire and struggle to be different from them, but often am almost an
exact likeness." Or as Clinton put it more than forty years later: "trying to
come to grips with what I did" with Lewinsky enabled me "to finally unify
my parallel lives."[220]

Many critics undoubtedly agree with Cal Thomas's assessment: "Clinton
feels about religion the way he feels about sex. He likes the kind that makes
him feel good but requires nothing of him." Near the end of his presidency,

a *Wall Street Journal*/NBC News poll reported that 43 percent of Americans considered Clinton "not that religious."[221] In the minds of many Americans, deeds trumped words. While such claims are impossible to prove, the evidence suggests, that more than most other presidents, Clinton, while having a meaningful personal faith, used religion to win votes, justify his policies, and try to create a positive image.

Barack Obama

"WE ARE OUR BROTHER'S KEEPER"

More than 2,000 years ago, a child born in a stable brought our world a redeeming gift of peace and salvation. It's a story with a message that speaks to us to this day—that we are called to love each other as we love ourselves, that we are our brother's keeper and our sister's keeper and our destinies are linked. It's a message that guides my Christian faith.

"REMARKS AT 'CHRISTMAS IN WASHINGTON,'" December 12, 2010

When I wake in the morning, I wait on the Lord, and I ask Him to give me the strength to do right by our country and its people. And when I go to bed at night I wait on the Lord, and I ask Him to forgive . . . my sins, and look after my family and the American people, and make me an instrument of His will.

"NATIONAL PRAYER BREAKFAST," February 4, 2011

Each and every time we've had to make a decision, my guiding principle, that north star, has been [that] I am my brother's keeper, I am my sister's keeper.

"REMARKS AT A DEMOCRATIC NATIONAL COMMITTEE FUNDRAISER IN CHICAGO," April 14, 2011

Introduction

Barack Obama's faith has significantly influenced his life, and it has been both widely misunderstood and highly controversial. Despite this fact and the major role that religious issues played in both the 2008 and 2012 elections, only one religious biography of Obama has been published.[1] Although both secular and Christian magazines have featured articles about the president's religious background and convictions, and he has talked about his faith in his two auto-biographies and dozens of speeches, many Americans are still confused about his faith. Numerous polls indicate that about 20 percent of Americans incorrectly think he is a Muslim. Others consider Obama to be an advocate of black liberation theology because of his long membership in Jeremiah Wright's church in Chicago. Many political and religious conservatives contend that his professions of faith are disingenuous and entirely politically motivated. Obama has been labeled "the most explicitly Christian president in American history" by historian John Fea and America's "Most Biblically-Hostile" president by evangelical author and activist David Barton.[2] Few presidents, argued a journalist in the *Los Angeles Times* in 2012, have spoken as often, deeply, or eloquently about their faith or faced such hostility over religious matters, including "charges that he is waging a 'war on religion,' widespread suspicion about the sincerity of his Christian faith, and the persistent legend that he is a practicing Muslim."[3] Many conservative Christian books and websites argue that Obama is trying to destroy the nation's Christian heritage and cannot possibly be a Christian because of his stances on abortion, gay marriage, and government redistribution of wealth. Some analysts and other Christians, by contrast, praise "Obama's Faith-Based Presidency," which has sought to help the poor, especially by providing universal healthcare.[4] Obama has repeatedly declared that Jesus is his savior and Lord and that he bases his life on Christ's teachings. He testifies that he prays and reads the Bible regularly and seeks to promote God's kingdom on earth. Obama's faith is difficult to decipher, however, because various streams—the African-American church, the Social Gospel movement, mainline progressive Protestantism, and evangelicalism—have all helped shape it.

Unlike Al Gore in 2000 and John Kerry in 2004, Obama made a concerted attempt in the 2008 election to win the votes of religiously committed Americans. During the campaign, he frequently discussed his faith journey and repeatedly labeled himself "a devout Christian." His staff reached out to religious groups, especially Catholics and evangelical Protestants. Obama insisted that religion could play a positive role in public life and that his religious convictions affected his approach to politics, understanding of political issues, and policies.[5] Despite claims that Obama is a Muslim, an advocate of black liberation theology, or a politically motivated pious pretender, considerable evidence indicates that his religious beliefs are mainstream Protestant ones and that faith is quite meaningful to him. Obama has frequently quoted Scripture, citing the Sermon on the Mount to undergird his economic positions, referring to the Golden Rule to explain his support for gay marriage, and often emphasizing that Christians are called to be their brother's keeper.

He has challenged Americans in dozens of speeches to work through both voluntary organizations and the government to help the impoverished, disabled, disadvantaged, and emotionally troubled. Obama relied on his faith to comfort Americans in the aftermath of shootings in Tucson, Aurora, Colorado, Newtown, Connecticut, and the Washington Navy Yard, tornados in Tuscaloosa, Alabama, Joplin, Missouri, and Moore, Oklahoma, the terrorist attack at the Boston Marathon, and the explosion at the fertilizer plant in West, Texas, by quoting Scripture and hymns, assuring Americans that God would bring good out of calamity, and underscoring the promise of heaven.[6]

The Faith of Barack Obama

Born in 1961, Barack Obama is the first American president who was not raised by Christian parents. The primary influences on him during his formative years were atheism, folk Islam, and secular humanism. His father, Barack Obama, Sr., returned to his native Kenya when the future president was 2. Obama's mother, Ann Dunham, attended the East Shore Unitarian Church in Bellevue, Washington, and was inspired by Unitarians' social activism. However, as a high school student, she declared herself to be an atheist. Dunham sometimes took her son to Christmas and Easter services, and she later lived briefly in a Buddhist monastery while working in India. Obama described his mother as an agnostic who believed that no religion had a corner on the truth.[7] She was a very spiritual person with an "enormous capacity for wonder" but was skeptical about "religion as an institution."[8] His mother, he wrote, was "a lonely witness for secular humanism, a soldier for the New Deal, [the] Peace Corps, [and] position-paper liberalism."[9] She was "instinctively guided by the Golden Rule," Obama asserted, and constantly emphasized honesty, hard work, kindness, and fair play.[10]

Adopting his mother's skepticism, Obama grew up religiously rootless. After Dunham remarried and moved her family to Indonesia, he was exposed to both Islam and Catholicism. His stepfather Lolo Soetoro occasionally took him to a mosque to worship, and Obama attended a Catholic elementary school for first and second grade. Soetoro's form of Islam made "room for the remnants of more ancient animist and Hindu faiths," Obama explained.[11] When he transferred to a public school for third grade, Obama studied the doctrines of Islam during the two hours of required religious instruction each week.[12] "In our household, the Bible, [t]he Koran and the Bhagavad Gita sat on the shelf alongside books of Greek and Norse and African mythology," Obama observed.[13]

Obama moved to Hawaii with his mother and sister in 1971. During his years at the highly regarded Punahou School in Honolulu, Occidental University in Los Angeles, and Columbia University in New York, Obama struggled to find his identity and determine his personal philosophy. While attending Columbia, Obama "did a lot of spiritual exploration." He fasted, went days without speaking to anyone, and read the works of Christian theologian Augustine, atheist philosopher Friedrich Nietzsche, and Roman Catholic novelist Graham Greene. He sometimes attended African-American congregations, most often Abyssinian Baptist Church in Harlem, attracted by its "exuberant worship," "family atmosphere," and "prophetic preaching."[14]

Hungering "for some sort of meaning" in life, Obama took a job in 1985 as a community organizer for a group of congregations in Chicago. "Inspired by the civil rights movement," he wanted to help "rebuild some of Chicago's poorest neighborhoods." Influenced by the ideas of Neo-Orthodox theologians Paul Tillich and Reinhold Niebuhr, Martin Luther King, Jr., and African-American and Roman Catholic liberation theologians, the religious leaders with whom Obama worked emphasized human sinfulness, Christian community, and Christ's call to help "the least of these."[15] Although Obama professed to know the Scriptures and to share their values, he gradually realized that "something was missing" in his life. He concluded that he needed "a commitment to a particular community of faith."[16]

This prompted Obama to attend Trinity United Church of Christ on the South Side of Chicago one Sunday in 1988 where he heard its pastor Jeremiah Wright, Jr. deliver a sermon titled "The Audacity to Hope." Wright's message convinced Obama that his "sins could be redeemed" and challenged him to acknowledge Christ as his savior and place his trust in Him. Obama soon came "to see faith as more than just a comfort to the weary or a hedge against death, but rather as an active, palpable agent in the world and in my own life." "These newfound understandings—that religious commitment did not require me to suspend critical thinking, disengage from the battle for economic and social justice, or otherwise retreat from the world"—led Obama to be baptized at Trinity Church to affirm his faith publicly. He described becoming a Christian "as a choice, and not an epiphany." His questions did not "magically disappear," and his "skeptical bent" did not "suddenly vanish." However, while kneeling beneath the cross at Trinity, Obama declared, "I heard God's spirit beckoning me. I submitted myself to His will, and dedicated myself to discovering His truth and carrying out His works."[17]

Obama and his wife Michelle Robinson, whom he married in 1992, attended Trinity Church fairly regularly until he ran for the Senate in 2004, had their children dedicated there, and supported the church financially.

This black megachurch sponsored several dozen ministries and educational institutions around the world. Its almost 10,000 members included wealthy businesspeople, physicians, politicians, and scores of college professors. After becoming its pastor in 1972, Wright built the church from eighty-seven members to the largest American congregation in the United Church of Christ denomination. Deeply influenced by James Cone, the nation's leading proponent of black liberation theology, Wright supported abortion rights and gay rights. More controversially, he exhorted the federal government to compensate blacks for their ancestors' enslavement and to greatly increase its aid to Africa.[18]

Obama was attracted to Trinity by Wright's sermons, its "upwardly mobile and politically active" black members, its "affirmation and celebration of his African heritage," its theological support for his political liberalism, its focus on social ministry, and the sense of belonging it provided.[19] Obama found Wright's interpretation of the Bible "as a story of the struggles of black people" and emphasis on social justice very appealing. He "imagined the stories of ordinary black people merging with the stories of David and Goliath, Moses and Pharaoh, the Christians in the lion's den, [and] Ezekiel's field of dry bones." Those accounts of survival, freedom, and hope "became our story, my story."[20]

As noted, Obama frequently asserted that he is a Christian. Examining his views of God, Jesus, humanity, faith, salvation, prayer, the Bible, church attendance, and the afterlife confirm this contention, although evangelicals criticize his understanding of scriptural authority, the nature of faith, and the basis of salvation. Obama explained that "I'm a Christian by choice," not upbringing. He embraced Christianity as an adult "because the precepts of Jesus Christ spoke to me in terms of the kind of life that I would want to lead—being my brothers' and sisters' keeper, treating others as they would treat me." "My public service is part of that effort to express my Christian faith." Obama often testified that he relied "heavily on my Christian faith in my job." "As Christians, my family and I remember the incredible sacrifice Jesus made for each and every one of us, how He took on the sins of the world, and extended the gift of salvation," the president declared in a 2013 address on Easter. "And we recommit ourselves to following His example here on Earth: to loving our Lord and Savior, to loving our neighbors, and to seeing everyone, especially 'the least of these,' as a child of God."[21]

For Obama, God is "awesome and loving." He often thanked God, "who holds the future in the hollow of His hand," for blessing and guiding America. Obama's call for a National Day of Prayer in 2011 asked "God for the sustenance and guidance" to meet the nation's great challenges. He explained that "failures and disappointments" had led him to inquire "what God had in store for me" and had reminded him "that God's plans for us may not always match our own short-sighted desires." While God controlled the course of events, people were often unable to discern His "heavenly plans." God, Obama insisted, "does great things beyond our understandings" (Job 37: 5).[22]

Obama affirmed that Jesus was both human and divine and that he had a personal relationship with Christ. "Our Savior, who suffered and died [and] was resurrected," he asserted, was "both fully God and also a man." Obama testified that Jesus Christ is his savior and Lord many times. In a 2008 interview in *Christianity Today*, he declared, "I am a devout Christian. I believe in the redemptive death and resurrection of Jesus Christ." "Accepting Jesus Christ," he added, powerfully affected his ideals, values, and conduct. At the 2011 National Prayer Breakfast, Obama explained that through "working with pastors and laypeople trying to heal the wounds of hurting neighborhoods" in Chicago "I came to know Jesus Christ for myself and embrace Him as my lord and savior." His faith in Christ's sacrifice and resurrection enabled him "to be cleansed of sin and have eternal life." At a 2010 breakfast, the president urged religious leaders to "continue the Easter celebration of our risen Savior." He discussed the lessons he derived "from Christ's sacrifice" "for the sins of humanity" and the inspiration His resurrection supplied. Christ's resurrection, Obama argued, forever changed the world. "As Christians," he proclaimed, "we believe that" our "faith in Jesus Christ" brings redemption and "eternal hope." The president insisted that like "our Lord and Savior," all Christians should "act justly," "love mercy and walk humbly with the Lord."[23] "The resurrection of our savior Jesus Christ," who "took on the sins of the world—past, present, and future—" and His "unfathomable gift of grace and salvation" put "everything else in perspective."[24] In his 2012 Easter message, Obama celebrated "the resurrection of a Savior who died so that we might live."[25] Christians had a "redeeming Savior, whose grace is sufficient for the multitude of our sins, and whose love is never failing."[26] Obama was deeply moved by his visit to Israel shortly before Easter in 2013. Visiting the Holy Land, he declared, "brings Scripture to life. It brings us closer to Christ." Christ's "lessons live on in our hearts and, most importantly, in our actions. When we tend to the sick, when we console those in pain, when we sacrifice for those in need, wherever and whenever we are there to give comfort and to guide and to love, then Christ is with us."[27]

Obama referred to Jesus in several major speeches early in his presidency. Speaking at Georgetown University, Obama used a parable from Jesus's Sermon on the Mount to support his economic policies; in his commencement address at the University of Notre Dame, he described his decision to follow

Christ; and in his speech in Cairo, Obama announced that he is a Christian. George W. Bush, by contrast, rarely mentioned Jesus except in his statements about Easter, Christmas, and the Salvation Army. Obama faced a very different political situation than Bush did. The Texan "was so closely politically identified with the Christian right that overt talk of Christ from the White House risked alienating mainstream and secular voters." However, Obama was often misidentified as a Muslim or a secularist, so using explicitly Christian rhetoric enabled him to connect with the 78 percent of Americans who identify themselves as Christians.[28]

Obama asserted that human beings are " 'wonderfully made' in the image of God" and have an "inherent dignity . . . that no earthly power can take away."[29] However, people are also "sinful," "flawed," and "fallible." They yield "to the temptations" of pride and power and sometimes to evil.[30] He attributed people's inability to work together to their selfishness, arrogance, acquisitiveness, stubbornness, and insecurities. All the world's "cruelties large and small" are "rooted in original sin." The Democrat lamented that people often sought to gain advantage over others, clung to "outworn prejudice," and viewed life "through the lens" of "self-interest and crass materialism." Many wealthy and powerful individuals, Obama complained, continually justified their privileges while ignoring poverty and injustice.[31] Speaking in Tucson at a memorial service for the six people killed in a January 2011 shooting, he declared, "the Scripture tells us that there is evil in the world, and that terrible things happen for reasons that defy human understanding."[32]

Much more than most public figures, Obama confessed that his faith "admits doubts, and uncertainty, and mystery." Like Danish philosopher Søren Kierkegaard, Obama asserted that "it's not faith if you are absolutely certain." People must take a "leap" to accept Christianity. Some biblical passages, he stated, "make perfect sense," but others are baffling.[33] Reflecting on his own faith journey, Obama declared, "I leave open the possibility that I'm entirely wrong."[34] When people questioned his faith, Obama strove to remember that what ultimately mattered was his fidelity to his conscience and to God. He sought to obey Christ's exhortation: "Seek first His kingdom and His righteousness and all these things will be given to you as well."[35]

Obama often stressed the benefits of prayer. Prayer, he argued, "has played an important role in the American story and in shaping our Nation's leaders." Obama asserted that he prayed every day and that his family said grace before dinner every night.[36] "For those of us who draw on faith as a guiding force in our lives, prayer has many purposes," including supplying "support when times are hard." Prayer "helps us find the vision and the strength to see the world that we want to build." Obama urged people to pray not only in times of trouble but also in times of "joy and peace and prosperity" to guard against conceit and complacency. Prayer, he maintained, could keep individuals "calm in a storm," help them overcome obstacles, and produce humility. Obama insisted that people living in a culture obsessed with wealth, power, and celebrity often needed "a brush with hardship or tragedy" to remind them of "what matters most."[37]

While praying for Billy Graham at the evangelist's home in 2009, Obama related, "the Holy Spirit interceded when I didn't know quite what to say." "I have fallen on my knees with great regularity since that moment—asking God for guidance not just in my personal life and my Christian walk, but in the life of this nation." God always has guided America, "and He always will." Like several of his predecessors, Obama quoted Abraham Lincoln's confession that "I have been driven many times upon my knees by the overwhelming conviction that I had nowhere else to go." "While the challenges that I've faced pale in comparison to Lincoln's," Obama added, "more than once I've been filled with the same conviction." At the 2010 National Prayer Breakfast, Obama declared, "I'm praying a lot these days." He prayed for patience, humility, wisdom, strength to help the struggling, and that he would "walk closer with God and make that walk my first and most important task." Obama declared in February 2011 that the events of the past two years had deepened his faith. "My Christian faith," he testified, has sustained "me over these last few years." "The challenges of the presidency," he added, prompted him to pray. Obama expected God to answer his prayers only if he worked hard, made sacrifices, and served others. Those who recognized that God had a larger purpose for their lives would be used in ways they "never fully know." Obama's faith kept him calm and peaceful when change was "painfully slow in coming" and his efforts seemed futile.[38]

Obama frequently asked Americans to pray for him, his family, and the United States, and he rejoiced that many were doing so. He reported that his spiritual advisors, especially megachurch pastors Joel Hunter and T. D. Jakes, periodically prayed with him in the Oval Office or on the phone. He thanked his children's godmother, Kaye Wilson, for organizing prayer circles for him throughout the nation.[39] "Keep praying" for me, Obama told South African Anglican Bishop Desmond Tutu. "I'll always need prayer."[40] The Democrat also frequently mentioned that he was praying for individuals.[41] For example, Obama told Israeli president Shimon Peres in 2013 that since he had assumed office, "I prayed that you would meet" your nation's "daunting and demanding challenges" "with wisdom and determination, without losing hope."[42]

The president testified that he received spiritual strength by reading the scriptural meditations aide Joshua DuBois sent him every morning. "I often search" the "Scripture to figure out how I can be a better man as well as a better President," Obama declared, and to "determine how best to balance" work and family life. He believed that the Bible "it is not a static text but the Living Word and that I must be continually open to new revelations—whether they come from a lesbian friend or a doctor opposed to abortion." Despite this assertion, which implies that other sources are equal in authority to Scripture, one evangelical claimed that Obama had a high view of the Bible, although whether he affirmed biblical infallibility or inerrancy is unclear.[43]

Obama argued that numerous paths lead to salvation and heaven. He could "have everlasting life," the Democrat averred, because Jesus Christ died for his sins. By confessing that Christ atoned for their sins, people "achieve salvation through the grace of God." However, Obama could not believe that God "would consign four-fifths of the world [those who had not accepted Jesus as their savior] to hell." "Jews and Muslims who live moral lives," the president added, "are just as much 'children of God' as he is." Moreover, he reasoned, because his mother was a kind and generous person, she is in heaven.[44]

Although Obama stated in a 2005 interview, "I don't presume to have knowledge of what happens after I die," as president he often professed belief in heaven. Obama concluded a eulogy for West Virginia Senator Robert Byrd in 2010, "May he be welcomed kindly by the Righteous Judge." In his Tucson remarks, the president referred to one murder victim as being in heaven and asked God to "bless and keep those we've lost in restful and eternal peace." Comforting mourners after the shootings in Aurora, Colorado, in July 2012, Obama quoted the promise of Revelation 21:4: God "will wipe away every tear from their eyes, and death shall be no more. Neither shall there be mourning, nor crying, nor pain anymore." Consoling those whose loved ones died at the Sandy Hook massacre five months later, Obama quoted 2 Corinthians 5:1: "For we know that if the earthly tent we live in is destroyed, we have a building from God, an eternal house in heaven, not built by human hands." "God has called them all home," he added. "May God bless and keep those we've lost in His heavenly place." "Scripture tells us to 'run with endurance the race that is set before us,'" Obama told mourners at a service for those who died when a bomb exploded at the 2013 Boston Marathon. "As we do, may God hold close those who've been taken from us too soon." In a 2013 Easter message, Obama asserted that Christ sacrificed his life "so that we might have eternal life." Five months later, he consoled grieving families whose members had been killed at the Washington Navy Yard by declaring, "May God hold close the souls taken from us and grant them eternal peace."[45]

After the tragedies in Aurora and Newtown, Obama spent time individually with every family who lost a member. The president's "incredibly appropriate and powerful message" at the Sandy Hook Interfaith Prayer Vigil prompted Atlanta megachurch minister Andy Stanley to dub him America's "Pastor-in-Chief."[46] Obama also provided comfort to Joel Hunter in 2010 after the Orlando pastor's 5-year-old granddaughter Ava was diagnosed with a deadly brain tumor. Obama phoned Hunter to tell him that he and Michelle were praying for Ava and her family and to offer spiritual counsel. "Joel," the president said, "I want you to remember that God has got you here. He's not going to let you go. He will walk all the way through this with you." When Ava died three months later, Obama called Hunter again to supply solace and spiritual reassurance. The president quoted several biblical passages and told Hunter that he was "trusting God to go through this with you."[47]

After Obama's election and during the early months of his presidency, many speculated about where he and his family would attend church, and numerous Washington congregations issued invitations. Obama said he might worship at "a number of different churches," but he has attended church in Washington infrequently, usually at Nineteenth Street Baptist Church or St. John's Episcopal Church.[48] Obama eventually decided not to join a Washington congregation and instead to worship primarily at the Evergreen Chapel at Camp David. Like William McKinley, Franklin Roosevelt, and Harry Truman, he complained about being on display when he worshipped (many people snapped pictures of him with their cell phones and pastors spoke directly to him). For example, when the Obamas attended the Metropolitan A.M.E. Church in Washington, DC to celebrate the legacy of Martin Luther King, Jr. in January 2013, large crowds gathered in the streets to watch the first family travel to and from the church. When Obama was formally introduced, parishioners applauded, and they also sang "Happy Birthday" to the first lady who had recently turned 49. In their opening prayers, pastors asked God to protect and guide the president.[49] Obama enjoyed the "powerful" sermons preached by Southern Baptist Carey Cash, the Navy chaplain assigned to lead Sunday worship services at Camp David. Cash, a great-nephew of singer Johnny Cash, previously served as a chaplain with a marine battalion in Iraq.[50] However, Obama spent little time at Camp David.[51] A CBS news reporter claimed that Obama attended church only eighteen times in his first five years as president, and the *New York Times* called attention to the Obamas not attending any Christmas services in 2013. Both Protestants and Catholics protested that the president's sporadic church attendance was a bad role model.[52]

Despite Obama's substantial use of Christian rhetoric and numerous professions that he is a Christian, millions of Americans continue to misunderstand his faith. Franklin Graham accused Obama of believing that he is a Christian simply because he attended church. Political analyst Peter Wehner countered that Obama had never claimed that attending church made some-one a Christian. Moreover, he had "been as explicit about his Christian faith as a public figure can be." Syndicated columnist Cal Thomas argued that no one who espoused universalism and works-based salvation and denied that Christ is "the sole mediator" between God and people as Obama did could be a Christian. Bob Jones University chancellor Bob Jones III simply stated, "I've no reason to think [Obama is] a Christian."[53]

On the other hand, Southern Baptist ethicist Richard Land labeled Obama "a very typical 21st-century mainline Protestant." Kirbyjon Caldwell, pastor of a huge United Methodist church in Houston, maintained that Obama's state-ments proved that "he is authentically Christian" and noted that citizens had not challenged the claim of any other recent president to be a Christian. Judd Birdsall contended in *Christianity Today* that Obama had provided "ample evi-dence for his repeated claim to be a devout Christian." Obama is "a committed Christian," and for evangelicals, he "is a brother in Christ." Hunter, Obama's closest spiritual mentor, insisted that Obama is "born again" and "has trusted in Jesus Christ with his whole heart."[54]

Despite Obama's own testimony and that of others who know him well, an August 2010 *Newsweek* poll found that 24 percent of Americans thought the president was a Muslim (a higher percentage than during the 2008 cam-paign), 42 percent believed he is a Christian, 10 percent believed he is "some-thing else," and 24 percent did not know what religion he espoused. Moreover, according to this poll, 31 percent of Americans agreed that the president "sym-pathizes with the goals of Islamic fundamentalists who want to impose Islamic law around the world."[55] Meanwhile, a Pew poll reported that the percentage of Americans who identified Obama as a Christian dropped from 48 percent to 34 percent. This misunderstanding prompted Obama's press secretary to declare that the president's "top priority" was not to ensure that "Americans know what a devout Christian he is." Rather, it was to improve the economy and create jobs. Another White House spokesperson characterized Obama as a man of "strong Christian faith," even though "he doesn't wear it on his sleeve." More than seventy Christian leaders, including Hunter, Jakes, Samuel Rodriguez of the National Hispanic Christian Leadership Conference, and World Vision president Rich Stearns, repudiated the contention that Obama is a Muslim and asserted that he unwaveringly confessed "Christ as Lord."[56] Stephen Mansfield, author of *The Faith of Barack Obama*, claimed that these polls were "a wake-up call to the White House," and thereafter Obama has frequently described his own spiritual journey, stated that he prayed daily, and talked explicitly about his Christian faith at prayer breakfasts and in his Easter and Christmas messages.[57]

Several factors help explain this persistent popular misperception that Obama is a Muslim. Franklin Graham maintained that "the president's problem is that he was born a Muslim" and had an Islamic name. Obama's 2009 visit to Egypt, quotations of the Qur'an, and sharing of his personal encounters with Islam also contributed to this misunderstanding. Others alleged that Obama's failure to attend church or to speak publicly about his faith (a patently false assertion) had produced this confusion.[58] Some blamed the conservative media. Pundits on the right, including Ann Coulter, David Limbaugh, and Chuck Norris, vociferously questioned Obama's claim to be a Christian. Other detractors repeatedly used the Internet to spread misinformation about the president. Writing in *Time*, Amy Sullivan pointed out that 60 percent of respondents in a 2010 Pew poll "who identified Obama's faith as Islam" reported "they learned the 'fact' from the media." Others reasoned that telling pollsters that Obama is a Muslim is a way of expressing disproval of him. The myth that the president is a Muslim, journalist Ross Douthat argues, became "rooted in the right-wing consciousness in part because Obama's prior institutional affiliation is with a church that seems far more alien to many white Christians than did the African-American Christianity of Martin Luther King Jr., or even Jesse Jackson."[59]

Others insisted that his giving so much credibility and prominence to Islam produced confusion about Obama's faith. In his first inaugural address, Obama labeled America a nation of "Christians and Muslims, Jews and Hindus and nonbelievers." Despite the Jews' longer history, larger numbers, and greater contributions to America, some protested, Obama placed Muslims second in this list.[60] Obama also stressed "civilization's debt to Islam." "Islamic culture has given us," he asserted, "timeless poetry and cherished music." Moreover, Muslims had demonstrated "religious tolerance and racial equality" through their words and deeds.[61] Like Clinton, Obama sent cordial messages to Muslims who were celebrating Ramadan, which enabled them to demonstrate their "devotion to God through prayer and through fasting." Ramadan inspired Americans to express "a spirit of love and respect, to renew our obligations to one another, as well as to renew our commitment to our neighbors and helping the most needy among us." "Throughout our history," the president added, "Islam has contributed to the character of our country," and Muslim Americans "have helped to build our Nation."[62]

Conservative Christians also objected to Obama's references in his Cairo address to "the Holy Koran" and to the Middle East as the region "where Islam was first revealed." Ken Blackwell, a former UN Human Rights commissioner, argued that labeling the scriptures of any other religion holy or revealed denied the uniqueness of Christianity. Although Obama was trying to improve relations with Muslim nations, making theological statements about Islam that many Christians considered unacceptable produced bewilderment about his own religious beliefs. The wide circulation of these statements on the Internet, Blackwell maintained, led many to reject Obama's claim to be a Christian.[63]

Obama's support in 2010 of the right of Muslims to build a mosque at Ground Zero in Manhattan also contributed to confusion about his religious commitments. The president insisted that Muslims had the same right "to practice their religion as anyone else in this country," which included "the right to build a place of worship and a community center" in lower Manhattan. After his statement evoked extensive criticism, Obama explained that he was not arguing that putting a mosque there was wise, only that the right to do so "dates back to our founding."[64]

While agreeing that American Muslims should have the freedom to worship how and where they pleased, many objected to constructing a mosque at this location. Conservative British author David Pryce-Jones complained that the quest to erect a "mosque in this site of mass murder committed by Muslims" expressed attitudes of "supremacy and conquest." He pointed out that non-Muslims were not permitted to establish places of worship in Saudi Arabia or to even enter Medina and Mecca.[65] Others denounced the plan to place a mosque at this site, led by an imam who refused to condemn Hamas, as "unseemly and ill-considered." They faulted the president for not counseling Muslim leaders to build their mosque in a different location.[66]

Two and a half years into Obama's presidency, others continued to hammer away at his long association with Trinity Church in Chicago. Joe Carter, the web editor of *First Things*, protested that for more than twenty years Obama belonged to this "apostate, racialist church" that failed to distinguish "between faith and politics." Trinity subordinated Christianity "to a twisted, racialist political ideology." Even if Obama knew nothing about Wright's "inflammatory rhetoric" and slept through his preaching of liberation theology, he had supported a church that promoted a "despicable," "divisive" theology. Tevi Troy, who served as George W. Bush's liaison to the Jewish community, criticized Obama for joining a church to gain political advantages while ignoring its theological positions.[67]

Meanwhile, some evangelicals still denied that Obama was a Christian. Writing in *Christianity Today* in 2012, Owen Strachan admitted that by professing Christ to be his savior and calling Scripture "an inspiration and moral guide" the president sounded like a Christian. However, Obama believed that "there are many paths" to an undefined eternal abode, "not one exclusive path to heaven." Moreover, for Obama, prayer was "a kind of Protestant Zen moment, a dialing-in to deeper currents and larger realities." In addition, the Democrat did not describe his conversion as saving him "from righteous damnation." Strachan also censured the "non-exclusivistic ecumenism" prevalent in Obama's religious pronouncements, which asserted that non-Christians could "answer the call" of God to fight against injustice. American culture, not the Bible, he argued, determined Obama's views. On abortion, "his own values matter, not Psalm 139"; on homosexuality and marriage, "his daughters' opinions matter, not Genesis 2 and Romans 1." "In the final analysis, what is missing from Obama's theology" was "the message of God-given righteousness grounded in the cross of Christ," which must be "received by faith and repentance."[68]

The Election of 2008

During their 2004 battle for a US Senate seat in Illinois, Republican Alan Keyes, a conservative Catholic, castigated Obama for discussing his faith only "when it's convenient to get votes." When faith must be followed, explained, and serve as a basis for policies, Keyes protested, Obama pled the "separation of church and state," a concept that is neither constitutional nor scriptural. "Christ would not vote for Barack Obama," Keyes asserted, because his behavior was so contrary to Christ's. Obama responded that he had a pastor, a Bible, and his prayers to teach him about Christianity; he did not need Keyes to lecture him on the subject. Obama easily defeated Keyes, but their heated campaign helped convince him that a candidate's faith was very important in politics. He later admitted that his typical responses to Keyes's charges—that "we live in a pluralistic society" and "I can't impose my own religious views" on others—had been inadequate.[69]

In July 2004 Obama gave a memorable keynote address at the Democratic National Convention in Boston. Asserting that many Democrats also had strong religious commitment and vibrant spiritual faith, Obama proclaimed, "We worship an awesome God in the Blue States." Democratic president nominee, Catholic John Kerry, generally avoided discussing his personal religious convictions during the campaign, but Obama's speech foreshadowed the approach that he and other Democrats would soon adopt. After losing the 2004 presidential election, Democrats made a concerted effort in 2006 to narrow the "God gap" by recruiting congressional candidates who had a staunch Christian commitment and accentuating the positive role faith and religious principles played in politics.[70]

Speaking at the 2006 Sojourners/Call to Renewal conference, Obama chided Democrats for avoiding talking about religious values because of their fear of offending people or their belief that religion had no place "in the public square." Ignoring "the power of faith" in the lives of Americans was "a mistake." Many great American reformers, including Frederick Douglass, Abraham Lincoln, William Jennings Bryan, Dorothy Day, and Martin Luther King, Jr., Obama avowed, were "motivated by faith" and "repeatedly used religious language to argue for their cause." The contention that people "should not inject their 'personal morality' into public policy debates is a practical absurdity; our law is by definition a codification of morality, much of it grounded in the Judeo-Christian tradition." "Secularists are wrong," Obama added, "when they ask believers to leave their religion at the door before entering into the public square." However, "the religiously motivated" must "translate their concerns into universal, rather than religion-specific, values." Their proposals, he maintained, must "be subject to argument, and amenable to reason." For example, individuals could oppose abortion for religious reasons, but they must not simply cite the teachings of their "church or evoke God's will." They must instead explain why abortion violates universally held principles.[71]

Obama's speech was widely acclaimed. E. J. Dionne, Jr. labeled it "the most important pronouncement by a Democrat on faith and politics since John F. Kennedy's Houston speech in 1960." He praised the Illinois senator for speaking honestly about his own faith, emphasizing "religion's need for independence from government," accentuating social justice, and insisting that social improvement "requires individual transformation." Amy Sullivan called Obama's address the first "affirmative statement from a Democrat about 'how to reconcile faith with our modern, pluralistic democracy' " in decades. Obama did not explain "his conversion in order to establish his religious" credentials, but rather to support his argument that religion has a vital role to play in public life. Journalist Michelle Goldberg applauded Obama for understanding "the spiritual void at the heart of American life, and the need for social movements to offer people meaning and existential solace along with practical policy solutions." *Christianity Today* commended Obama for discussing "his faith and religious values with earnestness and with ease." The editors argued, however, that Lincoln, King, and other Christian leaders had employed "a variety of reasons—some religious, some pragmatic—to motivate social change." They used God's justice and transcendent standards to critique societal laws and human behavior. While religious reasons may be insufficient by themselves to decide policy issues, so were considerations of power and rights.[72]

Obama challenged Americans to stop making religion "a divisive force in the body politic" and to instead harness "our deepest moral commitments" to remedy social ills. He challenged liberals and conservatives to quit debating whether private initiatives or government programs best helped raise children, reduce inner city poverty and AIDS, and improve the environment, and instead work together to achieve these ends.[73]

In his Call to Renewal speech Obama challenged Democrats to "reach out to people of faith," and during the 2008 election campaign, he did just that. Like Jimmy Carter and Bill Clinton, Obama frequently spoke the language of faith and courted the votes of religiously committed Americans. Many of Obama's campaign rallies began and ended with prayer, and he often gave talks in churches and quoted Scripture. During the South Carolina primary, Obama's staff distributed brochures picturing him standing at a pulpit in front of a large cross with the caption "Committed Christian."[74] Obama met with dozens of religious leaders, organized "Catholics for Obama," and advertised on many radio stations. Ronald Sider, head of Evangelicals for Social Action, contended that Obama understood "evangelicals better than any Democrat since Carter." Obama met with numerous evangelical luminaries including Jakes, Franklin Graham, Texas pastor and author Max Lucado, *Christianity Today* editor David Neff, and National Association of Evangelicals (NAE) executive Richard Cizik. Obama also sent weekly messages to the NAE, promising to confront problems the Bush administration had ignored, especially healthcare, and climate change. Republican nominee John McCain paid little attention to conservative social issues, prompting many evangelicals not to write off Obama immediately despite his pro-choice position on abortion and support of gay rights, and some evangelicals, including Bush supporter Kirbyjon Caldwell, endorsed him. To appeal to evangelicals, author and activist Tony Campolo was named to the Democratic Party's platform committee, which adopted a plank affirming the party's support for "a woman's decision to have a child by ensuring access to and availability of programs for pre- and post-natal healthcare, parenting skills, income support, and caring adoption programs." Joshua DuBois, a black Pentecostal pastor in Boston, led efforts to persuade religiously devout Americans to vote for Obama. He organized about 200 town hall meetings to provide a forum for evangelicals, mainline Protestants, Catholics, and Jews to discuss the relationship of faith and politics. Meanwhile, many Obama supporters held house parties to enable relatives, friends, and coworkers to dialogue about religion and public policy. In addition, Mara Vanderslice founded the Matthew 25 Network to urge Americans to vote for Obama because, like Jesus, he "cares for the least of these." This Internet network also sponsored commercials on Christian radio stations in hotly contested states.[75] The Democratic National Convention featured an ecumenical prayer service, substantial religious rhetoric, special meetings for religious groups, and a benediction by Joel Hunter.[76]

Obama participated in several faith and values forums (most notably one with other candidates for the Democratic nomination at Messiah College in Pennsylvania and another with John McCain hosted by Rick Warren at his Saddleback Church in California), spoke to numerous religious groups and gatherings, frequently described his faith journey, cited numerous scriptural concepts, and criticized the Republican agenda (especially tax cuts for the rich) as unbiblical. Obama protested that the Religious Right falsely claimed that Democrats disrespected churches and evangelical values and that religious Americans cared only about abortion, gay marriage, school prayer, and intelligent design.[77]

At an African Methodist Episcopal convention, Obama discussed his personal faith and promised to make "faith-based" social service "a moral center of my administration." While working as a community organizer in Chicago, he explained, "I learned that my sins could be redeemed and if I placed my trust in Jesus," "he could set me on a path to eternal life." Submitting to God's will and dedicating himself "to discovering His truth and carrying out His works," Obama added, had fortified his commitment to his work. Obama called for "an active faith, rooted in that most fundamental of all truths: that I am my brother's keeper." If elected, his faith would direct his efforts to combat "war and poverty, joblessness and homelessness, violent streets and crumbling schools," which were primarily "moral problems, rooted in both societal indifference and individual callousness." The nation's policies and laws should embody empathy, justice, and responsibility. Moreover, Obama endorsed the government funding of faith-based initiatives to feed the hungry, rehabilitate prisoners and drug addicts, and provide jobs.[78]

Obama offered a biblical basis for his policies on poverty, healthcare, immigration, and several other issues. He argued that their faith required Christians to help others through local congregations, parachurch ministries, and community organizations. However, the government also had a key role to play in combating such problems as racism, unemployment, illegal immigration, and war. Christians must work to reduce poverty and AIDS around the world and stop the genocide in Darfur. They must "heed the biblical call to care for 'the least of these,'" including America's 37 million poor, by expanding the Earned Income Tax Credit and increasing the minimum wage. The government, Obama insisted, also had a moral obligation to assist the 45 million Americans who did not have health insurance and the millions more who could not afford to pay their premiums. As "children of God," all people possessed "worth and dignity" regardless of where they "came from or what documents they have." Christian compassion necessitated giving the nation's 12 million undocumented immigrants "a chance to earn their citizenship by paying a fine and waiting in line behind all those who came here legally." Obama exhorted Christians to be good stewards of creation and promote "a consistent ethic of life." By bringing their convictions into the public arena and speaking in "universal terms" that everyone could understand, people of faith did "God's work here on Earth."[79]

Some socially liberal evangelicals applauded Obama's policies. Donald Miller, author of *Blue Like Jazz*, claimed that the Republican attempt to restrict abortion had failed. Their concern for aiding the marginalized, oppressed, and poor would prompt Democrats to create "better social conditions" so that fewer women "are put in situations where they feel like they need to have an abortion." Some younger evangelicals voted for Obama because his commitment to "social-justice issues like overcoming racism, combating poverty, and tackling global issues like AIDS . . . trumped abortion." *Sojourners'* editor Jim Wallis supported Obama because he would tackle "issues of injustice" while "articulating the politics of hope and even the possibility of racial unity." Others thought that Obama could heal the wounds that Bush's arrogant, bullying foreign policy caused and help citizens of other nations view Christianity more positively.[80]

Although many religious conservatives appreciated some of Obama's political positions, they deplored several of his other stances, especially on abortion and gay marriage. David O'Steen, the executive director of the National Right to Life Committee, argued that Obama was even more pro-choice than Hillary Clinton. As a member of the Illinois legislature, Obama had voted three times to defeat bills designed to help newborn survivors of abortion remain alive; as a US senator he had voted against a parental notification bill; and he promised that as president he would again legalize "partial-birth" abortion and authorize using tax funds to pay for abortions. In addition, pro-life advocates objected that the Democratic platform did not contain a "conscience clause" to allow healthcare workers to abstain from providing services they deemed unethical. Other evangelicals criticized Obama for opposing California's 2008 ballot referendum to ban gay marriage. Although Obama favored civil unions rather than marriage for gay couples, he contended that "referendums to amend federal and state constitutions" might be used "to undermine other legal protections." Explaining his support for civil unions, Obama insisted that the Christian position should be based on the Sermon on the Mount, not "an obscure line in Romans." Speaking for many evangelicals, Tom Minnery of Focus on the Family accused Obama of giving "lip service to the institution of marriage" but refusing to do anything to "ensure that traditional marriage survives."[81]

The inflammatory statements his pastor Jeremiah Wright made during the campaign also hurt Obama's efforts to win the votes of religious conservatives and eventually forced him to sever his relationship with Trinity Church. After video clips of some of Wright's most provocative sermons were posted online and shown on cable channels in March 2008, Obama criticized Wright's statements as "divisive" and "racially charged," but he refused to disown his pastor. He insisted that Trinity was "a very conventional black church" and argued that nine out of ten of Wright's sermons were not controversial. Its ministries were similar to those of thousands of other congregations across the nation.[82] However, Wright's continued diatribe against the US government, including claims that it had planted AIDS in black communities and incited the 9/11 attacks by its terrorist acts in other nations, prompted the Illinois senator to repudiate Wright's assertions and resign his Trinity membership in late May.[83]

Although the Wright controversy called considerable attention to Obama's church membership and he repeatedly referred to his Christian faith, a June 2008 Pew Research Center survey reported that only 57 percent of Americans correctly identified Obama as Christian, while 12 percent believed he was a Muslim. Moreover, some detractors repeatedly claimed on websites and Christian radio that the Democrat was a Muslim. Obama's staff worked vigorously to dispel this misperception. His campaign website featured the headline, "Obama Has Never Been a Muslim, and Is a Committed Christian."[84]

Obama's most vocal and caustic evangelical critic was Focus on the Family's James Dobson who accused him of "deliberately distorting the traditional understanding of the Bible" to suit "his own confused theology." Dobson lambasted Obama's abortion stance as "a fruitcake interpretation of the Constitution." Obama threatened "traditional family, life, and pro-moral values." In late October, Focus on the Family issued a provocative missive titled "Letter from 2012 in Obama's America" that envisioned the dire political, economic, and religious consequences Obama's policies might bring. The twenty-five developments it described included legalizing same-sex marriages in all fifty states, restricting home schooling, requiring training in gender identity in elementary schools, banning Christian radio stations, openly displaying pornography, and forcing churches to hire gays and perform same-sex weddings or lose their tax-exempt status. In addition, the letter warned, Obama was likely to heavily fund known terrorist allies, strengthen ties to communist nations, and do nothing if US cities were bombed. This could lead to communist revolutions in Latin America and to Russia regaining control over Eastern Europe and launching a nuclear attack against Israel. Equally inflammatory was Internet evangelist Bill Keller's contention that "pastors and churches who support Barack Hussein Obama are a stench in the nostrils of God!"[85]

Although most conservative Catholics did not support Obama because of his pro-choice position on abortion, many prominent Catholic politicians, activists, and theologians endorsed him. Gerald Beyer, a theology professor at St. Joseph's University, insisted that no candidate perfectly mirrored "Catholic teaching on issues such as abortion, war, stem-cell research, poverty, discrimination, gay marriage, and immigration," which made voting "a difficult matter of conscience for Catholics." However, Obama had "consistently opposed the war in Iraq," which many US bishops deemed unjust, and supported "a timely and responsible withdrawal." Moreover, Obama shared "the Catholic vision of a just internationalism guided by the principle of solidarity" and the bishops' belief that Americans "must more aggressively confront the enduring problem of racism." Obama agreed with the bishops that the children of minorities and the poor needed to have better educational opportunities, that racial disparities in the justice system must be eliminated, and that minorities must have better access to credit and housing. Obama's prochoice position contradicted Catholic teaching, Beyer noted, but he promised "to reduce the number of abortions by fostering socioeconomic conditions that favor choosing life and by promoting abstinence as a way of reducing unintended pregnancies," something that George W. Bush had failed to do.[86]

Although many criticized his positions, Obama's efforts to reach out to religious groups paid substantial dividends. Several other factors helped Obama defeat McCain, especially his stances on immigration, fighting poverty, and protecting the environment; the belief of many evangelicals that Bush had ignored or betrayed them and that McCain did not enthusiastically support their agenda; and the state of the economy. Obama had equal or higher levels of support among almost every religious group than John Kerry did in 2004. He received the votes of 43 percent of weekly churchgoers, while Kerry won only 39 percent of this group. Obama captured 54 percent of mainline Protestant votes compared with Kerry's 43 percent (significantly outpacing Democrat candidates generally), many of whom agreed with his progressive stances on social and moral issues and policy priorities.[87]

Obama's effort to win religiously committed voters was also aided by the decline and division of the Religious Right—Christian social conservatives who had strongly influenced American politics for almost three decades— and McCain's reluctance to discuss his personal faith or the religious basis for his policies. Jerry Falwell, who created the Moral Majority in 1979, and D. James Kennedy, the prominent pastor of Coral Ridge Presbyterian Church in Fort Lauderdale, had recently died. Ted Haggard, the president of the National Association of Evangelicals, had resigned from his church in disgrace after stories emerged about repeated encounters with a male prostitute, from whom he also bought methamphetamines. Pat Robertson, the founder of the Christian Broadcasting Network and Regent University, had discredited the Religious Right by his outlandish comments about world leaders. Other leading evangelicals such as Houston megachurch pastor Joel Osteen refused to take sides in the election, and Rick Warren and Bill Hybels commended aspects of Obama's agenda.[88]

Several issues posed challenges for Obama in gaining Jewish votes: his lack of foreign policy experience, especially as compared with McCain; his alleged Muslim background and blatantly Arab name, which some feared would lead him to sympathize more with Arabs nations than with Israel; Jeremiah Wright's harsh attacks on Israel; and the troubled relationship between Jews and blacks in the United States. Some Jews claimed that Obama was a covert Muslim who had sworn his senate oath of office on the Qur'an. Despite these obstacles, other factors helped Obama win 78 percent of the Jewish vote (almost identical to the percentage Clinton, Gore, and Kerry won). Many Jews admired his commitment to public service and social justice evident in his work as a community organizer, Illinois senator, and US senator. His effective rebuttal to attacks on his positions and character also convinced many Jews to continue their loyalty to the Democratic Party. Most Jews preferred Obama's stances on issues over those of McCain, particularly on education, health, the economy, and the war in Iraq as well as his likely choices for the Supreme Court. In addition, Republican vice presidential candidate Sarah Palin's religious background and commitments, which were very attractive to the evangelical wing of the party, repulsed many Jews. Meanwhile, his staff emphasized that many Illinois Jews who knew Obama well strongly supported him. The Democrat met with several hundred Jewish leaders in Cleveland, and an organization named "Rabbis for Obama" was formed to support his candidacy.[89]

Relations with Religious Groups

Following the example of many of his predecessors, the morning of his inauguration, Obama held a private ecumenical worship service at the Washington National Cathedral in which evangelicals, Catholics, Jews, Muslims, Buddhists, and Hindus all participated. T. D. Jakes, pastor of The Potter's House, a 30,000 member, nondenominational church in Dallas, preached a short sermon, and Orlando minister Joel Hunter, a registered Republican, led guests in lay-ing hands on the president-elect and praying that God would bless him and his administration.[90] While other recent presidents enlisted Billy Graham as a spiritual advisor, Obama sought counsel primarily from Hunter, Jakes, Kirbyjon Caldwell, and Jim Wallis.[91] Hunter sent Obama weekly devotionals and often prayed with the president.[92]

In March 2009 Obama named a group of religious leaders to advise the White House. After adding more members in May, this eclectic council of twenty-five included two Jews, a Muslim, a Hindu, a black Pentecostal bishop, and several other prominent Protestants and Catholics, most notably Hunter, Otis Moss, Jr., a retired Baptist pastor who had worked with Martin Luther King, Sr. at Ebenezer Church in Atlanta, and Vashti McKenzie, the first female bishop in the African Methodist Episcopal Church. Council members served one-year renewable terms and advised Obama on how government programs could best work with local community groups to alleviate poverty, reduce the number of abortions, promote responsible fatherhood, and increase interfaith dialogue abroad.[93]

No other president has so effusively praised the work of so many diverse religious communions or hosted such a wide variety of religious groups. "Part of the bedrock strength" of the United States, Obama insisted, "is that it embraces people of many faiths and of no faith." Although the nation "is still predominantly Christian," it had many Jews, Muslims, Hindus, atheists, agnostics, and Buddhist citizens, and each group's "path to grace" must be revered and respected "as much as our own."[94] "God's grace" and Americans' compassion is expressed, Obama asserted, through countless faith-based efforts, including those by evangelicals at World Relief, the American Jewish World Service, mainline Protestants, Catholic Relief Services, African-American churches, the United Sikhs, and Hindus. He contended that one law "binds all great religions together." Christians, Jews, Muslims, Buddhists, Hindus, followers of Confucius, and secular humanists all strove to love and understand one another and to treat others with dignity and respect. Like Christianity, Judaism, Islam, Hinduism, and Sikhism, all issued "a power-ful call to serve our brothers and sisters," to cultivate "a deep and abiding compassion for all, and to treat others as we wish to be treated ourselves."[95] "Our varied beliefs," Obama maintained, "can bring us together to feed the hungry and comfort the afflicted; to make peace where there is strife and rebuild what has broken; [and] to lift up those who have fallen on hard times." Through the White House Office of Faith-Based and Neighborhood Partnerships, he added, his administration promised to promote a productive "dialogue on faith." Although divisions would not "disappear overnight" and "long-held views and conflicts" would not suddenly vanish, if people talked to "one another openly and honestly," old rifts might "start to mend and new partnerships" might emerge.[96]

Like George H. W. Bush, Obama argued that Americans "are one nation under God." "That core tenet of our American experience," the president proclaimed in November 2013, "has guided us" since our founding and would lead us to an even brighter future. His use of this term, however, was more eclectic than Bush's: "We may call that God different names but we remain one nation." Even if adherents of other faiths "don't subscribe to the exact same notions that I do," Obama declared, "they are still good people" who "are fighting alongside us in our battles." Even Obama's Easter messages are inclusive. While "the story of Christ's triumph over death holds special meaning for Christians," he asserted in 2012, everyone could identify with its message of "the triumph of hope over despair" and "faith over doubt." These beliefs helped shape the values and guide the work of "Americans of all faiths and backgrounds." Obama also welcomed the leaders of major religions to the White House. He hosted a dinner to observe the end of the Muslim fast of Ramadan and a Seder to help Jews commemorate Passover. In addition, Obama invited dozens of prominent Christian clergy and laypeople to a breakfast celebrating Easter for four consecutive years.[97]

Although many black clergy disagreed with his stance on gay marriage, Obama's relationship with African-American churches has generally been positive. Like other African Americans, most black Christians were delighted to have a black president and heartily approved of his efforts to increase federal government funding and programming to provide jobs, increase healthcare, and reduce poverty, and Obama met several times with prominent black pastors to discuss these issues.[98] However, some black ministers complained that Obama was not doing enough in these areas. AME Bishop Don DiXon Williams praised the president for accentuating the themes Bread for the World stressed in its 2014 Hunger Report—"investing in good jobs . . . investing in people, strengthening the safety net, and encouraging community partnerships." On the other hand, he urged Obama to take a tougher stance against "further cuts to food stamps or poverty focused development." The National Black Church Initiative, a coalition of 34,000 congregations and 15.7 million African-American churchgoers belonging to fifteen denominations, protested in July 2013 that his administration had done very little for the black community in a variety of areas. They denounced his inactivity and "empty rhetoric" as "morally shameful and reprehensible" and implored him to do more to "eradicate racial disparities in healthcare, technology, education, housing, and the environment."[99]

Many mainline Protestants were delighted by Obama's election. It confirmed the success of the Civil Rights movement, brought into office a Protestant who shared many of their values, and made it likely that they would have greater access to the president and that policies they supported would be adopted.[100] In an open letter to Obama, National Council of Churches (NCC) executives pledged their "unstinting support" to a president-elect who faced immense challenges. The NCC's thirty-five member denominations, the letter declared, "stand ready to work with you" to provide greater justice and better housing, education, and healthcare. For the general secretary of the American Friends Service Committee, Obama's election increased hope for improved diplomatic relationship with Iran and for bringing American troops home from Iraq and Afghanistan. An Evangelical Lutheran Church in America bishop urged Obama to prioritize helping low-income Americans, restoring US credibility abroad, instituting "fair and humane immigration reform," and financing alternative energy research.[101]

White House policymakers regularly met with mainline Protestant leaders to discuss various issues and speechwriters sometimes used suggestions from leading progressive clergy to help craft major addresses. Obama's staff organized a two-hour conference call to discuss how the administration's proposed budget would affect the poor.[102] In April 2009 members of the president's domestic team asked more than 1,000 Christian progressives at the Mobilization to End Poverty in Washington to support the president's campaign to alleviate destitution. Sponsors of the conference included the Oxfam America, ELCA, the American Baptist Churches, and Wesley Theological Seminary.[103] In November 2010, Obama met with twenty NCC leaders to pray and discuss a variety of their concerns, including domestic poverty, Middle East disputes, and incivility in political life. Participants applauded the passage of healthcare reform. They also lauded Obama's efforts to resolve the conflict between Israelis and Palestinians. Katharine Jefferts Schori, presiding bishop of the Episcopal Church, praised the president's work to aid "so many people on the margins."[104] Jim Wallis commended the president for helping working families by extending unemployment benefits, providing various refundable tax credits, and passing a middle-class tax cut.[105]

Christian progressives were disappointed by some of Obama's actions and policies during his first term. However, encouraged by his support of gay marriage and calls for decisive action on climate change, they expressed confidence that the president would "claim the progressive legacy they believe he craves" during his second term. Leaders of the Christian Left argued that his convincing victory freed him to "pursue concrete progressive goals" such as immigration reform and greater government investment in infrastructure, clean energy, and the environment. Wallis protested that Obama was presiding over a huge redistribution of wealth that was producing the greatest "economic inequality in American history." Union Seminary theologian Gary Dorrien complained that Obama had missed his chance to break the power of the nation's large banks and to introduce a "public option for health care." Although bemoaning the "dramatic expansion of the notion of war" during Obama's first term, New York Theological Seminary professor Peter Heltzel pledged to work with the president for justice for the next four years and praised his "renewed push for gun control." "Through global counterterrorism activities and excessive reliance on drones and covert operations," Heltzel lamented, "we have normalized the use of violence and desensitized ourselves to the killing." Former Episcopal bishop Gene Robinson, the denomination's first openly gay bishop, commended Obama for connecting the rights of blacks, women, and gays in his second inaugural address. Dorrien and Robinson both insisted that Obama understood and sympathized with their agenda, but they felt compelled "to keep the president's feet to the fire on the issues they care about."[106]

The directors of many faith-based organizations were pleased that Obama maintained, and in some ways strengthened, the Office of Faith-Based and Neighborhood Partnerships. Under the leadership of Joshua Dubois, it expanded its focus from helping faith-based groups obtain government contracts to trying to motivate religious organizations to provide volunteers. It trained these volunteers in disaster preparedness and response and enlisted more than 1,000 congregations in a Job Clubs program to aid the unemployed.[107] Peg Chemberlin, a former NCC president, claimed in February 2012 that "the federal government's relationship with faith-based groups is stronger than ever."[108] Obama stressed that his administration had expanded faith-based initiatives, worked with Catholic Charities to abet indigent Americans, and partnered with numerous religious organizations to assist suffering people around the world. Moreover, thousands of college students participated in its Interfaith Campus Challenge to promote responsible fatherhood, increase adoption, help individuals find jobs, and serve veterans.[109]

While many conservatives applauded this increased federal aid to faith-based organizations that provided social services, some conservatives and many liberals criticized Obama's policy. Albert Mohler, Jr., president of the Southern Baptist Theological Seminary in Louisville, and some other conservatives warned that religious agencies could become dependent on funds that someday might be removed. Secularists and civil libertarians protested that Obama had not kept his promise to prohibit hiring discrimination or proselytizing by all religious organizations that received federal funds to supply social assistance. Mohler countered that the right of these organizations to hire individuals who shared their religious commitments and to evangelize while dispensing social aid was central to their mission. Stanley Carlson-Thies, who served in Bush's Office of Faith-Based and Community Initiatives, argued that "while the Bush administration tried to learn from successful faith-based poverty fighters," the Obama administration was using the office "to convince independent Christian and Jewish nonprofits to follow the administration's agenda." The approach of the Obama administration, he complained, was "we're the government, doing wonderful things, *you* can come join *us*."[110]

Obama's relationship with evangelicals has been mixed. The president has several evangelical spiritual advisors and has interacted frequently with prominent evangelicals.[111] However, several of his policies and actions have irritated large numbers of evangelicals. Obama met with NAE leaders in October 2011 and discussed international religious freedom, immigration reform, legal questions concerning whether religious organizations could receive federal funds if they hired employees based on religious beliefs, and proposed budget cuts, especially in funding for overseas development. These evangelicals disagreed with Obama positions on gay civil rights and requiring most religious organizations to offer insurance coverage for contraceptives.[112] In March 2013 Obama hosted fourteen influential religious leaders, including the presidents of the NAE, World Relief, and the National Hispanic Christian Leadership Conference, to discuss immigration policy. The president affirmed the importance of respect for "the dignity of individuals and focus on family reunification," principles evangelicals advocated.[113]

Evangelicals were very upset when Louie Giglio, an Atlanta pastor known for his ministry to victims of sex trafficking, was disinvited to give the benediction at Obama's second inaugural ceremony after gay and lesbian groups denounced a sermon he preached in the 1990s disapproving of homosexual acts. Giglio's invitation was rescinded because he did not fit the administration's commitment to "diversity." By this act, argued Mohler, the White House "declared historic, biblical Christianity to be out of bounds." This understanding of "diversity," he warned, would make all Protestant pastors who espoused traditional biblical orthodoxy, Roman Catholic prelates or priests, Orthodox Jewish rabbis, Muslim imams, and Mormon clergy unwelcome at the inaugural ceremony. Catholic ethicist Robert George of Princeton University and Southern Baptist theologian Russell Moore complained that this decision would lead "those who see marriage as a conjugal relationship—the union of husband and wife—and believe sexual conduct outside the marital bond" to be immoral to "be viewed as bigots, the equivalent of racists." Moral traditionalists were also disturbed that three of the pastors invited to speak at the

National Cathedral interfaith service the Obamas attended the day after his second inauguration were strong LGBT advocates.[114]

Religious conservatives were especially disappointed with Obama's handling of four issues—abortion, stem-cell research, relations with the Muslim world, and healthcare. In *The Audacity of Hope* Obama confessed that his support for abortion rights might not square with biblical teaching: "Jesus' call to love one another might demand a different conclusion"; in the future, "I may be seen as someone who was on the wrong side of history." Despite this possibility, Obama continued to strongly support the pro-choice position. Some religious conservatives accused Obama of failing to keep his promise to try to reduce the number of abortions. They also objected to his providing federal funding for both abortions and embryonic stem-cell research, which contradicted "the moral convictions of millions of ordinary Americans." Religious conservatives protested when Obama reversed a US policy that prohibited tax dollars from being used to fund abortion providers overseas, modified the Bush "conscience clause" that protected medical workers who refused to perform procedures that violated their religious convictions, and eliminated federal funding for abstinence-based sex education programs. Many Catholics and evangelicals also complained that Obama's healthcare plan required insurance plans to pay for all elective abortions.[115]

Obama's stance on abortion caused considerable controversy when the University of Notre Dame invited him to give its commencement address in May 2009. Many Catholics protested that Obama was unfit to speak because his position contradicted traditional Catholic teaching. By this action, philosophy professor Ralph McInerny protested, Notre Dame declared that the Catholic Church's teaching on abortion could be ignored and "forfeited its right to call itself a Catholic university." Upset that Obama's policies showed that he did not "hold human life as sacred," John D'Arcy, the Catholic bishop of the diocese that includes Notre Dame, declined to attend commencement. About 350,000 people signed an online petition posted by the Cardinal Newman Society—a group that sought to strengthen the ideals of the nation's 224 Catholic colleges and universities—urging Notre Dame to rescind its invitation. Labeling Obama's actions the "most anti-life" "of any American president," the petition asserted that his expanding of "federal funding for abortions" and for "research on stem cells from human embryos" clashed with traditional Catholic values. In addition, more than fifty bishops declared their opposition to Notre Dame's awarding Obama an honorary degree. They argued that Catholic institutions must not honor "those who act in defiance of our fundamental moral principles."

Notre Dame's president countered that the university's decision to invite Obama "should not be taken as condoning or endorsing his positions" on "abortion and embryonic stem cell research."[116]

The editors of *Commonweal*, a liberal Catholic journal, protested that Notre Dame's invitation to Obama had been wrongly "damned as a symptom of the school's craven desire for recognition and prestige, its slavish obedience to 'elite' liberal opinion, and its perverse determination to betray its Catholic identity." They maintained that "honorary degrees signify an institution's admiration for the accomplishments of the recipient. They do not signify blanket moral approbation." They added that the Catholic Church was much broader than the pro-life movement and argued that the church's interaction with the nation's political system must not be "held hostage to the demands of the most confrontational elements of that movement." If it did, "the church's social message, including its message about abortion," would "be marginalized and ineffectual." Notre Dame's invitation to the president was best understood as an illustration of "the willingness of Americans to live together peacefully, despite profound disagreement."[117]

In March 2011, the Obama administration rescinded facets of Bush's executive order that had made it easier for physicians and nurses to refuse to perform procedures they deemed morally objectionable, especially those dealing with contraception and abortion. Although these changes did not completely eliminate the previous protections, conservatives complained that they gave the Department of Health and Human Services (HHS) total discretion over the "enforcement of conscience protections." The new regulations stipulated that patients' rights trumped medical providers' protections of conscience. As a result, medical caregivers might be censured "for refusing either to refer patients to abortion providers" or to mention abortion as an option while counseling clients. The Christian Medical Association protested that since Obama had taken office, many physicians had been compelled to direct their patients to abortion suppliers and numerous medical students had jeopardized their future by declining to participate in abortion training. Moreover, these regulations might cause pro-life doctors to leave the profession and pro-life students to avoid practicing certain types of medicine.[118]

Both conservatives and liberals criticized Obama's decision to fund research on stem cell lines created from surplus embryos at fertility clinics but not on lines created in laboratories to study specific diseases. Conservatives argued that research should be limited to adult stem cells, while liberals protested that Obama's policy inhibited potentially promising research. Defending his decision, Obama declared, "As a person of faith, I believe we are called to care for each other and work to ease human suffering." God gave people the ability "to pursue this research and the humanity and conscience to do so responsibly."[119]

Religious conservatives also disliked Obama's approach to relations with the Muslim world. During the 2008 presidential campaign, the Democrat insisted that because he had lived in Indonesia, "the most populous Muslim country in the world," and had Muslim relatives, he could relate well with the world's Islamic community and challenge "Muslim countries to reconcile themselves to modernity." Many Muslims around the globe responded positively to Obama's speech in Cairo in June 2009. AlArabiya.net reported that "Egypt's officials saw in Obama's overtures to Islam and his usage of the Koran a sign of sincere respect and understanding of their religion while Muslim Brotherhood members said the speech highlighted values at the core of Islam's message." However, Joseph Loconte protested, the president had failed in his inaugural address, an interview on Al Arabiya television, and a speech to the Turkish parliament to point out "that Islamic societies are struggling with vast injustices and pathologies." Other religious conservatives, including American Values president Gary Bauer, criticized Obama for not discussing Muslims' persecution of Christians during his trip to the Middle East. The president praised Saudi Arabia for promoting "interfaith dialogue," Bauer complained, even though it was on the State Department's list of nations that severely violated religious freedom.[120]

In August 2011, HHS proposed that "all insurance plans, except those offered by churches or seminaries, cover the entire cost of prescription birth control pills, including abortion drugs . . . with no co-pays." HHS defined a religious organization as an entity that "primarily serves persons who share its religious tenets" and exists to inculcate its "religious values." If the Obama administration followed through, *World* magazine editor Marvin Olasky warned, thousands of religious hospitals, crisis pregnancy centers, and relief agencies that serve a variety of clients, not primarily their own members, would not be considered religious organizations and would be forced to follow these regulations. The U.S. Conference of Catholic Bishops complained that the proposed regulation "ignores the underlying principle of Catholic charitable actions: we help people because we are Catholic, not because our clients are." Some Catholics threatened to vote against Obama in 2012 if his administration did not back down. "Anyone who fails to grasp the constitutional issue" this regulation involved, Michael Sean Winter declared in the *National Catholic Reporter*, "probably should not be entrusted with the post of Chief Magistrate."[121]

On January 20, 2012, HHS did announce that all health plans must provide coverage at no cost for all contraceptives approved by the Food and Drug

Administration as part of preventive health services for women. Many leading Catholics and evangelicals criticized both the requirement that employers cover certain contraceptives such as Plan B ("the morning-after pill") and "the narrow religious exemption of churches." Prison Fellowship founder Chuck Colson and theologian Timothy George called this policy "an egregious, dangerous violation of religious liberty." They argued that neither Catholic hospitals, universities, and charitable organizations nor Protestant parachurch ministries could afford to pay fines ($2,000 per employee) for refusing to purchase insurance that violated their principles. They urged Christians to pray, contact their Congressmen, and sign a petition demanding that all religious employers be exempted from this "onerous mandate." Former Bush speechwriter Michael Gerson and others protested that the Obama administration claimed to have "the right to decide which religious institutions are religious and which are not." Its contention that church-sponsored hospitals, charities, and colleges should not be considered distinctly religious because they employed and served people of different faiths was a faulty, "highly privatized view of religious faith." The gospel, "which promises healing and hope to all people," required Christians to serve non-Christians.[122]

In early February 2012, the administration announced that the cost of paying for contraceptives for employees would be shifted from religiously affiliated charities and universities to health insurance companies. While the Catholic Health Association accepted this compromise, Catholic bishops still demanded that the mandate be rescinded.[123] More than 500 college professors, religious leaders of diverse faiths, and healthcare professionals sent Congress an open letter in mid-February denouncing this policy as "a grave violation of religious freedom." "This so-called 'accommodation' changes nothing of moral substance and fails to remove the assault on religious liberty and the rights of conscience." The New York Times commended Obama for refusing to yield to the "phony crisis over 'religious liberty'" orchestrated by the political Right and for strongly endorsing "an essential principle—free access to birth control for any woman." Its editors did fault the president for exempting "churches and their religious employees from the preventative care mandate" and argued that Catholic hospitals and universities, which employed thousands of non-Catholics, should not also be granted an exemption. On March 1, the Senate narrowly defeated the Blunt Amendment, which would have allowed "employers to refuse to include contraception in health care coverage if it violated their religious or moral beliefs."[124]

In June 2012, a coalition of almost 150 religious leaders, led by evangelicals, including Stanley Carlson-Thies, Samuel Rodriguez, David Neff, Ronald Sider, and Leith Anderson, president of the NAE, petitioned the Obama administration to exempt all religious organizations from its mandate that healthcare insurers provide free contraception coverage. The HHS definition created a "two-class system" of religious groups: churches, which qualified for an exemption, and "faith-based service organizations," which might or might not qualify. "Both worship-oriented and service-oriented religious organizations are authentically and equally religious organizations," these leaders argued. The federal government did not have the ability or authority to define "what constitutes true religion and authentic ministry." The heads of numerous Catholic groups and many priests also signed the letter. Dozens of religious organizations, primarily colleges, soon filed lawsuits to try to stop this mandate.[125]

On the other hand, some liberal Catholics censured the campaign of Catholic bishops to rescind the HHS mandate. Driven by their concerns about religious liberty, desire to regain influence after the church's sex abuse scandals, and anti-Obama prejudice, the bishops, Margaret O'Brien Steinfels argued, were "seemingly oblivious to the damage they are doing to their already diminished authority, as well as to their credibility on matters that need a vigorous and rational voice: immigration, unemployment, poverty, [and] the threat of war with Iran." Moreover, on the issues the bishops most cared about— "the legal right to contraception, abortion, and same-sex marriage"—they had "already lost the cultural argument, even with many Catholics."[126]

Some religious conservatives also criticized Obama's theology, lack of respect for the Bible, and attempt to remove religion from the public square. Ken Blackwell averred that Obama, who had belonged to the liberal United Church of Christ denomination (whose initials and doctrines led some to dub it "Unitarians considering Christ"), seemed to "believe in a Christless Christianity." Others protested that Obama considered "the Bible flawed and in need of modern revision," "unlike the Koran, which he has lavishly praised as a holy book." The Democrat allegedly "mocked passages from the Old Testament." Throughout his first term, Phyllis Schafly complained, Obama "waged a persistent campaign to secularize America," confine "religion behind church doors," and exclude religion from all public places, military facilities, and schools.[127]

Liberal Catholics, by contrast, applauded the president's approach to the economy, efforts to help the poor, and the Affordable Health Care Act, although they complained he did not sufficiently explain it to the American people.[128] They were also disappointed with aspects of Obama's approach to immigration problems, especially his deportation of "undocumented immigrants in record-breaking numbers" and his continuation of the war in Afghanistan.[129]

Obama maintained positive relations with Jews principally because of his progressive policies and appointment of many of them to key positions in his administration. Rahm Emanuel served as White House Chief of Staff from January 2009 until October 2010. David Axelrod was a Senior Advisor to the President. Lawrence Summers served as Director of the White House's National Economic Council and Ben Bernanke as chairman of the Federal Reserve Board. Obama named several Jews, most notably Richard Holbrooke, to important foreign policy positions in the Middle East and the State Department. Finally, the president selected Elena Kagan to be Solicitor General and then nominated her for the Supreme Court in 2010.[130]

The Election of 2012

The extensive media focus on the religious convictions of the candidates for the Republican nomination, concerns about the government's contraceptive mandate, and debates over the best way to address economic problems gave religion a prominent role in the 2012 presidential election.[131] Almost all the Republican hopefuls—evangelicals Texas Governor Rick Perry and Minnesota Congresswoman Michelle Bachman, Catholics Newt Gingrich and Rick Santorum, Texas Congressman Ron Paul, and the eventual nominee Mormon Mitt Romney—had strong faith commitments.[132] Unlike in 2008, the Obama campaign made little appeal to evangelicals. The president recognized that his Affordable Health Care Act, positions on abortion and same-sex marriage, and contraceptive mandate had upset many evangelicals, conservative Catholics, and other religious traditionalists, but he believed he could win without their votes.[133] Other major religious issues in the 2012 campaign were whether sizable numbers of evangelicals would support Romney, "Pulpit Freedom Sunday" (when pastors of almost 1,500 congregations challenged the IRS regulation that endorsing or opposing political candidates could cost them their tax-exempt status), and blatant Republican assaults on Obama's faith.[134] Although religious factors were "potentially explosive," in the final analysis, Romney's Mormonism did not matter as much as many pundits predicted and questions about Obama's faith were relevant "only to his most obdurate detractors."[135]

During the Republican primaries, Gingrich argued that Obama's policies were more "anti-religious" than those of any other president, while Romney accused him of implementing "a secular agenda" the "founders would not recognize." Santorum warned that if Obama were reelected, the federal government would dictate how Americans practiced their faith.[136] Obama, Santorum contended, was "leading the anti-Christian forces of what Pope Benedict XVI has called 'radical secularism.'"[137] Other conservatives protested that Obama "talks like a Christian while his actions scream secular-socialist." "His policies," they avowed, "are decidedly un-Christian."[138] Because Obama "is hostile and disdainful toward Christianity," Tony Perkins, president of the Christian Family Research Council, argued, Christians who voted for him in 2008 should repent and support Romney in 2012.[139]

These attacks prompted the release of a statement in February 2012 by fourteen Christian, Muslim, Jewish, Hindu, and Sikh organizations urging candidates to explain their religious conviction to voters but to avoid "deliberately encouraging division in the electorate along religious lines" or between religious and nonreligious Americans. The president of the Interfaith Alliance complained that some candidates seemed "to be running for 'pastor-in-chief'" and insisted that they crossed the line when they implied that people should vote for them "because of their faith."[140] Meanwhile, a large group of Christian leaders and pastors across the theological spectrum denounced Santorum's contention that Obama's theology was not "based on the Bible," the allegation that the president was a Muslim, and claims that he was waging "war on religion" as "cynical attempts to use faith as a weapon of political division" that hurt the country and harmed Christian witness. They exhorted politicians and the media "to stop using faith as a weapon to advance partisan politics and self-interest."[141]

Despite such admonitions, the 2012 campaign was one of the nastiest in American history. Its acrimony prompted Rick Warren to cancel a civil forum with Obama and Romney in August. Warren argued that a one-night respite from the campaign's "irresponsible personal attacks, mean-spirited slander, and flat-out dishonest attack ads" would be hypocritical. "The man who ran on hope four years ago," bemoaned *New York Times* columnist David Brooks, "is now running one of the most negative campaigns in history, aimed at disqualifying his opponent." Numerous conservatives objected that Obama ads assailed Romney's character and "even his basic humanity," while Democrats censured Romney's references to Obama as "a liar and a failed leader." On the other hand, Obama did praise Romney in a *Time* interview for taking "his faith very seriously." "As somebody who takes my Christian faith seriously," Obama added, "I appreciate that he seems to walk the walk and not just be talking the talk when it comes to his participation in his church."[142]

In August Obama and Romney responded to nine questions about their faith in *Cathedral Age*, the magazine of the Washington National Cathedral. Obama insisted that he could do little to counter claims that his faith was insincere. His job as president, he argued, did not include "convincing folks that my faith in Jesus is legitimate and real." Both candidates testified that their faith was central to their lives. "My Christian faith," Obama declared, "gives me a perspective and security . . . that I am loved" and that "God is in control." "Faith is integral to my life," Romney stated. "I have served as a lay pastor in my church. I faithfully follow its precepts." Obama praised the contributions Christianity had made to the suffrage, abolition, and civil rights movements and contended that faith supplied a "moral framework and vocabulary" that enabled Americans to deal with crises.[143]

Although disappointed with some of Obama's policies, most liberal Catholics backed the president. An Obama victory, economist Jeff Madrick argued, would best ensure that America cared for the poor, expanded middle-class opportunities, maintained its commitment to minority rights, and continued "its global responsibility" to model "values of fairness and good sense." *Commonweal* supported Obama's reelection because he believed that the federal government had a limited but indispensable role in "regulating commerce and the financial industry, protecting the environment, funding education, providing health-care coverage, and maintaining a safety net for the elderly and those who cannot provide for themselves." Pundit Jim Arkedis advised the Obama campaign that the best way to win Catholic swing voters was to emphasize social justice and economic solidarity and avoid driving "a wedge between the faithful and official church positions" on culture-war issues.[144]

Failing to heed this advice, the Obama administration's contraceptive mandate made the Catholic Church and its universities, schools, hospitals, and charities a significant election issue. By promising that insurers, rather than religious institutions, would be responsible for paying for the controversial procedures and products, the Obama administration satisfied some Catholic critics, but most bishops judged this modification to be "an accounting fiction," which did not change the substance of the policy.[145] Michael Gerson predicted that Obama's contraceptive mandate would cause him to lose his principal "political appeal to religious voters" of the 2008 election (which was "his support for faith-based social service providers"), "unite economic and social conservatives in outrage against government activism," and "energize religious conservatives in a way Mitt Romney could never manage."[146]

Both parties sought to influence Latino Catholic voters. Republicans aired a series of web videos featuring suave Mexican actor Eduardo Verástegui who starred in the 2006 pro-life film *Bella*. "Our values today are under attack by President Barack Obama," Verástegui claimed. "He is working hard to promote unlimited abortion and undermine traditional marriage" and "has unleashed an unprecedented attack on the church and its freedom." The video quickly cut to the Virgin Mary with a tear running down her cheek. Meanwhile, Obama dedicated a monument to César Chávez and quoted a prayer the activist wrote for farm workers: "Help us to love even those who hate, so we can change the world."[147]

In May Obama further antagonized religious traditionalists by announcing that he had decided that gay marriage was "consistent with his Christian beliefs." Christ's sacrifice "on our behalf" and "the Golden Rule" convinced him that gays and lesbians should have full civil rights, including marriage.[148] The reaction of religious leaders to Obama's statement was mixed. Some protested that the government was trying to force them "to accept a definition of marriage" that violated their convictions. If Obama had called him, Joel Hunter said, he would have tried to dissuade him from endorsing gay marriage because of his understanding of Scripture. Obama's stance would make it more difficult for him to vote for his friend for president. *Sojourners*, by contrast, backed Obama, stating that it supported "full legal rights for all people."[149]

Obama's endorsement of gay marriage provoked a variety of reactions among black clergy. The Sunday after Obama's announcement, many African-American ministers said nothing, while a few blasted both the president and his decision. Some pastors criticized Obama's position, while speaking favorably about him. Still others supported Obama's decision and tried to explain his change of heart. The 1,300-member Coalition of African American Pastors, many of whom were part of the nation's fifth largest denomination, the Church of God in Christ, claimed that "by embracing gay marriage," the president was "leading the country down an immoral path" and encouraged all black Christians to withhold support from him "until he corrects course." Harry Jackson, Jr., the senior pastor of the 3,000-member Hope Christian Church in Baltimore, argued that the president's position on gay marriage put black Christians in an adulterous relationship with him and forced them to choose between being black or godly. Jamal Bryant, the pastor of Baltimore Empowerment Temple, "absolutely, vehemently" disagreed with the president, but he insisted that he would still vote for Obama because he liked his other policies. African Americans were mature enough not to reject Obama because of a single issue, but the president must worship soon in black churches, clap his hands, and sing "Amazing Grace" to help motivate blacks to vote. Several ministers hosted a forum in Melbourne, Florida, to address concerns about Obama's gay marriage announcement at which they tried to reassure congregants that the president, despite being misguided on this issue, "demonstrated Christian values in his personal life and policy decisions." Bishop Timothy Clarke, pastor of the First Church of God, a large African-American congregation in Columbus, Ohio, declared, "I believe . . . the president made . . . his decision . . . in good faith . . . after much thought" and prayer.[150]

The president called eight prominent black pastors to explain his stance and solicit their aid. While several stated that Obama's position "might make it difficult for them to support his re-election," others promised to "work aggressively" for his campaign. Two dozen prominent black pastors in the Norfolk area discussed how to inspire their congregants to vote who were upset by Obama's endorsement of same-sex marriage. One minister maintained that "our president has declared Jesus Christ to be his Lord and savior, while his opponent denies the deity of Christ." These clergy produced a voter-education guide to distribute in churches and community centers that compared "Biblical Christianity" to Mormonism and pointed out that individuals of "African ancestry were not granted full access to Mormon priesthood and privilege until 1978." However, many other black pastors argued that attacking a candidate's religion was inappropriate, and Obama campaign officials declared that Romney's faith was "off limits." Obama's staff was confident that blacks would vote for the president because of his "historic health-care reform, investments in education," and "progress in getting people back to work."[151] Otis Moss, III and Charles Jenkins, a Grammy-winning song writer and head of the Fellowship Missionary Baptist Church in Chicago, urged black Christians and congregations to campaign for Obama. They praised the president's "clear vision" and "bold leadership." His administration had adopted economic policies that made the nation "less vulnerable to future economic catastrophes" and had produced "30 consecutive months of private sector job growth." Obama had also kept his promise on the critical healthcare issue. They claimed that Obama's opponents were exploiting the gay marriage issue "to distract us from the vision and accomplishments of this great President" who will continue to "guide our nation toward prosperity, opportunity and justice for all."[152] Although some African Americans, like many white evangelicals and Catholics, deplored Obama's support of abortion and same-sex marriage and alleged assault on religious liberties, 95 percent of black Protestants voted for him.[153]

Some religious leaders who backed Obama in 2008 complained that "through neglect and lack of focus," Democrats had "squandered the substantial gains they made with religious moderates" and worried that it might hurt the president's reelection. After the 2008 campaign, the Democratic National Committee reduced its faith outreach staff from six to one. Although its director, Derrick Harkins, the pastor of Nineteenth Street Baptist Church in Washington, claimed in June 2012 that the party still had strong relationships with numerous religious groups, many analysts insisted that Democrats had done little to explain the religious foundation for their policies.[154] That month the White House named Michael Wear, age 24, as head of the campaign's outreach to religious groups. Journalist Amy Sullivan noted that Wear had worked in the Office of Faith-Based and Neighborhood Partnerships, but argued that Republicans would have put somebody with "years of experience and a big Rolodex in that position," which "tells you something about how Democrats still view faith outreach and its importance." Unlike in 2008, Democrats did not mention "God" in their 2012 platform, while Republicans referred to God ten times in theirs.[155] However, Obama did devise a "faith platform" that listed his chief concerns as "economic recovery," "tax fairness," and "Wall Street reform." The platform stressed that the president believed that all people were connected; as Paul argued in 1 Corinthians, "If one part suffers, every part suffers with it." This led Obama to fight to provide "basic economic security for everyone who is willing and able to work," retirement security, and affordable healthcare. His campaign launched People of Faith for Obama in mid-September, which featured a video in which the president argued that major decisions in his first term, most notably his bailout of car companies and reform of the healthcare system, were motivated by moral concerns.[156] Some liberal clergy applauded Obama's support for same-sex marriage and sponsored ads praising Obama's plan to ensure that the poor received healthcare. Meanwhile, the "Nuns on the Bus" drove through the Midwest warning that Republican vice-presidential nominee Paul Ryan's proposed budget would greatly reduce "the social safety net."[157]

CNN journalist John Blake claimed that "when Obama invoked Jesus to support same-sex marriage" and "framed health care as a moral imperative to care for 'the least of these,'" he was echoing the Social Gospel movement of the late nineteenth and early twentieth century. Obama, Blake argued, effectively combined the activism of Social Gospelers who criticized churches for focusing on personal salvation and ignoring the conditions that produced poverty with "the emotional fire of the African-American church" and "the ecumenical outlook of contemporary Protestantism."[158]

Others contended that Obama's political priorities accorded much more with Scripture than those of his Republican adversaries. The Bible, political consultant Mike Lux asserted, accentuated "helping the poor, showing mercy to the weak, refraining from judging, treating others as you would treat yourself, calling on the wealthy to give their money to the poor," and other progressive values. Jesus discussed mercy in 24 verses, instructed people not to judge in 34 verses, exhorted individuals to love and forgive others in 53 verses and to treat others as they want to be treated in 19 verses, and "to help the poor and/ or spurn riches" in 128 verses. In these 258 verses "Rick Santorum's savior and George W. Bush's favorite philosopher sounds like a tried and true" "lefty liberal."[159]

Conservatives countered that Obama displayed "extraordinary disregard for society's most innocent and vulnerable members (babies in the womb)" and misinterpreted the Bible to justify a "radical redefinition of marriage."[160] They also argued that the president incorrectly cited the Bible to defend taking money from hard-working Americans and give it to the indolent. Scripture, they claimed, called for individual charitable acts, not using taxes to redistribute money from the prosperous to the poor.[161] Numerous religious conservatives accused Obama of subverting or at least not adequately defending religious freedom. Franklin Graham complained that Obama expressed too little "outrage over the plight of persecuted Christians," while Santorum called the president "particularly weak" on religious liberty. By forcing religiously affiliated institutions to offer health insurance to their employees that included abortion drugs, sterilization, and contraceptives, supporting various judicial decisions that limited the role of religious expression in the public square, and forbidding military practices that promoted religion, conservatives charged, the Obama administration had joined the ACLU and atheists in waging war on religion.[162]

The president's defenders protested that many religious conservatives defined religious freedom as the right "to impose one's own religious values on others." By charging Obama with undermining religious freedom, conservatives attempted to make American politics into "a Manichean battleground between two worldviews—red-blooded Christian America" and secularists.[163] Moreover, some conservatives praised Obama for allowing faith-based organizations that received federal funding for social services to hire only individuals who shared their faith, defending churches against municipal governments, and intervening in cases where prisoners were denied religious literature. "In word and in deed," Judd Birdsall added, "the Obama administration has demonstrated its commitment to promoting religious freedom." The president insisted that religious freedom is a "critical foundation of our Nation's liberty" and "a key to a stable, prosperous, and peaceful" world.[164]

Some conservative analysts argued that Romney could not win the vote of the faith community by simply highlighting his opposition to abortion and gay marriage. Republicans must also furnish "specific free-market solutions" for the environmental, healthcare, and poverty problems facing America, advocate aid for Africa, and combat human trafficking.[165] Led by Ralph Reed, the Faith and Freedom Coalition distributed 30 million voter guides in 117,000 churches, sent 24 million mailings to voters in battleground states, and made 26 million phone calls to promote Romney's campaign. Recognizing the importance of economic issues, the guide focused more on tax cuts and a balanced-budget amendment than on abortion and same-sex marriage.[166]

Obama lost votes because of his policies on abortion, same-sex marriage, and the HHS contraceptive mandate, his failure to deliver on his 2008 campaign promise that he could persuade Republicans and Democrats to work together to further the common good, and his inability to satisfy the very high expectations for his presidency his "Yes, We Can" campaign slogan created. Nevertheless, he decisively won the 2012 election.[167] Some commentators predicted that "Romney's Mormon faith would drive away evangelicals, many of whom consider his church a heretical cult."[168] However, encouraged by Billy Graham's unanticipated endorsement of Romney and upset by many of Obama's policies, 79 percent of the 22 percent of Americans who were white, self-described evangelicals voted for Romney.[169] This election, political analyst Robert Jones asserted, was the last one "where a white Christian strategy" was feasible. Obama received less than 40 percent of the votes of white Christians, but he still prevailed because of his overwhelming support from African Americans, Latinos, and religiously unaffiliated whites.[170]

Religious conservatives offered numerous explanations for Obama's victory: many Americans saw Democrats "as the 'caring' party" and the GOP as displaying little compassion for widows, children, or immigrants; Republicans were considered the party of "militarism, capitalism, [and] environmental destruction"; they were allegedly opposed to science, women, and "anything reasonable,"; Republicans made numerous nonsensical claims, including that Obama was a Muslim; and many evangelicals did not actively campaign for Romney because of his Mormonism.[171]

Al Mohler called the election a "catastrophe" for evangelicals. The reason social conservatives lost was especially disastrous. "An increasingly secularized America understands our positions"—that abortion and same-sex marriage are wrong—Mohler lamented, "and has rejected them." For Jim Wallis, the election was a debacle only for evangelicals who "had again tied their faith to the partisan political agenda of the Republican Party." This "conservative ideological agenda," he argued, harmed the poor, hindered immigration reform, "promoted endless wars, and neglected the environment."[172] The election outcome, especially Obama's winning of the Catholic vote 50 to 48 percent, was also painful for many Catholic bishops who loudly criticized numerous Obama policies.[173] Obama captured three-fourths of the Latino Catholic vote (many Latino Catholics favored Obama's use of government resources to aid the poor), which compensated for Romney capturing the white Catholic vote.[174]

Philosophy of Government

Numerous analysts argue that Obama is a philosophical pragmatist who has been strongly influenced by Reinhold Niebuhr, which the president himself also noted. Theologian Gary Dorrien contends that the Democrat "is pragmatic, nonideological," "and imbued with a Niebuhrian blend of idealism and realism." He seeks to combine "liberal internationalism and realism" because working with other nations best promotes America's interests. Like Niebuhr, Obama praises "the American experiment" while critiquing "American presumption." Historian James Kloppenberg insists that Obama is a philosopher president and a true intellectual, a rare breed among American chief executives. He believes in experimentation and assembling support "gradually, through compromise and painstaking consensus building" to achieve fruitful results. Kloppenberg, David Brooks, R. Ward Holder, Peter Josephson, and many others explain how Niebuhr's Christian realism has shaped Obama's worldview.[175] Kloppenberg also argues that Obama has been deeply affected by an American political theory known variously as civic republicanism, communitarianism, and deliberative democracy that emphasizes a "common good, emerging through the process of lively debates between champions of competing points of view."

Holder and Josephson argue that Obama's approach to politics, especially his economic, healthcare and foreign policies, is largely guided by Niebuhr's Christian realism. This has led Obama to insist that "the national interest is a necessary but not sufficient guide for policy" and to view America's purpose in the context of world history and God's providential direction of all events, as difficult as this is to discern. However, they also contend that Obama ignores Niebuhr's criticism of the social sciences and places tremendous faith in the solutions they supply for political problems. Social scientists and behavioral economists direct much of his administration's policy-making and have also tried to control decision-making in the private sector by expanding the federal government's regulatory power.[176]

"By conviction and temperament," *Christian Century* editorialized, Obama "seeks the middle ground. Though many of his opponents see him as a wild radical, intent on expanding the reach of government at all costs," his actions reveal instead that he is "a pragmatist interested in striking a bargain." Obama assumed that policy is best "made by getting smart people of good will in the same room and hammering out the best possible agreement." However, "as Niebuhr should have taught him, politics is not primarily about the exercise of intelligence and good will. It is about the exercise of power and self-interest." Obama needed "to take Niebuhrian realism from theory into practice" and use "the levers of power and mutual self-interest to get things done."[177]

Like other progressive Democrats, Obama favors an activist government. He agreed with Abraham Lincoln that individuals should "do what they do best for themselves," while government should do things it can do better than people can, including rebuilding the nation's infrastructure, helping create jobs, improving education, creating clean energy, and providing quality healthcare for all Americans.[178] Obama insisted that government cannot solve every problem. Hard-working individuals, "a rich and generous sense of community," and "parents taking responsibility for their kids" helped make America strong. To combat social ills, religious leaders must "mobilize their congregations to rebuild neighborhoods block by block" and civic organizations must help train the unemployed to prepare them for the jobs of the future. In addition, companies must provide "decent wages and salaries and benefits for their workers" and aid those who are down on their luck.[179]

Public Policy

Although a global recession, an uncooperative Republican opposition that controlled the House of Representatives, Arab Spring, renewed insurgency in Iraq and Afghanistan, upheaval in Egypt, and efforts to overthrow the Syrian government have inhibited his efforts, Obama has done little to unite or inspire Americans and has achieved few significant legislative successes except for the passage of the Affordable Health Care Act. In some ways, he has seemed aloof and indecisive. While often employing religious rhetoric to support his broad progressive agenda, Obama has rarely used biblical precepts to help justify specific policies including healthcare.

At the 2010 National Prayer Breakfast, Obama explained "the ways my faith informs who I am—as a President, and as a person." Crises like the earthquake in Haiti, he declared, reminded people "that life's most sacred responsibility," which "all of the world's great religions" affirm, is to help those in need. Unfortunately, Americans often ignored "the slow-moving tragedies" of hunger, homelessness, and "families without health care." Preoccupied by "abstract arguments," "ideological disputes," and "contests for power," many ignored "God's voice."[180]

Two years later, Obama asserted that faith played "an enormous role in motivating" Americans to aid the needy, solve "our most urgent problems," and keep "us going when we suffer setbacks." Obama's faith compelled him to ensure that America's financial institutions played "by the same rules as folks on Main Street," that insurance companies did not discriminate against the sick, and that "unscrupulous lenders" did not exploit the vulnerable. "God's command to 'love thy neighbor as thyself'" motivated him to improve the economy. Helping the indigent, he averred, "coincides with Jesus's teaching that 'for unto whom much is given, much shall be required.' It mirrors the Islamic belief that those who've been blessed have an obligation to use those blessings to help others" and "the Jewish doctrine of moderation and consideration for others." By dispensing foreign aid and striving to reduce human trafficking and prevent atrocities in strife-ridden nations, Obama sought to strengthen the nation's alliances, promote democratic values, and make Americans "safer and more secure." These actions were also motivated by the biblical command to care "for those at the margins of our society." Although Americans often earnestly disagreed about the best way to implement these scriptural directives, Obama avowed, they should strive to embody them in their policies. As C. S. Lewis argued, Christianity did not "have a detailed political program. It is meant for all men at all times, and the particular program which suited one place or time would not suit another." Therefore, Obama reasoned, no administration or party should declare its policies to be biblical. Because God alone is infallible, people of goodwill should promote their values and pursue "the common good" while respecting each other.[181]

Obama also insisted that his faith inspired him to put more people to work, preserve the "extraordinary planet" God created, and lessen the possibility of war. Loving spouses, supportive parents, good neighbors, and caring colleagues helped "bring His kingdom to Earth." "The Bible teaches us," Obama emphasized, to "be doers of the word and not merely hearers." "John tells us that, 'If anyone has material possessions and sees his brother in need but has no pity on him, how can the love of God be in him?'"[182]

Obama applauded the quest of Christians "to fix our broken immigration system," "protect our planet," and promote "responsible fatherhood and healthy marriage." Until God made everything as "it should be," he argued, Christians must express His justice, mercy, and compassion for "the most vulnerable." When his endeavors to strengthen the economy, reduce foreclosures, or improve healthcare seemed "profoundly inadequate," Obama declared, the "biblical injunction to serve the least of these" kept him going. Political officials, he averred, must seek to create a caring, just society. Americans' values and benevolence must be embodied not just in their families, workplaces, and houses of worship but also in their government. His administration was working through the Office of Faith-Based and Neighborhood Partnerships with religious nonprofits to feed hungry children, help parents nurture their children, and "improve the lives of people around the world." Guided by the biblical concepts of partnership and justice and Scripture's imperatives to aid the destitute, his administration strove to expand efforts to care "for the least of these."[183] Obama claimed that his attempt to help working-class and poor Americans by extending unemployment insurance, improving education, increasing the child tax credit, Pell grants for college students, and the earned-income tax credit, and doubling the funding for LIHEAP (a home heating assistance program) was motivated by his belief that "I am my brother's keeper." In his second inaugural address, Obama deplored the nation's excessive individualism and narcissism and challenged citizens to promote the common good by halting global warming, improving schools, strengthening the middle class, defending Medicare and Social Security, guaranteeing equal pay for women, and providing equal rights for gays and lesbians. He often insisted that his faith compelled him to "help our less fortunate citizens—our poor, our sick, [and] our neighbors in need."[184]

Tony Perkins applauded Obama's use of biblical language, but complained that he sometimes used it to defend anti-Christian policies, including abortion. Barry Lynn, the executive director of Americans United for Separation of Church and State, protested that citizens did not want to hear politicians explaining "how religious they are." David Kuo, who served in Bush's faith-based office, accused Obama of using religious rhetoric for political gain and of trying to resurrect the Religious Left as a powerful political force. The president, Joshua DuBois countered, "is a committed Christian" who is simply "being true to who he is."[185]

Obama's use of generic religious language abounds, but surprisingly he did little to connect biblical teaching with his signature program—the Affordable Health Care Act, which he signed on March 23, 2010, and which was upheld as constitutional by the Supreme Court on June 28, 2012. Obama repeatedly called this act the right thing to do, several times labeled it "a moral imperative," and quoted Ted Kennedy's assertion that healthcare "is above all a moral issue" that involved "fundamental principles of social justice and the character of our country."[186] However, he rarely provided explicit religious justification for it; he never cited the biblical obligation to care for the "least of these" or to be our "brother's keeper" or the story of the Good Samaritan so support this policy. In fact, in his presidential speeches, Obama did not quote a single biblical passage or precept to defend this policy or even mention God.

Obama's central argument was that healthcare was a right, not a privilege, which should be available to all citizens regardless of their economic resources. Millions had been unjustly "denied coverage because of preexisting conditions" or "had their policies canceled because of an illness." Many of them were working hard and meeting their responsibilities, but they were "held hostage" by health insurance companies that denied them coverage, dropped their coverage, or charged fees that they could not "afford for care that they desperately need." He strove to enable "Americans of every race, faith, and station" to "fulfill their God-given potential" by providing healthcare everyone could afford. The act would give citizens "more power, greater freedom, [and] stronger control of their health care." It would lower premiums, limit costs, rein in "the worst abuses of the insurance industry" by providing some of the nation's "toughest consumer protections," and give millions of Americans "a sense of security." When fully implemented in 2014, Obama promised, people could choose from "an array of quality, affordable, private health insurance plans."[187]

When Obama sought the support of the religious community for the Affordable Health Care Act, he sometimes did use religious language and arguments. In a conference call to about 1,000 rabbis in August 2009, he claimed that by passing this bill, "We are God's partners in matters of life and death." The president also told them that this plan would help fulfill "a core ethical and moral obligation"—"that I am my brother's keeper."[188] While Republicans worked to repeal the act, Department of Health and Human Services Secretary Kathleen Sebelius hosted a second conference call in January 2011 to a wide variety of religious leaders whose support the administration deemed essential to prevent this outcome. Many clergy, including Joel Hunter, promised to educate their parishioners about the benefits of the bill.[189]

Some Christian organizations strongly supported the Affordable Health Care Act. PICO National Network, Sojourners, Catholics in Alliance for the Common Good, Faith in Public Life, and Faithful America sponsored a "40 Days for Health Reform" campaign in 2009 to convince lawmakers that religious Americans considered "quality, affordable healthcare" "a moral issue." They encouraged citizens to sign a petition stating: "Over the next 40 days, I commit to . . . writing my representatives, attending events, and telling my friends about our efforts to make the faith community a positive force for health care reform."[190] Some Christians argued that "loving our neighbor as ourselves" demanded the creation of a just and equitable healthcare system. They strove to provide "at least minimal health insurance" for all Americans, require employers to contribute to health insurance coverage, and supply government assistance for those who could not afford coverage.[191]

Opponents of the bill protested that the Bible did not instruct government to use its coercive power to aid the disadvantaged. Pro-life proponents complained that the House version of the bill mandated federal funding of abortions and subsidizing health plans that covered abortions. This led the U.S. Conference of Catholic Bishops, Focus on the Family, the Christian Medical and Dental Associations, and the Southern Baptist Convention to predict that the bill would greatly expand the number of abortions.[192] Critics also warned that Obamacare would lead to rationing of healthcare and "death panels" that would decide who lived and died.[193]

Obama tied his denunciation of human trafficking more explicitly to biblical injunctions. Those who sought to end this evil—evangelicals, Catholics, the International Justice Mission, World Relief, and individual congregations—Obama argued, "are truly doing the Lord's work." "Groups like these," he insisted, "are answering the Bible's call—to 'seek justice' and 'rescue the oppressed.'" Obama praised the Passion Conference in Atlanta where thousands of young Christians worshipped "the God who sets the captives free" and pledged to work "to end modern slavery."[194] The president urged all faith communities to educate their constituents and join "coalitions that are bound by a love of God and a concern for the oppressed." Following the example of the "Good Samaritan on the road to Jericho," Americans must not "just pass by, indifferent." "Moved by compassion" and recognizing "we are our brother's keepers," he declared, "we've got to bind up" people's wounds. "Every life saved . . . is 'an act of justice,'" worthy of "the considerate judgment of mankind, and the gracious favor of Almighty God." In 2012 Obama promised that his Office of Faith-Based and Neighborhood Partnerships would zealously combat human trafficking and urged Congress to renew the Trafficking Victims Protection Act.[195]

Obama also connected a new program he announced in February 2014 to his most used biblical phrase—"My Brother's Keeper." He solicited the support of foundations, businesses, state and local political officials, religious leaders, and nonprofit organizations to create "more pathways to success" for Latino and African-American boys and young men. He reported that these groups promised to invest at least $200 million over the next five years to fund the initiative. Achieving its goals required giving all children "access to a world class education," creating more jobs, providing workers with skills, and paying a livable wage.[196]

Final Assessment

Some consider Obama's unconventional faith journey and religious commitments to be politically advantageous and beneficial to the nation, while others view them as "politically problematic" and detrimental to the country.[197] "For Obama," Stephen Mansfield argues, "faith is not simply political garb." Rather, it "is transforming, lifelong, and real." Obama seems to be "the Everyman in a heroic tale of spiritual seeking." Many Americans see him as "at least a fellow traveler and at most as a man at the vanguard of a new era of American spirituality."[198] Mansfield contends that Obama's "big-tent approach" to religion and spirituality "is perfectly in step with the country he now leads." Like the vast majority of Americans, he believes that people can travel many paths to reach God and that all religions contain fundamental truths.[199] Obama's faith animates "his life and leadership," and he seeks to help Americans "confront matters of race and public policy within a framework of religious values." By accentuating a "fully orbed social vision of Scripture" that neither the Religious Right nor Left completely understands, Mansfield hopes that Obama can bridge the divide between the two groups. Similarly, New York Times columnist Ross Douthat asserts that Obama represents America's "uncentered spiritual landscape in three ways." First, like 44 percent of Americans, the president switched his religion as an adult. Second, Obama was converted by Jeremiah Wright whose theological views differ substantially from historic Christian practice and belief. Third, as a Christian who does not belong to a congregation, Obama is part of one of America's fastest-growing religious constituencies—the "unchurched Christian" bloc.[200]

Many religious conservatives argue, by contrast, that Obama is not a Christian because his policies blatantly contradict the Bible. More than any other president, Obama's claim to be a Christian has been rejected. Although Obama professes to be a follower of Christ, a Liberty University School of Law professor declares, he "harbors tremendous animus toward all things Christian." Catholic political commentator Jerome Corsi contends that Obama's "Christianity is a religion of political convenience." Regardless of what he says in public, "his faith is essentially Marxism" expressed in a "watered-down version of Christianity."[201] Others allege that Obama employs religion to achieve his "socialist and libertine purposes" and is part of a long line of people who have used "Christ's words to justify a socialist agenda."[202]

Religious conservatives also complained about Obama's tendency to appeal to biblical values to solicit support for specific initiatives. The most egregious case was Obama's chastising the House for passing legislation reaffirming "In God We Trust" as the national motto while refusing to pass his jobs bill. "I trust in God," the president declared, "but God wants to see us help ourselves by putting people back to work." One critic protested that Obama argued that God expected Congress pass his jobs bill.[203]

For some, Obama's demeanor, identity, and actions have eschatological overtones. Analyzing the president's Cairo speech, a Newsweek editor declared, "in a way, Obama's standing" above the country and the world; "he's sort of God." Similarly, Michael Gerson denounced Obama's "Olympian" perspective.

Rather than participating in ideological struggles, "he aspires to be history's referee." "Our messianic president," Jonah Goldberg protested, sought to convince religious organizations to support his crusade to "expand the scope and role of government" to create the "Kingdom of God on Earth." Such a quest smacked of the Progressive concept that the state was the "march of God on earth," which was a major fascist theme.[204]

Numerous evangelicals find Obama's persona and policies very troubling. His internationalism, limited support for Israel, Nobel Peace Prize, and plan for universal healthcare coverage fit with expectations some have of the Antichrist's actions. Obama's enthralling promises of peace and prosperity make many religious conservatives suspicious. Mark Edward Taylor argues in *Branding Obamamessiah* (2011) that the Democrat acted and talked like "America's messiah" so that "people would recognize him as 'The One.' "[205]

Conservative Christians also criticize Obama for supporting pro-choice measures and same-sex marriage, authorizing the use of embryonic stem cells in research, and implementing policies that increase the national debt and weaken the United States. Obama's healthcare plan, Marvin Olasky protests, "will cost trillions and hurt millions. His foreign policy has heartened America's enemies." While Obama proposed to give failing public schools hundreds of millions of dollars, Joseph Loconte asserts, he refused to let poor families have vouchers to enable their children to "escape these mismanaged monstrosities and attend private religious schools." Other conservatives denounce Obama's "left-wing," ill-conceived, and poorly executed policies in books with provocative titles: Ken Blackwell and Ken Klukowski, *The Blueprint: Obama's Plan to Subvert the Constitution and Build an Imperial Presidency*; Robert Knight, *Radical Rulers: The White House Elites Who Are Pushing America Toward Socialism*; Stanley Kurtz, *Radical-in-Chief: Barack Obama and the Untold Story of American Socialism*; Hugh Hewitt, *The Brief against Obama: The Rise, Fall & Epic Fail of the Hope & Change Presidency*; David Limbaugh, *The Great Destroyer*; Edward Klein, *Amateur*; and George Neumayr and Phyllis Schlafly, *No Higher Power: Obama's War on Religious Freedom*. In short, to many religious conservatives, Obama is "a seething, alien radical bent on destroying America." Meanwhile, numerous progressives criticize Obama for other reasons: he has not removed all troops from Afghanistan, scaled back America's military empire, reduced the size of the nation's megabanks, campaigned vigorously for a public option in healthcare, terminated the Bush tax cuts, or devised a second stimulus bill to improve the economy and create jobs.[206]

Socially liberal Christians, on the other hand, generally applaud Obama's efforts to expand government programs to reduce poverty and provide jobs and universal healthcare and to increase gay civil rights. Dorrien credits Obama with restoring "the liberal internationalist approach to foreign policy," making "a historic outreach to the Muslim world," withdrawing troops from Iraq, helping inspire and adeptly responding to the democratic revolutions in the Arab world, helping end the "murderous regime of Muammar Qaddafi," orchestrating the death of Osama bin Laden, and representing the United States "with consummate dignity." Obama stabilized the economy, worked to improve the infrastructure, education, and housing, saved the automobile industry, and passed "the biggest antipoverty and job training bill since the Johnson administration." The Democrat stopped the mistreatment of gays and lesbians in the military, halted the Justice Department's legal challenges to the Defense of Marriage Act, restored federal funding to Planned Parenthood, and "suspended deportation proceedings against illegal immigrants lacking a criminal record." David Brooks praises Obama for moving "aggressively both to defeat enemies and to champion democracy."[207] In the final analysis, the disparate assessments of Obama by politically conservative and liberal Christians stem largely from their sharp disagreement over what responsibilities the Bible assigns to government and whether government programs or private initiatives and acts can best expand the economy and alleviate poverty.

Despite their differing evaluations of Obama's policies, Holder and Josephson argue, Obama's biblical language, Christian realism, and political pragmatism have not pleased either the Religious Right or the left wing of the Democratic Party. His repudiation of the United States' exceptionalism and righteousness offends religious conservatives, while his emphasis on the importance of religious faith and biblical values in the public sphere irritates liberal Democrats, most of whom are secularists. The Religious Right accuses Obama of using Scripture selectively to advance his liberal agenda. Most liberal Democrats dislike Obama's use of religious rhetoric, calls for a public faith, and denial of human goodness. Many of them also complain that his progressivism is too moderate. Moreover, Obama's Niebuhrian realism is too nuanced and prudential for many Americans who prefer stark contrasts and simple solutions to complex problems.[208] John Harris and James Hohmann contend that Obama's failure to clearly articulate his guiding philosophy and basing his policies on results-based pragmatism have produced bewilderment and disappointment among his supporters and enabled his enemies to distort his motives and agenda.[209]

Obama insists that "inauthentic expressions of faith" are blatantly transparent.[210] He argues that it is dangerous for public officials to "justify their actions by claiming God's mandate." They should not use their religious commitments "to insulate themselves from criticism, or avoid dialogue with people who disagree with them."[211] Although many of Obama's harshest critics contend that his faith is insincere, politically motivated, and biblically unorthodox, considerable evidence suggests that it is heartfelt and inspires his life and work. He has rarely employed it to escape criticism or evade discussions with individuals who espouse other religious perspectives or dispute his positions based on their understanding of the Bible. While religious conservatives are deeply disturbed by several policies he believes to be scripturally justified, his passion for aiding the poor and disadvantaged is commendable. Obama's faith has given him courage, confidence, and comfort and helped him cope with the immense challenges of the presidency.

Conclusion

*A man's religion is the chief fact with regard to him . . . [not]
the church-creed which he professes . . . [but] his vital relations
to this mysterious Universe, and his duty and destiny there.*

THOMAS CARLYLE, *On Heroes, Hero-Worship, and the Heroic
in History* (1907)

*None of has all the answers—none of us—no matter what
our political party or our station in life. The full breadth of
human knowledge is like a grain of sand in God's hands. . . .
The challenge . . . is to balance this uncertainty, this humility,
with the need to fight for deeply held convictions, to be open to
other points of view but firm in our core principles. And I pray
for this wisdom every day.*

BARACK OBAMA, "Remarks at the National Prayer
Breakfast," February 3, 2011

THIS EXAMINATION OF the lives of eleven presidents (twenty-two counting
the presidents profiled in my *Faith and the Presidency* [2006]) has shown that
many presidents were more deeply religious and had more vibrant personal
devotional lives than most scholars have recognized. In addition, faith had a
greater impact on their worldviews, leadership, actions, policies, and decision-
making than is typically acknowledged. This study leads to several conclusions
and questions.

First, it is difficult, if not impossible, to disentangle the personal religious
convictions of presidents from their use of religion to serve partisan political
purposes. Because of the expectations of citizens and the valuable ends that
religious rituals and rhetoric serve, presidents, regardless of the depth of their
scriptural understanding or their devoutness, have often exhibited public piety
and used religious language. Religious rhetoric resonates with millions of
Americans; it provides them with purpose, hope, reassurance, and solace. The

question William Inboden asks about Harry Truman is relevant to all presidents: Did he employ religious rhetoric simply for political profit? What better way can presidents gain the support of "politically skeptical but spiritually sensitive" citizens than by baptizing their policies "in sacred imagery and appealing to the will of God"?[1] These questions prompt many scholars, pundits, and ordinary Americans to inquire whether presidents' religious statements and practices express their true convictions or are employed primarily, or even completely, to win public approval and gain political advantages.

Presidents are very unlikely to admit that their religious assertions and activities purely or even primarily serve political goals. Therefore, we must judge whether their faith is authentic by examining their private correspondence as well as their public pronouncements and evaluating the testimonies of those who knew them best (although some of these people have incentives to make presidents appear more pious and moral than they actually are). We must also assess their behavior before, during, and after their presidencies (although most people's spiritual pilgrimage has high and low points, and, as noted, the pressures of their office prompted many chief executives to increase their church attendance, prayer, and Bible reading). Consequently, we can never be certain about the true faith commitments of any president. Depending on their view of the nature of a president's faith and the impact it has on his policies, some see him as a pious pretender and a holy hypocrite while others consider him a biblically sound, faithful follower of Christ. The evidence, however, does suggest that in many cases the public comments of these eleven presidents did reflect their genuine religious convictions.

Moreover, the faith of many presidents is difficult to decipher. The complexity and inconsistency of their convictions, changes in their beliefs over the years, their reticence to discuss their personal religious beliefs, and the incongruity between their words and deeds make assessing their faith very challenging. Jackson, McKinley, Nixon, Bush, Clinton, and Obama all professed to have had a Christian conversion experience either as a youth or an adult. However, it affected them differently, and their religious commitments, practices, and public policies differed substantially. Nine of the subjects of this book attended church regularly while in office. All of them affirmed the value of prayer and God's providential direction of history. The faith of the three early presidents who espoused Unitarianism—both Adamses and Madison—was especially complicated, and John Adams's and Madison's faith became less conventionally Christian as they aged. On the other hand, the beliefs of Jackson and Obama appear to have become more orthodox in later life. Nixon and Clinton are particularly perplexing because of the clash between their verbal profession and immoral actions. While some individuals and groups have criticized the faith of every president, Obama's has been especially controversial because of his association with Jeremiah Wright and alleged espousal of liberation theology. Countless Americans have trouble believing presidents are true Christians if they do not attend church regularly (Truman and Obama), engage in private behaviors widely considered sinful (Jackson, Truman, Nixon, and Clinton), or promote policies that seem immoral. For example, many religious conservatives questioned the genuineness of Clinton's and Obama's faith because of their support of abortion and gay rights, while numerous theological liberals doubted the authenticity of Nixon's and George H. W. Bush's faith because of their censure of abortion and homosexual acts and their military campaigns in Vietnam and the Middle East, respectively.

Second, although many of these presidents became more religious while in office, they all adopted an ecumenical religious perspective. John Adams and John Quincy Adams attended the Sunday services of different denominations, and their faith blended Unitarian rationalism with traditional Congregationalist and Presbyterian tenets. Andrew Jackson rejected numerous Presbyterian theological positions and espoused a more broadly Protestant view. Truman sought to enlist leaders of all world religions in a moral crusade to win the Cold War. Nixon identified with Quakerism his whole life, but during his political career he worshipped primarily with Presbyterian, Congregational, and Reformed Church of America congregations, and as president he sponsored nonsectarian services at the White House. While enthusiastically worshiping in Baptist, Methodist, Pentecostal, and African-American churches, Clinton also celebrated the teachings of Judaism and Islam. McKinley, Hoover, Truman, Nixon, George H. W. Bush, Clinton, and Obama strove to develop good relationships with Protestant leaders of all denominations and with Catholics. The latter five presidents also sought to cultivate cordial connections with Jews. They did so to help pass legislation and win elections but also because they saw themselves as representing Americans of all faith traditions. Moreover, as Will Herberg argued in *Protestant, Catholic, Jew* (1955), by the 1950s, the long-standing Protestant establishment had made room for Catholics and Jews. In some ways, all eleven presidents accommodated their personal religious convictions and practices to the expectations of the nation's civil religion.

Third, war or the threat of war played a major role in the presidencies of John Adams, Madison, McKinley, Truman, Nixon, Bush, and Obama. It always tested, and, in several cases, fortified their faith. Adams's tenure was preoccupied with the possibility of armed conflict with France. For almost two and one half years of Madison's presidency, the United States waged war with Britain. McKinley led the United States into a military clash with Spain that brought Cuba independence and the Philippines under American control. At the beginning of Truman's presidency, the United States defeated Germany and Japan to end World War II. The Baptist had to decide whether to use atomic bombs in Japan, how to wage the Cold War, and whether to send forces to fight in Korea. The unpopular conflict in Vietnam that Nixon inherited from his predecessors preoccupied his first term. Bush sent troops to the Middle East to liberate Kuwait and prevent Iraq from menacing other nations in the region. Clinton sought to halt the blood-letting in the Balkans between Serbs, Muslims, and Croats. Obama worked to end the military engagements George W. Bush initiated in Afghanistan and Iraq. All these presidents grappled with the morality of war, the effects of military engagements on the United States' welfare and international image, and the tragic deaths of American military personnel and innocent civilians. Most of them, as well as John Quincy Adams and Hoover, made the pursuit of world peace a priority of their presidencies. All eleven presidents testified that they relied on their faith in God to help them make difficult diplomatic decisions, cope with catastrophes, and provide consolation to those whose loved ones died in combat. Presidents' use of civil religious rhetoric helped sacralize America's deployment of troops and reduce criticism of their actions.

In the final analysis, does the faith of presidents have a positive or negative impact on their lives and administrations? When people's faith gives them confidence, assurance, comfort, consolation, and inspiration, it is generally positive. Their faith often stimulates individuals to be more compassionate, generous, and hopeful and supplies a constructive blueprint for bettering social conditions. As the leader of the world's wealthiest, most powerful, and most racially and ethnically diverse nation, presidents have daunting responsibilities and face immense pressures. Although the challenges confronting the United States significantly increased after World War I, earlier presidents also countered threats posed by foreign powers and internal dissension. A president's faith can greatly aid him in carrying out his demanding duties and playing the role of the nation's pastor-in-chief during crises and calamities. Every president has helped citizens cope with untimely deaths and tragic incidents, and many have sent American troops into battle. When doing so, they have usually relied on their faith and used civil religious discourse to defend their actions, unify Americans, assuage people's grief, provide hope of an afterlife, and contend that heartbreaking events serve a larger, if unknown, purpose.

Whether a president's faith plays a constructive role in his political decisions is more debatable. As previously argued, a president's faith is usually only one factor among others—strategic considerations, national security interests, party platform commitments, and his campaign promises, political philosophy, personal predilections and relationships, and reelection concerns—that affect his decisions. Americans' personal religious convictions strongly affect how they evaluate the faith of presidents. If a president's faith is similar to their own, people are much more likely to judge his faith favorably. If it differs substantially from their own, they are more inclined to view his faith negatively. When a president's faith does influence particular policies or decisions, Americans generally assess its role by whether they agree or disagree with his positions or acts in principle and by how they perceive their outcome. While the faith of all presidents has been both applauded and criticized, that of the last two has especially provoked debate and disagreement. Individuals espousing very different religious convictions have portrayed George W. Bush and Barack Obama as exemplars of Christian faith, as manipulative hypocrites, or even as the anti-Christ.

While many of these presidents possessed vibrant personal faith, worshipped regularly, prayed diligently, knew the Bible well, and pondered theological issues, none of them had a systemic, holistic understanding of scriptural teaching about government and politics. Although all of them quoted the Bible extensively and often cited its principles and parables in their speeches and letters, their philosophies of government were not consistently grounded in biblical theology and norms. Rather than basing their administrations and actions on a comprehensive biblical worldview, they tended to use scriptural passages as proof-texts to support their positions. Their political philosophies were not grounded on scriptural understandings of creation, human nature, sin, redemption, power, community, justice, and love.

Is it reasonable, however, to expect Christian politicians, especially presidents, to develop such a perspective given their backgrounds, education, responsibilities, and pressures? After all, only a small number of Christian political scientists, philosophers, theologians, historians, and policy analysts and a handful of politicians—most notably William Wilberforce, William Gladstone, Abraham Kuyper, William Jennings Bryan, Mark Hatfield, John Anderson, and Paul Henry—have consistently tried to do so.[2] Although both Adamses and Madison read widely in political theory and theology, they had limited sources, primarily the works of Augustine, Thomas Aquinas, John Calvin, John Knox, Theodore Beza, George Buchanan, John Wesley, and John Witherspoon as well as *Vindiciae contra Tyranno*, to help them think systematically about a biblical approach to politics. Jackson, McKinley (who had the models of Gladstone and Kuyper), and Truman all had limited formal education and read little political philosophy or theology.[3] As a result of their substantial political service, broad interests, wide travels, and extensive reading, both Quaker presidents, Hoover and Nixon, had a sophisticated understanding of political history and theory. However, influenced by their theological tradition and personal preferences, neither of them read much Christian political analysis. Although he was a faithful Episcopalian, George H. W. Bush was not by temperament and life experience particularly interested in theoretical reflection on the relationship between Christianity and politics. Despite his education at Georgetown, a Jesuit institution, and graduate study at Oxford, Clinton did not systematically explore biblical teaching about politics. Obama professes to be strongly influenced by Reinhold Niebuhr, but his political philosophy is not based on a coherent biblical framework.

All presidents since Hoover could have looked to Niebuhr for guidance in crafting a Christian perspective on politics. In his books, most notably *Moral Man and Immoral Society* (1932) and *The Structure of Nations and Empires* (1960), and hundreds of articles and essays, the Neo-orthodox theologian provided astute, biblically informed analysis of governance and politics.[4] Today a variety of theological traditions—Catholic, Reformed, mainline Protestant, and evangelical—provide helpful evaluations of biblical teaching on these issues.[5]

Is it possible in a nation that separates church and state and is comprised of dozens of groups that espouse different religions and ideologies for individuals who adopt a biblically grounded, comprehensive framework for politics to communicate their positions and policies in a way that appeals to enough citizens to be elected and govern effectively? Many Jews, Muslims, Hindus, Buddhists, agnostics, and secularists do not think the Bible (or, in the case of Jews, at least the New Testament) provides a proper basis for political philosophy and policy. Moreover, the different positions on issues advocated by America's non-Christian religious communities and competing Christian groups—Catholic, Orthodox, mainline Protestant, evangelical, black Protestant, Pentecostal, and charismatic (and often by different members of the same groups)—prevent presidents from pleasing or maintaining positive relationships with all of them. Some presidents have been more successful than others because of their personal religious convictions, personalities, political stances, cordial interactions with religious leaders and groups, and the effectiveness of their staff, especially their liaisons with religious bodies. In addition, Americans' perspectives on human dignity and rights, freedom, justice, and equality vary greatly. This, coupled with the nation's moral and cultural relativism, forces presidents (and other politicians) whose political perspective is guided by biblical principles to use arguments based on natural law, the common good, and potential beneficial outcomes to persuade lawmakers and citizens to support their policies.

Although our nation appears to be increasingly more secular, many Americans will probably continue to care deeply about the faith of their presidents and the impact it has on their policies. Numerous polls report that this is presently the case. For example, 67 percent of respondents to a 2012 Pew Research Religion & Public Life survey agreed that "it is important that a president have strong religious beliefs."[6] Their conviction that presidents believe that God directs history and seek His guidance in performing their duties and making decisions provides comfort to millions of Americans. On the other hand, many accuse chief executives of using religion as a tool to gain and consolidate power and accomplish their agendas. From 1789 to the present, the faith of many presidents has strongly influenced their political philosophy and practices. Although the founders wisely separated church and state, faith and the presidency and religious belief and politics, have been inextricably joined.[7] Therefore, the nature of presidents' faith and its effect on their positions, decisions, and actions is very likely to remain both captivating and controversial.

Notes

INTRODUCTION

1. E.g., John Blake, "Why a President's Faith May Not Matter," June 30, 2012, http://religion.blogs.cnn.com/2012/06/30/why-a-presidents-faith-may-not-matter/. Both Darrin Grinder and Niels Nielsen, whose books are cited below, give examples to support this argument.

2. Two edited collections stand out for their careful scholarship, use of archival materials, and judicious conclusions: Mark Rosell and Gleaves Whitney, eds., *Religion and the American Presidency* (New York: Palgrave Macmillan, 2007) and Gaston Espinosa, ed., *Religion and the American Presidency: George Washington to George W. Bush* (New York: Columbia University Press, 2009). See also Joseph Prud'homme, ed., *Faith and Politics in America: From Jamestown to the Civil War* (New York: Peter Lang, 2011). Two books continue earlier efforts to provide brief sketches of the faith of all presidents: Niels Nielsen, *God in the Obama Era: Presidents' Religion and Ethics from George Washington to Barack Obama* (New York: Morgan James, 2009) and Steve Shaw and Darrin Grinder, *The Presidents and Their Faith* (Boise, ID: Russell Media, 2012). Two books examine the faith of recent presidents: Randall Balmer, *God in the White House: A History: How Faith Shaped the Presidency from John F. Kennedy to George W. Bush* (New York: HarperOne, 2008) and David Holmes, *The Faiths of the Postwar Presidents: From Truman to Obama* (Athens: University of Georgia Press, 2012). Numerous recent books analyze the faith of individual presidents, most notably Michael Novak and Jana Novak, *Washington's God: Religion, Liberty, and the Father of Our Country* (New York: Basic Books, 2006); Malcolm Magee, *What the World Should Be: Woodrow Wilson and the Crafting of a Faith-Based Foreign Policy* (Waco, TX: Baylor University Press, 2008); Thomas Carty, *A Catholic in the White House?: Religion, Politics, and John F. Kennedy's Presidential Campaign*

(New York: Palgrave Macmillan, 2004); Larry Ingle, *Nixon's First Cover-up: The Religious Life of a Quaker President* (Columbia: University of Missouri Press, 2015); Randall Balmer, *Redeemer: The Life of Jimmy Carter* (New York: Basic Books, 2014); Paul Kengor, *God and Ronald Reagan: A Spiritual Life* (New York: ReganBooks, 2004); Kjell Lejon, *George H. W. Bush: Faith, Presidency, and Public Theology* (New York: Peter Lang, 2014); David Aikman, *A Man of Faith: The Spiritual Journey of George W. Bush* (Nashville, TN: W Pub. Group, 2004); Paul Kengor, *God and George W. Bush: A Spiritual Life* (New York: ReganBooks, 2005); Stephen Mansfield, *The Faith of Barack Obama* (Nashville, TN: Thomas Nelson, 2011); and R. Ward Holder and Peter Josephson, *The Irony of Barack Obama: Barack Obama, Reinhold Niebuhr and the Problem of Christian Statecraft* (Farnham, UK: Ashgate, 2012). While these religious biographies expand our knowledge of their subjects, they pay little attention to the role of religion in presidential campaigns, presidents' relationships with religious groups, or the influence of their faith on their policies. Other works that focus on the founders explore the faith of some early presidents, most importantly David Holmes, *The Faiths of the Founding Fathers* (New York: Oxford University Press, 2006); Jon Meacham, *American Gospel: God, the Founding Fathers, and the Making of a Nation* (New York: Random House, 2006); Steven Waldman, *Founding Faith: Providence, Politics, and the Birth of Religious Freedom in America* (New York: Random House, 2008); Daniel Dreisbach, Mark D. Hall, and Jeffry Morrison, eds., *The Forgotten Founders on Religion and Public Life* (Notre Dame, IN: University of Notre Dame Press, 2009); John Fea, *Was America Founded as a Christian Nation?* (Louisville, KY: Westminster John Knox Press, 2011); Gregg Frazer, *The Religious Beliefs of America's Founders: Reason, Revelation, Revolution* (Lawrence: University Press of Kansas, 2012); and Daniel Dreisbach and Mark D. Hall, eds., *Faith and the Founders of the American Republic* (New York: Oxford University Press, 2014). See also *Review of Faith and International Affairs* 9 (December 2011) and *Derecho y Religion* (*Right and Religion*) 6 (2011), two special editions of journals that analyze how the faith of presidents affected their foreign policy and the role of chief executives in defining and promoting civil religion. A very important book that analyzes the role of the faith of presidents in helping shape their foreign policy is Andrew Preston, *Sword of the Spirit, Shield of Faith: Religion in American War and Diplomacy* (New York: Anchor Books, 2012).

3. James David Barber, *The Presidential Character: Predicting Performance in the White House* (Englewood Cliffs, NJ: Prentice Hall, 1972), first quotation from 7–8, remainder from 8; Stephen Mansfield, *The Faith of Barack Obama* (Nashville, TN: Thomas Nelson, 2008), xxiii; Nathan Diament, "Obama's Religion Matters to Us If It Matters to Him," Aug. 31, 2010, http://newsweek.washingtonpost.com/onfaith/panelists/Nathan_Diament/2010/08/obamas_religion_matters_to_us_if_it_matters_to_him.html.

4. Michael Riccards, "The Moral Talk of American Presidents," in Moorhead Kennedy, R. Gordon Hoxie, and Brenda Repland, eds., *The Moral Authority of Government* (New Brunswick, NJ: Transaction Publishers, 2000), 22–23; Chris Cillizza, "Confusion Grows about Obama's Religion," Aug. 19, 2010, http://voices.washingtonpost.com/thefix/morning-fix/-1-2-3-1.html (quotation).

5. See Colleen Shogan, *The Moral Rhetoric of American Presidents* (College Station: Texas A&M University Press, 2006), 8, 10, 14.

6. E.g., Nicole Neroulias, "Poll: Americans Want Religious Presidents, but Are Vague on Details," *CC* Oct. 15, 2011, https://www.christian century.org/article/2011/poll-americans-want-religious-presidents. In a July 2011 poll conducted by Public Religion Research Institute, 56 percent of respondents said it was important for presidential candidates to have "strong beliefs." Cf. "Public Sees Religion's Influence Waning: Yet Americans' Appetite for Religion in Public Life Is Growing," in which 41 percent of respondents said that there had been "too little expression of religious faith and prayer" by political leaders. http://www.pew-forum.org/2014/09/22/public-sees-religions-influence-waning-press-release/.

7. See Vanessa Beasley, *You, the People* (College Station: Texas A&M University Press, 2004); Mary Stuckey, *Defining Americans: The Presidency and National Identity* (Lawrence: University Press of Kansas, 2004).

8. Robert Murray and Timothy Blessing, *Greatness in the White House: Rating the Presidents, George Washington through Ronald Reagan* (University Park: Pennsylvania State University Press, 1994), 29, 108.

9. Amy Sullivan, "The De Facto Religious Test in Presidential Politics," Oct. 21, 2011, http://swampland.time.com/2011/10/21/the-de-facto-religious-test-in-presidential-politics/#ixzz1c5AicH79.

10. S. Byron Wolf, "Separating Church and State: Vomit-Inducing or Necessary for Freedom of Religion?" Feb. 27, 2012, http://abcnews.go.com/blogs/politics/2012/02/separating-church-and-state-vomit-inducing-or-necessary-for-freedom-of-religion/. Responding to a Bloomberg National Poll conducted in March 2012, which asked how often "do you think a president's religious beliefs should influence his federal policy decisions," 8 percent said all of the time, 6 percent said most of the time, 25 percent some of the time, and 58 percent said never.

11. Barber, *Presidential Character*, 9; George Washington, "Inaugural Address," Apr. 30, 1789, online by Gerhard Peters and John Woolley, *The American Presidency Project*, http://www.presidency.ucsb.edu/ws/?pid=25800; Harry Truman, "Address in Milwaukee, Wisconsin," Oct. 14, 1948, http://www.presidency.ucsb.edu/ws/?pid=13049; Dwight Eisenhower, "Inaugural Address," Jan. 20, 1953, http://www.presidency.ucsb.edu/ws/?pid=9600; Barack Obama, "Address before a Joint Session of the Congress on the State of the Union," Jan. 25, 2011, http://www.presidency.ucsb.edu/ws/?pid=88928.

12. Ruth Morgan, "The Presidency and Moral Leadership," in Kennedy, Hoxie, and Repland, eds., *Moral Authority*, 13; Frank Keesler, "How 'Bully' Is the Pulpit?: Moral Authority of the American Presidents in the Twenty-First Century," in ibid., 62 (cf. Betty Glad, "When Governments Are Good," in ibid., 63ff.); Richard Pious, "Moral Action and Presidential Leadership," in ibid., 7–8.

13. E.g., Hugh Sidey, "The Presidency: Demand for 'Moral Leadership,'" *Life* 69 (Oct. 23, 1970), 2.

14. David Broder, *The Party's Over: The Failure of Politics in America* (New York: Harper and Row, 1972), 169; Ray Price, memorandum to Richard Nixon, reprinted in Joe McGuinness, *The Selling of the President, 1968* (New York: Trident, 1969), 193; Michael Genovese and Thomas Cronin, *The Paradoxes of the American Presidency* (New York: Oxford University Press, 2009), 134.

15. David McCullough, "Harry S. Truman, 1945–1953," in Robert Wilson, ed., *Character Above All: Ten Presidents from FDR to George Bush* (New York: Simon and Schuster, 1995), 41–42; Peggy Noonan, "Ronald Reagan," n.d., http://www.pbs.org/newshour/character/essays/reagan.html; William Bennett, *The Death of Outrage: Bill Clinton and the Assault on American Ideals* (New York: Free Press, 1998), 37–38; James Pfiffner, "Presidential Character: Multidimensional or Seamless?" in Mark Rozell and Clyde Wilcox, eds., *The Clinton Scandal and the Future of American Government* (Washington, DC: Georgetown University Press, 2000), 225 (cf. James Pfiffner, *The Character Factor: How We Judge America's Presidents* [College Station: Texas A&M Press, 2004], xii); Stanley Renshon, *High Hopes: The Clinton Presidency and the Politics of Ambition* (New York: New York University Press, 1996), 77.

16. John Adams, *A Dissertation on the Canon and Feudal Law* (1765), in Robert Taylor, Mary-Jo Kline, and Gregg Lint, eds., *Papers of John Adams*, 16 vols. (Cambridge, MA: Belknap Press of Harvard University Press, 1977–), 1:120–21; Robert Shogan, *The Double-Edged Sword: How Character Makes and Ruins Presidents, from Washington to Clinton* (Boulder, CO: Westview Press, 2000), 3 (third quotation); e.g., George Bush, "Remarks to the Kentucky Fried Chicken Convention in Nashville," Oct. 30, 1992, http://www.presidency.ucsb.edu/ws/?pid=21711; Bush, **"Remarks at a Rally in St. Louis,"** *Oct. 30, 1992*, http://www.presidency.ucsb.edu/ws/?pid=21713.

17. E.g., Gregory Koukl, "Does Presidential Character Count?" n.d., http://www.inplainsite.org/html/presidential_character.

18. Robert Dallek, "JFK's Intern Affair Tests Presidential Character," Feb. 9, 2012, http://www.thedailybeast.com/articles/2012/02/08/jfk-s-intern-affair-tests-presidential-character.html.

19. Donald Robinson, "The Authority of Presidents: Personal Morality and Political Effectiveness," in Kennedy, Hoxie, and Repland, eds., *Moral Authority*, 79 (first quotation); Klein quoted in "Shaggy Dog Tale," n.d., http://nymag.com/nymetro/

news/rnc/9733/; Cohen, quoted in Shogan, *Sword*, 117; Philip Wogaman, *From the Eye of the Storm: A Pastor to the President Speaks Out* (Louisville, KY: John Knox Press, 1998), 107–8; Bennett quoted in ibid., 110.

20. William Clinton, "Interview with Tom Brokaw of MSNBC's 'InterNight,'" July 15, 1996, http://www.presidency.ucsb.edu/ws/?pid=53067; Wendy Kaminer, letter to the editor, Oct. 11, 1998, http://www.nytimes.com/books/98/10/11/letters/letters.html; Mark Melcher, "'Character' in the First 'Post-Modern' Presidency," in Kennedy, Hoxie, and Repland, eds., *Moral Authority*, 160–62; first quotation from 160, second from 161.

CHAPTER 1

1. Richard Brown, "The Disenchantment of a Radical Whig," in Richard Ryerson, "John Adams and the Founding of the Republic: An Introduction," in Ryerson, ed., *John Adams and the Founding of the Republic* (Boston: Massachusetts Historical Society, 2001), 183 (first, third, and fourth quotations); Joseph Ellis, *Passionate Sage: The Character and Legacy of John Adams* (New York: W. W. Norton, 1993), 47 (second quotation).

2. John Patrick Diggins, *John Adams* (New York: Henry Holt, 2003), 157.

3. Stephen Kurtz, *The Presidency of John Adams: The Collapse of Federalism, 1795–1800* (Philadelphia: University of Pennsylvania Press, 1957), 334.

4. JA to Samuel Miller, July 8, 1820, in Charles Francis Adams, ed., *The Works of John Adams, Second President of the United States: With a Life of the Author* 10 vols. (Boston: Little, Brown, 1856), 10:390. Proclaimed by the Council of Chalcedon (451), this creed asserted that God the Father, Christ, and the Holy Spirit were "coeternal and coequal."

5. On Deism, see Peter Gay, *Deism: An Anthology* (Princeton, NJ: Van Nostrand, 1968); Herbert Morais, *Deism in Eighteenth Century America* (New York: Russell & Russell, 1960).

6. Paul Conklin, *Puritans and Pragmatists: Eight Eminent American Thinkers* (New York: Dodd, Mead, 1968), 120.

7. See Page Smith, *John Adams*, 2 vols. (Norwalk, CT: Easton Press, 1962), 1:29.

8. Anson Morse, "The Politics of John Adams," *American Historical Review* 4 (Jan. 1899), 304.

9. JA to Benjamin Rush, Jan. 21, 1810, *Works* 9:627. On Adams's strong dislike of Paine, see L. H. Butterfield, ed., *Diary and Autobiography of John Adams* (New York: Atheneum, 1964), 330–31. Adams declared, "The Christian religion is, above all the religions that ever prevailed or existed in ancient or modern times, the religion of wisdom, equity, and humanity, let the blackguard Paine say what he will" (July 26, 1796, *Diary* 3:234).

10. JA to TJ, July 17, 1813, *Works* 10:54.

11. JA to AA, Jan. 28, 1799, *Adams Family Papers: An Electronic Archive*, Massachusetts Historical Society, http://www.masshist.org/digitaladams/ (hereinafter cited as Adams Family Papers).

12. Diggins, *Adams*, 154–55.

13. Richard Ryerson, "John Adams and the Founding of the Republic: An Introduction," in Ryerson, ed., *Adams*, 28. No religious biography of Adams has been written. The best sources on the subject are C. Bradley Thompson, *Adams and the Spirit of Liberty* (Lawrence: University Press of Kansas, 1998), 3–24, 148–55; Conklin, *Puritans*, 113–23, 127–30, 134–38; James D. Grant, *John Adams: Party of One* (New York: Farrar, Straus and Giroux, 2005), 113–24, 152–59, 183–85; Peter Shaw, *The Character of John Adams* (New York: W. W. Norton, 1976), 15–24, 307–12; Edmund Morgan, "John Adams and the Puritan Tradition," *New England Quarterly* 34:4 (1961), 522–29; Howard Ioan Fielding, "John Adams: Puritan, Deist, Humanist," *Journal of Religion* 20 (Jan. 1940), 33–46; Zoltan Haraszti, *John Adams and the Prophets of Progress* (Cambridge, MA: Harvard University Press, 1952), 280–99; Edwin Gaustad, *Faith of the Founders: Religion and the New Nation, 1776–1826* (Waco, TX: Baylor University Press, 1993), 85–97, 107–9; and Warren Carroll, "John Adams, Puritan Revolutionist: A Study of His Part in Making the American Revolution, 1764–1776" (Ph.D. diss., Columbia University, 1959).

14. See George Marsden, "Introduction: Reformed and American," in David Wells, ed., *Reformed Theology in America: A History of Its Modern Development* (Grand Rapids, MI: Baker Books, 1997), 1–5; D. G. Hart, "Calvinism and American Politics," in Thomas Davis, ed., *John Calvin's American Legacy* (New York: Oxford University Press, 2010), 66–68; D. G. Hart, *Calvinism: A History* (New Haven, CT: Yale University Press, 2013), 105–15; Leland Ryken, *Worldly Saints: The Puritans as They Really Were* (Grand Rapids, MI: Academie Books, 1986).

15. Shaw, *Character*, 312.

16. Carroll, "John Adams," 32–42. During these years Adams made more references in his writings to Puritan leaders than to John Locke (32).

17. Shaw, *Character*, 65.

18. Thompson, *Adams*, 30.

19. JA to Charles Cushing, Apr. 1, 1756, in Robert Taylor, Mary-Jo Kline, and Gregg Lint, eds., *Papers of John Adams*, vol. 1: *September 1755–October 1773*, 16 vols. (Cambridge, MA: Harvard University Press, 1977), 1:12–13 (hereinafter cited as Papers).

20. JA to Jonathan Sewall, Feb. 1760, in Charles Francis Adams, *The Life of John Adams* (New York: Haskell House, 1871), 71.

21. JA to AA, Aug. 15, 1782, *Adams Family Papers*.

22. Butterfield, ed., *Autobiography*, 3:256.

23. See Smith, *Adams*, 1:3–8; John Ferling, "Before Fame: Young John Adams and Thomas Jefferson," in Ryerson, ed., *Adams*, 76; Steven Mintz and Susan Kellogg, *Domestic Revolutions: A Social History of American Family Life* (New York: Free Press, 1988), 1–23.

24. Smith, *Adams*, 1:11–17; quotation from 11; Robert Wilson III, *The Benevolent Deity: Ebenezer Gay and the Rise of Rational Religion in New England, 1696–1787* (Philadelphia: University of Pennsylvania Press, 1984), 63–66.

25. Thompson, *Adams*, 7. See Smith, *Adams*, 1:27–28. Adams was also influenced by the views of Jonathan Mayhew, the liberal pastor of Boston's West Church. In addition, Adams's views were also shaped by Mayhew's "Discourse Concerning Unlimited Submission and Non-Resistance to the Higher Powers" (1750). Its substance, he told Jefferson, "was incorporated into my Nature and indelibly engraved on my Memory" (JA to TJ, in Lester Cappon, ed., *The Adams–Jefferson Letters: The Complete Correspondence between Thomas Jefferson and Abigail and John Adams* [Chapel Hill: University of North Carolina Press, 1959], 2:527). See also Mar. 17, 1756, *Diary* 1:14–15.

26. John Fea, "John Adams and Religion," in David Waldstreicher, ed., *A Companion to John Adams and John Quincy Adams* (Chichester, UK: Wiley Blackwell, 2013), 186–88; Peter Rinaldo, *Atheists, Agnostics, and Deists in America: A Brief History* (Briarcliff Manor, NY: DorPete Press, 2000), 40; Wilson, *Benevolent Deity*, 128.

27. JA to Cushing, Apr. 1, 1756, *Papers* 1:13.

28. JA to Richard Cranch, Oct. 18, 1756, in Adams, *Life*, 46.

29. JA to Cushing, Oct. 19, 1756, *Papers* 1:21–22; quotation from 21.

30. Butterfield, ed., *Autobiography*, 3:262.

31. Ellis, *Sage*, 53.

32. Fielding, "John Adams," 38; Gregg Frazer, *The Religious Beliefs of America's Founders: Reason, Revelation, Revolution* (Lawrence: University of Kansas Press, 2012), 107–24. While Frazer argues persuasively that Adams should be considered a proponent of theistic rationalism—"a hybrid belief system" that mixes "elements of natural religion, Christianity, and rationalism, with rationalism as the predominate element" (14), it is simpler to label Adams a Unitarian. His views fit very well with the doctrines of this denomination, and he identified himself with it in his later years. The church Adams long belonged to in Quincy—The First Parish Church—incorrectly claims in its website (United First Parish Church, "A Brief History," http://www.ufpc.org) to have become officially Unitarian by 1750. Although the congregation was probably proto-Unitarian by 1800, it did not officially become Unitarian until 1825 when it joined the American Unitarian Association. See George Willis Cooke, *Unitarianism in America: A History of Its Origin and Development* (Boston: American Unitarian Association, 1902), 118, and the chapter on John Quincy Adams in my book. For a similar perspective on

Adams, see David Holmes who labels Adams a "Christian Deist" (*The Faiths of the Founding Fathers* [New York: Oxford University Press, 2006], 73).

33. David Robinson, *The Unitarians and Universalists* (Westport, CT: Greenwood Press, 1985), 4–5, 9–38; Conrad Wright, ed., *A Stream of Light: A Short History of American Unitarianism* (Boston: Skinner Book House, 1989), xi–xiv, 3–32; Conrad Wright, "The Election of Henry Ware: Two Contemporary Accounts, Edited with Commentary," *Harvard Library Bulletin* 17 (1969), 245–78; David Walker Howe, *Unitarian Conscience: Harvard Moral Philosophy, 1805–1861* (Cambridge, MA: Harvard University Press, 1970); John White Chadwick, *William Ellery Channing: Minister of Boston* (Boston: Houghton Mifflin, 1903); Wilson, *Benevolent Deity.*

34. JA to Miller, July 8, 1820, *Works* 10:389.

35. See Grant, *Adams*, 115–16.

36. On his study of the Bible, see July 21, 1756, *Diary* 1:35.

37. John Quincy Adams, *Memoirs of John Quincy Adams: Comprising Portions of His Diary from 1795 to 1848*, ed. Charles Francis Adams, 12 vols. (Freeport, NY: Books for Libraries Press, 1969), 8:414.

38. Thompson, *Adams*, 5 (quotation), 11–23.

39. Thompson argues that scholars who depict Adams as a Puritan or Calvinist because of his use in his diary of themes such as sin, self-examination, self-mastery, and the quest for salvation and his view of human nature are mistaken. He cites as examples Conklin, *Puritans*, 109; John Diggins, *The Lost Soul of American Politics: Virtue, Self-Interest, and the Foundations of Liberalism* (New York: Basic Books, 1984), 55, 71; Morgan, "Adams," 518–29; Bernard Bailyn, "Butterfield's Adams: Notes for a Sketch," *WMQ*, 3d ser., 19 (1962), 238–56; Shaw, *Character*, 23–24, 40, 65, 211–12; Ellis, *Sage*, 48, 52–53; and Smith, *Adams*, 1:262, 4:234. Thompson contends that Adams's understanding of these issues was markedly different than that of the Puritans (4–18). Although Adams repudiated many distinctively Reformed tenets, he was nevertheless deeply influenced by the Calvinist position on providence, sin, human nature, and morality.

40. Woody Horton, *Abigail Adams* (New York: Free Press, 2009), 45–46; Charles Akers, *Abigail Adams: An American Woman* (Boston: Little, Brown, 1980), 6–8. Both John and Abigail liked sermons that "reache[d] the Imagination and touche[d] the Passions," which did so "with great Propriety" (Oct. 23, 1774, *Diary* 2:156).

41. See Edith Gelles, *Portia: The World of Abigail Adams* (Bloomington: Indiana University Press, 1992), 14, 22, 139 (quotation), 147.

42. See Akers, *Abigail Adams*, 40–41, 63, 126–28; Phyllis Lee Levin, *Abigail Adams* (New York: St. Martin's Press, 1987), 5–6, 119, 179–81, 390, 443, 450, 454–55, 474; Paul Nagel, *The Adams Women: Abigail and Louisa Adams, Their Sisters*

and Daughters (Cambridge, MA: Harvard University Press, 1987), 74–75, 157; Paul Nagel, *Descent from Glory: Four Generations of the John Adams Family* (New York: Oxford University Press, 1983), 20, 28–31, 80–81; Gelles, *Portia*, 14, 22, 71, 129, 137–39, 147, 153, 166, 168, 168–69, 173, 205; and Clare Hodgson Meeker, *Partner in Revolution: Abigail Adams* (New York: Benchmark Books, 1998); G. J. Barker-Benfield, *Abigail and John Adams: The Americanization of Sensibility* (Chicago: University of Chicago Press, 2010), 32–42.

43. AA to JQA, Mar. 20, 1780, in Abigail Adams, *Letters of Mrs. Adams, Wife of John Adams*, ed. Charles Francis Adams, 2 vols. (Boston: C. C. Little and James Brown, 1840), 1:113.

44. E.g., AA to Isaac Smith, Jr., Oct. 30, 1777, in L. H. Butterfield, Marc Friedlaender, and Richard Ryerson, eds., *Adams Family Correspondence*, 9 vols. (Cambridge, MA: Harvard University Press, 1963), 2:363 (hereinafter cited as *AFC*).

45. AA to JQA, Mar. 20, 1780, *AFC* 3:310.

46. E.g., AA to JA, Oct. 9, 1775, *AFC* 1:297; AA to Louisa Adams, Jan. 30, 1813, Adams Papers, Massachusetts Historical Society, Boston, reel 415 (hereinafter cited as MHS).

47. Horton, *Abigail Adams*, 271, 307.

48. AA to JQA, May 5, 1816; AA to JQA, Oct. 12, 1815, Adams Papers, MHS, reel 431; quotations in that order.

49. E.g., JA to TJ, July 18, 1813, *Works* 10:56–57; JA to TJ, Sept. 22, 1813, ibid., 71–73; JA to TJ, Oct. 4, 1813, ibid., 75–78; JA to TJ, Dec. 25, 1813, ibid., 82–86; JA to TJ, Mar. 14, 1814, ibid., 89–94. See Haraszti, *Adams*, 280–99. John Howe, Jr. argues in *The Changing Political Thought of John Adams* (Princeton, NJ: Princeton University Press, 1966) that Adams read almost "every significant moralist of the day," including John Locke, Adam Smith, Jean-Jacques Rousseau, Bernard Mandeville, and Francis Hutcheson (15).

50. JA to TJ, July 18, 1813, *Works* 10:56.

51. Adams heard Priestley preach in London, and after he moved to the United States, Adams, while vice president, regularly attended his lectures on the "Evidences of Revealed Religion" in Philadelphia. When he published these lectures in 1796–97, Priestley dedicated them to Adams, praising his "steady attachment to the cause of Christianity" (*Discourses Relating to the Evidences of Revealed Religion* [Philadelphia: T. Dobson, 1796], 1:iii). Adams read numerous books by Priestley, including *Corruptions of Christianity* (1782), *Early Opinions Concerning Jesus Christ* (1786), *Institutions of Moses* (1799), and the *Doctrines of Heathen Philosophy Compared with Those of Revelation* (1804) (JA to TJ, July 18, 1813, *Works* 10:57; JA to TJ, Dec. 25, 1813, ibid., 82–86). See Haraszti, *Adams*, 280–81, 288–89. However, Adams told Jefferson: "I shall never be a disciple of Priestley. He is as absurd, inconsistent, credulous, and incomprehensible as Athanasius" (Mar. 14, 1814, *Works* 10:93).

52. JA to TJ, June 28, 1813, *Works* 10:45.

53. JA to TJ, Nov. 4, 1816, in Cappon, ed., *Letters*, 2: 493.

54. JA to TJ, Nov. 4, 1816, *Works* 10:229.

55. JA to TJ, Jan. 23, 1825, *Works* 10:416.

56. Frazer, *Religious Beliefs*, 113.

57. JA to Francis Van der Kamp, Dec. 27, 1816, *Works* 10:234.

58. July 26, 1796, *Diary*, 3:234.

59. Aug. 14, 1796, *Diary*, 3:240–41.

60. JA to TJ, Sept. 14, 1813, *Works* 10:67.

61. JA to Richard Cranch, Aug. 29, 1756, *Papers*, 1:15.

62. Aug. 22, 1756, *Diary* 1:43.

63. May 1, 1756, *Diary* 1:24.

64. Grant, *Adams*, 120.

65. May 24, 1756, *Diary* 1:29.

66. JA to Louisa Adams, Nov. 11, 1821, Adams Papers, MHS, reel 124.

67. Gaustad, *Founders*, 91–95.

68. JA to Stephen Peabody, Nov. 1, 1815, Adams Papers, MHS, reel 122.

69. JA to Elihu Marshall, Mar. 7, 1820, *Works* 10:389.

70. JA to Francis Van der Kemp, Feb. 18, 1809, *Works* 9:610.

71. E.g., JA to Rush, Apr. 18, 1808, in John Schutz and Douglass Adair, eds., *Spur of Fame: Dialogues of John Adams and Benjamin Rush, 1805–1813* (Indianapolis: Liberty Fund, 1966), 106; JA to Rush, Aug. 28, 1811, ibid., 192.

72. Conklin, *Puritans*, 118; Thompson, *Adams*, 23. E.g., Aug. 14, 1796, *Diary* 3:240–41.

73. Thompson, *Adams*, 211; May 29, 1756, *Diary*, 1:31 (quotation).

74. See Gordon Wood, "Religion and the American Revolution," in Harry Stout and D. G. Hart, eds., *New Directions in American Religious History* (New York: Oxford University Press, 1997), 173–74, and June 22, 1771, *Diary* 2:38: Adams described a landlord he stayed with as "a new Light—continually canting and whining in a religious Strain."

75. JA to Benjamin Waterhouse, Dec. 19, 1815, *Adams Papers*, Library of Congress, reel 122 (hereinafter cited as LC).

76. JA to TJ, Jan. 22, 1825, *Works* 10:415.

77. JA to Van der Kamp, Dec. 27, 1816, *Works* 10:234. Cf. JA to TJ, Feb. 2, 1816, Cappon, ed., *Letters*, 2:462. On at least one occasion, Adams referred to Jesus as "our Saviour" (JA to AA, Oct. 9, 1774, in L. H. Butterfield, ed., *The Book of Abigail and John: Selected Letters of the Adams Family, 1762–1784* [Cambridge, MA: Harvard University Press, 1975], 79).

78. JA to JQA, Mar. 28, 1816, Adams Papers, LC, reel 430.

79. John Adams, "Proclamation 8—Recommending a National Day of Humiliation, Fasting, and Prayer," Mar. 23, 1798, http://www.presidency.ucsb.edu/ws/?pid=65661; Adams, "Proclamation—Recommending a National Day of Humiliation, Fasting, and Prayer," Mar. 6, 1799, http://www.presidency.ucsb.edu/ws/?pid=65675.

80. JA to TJ, Sept. 14, 1813, *Works* 10:66–67.

81. JA to JQA, Nov. 3, 1815, Adams Papers, MHS, reel 122.

82. JA to TJ, Dec. 25, 1813, *Works* 10:85.

83. Aug. 1, 1761, *Diary* 1:220.

84. JA to Francis Van der Kemp, Jan. 23, 1813, Adams Papers, MHS, reel 121.

85. JA to JQA, Nov. 13, 1816, Adams Papers, MHS, reel 123.

86. JA to Francis Van der Kamp, July 13, 1815, *Works* 10:169–70; quotations in that order.

87. JA to Van der Kamp, July 13, 1815, *Works* 10:170.

88. Thompson, *Adams*, 18.

89. JA to Cranch, Aug. 29, 1765, *Papers* 1:16.

90. JA to TJ, Sept. 14, 1813, *Works* 10:69 (first and second quotations); JA to AA, May 2, 1775, in Butterfield, ed., *Book*, 82 (third, fourth, and fifth quotations); Adams, "Message in Reply to the Senate," Nov. 26, 1800, http://www.presidency.ucsb.edu/ws/?pid=65694 (sixth quotation).

91. *More Books: Being the Bulletin of the Boston Public Library*, vol. IX, no. 10 (Boston Public Library, Dec. 1934), 385 (first quotation); JA to Benjamin Rush, July 23, 1806, in Schutz and Adair, eds., *Spur*, 61–62 (second quotation).

92. JA to TJ, Dec. 25, 1813, *Works* 10:85.

93. JA to Rush, Feb. 2, 1807, in Schutz and Adair, eds., *Spur*, 75–76.

94. E.g., John Adams, "Governor Winthrop to Governor Bradford," Feb. 9 and 16, 1767, No. 11; in *The Revolutionary Writings of John Adams*, ed. C. Bradley Thompson (Indianapolis: Liberty Fund, 2000), 61, 63 (hereinafter cited as *RW*); JA to Unknown, Apr. 27, 1777, in Robert Taylor, Greg Lint, and Celeste Walker, eds., *Papers, August 1776–March 1778*, vol. 5 (Cambridge, MA: Harvard University Press, 1983), 163; JA to AA, May 4, 1775, in Butterfield, ed., *Book*, 83.

95. JA to TJ, June 28, 1813, *Works* 10:45.

96. Adams, *Works* 2:31; 10:66, 85; 9:396; quotations from Fielding, "Adams," 39. See also JA to TJ, Sept. 24, 1821, Cappon, ed., *Letters*, 2:576; JA to TJ, Jan. 23, 1825, *Works* 10:415–16.

97. Frazer, *Religious Beliefs*, 223.

98. JA to TJ, Dec. 25, 1813, *Works* 10:85.

99. JA to Benjamin Rush, Feb. 2, 1807, Schutz and Adair, eds., *Fame*, 76.

100. Feb. 22, 1756, *Diary*, 1:9.

101. Mar. 2, 1756, *Diary* 1:11.

102. JA to Cranch, Aug. 29, 1756, *Papers* 1:16; JA to Abigail Smith, Dec. 4, 1782, Abigail Adams Smith, *Correspondence of Miss Adams, Daughter of John Adams* (New York: Wiley and Putnam, 1842), 22.

103. E.g., JA to AA, Sept. 16, 1774, in Butterfield, ed., *Book*, 76; JA to Royall Tyler, Apr. 3, 1784, *Founding Families: Digital Editions of the Papers of the Winthrops and the Adamses*, ed. C. James Taylor (Boston: Massachusetts Historical Society, 2007), http://www.masshist.org/ff/; Adams, "To the Inhabitants of the Town

of Cincinnati," Aug. 11, 1798, *Works* 9:216 (cf. Adams, "To the Students of Dickinson College," June 29, 1798, *Works* 9:205; Adams, "To the Inhabitants of Harrison County, Virginia," Aug. 13, 1798, *Works* 9:217); JA to Pickering, Oct. 16, 1799, *Works* 9:39; Adams, "To the Mayor, Aldermen, and Citizens of the City of Philadelphia," Apr. 1798, *Works* 9:182 (cf. Adams, "To the Governor and the Legislature of Connecticut," *Works* 9:207–8); Adams, "Speech to Both Houses of Congress," Nov. 22, 1800, *Works* 9:143; JA to JQA, Feb. 18, 1825, *Works* 10:416.

104. E.g., JA to AA, Oct. 9, 1774, in Butterfield, ed., *Book*, 79; JA to AA, Aug. 4, 1776, ibid., 149; Apr. 23, 1786, *Diary* 3:190; Abigail Adams, March 30–May 1, 1788, ibid., 215. John Adams's diary contains many accounts of sermons he heard in various churches.

105. JA to Benjamin Rush, Aug. 28, 1811, *Works* 9:637.

106. E.g., June 9, 1771, *Diary* 2:30; Dec. 20, 1772, ibid., 2:71; Feb. 17, 1777, ibid., 2:259.

107. Oct. 23, 1774, *Diary*, 2:156.

108. David McCullough, *John Adams* (New York: Simon and Schuster, 2001), 20.

109. See Feb. 13, 1756, *Diary* 1:6; Apr. 25, 1756, ibid., 1:22. See Frazer, *Religious Beliefs*, 111. Adams did affirmatively recount the story of a Baptist pastor in rural Virginia who was brought before a magistrate for preaching that Anglican clergy taught that "Salvation was to be obtained by good Works, or Obedience," which was leading people to ruin. The magistrate discharged him, however, when the Baptist showed that the 18th or 20th article of the Anglican Thirty-Nine Articles asserted the same point he had made (Oct. 23, 1774, *Diary* 2:156). He also wrote that his religion was based on "the hope of pardon for my offences" and "contrition" (JA to Van der Kamp, July 13, 1815, *Works* 10:170).

110. May 7, 1756, *Diary*, 1:25.

111. May 28, 1756, *Diary* 1:31.

112. Thompson, *Adams*, 18. See May 29, 1756, *Diary*, 1:31.

113. JA to TJ, Dec. 12, 1816, in Cappon, ed., *Letters*, 2:499.

114. JA to Charlotte de Windt, Jan. 24, 1820, Adams Papers, LC, reel 124.

115. Aug. 14, 1796, *Diary*, 3:241.

116. Frazer, *Religious Beliefs*, 112.

117. Feb. 16, 1756, *Diary* 1:8.

118. JA to Miller, July 8, 1820, *Works* 10:390.

119. Butterfield, ed., *Autobiography*, 3:434–35.

120. JA to TJ, Dec. 12, 1816, *Works* 10:232. See Steven Waldman, *Founding Faith: Providence, Politics, and the Birth of Religious Freedom in America* (New York: Random House, 2008), 184. See also JA to TJ, Oct. 4, 1813, *Works* 10:76–78, where Adams praises the religious views of the Chaldeans, Egyptians, Persians, Indians, Chinese, Jews, and Greeks, and argues that Cleanthes, a Greek Stoic

philosopher, was "as good a Christian as [Joseph] Priestley" (78). On his views of Hinduism, see JA to TJ, Dec. 25, 1813, *Works* 10:85–86. In 1774 Adams described his attendance at St. Mary's Catholic Church in Philadelphia. He praised the short, moral homily on parents' duty to take care of their children's temporal and spiritual needs, but he protested that congregants fingered their beads and chanted Latin, which they did not understand. The service contained everything to "charm and bewitch the simple and ignorant" (JA to AA, Oct. 9, 1774, in Butterfield, ed., *Book*, 79). Cf. JA to William Tudor, Oct. 9, 1774, Robert Taylor, Mary-Jo Kline, and Gregg Lint, eds., *Papers of John Adams*, vol. 2: *December 1773–April 1775* (Cambridge, MA: Harvard University Press, 1977), 188. Reflecting on this service, Adams wrote, "I am amazed that Luther and Calvin, were ever able to break the Charm and dissolve the spell" of Catholicism. See also Oct. 9, 1774, *Diary* 2:150. For a similar critique of a Catholic service (in Brussels), see July 30, 1780, *Diary* 2:443. During the struggle against England, Adams frequently protested the Quakers' pacifism and failure to support the Revolution (e.g. Butterfield, ed., *Autobiography*, 3:313).

121. Feb. 18, 1756, *Diary*, 1:8.

122. John Adams, "A Dissertation on the Canon and the Feudal Law," August 1765, in *Works* 3:449–50, quotations in that order.

123. Aug. 1, 1761, *Diary* 1:219.

124. July 30, 1780, *Diary* 2:443. However, Adams added, "yet perhaps I was rash and unreasonable, and that it is as much Virtue and Wisdom in them to adore, as in me to detest and despise."

125. JA to TJ, Nov. 4, 1816, *Works* 10:229.

126. JA to TJ, Aug. 9, 1816, *Works* 10:225.

127. Thompson, *Adams*, 3–23, quotations from 5 and 10.

128. JA to TJ, Sept. 14, 1813, *Works* 10:67.

129. JA to Quincy, Apr. 22, 1761, *Papers* 1:49.

130. JA to TJ, Dec. 18, 1819, *Works* 10:386.

131. JA to Samuel Quincy, Apr. 22, 1761, *Papers*, 1:49. Cf. JA to Stephen Sewall, May 30, 1821, Adams Papers, MHS, reel 124, and JA to Joseph Thaxter, Aug, 28, 1822, ibid.

132. Aug. 15, 1756, *Diary*, 1:42.

133. JA to Francis van der Kemp, Feb. 23, 1815, Adams Papers, LC, reel 122. In another letter Adams professed: "I have an immense load of errors, weaknesses, follies, and sins to mourn over and repent of" (JA to Rush, May 1, 1807, Schutz and Adair, ed., *Spur*, 83–84).

134. JA to JQA, July 18, 1816, Adams Papers, MHS, reel 122.

135. JA to Rush, Jan. 21, 1810, *Works* 9:627.

136. Grant, *Adams*, 363.

137. JA to TJ, Mar. 2, 1816, *Works* 10:211–12.

138. Adams, marginal notes on Mary Wollstonecraft, *An Historical and Moral View of the Origin and Progress of the French Revolution* (1794), 230, quoted in Haraszti, *Adams*, 44.

139. JA to Rush, Apr. 18, 1808, Schutz and Adair, *Fame*, 106.

140. JA to Rush, Jan. 21, 1810, *Works* 9:627.

141. JA to TJ, Dec. 3, 1813, Cappon, ed., *Letters*, 2:406.

142. JA to Mordecai Noah, July 31, 1818, Adams Papers, MHS, reel 123.

143. Shaw, *Character*, 309.

144. Quoted in Howe, *Political Thought*, 46. See also Grant, *Adams*, 185.

145. July 22, 1756, *Diary* 1:35.

146. JA to Benjamin Rush, Apr. 12, 1809, *Works* 9:619.

147. JA to David Sewall, May 22, 1821, *Works* 10:399.

148. July 24, 1766, in *Diary* 1:316.

149. JA to Josiah Quincy, Oct. 6, 1775, *Papers* 3:186.

150. JA to Samuel Chase, June 24, 1776, *Works* 9:413. Cf. JA to Josiah Quincy, July 29, 1775, *Works* 9:361.

151. JA to AA, July 3, 1776, *Works* 9:420 (first quotations), 418 (remainder of the quotations).

152. JA to Edmund Jenings, Apr. 28, 1782, Adams Papers, MHS, reel 356.

153. John Adams, "Inaugural Address," Mar. 4, 1797, http://www.presidency.ucsb.edu/ws/?pid=25802.

154. John Adams, "First Annual Message," Nov. 22, 1797, http://www.presidency.ucsb.edu/ws/?pid=29439. Cf. Adams, "Special Session Message," May 16, 1797, http://www.presidency.ucsb.edu/ws/?pid=65636; Adams, "Third Annual Message," Dec. 3, 1799, http://www.presidency.ucsb.edu/ws/?pid=29441.

155. Adams, "Proclamation," Mar. 23, 1798. On Adams's copious use of providential language, also see Arthur Scherr, "John Adams, Providential Rhetoric and Party Warfare: A Note on Massachusetts Politics in the Late 1790s," *Mid-America* 73 (Jan. 1991), 7–27.

156. Adams, "Proclamation," Mar. 23, 1798.

157. John Adams, "Second Annual Message," Dec. 8, 1798, http://www.presidency.ucsb.edu/ws/?pid=29440.

158. Adams, "Proclamation," Mar. 6, 1799.

159. John Adams, "Reply to the Address of the Senate, on the Death of George Washington," Dec. 23, 1799, http://www.presidency.ucsb.edu/ws/index.php?pid=65683.

160. John Adams, "To the Soldier Citizens of New Jersey," May 31, 1798, *Works* 9:196.

161. Adams, "Message in Reply to the Senate," Nov. 26, 1800. Cf. John Adams, "To the Legislature of Massachusetts," June 15, 1798, *Works* 9:201.

162. John Adams, "To the Printers of the Boston Patriot," June 10, 1809, Letter XVIII, *Works* 9:311.

163. JA to Francis Van der Kemp, Dec. 28, 1800, *Works* 9:577; JA to Elbridge Gerry, Dec. 30, 1800, *Works* 9:578; quotations in that order. Adams responded similarly when he and Abigail lost a stillborn daughter in 1777 (Smith, *Adams*, 1:332).

164. Aug. 14, 1756, in *Diary*, 1:41.

165. JA to John Lathrop, Mar. 22, 1813, *Works* 10:34.

166. Summer 1759, *Diary*, 1:113; it is possible this letter was never sent (122).

167. JA to Francis Van der Kamp, May 26, 1816, *Works* 10:220.

168. JA to TJ, May 6, 1816, *Works* 10:218.

169. E.g., JA to AA, May 2, 1775, July 3, 1776, June 2, 1777, Oct. 12, 1782, all in *Adams Family Papers*.

170. Marginalia in *Winthrop's Lecture on Earthquakes*, Dec. 1758(?), *Diary* 1:62.

171. JA to James Warren, July 15, 1776, in *Warren–Adams Letters: Being Chiefly a Correspondence among John Adams, Samuel Adams, and James Warren*, vol. 1: *1743–1777* (Boston: Massachusetts Historical Society, 1917), 260.

172. George Washington Corner, ed., *Autobiography of Benjamin Rush* (Philadelphia: American Philosophical Society, 1948), 142. See also Benjamin Rush to JA, Feb. 24, 1790, in L. H. Butterfield, ed., *Letters of Benjamin Rush*, 2 vols. (Princeton, NJ: American Philosophical Society, 1951), 1:532–36.

173. Diary, Feb. 21, 1765, Adam Family Papers, MHS. Adams did declare that "America is the City, set upon a hill," but he made no reference to Winthrop. See JA to Nathanael Greene, Mar. 18, 1780, *Papers of John Adams*, vol. 9: *March 1780–July 1780*, ed. Gregg Lint et al. (Cambridge, MA: Harvard University Press, 1996), 62.

174. JA to General Benjamin Lincoln, June 19, 1789, quoted in John Robert Irelan, *The Republic; or, A History of the United States of America* (Chicago: Fairbanks and Palmer, 1888), 448.

175. John Adams, *A Defence of the Constitutions of the Governments of the United States of America* (1786) in *Works* 4:401.

176. JA to Benjamin Rush, Oct. 22, 1812, in *Old Family Letters: Contains Letters of John Adams* (Philadelphia: J. B. Lippincott, 1892), 311.

177. Sarah Beth Vosburg, "American Exceptionalism, Responsibility and the Limits of Politics: America's Purpose and Liberty's Progress in the Political Thought of John Adams," 14, http://papers.ssrn.com/sol3/papers.cfm?abstract_id=2111008.

178. John Adams, *Defence*, in *Works* 4:290.

179. John Adams, "The Earl of Clarendon to William Pym," No II, *Works* 3:475.

180. Adams, "Dissertation," *Works* 3:452.

181. Adams, "Dissertation," *Works* 3:453–54; first quotation from 454, remainder from 453.

182. Adams, "Dissertation," No. 2, Aug. 19, 1765, *Papers* 1:116. Cf. Adams, "Governor Winthrop to Governor Bradford," No. 1, Jan. 26, 1767, in *RW*, 59.

183. Smith, *Adams*, 1:235; Gordon Wood, *The Creation of the American Republic, 1776–1787* (New York: Norton, 1969), 575–76, 579.

184. JA to AA, Apr. 11, 1764, Adams Papers, LC, reel 343.

185. JA to TJ, July 18, 1813, *Works* 10:58.

186. JA to Francis Van Der Kamp, July 13, 1815, *Works* 10:170.

187. JA to Benjamin Rush, Nov. 29, 1812, Schutz and Adair, eds., *Spur*, 255.

188. See JA to TJ, May 3, 1816, *Works* 10:215.

189. JA to Mrs. Rush, Apr. 24, 1813, in Schutz and Adair, eds., *Spur*, 281.

190. Quoted in Nagel, *Adams Women*, 157.

191. JA to Miller, July 8, 1820, *Works* 10:390. Cf. JA to the Freemasons of the State of Maryland, July 14, 1798, *Works* 9:213.

192. JA to TJ, May 29, 1818, *Works* 10:314.

193. JA to Sewall, May 22, 1821, *Works* 10:399.

194. JA to Benjamin Rush, Sept. 19, 1806, in Schutz and Adair, eds., *Spur*, 65.

195. JA to Alexander Johnson, April 1823, Adams Papers, reel 124. Cf. JA to TJ, Aug. 9, 1816, Cappon, ed., *Letters* 2:486.

196. JA to Van Der Kamp, Dec. 27, 1816, *Works* 10:236.

197. JA to TJ, Dec. 8, 1818, *Works* 10:363.

198. Aug. 22, 1770, *Diary* 1:365.

199. Adams, "Thoughts on Government," in *Works* 4:193.

200. Conklin, *Puritans*, 122, 127–28.

201. Adams, "Inaugural Address."

202. JA to TJ, June 28, 1813, *Works* 10:45–46; Grant, *Adams*, 222. See the constitution he drafted for Massachusetts in 1779, *Papers*, 8:238ff.

203. John Fea, *Was America Founded as a Christian Nation?: A Historical Introduction* (Louisville, KY: Westminster John Knox Press, 2011), 3–4.

204. JA to Francis Van Der Kemp, Feb., 16, 1809, *Works* 9:610.

205. Adams's marginal note on Condorcet's *Outlines of an Historical View of the Progress of the Human Mind* (1795), as quoted in Haraszti, *Adams*, 252.

206. Smith, *Adams*, 1:380.

207. Adams, "Discourses on Davila," in *Works* 6:281.

208. Thompson, *Adams*, 149; Diggins, *Adams*, 100.

209. Richard Samuelson, "John Adams and the Republic of Laws," in Bryan-Paul Frost and Jeffrey Sikkenga, eds., *History of American Political Thought* (Lanham, MD: Lexington Books, 2003), 116. See also, Adams, *Defence*, in *Works* 6:43.

210. Ellis Sandoz, *Republicanism, Religion, and the Soul of America* (Columbia: University of Missouri Press, 2006), 49. Adams, "Dissertation," *Works* 3:462–63.

211. JA to TJ, Apr. 19, 1817, *Works* 10:254.

212. *Works* 4:406, 4:206.

213. Adams, "On Private Revenge," no. III, in *RW*, 17; Adams, *Defence*, in *Works* 6:61; JA to Waterhouse, Dec. 19, 1815.

214. Adams, *Works* 4:286, 409.

215. JA to AA, Aug. 5, 1776, in Butterfield, ed., *Book*, 151.

216. Adams, "On Self-Delusion," no. II, in *RW*, 9.

217. JA to James Warren, Feb. 25, 1779, in Taylor, ed., *Papers* 7:429.

218. Feb. 19, 1756, *Diary* 1:8.

219. Adams, *Works* 4:408.

220. Thompson, *Adams*, 149.

221. E.g., Adams, *Works* 4:406, 408; 6:182–83.

222. Thompson, *Adams*, 152. See *Works* 6:234; 4:407. On Adams's view of Hobbes, see John Payner, "John Adams' 'Hobbism'," in Ronald Pestritto and Thomas West, eds., *The American Founding and the Social Compact* (Lanham, MD: Lexington Books, 2003), 231–53.

223. *Works* 6:141; Thompson, *Adams*, 152.

224. Adams, *Defence*, in *Works* 6:115.

225. *Works* 6:114–15, 141, 234 (quotations).

226. Adams, "Discourses on Davila," in *Works* 6:232.

227. JA to AA, May 22, 1777, *Adams Family Papers*.

228. *Works* 6:234; Thompson, *Adams*, 150–55.

229. Shaw, *Character*, 21.

230. *Works* 6:279.

231. Shaw, *Character*, 21.

232. Adams, "Discourses on Davila," in *Works* 6:246.

233. Ralph Adams Brown, *The Presidency of John Adams* (Lawrence: University of Kansas Press, 1975), 211. See John Adams, "Conclusion," in *Defence*, in *Works* 4:579–88; Adams, "Three Letters to Roger Sherman on the Constitution of the United States," II, July 18, 1789, in *Works* 6:431; JA to Thomas McKean, Sept. 20, 1779, in Taylor, ed., *Papers* 8:485.

234. Howe, *Political Thought*, 89–99; Wood, *Creation*, 574–80.

235. JA to James Sullivan, Sept. 17, 1789, *Works* 9:562.

236. Adams, *Defence*, in *Works* 4:290.

237. Taylor, ed., *Papers* 1:109. Cf. ibid., 117, 120. See also *Works* 3:449; 4:220.

238. JA to Brand-Hollis, June 11, 1790, *Works* 9:570.

239. Brown, *Presidency*, 212.

240. Taylor, ed., *Papers* 1:121.

241. Brown, *Presidency*, 214.

242. JA to Brand-Hollis, June 11, 1790, *Works* 9:570.

243. John Adams, "Discourses on Davila," in *Works* 6:396.

244. JA to James Warren, June, 17, 1782, *Works* 9:512.

245. JA to Mercy Otis Warren, May 29, 1789, *Warren–Adams Letters*, vol. 2: *1778–1814* (Boston: Massachusetts Historical Society, 1925), 314. Cf. JA to AA, Jan. 24, 1793, in Charles Francis Adams, ed., *Letters of John Adams Addressed to His Wife*, 2 vols. (Boston: Charles Little and James Brown, 1841), 2:121: "I never in my Life . . . sacrificed my Principles or Duty to Popularity, or Reputation."

246. JA to Benjamin Rush, May 1, 1807, in Schutz and Adair, eds., *Spur*, 83.

247. Adams, "Clarendon to Pym," no. III, Jan. 27, 1766, in *RW*, 53.

248. JA to Mercy Otis Warren, Apr. 16, 1776, Robert Taylor, Greg Lint, and Celeste Walkers, eds., *Papers*, vol. 4: *February–August 1776* (Cambridge, MA: Harvard University Press, 1979), 124.

249. John Adams, "To the Inhabitants of the Borough of Harrisburgh Pennsylvania," May 12, 1798, *Works* 9:193.

250. John Adams, *Novanglus; or a History of the Dispute with America, from Its Origin, in 1754, to the Present Time*, no. IV, in *RW*, 185.

251. JA to Warren, Apr. 16, 1776, *Papers* 4:124–25; quotation from 124.

252. Adams, "Dissertation," *Works* 3:463, 456; quotations in that order.

253. Adams, "Dissertation," in *RW*, 33.

254. See, Howe, Jr., *Political Thought*, 17–19; Wood, *Creation*, 18–28 and passim.

255. Adams, "Dickinson College," *Works* 9:205.

256. JA to Rush, Aug. 28, 1811, *Works* 9:636.

257. John Adams, "To the Students of New Jersey College," June 29, 1798, *Works* 9:206.

258. JA to Zabdiel Adams, June 21, 1776, *Works* 9:401.

259. John Adams, "To the Officers . . . of the Militia of Massachusetts," Oct. 11, 1798, *Works* 9:229.

260. Susan Dunn, *Jefferson's Second Revolution: The Election Crisis of 1800 and the Triumph of Republicanism* (Boston: Houghton Mifflin, 2004), 11. See the titles of the books below as well as Charles Lerche, Jr., "Jefferson and the Election of 1800: A Case Study in Political Smear," *William and Mary Quarterly*, 3d ser., 5 (Oct. 1948), 467–91.

261. AA to Mary Smith Cranch, May 5, 1800, in Stewart Mitchell, ed., *New Letters of Abigail Adams* (Boston: Houghton Mifflin, 1947), 251–52.

262. Dunn, *Jefferson's Second Revolution*, 2.

263. John Mason, *The Voice of Warning, to Christians, on the Ensuing Election of a President of the United States* (New York, 1800), 8; Theophilus Parsons to John Jay, May 5, 1800, in Henry Johnson, ed., *The Correspondence and Public Papers of John Jay*, 4 vols. (New York: G. P. Putnam's Sons, 1893), 4:270; *Connecticut Courant*, Sept. 20, 1800.

264. *New York Commercial Advertiser*, July 11, 1800.

265. William Linn, *Serious Considerations on the Election of a President* (New York: John Furman, 1800), 28.

266. John Miller, *The Federalist Era, 1789–1801* (New York: Harper, 1960), 264–65. See also John Ferling, *Adams vs. Jefferson: The Tumultuous Election of 1800* (New York: Oxford University Press, 2004), 154.

267. AA to Mary Smith Cranch, Feb. 7, 1801, *New Letters*, 266.

268. Edward Larson, *A Magnificent Catastrophe: The Tumultuous Election of 1800, America's First Presidential Campaign* (New York: Free Press, 2007), 166, 176.

269. Larson, *Magnificent Catastrophe*, 174; *Independent Chronicle*, July 17–21, 1800, 2.

270. *Aurora*, Oct. 14, 1800, 2.

271. Dunn, *Jefferson's Second Revolution*, 149–50; Fisher Ames to Rufus King, Sept. 24, 1800, in Charles King, ed., *Life and Correspondence of Rufus King*, 6 vols. (New York: G. P. Putnam's Sons, 1894–1900), 3:304; JA to John Trumbull, Sept. 10, 1800, in *Works*, 9:83.

272. JA to John Trumbull, Sept. 10, 1800, *Works* 9:83.

273. Thomas Jefferson to Benjamin Rush, Sept. 23, 1800, in Julian Boyd et al., eds., *The Papers of Thomas Jefferson*, 40 vols. to date (Princeton, NJ: Princeton University Press, 1950–), 32:168.

274. *Letter from Alexander Hamilton Concerning the Public Conduct and Character of John Adams, Esq., President of the United States* (New York: John Lang, 1800), 4 (first phrase), 12 (remainder of the phrases); James Roger Sharp, *The Deadlocked Election of 1800: Jefferson, Burr, and the Union in the Balance* (Lawrence: University Press of Kansas, 2010), 105–6; Bernard Weisberger, *American Afire: Jefferson, Adams, and the Revolutionary Election of 1800* (New York: William Morrow, 2000), 249–50.

275. Weisberger, *American Afire*, 252.

276. Larson, *Magnificent Catastrophe*, 177; Dunn, *Jefferson's Second Revolution*, 6.

277. John Adams, "The Report of a Constitution, or a Form of Government, for the Commonwealth of Massachusetts," in *RW*, 298–99. Adams called establishment of the Congregational Church in colonial Massachusetts "a most mild and equitable establishment of religion," an arrangement that was largely preserved in the 1780 Constitution (*Diary*, Oct. 14, 1774, *Works*, 2:399).

278. See John Witte, Jr., "'A Most Mild and Equitable Establishment of Religion': John Adams and the Massachusetts Experiment," *JCS* 41 (Spring 1999), 213–52.

279. E.g., Adams, "Speech to Both Houses of Congress," Nov. 22, 1800, *Works* 9:144.

280. E. H. Gillett, *History of the Presbyterian Church in the United States of America*, 2 vols. (Philadelphia: Presbyterian Publication Committee, 1873), 1:296–97.

281. JA to Benjamin Rush, June 12, 1812, Schutz and Adair, eds., *Spur*, 224.

282. Adams, "To the Printers of the Boston Patriot," June 10, 1809, Letter XIII, *Works* 9:291. See also Charles Ellis Dickson, "Jeremiads in the New American Republic: The Case of the National Fasts in the John Adams Administration," *New England Quarterly* 60 (June 1987), 187–207.

283. Grant, *Adams*, 157.

284. JA to AA, Nov. 18, 1775, in *AFC*, 1:327.

285. Thompson, *Adams*, 22. E.g., May 14–Aug. 22, 1756, *Diary* 1:33–44.

286. "A Proclamation By the Great and General Court of the Colony of Massachusetts Bay," in Adams, *Life*, 1:273.

287. Mercy Otis Warren, *History . . . of the American Revolution*, 3 vols. (Boston: Manning and Loring, 1805), 3:395.

288. Thompson, *Adams*, 31–32; quotations in that order.

289. JA to Richard Price, Apr. 19, 1790, *Works* 9:564.

290. Brown, *Presidency*, 179 (quotation), 186. See, for example, Alexander Hamilton, *Letter concerning the Public Conduct and Character of John Adams* (New York: John Lang, 1800).

291. JA to Rush, Aug. 28, 1811, *Works* 9:636–37; all quotations except the last one from 636.

292. Shaw, *Character*, 19; Feb. 16, 1756, *Diary*, 1:7–8; quotations in that order.

293. May 3, 1756, *Diary*, 1:25.

294. Shaw, *Character*, 23.

295. Smith, *Adams*, 1:263.

296. Diggins, *Adams*, 174.

297. JA to Edmund Jenings, Sept. 27, 1782, Adams Papers, MHS, reel 358.

298. JA to James Warren, Jan. 9, 1787, *Warren–Adams Letters* 2:281.

299. Brown, *Presidency*, 22.

300. Stanley Elkins and Eric McKitrick, *The Age of Federalism: The Early American Republic, 1788– 1800* (New York: Oxford University Press, 1993), 529; Kurtz, *Presidency*, 403–4 (see also Steven Kurtz, "President Adam Chooses Peace," in *The Federalists: Creators and Critics of the Union, 1780–1801*, ed. Kurtz [New York: Wiley, 1972], 185–97; Brown, *Presidency*, 174; JA to James Lloyd, Jan. 1815, *Works* 10:113).

301. Adams, "Proclamation," Mar. 6, 1799; Adams: "Message in Reply to the House of Representatives," Dec. 14, 1798, http://www.presidency.ucsb.edu/ws/?pid=65664 (quotation). Cf. Adams: "Message in Reply to the House of Representatives," Dec. 10, 1799, http://www.presidency.ucsb.edu/ws/?pid=65679.

302. Adams, "Special Session Message," May 16, 1797; Adams, "First Annual Message"; Adams, "Inaugural Address."

303. John Ferling, *John Adams: A Life* (Knoxville: University of Tennessee Press, 1992), 342–45; quotation from 342.

304. John Adams, "**Message in Reply to the Senate**," May 24, 1797, http://www.presidency.ucsb.edu/ws/index.php?pid=65647.

305. Adams, "First Annual Message."

306. Adams, "To the Inhabitants of Bridgeton," May 1, 1798, *Works* 9:186.

307. JA to John Marshall, Oct. 3, 1800, *Works* 9:86.

308. John Adams, "Speech to Both Houses of Congress," Nov. 23, 1797, *Works* 9:122.

309. John Adams, "To the Cincinnati of South Carolina," Sept. 15, 1798, *Works* 9:222–23.

310. JA to Timothy Pickering, Sept. 19, 1799, *Works* 9:32.

311. Brown, *Presidency*, 31, 102–3; quotation from 31.

312. John Adams, "Speech to Both Houses of Congress," Dec. 8, 1798, *Works* 9:130.

313. Brown, *Presidency*, 91, 101; quotations in that order. On the divisions among the Federalists, see Manning Dauer, *The Adams Federalists* (Baltimore: Johns Hopkins University, 1953), 172–237.

314. Adams, "Speech to Both Houses of Congress," May 16, 1797, *Works* 9:119.

315. Adams, "To the Legislature of Massachusetts," June 15, 1798, *Works* 9:201.

316. Adams, "Proclamation," Mar. 23, 1798.

317. Adams, "Proclamation," Mar. 6, 1799.

318. Adams, "To the Printers of the Boston Patriot," June 10, 1809, Letter XIII, *Works* 9:291.

319. John Adams, "To the Boston Marine Society," Sept. 7, 1798, *Works* 9:221.

320. Adams, "Harrison County," *Works* 9:217.

321. John Adams, "To the Grand Jurors of the County of Hampshire, Massachusetts," Oct. 3, 1798, *Works* 9:227.

322. Adams, "Legislature of Massachusetts," *Works* 9:201.

323. John Adams, "To the Inhabitants of Washington County, Maryland," July 14, 1798, *Works* 9:214.

324. JA to Timothy Pickering, Aug. 6, 1799, *Works* 9:11.

325. Ferling, *Life*, 379; Alexander DeConde, *The Quasi-War: The Politics and Diplomacy of the Undeclared War with France, 1797–1801* (New York: Scribner, 1966), 170, 179–80; JA to George Washington, Feb. 21, 1799, *Works* 8:626.

326. Ferling, *Life*, 372–73.

327. James Morton Smith, *Freedom's Fetters: The Alien and Sedition Laws and American Civil Liberties* (Ithaca, NY: Cornell University Press, 1966), 20.

328. Leonard Levy, *Freedom of Speech and Press in Early American History: Legacy of Suppression* (New York: Harper and Row, 1960), 198. For a condemnation of Adams's role in the Alien and Sedition Acts, see John Miller, *Crisis in Freedom: The Alien and Sedition Acts* (Boston: Little, Brown, 1951). For a defense of the Federalist position, see James Martin, "When Repression Is Democratic and Constitutional: The Federalist Theory of Representation and the Sedition Act of 1798," *University of Chicago Law Review* 66 (Winter 1999), 117–82.

329. Kurtz, *Presidency*, 374.

330. Ferling, *Life*, 379–80; quotation from 379.

331. Brown, *Presidency*, 113.

332. Ryerson, "Introduction," 28–29; both quotations from 28.

333. Conklin, *Puritans*, 123.

334. Thompson, *Adams*, xiv.

335. Corner, ed., *Autobiography*, 140; Thomas Jefferson, conversation with Daniel Webster, 1824, http://history.wisc.edu/csac/founders/john_adams.htm#webster1824.

336. Edmund Morgan, "John Adams and the Puritan Tradition," *New England Quarterly* 34 (Dec. 1961), 522.

337. McCullough, *Adams*, 384.

338. Conklin, *Puritans*, 112, 114; quotations in that order.

339. Kurtz, *Presidency*, 407.

340. Brown, *Presidency*, 210.

341. Smith, *Adams*, 2:673.

342. Brown, *Presidency*, 215. For a much more negative appraisal of Adams's presidency that portrays him as a weak executive who was hampered by his own lack of political acumen, isolation, the absence of moderate advice, see Douglas Bradbury, "The Presidency of John Adams," in Waldstreicher, ed., *Companion*, 166–83.

343. JA to Francis Van der Kemp, Dec. 28, 1800, *Works* 9:577.

344. Brown, *Presidency*, 215.

345. Conklin, *Puritans*, 145.

346. Bowditch, as quoted in Ellis, *Sage*, 210; Rush is quoted in the *Niles' Weekly Register*, July 22, 1826. See also Merrill Peterson, *The Jefferson Image in the American Mind* (New York: Oxford University Press, 1960), 2–10.

347. Conklin, *Puritans*, 118.

CHAPTER 2

1. John Vile, William Pederson, and Frank Williams, "Introduction: More Than Just a President," in Vile, Pederson, and Williams, ed., *James Madison: Philosopher, Founder, and Statesman* (Athens: Ohio University Press, 2008), vii.

2. Irving Brant, *James Madison: The Nationalist, 1780–1787* (Indianapolis: Bobbs-Merrill, 1948), 352 (first quotation); Ralph Ketcham, *James Madison: A Biography* (Charlottesville: University of Press of Virginia, 1990), 163, 165 (second quotation).

3. Garrett Ward Sheldon, "Religion and the Presidency of James Madison," in Gaston Espinoza, ed., *Religion and the American Presidency: George Washington to George W. Bush* (New York: Columbia University Press, 2009), 112.

4. E.g., Jack Rakove, ed., *Writings/James Madison* (New York: Library of America, 1999); Ralph Ketcham, ed., *Selected Writings of James Madison* (Indianapolis: Hackett, 2006); Jack Rakove, *James Madison and the Creation of the American Republic* (New York: Pearson Longman, 2007).

5. Garry Wills, *James Madison* (New York: Times Books, 2002), 2–4, 5–7; quotation from 4.

6. Norman Cousins, ed., *The Republic of Reason: Personal Philosophies of the Founding Fathers* (San Francisco: Harper and Row, 1988), 296.

7. Lance Banning, *The Sacred Fire of Liberty: James Madison and the Founding of the Federal Republic* (Ithaca, NY: Cornell University Press, 1995), 80. See also Lance Banning, "James Madison and the Statute for Religious Freedom and

the Crisis of Republican Conviction," in Merrill Pederson and Robert Vaughn, ed., *The Virginia Statute for Religious Freedom: Its Evolution and Consequences in American History* (New York: Cambridge University Press, 1988), 109.

8. Edmund Randolph to JM, Mar. 18, 1790, William Hutchinson and William Rachel, eds., *The Papers of James Madison*, 17 vols. (Chicago: University of Chicago Press), 13:108–9 (hereinafter cited as *Papers*).

9. Irving Brant, *James Madison*, 6 vols. (Indianapolis: Bobbs Merrill, 1941–64), 1:118, 295.

10. Craig Grau, "More than an Intellectual Scribe: The Political Drives and Traits of James Madison," in Vile, Pederson, and Williams, ed., *Madison*, 27.

11. Douglass Adair, ed., "James Madison's Autobiography," *William and Mary Quarterly*, 3d ser., 2 (1945), 197.

12. Mary-Elaine Swanson, *The Education of James Madison: A Model for Today* (Montgomery, AL: Hoffman Education Center, 1992), 2; Brant, *Madison*, 1:62, 58; Sheldon, "Madison," 114.

13. Brant, *Madison*, 1:68–70, 73, 77; Sheldon, "Madison," 114; Mary-Elaine Swanson, "James Madison and the Presbyterian Idea of Man and Government," in Garrett Ward Sheldon and Daniel Dreisbach, eds., *Religion and Political Culture in Jefferson's Virginia* (Lanham, MD: Rowman and Littlefield, 2000), 121; Adair, ed., "Autobiography," 197; Mark Noll, *Princeton and the Republic, 1768–1872* (Princeton, NJ: Princeton University Press, 1989), 32 (quotation).

14. Sheldon, "Madison," 115; Swanson, *Education*, 107; Francis Broderick, "Pulpit, Physics, and Politics: The Curriculum of the College of New Jersey, 1746–1794," *William and Mary Quarterly*, 3d ser., 6 (Jan. 1949), 42–68.

15. William Meade, *Old Churches, Ministers and Families of Virginia*, 2 vols. (Philadelphia: Lippincott, 1872), 2:99. Brant argued that it was very unlikely that Madison was influenced by the Princeton revival in 1770 (*Madison*, 1:114–17).

16. Jeff Broadwater, *James Madison: A Son of Virginia and a Founder of the Nation* (Chapel Hill: University of North Carolina, Press, 2012), 4.

17. Brant, *Madison*, 1:84.

18. On Princeton during these years, see Noll, *Princeton*, 26–27, 29–32. Madison secretly read Voltaire at Princeton, but as a young man he was very critical of those who attacked Christianity, accusing them of citing passages out of context and seeking to destroy "the most essential truths" (Brant, *Madison*, 1:119).

19. Broadwater, *Madison*, 4.

20. Wills, *Madison*, 18.

21. Broadwater, *Madison*, 4.

22. Catherine Allgor, *A Perfect Union: Dolley Madison and the Creation of the American Republic* (New York: Henry Holt, 2006), 20.

23. Allgor, *Union*, 5, 32, 387 (quotation); Steven Waldman, *Founding Faith: Providence, Politics, and the Birth of Religious Freedom in America* (New York: Random House, 2008), 184.

24. Allgor, *Union*, 8, 33; Gaillard Hunt, *The Life of James Madison* (New York: Russell and Russell, [1902] 1968), 245.

25. William Rives, *History of the Life and Times of James Madison, 1859–1868*, 4 vols. (Freeport, NY: Books for Libraries Press, 1970), 1:34–35; first and second quotations from 34, third from 35. Madison took many notes on William Burkitt's *Expository Notes, with Practical Observations, on the New Testament of our Lord and Savior Jesus Christ* (1724). Madison's list included the works of many church fathers, including Tertullian, Athanasius, and Augustine. His other authors included Thomas Aquinas, Martin Luther, John Calvin, Isaac Newton, Cotton Mather, William Penn, Jonathan Edwards, Gottfried Wilhelm Leibnitz, and John Wesley. See Rives, *History*, 1:642–44.

26. James Smylie, "Madison and Witherspoon: Theological Roots of American Political Thought," *Princeton Library Chronicle* 22 (Spring 1961), 124, 125 (quotation), 127; Michael Novak, *On Two Wings: Humble Faith and Common Sense at the American Founding* (San Francisco: Encounter Books, 2003), 139; Garrett Ward Sheldon, "Religion and Politics in the Thought of James Madison," in Daniel Dreisbach, Mark D. Hall, and Jeffry Morrison, eds., *The Founders on God and Government* (Lanham, MD: Rowman and Littlefield, 2004), 84; Sheldon, "Madison," 111 (see also Sheldon, *The Political Philosophy of James Madison* [Baltimore: Johns Hopkins University Press, 2001], xi–xvi, 6–37); Sheldon, *Philosophy*, 10; quotations in that order. On Witherspoon, see L. Gordon Tait, *The Piety of John Witherspoon: Pew, Pulpit, and Public Forum* (Louisville, KY: Geneva Press, 2001), and Jeffry Morrison, *John Witherspoon and the Founding of the American Republic* (Notre Dame, IN: University of Notre Dame Press, 2005).

27. Sheldon, "Madison," 112–13 (first quotation); Sheldon, *Philosophy*, xv (second quotation), 2 (third quotation).

28. Sheldon, "Madison," 112–13. See James Madison, "Commentary on the Bible, 1770," *Papers*, 1:58.

29. Sheldon, "Madison," 112 (first quotation), 133, (third and fourth quotations); Sheldon, *Philosophy*, xii (second quotation).

30. Sheldon, "Madison," 117. Madison argued "it is not the *talking*, but the *walking* and *working* person that is the true Christian" ("Commentary on the Bible," 1:58).

31. Sheldon, "Madison," 111.

32. Swanson, *Education*, 126.

33. Swanson, *Education*, 71. See Madison, "Notes on a Brief System of Logick," *Papers* 1:32–42.

34. Swanson, "Madison," 119, 122–23 (quotation from 122); Swanson, *Education*, 87.

35. John Noonan, Jr., *The Lustre of Our Country: The American Experience of Religious Freedom* (Berkeley: University of California Press, 1998), 89 (quotation), 64–65, 87. "Precious gift" and "light": James Madison, *Memorial and Remonstrance*

against Religious Assessments, Papers 8:303; "Xn principle," Madison, "Detached Memorandum," in Elizabeth Fleet, ed., *William and Mary Quarterly*, 3d ser., 3 (Oct. 1946), 554.

36. Noonan, *Lustre*, 87 (first quotation), 88 (second and third quotations).

37. Scott Kester, *The Haunted Philosophe: James Madison, Republicanism, and Slavery* (Lanham, MD: Lexington Books, 2008), 29 (quotation); Ralph Ketcham, "James Madison and Religion—A New Hypothesis," in Robert Alley, ed., *James Madison on Religious Liberty* (Buffalo, NY: Prometheus Books, 1985), 182; Gregg Frazer, *The Religious Beliefs of America's Founders: Reason, Revelation, Revolution* (Lawrence: University Press of Kansas, 2012), 186.

38. See Swanson, *Education*, 77, 82–84, 165, 296, 319–20; Sheldon, *Philosophy*, 14; Kester, *Philosophe*, 30.

39. Meade, *Churches*, 2:99–100. However, Meade reported that when Madison died, his pastor William Jones and some of his neighbors "openly expressed their conviction, that, from his conversation and bearing during the latter years of his life, he must be considered as receiving the Christian system to be divine" (100). David Holmes counters that no other evidence directly supports this testimony (*The Faiths of the Founding Fathers* [New York: Oxford University Press, 2006], 97).

40. Brant, *Madison*, 1:77 (first quotation), 277 (second quotation), 118 (third quotation); George Ticknor et al., *Life, Letters and Journal of George Ticknor* (Boston: J. R. Osgood, 1876), 1:30; Douglass Adair, *Fame and the Founding Fathers: Essays* (Indianapolis: Liberty Fund, [1964] 1998), 145; Franklin Steiner, *The Religious Beliefs of Our Presidents* (Girard, KS: Haldeman-Julius, 1936), 91; Frank Lambert, *The Founding Fathers and the Place of Religion in America* (Princeton, NJ: Princeton University Press, 2003), 263 (see also 177–78); Holmes, *Faiths*, 97; Vincent Phillip Munoz, "Religion in the Life, Thought, and Presidency of James Madison," in Mark Rozell and Gleaves Whitney, eds., *Religion and the American Presidency* (New York: Palgrave Macmillan, 2007), 56; John West, Jr., *The Politics of Revelation and Reason: Religion and Civic Life in the New Nation* (Lawrence: University of Kansas Press, 1996), 67–68.

41. James Hutson, *Forgotten Features of the Founding* (Lanham, MD: Lexington Books, 2003), 158 (first quotation), 159 (third, fourth, and fifth quotations); JM to TJ, Dec. 31, 1824, in James Smith, ed., *The Republic of Letters: The Correspondence between Thomas Jefferson and James Madison, 1776–1826*, 3 vols. (New York: W. W. Norton, 1995), 3:1913 (second quotation).

42. Kester, *Philosophe*, 18 (first and second quotations), 17, 21 (third quotation), 29. Munoz adds that brief assertions in letters written in his last years display "a more detached, philosophical" perspective that does not "affirm or deny the existence of God or an afterlife" ("Madison," 53).

43. Frazer, *Religious Beliefs*, 166, 172; quotations in that order. Cushing Stout, *The New Heavens and New Earth: Political Religion in America* (New York: Harper

and Row, 1974), 78–79, and Robert Kraynak, *Christian Faith and Modern Democracy: God and Politics in the Fallen World* (Notre Dame, IN: University of Notre Dame Press, 2001), 126–27, also portray Madison as a proponent of "rational religion." According to Stout, these rationalists based their idea of toleration on "a shared conception of 'enlightened religion,' purified of the corruptions" of historic faiths (79). Kraynak avers that these rationalists rejected belief in the Bible as God's revealed word, original sin, divine redemption, the deity and resurrection of Christ, miracles, and eternal punishment in hell.

44. JM to Frederick Beasley, in Gaillard Hunt, ed., *Writings of James Madison*, 9 vols. (New York: G. P. Putnam's Sons, 1910), 9:230–331; Madison, *Memorial*, 8:304; Madison, "Detached Memoranda," 559.

45. JM to Charles Caldwell, Nov. 23, 1826, http://memory.loc.gov/cgi-bin/ampage?collId=mjm&fileName=21/mjm21.db&recNum=734&itemLink=D?mjm:3:./temp/~ammem_aCfH::.

46. Joseph Loconte, "Faith and the Founding: The Influence of Religion on the Politics of James Madison," *JCS* 40 (Autumn 2003), 700.

47. Ketcham, *Madison*, 47; Ketcham, "Hypothesis," 184; quotations in that order.

48. Ketcham, "Hypothesis," 192 (first and second quotations), 175, 176 (third quotation).

49. Ketcham, "Hypothesis," 180.

50. Rives, *History*, 2:518.

51. Ketcham, "Hypothesis," 177–78.

52. Samuel Stanhope Smith to JM, between Nov. 1777 and Aug. 1778, *Papers* 1:194–97, 209–11; Smith to Madison, Sept. 15, 1778, *Papers* 1:256–57. See Noll, *Princeton*, 69–72.

53. Noonan, *Lustre*, 86–87.

54. JM to Jasper Adams, Sept. 1833, in Daniel Dreisbach, ed., *Religion and Politics in the Early Republic: Jasper Adams and the Church–State Debate* (Lexington: University of Kentucky Press, 1996), 117; Madison, *Memorial, Papers* 8:303; quotations in that order.

55. Madison, *Memorial, Papers* 8:301; Frazer, *Religious Beliefs*, 171.

56. JM to Bradford, Sept. 25, 1773, *Papers* 1:96.

57. Frazer, *Religious Beliefs*, 174. E.g., Madison, "Detached Memorandum," 560–61; JM to Edmund Pendleton, Oct. 28, 1787, in Hunt, ed., *Writings*, 5:44–45.

58. Madison, *Memorial, Papers* 8:303.

59. Banning, *Sacred Fire*, 436.

60. JM to Frederick Beasley, Nov. 20, 1825, in Hunt, ed., *Writings*, 9:230–31.

61. Munoz, "Madison," 55.

62. On Witherspoon's emphasis on God's providence, see his *The Dominion of Providence over the Passions of Men* (Philadelphia: R. Aitken, 1776).

63. James Madison, "Fourth Annual Message," Nov. 4, 1812, http://www.presidency. ucsb.edu/ws/?pid=29454.

64. James **Madison, "Proclamation 20—Recommending a Day of Public Thanksgiving for Peace,"** *Mar. 4, 1815,* http://www.presidency.ucsb.edu/ ws/index.php?pid=65984; Madison, "Proclamation—Recommending a Day of Prayer," July 23, 1813, http://www.presidency.ucsb.edu/ws/?pid=65959; Madison, "Weaknesses of the Confederation," June 7, 1788, *Papers* 11:96; quotations in that order.

65. Robert Rutland, "Introduction" in Merrill Peterson, ed., *James Madison: A Biography in His Own Words,* 2 vols. (New York: Newsweek Book Division, 1974), 1:9.

66. James Madison, Federalist 37. Because Madison did not similarly stress the role of providence in a private letter, some scholars conclude that Madison used providentialist language merely to please the public. E.g., Richard Matthews, *If Men Were Angels: James Madison and the Heartless Empire of Reason* (Lawrence: University Press of Kansas, 1995), 138.

67. "Address of the House of Representatives to the President," May 5, 1798, *Papers* 12:133.

68. James Madison, "Inaugural Address," Mar. 4, 1809, http://www.presidency. ucsb.edu/ws/?pid=25805; Madison, "Special Message," Mar. 9, 1812; Madison, "First Annual Message," Nov. 29, 1809, http://www.presidency.ucsb.edu/ ws/?pid=29451.

69. Madison, "Public Thanksgiving."

70. Madison, "Fourth Annual Message."

71. James Madison, "Fifth Annual Message," Dec. 7, 1813, http://www.presidency. ucsb.edu/ws/?pid=29455. Cf. Madison, "Eighth Annual Message," Dec. 3, 1816, http://www.presidency.ucsb.edu/ws/?pid=29458.

72. James Madison, "Special Message," Feb. 18, 1815, http://www.presidency.ucsb. edu/ws/?pid=65976.

73. JM to DM, Aug. 17, 1809, Lucia Beverly Cutts, ed., *Memoirs and Letters of Dolly Madison* (Boston: Houghton Mifflin, 1896), 67; JM to Eliza House Trist, Feb. 10, 1787, *Papers* 9:259; JM to Philip Mazzei, Oct. 8, 1788, *Papers* 11:279. Many of Madison's personal letters have not been preserved so he may have used religious language much more often.

74. JM to William Bradford, June 10, 1773, in *Papers,* 1:89.

75. JM to William Bradford, Sept. 25, 1773, in *Papers,* 1:96. Frazer claims that this is the only time Madison mentioned Jesus (*Religious Beliefs,* 183).

76. JM to Bradford, Sept. 25, 1773, *Papers,* 1:96; Madison, *Memorial, Papers* 8:301; Madison, "Detached Memoranda," 556.

77. E.g., Frazer, *Religious Beliefs,* 185.

78. Madison, Federalist 37.

79. Madison, Federalist 55 (first quotation); Madison, Federalist 10 (second quotations); Smylie, "Madison," 129.

80. JM to William Bradford, June 19, 1775, *Papers* 1:151.

81. Madison, "Address to Virginia General Assembly," Jan. 1799, in Alley, ed., *Madison*, 78.

82. Madison, Federalist 10.

83. JM to Bradford, Nov. 9, 1772, *Papers* 1:74.

84. E.g., Smylie, "Madison," 121–22; Sheldon, "Madison," 115–19, 124–26; and Mary-Elaine Swanson, "Madison," 122–28. See also John Witherspoon, "All Mankind by Nature under Sin," *The Works of the Rev. John Witherspoon*, 4 vols. (Philadelphia: William W. Woodward, 1802), 1:277.

85. Frazer, *Religious Beliefs*, 184. Madison does use the word "sins" in "Proclamation 18—Recommending a Day of Public Humiliation, Fasting, and Prayer," Nov. 16, 1814, http://www.presidency.ucsb.edu/ws/?pid=65981, and the word "transgressions" in this proclamation, his "Proclamation—Recommending a Day of Prayer," July 9, 1812, http://www.presidency.ucsb.edu/ws/?pid=65944, and his July 23, 1813 proclamation.

86. The first two quotations are from Madison, Federalist 55; the last one is Clinton Rossiter, *The Political Thought of the American Revolution* (New York: Harcourt, Brace, and World, 1963), 102. See Frazer, *Religious Beliefs*, 184.

87. Ralph Ketcham, "James Madison and the Nature of Man," *Journal of the History of Ideas* 19 (Jan. 1958), 67.

88. Kester, *Philosophe*, 85.

89. JM to Nicholas Trist, April 1827, in Peterson, ed., *Madison*, 2:387–88.

90. Madison, "Proclamation 18."

91. JM to Caldwell, Nov. 23, 1825; Madison, *Memorial, Papers* 8:303 (quotation).

92. Madison, Federalist 37.

93. James Madison, "Who Are the Best Keepers of the People's Liberties?" Dec. 20, 1792, *National Gazette, Papers* 14:427.

94. James Madison, "Universal Peace," Jan. 31, 1792, *National Gazette, Papers* 14:208; Madison, "The Report of 1800," Jan. 7, 1800, *Papers* 17:338; quotations in that order.

95. JM to Edmund Randolph, May 27, 1783, *Papers* 7:90; JM to Lafayette, Mar. 20, 1785, *Papers* 8:251; Madison, "Property," Mar. 27, 1792, *National Gazette, Papers* 14:267; JM to Randolph, July 16, 1782, *Papers* 4:419; Madison, essay in *Dunlap's American Daily Advertiser*, Oct. 20, 1792, *Papers* 14:387; Madison, "Advice to My Country," 1834, http://www.constitution.org/jm/jm.htm. Kester, *Philosophe*, 24, 41, called my attention to all these references except the last one.

96. Written by Isaiah Woodward and published in 1768, this book included scriptural readings and stories for daily use (Ketcham, "Hypothesis," 181).

97. JM to William Bradford, Jan. 24, 1774, *Papers* 1:105.

98. Meade, *Churches*, 2:99; JM to James Madison, Sr., Oct. 5, 1794, *Papers* 15:361–62; JM to the Ursuline Convent, in Robert Rutland et al., eds., *The Papers of James*

Madison, Presidential Series, 7 vols. (Charlottesville: University Press of Virginia, 1984–2012), 1:136, Madison, *Memorial, Papers* 8:304, Madison, "First Inaugural Address"; Madison, "Special Session Message," May 23, 1809, http://www.presidency.ucsb.edu/ws/?pid=65920; Madison, "Eighth Annual Message."

99. JM to Thomas Kenney, Mar. 18, 1809, in William Rives, ed., *Letters and Other Writings of James Madison,* 4 vols. (Philadelphia: J. B. Lippincott & Co., 1865), 2:433.

100. James Madison, "To the Inhabitants of the Town of Milton, in Massachusetts," May 18, 1812, *Papers, Presidential,* 1:394.

101. Madison, "Eighth Annual Message."

102. See Ketcham, "Hypothesis," 176, 184, and Meade, *Churches,* 2:99.

103. Broadwater, *Madison,* 5.

104. Hutson, *Features,* 159–60; quotation from 160.

105. Broadwater, *Madison,* 26.

106. James Madison, "Journal of the Virginia Convention," [1776], in Hunt, ed., *Writings,* 1:40.

107. JM to Beasley, Nov. 20, 1825.

108. JM to Bradford, Nov. 9, 1772.

109. JM to Jasper, 1833, 117.

110. Broadwater, *Madison,* 5.

111. Ketcham, *Madison,* 56–57, 167; Banning, "James Madison," 109 (quotation).

112. Ketcham, "Hypothesis," 184–86; quotation from 184. See Lyman Butterfield, "Elder John Leland, Jeffersonian Itinerant," *Proceedings of the American Antiquarian Society* 62 (Oct. 1952), 155–242.

113. "Naturalization," Jan. 1, 1795, *Papers* 15:432–33; JM to Jacob de la Motta, Aug. 1820, Madison Papers, LC.

114. Grau, "Intellectual Scribe," 27; Ketcham, "Hypothesis," 187 (quotation); Ketcham, *Madison,* 58.

115. Ketcham, "Hypothesis," 191, 187 (quotation); Ketcham, *Madison,* 58.

116. JM to Adams, Sept. 1833, 117.

117. JM to Edward Everett, Mar. 19, 1823, in Hunt, ed., *Writings,* 9:127.

118. Broadwater, *Madison,* 6.

119. Grau, "Intellectual Scribe," 25.

120. Ketcham, *Madison,* 57.

121. Ketcham, *Madison,* 58.

122. Ketcham, *Madison,* 58.

123. JM to William Bradford, Apr. 1, 1774, *Papers* 1:113.

124. JM to William Bradford, Dec. 1, 1773, *Papers* 1:101.

125. Wills, *Madison,* 15; JM to Bradford, Apr. 1774, 1:112–13 (first quotation); JM to Bradford, Jan. 24, 1774, *Papers* 1:105–6 (second and fourth quotations from 106, third from 105).

126. Broadwater, *Madison,* 9.

127. Sheldon, *Political Philosophy*, 31–32.

128. Brant, *Madison*, 2:352; Rodney Grunes, "James Madison and Religious Freedom," in Vile, Pederson, and Williams, ed., *Madison*, 109.

129. JM to Jacob de la Motta, Aug. 1820, in Hunt, ed., *Writings*, 9:30.

130. Madison, *Memorial, Papers* 8:300, 299; quotations in that order.

131. Madison, "Journal of the Virginia Convention," http://oll.libertyfund. org/?option=com_staticxt&staticfile=show.php%3Ftitle=1932&chapter=11812 5&layout=html&Itemid=27. Cf. Madison, "Essay" in *National Gazette*, Mar. 27, 1792, in Alley, *Madison*, 77.

132. Madison, *Memorial, Papers*, 8:303.

133. Ketcham, 165, see his note.

134. Lance Banning, "James Madison and the Statue for Religious Freedom and the Crisis of Republican Conviction," in Pederson and Vaughn, eds., *Virginia Statute*, 113.

135. *Papers*, 12:201–2.

136. *Papers* 12:757.

137. Donald Drakeman, "Religion and the Republic: James Madison and the First Amendment," *JCS* 25 (Autumn 1983), 430–31. See also Clifton Kruse, "The Historical Meaning and Judicial Construction of the Establishment of Religion Clause of the First Amendment," *Washburn Law Journal* 2 (Winter 1962), 65–144; Michael J. Malbin, *Religion and Politics: The Intentions of the Authors of the First Amendment* (Washington, DC: American Enterprise Institute, 1978).

138. James Madison, Journals, June 12, 1788, in Cousins, ed., *Republic*, 314.

139. Broadwater, *Madison*, 25.

140. JM to Robert Walsh, Mar. 2, 1819, in Alley, ed., *Madison*, 81.

141. JM to F. L. Schaffer, Dec. 3, 1821, in Alley, ed., *Madison*, 82.

142. JM to Mordecai Noah, May 15, 1818, in Hunt, ed., *Writings*, 8:412.

143. JM to Edward Livingstone, July 10, 1822, in Hunt, ed., *Writings*, 9:103. See also JM to Edward Everett, March 19, 1823, in ibid., 9:125–28.

144. Ravoke, *Madison*, 227–28; quotations from 228.

145. *Herald of Gospel Liberty*, May 8, 1812, and Dec. 11, 1812; quotations in that order. Smith also published a tract titled *Madison and Religion* (Philadelphia, 1811) to assist in Madison's reelection.

146. Sheldon, "Madison," 120.

147. Noll, *Princeton*, 8–9; Sheldon, "Madison," 115.

148. Sheldon, "Madison," 117.

149. John Witherspoon, *Lectures on Moral Philosophy*, ed. Jack Scott (Newark: University of Delaware Press, 1982), 123, 87, 64 (quotation), 85, 102–3. On Witherspoon's worldview, see Noll, *Princeton*, 44–58, and Morrison, *Witherspoon*.

150. Sheldon, "Madison," 118, 112 (quotation).

151. On Witherspoon's view of depravity, Smylie, "Madison," 121. The quotation is from Witherspoon, *Works*, 3:435.

152. Sheldon, *Philosophy*, xii.

153. James Madison, Federalist 51, http://www.constitution.org/fed/federa51.htm.

154. Madison, Federalist 51; Sheldon, "Madison," 121; quotations in that order.

155. Ketcham, *Madison*, 65.

156. Madison, Federalist 55.

157. Madison, Federalist 51.

158. Hutson, *Features*, 167.

159. "Commonplace Book," Abstracts from the Memoirs of the Cardinal de Retz, Dec. 24, 1759, *Papers* 1:7.

160. Madison, Federalist 10 (first quotation); JM to TJ, Oct. 24, 1787, *Papers* 10:214 (second quotation).

161. Madison, "Eighth Annual Message."

162. Madison, "Third Annual Message."

163. Madison, Federalist 43.

164. Ravoke, *Madison*, 222.

165. James Madison, "House Address to the President," Nov. 27, 1794, *Papers* 15:391 (first quotation); Kester, *Philosophe*, 84, 86 (second quotation).

166. Madison, "Universal Peace."

167. Kester, *Philosophe*, 27, 12; Madison, Federalist 46.

168. Madison, "Proclamation," July 23, 1813.

169. Munoz, "Madison," 65.

170. As quoted or cited by Brant, *Madison*, 6:199. See *Federal Republican*, July 30, Aug. 2, and Aug. 27, 1813.

171. Grunes, "Madison," 104–5.

172. Madison, "Detached Memorandum," 560–61.

173. Hutson, *Features*, 174.

174. JM to Edward Livingston, July 10, 1822, Hunt, ed., *Writings*, 9:101.

175. Madison, "Detached Memorandum," 560–61.

176. Munoz, "Madison," 64.

177. Drakeman, "Religion and the Republic," 443.

178. James Hutson, "James Madison and the Social Utility of Religion: Risks vs. Rewards," http://www.loc.gov/loc/madison/hutson-paper.html.

179. Madison, "Detached Memoranda," 558–62; quotation from 558; Rakove, *Writings*, 762–64. See also Irving Brant, "Madison: On the Separation of Church and State," *William and Mary Quarterly*, 3d ser., no. 8 (1951), 21–24.

180. JM to Livingston, July 10, 1822, Hunt, ed., *Writings*, 9:100.

181. James Madison, "Veto Message," Feb. 21, 1811, http://www.presidency.ucsb.edu/ws/?pid=65921; Madison, "Veto Message," Feb. 28, 1811, http://www.presidency.ucsb.edu/ws/?pid=65922.

182. Madison, "Eighth Annual Message." On the other hand, Madison allowed two other tax exemptions for churches to become law. See Leo Pfeiffer, "Madison's 'Detached Memoranda': Then and Now," in Merrill Peterson and Robert Vaughan, eds., *The Virginia Statutes for Religious Freedom* (New York: Cambridge University Press, 1988), 293–95.

183. Madison, "Detached Memoranda," 554–57; first two quotations from 554, third from 557.

184. E.g., *Everson v. Board of Education*, 330 U.S. 1, 15–16, 39 (1947).

185. Grunes, "Madison," 116–21.

186. JM to Adams, Sept. 1833, 120.

187. Vincent Phillip Munoz, "James Madison's Principle of Religious Liberty," *American Political Science Review* 97 (Feb. 2003), 17–32, and Munoz, "Religion and the American Founding," *Intercollegiate Review* 38 (Spring/Summer 2003), 33–43.

188. Munoz, "Madison," 59.

189. Ketcham, "Hypothesis," 189.

190. Madison, "Detached Memoranda," 566.

191. JM to Robert Walsh, Mar. 2, 1819, in Alley, ed., *Madison*, 81.

192. Robert Allen Rutland, *The Presidency of James Madison* (Lawrence: University Press of Kansas, 1990), 5.

193. The best account of the war's military, political, and economic aspects is J. C. A. Stagg, *Mr. Madison's War: Politics, Diplomacy and Warfare in the Early American Republic, 1783–1830* (Princeton, NJ: Princeton University Press, 1983). See also John Mahon, *The War of 1812* (Gainesville: University Presses of Florida, 1972), and Donald Hickey, *The War of 1812: A Forgotten Conflict* (Urbana: University of Illinois Press, 1989).

194. Madison, "Special Session Message," May 23, 1809.

195. JM to Kenney, Mar. 18, 1809.

196. JM to TJ, Apr. 3, 1812, Rives, ed., *Letters*, 2:531.

197. James Madison, "Special Message," June 1, 1812, http://www.presidency.ucsb.edu/ws/?pid=65936.

198. http://www.pbs.org/opb/historydetectives/feature/british-navy-impressment/; *Annals of the Congress of the United States*, 12th Congress, 1st Session, Part I (Washington, DC: Gales and Seaton, 1853), 599, 519, 686–87, 600–601 (Clay), 414–15 (Porter); J. Leitch Wright, Jr., *Britain and the American Frontier, 1783–1815* (Athens: University of Georgia Press, 1975). See also Ralph Beebe, "The War of 1812," in Ronald Wells, ed., *The Wars of America: Christian Views* (Grand Rapids, MI: Eerdmans, 1981), 35–37.

199. Beebe, "War," 37.

200. E.g., Madison, "Special Message," June 1, 1812; Madison, "Fourth Annual Message."

201. James Madison, "Proclamation—Announcement of a State of War between the United States and the United Kingdom," June 19, 1812, http://www.presidency.ucsb.edu/ws/?pid=65943.

202. Madison, "Fourth Annual Message."

203. Madison, "Fifth Annual Message."

204. James Madison, "Special Message," Feb. 24, 1813, http://www.presidency.ucsb.edu/ws/?pid=65951.

205. James Madison, "Special Session Message," May 25, 1813, http://www.presidency.ucsb.edu/ws/?pid=65955.

206. Madison, "Inaugural Address," Mar. 4, 1813.

207. Madison, "Proclamation," July 23, 1813.

208. James Madison, "Sixth Annual Message," Sept. 20, 1814, http://www.presidency.ucsb.edu/ws/?pid=29456.

209. William Gribbin, *The Churches Militant: The War of 1812 and American Religion* (New Haven, CT: Yale University Press, 1973), 62, 40–41, 27–28 (quotations). See Channing, *A Sermon Preached in Boston, July 23, 1812* (Boston: Greenough and Stebbins, 1812), 13.

210. Ketcham, *Madison*, 537 (first quotation); Rutland, *Presidency*, 116 (second quotation); Gribbin, *Churches*, 20.

211. Quoted by Brant, *Madison*, 6:28.

212. Gribbin, *Churches*, 78.

213. John Stevens, Apr. 8, 1813, and Solomon Froeligh, Sept. 22, 1812, *Centinel of Freedom*, as quoted in Gribbin, *Churches*, 61, 74.

214. Gribbin, *Churches*, 67, 72–77.

215. Daniel Merrill, *Balaam Disappointed: A Thanksgiving Sermon* (Concord, NH: Isaac & W.R. Hill, 1815), 9.

216. William Parkinson, *A Sermon Preached in . . . New York* (New York: J. Tiebout, 1812), 27.

217. Madison, "Proclamation," July 9, 1812.

218. John Fiske, *A Sermon Delivered at New-Braintree* (Brookfield, MA: E. Merriam, 1812), 17.

219. *Boston Gazette*, in the *Washingtonian*, Aug. 24, 1812.

220. Beebe, "War," 34–35.

221. Wills, *Madison*, 121.

222. Beebe, "War," 41.

223. Wills, *Madison*, 97–99.

224. Rutland, *Presidency*, 110; Beebe, "War," 41.

225. Rutland, *Presidency*, 209.

226. Wills, *Madison*, 143–44.

227. Beebe, "War," 41, 38.

228. *Rutland Herald*, Aug. 23, 1815, as quoted in Gribbin, *Churches*, 134. Cf. *Niles Weekly Register*, Feb. 18, 1815, 1.

229. Madison, "Public Thanksgiving."

230. E.g. James Madison, "Seventh Annual Message," Dec. 5, 1815, http://www.presidency.ucsb.edu/ws/index.php?pid=29457&st=&st1=.

231. Rutland, *Presidency*, 211.

232. Gribbin, *Churches*, 137–40; An American Layman [Elias Boudinot], *The Second Advent, or the Coming of the Messiah in Glory* (Trenton, NJ: D. Fenton and S. Hutchinson, 1815), 528–31.

233. Wills, *Madison*, 164. Cf. Richard Brookhiser, *James Madison* (New York: Basic Books, 2011), 249.

234. Grunes, "Madison," 105.

235. Wills, *Madison*, 164.

236. Noonan, *Lustre*, 4.

237. Henry Adams, *History of the United States of America during the Administrations of Thomas Jefferson and James Madison*, vol. 2, ed. Earl Harbert (New York: Library of America, 1986), passim; Samuel Morison et al., *A Concise History of the American Republic*, 2 vols. (New York: Oxford University Press, 1977), 1:160.

238. Byron Daynes and Mark Hopkins, "James Madison: Brilliant Theorist, Failed Tactician," in Vile, Pederson, and Williams, ed., *Madison*, 229; Banning, *Sacred Fire*, 374 (quotation).

239. Wills, *Madison*, 2; James David Barber, *The Presidential Character* (Englewood Cliffs, NJ: Prentice Hall, 1992), 11. For examples of scholarly rankings of Madison, see Arthur Schlesinger, Jr., "Rating the Presidents: Washington to Clinton," *Political Science Quarterly* 112:2 (1997), 179–90; University C-Span Survey of Presidential Leadership, March–December 1999, http://www.americanpresidetns.org/survey/historians/04.asp.

240. Vile, Pedersen, and Williams, "Introduction," xiii; Daynes and Hopkins, "Madison," 244–45.

241. Edward Coles to Hugh Blair Grigsby, Dec. 23, 1854, as quoted in Drew McCoy, *The Last of the Fathers: James Madison and the Republican Legacy* (Cambridge: Cambridge University Press, 1989), 20.

242. Thomas Jefferson to Thomas Flournoy, Oct. 1, 1812, http://memory.loc.gov/cgi-bin/query/P?mtj:7:./temp/~ammem_V8rr::.

243. Max Farrand, ed., *Records of the Federal Convention of 1787*, 3 vols. (New Haven, CT, 1911), 3:94–95.

244. John Quincy Adams, *The Lives of James Madison and James Monroe* (Buffalo, NY: George Derby, 1850), 46.

245. Rakove, *Madison*, 218, 220; quotations in that order.

246. Rutland, *Presidency*, 210; Wills, *James Madison*, 153; quotations in that order.

247. Rutland, *Presidency*, xii.
248. Lester Cappon, ed., *The Adams–Jefferson Letters*, 2 vols. (Chapel Hill: University of North Carolina Press, 1959), 2:508.
249. Rutland, *Presidency*, 208, 2; quotations in that order.
250. Brant, "Madison," 5.

CHAPTER 3

1. John Quincy Adams, *Memoirs of John Quincy Adams: Comprising Portions of His Diary from 1795 to 1848*, ed. Charles Francis Adams, 12 vols. (Freeport, NY: Books for Libraries Press, 1969), 7:27–29, June 13, 1825; quotations from 28 (hereinafter cited as *Memoirs*). See also Paul C. Nagel, *John Quincy Adams: A Public Life, A Private Life* (New York: Alfred Knopf, 1998), 309–10.
2. William Weeks, *John Quincy Adams and the American Global Empire* (Lexington: University Press of Kentucky, 1992), 1.
3. Harlow Giles Unger, *John Quincy Adams* (Boston: De Capo Press, 2012), 3.
4. *National Intelligencer* 49, Feb. 24 and 26, 1848.
5. See Sara Georgini, "John Quincy Adams at Prayer," *Church History* 82 (Sept. 2013), 650.
6. Georgini, "Adams," 654, 651.
7. Adams, *Memoirs* 2:497, July 31, 1813.
8. Adams, *Memoirs* 2:452, Mar. 17, 1813 (first quotation); Adams, *Memoirs* 7:20, May 31, 1825 (second and third quotations). Only about half of Adams's diary has been published. The remainder, titled the *Diaries of John Quincy Adams: A Digital Collection* (hereinafter cited as *Diary*) is available online at http://www.masshist.org/jqadiaries/php/.
9. E. H. Chapin, *The Truly Great: A Discourse, Appropriate to the Life and Character of John Quincy Adams* (Boston: A. Thompkin, 1848), 11, 15–16; Richard S. Storrs, *On the Occasion of the Inauguration of John Quincy Adams* (Boston: Monroe and Francis, 1825), 18–19; Joseph Henry Allen, *The Statesman and the Man* (Washington: J. and G. S. Gideon, 1848), 16–17; Joshua Bates, *A Discourse on the Character, Public Services and Death of John Quincy Adams* (Worcester, MA, 1848), 18–19; R. C. Waterston, *Discourse on the Life and Character of John Quincy Adams* (Boston: William Ticknor, 1848), 16–22; "Notice of Recent Publications," *Christian Examiner and Religious Miscellany* 44 (May 1848), 470–73.
10. Theodore Parker, *A Discourse Occasioned by the Death of John Quincy Adams* (Boston: Bela Marsh, 1848), 45.
11. E.g., A. A. Livermore, *The Ancient and Honorable Man* (Keane, NH: J. W. Prentice, 1848), 16.
12. Richard Storrs, *God Determines the Rise and Fall of Princes* (Boston: T. R. Martin, 1848), 16; Charles Hudson, in *Token of a Nation's Sorrow: Addresses in the*

Congress of the United States and Funeral Solemnities (Washington: G. S. Gideon, 1848), 12.

13. George A. Lipsky, *John Quincy Adams: His Theory and Ideas* (New York: Thomas Crowell Co., 1950), 75; Weeks, *Adams*, 11, 16–17; first quotation from 11, second and third from 17. On Adams's faith, see also Boardman Kathan, "The Spiritual Growth, Religious Beliefs and Church Affiliation of John Quincy Adams," *Prism: A Theological Journal of the United Church of Christ* 16 (Spring 2001), 22–33.

14. Adams, *Memoirs* 5:129, May 22, 1820; 6:503, Feb. 9, 1825; quotations in that order. See also David Thibault, "The Religious-Political Mindset of John Quincy Adams" (M.A. thesis, California State University, Fullerton, 1988), 34 and passim. Thibault called my attention to numerous discussions of religious topics in Adams's *Memoirs* and letters.

15. Paul C. Nagel, *The Adams Women: Abigail and Louise Adams, Their Sisters and Daughters* (Cambridge, MA: Harvard University Press, 1987); Marie B. Hecht, *John Quincy Adams: A Personal History of an Independent Man* (New York: Macmillan, 1972); and Samuel Flagg Bemis, *John Quincy Adams and the Union* (Norwalk, CT: Easton Press, 1987); chapter titles in that order.

16. Samuel Flagg Bemis, *John Quincy Adams and the Foundations of American Foreign Policy* (Norwalk, CT: Easton Press, 1987), ix. See also Padraig Riley, "The Presidency of John Quincy Adams," in David Waldstreicher, ed., *A Companion to John Adams and John Quincy Adams* (Chichester, UK: Wiley Blackwell, 2013), 329.

17. Walter LaFeber, "John Quincy Adams: An Introduction," in LaFeber, ed., *John Quincy Adams and the American Continental Empire: Letters, Speeches, and Papers* (Chicago: Quadrangle Books, 1965), 15; Bemis, *Union*, 9.

18. Bemis, *Union*, 523.

19. Bemis, *Foreign Policy*, 154.

20. Lynn Hudson Parsons, *John Quincy Adams* (Madison, WI: Madison House, 1998), 100–101, quotation from 101; Adams, "Inaugural Address," Mar. 4, 1825, in *A Compilation of the Messages of and Papers of the Presidents, 1789–1897*, ed. James Richardson, 10 vols. (New York: Bureau of National Literature and Art, [1896–99] 1901–6), 2:865.

21. Jack Shepherd, *Cannibals of the Heart: A Personal Biography of Louisa Catherine Adams and John Quincy Adams* (New York: McGraw Hill, 1980), 16–17.

22. AA to JQA, Nov. 1783, in Abigail Adams, *Letters of Mrs. Adams, Wife of John Adams*, ed. Charles Francis Adams, 2 vols. (Boston: C. C. Little and James Brown, 1840), 1:191; John Adams, as quoted in Paul Nagel, *Descent from Glory: Four Generations of the John Adams Family* (New York: Oxford University Press, 1983), 53.

23. Quotations from Weeks, *Adams*, 9.

24. Bemis, *Union*, 3–4.

25. Nagel, *Descent*, 7.

26. See JA to AA, June 29 and Aug. 28, 1774, and July 17, 1775, in L. H. Butterfield, ed., *Adams Family Correspondence*, 6 vols. (Cambridge, MA: Harvard University

Press, 1963–93), 1:113–14, 145, 252; Louis Albert Banks, *The Religious Life of Famous Americans* (New York: American Tract Society, 1904), 199–208.

27. AA to JQA, June 1778, in Adams, *Letters*, 1:95; AA to JQA, Mar. 20, 1780, in ibid., 1:113.

28. JQA, as quoted in Shepherd, *Cannibals*, 32.

29. Weeks, *Adams*, 10, 14; JQA to AA, Feb. 8, 1810, in Worthington Chauncey Ford, ed., *Writings of John Quincy Adams*, 7 vols. (New York: Greenwood Press, Publishers, 1968), 3:393–94 (hereinafter cited as *Writings*).

30. Nagel, *Descent*, 199, 338, 341; Shepherd, *Cannibals*, 26–27, 163–64, 359–60; Nagel, *Adams Women*, 188–89, 194–95, 218, 224, 228, 240, 268–69, 281, 283–84, 290–91.

31. Parsons, *Adams*, 105. Parsons claims that Adams seldom mentioned religious or theological issues in his diary before 1803, but it is filled with comments on religious matters. He contends that Adams "approached the Scriptures, not as the Word of God, but [only] as divinely inspired literature." Ample evidence, however, indicates that Adams viewed the Bible as God's unique revelation to humanity.

32. Adams, *Diary*, Dec. 31, 1800, http://www.masshist.org/jqadiaries/php/doc?id=jqad24_314.

33. Nagel, *Adams*, 124.

34. Adams, *Diary*, Dec. 31, 1812, http://www.masshist.org/jqadiaries/php/doc?id=jqad28_443; Adams, *Memoirs* 11:340, Mar. 19, 1843, quotations in that order. Despite his daughter's death, Adams added to his earlier entry, "I offer to a merciful God at the close of the year my humble tribute of gratitude for the blessings with which he has in the course of it favored me and those who are dear to me." See also his entry for September 17, 1812, http://www.masshist.org/jqadiaries/php/doc?id=jqad28_413.

35. See Adams, *Memoirs* 4:425, Oct. 24, 1819.

36. Adams, *Memoirs* 11:341, Mar. 19, 1843. Along with twenty-six others, Adams helped found All Souls' Church in 1821. See George Willis Cooke, *Unitarianism in America: A History of Its Origin and Development* (Boston: American Unitarian Association, 1902), 119, 376, 380.

37. Parker, *Discourse*, 45.

38. Adams, *Memoirs* 11:340–41; *Memoirs* 9:289, May 29, 1836; quotations in that order.

39. Adams, *Memoirs* 7:147–49. "It is right," he declared, "that I should make a public profession of my faith and hope as a Christian" (147–48). After joining the church that morning, Adams took communion for the first time in his life. Cooke lists the First Parish Church in Quincy, also called the First Congregationalist Church and Society, as one of the 125 congregations that had associated with the Unitarian faith by 1825 (*Unitarianism in America*). William Lunt, who became a co-pastor of this church in 1835, had previously pastored the Second Unitarian Church in New York City, was a member of the American Unitarian Association,

and wrote several tracts defending Unitarian beliefs. See Kathan, "John Quincy Adams," 32.

40. Quotation from Adams, *Memoirs* 7:147. See also Dean Grodzins, *American Heretic: Theodore Parker and Transcendentalism* (Chapel Hill: University of North Carolina Press, 2002), 88.

41. John Quincy Adams, *Lectures on Rhetoric and Oratory,* 2 vols. (New York: Russell and Russell, [1810] 1962), 1:326–27; quotations from 327.

42. First two quotations from Adams, *Memoirs* 7:376, Dec. 9, 1827; third quotation from Adams, *Memoirs* 9:543, May 27, 1838.

43. Allen, *Statesman,* 5–6.

44. Adams disliked sermons that focused more on style than substance (*Memoirs* 11:69, Jan. 23, 1842).

45. Adams, *Lectures on Rhetoric,* 1:323–24, 336–67, 338; first quotation from 323, second from 338.

46. See Adams, *Memoirs* 7:471, Mar. 9, 1828.

47. William Seward, "John Quincy Adams," *Boston Recorder,* 1848, in Edward J. Giddings, comp., *American Christian Rulers or Religion and Men of Government* (New York: Bromfield, 1889), 12.

48. E.g., *Letters of Mrs. Adams . . . Containing the Letters Addressed by John Q. Adams to His Son on the Study of the Bible* (Boston: Wilkins, Carter and Co., 1848), 428.

49. Edward Everett, *A Eulogy on the Life and Character of John Quincy Adams* (Boston: Dutton and Wentworth, 1848), 66; G. F. Disoway, "John Quincy Adams," *The Ladies Repository* 10 (Feb. 1850), 54; quotations in that order.

50. Adams, *Memoirs* 2:352, Mar. 13, 1812.

51. Adams, *Bible,* 431.

52. Adams, *Memoirs* 8:89, Jan. 1, 1829; Adams, 1844 address to the American Bible Society, in Samuel Cox, *Interviews: Memorable and Useful* (New York: Harper and Brothers, 1853), 271; quotations in that order.

53. See John Gibson, *Soldiers of the Word: The Story of the American Bible Society* (New York: Philosophical Library, 1858), 69, 107.

54. Adams, *Memoirs* 2:334, Jan. 12, 1812.

55. *Christian Register* as cited by Livermore, *Honorable Man,* 13–14.

56. E.g., Seward, "Adams," 11.

57. Hecht, *Adams,* 454.

58. Quoted in Seward, "Adams," 9.

59. Adams also read many collections of sermons (Josiah Quincy, *Memoir of the Life of John Quincy Adams* [Boston: Phillips, Sampson, 1859], 52; Adams, *Memoirs* 2:379, June 21, 1812; 2:388, July 12, 1812).

60. Adams, *Bible,* 428, 472, 440; first quotations from 428, last two from 440.

61. Adams, *Bible,* 428, 440; first three quotations from 428, last two from 440.

62. Adams, *Bible,* 435, 465, 467; all quotations from 465.

63. Adams, *Memoirs* 6:518–15, Mar. 4, 1825; 8:149, Apr. 30, 1829; quotations in that order.

64. E.g., *Memoirs* 7:149, Sept. 13, 1826; William Lunt, *A Discourse Delivered in Quincy* (Boston, 1848), 11.

65. Nagel, *Adams*, 306 (first quotation), 405; *Adams*, 449 (second quotation); Lunt, *Discourse*, 37.

66. Adams, *Memoirs* 7:53–54, Nov. 15–16, 1825; quotations from 54.

67. Lunt, *Discourse*, 11.

68. Livermore, *Honorable Man*, 11.

69. John Quincy Adams, *Poems of Religion and Society* (Buffalo, NY: Miller, Orton, and Mulligan, 1854). These poems express Adams's deep sense of piety, reverence, and worship.

70. John Quincy Adams, "On Faith," hand-written draft in the Adams Family Papers at the Massachusetts Historical Society in Boston. See also Seward, "Adams," 10; Stedman Hanks, *Sermon on the Occasion of the Death of John Quincy Adams* (Lowell, MA: W. H. Waldron, 1848), 20; Bates, *Discourse*, 18.

71. Adams, American Bible Society address, 272.

72. Adams, *Memoirs* 11:341, Mar. 19, 1843.

73. John Quincy Adams, *A Discourse on Education* (Boston: Perkins and Marvin, 1840), 17; Adams, "Lord of All Worlds," in *Poems*, 92–93.

74. JQA to Thomas Boylston Adams, Aug. 7, 1809, in Ford, ed., *Writings* 2:354–55; JQA to AA, Mar. 12, 1814, in ibid., 5:42; Adams, *Memoirs* 2:602, Apr. 28, 1814; Adams, *Memoirs* 4:275, Feb. 22, 1819; *Memoirs* 6:418, Oct. 30, 1824; Adams, "Inaugural Address," 2:865; Adams, "First Annual Message," Dec. 6, 1825, in Ford. ed. *Writings* 3:865. Cf. Adams, *Memoirs* 8:246, Nov. 7, 1830.

75. Adams, *Diary*, June 10, 1829, http://www.masshist.org/jqadiaries/php/doc?id=jqad36_191.

76. Adams, *Memoirs* 7:176, Nov. 12, 1826.

77. John Quincy Adams, "Society and Civilization," *American Whig Review* 2 (July 1845), 88.

78. Quoted in Nagel, *Adams*, 261.

79. Nagel, *Descent*, 184.

80. Adams, *Rhetoric*, 1:333.

81. Adams, *Memoirs* 2:357, Apr. 12, 1812.

82. Adams, *Bible*, 439. Yet Adams wrote to his mother in 1815, "If I must choose" between "the belief that Christ was a mere man" or proclaim him the Son of God, he would not hesitate to affirm Christ's deity (JQA to AA, Dec. 5, 1815, in Ford, ed., *Writings* 5:432). While he did not fully believe that the Bible taught the Athanasian Trinity, Adams added, the texts declaring Christ to be God were "too numerous," from too diverse parts of Scripture, connected by too strong a chain of argument, and contained too "direct and irresistible inferences" to accept the

explanations Unitarians offered of them or the evasions others used to escape them. Jesus allowed His disciples to call Him God; two apostles "expressly and repeatedly" declared Him to be the Creator of the world; and Isaiah called Him "the mighty God" (432–33).

83. Adams added, "You think it blasphemous to believe that the omnipotent Creator could be crucified. God is a spirit. The spirit was not crucified. The body of Jesus of Nazareth was crucified. . . . You see my orthodoxy grows upon me" (JQA to JA, Jan. 3, 1817, in Ford, ed., *Writings* 6:135–36). See also JQA to JA, Jan. 5, 1816, Ford, ed., *Writings* 5:459.

84. Adams, *Memoirs* 7:229, Feb. 18, 1827; Adams, *Memoirs* 7:324, Aug. 13, 1827.

85. Adams, *Memoirs* 7:477, Mar. 17, 1828.

86. Quoted in Nagel, *Adams*, 261; see also Adams, *Memoirs* 4:130, Sept. 19, 1818.

87. Nagel, *Adams*, 261. Cf. Adams, *Memoirs* 9:507, Mar. 11, 1838.

88. Adams, *Memoirs* 7:477, Mar. 17, 1828. Adams added that Baker lent him a pamphlet by Lewis Tappan who had been "converted from Unitarianism to Orthodoxy" (*Memoirs* 7:481, Mar. 21, 1828).

89. Adams, *Bible*, 439, 462; first quotation from 439, second and third from 462.

90. Adams, *Memoirs* 9:117–18, Mar. 30, 1834.

91. Adams, *Education*, 13, 15, 18, quotation from 18.

92. Adams, "Society and Civilization," 89.

93. JQA to JA, Aug. 31, 1815, in Ford, ed., *Writings* 4:362.

94. Adams, *Memoirs* 7:459, Mar. 2, 1828.

95. Quoted in Nagel, *Adams*, 407.

96. JQA to George Sullivan, Jan. 20, 1821, in Ford, ed., *Writings*, 7:90–91.

97. Adams, *Memoirs* 7:268, May 6, 1827; Adams, *Rhetoric*, 1:344.

98. Adams, *Memoirs* 8:89, Jan. 1829; Adams, *Education*, 16; quotations in that order.

99. Adams, American Bible Society address, 271.

100. Adams refused to submit to a religious test to become a professor at Harvard. He argued that the precise nature of his faith was between God and him alone (JQA to Samuel Dexter, Oct. 6, 1805, Ford, ed., *Writings* 3:125).

101. Adams, *Memoirs* 10:345, Aug. 2, 1840.

102. Adams, *Memoirs* 8:353, Apr. 3, 1831. See also *Memoirs* 9:438–39, Dec. 3, 1837.

103. Adams, *Memoirs* 9:435, Nov. 26, 1837.

104. Adams, *Memoirs* 8:214, Apr. 4, 1830; 9:340, Jan. 1, 1837; quotations in that order.

105. Quoted in Nagel, *Adams*, 407.

106. The first quotation is from Adams, *Diary*, June 18, 1829, http://www.masshist.org/ jqadiaries/php/doc?id=jqad36_197; the second is quoted by Nagel, *Adams*, 203.

107. E.g., Adams, *Bible*, 432. See also Adams, *Rhetoric*, 1:335.

108. Adams, *Memoirs* 7:459, Mar. 1, 1828. See also Bemis, *Union*, 105; and Greg Russell, *John Quincy Adams and the Public Virtues of Diplomacy* (Columbia: University of Missouri Press, 1995), 81–87.

109. JQA to JA, Dec. 24, 1804, in Ford, ed., *Writings*, 3:104; Adams, *Memoirs* 9:263, Nov. 23, 1835; 9:439, Dec. 3, 1837, quotations in that order.

110. Quoted in Nagel, *Adams*, 407.

111. Adams, *Memoirs* 7:268–69; second quotation from 268, the rest from 269.

112. During the last twenty-five years of his life Adams frequently worshipped at the Second Presbyterian Church (Hanks, *Sermon*, 22). Near the end of his life, Adams allegedly told a minister, "I should not, I suppose, be considered fully orthodox, according to the standard of the Presbyterian Church; but I am not so far from them as people generally imagine" (ibid., 21).

113. See Adams, *Diary*, Apr. 26, 1829, http://www.masshist.org/jqadiaries/php/doc?id=jqad36_170; June 18, 1829, http://www.masshist.org/jqadiaries/php/doc?id=jqad38_170 (all quotations).

114. Nagel, *Descent*, 150; first and second quotations from Adams, Diary, June 16, 1829, http://www.masshist.org/jqadiaries/php/doc?id=jqad36_195; third and fourth from Adams, *Memoirs* 8:159–60, Dec. 30, 1829.

115. Bemis, *Union*, 200; Adams, *Bible*, 460.

116. Parsons, *Adams*, 220; Adams, *Memoirs* 12:206, July 26, 1845.

117. See Adams, *Diary*, Apr. 25, 1831, http://www.masshist.org/jqadiaries/php/doc?id=jqad36_197; *Memoirs* 7:340, Oct. 18, 1827; and Keith Sprunger, "Cold Water Congressmen: The Congressional Temperance Society before the Civil War," *The Historian* 38 (Aug. 1965), 498–515.

118. John Quincy Adams, *Address to the Norfolk County Temperance Society* (Boston: Gould, Kendall, and Lincoln, 1842), 4, 12, 19, 20; first quotation from 12, second from 19.

119. Russell, *Adams*, 3–4, 8, 137, 173; quotation from 3.

120. Adams, *Address of John Quincy Adams to his Constituents* (Boston: J. H. Eastburn, 1842), as quoted by Quincy, *Memoir*, 376.

121. John Quincy Adams, *An Oration Delivered [at] Newburyport* (Newburyport, MA: Morss and Brewster, 1837), 31.

122. JQA to Joseph Hall, in Ford, ed., *Writings*, 1:33; quotation from Adams, *Memoirs* 2:581, Mar. 6, 1814.

123. John Quincy Adams, "Letters of Publicola," Ford, ed., *Writings*, 1:70.

124. JQA to Skelton Jones, Apr. 17, 1809, in Ford, ed., *Writings*, 3:300.

125. See Lipsky, *Adams*, 139–62.

126. Weeks, *Adams*, 19.

127. John Quincy Adams, *An Oration, Delivered before the Cincinnati Astronomical Society* (Cincinnati: Shepard, 1843), 13–14.

128. John Quincy Adams, *Lives of James Madison and James Monroe, Fourth and Fifth Presidents of the United States* (Buffalo, NY: G. H. Derby, 1850), 35 (quotation); Adams, "Inaugural Address," 2:865; Adams, "First Annual Message," 882.

129. Adams, *Education*, 18 (first quotation), 25 (second quotation); Adams, *Temperance Society*, 23 (third quotation); Adams, *Memoirs* 10:126, June 27, 1839.

130. Quoted in John F. Kennedy, *Profiles in Courage* (New York: Harper and Brothers, 1955), 43.

131. Lipsky, _Adams_, 67.

132. Adams, _Memoirs_ 1:434, Apr. 17, 1806; Bemis, _Union_, 544; Adams, _Memoirs_ 9:58.

133. JQA to AA, July 25, 1810, in Ford, ed., _Writings_ 3:456.

134. John Quincy Adams, _Discourse Delivered before the Massachusetts Historical Society_ (Boston: Charles Little and James Brown, 1843), 43, 47; first quotation from 43, the rest from 47. See also Adams, _Rhetoric_, 1:330.

135. Quoted in Weeks, _Adams_, 20.

136. Adams, _Constituents_, as quoted by Quincy, _Memoir_, 382; Adams, "First Annual Message," 2:882; quotations in that order.

137. _Congressional Globe_, 29th Cong., 1st Session (1845–46), 338–42 (Feb. 9, 1846) (quotations) (see also Adams, _Memoirs_ 12:259); _Hansard's Parliamentary Debates_ 84:1321–322 (Mar. 20, 1846), as quoted in Richards, _Life and Times_, 185.

138. John Quincy Adams, _Address [on] the Declaration of Independence_ (Washington, DC: Davis and Force, 1821), http://www.archive.org/stream/addressdelivered-00adamiala/addressdelivered00adamiala_djvu.txt.

139. Parsons, _Adams_, 149–50.

140. John Quincy Adams, "The Opium War and the Sanctity of Commercial Reciprocity," _Proceedings of the Massachusetts Historical Society_ 42 (October 1909–June 1910, 295–325), in LaFeber, ed., _Adams_, 48–51; first four quotations from 49, fifth from 50.

141. Adams, _Newburyport Oration_, 17; Adams, "Columbus," III, in Ford, ed., _Writings_ 1:164, quotations in that order.

142. Lipsky, _Adams_, 74; quotation from Banks, _Religious Life_, 44.

143. Wendell Glick, "The Best Possible World of John Quincy Adams," _New England Quarterly_ 37 (Mar. 1964), 3–17; quotation from 4.

144. Lipsky, _Adams_, 71.

145. Adams, _Memoirs_ 5:47–48, Mar. 29, 1820.

146. Lipsky, _Adams_, 69, 71; quotation from 71; see JQA to Edward Everett, in Ford, ed., _Writings_ 7:202.

147. JQA to William Vans Murray, July 22, 1798, in Ford, ed., _Writings_ 2:344.

148. See William G. Morgan, "John Quincy Adams versus Andrew Jackson: Their Biographers and the 'Corrupt Bargain' Charge," _Tennessee Historical Quarterly_ 26 (Spring 1967), 43–58, and Morgan, "The 'Corrupt Bargain' Charge against Clay and Adams," _Filson Club Historical Quarterly_ 42 (Apr. 1968), 132–49. Most biographers of Adams and Jackson repudiate this charge.

149. Bemis, _Union_, 11, 71.

150. Lipsky, _Adams_, 75; Adams, _Education_, 13.

151. JQA to James Lloyd, Oct. 1, 1822, in Ford, ed., _Writings_, 7:311.

152. Adams, _Memoirs_ 5:364, Oct. 20, 1821. See also _Memoirs_ 5:281, Feb. 16, 1821.

153. Daniel Walker Howe, _What God Hath Wrought: The Transformation of America, 1815–1848_ (New York: Oxford University Press, 2007), 251–52; Adams,

Massachusetts Historical Society, 12–13; Adams, *Memoirs* 2:283, July 30, 1811, 11:441; Adams, *Cincinnati Oration*, 34, 38; Quincy, *Memoir*, 265, 306.

154. Adams, "Inaugural Address," 2:864; Adams, "First Annual Message," 2:877.

155. Adams, "First Annual Message," 2:882.

156. Adams as quoted in William Seward, *Life and Public Services of John Quincy Adams* (Auburn, NY: Derby, Miller, 1849), 221 (first quotation), 223 (second quotation). See also Adams, *Memoirs* 8:48–49.

157. Adams, *Memoirs* 7:59, Nov. 23, 1825.

158. LaFeber, "Adams," 24–25; Bemis, *Union*, 76–78; Mary Hargreaves, *The Presidency of John Quincy Adams* (Lawrence: University Press of Kansas, 1985), 30–40, 257–78.

159. JQA to Charles Upham, Feb. 2, 1837, *Huntington Library Quarterly* 4 (April 1941), 381–82, in Lefeber, ed., *Adams*, 147. See also Adams, *Memoirs* 9:162, July 30, 1834, 8:100–101, Feb. 28, 1829; 8:486, Mar. 3, 1832. On Adams's attempt to have the federal government fund internal improvements, see also Sean Patrick Adams, "John Quincy Adams and the Nation State," in Waldstreicher, ed., *Companion*, 348–65, and John Larson, *Internal Improvements: National Public Works and the Promise of Popular Government in the Early United States* (Chapel Hill: University of North Carolina Press, 2001).

160. See JQA to George William Erving, Nov. 28, 1818, in Ford, ed., *Writings* 6:498–99; George Dangerfield, *The Era of Good Feelings* (New York: Harcourt, Brace and World), 137–38; and Bemis, *Foreign Policy*, 200–208, 315–16.

161. Adams to the Senate, Jan. 31, 1826, and Apr. 25, 1826, in Richardson, ed., *Messages and Papers*, 2:324–26, 345; Adams to the Senate, Feb. 5, 1827, in ibid., 2:370–73.

162. Lynn Hudson Parsons, "'A Perpetual Harrow upon My Feelings': John Quincy Adams and the American Indian," *New England Quarterly* 46 (September 1973), 358.

163. See Richard Hryniewicki, "The Creek Treaty of November 15 1827," *Georgia Historical Quarterly* 52 (March 1968), 1–15, and Adams, *Memoirs* 7:370–71, Dec. 6, 1827.

164. Parsons, "Perpetual Harrow," 356; John Quincy Adams, "Fourth Annual Message," Dec. 2, 1828, in Richardson, ed., *Messages and Papers*, 2:416.

165. Adams, *Memoirs* 7:465, Mar. 7, 1828.

166. Parsons, *Adams*, 181–83.

167. Parsons, "Perpetual Harrow," 357, 341; quotations in that order. See Adams, *Memoirs* 7:89–90, Dec. 22, 1825, and Bemis, *Union*, 83–84. Adams insisted that Americans had a "moral and religious duty" to "cultivate their territory" by terminating "the rights of savage tribes, by fair and amicable means" (*Memoirs* 3:39–42, Sept, 23, 25, 1814; quotation from 40).

168. Adams, *Memoirs* 8:206, Mar. 22, 1830.

169. Parsons, "Perpetual Harrow," 364; Richards, *Life and Times*, 148.

170. Richards, *Life and Times*, 150.

171. Parsons, "Perpetual Harrow," 374.

172. Adams, *Memoirs* 10:491–92, June 30, 1841 (first quotation from 492); Adams as quoted in Seward, *Life and Public Services*, 312–13 (second quotation).

173. Matthew Mason, "John Quincy Adams and the Tangled Politics of Slavery," in Waldstreicher, ed., *Companion*, 404.

174. Bemis, *Union*, 54; Weeks, *Adams*, 193. See also *Memoirs* 6:375, June 4, 1824.

175. Weeks, *Adams*, 193.

176. Adams, *Memoirs* 5:4, 11, Mar. 3, 1820; first three quotations from 11, fourth from 4.

177. Adams did urge Congress to prohibit the introduction of slaves in new territories (*Memoirs* 4:530, Feb. 23, 1820).

178. Adams, *Memoirs* 4:531, Feb. 24, 1820 (first quotation); 5:11–12, Mar. 3, 1820 (second and third quotations). Cf. *Memoirs* 5:205–11.

179. JQA to Moses Brown, Dec. 9, 1833, Adam MSS, as cited by Bemis, *Union*, 331.

180. Adams, *Memoirs* 6:376, June 6, 1824; *Congressional Globe*, 28th Congress, 1st session, Dec. 29, 1843, 88–89; ibid., 27th Cong., 2nd session, 569–70; Richards, *Life and Times*, 99.

181. Richards, *Life and Times*, 98.

182. Adams, *Memoirs* 5:11–12, Mar. 2, 1820; quotation from 9:544, May 27, 1838.

183. Adams, *Letter from the Hon. John Quincy Adams* (Quincy, MA: privately printed, 1843), 1–2; Adams, *Education*, 13.

184. Quotation from Adams, *Memoirs* 4:492, Dec. 27, 1819; Adams, "Introduction," *Memoir of the Rev. Elijah P. Lovejoy* (New York: J. S. Taylor, 1838), 3–4.

185. Adams, *Constituents*, quoted in Quincy, *Memoir*, 384–85.

186. Adams, *Memoirs* 12:171, Feb. 19, 1845; 11:180, June 20, 1842.

187. Adams, *Memoirs* 10:63, Dec. 13, 1838 (first quotation); Adams, *Constituents*, 51–52 (second, third, and fourth quotations).

188. Lipsky, *Adams*, 127.

189. Story as cited by Richards, *Life and Times*, 137; see also 135–39; quotation from 138.

190. Adams, *Memoirs* 10:453–54, Mar. 29, 1841.

191. Richards, *Life and Times*, 99, 104–5 (first quotation); Weeks, *Adams*, 194 (second quotation).

192. Adams, 1827 poem. Most were from southerners.

193. See also William Lee Miller, *Arguing about Slavery: John Quincy Adams and the Great Battle in the United States Congress* (New York: Alfred Knopf, 1996), 153–78.

194. Hargreaves, *Presidency*, 114 (see also J. Orin Oliphant, "The Parvin-Brigham Mission to Spanish America, 1823–26," *Church History* 14 [June 1945] 85–103); Adams, "Message to the House of Representatives of the United States," Mar. 15, 1826, in Richardson, ed., *Messages and Papers*, 2:898.

195. See Wilkins Winn, "The Efforts of the United States to Secure Religious Liberty in a Commercial Treaty with Mexico, 1825–1831," *The Americas* 28 (January 1972), 311–32.

196. JQA to Richard Anderson, May 27, 1823, in Ford, ed., *Writings* 7:465–67; quotation from Adams, *Massachusetts Historical Society*, 46–47.

197. JQA to Anderson, May 27, 1823, 7:465–66 (quotation from 466).

198. Nagel, *Descent*, 100; Adams, *Memoirs* 2:387, July 11, 1812; 9:14, Sept. 9, 1833; quotations in that order.

199. Quoted in Nagel, *Descent*, 194.

200. Adams, *Memoirs* 12:276–77, Oct. 31, 1846.

201. Lynn Hudson Parsons, "The 'Splendid Pageant': Observations on the Death of John Quincy Adams," *New England Quarterly* 53 (December 1980), 473.

202. Bemis, *Union*, 8.

203. Nagel, *Adams*, 304–5.

204. E.g., Parker, *Discourse*, 42.

205. Bemis, *Foreign Policy*, 571.

206. Disoway, "Adams," 54.

207. Nagel, *Adams Women*, 211.

208. Allen, *Statesman*, 7; Disoway, "Adams," 28; quotations in that order.

209. Bemis, *Union*, 326; Richards, *Life and Times*, 3.

210. "Recent Publications," 473 (first and second quotations); Disoway, "Adams," 54, 28 (third and fourth quotations).

211. Weeks, *Adams*, 126; JQA to Lloyd, Oct. 1, 1822, in Ford, ed., *Writings*, 7:313; Adams, *Memoirs* 4:107, July 11, 1818; JQA to JA, Aug. 1, 1816, in *Adams Family Papers*.

212. Weeks, *Adams*, 125, 187, 139; first and third quotations from 125, second from 187, fourth from 139.

213. Weeks, *Adams*, 187 (first and third quotations); John Quincy Adams, "The Macbeth Policy," in Ford, ed., *Writings*, 7:357–58 (second quotation from 357, fourth quotation from 358).

214. Weeks, *Adams*, 187–88.

215. Bemis, *Union*, 58 (for a discussion of these deals, see 36–47); Dangerfield, *Good Feelings*, 345 (second quotation); Weeks, *Adams*, 189 (third quotation).

216. Gail Collins, *Scorpion Tongues: Gossip, Celebrity, and American Politics* (New York: Morrow, 1998), 31 (first quotation); Nagel, *Adams*, 317, 319 (second quotation).

217. For analysis of the elections of 1824 and 1828, see Robert Remini, *Andrew Jackson and the Course of American Freedom, 1822–1832* (New York: Harper and Row, 1981), 74–100, 143–55; Hargreaves, *Presidency*, 19–40; and my chapter on Jackson.

218. Allen, *Statesman*, 6, 8; Chapin, *Truly Great*, 12, 16.

219. Parsons, "Splendid Pageant," 464–78, first quotation from 465, second from 469, third from 478.

220. "Recent Publications," 468–69.

221. E.g., Hanks, *Sermon*, 22; Allen, *Statesman*, 16; Lunt, *Discourse*, 35; Timothy Walker, *An Oration on the Life and Character of John Quincy Adams* (Cincinnati: J. F. Desilver, 1848), 5, 17; Bates, *Discourse*, 18; Livermore, *Honorable Man*, 6, 10; Disoway, "Adams," 28.

222. See Lee Benson, *Concept of Jacksonian Democracy: New York as a Test Case* (Princeton NJ: Princeton University Press, 1961), 198–207 and Ronald Formisano, *The Birth of Mass Political Parties* (Princeton, NJ: Princeton University Press 1971), 137–64.

223. William Furness, *The Memory of the Just: A Discourse* (Philadelphia: Crissy and Markley, 1848), 10; Chapin, *Truly Great*, 9; quotations in that order.

224. Lunt, *Discourse*, 32, 35; quotations in that order; William Seward, *Oration on the Death of John Quincy Adams* (Albany, NY: Charles Van Benthuysen, 1848), 32.

225. Parsons, "Splendid Pageant," 481. For this assessment of Adams, see Lewis, *Adams*, 141–42; Bemis, *Foreign Policy*, 571; Walter LaFeber, *The American Age: United States Foreign Policy at Home and Abroad since 1750* (New York: Norton, 1989), 72; Weeks, *Adams*, 1; H. W. Brands, *The United States in the World: A History of American Foreign Policy* (Boston: Houghton Mifflin, 1994), 102–3; and Russell, *Adams*, 3–4. For a dissenting view, see James Lewis, Jr., *John Quincy Adams: Policy Maker for the Union* (Wilmington, DE: Scholarly Resources, 2001), xiii–xvii, 141–45.

226. Bemis, *Foreign Policy*, 567–71; quotation from 570.

227. Adams, *Memoirs* 8:100–101, Feb. 28, 1829.

228. James Truslow Adams, *The Adams Family* (Boston: Little, Brown, 1930), 188, 212, 481; first quotation from 481, second 188.

229. Harlow, *Adams*, 240–48; quotation from 240.

230. Russell, *Adams*, 53–54.

231. Hargreaves, *Presidency*, xiii; Bemis, *Foreign Policy*, 127; Lipsky, *Adams*, 328.

232. Quoted in Parsons, *Adams*, 271.

233. Parsons, *Adams*, 271.

234. Hecht, *Adams*, 488; Bemis, *Union*, 106.

235. Nagel, *Adams*, 418–19; quotation from 419.

CHAPTER 4

1. In the Jackson Manuscripts in the Library of Congress, many endorsements have become separated from the letters they accompanied; editor's note in John Spencer Bassett, ed., *The Correspondence of Andrew Jackson*, 7 vols. (Washington, DC: Carnegie Institution of Washington, 1926–1933), 5:1 (hereinafter cited as *CAJ*).

2. Pauline Burke, *Emily Donelson of Tennessee*, 2 vols. (Knoxville: University of Tennessee Press, [1941] 2001), 1:214.

3. Jon Meacham, *American Lion: Andrew Jackson in the White House* (New York: Random House, 2008), 16.

4. Sean Patrick Adams, "The President and His Era," in Adams, ed., *A Companion to the Era of Andrew Jackson* (Chichester, UK: Wiley-Blackwell, 2013), 2.

5. Nathan Hatch, *The Democratization of American Christianity* (New Haven, CT: Yale University Press, 1989), 3–11 and passim. On the Second Great Awakening, see Jon Butler, *Awash in a Sea of Faith: Christianizing the American People* (Cambridge, MA: Harvard University Press, 1990); Richard Carwardine, *Evangelicals and Politics in Antebellum America* (Knoxville: University of Tennessee Press, 1997); Paul Johnson, *A Shopkeeper's Millennium: Society and Revivals in Rochester, New York, 1815–1837* (New York: Hill and Wang, 1978); Charles Hambrick-Stowe, *Charles G. Finney and the Spirit of American Evangelicalism* (Grand Rapids, MI; Eerdmans, 1996); Eric Schlereth, "Religious Revivalism and Public Life," in Adams, ed., *Companion*, 111–29.

6. Meacham, *Lion*, 9; James Parton, *Life of Andrew Jackson*, 3 vols. (Boston: James Osgood and Co., 1876), 1:58–69; Hendrik Booraem, *Young Hickory: The Making of Andrew Jackson* (Dallas: Taylor Trade, 2001), 17–22; Robert Remini, *Andrew Jackson: The Course of American Empire, 1767–1821* (Baltimore: Johns Hopkins University Press, [1977] 1998), 1:5–11 (hereinafter cited as *Course*, 1).

7. Meacham, *Lion*, 17. See William Bynum, "The Genuine Presbyterian Whine: Presbyterian Worship in the Eighteenth Century," *Journal of Presbyterian History* 74 (Fall 1996), 157–69.

8. Remini, *Course*, 1:6.

9. Peter Cartwright, *Autobiography of Peter Cartwright* (New York: Abingdon Press, 1956), 134.

10. Remini, *Course*, 1:7. See, for example, Sean Wilentz, *Andrew Jackson* (New York: Times Books, 2005), 160, who asserts that Jackson was "never an especially pious man."

11. Meacham, *Lion*, 18.

12. Robert Remini, *Andrew Jackson and the Course of American Democracy, 1833–1845* (New York: Harper and Row, 1984), 519 (hereinafter cited as *Course*, 3).

13. Remini, *Course*, 3:91.

14. AJ to John Coffee, Mar. 19, 1829, in Sam Smith and Harriet Chappell Owsley, eds., *The Papers of Andrew Jackson*, 8 vols. (Knoxville: University of Tennessee Press, 1980–), 7:104 (hereinafter cited as *PAJ*).

15. New York *Evening Post*, July 1853, as cited by Parton, *Life*, 3:602.

16. AJ to Mary Coffee, Aug. 15, 1833, *CAJ* 5:158.

17. E.g., AJ to Andrew Hutchins, Mar. 2, 1840, *CAJ* 6:53.

18. Parton, *Life*, 3:644–45.

19. Parton, *Life*, 3:646–48; quotation from 646. Also see Remini, *Course*, 3:444–47.

20. Rachel Jackson Lawrence, "Andrew Jackson at Home: Reminiscences by His Granddaughter," *McClure's Magazine* 9 (July 1897), 793.

21. Diary of William Tyack, May 31 (first two quotations) and June 2 (third quotation) in Parton, *Life*, 3:674–75.

22. Tyack diary, May 30, 1845, in Parton, *Life*, 3:673.

23. Robert Remini, *Andrew Jackson and the Course of American Freedom, 1822–1832* (New York: Harper and Row, 1981), 2:10 (hereinafter cited as *Course*, 2).

24. Remini, *Course*, 2:6, 85; quotations in that order.

25. AJ to John Coffee, Jan. 23, 1825, *CAJ* 3:275.

26. RJ to Eliza Kingsley, Apr. 27, 1821, in Parton, *Life*, 2:595.

27. RJ to John Donelson, Aug. 25, 1821, Miscellaneous Jackson Papers, Tennessee Historical Society, as cited by Remini, *Course*, 2:6–7.

28. RJ to Louise Livingston, Dec. 1, 1828, *PAJ* 6:536–37.

29. RJ to Mrs. L. A. Douglas, Dec. 3, 1828, *PAJ* 6:538.

30. Remini, *Course*, 2:153. See also Marquis James, *The Life of Andrew Jackson* (New York: Bobbs-Merrill, 1938), 482.

31. Edward Livingston to AJ, Jan. 3, 1829, *PAJ* 7:6.

32. Thomas Hart Benton, *Thirty Years' View: Or, A History of the Working of American Government for Thirty Years, from 1820 to 1850*, 2 vols. (New York: D. Appleton, 1854), 738.

33. Charles Coffin to AJ, Jan. 21, 1829, *PAJ* 7:16.

34. Ely to AJ, July 3, 1829, *PAJ* 7:322.

35. Ezra Stiles Ely, *The Duty of Christian Freemen to Elect Christian Rulers, A Discourse Delivered on the Fourth of July, 1827* (Philadelphia, 1828), appendix.

36. Benton, *Thirty Years' View*, 737.

37. Francis Blair to AJ, May 20, 1839, *CAJ* 6:14.

38. Quoted in Sam Houston to James Polk, June 8, 1845, *CAJ* 6:415.

39. AJ to Emily Tennessee Donelson, Nov. 28, 1830, *PAJ* 8:640; e.g., Tyack diary, May 29, 1845, in Parton, *Life*, 3:673.

40. E.g., AJ to Andrew Hutchings, Aug. 2, 1838, *CAJ* 5:561.

41. E.g., AJ to Ezra Stiles Ely, Mar. 23, 1829, *PAJ* 7:117; AJ to Coffee, *CAJ* 5:158.

42. AJ to John Coffee, Jan. 17, 1829, *PAJ* 7:12.

43. AJ to Hutchins, Sept. 20, 1838, *CAJ* 5:566. Cf. AJ to Nicholas Trist, Sept. 19, 1838, *CAJ* 5:566; AJ to Jesse Duncan Elliott, Mar. 27, 1845, *CAJ* 6:391–92.

44. AJ to Andrew Hutchins, Dec. 3, 1839, *CAJ* 6:41.

45. William Shaw as quoted in Parton, *Life*, 3:633.

46. William Allen Butler, *A Retrospect of Forty Years, 1825–1865* (New York: Charles Scribner's Sons, 1911), 122–23; quotation from 123.

47. AJ to Ellen Hanson, Mar. 25, 1835, *CAJ* 5:333.

48. As quoted in Tyack diary, May 29, in Parton, *Life*, 3:673.

49. Andrew Jackson, Jr. to A. O. P. Nicholson, June 17, 1845, Miscellaneous Jackson Papers, New York Historical Society, as cited by Remini, *Course*, 3:521.

50. John Esselman to Francis Blair, June 9, 1845, in "Account of Gen. Jackson's Last Moments From His Family Physician," *Niles National Register*, July 5, 1845, 384.

51. Parton, *Life*, 647–48; quotations in that order.

52. General Jackson's Will, June 7, 1848, in Parton, *Life*, 3:650.

53. H. W. Brands, *Andrew Jackson: His Life and Times* (New York: Doubleday, 2005), 548.

54. "Statement of an Interview with John Nicholson Campbell," Sept. 1829, *PAJ* 7:410. Jackson claimed that he had read at least three chapters of the Bible every day for the thirty-five years before he became president (testimony of William Shaw in Parton, *Life*, 3:633). Dozens of books quote Jackson's alleged comment that "the Bible is the Rock on which this Republic rests," but I cannot find a reliable source to authenticate this statement.

55. Francis Blair to Mrs. Benjamin Gratz, Apr. 20, 1831, in Thomas Clay, "Two Years with Old Hickory," *Atlantic Monthly* 60 (Aug. 1887), 193. See also Parton, *Life*, 3:674.

56. Parton, *Life*, 3:648. The volume is titled *The Comprehensive Commentary on the Holy Bible . . . Designed to Be a Digest . . . of the Best Bible Commentaries* (Boston: Shattuck, 1834–38).

57. AJ to John Donelson, June 7, 1829, *CAJ* 4:41.

58. Jackson, Jr. to Nicholson, June 17, 1845. The Jacksons adopted Andrew Jackson, Jr., the child of Rachel's younger brother Severn and his wife Elizabeth, in 1809.

59. Meacham, *Lion*, 17–18; both quotations from 18. See also Booraem, *Young Hickory*, 20–21; Arda Walker, "The Educational Training and Views of Andrew Jackson," *East Tennessee Historical Society's Publications* 16 (1944), 22.

60. E.g., AJ to Jesse Bledsoe, Jan. 18, 1826, *PAJ* 6:133; AJ to Martin Van Buren, Mar. 31, 1829, *PAJ* 7:133; AJ to John Nicholson Campbell, Sept. 10, 1829, *PAJ* 7:423; AJ to Ely, Jan. 12, 1830, *PAJ* 8:29.

61. AJ to William Berkeley Lewis, Feb. 14, 1825, *PAJ* 6:29–30.

62. AJ to William Lawrence, Aug. 24, 1838, *CAJ* 5:565.

63. AJ to Hardy Cryer, Apr. 7, 1833, *CAJ* 5:53.

64. AJ to John Coffee, May 30, 1829, *PAJ* 7:249.

65. AJ to John Christmas McLemore, Sept. 1829, *PAJ* 7:430. Cf. AJ to Coffee, *PAJ* 7:12.

66. AJ to Coffee, *CAJ* 3:274.

67. AJ to RJ, Aug. 28, 1814, *CAJ* 2:35. Cf. AJ to RJ, Oct. 11, 1814, *CAJ* 2:72.

68. AJ to Robert Hays, Jan. 26, 1815, *PAJ* 3:258.

69. AJ to David Holmes, Jan. 18, 1815, *CAJ* 2:145.

70. General Jackson's Reply to Louis Dubourg, in John Reid and John Henry Eaton, *The Life of Andrew Jackson*, ed. Frank Lawrence Owsley, Jr. (Tuscaloosa: University of Alabama Press), 407.

71. Brands, *Jackson*, 64–65.

72. AJ to Duane Morgan, Jan. 3, 1829, *PAJ* 7:5. Cf. AJ to Henry Conwell, Apr. 25, 1829, *PAJ* 7:182.

73. Quoted in Henry Wise, *Seven Decades of the Union* (Philadelphia: J. B. Lippincott, [1871] 1876), 116.

74. AJ to Donelson, *CAJ* 4:42.

75. AJ to Hardy Cryer, May 16, 1829, *PAJ* 7:223.

76. AJ to William Branch Giles, Mar. 13, 1830, *PAJ* 8:130.

77. AJ to Andrew Jackson, Jr., Oct. 23, 1834, Jackson Papers, Library of Congress (hereinafter cited as LC). Jackson's papers, books, valuables, and most of the furniture were saved.

78. AJ to Emily Donelson, Nov. 27, 1836, *CAJ* 5:439.

79. AJ to Coffee, Oct. 3, 1831, Coffee Papers, Tennessee Historical Society.

80. AJ to Robert Chester, Aug. 8, 1833, *CAJ* 5:149.

81. AJ to Cryer, *CAJ* 5:53.

82. AJ to Andrew Jackson Hutchings, Jan. 25, 1835, *CAJ* 5:322.

83. Andrew Jackson, "First Inaugural Address," Mar. 4, 1829, *PAJ* 7:75 (first two quotations), 79 (third quotation). Meacham argues that Jackson saw himself as the "national pastor" who was "leading the largest possible flock" in America (*Lion*, 61).

84. Andrew Jackson, "First Annual Message," Dec. 8, 1829, http://www.presidency.ucsb.edu/ws/?pid=29471.

85. Draft by Andrew Jackson, First Annual Message to Congress, Dec. 1829, *PAJ* 7:601–2.

86. Andrew Jackson, "Farewell Address," Mar. 4, 1837, http://www.presidency.ucsb.edu/ws/?pid=67087.

87. AJ to Richard Keith Call, July 26, 1826, *PAJ* 6:191.

88. AJ to Francis Blair, Apr. 19, 1841, *CAJ* 6:105.

89. AJ to RJ, Dec. 21, 1823, *CAJ* 3:218. See also AJ to the Synod of the Reformed Church, June 12, 1832, *CAJ* 4:447.

90. E.g., AJ to Mary Coffee, Aug. 15, 1833, *CAJ* 5:159; AJ to Chester, Aug. 8, 1833, *CAJ* 5:150; AJ to Andrew Jackson Hutchings, June 13, 1829, *PAJ* 7:280.

91. AJ to Sarah Jackson, Jan. 5, 1834, *CAJ* 5:239.

92. AJ to Francis Blair, Apr. 9, 1845, *CAJ* 6:398. Cf. AJ to Amos Kendall, May 20, 1845, *CAJ* 6:407; AJ to William Donelson, Jan. 30, 1830, *PAJ* 8:60.

93. Parton, *Life*, 3:648.

94. AJ to John Overton, July 5, 1829, *PAJ* 7:328.

95. Quoted in Wise, *Seven Decades*, 116.

96. AJ to Hugh Lawson White, Oct. 12, 1829, *PAJ* 7:492.

97. AJ to Mary Fogg, Jan. 17, 1829, *PAJ* 7:14.

98. AJ to Hutchings, *CAJ* 5:322.

99. AJ to John Coffee, Sept. 21, 1829, *PAJ* 7:444.

100. AJ to William Lewis, Apr. 29, 1833, *CAJ* 5:66.

101. AJ to Kendall, *CAJ* 6:406–7. Cf. AJ to Andrew Donelson, May 24, 1845, *CAJ* 6:408.

102. AJ to Sarah Jackson, June 21, 1832, Jackson Papers, Ladies Hermitage Association, Hermitage, Tennessee, as cited by Remini, *Course*, 2:387. Cf. AJ to Francis Blair, Mar. 18, 1845, *CAJ* 6:386, and AJ to Blair, Apr. 9, 1845, *CAJ* 6:395.

103. AJ to Donelson, *CAJ* 5:439–40.

104. AJ to John Donelson, Dec. 31, 1836, *CAJ* 5:442–43. Cf. AJ to Andrew Hutchings, Jan. 26, 1838, *CAJ* 5:533; AJ to Hutchins, Dec. 19, 1839, *CAJ* 6:42.

105. AJ to Donelson, *CAJ* 4:41.

106. AJ to Coffee, *CAJ* 5:158.

107. Columbia, Tennessee *Democrat*, Mar. 27, 1845, Jackson Papers Project, Hermitage, Tennessee.

108. "Old Hannah's Narrative of Jackson's Last Days," *CAJ* 6:415; John Esselman, as cited in Parton, *Life*, 3:676; quotations in that order.

109. E.g., AJ to RJ, Dec. 7, 1823, *CAJ* 3:215; AJ to RJ, Dec. 21, 1823, *CAJ* 3:218; AJ to RJ, Jan. 5, 1824, *CAJ* 3:222; AJ to RJ, Dec. 28, 1831, *CAJ* 2:220. See also John Eaton to RJ, Feb. 8, 1824, *CAJ* 3:226.

110. Brands, *Jackson*, 449. See "Jackson's Pew Rent," for 2nd P.C., Apr. 1, 1831, *CAJ* 4:255.

111. Gaillard Hunt, ed., *First Forty Years of Washington Society* (New York: Scribner, 1906), 289.

112. James Stuart, *Three Years in North America*, 2 vols. (Edinburgh, 1833), 2:75–76.

113. Remini, *Course*, 2:385.

114. Parton, *Life*, 3:101–2.

115. AJ to John Coffee, Feb. 20–24, 1828, *PAJ* 5:419. See also AJ to Coffee, late 1827/ early 1828, *CAJ* 3:388.

116. Parton, *Life*, 3:647.

117. AJ to Lawrence, *CAJ* 5:565.

118. Parton, *Life*, 3:641.

119. Andrew Burstein, *The Passions of Andrew Jackson* (New York: Alfred Knopf, 2003), 39, 229.

120. Wilkins Tannehill, *The Masonic Manual, or, Freemasonry Illustrated* (Nashville, TN: G. Wilson, 1824), 70–73.

121. AJ to William Hess and the Masons of Lodge 45, Jackson, Tennessee, Sept. 19, 1825, *PAJ* 6:102.

122. Carwardine, *Evangelicals and Politics*, 121. The Antimason Party, which played a significant role in New England politics from 1826 to 1836, criticized numerous Jackson policies, but it did not directly attack Jackson for being a mason. See Paul Goodman, *Towards a Christian Republic: Antimasonry and the Great Transition in New England, 1826–1836* (New York: Oxford University Press, 1988), 122–23, 141, 217, 29–30.

123. Remini, *Course*, 1:26.

124. Quoted in James M'Cabe, Jr., *The Great Republic* (Toledo, OH: O. A. Browning, 1871), 793.

125. Parton, *Life*, 1:253.

126. Burstein, *Passions*, 143. See also Bertram Wyatt-Brown, *The Shaping of Southern Culture: Honor, Grace, and War, 1760s–1880s* (Chapel Hill: University of North Carolina Press, 2001), 56–80.

127. AJ to John Coffee, June 18, 1824, *CAJ* 3:255–56.

128. Parton, *Life*, 3:101.

129. Benton, *Thirty Years' View*, 738.

130. Levi Woodbury, eulogy, in B. M. Dusenbery, *Monument to the Memory of the General Andrew Jackson* (Philadelphia: Walker & Gillis, 1846), 75.

131. Burstein, *Passions*, 175.

132. Remini, *Course*, 2:142.

133. Mary Donelson Wilcox, *Christmas under Three Flags* (Washington, DC: Neale, 1900), 17–45.

134. Benton, *Thirty Years' View*, 737.

135. AJ to Coffee, *PAJ* 7:249.

136. AJ to Morgan Lewis, Mar. 31, 1829, *PAJ* 7:134.

137. Brands, *Jackson*, 149.

138. AJ to Egbert Harris, Apr. 13, 1822, *PAJ* 5:170.

139. Brands, *Jackson*, 150.

140. Remini, *Course*, 2:250.

141. AJ to Andrew Jackson, Jr., July 4, 1829, *CAJ* 4:49–50.

142. Brands, *Jackson*, 149–51; first quotation from 149, second from 150.

143. Brands, *Jackson*, 554.

144. Burstein, *Passions*, 226.

145. Remini, *Course*, 3:484.

146. Norma Basch, "Marriage, Morals, and Politics in the Election of 1828," *Journal of American History* 80 (Dec. 1993), 892.

147. Parton, *Life*, 3:141.

148. Brands, *Jackson*, 397.

149. Burstein, *Passions*, 227.

150. *National Banner and Nashville Whig*, Aug. 2, 1828, quoted in *PAJ* 6:486. See also Andrew Ervin, *Gen. Jackson's Negro Speculations, and His Traffic in Human Flesh, Examined and Established by Positive Proof* (n.p., 1828).

151. Brands, *Jackson*, 398.

152. Remini, *Course*, 2:122; handbill in Huntington Library.

153. [Charles Hammond], *View of General Jackson's Domestic Relations, in Reference to his Fitness for the Presidency* (Cincinnati, 1828), 15. See also *An Appeal to the Moral and Religious of All Denominations; or, An Exposition of Some of the Indiscretions of General Andrew Jackson* (New York, 1828), 4.

154. Basch, "Marriage," 891.

155. Frankfort *Argus*, Apr. 18, 1827, quoting Frankfort *Commentator*, in *PAJ* 6:344 n. 2.

156. Basch, "Marriage," 891.

157. Basch, "Marriage," 894–95; first and second quotation from 895, third and fourth from 895.

158. Hammond, *Domestic Relations*, esp. 11–12, 18.

159. Basch, "Marriage," 900; *Daily National Journal*, Oct. 14, 1828; *We the People*, Apr. 12, 1828.

160. Basch, "Marriage," 895 (all quotations), 891.

161. Basch, "Marriage," 894 (first quotation), 895 (second quotation), 900.

162. Parton, *Life*, 3:140.

163. July 4, 1821. See Florence Weston, *The Presidential Election of 1828* (Washington, DC: Ruddick Press 1938), 168. Also see John Quincy Adams, "Special Message," Dec. 26, 1825, http://www.presidency.ucsb.edu/ws/?pid=66660.

164. Lynn Hudson Parsons, *The Birth of Modern Politics: Andrew Jackson, John Quincy Adams, and the Election of 1828* (New York: Oxford University Press, 2009), 174.

165. *A History of the Life and Public Services of Major General Andrew Jackson* (n.p., 1828), 19.

166. As quoted in Hudson, *Modern Politics*, 175.

167. Remini, *Course*, 2:133. See also Robert Remini, *The Election of Andrew Jackson* (Philadelphia: Lippincott, 1963), 117–19.

168. *Weekly Marylander*, Nov. 6, 1828.

169. Basch, "Marriage," 896 (first and second quotation), 908 (third quotation).

170. AJ to Robert Paine et al., Sept. 30, 1826, *PAJ* 5:220.

171. See Joseph Blau, "The Christian Party in Politics," *Review of Religion* 11 (November 1946), 18–35; Bertram Wyatt-Brown, "Prelude to Abolitionism: Sabbatarian Politics and the Rise of the Second Party System," *Journal of American History* 58 (Sept. 1971), 316–41.

172. Ely, *Christian Freemen*, 11, 6, 4; quotations in that order.

173. Carwardine, *Evangelicals and Politics*, 120; Lorenzo Dow, *The Dealings of God, Man and the Devil* (New York: Sheldon, Lamport, and Blakeman, 1854), 181–82. On the political allegiances of Protestants during this period, see Lee Benson, *The Concept of Jacksonian Democracy: New York as a Test Case* (Princeton, NJ: Princeton University Press, 1961), 284–86, and Carwardine, *Evangelicals and Politics*, 106–20.

174. AJ to Ezra Stiles Ely, July 12, 1827, *PAJ* 6:358–59.

175. Remini, *Election*, 152.

176. Remini, *Course*, 2:119.

177. AJ to John Christmas McLemore, Dec. 25, 1830, *PAJ* 8:707.

178. Hammond, *Domestic Relations*, 11; Basch, "Marriage," 906.

179. RJ to Elizabeth Watson, July 18, 1828, *CAJ* 3:415–16.

180. AJ to McLemore, *PAJ* 8:707.

181. Brands, *Jackson*, 65.

182. Arthur Schlesinger, Jr., *The Age of Jackson* (Boston: Little, Brown, 1945), 350.

183. Quoted in John Andrews, *From Revivals to Removal: Jeremiah Evarts, the Cherokee Nation, and the Search for the Soul of America* (Athens: University of Georgia Press, 1992), 56.

184. Charles Coffin to AJ, Jan. 21, 1829, *PAJ* 7:17.

185. Ezra Stiles Ely to AJ, Jan. 28, 1829, *PAJ* 7:17, 20, 21; quotations in that order.

186. New York *Journal of Commerce*, June 15, 1833 (quotation) and *National Intelligencer*, June 20, 1833, both as cited by Remini, *Course*, 3:74. See also Richard John, "Taking Sabbatarianism Seriously: The Postal System, the Sabbath, and the Transformation of American Political Culture," *Journal of the Early Republic* 10 (Winter 1990), 517–67; Steven Green, *The Second Disestablishment: Church and State in Nineteenth Century America* (New York: Oxford University Press, 2010), 84.

187. *Register of Debates*, 22nd Congress, 1st session, 1130–31; Parton, *Life*, 3:418–20; Brands, *Jackson*, 450; Adam Jortner, "Cholera, Christ, and Jackson: The Epidemic of 1832 and the Origins of Christian Politics in Antebellum America," *Journal of the Early Republic* 27 (Summer 2007), 247–62.

188. Jortner, "Cholera," 239.

189. AJ to the Synod of the Reformed Church, June 12, 1832, *CAJ* 4:447.

190. Van Buren Papers, LC.

191. Theodore Frelinghuysen, *An Inquiry into the Moral and Religious Character of the American Government* (New York: Wiley and Putman, 1838), 10 (first quotation), 14, 18, 19, 89, 92, 109, 206, 133; Schlesinger, *Jackson*, 352 (second quotation).

192. Quoted in Charles Rosenberg, *The Cholera Years: The United States in 1832, 1849, and 1866* (Chicago: University of Chicago Press, 1962), 50.

193. AJ to William Conway, Apr. 4, 1831, *CAJ* 4:256.

194. AJ to Ely, *PAJ* 6:358. Cf. AJ to Ellen Hanson, Mar. 25, 1835, *CAJ* 5:333.

195. Carwardine, *Evangelicals and Politics*, 125.

196. Andrew Jackson, "Proclamation 43—Regarding the Nullifying Laws of South Carolina," Dec. 10, 1832, http://www.presidency.ucsb.edu/ws/?pid=67078. Cf. Jackson, "Special Message," Jan. 16, 1833, http://www.presidency.ucsb.edu/ws/index.php?pid=66895&st=&st1=; Jackson, "Fourth Annual Message," Dec. 4, 1832, http://www.presidency.ucsb.edu/ws/index.php?pid=29474&st=&st1=.

197. Andrew Jackson, "Third Annual Message," Dec. 6, 1831, http://www.presidency.ucsb.edu/ws/index.php?pid=29473&st=&st1=.

198. Andrew Jackson, "Sixth Annual Message," Dec. 1, 1834, http://www.presidency.ucsb.edu/ws/index.php?pid=29476&st=&st1=.

199. Richard Latner, *The Presidency of Andrew Jackson: White House Politics, 1829–1837* (Athens: University of Georgia Press, 1979), 3, 24, 86; quotations in that order.

200. Latner, *Presidency*, 142.

201. AJ to Taney, Oct. 13, 1836, *CAJ* 5:429.

202. Jackson, "Farewell Address."

203. AJ to Elliott, *CAJ* 6:391.

204. Jackson, "First Annual Message."

205. Remini, *Course*, 3:338–39, 342.

206. AJ to Elliott, *CAJ* 6:391. See also Remini, *Course*, 3:340.

207. AJ to Francis Blair, May 2, 1839, Jackson Papers, LC.

208. AJ to Elliott, *CAJ* 6:391.

209. Latner, *Presidency*, 123. See AJ to Roger Taney, Oct. 13, 1836, *CAJ* 5:430.

210. AJ to James Hamilton, Jr., June 29, 1828, *CAJ* 3:412.

211. Andrew Jackson, Veto Message, July 10, 1832, http://www.presidency.ucsb.edu/ws/index.php?pid=67043&st=&st1=.

212. Jackson, "First Inaugural Address," 7:79.

213. AJ to James Alexander Hamilton, Sept. 11, 1829, *PAJ* 7:427.

214. Meacham, *American Lion*, 121; Marvin Meyers, *The Jacksonian Persuasion: Politics and Belief* (Stanford, CA: Stanford University Press, 1957), 12–17.

215. AJ to James Hamilton, Dec. 19, 1829, *PAJ* 7:642–43.

216. AJ to Senator John Branch, June 24, 1828, Andrew Jackson Papers, LC, Microfilm, reel 35, as cited in Burstein, *Passions*, 169.

217. Latner, *Presidency*, 143, 145.

218. AJ to Taney, *CAJ* 5:430. See also Burstein, *Passions*, 154.

219. Burstein, *Passions*, 199; Meacham, *American Lion*, 121; quotations in that order.

220. Andrew Jackson, "Seventh Annual Message," Dec. 7, 1835, http://www.presidency.ucsb.edu/ws/?pid=29477.

221. Latner, *Presidency*, 99, 106. See "Notes for the Maysville Road Veto," May 19–26? 1830, *CAJ* 4:138.

222. Donald Cole, *The Presidency of Andrew Jackson* (Lawrence: University Press of Kansas, 1993), 63.

223. AJ to John Coffee, July 17, 1832, *CAJ* 4:462–63; AJ to Coffee, Apr. 9, 1833, *CAJ* 5:56; quotations in that order.

224. AJ to Joel Poinsett, Dec. 9, 1832, *CAJ* 4:498.

225. Remini, *Course*, 3:343.

226. Cole, *Presidency*, 109. See AJ to John Coffee, Nov. 6, 1832, *CAJ* 4:483.

227. Latner, *Presidency*, 89; Remini, *Course*, 2:258. See also Francis Prucha, "Andrew Jackson's Indian Policy: A Reassessment," *Journal of American History* 56 (December 1969), 527–39; Ronald Satz, *American Indian Policy in the Jacksonian Era* (Norman: University of Oklahoma Press, 2002), 9–10.

228. Remini, *Course*, 2:201.

229. AJ to James Monroe, Mar. 4, 1817, *CAJ* 2:280–81; quotations in that order.

230. AJ to Monroe, *CAJ* 2:279–81.

231. AJ to Captain James Gadsden, Oct. 12, 1829, *CAJ* 4:81.

232. Jackson, "First Annual Message." Also see Remini, *Course*, 2:221.

233. AJ to John Coffee, Oct. 16, 1830, Microfilm Supplement to the Andrew Jackson Papers (Wilmington, DE: Scholarly Resources, 1986).

234. Andrew Jackson, "Second Annual Message," Dec. 6, 1830, http://www.presidency.ucsb.edu/ws/?pid=29472.

235. Jackson, "Seventh Annual Message."

236. Jackson, "Farewell Address."

237. Francis Prucha, *The Great Father: The United States Government and the American Indians*, 2 vols. (Lincoln: University of Nebraska Press, 1984), 1:201–2; Meacham, *Lion*, 75. See Jeremiah Evarts, *Cherokee Removal: The William Penn Essays and Other Writings*, ed. Francis Prucha (Knoxville: University of Tennessee Press, 1981).

238. Prucha, *Great Father*, 1:205; Evarts, *Removal*, 8, 49, 51.

239. Satz, *Indian Policy*, 54–55.

240. Latner, *Presidency*, 92. See *Register of Debates*, 21 Cong., 1 Sess., 319–20, 380–82, 997, 1026, 1111.

241. See Cole, *Presidency*, 72; *Speeches on the Passage of the Bill for the Removal of the Indians Delivered in the Congress of the United States, April and May, 1830* (Millwood, NY: Kraus, 1973), 1–78; *Registry of Debates*, 21 Cong., 1st sess., 325–29.

242. *Speech of Mr. Frelinghuysen of New Jersey, delivered in the Senate of the United States, April 6, 1830* (Washington, DC: National Journal, 1830), 7–9.

243. Cole, *Presidency*, 73. See Wilcomb Washburn, ed., *The American Indian and the United States: A Documentary History*, 4 vols. (Westport, CT: Greenwood Press, 1973), 2:1017–93, and Wilson Lumpkin, *The Removal of the Cherokee Indians from Georgia*, 2 vols. (New York: Dodd, Mead and Co. 1907). On the connection between Indian removal and abolitionism, see D. Laurence Rogers, *Apostles of Equality: The Birneys, the Republicans, and the Civil War* (East Lansing: Michigan State University Press, 2011).

244. "Removal of the Indians," *North American Review* 30 (1830), 77.

245. *Congressional Globe*, 27 Cong., 3 sess., Appendix.

246. *Journal of the House of Representatives of the State of Georgia*, 1830, quoted in Prucha, *Great Father*, 1:196.

247. Satz, *Indian Policy*, 13–19; Prucha, *Great Father*, 1:201–5; Cole, *Presidency*, 70; Herman Viola, *Thomas L. McKenney: Architect of America's Early Indian Policy, 1816–1830* (Chicago: Swallow Press, 1974), 206–22.

248. Satz, *Indian Policy*, 54–56.

249. Prucha, *Great Father*, 1:207; Francis Prucha, *American Indian Policy in the Formative Years: The Indian Trade and Intercourse Acts, 1790–1834* (Cambridge, MA: Harvard University Press, 1962), 243.

250. Meacham, *Lion*, 96.

251. Cole, *Presidency*, 114–15; Brands, *Jackson*, 493.

252. AJ to Coffee, *CAJ* 4:483.

253. Cole, *Presidency*, 117.

254. Remini, *Course*, 3:303. See Grant Foreman, *Indian Removal: The Emigration of the Five Civilized Tribes* (Norman: University of Oklahoma Press, 1966); Mary Elizabeth Young, *Redskins, Ruffians, Ruffleshirts, and Rednecks: Indian Allotments in Alabama and Mississippi, 1830–1860* (Norman: University of Oklahoma Press, 1961), 47–72; Satz, *Indian Policy*, 83–87.

255. Clay as quoted in Adams, *Memoirs*, Dec. 22, 1825, 7:89–90; Wilentz, *Jackson*, 68–69; quotations in that order.

256. Cole, *Presidency*, 117. See also Edward Pessen, *Jacksonian America: Society, Personality, and Politics* (Homewood, IL: Dorsey Press, 1978), 296–301, and Michael Paul Rogin, *Fathers and Children: Andrew Jackson and the Subjugation of the American Indian* (New York: Alfred Knopf, 1975), 4–15, 165–69, 179–85.

257. Latner, *Presidency*, 90; Rogin, *Fathers*, 4, 13 (quotation), 179; Meacham, *Lion*, 97.

258. Meacham, *Lion*, 93, 318 (quotation). See also Prucha, *Great Father*, 1:242.

259. Satz, *Indian Policy*, 9–10 (e.g., AJ to John Coffee, Sept. 2, 25, 1826, *CAJ* 3:312, 315); Remini, *Course*, 2:264; Prucha, *Great Father*, 1:191 (cf. Prucha, "Indian Policy," 527–39); Brands, *Jackson*, 492 (quotation), 310, 321.

260. Meacham, *Lion*, 123.

261. Cole, *Presidency*, 115, 118. On Indian removal, also see Anthony Wallace, *The Long Bitter Trail: Andrew Jackson and the Subjugation of the Indian* (New York: Hill and Wang, 1993); Andrew Frank, "Native American Removal," in Adams, ed., *Companion*, 391–411; Dona Akers, *Living in the Land of Death: The Choctaw Nation, 1830–1860* (East Lansing: Michigan State University Press, 2004); Stuart Banner, *How Indians Lost Their Land: Law and Power on the Frontier* (Cambridge, MA: Harvard University Press, 2005).

262. Remini, *Course*, 3:227 (quotation); Cole, *Presidency*, 272–73. See also Charles Sellers, *The Market Revolution: Jacksonian America, 1815–1846* (New York: Oxford University Press, 1991), and Jama Lazerow, *Religion and the Working Class in Antebellum America* (Washington, DC: Smithsonian Institution Press, 1995).

263. Cole, *Presidency*, 220–21.

264. Jan. 21, 1834.

265. Parker to AJ, Feb. 26, 1836, Andrew Jackson Papers, LC, cited in Cole, *Presidency*, 269.

266. *Washington Union*, June 16, 30, 1845, quoted in Remini, *Course*, 3:527.

267. Quoted in "Mr. Webster's Remarks," *Niles National Register*, July 5, 1845, 382.

268. Hendrick Wright, eulogy, in Dusenbery, *Monument*, 248.

269. Remini, *Course*, 3:412–13, 337; first and second quotations from 412, third from 337.

270. Jackson, "Farewell Address."

271. Robert Remini, *Andrew Jackson* (New York: Twayne, 1966), 14 (first quotation); Meacham, *Lion*, 83 (second quotation).

272. Remini, *Course*, 2:184 (first quotation); "Memorandum on Appointments," Feb. 23, 1829, *PAJ* 7:60 (second quotation from 61). See also Albert Somit, "Andrew Jackson as Administrative Reformer," *Tennessee Historical Quarterly* 13:3 (1954), 204–33.

273. Matthew Warshauer, "Andrew Jackson and the Legacy of the Battle of New Orleans," in Adams, *Companion*, 80; George Bancroft, eulogy, in Dusenbery, *Monument*, 41–43.

274. Anonymous, *An Impartial and True History of the Life and Service of Major General Andrew Jackson* (n.p., n.d.), 40, quoted in John William Ward, *Andrew Jackson: Symbol for an Age* (New York: Oxford University Press, 1955), 64.

275. Adams, *Memoirs*, June 17, 1833, 8:546.

276. Burnstein, *Passions*, 234.

277. Glyndon Van Deusen, *William Henry Seward* (New York: Oxford University Press, 1967), 44.

278. *New York American* as quoted by Parton, *Life*, 3:627.

279. Adams, *Memoirs*, Oct. 11, 1836, 9:311.

280. AJ to Blair, July 19, 1838, *CAJ* 6:557.

281. AJ to D. G. Goodlett, Mar. 12, 1844, *CAJ* 6:273.

282. Adams *Diary*, June 18, 1845, Adams Papers Microfilm, reel 48, MA Historical Society, Boston. See also Adams, *Memoirs*, Feb. 16, 1831, 8:319.

283. Remini, *Course*, 3:413–14.

284. Wilentz, *Jackson*, 8.

285. Burstein, *Passions*, 231 (quotation), 236.

286. Ward, *Jackson*, 140.

287. Parsons, *Modern Politics*, 187.

288. Burstein, *Passions*, 183, 231 (quotation).

289. Wilentz, *Jackson*, 8.

290. Parton, *Life*, 1:vii.

291. Burstein, *Passions*, 235.

292. Wyatt-Brown, *Shaping*, 58.

293. Tyack diary, May 29, 1845, in Parton, *Life*, 3:673.

CHAPTER 5

1. Edwin Andrews, eulogy, in Murat Halstead, *The Illustrious Life of William McKinley, Our Martyred President* (Chicago: n.p., 1901), 284.

2. See "The Mother's Story," in Charles Grosvenor, *William McKinley: His Life and Work* (Washington, DC: Continental Assembly, 1901), 175–79.

3. Frederick Barton, "A Christian Gentleman: William McKinley," *The Chautauquan* 34 (Nov. 1901), 134. Historians and contemporaries disagree

about when McKinley had his conversion experience. Richard Pierard and Robert Linder, *Civil Religion and the Presidency* (Grand Rapids, MI: Academie Books, 1988), 115, and Margaret Leech, *In the Days of William McKinley* (New York: Harper and Brothers, 1959), 5, claim he was 10; Halstead (*Illustrious Life*, 422) maintained he was about 14; and Frank Gunsaulus, "The Religious Life of William McKinley," *Interior*, Sept. 26, 1901, 1205, alleged he was 15.

4. Charles Olcott, *The Life of William McKinley*, 2 vols. (Boston: Houghton Mifflin Co., 1916), 1:18–19; Robert Porter, *Life of William McKinley, Soldier, Lawyer, Statesman* (Cleveland: N. G. Hamilton, 1896), 53ff.

5. James Rusling, "Interview with President McKinley," *CA* 78 (Jan. 22, 1903), 17.

6. Quoted in Joseph Butler, Jr., *Recollection of Men and Events* (New York: Putnam, 1927), 26.

7. H. Wayne Morgan, ed., "A Civil War Diary of William McKinley," *Ohio History* 69 (July 1960), 283.

8. *Speeches and Addresses of William McKinley from His Election to Congress to the Present Time* (New York: D. Appleton, 1893), 606; "Notable Public Utterances of President McKinley; Outspoken and Eloquent Championship of the Christian Religion," *PB*, Oct. 3, 1901, 13; William McKinley Papers, Manuscript Division, Library of Congress, reel 18, vol. 90, p. 425; quotations in that order (hereinafter cited as WMP).

9. Halstead, *Illustrious Life*, 387.

10. Barton, "Christian Gentleman," 135.

11. Halstead, *Illustrious Life*, 370.

12. *Epworth Herald*, Sept. 24, 1901, quoted in Halstead, *Illustrious Life*, 395; T. DeWitt Talmage and Eleanor Talmage, *T. DeWitt Talmage As I Knew Him* (New York: E. P. Dutton, 1912), 307; "Faith during the Crisis in Peking," *The Chautauquan* 34 (Nov. 1901), 137–38, quotation from 138.

13. Vernon B. Hampton, *Religious Background of the White House* (Boston: Christopher Publishing House, 1932), 356–58.

14. Carl Sferrazza Anthony, *America's First Families* (New York: Touchstone, 2000), 224 (first quotation); Barton, "Christian Gentleman," 135 (second quotation). See also Edward Thornton Heald, *The William McKinley Story* (Canton, OH: Stark County Historical Society, 1964), 84.

15. Manchester wrote McKinley frequently about a variety of church, political, and personal matters. See especially Manchester to WM, Apr. 7, 1897, reel 58; Oct. 8, 1897, reel 2; Sept. 21, 1899, reel 8; July 9, 1898, reel 61; Jan. 20, 1899, reel 5; and WM to Manchester, Apr. 14, 1899, reel 39, all in WMP.

16. John Long, "Some Personal Characteristics of President McKinley," *Century Magazine* 63 (1901), 145.

17. Halstead, *Illustrious Life*, 423.

18. See James Norr to WM, June 26, 1899, WMP, reel 2. McKinley's papers contain numerous letters thanking the president for his contributions to the YMCA and various congregations.

19. Quoted in Barton, "Christian Gentleman," 136.

20. Barton, "Christian Gentleman," 135.

21. E.g., Bliss Isely, *The Presidents, Men of Faith* (Boston: W. A. Wilde, 1953), 191.

22. McKinley as quoted in an American Bible Society tract.

23. Leech, *McKinley*, 462, 132 (quotation).

24. Barton, "Christian Gentleman," 134 (cf. A. Ellwood Corning, *William McKinley: A Biological Study* [New York: Broadway, 1907], 170–71); Pepper, as quoted in Halstead, *Illustrious Life*, 386; Barton, "Christian Gentleman," 135; *Speeches and Addresses of William McKinley from March 1, 1897 to May 30, 1900* (New York: Doubleday and McClure, 1900), 2 (first quotation), 15 (second quotation); *Speeches and Addresses* (1900), 229.

25. William McKinley, "Proclamation 441—Thanksgiving Day, 1899," Oct. 25, 1899, http://www.presidency.ucsb.edu/ws/?pid=69264. Cf. McKinley, "First Annual Message," Dec. 6, 1897, http://www.presidency.ucsb.edu/ws/?pid=29538.

26. *Speeches and Addresses* (1900), 319.

27. *Speeches and Addresses* (1893), 607.

28. *Speeches and Addresses* (1900), 66–67; quotation from 66.

29. *Speeches and Addresses* (1893), 607; May 22, 1901, speech in San Francisco, as cited in "The First Anniversary!" *CA* 77 (Sept. 18, 1902), 1483; Leech, *McKinley*, 10; quotations in that order.

30. See *UP*, Sept. 19, 1901, 4.

31. *Speeches and Addresses* (1900), 367–68. See also "The Ecumenical Missionary Conference," *Watchman*, Apr. 26, 1900, 12; "The Ecumenical Missionary Conference," *UP*, May 3, 1900, 8–9; and "Annual Cosmopolitan Survey," *CA* 74 (Nov. 14, 1901), 1–2.

32. McKinley and his wife Ida had two daughters, one of whom died at age 3 and the other at four months. Never recovering from these crushing blows, Ida developed a nervous disorder that made her a semi-invalid for the rest of her life.

33. Pepper, as cited in Halstead, *Illustrious Life*, 388; e.g., McKinley, 1899 Thanksgiving Proclamation; Hill, as quoted in Corning, *McKinley*, 170; on the McKinleys' relationship, see Leech, *McKinley*, 28–30, 432–61.

34. Halstead, *Illustrious Life*, 425.

35. Quoted in Barton, "Christian Gentleman," 136.

36. *Epworth Herald*, Sept. 24, 1901, quoted in Halstead, *Illustrious Life*, 395.

37. George McClellan Fiske, *William McKinley: President, Patriot, and Martyr* (Providence, RI: Snow and Farnham, 1901), 11.

38. Leslie Shaw, cited in Grosvenor, *McKinley*, 127. Cf. *PB*, Sept. 19, 1901, 4.

39. Edward Ransom, "Electing the President, 1896," *Annual Editions, American History*, vol. 2: *Reconstruction through the Present* (Guilford, CT: Dushkin/McGraw Hill, 1999), 51.

40. Stanley Jones, *The Presidential Election of 1896* (Madison: University of Wisconsin Press, 1964), 143; Leech, *McKinley*, 76–77.

41. WM to William Osborne, Apr. 17, 1896, WMP, as cited by Jones, *Presidential Election*, 143. After McKinley secured the nomination, the APA decided that his qualifications and record were satisfactory and endorsed him (ibid., 169–70, 144).

42. See "Archbishop Ireland Opposes the Chicago Platform," *Literary Digest*, Oct. 24, 1896, 806–807; *New York Journal*, Oct. 12, 1896, 1; James Moynihan, *The Life of Archbishop John Ireland* (New York: Harper and Brothers, 1953), 261–62. Moynihan contended that Ireland "spared no effort to aid in the election of McKinley" (262).

43. *New York Herald*, Oct. 17, 1896; *NYT*, Oct. 9, 1896, as cited by Robert F. Durden, *The Climax of Populism: The Election of 1896* (Lexington: University of Kentucky Press, 1965), 149–50.

44. Ransom, "Electing the President," 51; *NYT*, Aug. 17, 1896. Cf. "Strong Pulpit Attack on the Silver Delusion," "Silver and Common Sense," "A Drift toward Anarchy," all in ibid., Oct. 5, 1896. These are excerpts of sermons by some of the nation's leading ministers.

45. *NYT*, Aug. 23, 1896.

46. "Dr. MacArthur Denounces the Chicago Platform," *NYT*, Aug. 3, 1896.

47. *New York Tribune*, Nov. 2, 1896, 2, as quoted by Jones, *Presidential Election*, 340. See also "Mr. Dixon Talks of Mr. Bryan," *NYT*, Oct. 12, 1896.

48. Leech, *McKinley*, 463.

49. E. Berkeley Tompkins, *Anti-Imperialism in the United States: The Great Debate, 1890–1920* (Philadelphia: University of Pennsylvania Press, 1970), 236.

50. Quoted in William Harbaugh, *Power and Responsibility: The Life and Times of Theodore Roosevelt* (New York: Farrar, Straus and Cudahy, 1961), 139.

51. "Mr. Bryan's Indianapolis Speech," *Watchman*, Aug. 16, 1900, 6.

52. E.g., "President McKinley's Letter," *Watchman*, Sept. 13, 1900, 1.

53. E.g., "McKinley Must Be Beaten," *New York Freeman's Journal*, Oct. 12, 1900, 2. For the larger context, see Frank Reuter, *Catholic Influence on American Colonial Policies, 1898–1904* (Austin: University of Texas Press, 1967), 70–72.

54. Harbaugh, *Power*, 140.

55. "A Resolution adopted by the Chicago Preachers' Meeting of the MEC," Mar. 8, 1897, WMP, reel 2 (the Baltimore and Kansas conferences of the MEC sent similar statements, which are also in reel 2); "Thanks to President McKinley," *CA* 74 (Nov. 30, 1899), 1928; Fiske, *McKinley*, 12–13; see "Programme of the Seventh Council," WMP, reel 68.

56. See Frontispiece, *Christian Endeavor World*, July 1899; Francis Clark to WM, WMP, reel 67; WM to William Cozens, Nov. 27, 1898, reel 17; Frederick Tucker to WM, Jan. 25, 1898, reel 60; Tucker to WM, Dec. 9, 1898, reel 64; J. Wilbur Chapman to WM, Aug. 13, 1899, reel 73.

57. See "Letters to the President . . . from Sixty-Two Clergymen" (WMP, reel 71); "Letters to the President . . . from Presidents of Thirteen Universities" (reel 70); "Letters to the President . . . from Twenty-Seven Instructors" (reel 70); and "Letters to the President . . . from Thirty-One College Presidents" (reel 70).

58. The United Presbyterian Church of North America and the Presbyterian Church in the U.S.A. both adopted resolutions in May 1899 (see William Reid to WM, Jan. 24, 1900, WMP, reel 71, and William Henry Roberts to WM, Jan. 20, 1900, reel 71). Reel 70 contains dozens of letters from local WCTUs and individual congregations.

59. Bishop Fitzgerald, "Thanks for President McKinley," *CA* 74 (Dec. 21, 1899), 2073.

60. O. F. Gregory to WM, Jan. 31, 1900, WMP, reel 71.

61. Alice Brown to WM, Jan. 30, 1900, WMP, reel 71.

62. Doherty to WM, Jan. 31, 1900, WMP, reel 71.

63. Milton Buck to WM, Jan. 16, 1900, WMP, reel 71.

64. H. H. Bowen to WM, Jan. 30, 1900, WMP, reel 71; A. Baker to WM, Jan. 22, 1900, reel 71; Vaughan Colins to WM, Jan. 5, 1900, reel 70.

65. Karl Harrington to WM, Jan. 16, 1900, WMP, reel 70.

66. On his temperance activities in Ohio, see H. Wayne Morgan, *William McKinley and His America* (Syracuse, NY: Syracuse University Press, 1963), 46. On this episode, see Gaines M. Foster, *Moral Reconstruction: Christian Lobbyists and the Federal Legislation of Morality, 1865–1920* (Chapel Hill: University of North Carolina Press, 2002), 168–70.

67. WM to T. C. Evans, Nov. 30, 1895, WMP, reel 17.

68. Moynihan, *John Ireland*, 261–63. On Gibbons, see especially John Addison Porter to Gibbons, Apr. 13, 1899, reel 18; Gibbons to WM, Mar. 14, 1900, reel 9.

69. See *NYT*, Mar. 1, 1898, 1; *New York Freeman's Journal*, Mar. 5, 1898, 1.

70. Reuter, *Catholic Influence*, 8.

71. John Ireland, "His Memory Will Live," in Alexander McClure, *The Authentic Life of William McKinley, Our Third Martyr President* (Washington, DC: Scull, 1901), 403. See also Gibbons's eulogy, "His Characteristic Virtues," in ibid., 401–2.

72. See Ireland to WM, Nov. 9, 1900, WMP, reel 14; John Addison Porter to Ireland, Feb. 19, 1898, reel 26.

73. Richard Purcell, "Catholics in the President's Cabinet," *America* 48 (Dec. 17, 1932), 253; e.g., "Evils of Romanism," a newspaper account of a speech by J. C. Hardenbergh, WMP, reel 70.

74. Reuter, *Catholic Influence*, 68–79, 84–86; quotation from 79.

75. Morgan, *McKinley*, 335.

76. Lewis Gould, *The Spanish-American War and President McKinley* (Lawrence: University Press of Kansas, 1982), 19 (quotations), 25.

77. Augustus Cerillo, Jr., "The Spanish-America War," in Ronald Wells, ed., *The Wars of America: Christian Views* (Grand Rapids, MI: Eerdmans, 1981),

92–94, quotations from 94. Also see David Healy, *U.S. Expansionism: The Imperialist Urge in the 1890s* (Madison: University of Wisconsin Press, 1970); Ernest May, *American Imperialism: A Speculative Essay* (New York: Atheneum, 1968); and Robert L. Beisner, *From the Old Diplomacy to the New, 1865–1900* (New York: Thomas Y. Crowell, 1975).

78. Ian Tyrell, *Reforming the World: The Creation of America's Moral Empire* (Princeton, NJ: Princeton University Press, 2010); Susan Harris, *God's Arbiters: Americans and the Philippines, 1898–1902* (New York: Oxford University Press, 2011); Andrew Preston, *Sword of the Spirit, Shield of Faith: Religion in American War and Diplomacy* (New York: Knopf, 2012), 155–59, 207–32.

79. Cerillo, "Spanish-America War," 98–105, quotations from 105.

80. Charles Dawes, *A Journal of the McKinley Years*, ed. Bascom Timmons (Chicago: Lakeside Press, 1950), 115; George Parker, *Recollections of Grover Cleveland* (New York: Century, 1909), 249–50.

81. William McKinley: "Inaugural Address," Mar. 4, 1897. http://www.presidency. ucsb.edu/ws/?pid=25827.

82. Lewis Gould, *The Presidency of William McKinley* (Lawrence: University Press of Kansas, 1980), 33.

83. Cerillo, "Spanish-American War," 107–8.

84. McKinley, "First Annual Message."

85. Cerillo, "Spanish-American War," 109.

86. Quoted in Ernest May, *Imperial Democracy: The Emergence of America as a Great Power* (New York: Harper Torch-books, 1961), 141.

87. Gould, *Spanish-American War*, 40.

88. Cerillo, "Spanish-American War," 112.

89. James Richardson, ed., *Compilation of the Message and Papers of the Presidents* (New York: Bureau of National Literature, 1917), 13:6289–90, 92; first quotation from 6292, the rest from 6289.

90. Ibid., 13:6289, 6292; first two quotations from 6292, the last two from 6289.

91. Preston, *Sword*, 208–18; Benjamin Wetzel, "A Church Divided: American Catholics Debate the Spanish-American War," unpublished paper.

92. Cerillo, "Spanish-American War," 113–14, quotations in that order.

93. See James Moorhead, "The American Israel: Protestant Tribalism and Universal Mission," in William Hutchison and Harmut Lehman, eds., *Many Are Chosen: Divine Election and Western Nationalism* (Minneapolis: Fortress Press, 1994), 145–53; Russel Nye, *This Almost Chosen People: Essays in the History of American Ideas* (East Lansing: Michigan State University Press, 1966); and Conrad Cherry, ed., *God's New Israel: Religious Interpretations of American Destiny* (Chapel Hill: University of North Carolina Press, 1998).

94. Pierard and Linder, *Civil Religion*, 132.

95. "Sermon to the President," *NYT*, Mar. 14, 1898, 2; Resolution to McKinley, Apr. 6, 1898, WMP, reel 60; see Diary, Mar. 26, 1898, Cortelyou Papers, box 52;

New York Tribune, Apr. 1, 1898; Hermann Hagedorn, *Leonard Woods*, 2 vols. (New York: Harper and Brothers, 1931), 1:141; Behrends quoted in "He Trusts the President," *NYT*, Apr. 18, 1898, 12; "Dr. Lyman Abbott Says the Time to Stop Spanish Inhumanity in Cuba Has Come," *NYT*, Mar. 14, 1898, 2. In a March 6, 1898, letter to McKinley, Abbott praised the president's "courageous patience" in dealing with the crisis and maintained that most "religious people are with you in this course" (WMP, reel 60).

96. MacArthur quoted in "A Plea for United Action," *NYT*, Apr. 18, 1898, 12 (cf. "A War for Civilization," ibid.; "Father Malone for Action," ibid.); CMA editorial quoted in John Lukacs, "The Meaning of '98," in *Annuals Editions: American History*, 2:55.

97. Pierard and Linder, *Civil Religion*, 127.

98. These three clergymen are quoted in John E. Smylie, "Protestant Clergymen and America's World Role, 1865–1900: A Study of Christianity, Nationality, and International Relations" (Th.D. diss., Princeton Theological Seminary, 1959), 431–32, as cited in Pierard and Linder, *Civil Religion*, 125–26. See David Gregg, *The National Crisis, or God's Purposes Worked Out Through International Relations* (Brooklyn, NY: Brooklyn Citizen, 1898), esp. 2, 5, 13. See also Charles Eaton, "Stay-at-Home Patriots," *NYT*, May 2, 1898, 12; "Rev. Dr. J. O. Wilson's Sermon," ibid.

99. Peters is quoted in "Services of Thanksgiving," *NYT*, July 11, 1898, 10; "The Rev. Henry Van Dyke Justifies the Position Taken by the United States," *NYT*, May 2, 1898, 12; Gladden to WM, June 1, 1898, WMP, reel 3.

100. "A Day of Thanksgiving," *NYT*, July 7, 1898, 1; "German-American Attitude: A Hearty Response to the President's Proclamation at the Lutheran Churches in Brooklyn," *NYT*, July 11, 1898, 10; "Thanksgiving for Victory," *NYT*, July 11, 1898, 10. Bristol sent McKinley many letters between July 1898 and June 1901.

101. "Peace!" *CA* 73 (Aug. 18, 1898), 1322; William McKinley, "Proclamation 426— Thanksgiving Day, 1898," Oct. 28, 1898, http://www.presidency.ucsb.edu/ws/index.php?pid=69247&st.

102. Joseph Fry, "William McKinley and the Coming of the Spanish-American War: A Study of the Besmirching and Redemption of an Historical Image," *Diplomatic History* 3 (Jan. 1979), 77, 96 (quotations); Roosevelt as quoted in ibid., 77. Louis Perez, Jr. provides a succinct overview of various historians' interpretations of McKinley's role in declaring war on Spain in *The War of 1898: The United States and Cuba in History and Historiography* (Chapel Hill: University of North Carolina Press, 1998), 75–80.

103. Cerillo, "Spanish-American War," 95 (first four quotations), 96 (fifth and sixth quotations), 97 (seventh quotation); Gulick, as quoted in Robert Handy, *A Christian America: Protestant Hopes and Historical Realities* (New York: Oxford University Press, 1971), 123. See also Paul Varg, "Motives in Protestant Missions, 1890–1917," *CH* 23 (Mar. 1954), 68–82.

104. Cerillo, "Spanish-American War," 114–15; quotations from 114.

105. "Richard Olney on Cuba," *Watchman*, Mar. 1, 1900, 8.

106. Cerillo, "Spanish-American War," 117–18; quotations are from the Platt Amendment of 1902.

107. Michael Walzer, *Just and Unjust Wars* (New York: Basic Books, 1977), 104.

108. Fry, "Spanish-American War," 77.

109. Gould, *Presidency*, 34; Gould, *Spanish-American War*, 136 (all quotations).

110. See Gould, *Spanish-American War*, 44–45, and Moynihan, *John Ireland*, 162–76.

111. Morgan, *McKinley*, 335; Gould, *Spanish-American War*, 52–53; all quotations from 52.

112. William McKinley, "To the Congress of the U.S.," Apr. 11, 1898, in James Richardson, ed., *Messages and Papers*, 13:6288–89, quotation from 6289.

113. John Grenville and George Young, *Politics, Strategy, and American Diplomacy: Studies in Foreign Policy, 1873–1917* (New Haven, CT: Yale University Press, 1966), 242–43, 265–66.

114. McKinley, "To the Congress," 13:6283–85, quotation from 6283.

115. Beisner, *Diplomacy*, 114.

116. Cerillo, "Spanish-American War," 120.

117. Quoted in Smylie, "Protestant Clergymen," 490.

118. "Bible Work in the Philippine Islands," WMP, reel 68, 18–22, quotations from 20; W. Henry Grant to WM, Apr. 18, 1900, WMP, reel 71. See also Kenton Clymer, *Protestant Missionaries in the Philippines, 1898–1916: An Inquiry into the American Colonial Mentality* (Urbana: University of Illinois Press, 1986).

119. Quoted in Leech, *McKinley*, 326; Ivan Musicant, *Empire by Default: The Spanish-American War and the Dawn of the American Century* (New York: Henry Holt, 1998), 600.

120. A poll published in *Public Opinion* in August 1898 revealed that 43 percent of respondents favored keeping the island, 25 percent were opposed, and 32 percent were leaning toward retention. McKinley paid close attention to the telegrams and letters about the Philippines that poured into the White House. See Musicant, *Empire*, 614, 591.

121. Quoted in Musicant, *Empire*, 614.

122. Some businessmen opposed annexation, but the majority of them supported it. See Julius Pratt, *Expansionists of 1898: The Acquisition of Hawaii and the Spanish Islands* (Baltimore: Johns Hopkins University Press, 1936), 265–70.

123. Musicant, *Empire*, 591.

124. H. Wayne Morgan, *America's Road to Empire: The War with Spain and Overseas Expansion* (New York: John Wiley and Sons, 1965), 89. The Philippines contained eighty different tribes that spoke more than sixty different languages (Reuter, *Catholic Influences*, 61–62). In his second inaugural address, McKinley argued that the great majority of Filipinos welcomed American control "as a guarantee of order and of security for life, property, liberty, freedom of

conscience, and the pursuit of happiness" (Mar. 4, 1901, http://www.presi-dency.ucsb.edu/ws/?pid=25828).

125. In a memo to McKinley on August 30, 1898, General Francis Vinton Greene labeled Aguinaldo's insurgent regime a "pure despotism." The "intelli-gent classes" of Filipinos preferred a republic under American protection ("Memoranda Concerning the Situation in the Philippines," 422–25, as cited by Musicant, *Empire*, 613–14).

126. Theodore Roosevelt, "Introductory Address," in Corning, *McKinley*, vi.

127. Musicant, *Empire*, 601.

128. Gould, *Spanish-American War*, 104.

129. *Speeches and Addresses* (1900), 105 (first and second quotations), 118 (third quo-tation), 134 (fourth and fifth quotations).

130. *Speeches and Addresses* (1900), 161, 288, 186–87; quotations in that order.

131. Ibid., 192.

132. Ibid., 187–89.

133. Ibid., 193.

134. Ibid., 269.

135. Ibid., 318–19; quotations from 318.

136. Rusling, "Interview with McKinley," 137.

137. Gould, *Spanish-American War*, 108. Cf. Morgan, *McKinley*, 412.

138. Preston, *Sword*, 156. One such criticisms of McKinley is Akira Iriye, *Estrangement: Japanese and American Expansion, 1897–1911* (Cambridge, MA: Harvard University Press, 1972), 119.

139. Gould, *Spanish-American War*, 109–10; first quotation 109; Gould, *Presidency*, 142 (second quotation). See James F. Rusling, *Men and Things I Saw in Civil War Days* (New York: Eaton and Mains, 1899), 15. Ephraim Smith also ques-tions the authenticity of this quotation in "'A Question from Which We Could Not Escape': William McKinley and the Decision to Acquire the Philippine Islands," *Diplomatic History* 9 (Fall 1985), 364.

140. Pierard and Linder, *Civil Religion*, 130; Preston, *Sword*, 157.

141. Schurz, Carnegie, Cleveland, and Edward Atkinson all served as vice presi-dents of the Anti-Imperial League (founded in November 1898), along with Charles Francis Adams, Jr., labor leader Samuel Gompers, and Episcopal rec-tor Henry Codman Potter. See also Robert Beisner, *Twelve Against Empire: The Anti-Imperialists, 1898–1900* (New York: McGraw-Hill, 1968).

142. Morgan, *America's Road*, 103 (first quotation), 104 (second and third quotations).

143. E.g., F. H. Agnew, "The President's Pittsburg Address, and His Responsibility," *CA* 74 (Nov. 30, 1899), 1921–22; W. H. Larrabee, "Some Thoughts of an Anti-Imperialist," *CA* 74 (Dec. 28. 1899), 2105–6.

144. Tompkins, *Anti-Imperialism*, 125.

145. Ibid., 146. See, for example, Anti-Imperialist League, *Arguments Against a So-Called Imperial Policy* (Washington, 1898); and Andrew Carnegie, "Distant

Possessions—The Parting of the Ways," *North American Review* 167 (Aug. 1898), 239–48.

146. Tompkins, *Anti-Imperialism*, 205. He concludes that anti-imperialists were unsuccessful because their "arguments tended to be too academic and their speeches too erudite for widespread popular consumption." Moreover, their "position was negative, restrictive, and self-denying" (250).

147. Henry Van Dyke, *The American Birthright and the Philippine Pottage* (New York: Scribner's, 1898), esp. 4, 11, 14, 16.

148. Wallace Radcliffe, "Presbyterian Imperialism," *Assembly Herald* 1 (1899), 6; Gladden as quoted in Smylie, "Protestant Clergymen," 520; e.g., J. B. Van Petten, "The President's Pittsburg Address and His Responsibility," *CA* 74 (Dec. 28, 1899), 2106–7.

149. Morgan, *America's Road*, 109. Although Bryan was an anti-imperialist, he supported the treaty as the fastest way to stop the bloody fighting. On the debate over ratification, see Brian P. Damiani, *Advocates of Empire: William McKinley, the Senate, and American Expansion, 1898–99* (New York: Garland, 1987), especially 183–215.

150. Richardson, ed., *Messages and Papers* (1917), 13:6582; Gould, *Presidency*, 180.

151. Gould, *Presidency*, 182.

152. Carl Schurz, *Speeches, Correspondence and Political Papers of Carl Schurz*, ed. Frederick Bancroft, 6 vols. (New York: G. P. Putnam's Sons. 1913), 6:115; Gould, *Presidency*, 189, 237; quotations in that order.

153. Morgan, *America's Road*, 97; Thompkins, *Anti-Imperialism*, 293; Cerillo, "Spanish-American War," 123–25; first quotation from 123, second, third, and fourth quotations from 124, fifth from 125.

154. Preston, *Sword*, 223–32. See also Harris, *God Arbiters*, 28–29 and passim, and Stuart Creighton Miller, *"Benevolent Assimilation": The American Conquest of the Philippines, 1899–1900* (New Haven, CT: Yale University Press, 1982).

155. See Pierard and Linder, *Civil Religion*, 134. Many ministers discussed this theme in their sermons.

156. Preston, *Sword*, 158.

157. Henry Pritchett, "Some Recollections of President McKinley and the Cuban Intervention," *North American Review* 189 (1909), 401; Cerillo, "Spanish-American War," 125.

158. "The Attempted Assassination of the President," *PB*, Sept. 12, 1901, 5.

159. Fiske, *McKinley*, 10.

160. Farquhar to Cortelyou, Sept. 7, 1901, WMP, reel 16; see Allan Sutherland, "Our Martyred President's Favorite Hymns," *PB*, Oct. 3, 1901, 12; e.g., "Last Words of President McKinley," *CA* 77 (Sept. 18, 1902), 1493–94; Barton, "Christian Gentleman," 137; "The President is Dead," *WP*, in Grosvenor, *McKinley*, 26; "The Death of the President," *Baltimore Sun*, in ibid., 29; "The Dead President," *News and Courier*, in ibid., 57.

161. McCook as quoted in George Washington Townsend, *Our Martyred President* (Philadelphia?, 1902), 417; DeWitt Talmage, "Our Dead President," *Christian Herald*, quoted in Halstead, *Illustrious Life*, 388–89; "God's Will, Not Ours, Be Done," *Rocky Mountain News*, in Grosvenor, *McKinley*, 66; "The Man and His Faith," *New York Herald*, in ibid., 72; W. J. Bryan, "Address," in Halstead, *Illustrious Life*, 266; Halstead, *Illustrious Life*, 370; Grosvenor, *McKinley*, 272.

162. "The Nation's Sorrow," *Interior*, Sept. 19, 1901, 1175; "The Meaning of the Tragedy," *PB*, Sept. 19, 1901, 6; Huntingdon as cited in Halstead, *Illustrious Life*, 280; Harry Edwards of Macon, Georgia, quoted in Edward Parks, "The Progress of Sentiment in the South," *CA* 76 (Nov. 28, 1901), 1898.

163. Fiske, *McKinley*, 13.

164. Andrews, "Eulogy," in Halstead, *Illustrious Life*, 284; Chapman as quoted in ibid., 287.

165. *Providence Journal*, in Grosvenor, *McKinley*, 59; e.g., "A Nation Mourns," *Milwaukee Sentinel*, in ibid., 82.

166. "The Death of President McKinley," *UP*, Sept. 19, 1901, 4 (cf. Halstead, *Illustrious Life*, 288); Gunsaulus, quoted in ibid., 259.

167. E.g., "The President is Dead," *Ohio State Journal*, in Grosvenor, *McKinley*, 124.

168. *Daily Inter Ocean*, Sept. 19, 1901, 1.

169. Fiske, *McKinley*, 9.

170. "Secularization Far Overdone," *Interior*, Sept. 26, 1901.

171. Manchester as quoted in Halstead, *Illustrious Life*, 251–52; Theodore Roosevelt, "Proclamation, 465—Announcing the Death of William McKinley," Sept. 14, 1901, http://www.presidency.ucsb.edu/ws/?pid=69370.

172. "The President is Dead," *WP*, 26; "Our Dead President," *Indianapolis Journal*, in Grosvenor, *McKinley*, 35; "President McKinley's Death," *Buffalo Courier*, in ibid., 52.

173. Fiske, *McKinley*, 5, 7–9; "The Death of the President," *Baltimore Sun*, 30; "President McKinley," *Springfield Union*, in Grosvenor, *McKinley*, 49; Aaron T. Bliss, quoted in ibid., 155; Cardinal James Gibbons, "Eulogy," in Halstead, *Illustrious Life*, 264; McClure, *Authentic Life*, 204; Corning, *McKinley*, 162.

174. "McKinley-Roosevelt," *Century Magazine* 63 (1901), 148; Roosevelt, "Introduction," viii; the first quoted word is from Iowa Senator Jonathan Dolliver in Halstead, *Illustrious Life*, 271; the second is from Locke in Halstead, *Illustrious Life*, 276; the third is from Leech, *McKinley*, 10.

175. "William McKinley," *Times-Star*, in Grosvenor, *McKinley*, 54; "Death of the President," *Philadelphia North-American*, in ibid., 38; Bristol, as cited in Corning, *McKinley*, 167; "Our President," *Buffalo Express*, in Grosvenor, *McKinley*, 106; "McKinley's Death," 52; Gibbons, "Eulogy," 263; Long, "Personal Characteristics," 144–45.

176. Quoted in Fiske, *McKinley*, 6; "The President is Dead," *Ohio State Journal*, 124; "President McKinley," *Springfield Union*, in Grosvenor, *McKinley*, 50.

177. "President William McKinley," *PB*, Sept. 19, 1901, 5.

178. Fiske, *McKinley*, 10–13; first two quotations from 10, third from 12.

179. Halstead, *Illustrious Life*, 281.

180. "William McKinley," 55–56, quotations in that order; "The Nation's Grief," *Constitution*, in Grosvenor, *McKinley*, 97; "Death of the President," *Baltimore Sun*, 30; "Death of the President," *Chicago Tribune*, in Grosvenor, *McKinley*, 61.

181. "Nation Mourns," 82; "Death of President McKinley," *Age-Herald*, in Grosvenor, *McKinley*, 69; "President McKinley Dead," *Philadelphia Inquirer*, in ibid., 80–81; Olcott, *McKinley*, 2:336.

182. Gould, *Presidency*, 252.

183. Morgan, *McKinley*, 528. See also John Offner, *An Unwanted War: The Diplomacy of the United States and Spain over Cuba, 1895–1898* (Chapel Hill: University of North Carolina Press, 1992).

184. Gould, *Presidency*, vii (quotation); Gould, *Spanish-American War*, 5, 137.

185. Gould, *Presidency*, 17, 1, 137–38, vii, 56; first quotation from viii, second from 56. See also Robert C. Hilderbrand, *Power and the People: Executive Management of Public Opinion and Foreign Affairs, 1877–1921* (Chapel Hill: University of North Carolina Press, 1981).

186. *Speeches and Addresses* (1900), 129; Morgan, *McKinley*, 527–28.

187. Morgan, *McKinley*, 529.

188. Gould, *Presidency*, 253, 5–6; quotation from 253. See also Lewis Gould, "William McKinley and the Expansion of Presidential Power," *Ohio History* 87 (1978), 5–20.

189. Quoted in Morgan, *McKinley*, 12.

190. Barton, "Christian Gentleman," 134; Pierard and Linder, *Civil Religion*, 135; *Speeches and Addresses* (1900), 210.

191. Quoted in Leech, *McKinley*, vi, frontispiece.

CHAPTER 6

1. William Leuchtenburg, *Herbert Hoover* (New York: Henry Holt, 2009), 3.

2. David Hinshaw, *Herbert Hoover: American Quaker* (New York: Farrar, Straus, 1950), 34.

3. Martin Fausold, *The Presidency of Herbert C. Hoover* (Lawrence: University Press of Kansas, 1985), 4; Kendrick Clements, *The Life of Herbert Hoover: Imperfect Visionary, 1918–1928* (New York: Palgrave Macmillan, 2010), xii. See also J. William Frost, "The Dry Bones of Quaker Theology," *CH* 39 (Dec. 1970), 503–23.

4. *Chicago Daily News*, Nov. 8, 1928.

5. Leuchtenburg, *Hoover*, 3, 111.

6. Glen Jeansonne, *The Life of Herbert Hoover: Fighting Quaker, 1928–1933* (New York: Palgrave Macmillan, 2012), 455.

7. E.g., Lydia Murray Huneke, transcript, Oral History Interview, Oct. 11, 1967, 10, Herbert Hoover Presidential Library (hereinafter cited as HL); D. Elton Trueblood, transcript, ibid., July 12, 1971, 12, HL; Joan Hoff Wilson, *Herbert Hoover: Forgotten Progressive* (Boston: Little and Brown, 1975), 4.

8. John Hoover was nationally known for his support of peace and wrote a memoir titled *History of the Life and Labors of J. Y. Hoover: A Minister of the Gospel of our Lord Jesus Christ* (West Branch, IA?, 1909?).

9. Fausold, *Presidency*, 2–3; Herbert Hoover, "Boyhood in Iowa," *The Palimpsest* 43 (Aug. 1962), 337–43.

10. Richard Norton Smith, *An Uncommon Man: The Triumph of Herbert Hoover* (New York: Simon and Schuster, 1984), 66 (quotation); David Burner, *Herbert Hoover: A Public Life* (New York: Knopf, 1979), 15.

11. George Nash, "Social Philosophy of Herbert Hoover," in *Herbert Hoover Reassessed: Essays Commemorating the Fiftieth Anniversary of the Inauguration of our Thirty-first President* (Washington, DC: G.P.O., 1981), 93.

12. Alexander DeConde, "Herbert Hoover and Foreign Policy: A Retrospective Assessment," in *Hoover Reassessed*, 317.

13. See William Wister Comfort, *Just among Friends: The Quaker Way of Life* (New York: Macmillan, 1941); William Wister Comfort, *Quakers in the Modern World* (New York: Macmillan, 1949); and Daisy Newman, *A Procession of Friends: Quakers in America* (Garden City, NY: Doubleday, 1972).

14. Many others support Hinshaw's interpretation. E.g., John Richelsen, "Herbert Hoover and the Quakers," *Current History* 30 (April 1929), 79–83; Raymond Moley, "Hoover—the Great Quaker," *Newsweek*, Apr. 10, 1950, 88; Elizabeth Gray Vining, *Friend of Life: The Biography of Rufus M. Jones* (Philadelphia: J. B. Lippincott, 1958), 169; David Burner, "The Quaker Faith of Herbert Hoover," in Lee Nash, ed., *Understanding Herbert Hoover: Ten Perspectives* (Stanford, CA: Hoover Institution, 1987), 53–64; James Johnson, "Herbert Hoover: The Orphan as Children's Friend," *Prologue* 12 (Winter 1980), 193–206; and Fausold, *Presidency*, 1–19. On Hoover's moral convictions, also see David Burner and Thomas West, "A Technocrat's Morality: Conservatism and Hoover the Engineer," in Stanley Elkins and Eric McKitrick, eds., *The Hofstadter Aegis* (New York: Knopf, 1974), 235–56.

15. Hinshaw, *Hoover*, 27, 38–39, 28; first two quotations from 27, third and fourth from 38–39.

16. To Quakers, the Bible was a spiritual guidebook that should direct daily conduct. Because of their belief in the inner light, Friends considered revelation to be continuing. See Comfort, *Friends*, 26–27.

17. Fausold, *Presidency*, 4; Frost, "Quaker Theology," 503–23.

18. George Nash, *The Life of Herbert Hoover*, vol. 2: *The Humanitarian, 1914–1917* (New York: W. W. Norton, 1988), 255. However, when they lived in Washington,

DC, in the late 1910s the Hoovers sent their sons to the Friends School (Helen Pryor, *Lou Henry Hoover: Gallant First Lady* [New York: Dodd Mead, 1969], 106).

19. Fausold, *Presidency*, 4. See also "Hoovers Attend Friends' Services," *NYT*, Mar. 11, 1929, 10. Hoover was embarrassed by the fact that there were three Friends groups in Washington—Hicksite, Independent, and Orthodox, in which the president had been reared. Unable to convince them to combine, Hoover persuaded the Orthodox group to build a new meetinghouse. See Henry Cadbury, "Individual Faithfulness," *Friends Journal*, Nov. 15, 1964, 525. "The President habitually attends divine service at the Friends Meeting House here in Washington" (French Strother to William Brown, Apr. 29, 1931, Churches, Protestant, 1931, HL). When he was at his Rapidan camp or on a ship, Hoover attended a Sunday service conducted by a Navy chaplain. He also sometimes worshipped with other congregations when he was traveling. See Harry Earl Woolever, "President Hoover at Church," *CA* 107 (Apr. 7, 1932), 375. While agreeing with most Quaker principles, Hoover's wife Lou remained an Episcopalian throughout her life. See Pryor, *Lou Henry Hoover*, 245.

20. Hoover belonged to the branch of Friends that had ordained ministers and weekly sermons. Worshippers were given time to meditate before and after the sermon and sang hymns only as requested by members. See Pontiac *Press*, Nov. 11, 1929, and "Shining Example," Waltham (MA) *News Tribune*, Nov. 25, 1929, in President's Personal File, Murray, Augustus T., 1929–32, HL (hereinafter cited as PPF).

21. Nevertheless, Hoover frequently mentioned the importance of prayer, urged people to pray, and thanked individuals for praying for him.

22. Hinshaw, *Hoover*, 359.

23. Herbert Hoover, "Address to the Convention of the International Christian Endeavor Societies," July 16, 1931, *The Presidential Papers of Herbert Hoover*, 4 vols. (Washington, DC: GPO, 1974–77), 356 (hereinafter cited as *PP*). See also Merlin Gustafson, "President Hoover and the National Religion," *JCS* 16 (Winter 1974), 92.

24. Herbert Hoover, "Acceptance of the Nomination," Aug. 11, 1928, *PP*, 519.

25. Hinshaw, *Hoover*, 39; Jeansonne, *Hoover*, 180.

26. Herbert Hoover, *American Individualism* (Garden City, NY: Doubleday, Doran, 1922), 26. Hoover expressed this point many times. E.g., Herbert Hoover, "This I Believe," in *Addresses upon the American Road, 1950–1955* (Stanford, CA: Stanford University Press, 1955), 317 (hereinafter cited as *Addresses, 1950–55*); Hoover, "Concerning Honor in Public Life," in ibid., 117; Hoover, "The Government Cannot Do It All," in *Addresses upon the American Road, 1948–1950* (Stanford, CA: Stanford University Press, 1951), 175); Hoover, "We'll Have to Feed the World Again," in *Addresses upon the American Road, 1941–1945* (New York: D. Van Nostrand Co., 1946), 294 (hereinafter cited as *Addresses, 1941–45*).

27. Hoover, *Individualism*, 31.

28. Herbert Hoover, "Message to the American Bible Society on Universal Bible Sunday," Dec. 4, 1931, *PP*, 578. Cf. Hoover, "Address to . . . the World Alliance for Friendship through the Churches," Nov. 11, 1930, *PP*, 477.

29. Herbert Hoover, "Radio Address to the World's Conference of the YMCA," Aug. 8, 1931, *PP*, 380. Cf. Hoover, "Message . . . in the Washington Cathedral," Dec. 27, 1929, *PP*, 490.

30. Herbert Hoover, "Radio Address to the Women of America," Oct. 7, 1932, *PP*, 500. See also Hoover, "The Front of Human Decency," *Addresses, 1941–45*, 396.

31. Herbert Hoover, "Annual Message to the Congress on the State of the Union," Dec. 8, 1931, *PP*, 580. Cf. Hoover, "YMCA," 381.

32. Herbert Hoover, "Memorial Day Address," May 30, 1930, *PP*, 210. See HH to George Wysor, June 19, 1929, Church Matters, 1929, HL (hereinafter cited as CM); HH to Frank Richards, CM, 1930; HH to Daniel Poling, Aug. 22, 1932, Hoover, Herbert, Philosophy, Personal; Hoover, "Women of America," 499; Hoover, "Address Accepting the Republican Presidential Nomination," Aug. 11, 1932, *PP*, 361. See Kendrick Clements, *Hoover, Conservation, and Consumerism: Engineering the Good Life* (Lawrence: University Press of Kansas, 2000).

33. Hoover, *Individualism*, 16.

34. Herbert Hoover, "In the Name of Humanity," *Addresses 1941–45*, 311; Hoover, "When Winter Comes to Europe," *Further Addresses upon the American Road, 1938–1940* (New York: C. Scribner's Sons, 1940), 145.

35. Hoover, "Women of America," 500. Cf. Hoover, "This I Believe," 316; HH to John Albert Jay, Feb. 18, 1933, CM, 1932–1933. In his Greeting to the Methodist Episcopal Churches of Newark, Dec. 22, 1932 (CM, 1932–33), Hoover proclaimed that "peace of mind" comes from "acquiescence in the divine purpose and the unquenchable hope that comes from faith in the wisdom and beneficence of providence."

36. Hoover, "YMCA," 381. Cf. Hoover, "Address on the 150th Anniversary of the Battle of Kings Mountain," Oct. 7, 1930, *PP*, 424.

37. Herbert Hoover, "Resistance to Communism," *Addresses, 1950–55*, 98.

38. Hoover, "Kings Mountain," 420.

39. Herbert Hoover, "United Church Canvass," *Addresses, 1941–45*, 378.

40. PPL, Bible, 1929–32. This statement was repeatedly put forth as his definitive statement on the Bible.

41. Herbert Hoover, "Inaugural Address," Mar. 4, 1929, http://www.presidency. ucsb.edu/ws/?pid=21804. Hoover, "Name of Humanity," 311. Cf. Hoover, "When Winter Comes," 145, and Hoover, "Challenge to Liberty, 1938," *Addresses upon the American Road, 1933–1938* (New York: Charles Scribner's Sons, 1938), 327 (hereinafter cited as *Addresses, 1933–38*).

42. HH to William S. Kenyon, May 21, 1931, CM, 1931.

43. Hoover, "Nomination," 503.

44. Hoover, "Resistance to Communism," 98.

45. Herbert Hoover, "Message to the Quadrennial General Conference of the Methodist Episcopal Church," May 19, 1932, *PP*, 221. Cf. Hoover, "Message to the Southern Baptist Convention," May 13, 1932, *PP*, 217; HH to John C. Broomfield, May 12, 1931, CM, 1931.

46. Hoover, "Public Life," 116–17. Cf. Hoover, "Moral and Spiritual Recovery from War," *Addresses, 1941–45*, 40, and Hoover, "True Liberalism in America," *Addresses, 1933–38*, 134.

47. Herbert Hoover, "Radio Remarks to the Methodist Ecumenical Congress," Oct. 25, 1931, *PP*, 503.

48. Hoover, "United Church Canvass," 378.

49. Hoover, "This I Believe," 316. Hoover was fond of quoting James 2:17, "Even so faith, without works, is dead" (e.g., Hoover, "Resistance to Communism," 97).

50. Cadbury, "Individual Faithfulness," 525.

51. Smith, *Uncommon Man*, 96.

52. Hoover, *Individualism*, 5.

53. Hoover, "Government Cannot Do It All," 176.

54. Hoover, "Nomination," 517.

55. Herbert Hoover, commencement address at William Penn College, Oskaloosa, Iowa, June 12, 1925, in *Penn College Bulletin* 19 (July 1925), quoted in Nash, "Social Philosophy," 97.

56. Hoover, "Kings Mountain," 424.

57. James Olson, "Herbert Hoover and Twentieth Century America," in *Hoover Reassessed*, 151.

58. See Hoover, "Kings Mountain," 426.

59. Hoover, *Individualism*, 26. See also Eckley, *Hoover*, 53.

60. Hoover, *Individualism*, 17.

61. Olson, "Herbert Hoover," 149.

62. Vaughn Davis Bornet, "An Uncommon President," in *Hoover Reassessed*, 79–80.

63. Olson, "Hoover," 151–52. See Ellis Hawley, "Herbert Hoover, the Commerce Secretariat, and the Vision of an 'Associative State,'" *JAH* 61 (June 1974), 116–40.

64. Olson, "Hoover," 153.

65. Gary Koerselman, "The Significance of Herbert Hoover," in *Hoover Reassessed*, 46–47.

66. Hoover, "Government Cannot Do It All," 176. Cf. Hoover, "Humanity," 311.

67. Hoover, "Community Chest," 298–99.

68. See Hoover, "Salvation Army Appeal," 380–81; HH to D. C. Hiebert, June 25, 1929, CM, 1929, Box 14; Hoover, "Message to the Federal Council of the Churches of Christ in America," Dec. 6, 1932, *PP*, 854–55; and Hoover, "YMCA," 380–81.

69. Wilson, *Hoover*, 124–25.

70. Herbert Hoover, "Nomination," 503.

71. Wilson, *Hoover*, 129, 131; quotation from 129.

72. For the context, see Mark Massa, *Anti-Catholicism in America: The Last Acceptable Prejudice* (New York: Crossroad, 2003); Philip Jenkins, *The New Anti-Catholicism: The Last Acceptable Prejudice* (Oxford: Oxford University Press, 2003); and Robert Lockwood, ed., *Anti-Catholicism in American Culture* (Huntington, IN: Our Sunday Visitor, 2000).

73. "A Test for Governor Smith," *NR*, Apr. 6, 1927, 183. Cf. "More about Catholicism and the Presidency," *NR*, May 11, 1927, 315–16; Dixon Merritt, "Six Questions for Governor Smith," *Outlook* 147 (Dec. 7, 1927), 428–29.

74. Charles Marshall, "An Open Letter to the Honorable Alfred E. Smith," *AM* 139 (Apr. 1927), 540–49, quotation from 540.

75. Alfred Smith, "Catholic and Patriot: Governor Smith Replies," *AM* 139 (May 1927), 721–28; first quotation from 722, second from 727. Smith cited many leading American Catholics, including John Ryan, Archbishop John Ireland, and James Cardinal Gibbons, to support his interpretation of the church's position on civil authority. He argued that as governor of New York he had greatly increased state appropriations for public education and that he had appointed people to public office on the basis of merit without inquiring about their religious convictions. Smith insisted that if a conflict arose between his faith and his political duty, he would resolve it by the "dictates of his conscience" (as would any Protestant), not by the pronouncements of his church (726).

76. Pierre Crabites, "Is It Time for a Catholic President?" *Outlook* 146 (Aug. 17, 1927), 504–8; quotation from 507.

77. "It Seems to Heywood Broun," *Nation* 126 (Feb. 8, 1928), 142.

78. See John Wilson, "The Quaker and the Sword: Herbert Hoover's Relations with the Military," *Military Affairs* 38 (April 1974), 41–47.

79. John Gummere, "Quakers and Catholics—Two Horns of One Dilemma," *AM* 142 (Sept. 1928), 428–30. See also Louis Liebovich, *Bylines in Despair: Herbert Hoover, the Great Depression, and the U. S. News Media* (Westport, CT: Praeger, 1994), 75–76.

80. "Herbert Hoover as a Quaker," *Nation* 127 (Oct. 17, 1928), 388. The editors also discussed the September 13 issue of the *American Friends*, which complained that the man who they had expected to lead the world toward disarmament was leading it toward preparedness instead. Cf. "Cites Hoover's Faith in Comparing Smith's," *NYT*, Sept. 14, 1928.

81. Herbert Hoover, *Memoirs of Herbert Hoover*, vol. 2: *The Cabinet and the Presidency* (New York: Macmillan, 1952), 207. Cf. "Tolerance in Question," New York *Herald*, Sept. 16, 1928.

82. Hoover, *Memoirs*, 2:207.

83. Smith, *Uncommon Man*, 104.

84. Burner, *Hoover*, 205.

85. Burner, *Hoover*, 205. See "Hoover and the Religious Issue," *Independent* 121 (Oct. 13, 1928), 341. The editors pointed out that a Catholic had served as Hoover's private secretary for the last eight years.

86. Hoover, *Memoirs*, 2:208. See also "It Seems to Heywood Broun," *Nation* 129 (Sept. 11, 1929), 207; "Hoover: Conservative," *NR* 56 (Oct. 31, 1928), 287; "Herbert Hoover's Great Illusion," *NR* 56 (Aug. 22, 1928), 3–5; "Hoover, the Economist," ibid., 5–6. Most political commentators blamed others, not Hoover, for the "whispering campaign" against Smith. E.g., "Tilson Denies Importing Issue of Catholicism into Campaign," New York *World*, Sept. 17, 1928; "The Naïve Dr. Work: His Disclaimer of 'Whispering' Tactics Does Not Wholly Satisfy," *NYT*, Sept. 17, 1928.

87. Quoted in Albert Bushnell Hart, "Religion and Prohibition as Issues in the Presidential Election," *Current History* 29 (November 1928), 314.

88. "Politics and Bigotry," *America* 40 (Nov. 3, 1928), 77; "Religious Bigotry in the Campaign," *America* 40 (Nov. 10, 1928), 102. They protested that thousands of ministers had urged their parishioners to vote for Hoover because Smith was a papist and that Republicans had disseminated large amounts of anti-Catholic propaganda in every state. The Episcopal *Churchman* also denounced the campaign of slander directed against Smith. See 138 (Sept. 22, 1928), 1.

89. "Church Affiliations and the Presidency of the United States," *Lutheran*, Sept. 20, 1928, 6–7, 22.

90. See "Two Views of Hoover," Reprint File, Sept. 1928–Oct. 1928, HL. See also "Preacher Politicians," *Outlook* 149 (Aug. 8, 1928), 571, and George Hinman, Jr., "Protestantism in Politics," *Outlook* 149 (Aug. 29, 1928), 683–85, 716.

91. Other Presbyterians urged pastors and laypeople to join them in "a valiant, unfaltering and enthusiastic defense" of National Prohibition and, by implication, in voting for Hoover. See "The Church and the Political Situation," *Presbyterian*, Nov. 1, 1928, 15–16.

92. Hart, "Religion and Prohibition," 312–14; all quotations from 313.

93. "Close of the Campaign," *PB*, Nov. 1, 1928, 8. On the role of religion in the 1928 campaign, see Berton Dulce and Edward Richter, *Religion and the Presidency: A Recurring American Problem* (New York: Macmillan 1962), 81–97.

94. Quoted in Hart, "Religion and Prohibition," 315.

95. "Religion in the Campaign," *America* 40 (Oct. 20, 1928), 29.

96. John Ryan, "A Catholic View of the Election," *Current History* 29 (December 1928), 377–78, quotation from 378.

97. Ryan, "Catholic View," 378–79; quotation from 379. See also Rembert Smith, *Politics in a Protestant Church* (Atlanta: Ruralist Press, 1930).

98. "The Religious Issues," *CC* 55 (Oct. 18, 1928), 1251. Others argued that "Protestants hesitated to vote for Catholics" because they held "a political creed" which "is opposed to liberty of conscience, liberty of worship, liberty of

speech, and liberty of the press." See W. L. Lingle, "Tolerance and Intolerance," *Presbyterian*, Sept. 20, 1928, 22–23; quotation from 23. Cf. "Bigotry," *Lutheran*, Aug. 16, 1928, 6–7.

99. Ryan, "Catholic View," 379–80; quotations from 380.

100. Hoover, *Memoirs*, 2:208–9; quotation from 208.

101. Jeansonne, *Hoover*, 32.

102. See Kent Schofield, "The Public Image of Herbert Hoover in the 1928 Campaign," *Mid-America* 51 (October 1969), 278–93; Matthew and Hannah Josephson, *Al Smith: Hero of the Cities* (Boston: Houghton Mifflin, 1969), chap. 14; Edmund Moore, *A Catholic Runs for President: The Campaign of 1928* (New York: Ronald Press, 1956); Allan Lichtman, *Prejudice and Old Politics: The Presidential Election of 1928* (Chapel Hill: University of North Carolina Press, 1979); Roy Victor Peel and Thomas Donnelly, *The 1928 Campaign: An Analysis* (New York: R. R. Smith, 1931); Oscar Handlin, *Al Smith and His America* (Boston: Little, Brown, 1958), 112–36; James Smylie, "The Roman Catholic Church, the State, and Al Smith," *CH* 69 (September 1960), 321–43; and Robert Slayton, *Empire Statesman: The Rise and Redemption of Al Smith* (New York: Free Press, 2001).

103. Wilson, *Hoover*, 129–33; quotation from 133. Jewish supporters distributed thousands of pamphlets throughout New York state titled "The Modern Moses of War-Stricken Europe—Herbert Hoover" (Burstein, Rabbi Abraham, Aug. 6, 1929, Churches, Jewish, Aug.–Dec. 1929, HL). Many religious groups were quite pleased with Hoover's election. "Never has there been a more auspicious and happier inauguration," declared the *Presbyterian Banner* (Mar. 7, 1929, 5). *The Presbyterian* rejoiced that a Quaker had been "called in God's good guidance into national leadership" ("Hopeful Inferences from the National Election," Nov. 15, 1928, 13).

104. See D. G. Hart, "Mainstream Protestantism, 'Conservative' Religion, and Civil Society," in Hugh Heclo and Wilfred McClay, eds., *Religion Returns to the Public Square: Faith and Policy in America* (Baltimore: Johns Hopkins University Press, 2003), 202. The Catholic Church affirmed these five points—biblical inerrancy, the Virgin Birth, and Christ's vicarious atonement, bodily resurrection, and miracles.

105. See Daniel Poling to HH, Feb. 20, 1933, PPF. Robins carried on an extensive correspondence with Hoover and occasionally stayed at the White House. See Individual File, Robins, Raymond, 1929, Robins, Mr. and Mrs. Raymond Robins, 1929–33, HL. Two other close friends of Hoover's—H. J. Heinz, the Pittsburgh industrialist, and Bruce Barton, the Madison Avenue advertising executive—had strong religious commitments.

106. E.g., "Dr. Daniel A. Poling Makes an Announcement," *PB*, Sept. 1, 1932, 3–4.

107. See Kenneth Vines, "The Role of the F.C.C.C.A. in the Formation of American National Policy" (Ph.D. diss., University of Minnesota, 1953), 211–32; Pryor, *Lou Henry Hoover*, 191; Gustafson, "Hoover," 90.

108. Cadman sermon, PPL, Cadman, Rev. S. Parkes, 1929–30, 9–10. See also Cadman to HH, July 26, 1929, PPL, Cadman, Rev. S. Parkes, 1929–30.

109. See Churches, Conferences, and Assemblies Presbyterian, PC, General Assembly of the U.S., 1931. Cf. "A Disciple of George Fox," *Presbyterian*, Aug. 13, 1931, 6–7.

110. William McDowell to HH, May 17, 1932, Churches—Conferences and Assemblies, Methodist Episcopal Church, 1931–32.

111. Charles Clayton Morrison, "Open Letter to Herbert Hoover," *CC* 46 (Mar. 21, 1929).

112. E.g., *Religious Press Digest*, 1929–1930, "Mr. Hoover Stands on Solid Ground," *CC* 48 (May 13, 1931), 635.

113. See George Hastings to Samuel Cavert, July 21, 1931, Churches, Protestant, 1931. See also Hastings to Frederick Fisher, Oct. 27, 1931, ibid.; George Akerson to C. W. Buschgen, Mar. 6, 1929, ibid., 1929; Akerson to E. S. Dreher, Sept. 19, 1929, ibid., 1929, July–Dec. For these congratulatory statements, see PPL, CM 1929, 1930, 1931, 1932.

114. George Akerson to Paul Radenhausen, May 19, 1929, Churches, Protestant, 1929, March–June.

115. Herbert Hoover, "Message to American Lutherans on the Anniversary of the Protestant Reformation," Oct. 9, 1930, *PP*, 427–28.

116. Quoted in "A Presidential Greeting and Its Catholic Criticism," *Lutheran Witness*, Oct. 28, 1930, 362. See also G. K. Chesterton, "Luther and Mr. Hoover," *America* 44 (Nov. 29, 1930), 176–77.

117. "Presidential Greeting," 362–63.

118. "Hoover and the Lutherans," Haverhill *Gazette*, Oct. 17, 1930.

119. See "Mr. Hoover's Lutheran Greeting," *New York World*, Oct. 15, 1930, "Hoover under Catholic Fire for Message," *San Antonio Evening News*, Oct. 14, 1930, 4. See also J. F. Nickelsburg to HH, Sept. 22, 1930, CM 1930 and PPL, Lutheran Message Controversy, 1930, Sept. 9–Oct. 15.

120. E.g., "The New Administration," *America* 40 (Nov. 17, 1928), 126. The editors challenged Hoover to ensure religious freedom, reexamine Prohibition, and stop the plunder of the nation's resources by big business.

121. Gustafson, "Hoover," 94.

122. "Rumor That There May Be a Catholic in the Cabinet," *Catholic News*, Apr. 26, 1930.

123. *New York World*, Jan. 10, 1930.

124. Gustafson, "Hoover," 96.

125. One of Coughlin's radio addresses, "Hoover Prosperity Means Another War," evoked 1.2 million letters. See Ruth Mugglebee, *Father Coughlin* (Boston: L. C. Page, 1933); Louis Ward, *Father Charles Coughlin* (Detroit: Tower Publications, 1933); and John Richelsen, "Herbert Hoover and the Quakers," *Current History*, 30 (April 1929), 79–83.

126. Gustafson, "Hoover," 97.

127. Merlin Gustafson, "How a President Uses Religion and How It Uses Him," 6–7, unpublished paper, Eisenhower Presidential Library.

128. Nash, "Social Philosophy," 93.

129. Hoover, "Republican Presidential Nomination," 370–71. For a discussion of the reforms Hoover undertook, see David Burner, "Before the Crash: Hoover's First Eight Months in the Presidency," in Martin Fausold and George Mazuzan, eds., *The Hoover Presidency: A Reappraisal* (New York: State University of New York Press, 1974), 50–65.

130. Hoover, "Methodist Ecumenical Congress," 504.

131. Hoover, "Nomination," 514.

132. See "White House Statement on Committees and Commissions," Apr. 24, 1932, *PP*, 174–77.

133. Hoover, "Nomination," 515. See also Hoover, "Radio Address to the Women's Conference on Current Problems," Sept. 29, 1932, *PP*, 446–49; Hoover, *Memoirs*, 2:259–65.

134. These women included the wives of Julius Rosenwald, Edward Bok, Thomas Edison, Henry Ford, and Lewis Strauss, as well as Ada Comstock, and M. Carey Thomas.

135. Herbert Hoover, "Message to the Christian Family Crusade," June 16, 1931, *PP*, 313.

136. See Herbert Hoover, "White House Conference on Child Health and Protection," July 2, 1929, *PP*, 208–10; Hoover, "White House Conference on Child Health and Protection," Nov. 14, 1930, *PP*, 481. Cf. Hoover, "Excerpts from an Interview with the President," Nov. 25, 1930, *PP*, 683–84.

137. Herbert Hoover, "Address to the White House Conference on Child Health and Protection," Nov. 19, 1930, *PP*, 491.

138. Ibid., 490–91; Jeansonne, *Hoover*, 98–99.

139. Hinshaw, *Hoover*, 46–47.

140. Hoover, *Memoirs*, 2:317.

141. See Jeansonne, *Hoover*, 316–21; Randolph Downes, "A Crusade for Indian Reform, 1929–1934," *Mississippi Valley Historical Review* 32 (Dec. 1945), 331–45; Burner, *Hoover*, 224–27; "President's News Conference," Jan. 3, 1930, *PP*, 3–4; Hoover, *Memoirs*, 2:317–19.

142. See Clements, *Hoover*, 371–94.

143. Herbert Hoover, "Statement on Equality of Opportunity in Employment," Oct. 26, 1932, *PP*, 599. On the other hand, while campaigning for president in 1928, Hoover denied he opposed Jim Crow laws, permitted subordinates to make racist remarks, and refused to denounce the Ku Klux Klan (Leuchtenburg, *Hoover*, 75, 99). See also Donald Lisio, *Hoover, Blacks, and Lily-Whites: A Study of Southern Strategies* (Chapel Hill: University of North Carolina Press, 1985), 282.

144. Herbert Hoover, "Message Condemning Lynching," Sept. 23, 1930, *PP*, 301.

145. See Pryor, *Lou Henry Hoover*, 179–80; Jeansonne, *Hoover*, 305–7.

146. See Herbert Hoover, "Message to the National Association of Teachers in Colored Schools," July 29, 1931, *PP*, 363–64; Hoover, "Radio Address on . . .

the Founding of Tuskegee Institute," Apr. 14, 1931, *PP*, 185–87; and Hoover, "Commencement Address at Howard University," June 10, 1932, *PP*, 255–56.

147. See Burner, *Hoover*, 194–97, 214–17, on which this section heavily depends. See also George Garcia, "Herbert Hoover and the Issue of Race," *Annals of Iowa* 64 (Winter 1979), 507–17.

148. See Burner, *Hoover*, 218–19; Hoover, *Memoirs*, 2:274–75; Jeansonne, *Hoover*, 106–7; Hoover, "Annual Message to the Congress on the State of the Union," Dec. 3, 1929, *PP*, 429.

149. See Burner, *Hoover*, 213–14, quotation from 214; and Wilson, *Hoover*, 135–36.

150. Jeansonne, *Hoover*, 155.

151. "Hoover wanted to be, and usually was, in direct command of foreign policy" (DeConde, "Hoover," 314). See also Fausold, *Presidency*, 167; Selig Adler, "Hoover's Foreign Policy and the New Left," 153–63; and Joan Hoff Wilson, "A Reevaluation of Herbert Hoover's Foreign Policy," 164–86, in Fausold and Mazuzan, eds., *Hoover Presidency*.

152. See Melvyn Leffler, "Open Door Expansionism, World Order, and Domestic Constraints," in Thomas Paterson, ed., *Major Problems in American Foreign Policy*, vol. 2: *Since 1914* (Lexington, MA: D. C. Heath, 1989), 142–47.

153. DeConde, "Hoover," 327.

154. Hoover, "Nomination," 516.

155. Hoover, *Memoirs*, 2:330.

156. Hoover, "Methodist Ecumenical Congress," 505.

157. Herbert Hoover, "Address to . . . the World Alliance for Friendship Through the Churches," Nov. 11, 1930, *PP*, 474. On Hoover's concern for peace, also see Herbert Hoover and Hugh Gibson, *The Problems of Lasting Peace* (Garden City, NY: Doubleday, Doran, 1942), and Hoover and Gibson, *The Basis of Lasting Peace* (New York: D. Van Nostrand, 1945).

158. In *American Diplomacy in the Great Depression: Hoover-Stimson Foreign Policy, 1929–1933* (New Haven, CT: Yale University Press, 1957), Robert Ferrell argued that during the 1920s American diplomats were directed by four assumptions: the Great War was an aberration; Europe could take care of itself; East Asia could function peacefully with only occasional guidance from the United States; and "the real force for peace in the world was moral, not military" (20). The Hoover administration negotiated twenty-five new arbitration treaties and seventeen new conciliation agreements (32).

159. Herbert Hoover, "When Disarmament Can Come," *Addresses, 1948–50*, 100–101, quotation from 101.

160. Hoover, "Nomination," 517.

161. See "House of Bishops of the Protestant Episcopal Church," Oct. 2, 1929, Churches, Protestant, July–Dec. 1929; William McDowell to HH, May 17, 1930, ibid., Jan.–May 1930; Francis McConnell to HH, July 14, 1931, ibid., 1931; Joseph Sizoo to HH, Nov. 27, 1931, ibid.; National Council of the Congregationalist Churches in the United States, May 26, 1930, CM, 1930; William McDowell to

HH, May 16, 1931, ibid., 1931; W. J. McGlothlin to HH, May 15, 1931, ibid.; Indiana Yearly Meeting of the Religious Society of Friends to HH, Sept. 26, 1931, ibid.; Resolution of the Board of Bishops of the Methodist Episcopal Church, May 9, 1931, Churches—Conferences and Assemblies, MEC, 1931–32. See also Mark Mohler, "Mixing Religion and Politics," *Current History* 32 (Mar. 1930), 674–78.

162. Hoover, "Republican Presidential Nomination," 371. See "The President's News Conference," June 22, 1932, *PP*, 267–70. Hoover proposed that all bombers be abolished and the number and tonnage of all naval vessels be reduced by either one-third or one-fourth (269). Hoover lamented in 1931 that the world's armies were larger than they had been before World War I, and the next year he complained that the American government was spending about 75 percent of its budget on the military (*Memoirs*, 2:353).

163. Hoover, "Women of America," 498. Cf. Hoover, "Good-Will Congress," 475.

164. Hoover, *Memoirs*, 2:332–79. Various presidential speeches highlight his achieving aspects of this agenda. E.g., "State of the Union," 1929, 404–8, and "Statement about the London Naval Conference," Apr. 11, 1930, *PP*, 124–26. The editors of *Christian Century* praised Hoover's moratoriums on war reparation and debts. See "A Year of Grace" 48 (July 1, 1931), 863–64; "Next Winter" 48 (July 8, 1931), 894–95; and "Mr. Hoover Assumes World Leadership" 48 (July 15, 1931), 916.

165. See "To the Secretary of State, Washington," Sept. 17, 1929, *Papers Relating to the Foreign Relations of the United States, 1929*, 3 vols. (Washington, DC, 1943), 1:24.

166. The first quotation is from Herbert Hoover, "Armistice Day Address," Nov. 11, 1929, *PP*, 375; the second is from DeConde, "Hoover," 318.

167. Herbert Hoover, "Address to the American Legion," Oct. 6, 1930, *PP*, 406. Cf. Hoover, "Radio Address to the Nation on the Peace Efforts and Arms Reduction," Sept. 18, 1929, *PP*, 295.

168. Hoover's statement for the *Christian Science Monitor*, Aug. 26, 1929, PPF, Peace, 1929–32.

169. Hoover, "King's Mountain," 425.

170. Hoover, "Republican Presidential Nomination," 371.

171. Hoover, "Good-Will Congress," 477.

172. Herbert Hoover, "National Defense," *Addresses upon the American Road, 1940–1941* (New York: Charles Scribner's Sons, 1941), 5.

173. Hoover, "American Legion," 406; Oswald Villard, "The Pot and the Kettle: Roosevelt and Hoover Militarists Both," *Nation* 26 (October 1932), 390.

174. DeConde, "Hoover," 327.

175. He also began a process that led to the removal of troops from Haiti shortly after he left the presidency. Frank Freidel, Jr. contends that Franklin Roosevelt's "Good Neighbor" policy built on "what Hoover had worked long and hard in developing." See "Hoover and Roosevelt in Historical Continuity," in *Hoover Reassessed*, 288–89.

176. DeConde, "Hoover," 327 (first and second quotations), 329 (third and fourth quotations). *Christian Century* praised Hoover for his leadership in reducing arms and for sending a representative to consult with the League of Nations. See "Preparing for the Geneva Conference," 48 (Nov. 25, 1931), 1476–77 and "Mr. Hoover Breaks the Taboo," 48 (Oct. 28, 1931), 1337–38. Cf. "Cutting through the Brush," *Time* 20 (July 4, 1932), 11, and "America's Future Foreign Policy—Retreat or Advancement?" *CA* (Dec. 29, 1932), 1406–7.

177. Gary Dorrien, *The Making of American Liberal Theology: Idealism, Realism, and Modernity, 1900–1950* (Louisville, KY: Westminster John Know Press, 2003), 3. On the Social Gospel, see Charles Howard Hopkins, *The Rise of the Social Gospel in American Protestantism, 1865–1915* (New Haven, CT: Yale University Press, 1940), and Gary Scott Smith, *The Search for Social Salvation: Social Christianity and America, 1880–1925* (Lanham, MD: Lexington Books, 2000).

178. Dorrien, *Making*, 147.

179. Charles Clayton Morrison, *The Social Gospel and the Christian Cultus* (New York: Harper and Brothers, 1933), 20, 13, 15; quotations in that order.

180. See Paul Carter, *The Decline and Revival of the Social Gospel: Social and Political Liberalism in American Protestant Churches, 1920–1940* (Ithaca, NY: Cornell University Press, 1956); Kenneth Cauthen, *The Impact of American Religious Liberalism* (New York: Harper & Row, 1962); William Hutchison, *The Modernist Impulse in American Protestantism* (Cambridge, MA: Harvard University Press, 1976); William Hutchison, ed., *Between the Times: The Travail of the Protestant Establishment in America, 1900–1960* (Cambridge: Cambridge University Press, 1989); Leigh Schmidt and Sally Promey, eds., *American Religious Liberalism* (Bloomington: Indiana University Press, 2012).

181. E.g., Maurice Sheehy to George Akerson, Mar. 27, 1930, Churches, Catholic, 1930, which discusses a meeting of the National Catholic Alumni Federation with Hoover. They pledged to Hoover their "earnest support in the execution of the onerous burdens" he had assumed. See also Hoover, "Message to the Annual Convention of the National Council of Catholic Women," Oct. 6, 1931, *PP*, 462.

182. Herbert Hoover, "Remarks on the Unveiling of a Memorial Statue of James Cardinal Gibbons," Aug. 14, 1932, *PP*, 380. Protestants protested the undue influence Catholics had on Hoover, the alleged Catholic crusade to undermine the public school system, and efforts to establish diplomatic relations with the Vatican. E.g., "Our Public School System Threatened," *The Civic Forum*, Mar. 1932, 1; H. Lee McLendon to HH, Feb. 18, 1930, Churches, Catholic, 1930; Arthur J. Barton to HH, July 2, 1929, Churches, Catholic, 1929; Edward J. Lee to HH, Mar. 9, 1929, ibid.

183. E.g., "The End of an Era," *America* 48 (Nov. 19, 1932), 149.

184. Fred Payne to Walter Newton, Oct. 24, 1932, Churches, Catholic, 1931–33.

185. "Klan Sheet Would Save Hoover," *Courier-Journal*, Oct. 28, 1932, Churches, Catholic, 1931–33.

186. E.g., Wilfrid Parsons, "The Pope, the President, and the Governor," *America* 47 (Sept. 3, 1932), 517–19.

187. PPF, Prohibition contains scores of letters endorsing Hoover. See also "Mr. Hoover Is a Dry!" *CC* 48 (Feb. 11, 1931), 198–200. The editors urged Hoover to explain why he was a dry. Doing so would be "a great act of patriotism, a supremely vital service to prohibition," and the best political strategy (199). See also "Hoover and Curtis Again," *CA* 107 (June 23, 1932), 650; "President Hoover Presents Program," ibid. (Aug. 25, 1932), 890; "Supporting Mr. Hoover," ibid. (Oct. 6, 1932), 1057; and "Who Will Be Our Next President?" ibid. (Nov. 3, 1932), 1171.

188. "The Stakes in the Election," *CC* 49 (Oct. 26, 1932), 1294–8. Although the editors endorsed Hoover, they often criticized the way he handled the Depression, calling for less emphasis on individual initiative and voluntary charity and more focus on government programs. E.g., "Two Years of Mr. Hoover," 48 (Mar. 18, 1931), 366–67; "Charity Is Needed and Something More," 48 (Apr. 22, 1931), 531–32; "Our Valley Forge," 48 (June 10, 1931), 767–69. The second editorial complained that Hoover had never gotten "beyond the purely individualistic point of view" (367).

189. "Mr. Hoover's Peace Record," *CC* 49 (Sept. 28, 1932), 1158–59.

190. "Stakes in the Election," 1294–98, quotations from 1297. The editors argued that the ideals and program of the socialist party were "far more closely in accord with the ideals of Christianity" than those of the two major parties. Since the socialist candidate Norman Thomas was unelectable and relief of human suffering would have to come through the capitalist system, Hoover would do a better job than Roosevelt (1294). The editors concluded that Hoover possessed "one of the most admirable characters" of all the presidents. "We disagree with many of his policies and with his philosophy of government, but we have great faith in the man" (1381). See also Reinhold Niebuhr, "A Communication: The Stakes in the Election," *CC* 49 (Nov. 9, 1932), 1379–81, and the editors' reply, 1381; "It Is the Church's Opportunity," *CC* 49 (June 15, 1932), 758–60; "The Growing Platforms," *CC* (July 20, 1932), 902–4; and "Mr. Roosevelt and Foreign Policy," *CC* (Oct. 5, 1932), 1192–93.

191. "Mr. Roosevelt's Free Hand," *CC* 49 (Nov. 23, 1932), 1430.

192. *Jewish Leader*, Nov. 4, 1932, PPF, Newspapers, 1932. Other Jewish publications also supported Hoover. While Hoover did not appoint as many Jews to significant positions as Roosevelt, he did name Benjamin Cardozo to the Supreme Court, Eugene Meyer as the Governor of the Federal Reserve System, and seven other Jews as judges or foreign ambassadors or ministers. See Henry Allen to Lawrence Richey, Aug. 6, 1932, Churches, Jewish, 1932–33.

193. E.g., "Faith in God," *PB* 119 (Oct. 6, 1932), 3; "Campaign Slander," *Presbyterian* 102 (Sept. 22, 1932), 5.

194. "Quiet Chicago," *PB*, July 14, 1932, 3. Others regretted that both Hoover and Roosevelt had suffered extensive personal abuse during the campaign. See "Campaign Slander," 5.

195. Smith, *Uncommon Man*, 52.

196. Henry Graff, "Reassessing the Depression Chief," in *Hoover Reassessed*, 44.

197. Villard, "Pot and the Kettle," 390.

198. Smith to HH, Nov. 18, 1932, PPF, Smith, Fred B., 1929–32. Expressing the dismay of many other religious leaders, Harry Dewey of Minneapolis, preached a sermon entitled "Losing and Winning," as a tribute to Hoover. See Dewey, Rev. Dr. Harry, Hoover, Herbert, Philosophy, Personal.

199. Eckley, *Hoover*, 154.

200. Graf, "Depression Chief," 43; Hinshaw, *Hoover*, 350, 386–87; Jeansonne, *Hoover*, xvii (quotation), xix. William Leuchtenburg, on the other hand, accused Hoover of deceiving both the Allies and the Central Powers and sometimes telling "outright lies" while providing relief to Europeans during World War I (*Hoover*, 30).

201. Graf, "Depression Chief," 45.

202. William Appleman Williams, "The Shattered Dream: Herbert Hoover and the Great Depression," in *Hoover Reassessed*, 439; Ellis Hawley, "Herbert Hoover and Modern American History," in ibid., 450.

203. Eugene Lyons, *Our Unknown Ex-President: A Portrait of Herbert Hoover* (Garden City, NY: Doubleday, 1949), 18.

204. Hinshaw, *Hoover*, 349–50; J. E. Wallace Sterling, "Herbert Hoover," in *Hoover Reassessed*, 8.

205. DeConde, "Hoover," 317. Cf. Gene Smith, *The Shattered Dream: Herbert Hoover and the Great Depression* (New York: Morrow, 1970).

206. Hawley, "Hoover," 450.

207. Andrew Fairfield, "Mr. Hoover's Credo," *Nation* 133 (Sept. 30, 1931), 330–32; first two quotations from 331, second two from 332. Cf. Robert Herrick, "Our Super-Babbitt: A Recantation," *Nation* 131 (July 16, 1930), 60–62, and "Christian Science Economics," *Nation* 134 (Feb. 17, 1932), 185.

208. Arthur M. Schlesinger, Jr., *The Cycles of American History* (Boston: Houghton Mifflin Co., 1986), 387.

209. Theodore Joslin, Hoover's personal secretary from 1931 to 1933, provides a different picture. He argued that "the trials of a harassed people haunted him from the eighth month of his administration down to the day he again became a private citizen." See *Hoover off the Record* (Garden City, NY: Doubleday, Doran., 1934), 9.

210. Hinshaw, *Hoover*, 349.

211. "Two Years of Mr. Hoover," 367.

212. Wilson, *Hoover*, 163.

213. Bornet, "Uncommon President," 83.

214. Frederick Tolles argued that some Quakers felt impelled to enter politics to remove obstacles to human equality and eliminate causes of war. Their antipathy toward manipulating others and compromising their principles, however, made political participation very difficult for Friends (*Quakerism and the Atlantic Culture* [New York: Macmillan, 1960], 36). See also Rufus Jones, *Quakers in the American Colonies* (London: Macmillan, 1911), 175.

215. Fausold, *Presidency*, 244–45, first three quotations from 244, fourth from 245.

216. Burner, "Quaker," 14.

217. Jeansonne, *Hoover*, 198.

218. Wilson, *Hoover*, 163, 166, quotation from 166.

219. "Two Years of Mr. Hoover," 367.

220. Willis Abbot, *Watching the World Go By* (Boston: Little, Brown, 1934), 345. See also "The New Pilot Comes Aboard," *CC* 50 (Mar. 1, 1933), 278.

221. Fausold, *Presidency*, 245.

222. Smith, *Uncommon Man*, 30, 17; Wilson, *Hoover*, 167.

223. Vaughn Davis Bornet and Edgar Eugene Robinson, *Herbert Hoover: President of the United States* (Palo Alto, CA: Hoover Institution Press, 1975), 186.

224. Bornet, "Uncommon President," 88.

225. Jeansonne, *Hoover*, 453.

226. Williams, "What This Country Needs," 440. See also James Olson, "The Philosophy of Herbert Hoover: A Contemporary Perspective," *Annals of Iowa* 43 (Winter 1976), 181–91.

227. Olson, "Hoover," 150, 155 (first quotation), 157 (second quotation).

228. Freidel, "Historical Continuity," 279–90. Freidel argues that the Hoover administration provided numerous "precedents for the New Deal" (289).

229. Smith, *Uncommon Man*, 127, 197 (quotation).

230. Olson, "Hoover," 145.

231. E.g., Jeansonne, *Hoover*, 452–54.

232. Jeansonne, *Hoover*, 459.

233. E.g., P. B. Mather, "Quaker Requiem," *CC* 81 (Nov. 18, 1964), 1446.

CHAPTER 7

1. Alonzo Hamby, "The Mind and Character of Harry S. Truman," in Michael Lacey, ed., *The Truman Presidency* (New York: Cambridge University Press, 1989), 25.

2. David McCullough, "Harry S. Truman, 1945–1953," in Robert Wilson, ed., *Character above All: Ten Presidents from FDR to George Bush* (New York: Simon & Schuster, 1995), 47.

3. Harry Truman, *Memoirs by Harry S. Truman*, vol. 2: *Years of Trial and Hope* (Garden City, NY: Doubleday, 1956), 105. Moreover, speechwriter George Elsey

asserted that with regard to spiritual and religious ideas, Truman "led and the staff followed." Such phrases and sentences expressed "Truman's own personal belief and feeling," and he added many of them "in longhand very near the final draft of a speech." See Oral History, George Elsey, Mar. 9, 1965, interviewed by Carol Hoffecker and Charles Morrissey, http://www.trumanlibrary. org/oralhist/elsey.htm, 94–95; quotations from 95. Surprisingly, Truman's numerous post-presidential books, including his memoirs and interviews, contain few expressions of his faith.

4. William Inboden, *Religion and American Foreign Policy, 1945–1960: The Soul of Containment* (Cambridge: Cambridge University Press, 2008), 107.

5. Elizabeth Edwards Spalding, "'We Must Put on the Armor of God': Harry Truman and the Cold War," in Mark Rozell and Gleaves Whitney, eds., *Religion and the American Presidency* (New York: Palgrave Macmillan, 2007), 95. See also Merlin Gustafson, "Harry Truman as a Man of Faith," *CC* 90 (Jan. 17, 1973), 75–78.

6. Inboden, *Containment*, 106–7.

7. Spalding, "Truman," 95–96. On Truman's religious views, see Robert Ferrell, *Harry S. Truman: A Life* (Columbia: University of Missouri Press, 1994), 49, 134; David McCullough, *Truman* (New York: Simon and Schuster, 1992), 83; and Alonzo Hamby, *Man of the People: A Life of Harry S. Truman* (New York: Oxford University Press, 1995), 21, 474.

8. McCullough, *Truman*, 47, 54; Robert H. Ferrell, ed., *The Autobiography of Harry S. Truman* (Boulder: University Press of Colorado, 1980), 127 (quotation); Hamby, "Mind and Character," 21; Alfred Steinberg, *The Man from Missouri: The Life and Times of Harry S. Truman* (New York: Putman, 1962), 18, 23.

9. Harry Truman, *Mr. Citizen* (New York: Random House, 1960), 127–29; Ferrell, ed., *Autobiography*, 33 (quotation).

10. Harry Truman composition books, Collection of James and Mary Ann Truman Swoyer, as quoted by McCullough, *Truman*, 60.

11. Hamby, *Truman*, 21; Ferrell, *Truman*, 49; William Pemberton, *Harry S. Truman, Fair Dealer and Cold Warrior* (Boston: Twayne, 1989), 2–3, 11; A. C. Chism to HST, Apr. 29, 1942, Official File 200, Invitations, Kansas City, Harry S. Truman Library (hereinafter cited as TL). Glen Stassen argues that Truman's faith is evident in his biblical understanding, valuing of prayer, integrity, attack on corruption, support for public justice, promotion of civil rights, and quest for peacemaking. See "Harry Truman as Baptist President," *Baptist History and Heritage*, Summer 1999, http://findarticles.com/p/articles/mi_moNXG/is_3_34/ai_94161025/.

12. Quoted in Charles Rodeffer, "Truman's Faith Respected by His Preacher," unknown newspaper, Oct. 1950, President's Personal File 627, Box 490.

13. Robert Phillips, "Another Look—Give 'Em Heaven, Harry!" *Kansas City Star*, Dec. 21, 1976, 1, 5.

14. Thomas Murray interview, Mar. 16, 1955, Post-Presidential Papers, Memoir Files, Box 641.

15. E.g., HST to John Noll, Aug. 16, 1945, President's Personal File 260, Box 449 (hereinafter cited as PPF).

16. E.g., William Hassett to Floyd Johnson, Sept. 25, 1945, Official File 76, 1945–46, 1 of 2, Box 424 (hereinafter cited as OF); Joseph Short to Robert McMichael, Jan. 29, 1951, OF 76, 1951–53, 1 of 3, Box 425.

17. William Hassett to Harry Denman, May 14, 1945, OF 76, 1945–46, 1 of 2, Box 424.

18. E.g., Charles Ross to Marian Beatty, Feb. 27, 1950, OF 76, 1949–59, 1 of 2, Box 425.

19. Mr. and Mrs. James Boylan, Oct. 20, 1949, OF 76 "A," Box 425 (2 of 2). Cf. Doris Bridwell, Feb. 28, 1950, OF 76 "A," Box 425 (2 of 2).

20. Truman, Pickwick Papers, as quoted in Andrew Dunbar, *The Truman Scandals and the Politics of Morality* (Columbia: University of Missouri Press, 1984), 11 (first and third quotations); a handwritten manuscript found in Truman's desk after he died, Post-Presidential Papers (second quotation).

21. Truman, *Mr. Citizen*, 139; HST to Seth Brooks, Mar. 13, 1948, PPF 217-A, Box 448. Cf. HST to Pope Pius XII, Dec. 17, 1949, PPF 108, Box 175; HST to Joseph Gedra, Mar. 7, 1947, PPF 217-A, Box 448.

22. Truman, *Mr. Citizen*, 140. See his various Christmas messages including "Lighting of the National Community Christmas Tree," Dec. 24, 1945, http://www.trumanlibrary.org/publicpapers/index.php?pid=517&st.

23. HST to J. Warren Hastings, Mar. 27, 1950, PPF 217-A, Box 448.

24. HST to J. Warren Hastings, Mar. 8, 1951, PPF 217-A, Box 448. Cf. HST to J. L. Williams, Apr. 4, 1949, PPF 217-A, Box 448.

25. Harry Truman, "Lighting the National Community Christmas Tree," Dec. 24, 1952, http://www.trumanlibrary.org/publicpapers/index.php?pid=2092&st.

26. HST, June 1, 1952, in Robert Ferrell, ed., *Off the Record: The Private Papers of Harry S. Truman* (New York: Harper and Row, 1980), 251–52; all quotations except the second from 252.

27. HST to EW, Mar. 19, 1911, Papers Relating to Family, Business, and Personal Affairs.

28. HST to EW, Feb. 7, 1911, in Robert Ferrell, ed., *Dear Bess: The Letters from Harry to Bess Truman, 1910–1959* (New York: Norton, 1983), 22.

29. HST to EW, Mar. 28, 1918, in Ferrell, ed., *Dear Bess*, 256.

30. HST to G. Bromley Oxnam, May 13, 1948, OF 213, Box 943.

31. Autobiographical sketch, President's Secretary's File, as cited by Niel Johnson, interviewer in Oral History, Welbern Bowman, http://www.trumanlibrary.org/oralhist/bowmanw.htm, 47–48.

32. HST to the Northern Baptist Convention, Apr. 16, 1946, PPF 260-A, Box 449.

33. Diary, June 1, 1945, in Ferrell, ed., *Record*, 41.

34. Joseph Short to Mary Ellen Juiles, July 19, 1951, OF 76, 1951, Box 646. Pruden claimed that Truman "came fairly regularly, though his visits were spaced according to particular crises and responsibilities" he faced (Oral History Interview with Edward Hughes Pruden by Jerry Hess, Feb. 17, 1971, http://www.truman-library.org/oralhist/prudeneh.htm, 2).

35. HST to Russell Stroup, Nov. 25, 1952, Vertical File, Religion; HST to Rev. Herbert Baucom, Jr., May 13, 1949, PPF 4839, Box 591. Truman added that he did not attend political meetings on Sunday (HST to Edward Pruden, Oct. 28, 1949, OF 76, 1949–50, 1 of 2, Box 425). Years later, however, Truman wrote, "I work every day and Sunday too even if Exodus 2–8.9.10 and 11 and Deuteronomy 5–13 and 14 say I shouldn't" (HST to Dean Acheson, Apr. 10, 1968, TL).

36. HST to Edward Pruden, May 14, 1948, PPF 627, Box 490.

37. Truman, *Mr. Citizen*, 127.

38. Harry Vaughan to Robert Hambrook, OF 76, 1949–50, 2 of 2, Box 425. Truman reportedly told Vaughan that people made such a spectacle of his presence that "it spoiled the solemnity of the service for the regular communicants" (quoted in Joseph Lastelic, "Presidential Churchgoing Can Be an Ordeal," *Kansas City Star*, April 10, 1977).

39. HST to John Briggs, May 15, 1948, PPF 3857, Box 578. Cf. Diary, Feb. 8, 1948, in Ferrell, ed., *Record*, 123: When Truman went to Foundry Methodist Church the pastor Frederick Brown Harris made such a "show of the occasion" that he would "never go back."

40. Larston Farrar, "When Mr. Truman Goes to Church," *Washington News Digest* 4 (Oct. 1946), 13.

41. HST to Pruden, Nov. 23, 1945, Vertical File, Religion.

42. HST, June 1, 1952, Ferrell, ed., *Record*, 252.

43. Clinton Howard to HST, Apr. 17, 1945, PPF 675, Box 491.

44. K. Owen White to HST, Apr. 23, 1945, PPF 1023, Metropolitan Baptist Church, Box 497.

45. Welbern Bowman served as the pastor of the Grandview Baptist Church from 1941 to 1969. When Truman's mother Martha was gravely ill in 1947, he frequently prayed and discussed spiritual matters with the president (Bowman Oral History, 48–49). Truman contributed $20,000 for the building of the new church and participated in the dedication service on December 24, 1950 (see Bowman Oral History, 17; Dedication Service, VF Religion). Bowman also met several times with Truman at the White House and in Kansas City (Cross Reference Sheet, Oct. 29, 1950, PPF 364, Box 482; Bowman Oral History, 1). Truman claimed in his memoirs that he stopped attending the church in Washington because his presence, combined with the journalists, photographers, and curiosity seekers who accompanied him, diverted attention from the services. Thereafter he worshipped at the chapels of Walter Reed Hospital or Bethesda, which barred the news media (*Mr. Citizen*, 130–31). However, "Churches Attended by President Truman in Washington" in the Vertical File at the Truman Library lists Truman as attending church twenty times during his presidency, including eleven times at First Baptist and four times at St. John's Episcopal Church, and only once at either chapel. However, this list is not complete as correspondence indicates that Truman also attended First Baptist Church on at least five other occasions not

listed on this sheet. Truman also attended services in other communities while traveling.

46. Edward Pruden to HST, Nov. 26, 1945, VF, Religion. First Baptist Church belonged to both the American Baptist Churches and the Southern Baptist Convention.

47. HST to Jesse Bader, Sept. 29, 1947, PPF 33, Box 133.

48. HST to Charles Wilson, Oct. 26, 1950, PPF 260, Box 449.

49. Joseph Short to W. Ware Lynch, Sept. 3, 1952, OF 76, 1951–53, 3 of 3, Box 425.

50. E.g., Ohio Independent Fundamentalist Churches of America to HST, Apr. 8, 1951, PPF 1-H Con, Box 20.

51. Bill Henry, "The President Goes to Church," *LAT*, Feb. 1, 1949.

52. HST to George McNeill Ray, Mar. 16, 1951, PPF 5689, Box 602.

53. Edward Pruden, "HST—'Good Baptist,'" letter to the *Washington Post*, Jan. 11, 1973 (quotation); HST to Edward Pruden, Nov. 23, 1945, VF, Religion. Pruden, however, admitted that he prepared every sermon with Truman in mind (Farrar, "Truman Goes to Church," 14).

54. Pruden Oral History, 5.

55. HST to EWT, July 22, 1945, TL, as cited by McCullough, *Truman*, 436. Like many other presidents, Truman held a special service at St. John's Episcopal Church the morning of his inauguration on January 20, 1949.

56. See Ralph Weber, ed., *Talking with Harry: Candid Conversations with President Harry S. Truman* (Wilmington, DE: SR Books, 2001), 319 (first quotation); Merle Miller, *Plain Speaking: An Oral Biography of Harry S. Truman* (New York: Berkley, 1974), 214 (second quotation). See also Truman, *Mr. Citizen*, 203; HST to Orville Freeman, Feb. 7, 1958, in Ferrell, ed., *Record*, 355. This claim seems suspect. On a number of other occasions, Truman said he had read the Bible through twice by age 16 (e.g., HST to EWT, Aug. 15, 1941, in Ferrell, ed., *Dear Bess*, 460).

57. Bliss Isely, "Our Presidents, Men of Faith: Harry S. Truman," *Classmate*, Oct 21, 1951, 4.

58. "Truman Knows His Bible, Says Rabbi Herzog," newspaper article, May 10, 1949, VF, Religion.

59. "Religion: Israel's Rabbi," *Time*, May 23, 1949, http://www.time.com/time/magazine/article/0,9171,794774,00.html.

60. Matthew Connelly to Raymond Willis, Sept. 6, 1946, PPF 260, Box 449.

61. Truman, *Mr. Citizen*, 203.

62. HST to Reginald R. Belknap, Sept. 24, 1946, OF 76, 1947, 1 of 2, Box 424 (quotation); HST to James Claypool, Sept. 9, 1950, PPF 260, Box 449; HST to Claypool, Oct. 24, 1947, PPF, 260, Box 449.

63. Harry Truman, "Remarks to the President's Conference on Community Responsibility to Our Peacetime Servicemen and Women," May 25, 1949, http://www.presidency.ucsb.edu/ws/index.php?pid=13195&st=&st1=. Truman explained that his commitment to the Sermon on the Mount prevented him

from cheating people in trade, browbeating workers, and being "a good banker." "Maybe I'm crazy," he concluded, "but so is the Sermon on the Mount if I am" (HST to EWT, Feb. 7, 1937, in Ferrell, ed., *Dear Bess*, 396 [first quotation]; HST to EWT, Feb. 25, 1937, in ibid., 398 [second quotation]).

64. HST to William Lipphard, July 9, 1947, OF 76, 1947, 2 of 2, Box 424.

65. Harry Truman, "Radio Address as Part of the Program 'Religion in American Life,'" Oct. 30, 1949, http://www.presidency.ucsb.edu/ws/?pid=13345. Cf. Truman, "Address in Columbus at a Conference of the Federal Council of Churches," Mar. 6, 1946, http://www.trumanlibrary.org/publicpapers/index.php?pid=1494&st; "The Kidding Stopped," *Time*, July 24, 1950, http://www.time.com/time/magazine/article/0,9171,812794,00.html. Truman also made this point in dozens of letters.

66. Truman, "Christmas Tree," Dec. 24, 1945.

67. Elizabeth Edwards Spalding, *The First Cold Warrior: Harry Truman, Containment, and the Remaking of Liberal Internationalism* (Lexington: University Press of Kentucky, 2006), 219.

68. HST to James Claypool, Oct. 4, 1948, PPF 260, Box 449. Cf. HST to Daniel Poling, Dec. 9, 1947, PPF 260-A, Box 449; HST to Martin Weitz, May 5, 1947, PPF 260, Box 449.

69. Harry Truman, "Address to the Washington Pilgrimage of American Churchmen," Sept. 28, 1951 http://www.trumanlibrary.org/publicpapers/index.php?pid=457&st.

70. HST to Sid McMath, Dec. 5, 1950, PPF 260, Box 449. Cf. Diary, June 15, 1952, Ferrell, ed., *Record*, 256.

71. Harry Truman, *Memoirs by Harry S. Truman*, vol. 1: *Years of Decisions* (Garden City, NY: Doubleday, 1955), 19.

72. Harry Truman, "Inaugural Address," Jan. 20, 1949, http://www.trumanlibrary.org/publicpapers/index.php?pid=1030&st); HST to Edmond Butler, Apr. 18, 1945, PPF 260, Box 449. Cf. HST to Samuel McCrea Cavert, Apr. 19, 1945, PPF 33, Box 130; HST to Richard Cushing, Apr. 23, 1945, PPF 119, Box 175.

73. HST to Frederick Curtis Fowler, Apr. 29, 1950, PPF 5307, Box 597.

74. Harry Truman, "Remarks at the 91st Annual National Convention of the Augustana Lutheran Church," June 7, 1950, http://www.trumanlibrary.org/publicpapers/index.php?pid=785&st.

75. Diary, May 27, 1945, in Ferrell, ed., *Record*, 38; Diary, Mar. 4, 1952, in ibid., 245.

76. A handwritten manuscript in Post-Presidential papers found in Truman's desk after he died.

77. Diary, Apr. 13, 1952, in Ferrell, ed., *Record*, 247.

78. Joseph Short to Maurice Sheehy, Feb. 9, 1952, PPF 260, Box 449.

79. HST to Edward Pruden, June 13, 1952, with August 15, 1950, memo attached, Miscellaneous Historical Documents Collection No. 517. See William Hillman, ed., *Mr. President* (New York: Farrar, Straus and Young, 1952), frontispiece.

80. Harry Truman, "Proclamation 2660—Victory in the East—Day of Prayer," Aug. 16, 1945, http://www.trumanlibrary.org/publicpapers/index.php?pid=112&st. Truman referred to the help of God at least thirty times in his addresses and proclamations.

81. Harry Truman, "Proclamation 2978—National Day of Prayer, 1952," June 17, 1952, http://www.presidency.ucsb.edu/ws/?pid=87332.

82. A handwritten manuscript, about 1931, from the so-called "Pickwick Papers," TL.

83. Diary, July 16, 1945, in Ferrell, ed., *Record*, 52.

84. Diary, Sept. 26, 1946, in Ferrell, ed., *Record*, 99.

85. HST, handwritten draft, n.d., Oct. 14, 1946, folder, PSF, Speech File. See also Margaret Truman, ed., *Where the Buck Stops: The Personal and Private Writings of Harry S. Truman* (New York: Warner Books, 1989), 203; Weber, ed., *Talking with Harry*, 291.

86. McCullough, *Truman*, 325; Weber, ed., *Talking with Harry*, 284; quotations in that order.

87. HST, May 23, 1945, PSF, Longhand Notes, Box 333.

88. Weber, ed., *Talking with Harry*, 256.

89. Spalding, *Cold Warrior*, 201.

90. HST to EW, July 31, 1918, in Ferrell, ed., *Dear Bess*, 268.

91. Harry Truman, "Informal Remarks in Nebraska," June 5, 1948, http://www.trumanlibrary.org/publicpapers/index.php?pid=1647&st.

92. Harry Truman, "Remarks at the Armed Forces Dinner," May 19, 1950, http://www.trumanlibrary.org/publicpapers/index.php?pid=762&st; diary, Feb. 2, 1955, in Ferrell, ed., *Record*, 313; author's interview of Margaret Truman Daniel, McCullough, *Truman*, 986.

93. E.g., Edgar Hinde, Oral History, Mar. 15, 1962, interviewed by James R. Fuchs, http://www.trumanlibrary.org/oralhist/hindeg.htm, 14: "Harry is one of the cleanest" men "I ever saw—or knew."

94. Ferrell, *Truman*, 182–83; quotations from 183.

95. Robert Donovan, *Tumultuous Years: The Presidency of Harry S Truman, 1949–1953* (New York: W. W. Norton, 1982), 14.

96. See Ferrell, ed., *Dear Bess*. E.g., HST to EWT, Aug. 15, 1941, 460.

97. McCullough, *Truman*, 556.

98. Truman, *Mr. Citizen*, 196.

99. HST Memorandum, 1954 (?), in Ferrell, ed., *Record*, 310.

100. Miller, ed., *Plain Speaking*, 137.

101. See McCullough, "Truman," 54; Robert Ferrell, *Truman and Pendergast* (Columbia: University of Missouri Press, 1999), 1; Dunbar, *Truman Scandals*, 1–17.

102. Pemberton, *Truman*, 20.

103. At age 18, Truman claimed that he did not drink, and never gambled, played cards for money, or "speculated in any way" (Apr. 24, 1903, document, TL, as cited by McCullough, *Truman*, 68).

104. Edwin Stearns to HST, Aug. 18, 1945; Irene Lockridge to HST, Sept. 30, 1945; e.g., W. G. Webb to HST, Oct. 4, 1945; Lynn Sheeley to HST, Oct. 8, 1945, all in PPF 1-H Con, Box 20; quotations/citations in that order.

105. "Harry Truman Takes a Trip," *Life* 18 (Oct. 22, 1945), 31, 33; quotations in that order. See also "Push and Pull," *Time* 46 (Oct. 22, 1945), http://www.time.com/time/magazine/article/0,9171,778412,00.html.

106. J. R. McLarty to HST, Oct. 30, 1945; August Mintz, C. C. Caldwell, and Alice Graber to HST, Nov. 11, 1945; Floyd Looney to HST, Nov. 12, 1945, all in PPF 1-H Con, Box 20; "Texas Baptists Assail Truman on 'Drinking and Gambling,'" *Courier-Journal*, Nov. 16, 1945, 1; quotations in that order.

107. B. Tunstall to HST, Nov. 9, 1945, PPF 1-H Pro, Box 20; Virginia T. McCormick to HST, Nov. 16, 1945, ibid.

108. A. C. Shuler to HST, Dec. 21, 1945, PPF 2306, Box 548. Similarly, a Kansas City pastor declared: "I am one of many Baptists" "who are ashamed of those Texas Baptists who 'flew off the handle'" (Homer Huff to HST, Jan. 2, 1946, PPF 2344, Box 549).

109. S. J. Starnes to HST, July 15, 1946; Mrs. C. R. Little to HST, June 27, 1946; to HST, Sept. 22, 1949; Ruth Stanley, Jr. to HST, Jan. 11, 1950; Harry Denman to HST, Apr. 24, 1950, all in PPF 1-H Con, Box 20; quotations in that order.

110. E.g., Howard Bishop to HST, Jan. 11, 1951; Robert Condon to HST, Jan. 16, 1951; Jessie Burwell to HST, Oct. 1, 1951, all in PPF 1-H Con, Box 20.

111. E.g., Nora Forrester to HST, Feb. 19, 1951; Mrs. John Labout to HST, June 17, 1951, both in PPF 1-H Con, Box 20.

112. E.g., Betty Carlisle to HST, Apr. 18, 1951; e.g., Joseph Short to Mrs. John Labout, July 13, 1951; cf. Short to Nora Forrester, Feb. 26, 1951, all in PPF 1-H Con, Box 20.

113. "Pastor Defends Truman," UP, June 30, 1951. "When history is written," he added, "your statement will be the correct one" (HST to Ray, July 14, 1951, Box 602, PPF 5689).

114. Quoted in "Truman, 33rd President Is Dead," *NYT*, Dec. 27, 1972.

115. Diary, Nov. 1, 1949, in Ferrell, ed., *Record*, 168.

116. Philip Lagerquist, "The Masonic Biography of Harry S. Truman," Miscellaneous Historical Documents Collection, No. 177; "The Masonic History of Harry S. Truman," *Virginia Masonic Herald*, April 1949, PPF 13, 1949–53, Box 122; HST to Solon Cameron, Sept. 18, 1950, PPF 13-B, Missouri Lodge of Research, Box 122; HST to Ray Bond, Nov. 10, 1950, ibid.; HST to Franklin Bright, Mar. 23, 1949, PPF 13-E, Box 122.

117. McCullough, *Truman*, 78; Richard Lawrence Miller, *Truman: The Rise to Power* (New York: McGraw Hill, 1986), 68–72.

118. Harry Truman, "Remarks at a Masonic Breakfast," Feb. 21, 1952, http://www.trumanlibrary.org/publicpapers/index.php?pid=927&st.

119. "Exchange of Messages with Pope Pius XII," Aug. 28, 1947, http://www.trumanlibrary.org/publicpapers/index.php?pid=1902&st. Cf. HST to Edward Pruden, Sept. 9, 1949, PPF 627, Box 490.

120. Truman, "Federal Council." Cf. HST to William Lipphard, July 23, 1947, PPF 260, Box 449; HST to Samuel McCrea Cavert, May 21, 1948, PPF 33, Box 130; HST to Charles Taft, Nov. 24, 1948, ibid.

121. Diary, Apr. 4, 1948, in Ferrell, ed., *Record*, 129. Cf. Truman, "Remarks at the Young Democrats Dinner," May 14, 1948, http://www.trumanlibrary.org/publicpapers/index.php?pid=1624&st=.

122. E.g., William Hassett to Mrs. C. E. Beacom, Oct. 28, 1949, OF 76 "A," 2 of 2, Box 425; Hassett to Adrian Burkard, Oct. 27, 1949, ibid.; Hassett to Jack Brown, Feb. 5, 1952, ibid.

123. E.g., Richard Bennett to HST, Dec. 18, 1951, OF 76 "A," 2 of 2, Box 425.

124. Mrs. W. R. Alexander to HST, Jan. 30, 1952, OF 76 "A," 2 of 2, Box 425. Cf. M. W. Beadle to HST, Feb. 21, 1952, OF 76, Revival B, 2 of 2, Box 425.

125. "Our Weekly Chat with You," *Huntington Catholic*, Oct. 16, 1949, OF 76, Revival B, 1 of 2, Box 425. Cf. "God and the Atom," an open letter to Truman from Ferris Booth, in *NYT*, Oct. 3, 1949.

126. "Exchange of Messages with Pope Pius XII," Aug. 28, 1947 (first quotation); Truman, "Washington Pilgrimage" (second and third quotations); HST to the 164th General Assembly, Presbyterian Church (USA), May 19, 1952, PPF 260, Box 449 (fourth quotation); HST to William Lampe, Apr. 29, 1946, ibid. (fifth quotation).

127. Truman, "Washington Pilgrimage" (first, second, and fourth quotations); Imboden, *Containment*, 115 (third quotation).

128. Harry Truman, "Address at the Cornerstone Laying of the New York Avenue Presbyterian Church," Apr. 3, 1951, http://www.trumanlibrary.org/publicpapers/index.php?pid=280&st (first and third quotations); HST to Seth Brooks, Mar. 13, 1948, PPF 217-A, Box 448 (second quotation); Harry Truman, "Radio Address as Part of Interdenominational Program, 'One Great Hour,'" Mar. 26, 1949, http://www.trumanlibrary.org/publicpapers/index.php?pid=1080&st=&st1= (fourth quotation).

129. Harry Truman, "Remarks in Alexandria, Va., at the Cornerstone Laying of the Westminster Presbyterian Church," Nov. 23, 1952, http://www.trumanlibrary.org/publicpapers/index.php?pid=2230&st.

130. Harry Truman, "Address at . . . Arlington National Cemetery," Dec. 21, 1949, http://trumanlibrary.org/publicpapers/viewpapers.php?pid=1351.

131. Truman, "New York Avenue."

132. Truman, *Memoirs*, 1:418; Truman, "Radio Address to the American People after the Signing of the Terms of Unconditional Surrender by Japan," Sept. 1, 1945, http://www.trumanlibrary.org/publicpapers/index.php?pid=129&st (all quotations). Truman wrote to Bess in 1918 that he "had shells fall on all sides and I am sure" "that the Lord was and is with me" (Oct. 6, 1918, Ferrell, ed., *Dear Bess*, 271).

133. HST to Samuel McCrea Cavert, Aug. 20, 1945, OF 213, Box 943.

134. E.g., HST to G. Bromley Oxnam, May 13, 1948, OF 213, Box 943.

135. E.g., HST to Jacob Weinstein, Oct. 13, 1947, PPF 260, Cross Reference 45–53, Box 449.

136. HST to Ivan Lee Holt, June 23, 1947, OF 76, 1947, 2 of 2, Box 424. Cf. HST to Holt, Aug. 4, 1947, PPF 260, Box 449.

137. "Exchange of Messages," Aug. 28, 1947; Harry Truman, longhand notes, longhand personal memos, 1952, PSF, folder 1, Box 333; quotations in that order.

138. Harry Truman, "Faith in Our Time," 4, Sept. 20, 1946, PPF 260, Box 449.

139. Truman, "One Great Hour."

140. Truman, "Federal Council"; Truman, "Radio Address Opening the Community Chest," Sept. 26, 1947, http://www.trumanlibrary.org/publicpapers/index.php?pid=1894&st=&st1= (quotation).

141. Harry Truman, "Lighting of the National Community Christmas Tree," Dec. 24, 1951, http://www.trumanlibrary.org/publicpapers/index.php?pid=569&st.

142. HST to the National Stewardship Conference, Oct. 28, 1947, PPF 2903, Box 641. Dozens of organizations and individuals asked Truman for donations.

143. Matthew Connelly to Laurie Battle, Sept. 19, 1951, PPF 1-A, VF, Religion.

144. Truman, "Westminster Presbyterian Church."

145. Harry Truman, "Address at a Luncheon of the National Conference of Christians and Jews," Nov. 11, 1949, http://www.trumanlibrary.org/publicpapers/index.php?pid=1335&st=&st1=; Scripture quotation from Truman, "Address in Buffalo," Oct. 8, 1948, http://www.trumanlibrary.org/publicpapers/index.php?pid=1979&st.

146. HST to William Lampe, Apr. 29, 1946, PPF 260, Box 449.

147. Harry Truman, "Veto of Bill to Revise the Laws Relating to Immigration, Naturalization, and Nationality," June 25, 1952, http://www.trumanlibrary.org/publicpapers/index.php?pid=2389&st; cf. Truman, "Address in Buffalo."

148. Truman, "Federal Council."

149. HST to Douglas Horton, Oct. 10, 1945, OF 76, 1945–46, 2 of 2, Box 424.

150. OF 76, 1945–46, Oxnam, G. Bromley, 2 of 2, Box 424.

151. OF 213, Patterson, Robert, Feb. 13, 1946, Box 943, details the correspondence involved in facilitating this.

152. Samuel McCrea Cavert to HST, Mar. 9, 1948, OF 213, Box 943. See also HST to Cavert, Mar. 12, 1948, ibid.

153. PPF 260, Cavert, Samuel McCrea, Apr. 27, 1948, Box 449.

154. OF 2953, Cavert, Samuel McCrea, Box 2953, details the correspondence between the leaders of the National Council and Truman between December 6 and 14, 1950.

155. HST to Henry Knox Sherrill, Mar. 15, 1952, OF 76, 1951–53, 2 of 3, Box 425.

156. Matthew Connelly to Mrs. James Wyker, May 23, 1951, PPF 2953, Box 1743.

157. E.g., Edna Stone to HST, Mar. 7, 1946, OF 213, FCC, Box 943.

158. Bernard Stanton to HST, Oct. 10, 1951, OF 2953, Box 1743.

159. E.g., Pruden to HST, Nov. 10, 1945; Pruden to HST, Dec. 6, 1946; HST to Pruden, June 2, 1947, all in PPF 627, Box 490. Pruden frequently applauded Truman's addresses (e.g., Pruden to HST, Oct. 25, 1949, OF 76, 1949–50, 1 of

2, Box 425; Pruden to HST, Sept. 20, 1951, PPF 260, Box 449), and Truman thanked Pruden for sending him copies of his talks and sermons (e.g., HST to Pruden, Nov. 15, 1949, PPF 627, Box 490; HST to Pruden, July 10, 1951, ibid.).

160. E.g., Charles Ross to Edward Pruden, Dec. 2, 1946, PPF 627, Box 490.

161. See HST to Matthew Connelly, n.d., PPF 260, Box 449.

162. Edward Pruden to HST, July 22, 1948, PPF 627, Box 490.

163. HST to Pruden, Oct. 19, 1950, PPF 627, Box 490; Rodeffer, "Truman Faith."

164. HST to Pruden, Apr. 19, 1951, PPF 627, Box 490.

165. See also HST to Pruden, May 4, 1950, PPF 627, Box 490. Pruden wrote an article for *Presbyterian Life* opposing Mark Clark being appointed to this position.

166. Pruden Oral History, 12–13; first quotation from 12, second from 12–13.

167. HST, memorandum for Dean Acheson, June 3, 1952 (quotations). See also HST to Poling, May 1, 1946; HST to Poling, Oct. 14, 1947; HST to Poling, Dec. 5, 1950; all in PPF 1677, Box 530.

168. Billy Graham, *Just As I Am: The Autobiography of Billy Graham* (Grand Rapids, MI: Zondervan, 1997), xix–xxiii; Gerald Strober, *Billy Graham: His Life and Faith* (Waco, TX: Word Books, 1977), 105–6. In *Just As I Am*, Graham reported that he asked Truman about his "religious background and leanings." Truman responded that he tried "to live by the Sermon on the Mount and the Golden Rule." Graham countered that more was required: "It's faith in Christ and His death on the Cross that you need" (xxii).

169. William Hassett to Mathew Connelly, Dec. 28, 1951, OF 76, Revival, Box 425. See also Connelly to Graham, Dec. 31, 1951, and Feb. 1, 1952, OF 1952, Jan. 13–Feb. 9.

170. Richard Pierard, "Billy Graham and the U.S. Presidency," *JCS* 22:1 (1980), 114–15; Billy Graham, "Program for Peace," 1952 sermon, 1; *United Evangelical Action*, Aug. 15, 1952, 1 (quotation).

171. E.g., HST to Howard Carroll, Sept. 17, 1945, PPF 1935, Box 539; HST to Karl Alter, Nov. 10, 1945, PPF 1936, Box 539; HST to Leo Mooney, Dec. 1, 1948, PPF 260, Box 449; HST to Angelus Delahunt, Sept. 9, 1949, PPF 260, Box 449.

172. Jozach Miller III to Hassett, June 6, 1948, PPF 260, Box 449. Truman's staff implemented this suggestion.

173. See George Gill, "The Truman Administration and Vatican Relations," *The Catholic Historical Review* 73 (July 1987), 408–23; George Flynn, *Roosevelt and Romanism: Catholics and American Diplomacy, 1937–1945* (Westport, CT: Greenwood Press, 1976), 111–14.

174. Harry Truman, "Myron C. Taylor's Mission to the Vatican," Aug. 15, 1947, http://www.trumanlibrary.org/publicpapers/index.php?pid=1909&st=&st1= (first quotation); Truman, "Reappointing Myron Taylor," May 3, 1946, http://www.trumanlibrary.org/publicpapers/index.php?pid=1542&st= (second quotation). See also HST to Pius XII, Apr. 19, 1946, PPF 108, Box 175; Pius XII to HST, May 20, 1946, ibid.

175. Gill, "Truman Administration," 410–12; quotation from 410.

176. "The Vatican Embassy Fraud," *CC* 63 (Apr. 3, 1946), 422–24; first quotation from 423, second and third from 422.

177. J. R. Cunningham to HST, June 14, 1947, OF 213, Box 943; "Mr. Truman: Recall Myron C. Taylor," *CC* 63 (Dec. 4, 1946), 1460. Truman met with a group of influential Protestant leaders on June 5, 1946 and November 14, 1947 about this issue and exchanged many letters with FCC executives. FCC leaders grew increasingly irritated as Taylor's mission continued. See G. Bromley Oxnam to HST, Nov. 15, 1947; HST to Oxnam, Nov. 20, 1947; Oxnam to HST, June 13, 1949, all in PPF 2838, Box 560; "Pray—and Watch," *CC*, June 19, 1946, 774–75.

178. The Cross Reference Sheet of September 12, 1950 (PPF 2838, Box 560) details numerous exchanges between Oxnam and the White House on this issue.

179. Joseph Short's explanation of Truman's position in footnote to "The President's News Conference," Oct. 25, 1951, http://www.trumanlibrary.org/publicpapers/index.php?pid=535&st=&st1=.

180. HST to Leland Stark, Oct. 29, 1951, PPF 260, Box 449.

181. "President Surrenders to the Pope," *CC* 68 (Oct. 31, 1951), 1243; "Why Did He Do It?" *CC* 68 (Nov. 7, 1951), 1269–71; "Protesting Protestants," *Time* 58 (Dec. 10, 1951), 77; Paul Blanshard, "One-Sided Diplomacy," *Atlantic Monthly* 189 (Jan. 1952), 52–54; Gill, "Truman Administration," 420.

182. Spellman to HST, Aug. 21, 1947; HST to Spellman, Aug. 25, 1947, PPF 214, Box 448; J. Frank Norris to Myron Taylor, July 25, 1947, PPF 2565, Myron Taylor, Box 554; Norris to HST, July 26, 1947, OF 213, Box 943. Charles Lowry preached a sermon titled "Should America Be Represented at the Vatican?: An Episcopal Viewpoint" in late October 1951, which received substantial publicity.

183. Alan Berger, "Harry S. Truman and Jewish Refugees," in Michael Devine, Robert Watson, and Robert Wolz, eds., *Israel and the Legacy of Harry S. Truman* (Kirksville, MO: Truman State University Press, 2008), 8–9; quotation from 8.

184. Truman, July 21, 1947, in Bruce Warshal, "Truman's 1947 'Anti-Semitic' Diary Entry," in Devine, Watson, and Wolz, eds., *Israel*, 11–20.

185. July 30, 1946, cabinet meeting, as recorded by Henry Wallace, in John Morton Blum, ed., *The Price of Vision: The Diary of Henry A. Wallace* (Boston: Houghton Mifflin, 1973), 607. The pressure on Truman increased in 1947–48 as the White House was inundated by telegrams, postcards, and letters about Palestine (Raymond Geselbracht, "The Truman Administration and U.S. Recognition of Israel," in Devine, Watson, and Wolz, eds., *Israel*, 98).

186. Harry Truman, "A Task for Men of Good Will," PSF 253.

187. HST to Jacob Aronson, Oct. 27, 1947, PPF 2418, Box 550. Cf. HST to Maurice Eisendrath, Feb. 11, 1947, ibid.

188. HST to Jacob Aronson, Oct. 9, 1948, PPF 2418, Box 550.

189. HST to Stephen Wise, Feb. 8, 1949, PPF 1058, Box 498.

190. Weber, ed., *Talking with Harry*, 319.

191. Truman, "New York Avenue."

192. Harry Truman, "Address at the Columbia Scholastic Press Association," Mar 15, 1952, http://www.trumanlibrary.org/publicpapers/index.php?pid=945&st.

193. E.g., "The President's News Conference," Oct. 13, 1949, http://www.trumanlibrary.org/publicpapers/index.php?pid=1249&st.

194. Truman, "Augustana Lutheran Church."

195. Truman, "Washington Pilgrimage."

196. HST to John Swift, Aug. 2, 1950, PPF 260, Box 449; HST to Wallace Speers, Oct. 10, 1945, ibid.; quotations in that order.

197. Truman, *Mr. Citizen*, 139.

198. Harry Truman, "Address in Mexico City," Mar. 3, 1947, http://www.trumanlibrary.org/publicpapers/index.php?pid=2194&st.

199. "Exchange of Messages with Pope Pius XII," Dec. 23, 1949, http://www.trumanlibrary.org/publicpapers/index.php?pid=1353&st.

200. Truman," Scholastic Press Association."

201. HST to Jesse Bader, July 14, 1947, PPF 33, Box 133.

202. Ferrell, *Truman*, xii.

203. Truman, "Press Association."

204. Weber, ed., *Talking with Harry*, 100.

205. See, for example, Ferrell, *Truman*, 285–305; William Berman, *The Politics of Civil Rights in the Truman Administration* (Columbus: Ohio State University Press, 1970); Donald McCoy and Richard Ruetten, *Quest and Response: Minority Rights and the Truman Administration* (Lawrence: University Press of Kansas, 1973); Richard Dalfiume, *Desegregation of the U.S. Armed Forces: Fighting on Two Fronts, 1939–1953* (Columbia: University of Missouri Press, 1969).

206. Edwards, "Truman," 100–107; quotation from 100. To win the propaganda war, Truman established the Campaign for Truth in 1950 and expanded the work of Voice of America (101–2). Surprisingly, Truman made few references to his faith in discussing his decision to use the atomic bomb in Japan and, therefore, it is not analyzed as one of the issues illustrating how his faith affected his policies.

207. Spalding, *Cold Warrior*, 218–20; quotation from 218.

208. Richard Kirkendall, "The Truman Period as a Research Field," in Michael Devine, ed., *Harry S. Truman, the State of Israel, and the Quest for Peace in the Middle East* (Kirksville, MO: Truman State University Press, 2009), 18. See also Kirkendall, "Faith and Foreign Policy: An Exploration into the Mind of Harry Truman," *Missouri Historical Review* 102 (July 2008), 214–24.

209. Harry Truman, "Address in Little Rock at the Dedication of the World War Memorial Park," June 11, 1949, http://www.presidency.ucsb.edu/ws/?pid=13206.

210. Truman, *Mr. Citizen*, 98; longhand notes, 1952; Inboden, *Containment*, 107; Spalding, "Truman," 112–13.

211. Truman, "Federal Council."

212. Truman, "Washington Pilgrimage." Cf. HST to John Noll, Oct. 18, 1951, PPF 260-A, Box 449.

213. Harry Truman, "Midcentury White House Conference on Children and Youth," Dec. 5, 1950, http://www.trumanlibrary.org/publicpapers/index.php?pid=989&st=.

214. Truman, "New York Avenue."

215. Truman, "Westminster Presbyterian Church."

216. Harry Truman, "Dedication of the Credit Union National Association's Filene House, Madison, Wisconsin," May 14, 1950, http://www.trumanlibrary.org/publicpapers/index.php?pid=756&st.

217. Harry Truman, "Farewell Address to the American People," Jan. 15, 1953, http://www.trumanlibrary.org/publicpapers/index.php?pid=2059.

218. HST to the American Baptist Convention, June 6, 1951, PPF 2582, Box 554.

219. HST to John Callan, Nov. 15, 1945, PPF 260, Box 449.

220. Harry Truman, "Address at the Jefferson Day Dinner," Apr. 5, 1947, http://www.trumanlibrary.org/publicpapers/index.php?pid=2177&st=&st1=; Truman, "Address in New York City Before the United Nations General Assembly," Oct. 24, 1950, http://www.trumanlibrary.org/publicpapers/index.php?pid=901&st=.

221. HST to Pope Pius XII, Aug. 11, 1948, Myron Taylor Papers, Box 1; TL; Truman, *Memoirs*, 2:110; quotations in that order.

222. Harry Truman, "Address on Foreign Policy at the Navy Day Celebration," Oct. 27, 1945, http://www.trumanlibrary.org/publicpapers/index.php?pid=187&st; Truman, "Remarks at a Meeting . . . Conducted by the CIA," Nov. 21, 1952, http://www.trumanlibrary.org/publicpapers/index.php?pid=2232&st; quotations in that order.

223. "Exchange of Messages," Dec. 23, 1949.

224. Harry Truman, "Lighting of the National Community Christmas Tree," Dec. 24, 1946, http://www.trumanlibrary.org/publicpapers/index.php?pid=1841&st. Cf. HST to Donald McQuade, Oct. 7, 1950, PPF 260, Box 449.

225. Harry Truman, "Address in Spokane at Gonzaga University," May 11, 1950, http://www.trumanlibrary.org/publicpapers/index.php?pid=750&st=).

226. Truman, "Inaugural Address."

227. Truman, "Gonzaga University."

228. Truman, "United Nations"; "Disarmament—Last Call!" *CC* 67 (Nov. 8, 1950), 1320–21.

229. HST to Charles Wilson, Oct. 26, 1950, PPF 260, Box 449.

230. "Exchange of Messages," Aug. 28, 1947. Cf. HST to A. G. Cieognani, Jan. 22, 1949, PPF 108, Box 175; "Reappointing Myron Taylor."

231. Inboden, *Containment*, 110.

232. HST to the 164th General Assembly (second quotation); HST to Bader, Sept. 29, 1947 (first and third quotations).

233. Truman, "Federal Council."

234. Truman, *Mr. Citizen*, 134.

235. HST to EWT, Oct. 2, 1947, in Ferrell, ed., *Dear Bess*, 554.

236. Harry Truman, "Remarks to a Group of Bishops of the Church of England," Sept. 9, 1949, http://www.trumanlibrary.org/publicpapers/index. php?pid=1225&st=.

237. HST to Pope Pius XII, Mar. 26, 1948, PPF 766, Box 1676.

238. Harry Truman, "Remarks in Kansas City," Dec. 22, 1950, http://www.truman-library.org/publicpapers/index.php?pid=1003&st.

239. See Francis Spellman, "Communism Is Unamerican"; Fulton Sheen, *Communism and the Conscience of the West* (Indianapolis: Bobbs-Merrill, 1948). On Truman's crusade, see also Inboden, *Containment*, 119–55.

240. Truman, "Washington Pilgrimage."

241. "Truman Calls Sermon on the Mount Our Guide," *CC* 66 (Sept. 21, 1949), 1091.

242. "Mr. Truman's Spiritual Blindness," *CC* 67 (June 28, 1950), 782–83; first and second quotations from 782, third from 783. Cf. "The President Lays a Cornerstone," *CC* 58 (Apr. 18, 1951), 483; "The President at His Best and Worst," *CC* 58 (Oct. 3, 1951), 1115.

243. Truman, "Washington Pilgrimage." Cf. HST to Levi Strauss, Feb. 15, 1951, PSF; Truman, "Message to Dr. Daniel Poling," July 21, 1950, http://www.presi-dency.ucsb.edu/ws/index.php?pid=13564&st.

244. HST to Edward Pruden, Aug. 28, 1952, PPF 627, Box 490; Weber, ed., *Talking with Harry*, 290. Truman complained that some Protestant leaders were much more interested in battling with the Catholic Church than in joining a moral crusade (HST to Lewis Strauss, Feb. 15, 1951, PSF, Box 250, Chronological Name File, Strauss, Levi). See also Diary, Feb. 26, 1952, in Ferrell, ed., *Record*, 241–42.

245. Truman, *Mr. Citizen*, 134.

246. Spellman to HST, Oct. 25, 1946, PPF 214, Box 448.

247. Truman, "Inaugural Address."

248. Truman, "Washington Pilgrimage."

249. Truman, "Christmas Tree," Dec. 24, 1945. Cf. Truman, "Christmas Tree," Dec. 24, 1951.

250. "68 Senators Back Palestine Refuge," *NYT*, Apr. 20, 1941, 28.

251. Harry Truman, "Speech . . . Before the United Rally to Demand Rescue of Doomed Jews," Apr. 14, 1943, HST Senate File, Box 108.

252. Hamby, *Truman*, 404.

253. HST, Memorandum for David Niles, May 13, 1947, PSF, Chronological Name File Niles, Box 247.

254. McCullough, *Truman*, 597–98; Truman, *Memoirs*, 2:158 (quotation).

255. E.g., Harry Truman, "Remarks to a Delegation from the United Jewish Appeal," Feb. 25, 1946, http://www.trumanlibrary.org/publicpapers/index. php?pid=1484&st=&st1=.

256. Hamby, *Truman*, 406.

257. Truman, *Memoirs*, 2:132.

258. HST to Myron Taylor, May 27, 1946, OF 204, Box 913. See also Truman, *Memoirs* 2:143–46, 152–55.

259. "Statement by the President on Palestine," June 5, 1947, http://www.trumanli-brary.org/publicpapers/index.php?pid=2137&st=&st1=.

260. J. Frank Norris to HST, Oct. 2, 1947, PPF 3386, Box 570; HST to J. Frank Norris, Oct. 7, 1947, ibid.

261. Truman, *Memoirs*, 2:160–61; Miller, ed., *Plain Speaking*, 215–18; McCullough, *Truman*, 606–9, 612.

262. McCullough, *Truman*, 609 (all quotations). See *NYT*, Mar. 21, 1948.

263. Samuel and Katherine Sloan to HST, Mar. 19, 1948, OF 204, March 1948, Box 916.

264. George Gallup, *The Gallup Poll: Public Opinion, 1935–71* (New York: Random House, 1972), 727; Michael Straight, "Truman Should Quit," *New Republic* 118 (Apr. 5, 1948), 1–5. Cf. Dale Kramer, "Must It Be Truman?" *Nation* 166 (Mar. 13, 1948), 295–96. See also Bruce Evensen, "A Story of 'Ineptness': The Truman Administration's Struggle to Shape Conventional Wisdom on Palestine at the Beginning of the Cold War," *Diplomatic History* 15 (July 1991), 339–59.

265. Truman, *Memoirs*, 2:149, 162.

266. Clark Clifford and Richard Holbrooke, "President Truman's Decision to Recognize Israel," http://rslissak.com/content/president-trumans-decision-recognize-israel-clark-clifford-richard-holbrooke; Clark Clifford, *Counsel to the President: A Memoir* (New York: Doubleday, 1992), 7–8. See also Miller, ed., *Plain Speaking*, 230–32; and Ronald Radosh and Allis Radosh, "Truman, Jews, and Zionists," in Devine, ed., *Truman*, 110–11.

267. Interview with Clark Clifford by Richard Holbrooke, May 4, 1988, Holbrooke Papers, TL.

268. Alfred M. Lilienthal, "Remembering General George Marshall's Clash with Clark Clifford over Premature Recognition of Israel," *Washington Report on Middle Eastern Affairs*, June 1999, 49–50.

269. Eliahu Elath, "Harry S. Truman—The Man and the Statesman," May 18, 1977, lecture, Hebrew University, 48.

270. Michael Benson, *Harry S. Truman and the Founding of Israel* (Westport, CT: Praeger, 1997), 25.

271. Miller, ed., *Plain Speaking*, 213–14.

272. Michael Benson, "A Little Touch of Harry in the Night," in Devine, Watson, and Wolz, eds., *Israel*, 24. For the case that Truman recognized Israel to win the Jewish vote in the 1948 election, see Harold Gosnell, *Truman's Crises: A Political Biography of Harry S. Truman* (Westport, CT: Greenwood Press, 1980), 363, and McCullough, *Truman*, 596. McCullough insists, however, that for Truman, humanitarian considerations trumped foreign policy concerns (596). See also

John Snetsinger, *Truman, the Jewish Vote, and the Creation of Israel* (Stanford, CA: Hoover Institution Press, 1974), 119–36.

273. Truman, *Memoirs*, 2:132–33, 156 (quotation).

274. As quoted by Wallace, *Vision*, 607.

275. David McCullough interview with Benson, May 27, 1993, cited in Benson, "Little Touch," 24.

276. Hamby, *Truman*, 417.

277. Pemberton, *Truman*, 118–19; quotation from 118.

278. In his *Memoirs*, Truman repeatedly emphasized that he strove to relieve misery and provide justice in Palestine (2:137–40, 145, 156–57, 160, 163).

279. Quoted in Benson, *Truman*, 188.

280. David Niles, as quoted in Steinberg, *Man from Missouri*, 308.

281. Gosnell, *Truman's Crises*, 281, 541; quotations in that order. Gosnell is summarizing the views of others such as Bert Cochran, *Truman and the Crisis Presidency* (New York: Funk & Wagnalls, 1973), 396–99 and Barton Bernstein, ed., *Politics and Policies of the Truman Administration* (Chicago: Quadrangle Books, 1970), 3–14.

282. Pemberton, *Truman*, 96, 167; quotations in that order; McCullough, *Truman*, 472, 325 (quotations).

283. Kirkendall, "Truman Period," 12. See, for example, Arthur Schlesinger, Jr., "The Ultimate Approval Rating," *NYT Magazine*, Dec. 15, 1996, 46–51.

284. Donovan, *Tumultuous Years*, 14; McCullough, *Truman*, 991; McCullough, "Truman," 58–59; quotations in that order.

285. Ferrell, *Truman*, 179; McGrory as quoted by McCullough, *Truman*, 989–90; Gosnell, *Truman's Crises*, 566.

286. Abba Eban, "My First Forty-five Minutes with Harry S. Truman," in Devine, Watson, and Wolz, eds., *Israel*, 94–95; Elizabeth Edwards Spalding, "True Believers," *The Wilson Quarterly* 30 (Spring 2006), 47. See also Spalding, *Cold Warrior*, 76–79; Ferrell, *Truman*, 246; Donald McCoy, *The Presidency of Harry S. Truman* (Lawrence: University Press of Kansas, 1984), 319; Arnold Offner, *Another Such Victory: President Truman and the Cold War, 1945–1953* (Stanford, CA: Stanford University Press, 2002), 470.

287. Inboden, *Containment*, 109, 113 (quotation).

288. Truman, "New York Avenue" (first and second quotations); Truman, "Washington Pilgrimage" (third quotation).

289. Pruden Oral History, 18.

290. Inboden, *Containment*, 108.

CHAPTER 8

1. Jonathan Aitken, *Nixon: A Life* (Washington, DC: Regnery, 1993), 58; Charles Henderson, Jr., *The Nixon Theology* (New York: Harper and Row, 1972), 41. A fellow lieutenant recalled that during the war Nixon "was an absolutely straight

arrow and a true Quaker," who did not smoke or drink and "spent a lot of time reading his Bible" (James Stewart, interview with Aitken, January 1990, *Nixon*, 104).

2. Henderson's *Nixon Theology* is the only book that examines this subject. Of Nixon's numerous biographers, only Jonathan Aitken and Roger Morris discuss his religious background in detail. Aitken claims that "Nixon's intensely private religious beliefs" were "an important dimension in his life" (46). Aitken relies primarily on interviews with Nixon and some residents of Whittier for his information about Nixon's religion. See Roger Morris, *Richard Milhous Nixon: The Rise of an American Politician* (New York: Henry Holt, 1990), 77, 86–87, 127–29, 175, 220, 799. Nixon insisted in 1989 that "the impact of my Quaker heritage on my personality has been underestimated" (RN, memorandum to Aitken, Aug. 8, 1989, *Nixon*, 46). See Stephen Ambrose, *Nixon: The Education of a Politician, 1913–1962* (New York: Simon and Schuster, 1987), 31, on how Nixon's Quaker background helped shape his personality.

3. Quoted in David Gergen, *Eyewitness to Power: The Essence of Leadership, Nixon to Clinton* (New York: Simon and Schuster, 2000), 20. Many others who knew Nixon well also referred to him as a complicated man who could not truly be known: William Safire, *Before the Fall: An Inside View of the Pre-Watergate White House* (New York: Doubleday, 1975), 97–106; Stephen Ambrose, *Comrades: Brothers, Fathers, Heroes, Sons, Pals* (New York: Simon and Schuster, 1999), 67–73; H. R. Haldeman, "High School Colloquium," in Leon Friedman and William Levantrosser, eds., *Richard M. Nixon: Politician, President, Administrator* (New York: Greenwood Press, 1991), 49; John Ehrlichman, "The White House and Policy Making," in ibid., 140; Garry Wills, *Confessions of a Conservative* (Garden City, NY: Doubleday, 1979), 81.

4. Milton Mayer argued that most members of this branch of Friends supported the war in Vietnam ("Disownment: The Quakers and Their President," *CC*, Oct. 10, 1973, 1001). Nixon also refused to meet with several groups of Quakers who asked to consult with him (Henderson, *Nixon Theology*, 32–33).

5. William Bundy, *A Tangled Web: The Making of Foreign Policy in the Nixon Presidency* (New York: Hill and Wang, 1998), 517; Tom Wicker, "Richard M. Nixon, 1969–1974," in Robert Wilson, ed., *Character above All* (New York: Simon & Schuster, 1995), 130.

6. Daniel Williams, *God's Own Party: The Making of the Christian Right* (New York: Oxford University Press, 2010), 88–90; quotation from 88. See also Nixon, "What Has Happened in America?" *Reader's Digest*, October 1967, 49–54.

7. Daniel Williams, "Richard Nixon's Religious Right: Catholics, Evangelicals, and the Creation of an Antisecular Alliance," in Daniel Williams and Laura Jane Gifford, eds., *The Right Side of the Sixties: Reexamining Conservatism's Decade of Transformation* (New York: Palgrave Macmillan, 2012), 150, 141. On the broader religious context of the years of Nixon's presidency, see Dean Kelley, *Why Conservative Churches Are Growing* (New York: Harper and Row, 1972);

Robert Bellah, *The Broken Covenant* (New York: Seabury Press, 1975); Dean Hoge and David Roozen, ed., *Understanding Church Growth and Decline, 1950–1978* (New York: Pilgrim Press, 1979); and Lowell Streiker and Gerald Strober, *Religion and the New Majority: Billy Graham, Middle America, and the Politics of the 70s* (New York: Association Press, 1972).

8. Richard Nixon, "Annual Message to the Congress on the State of the Union," Jan. 22, 1970, http://www.presidency.ucsb.edu/ws/?pid=2921; Gergen, *Eyewitness*, 77.

9. Gergen, *Eyewitness*, 85.

10. "Remarks by Dr. Billy Graham at Richard Nixon's Funeral," Apr. 27, 1994, http://watergate.info/nixon/94-04-27_funeral-graham.shtml.

11. Aitken, *Nixon*, 46–47.

12. Richard Nixon, "Remarks at . . . the Birthplace of the President's Mother," June 24, 1971, http://www.presidency.ucsb.edu/ws/?pid=3053.

13. Richard Nixon, *RN: The Memoirs of Richard Nixon* (New York: Grosset & Dunlap, 1978), 117, 8; quotations in that order; Jonathan Aitken, "The Nixon Character," *Presidential Studies Quarterly* 26 (Winter 1996), 241.

14. Billy Graham, Memorial Service for Hannah Milhous Nixon, Oct. 3, 1967, Post Pres. Correspondence, Special People, A–K, Graham, Billy and Ruth, 1990, 4 of 4.

15. Henderson, *Nixon Theology*, 11; Jessamyn West, *To See the Dream* (New York: Harcourt, Brace, 1956), 221; Stephen Ambrose, *Nixon: The Education of a Politician* (New York: Simon and Schuster, 1987), 14; David Le Shana, *Quakers in California* (Newberg, OR: Barclay Press, 1969), 109–26.

16. Joseph Dmohowski, "From a Common Ground: The Quaker Heritage of Jessamyn West and Richard Nixon," *California History* 73 (Fall 1994), 217; Ambrose, *Nixon: Education*, 19.

17. RN to Samuel Gressitt, June 6, 1972, Religious Matters 6 (hereinafter cited as RM), Prayer-Prayer Periods, 1/1/71 (hereinafter cited as PPP); RN to Mrs. Donald Lee, June 6, 1972, RM2, 1/1/72–7/31/72.

18. Richard Nixon, "A Nation's Faith in God," *Decision*, Nov. 1962, 4 (quotation); "A Worshiper in the White House," *Time*, Dec. 6, 1968, http://www.time.com/time/printout/0,8816,844670,00.html# (quotation); Nixon, *Memoirs*, 13–14; West, *To See the Dream*, 130; Dmohowski, "Common Ground," 219; Aitken, *Nixon*, 48; Morris, *Nixon*, 30–31, 86–87. On Quakers, see Le Shana, *Quakers*, esp. 63–135; Thomas Hamm, *The Transformation of American Quakerism: Orthodox Friends, 1800–1907* (Bloomington: Indiana University Press, 1988), 102–43; Thomas Hamm, *The Quakers in America* (New York: Columbia University Press, 2003), 49–61, 64–119.

19. Nixon, "Nation's Faith," 4 (quotation); Aitken, *Nixon*, 48; Dmohowski, "Common Ground," 220.

20. Tom Bewley interview, The Richard Nixon Project, California State University at Fullerton, http://www.yorbalindahistory.org/gsdl/cgi-bin/library?e), as cited by Aitken, *Nixon*, 47.

21. Richard Nixon, *In the Arena* (New York: Simon and Schuster, 1990), 89.

22. Dmohowski, "Common Ground," 226; Aitken, *Nixon*, 26; Hannah Nixon, "A Mother's Story, as Told to Flora Rheta Schreiber," *Good Housekeeping* 150 (June 1960), 212.

23. Nixon, "Mother's Story," 212. See also Aitken, *Nixon*, 54.

24. Richard Nixon, *Six Crises* (Garden City, NY: Doubleday, 1962), 295; Martin Goldman, *Richard M. Nixon: The Complex President* (New York: Facts on File, 1998), 4; Ambrose, *Nixon: Education*, 58.

25. Nixon interview with Aitken, *Nixon*, 42.

26. Mildred Mendenhall, Richard Nixon Project, 2, as cited in Morris, *Nixon*, 220.

27. Morris, *Nixon*, 243; Nixon, *Memoirs*, 26. However, Henry Spalding maintained that Nixon enlisted only after "many months of agonized soul-searching" (*The Nixon Nobody Knows* [Middle Village, NY: J. David, 1972], 132); and Bela Kornitzer quotes Pat Nixon as saying that "because of Richard's upbringing, he did much soul-searching before he made his decision" (*The Real Nixon: An Intimate Biography* [New York: Rand McNally, 1960], 140).

28. Nixon, *Memoirs*, 27.

29. Ambrose, *Nixon: Education*, 106.

30. Ambrose, *Nixon: Education*, 100.

31. Quoted in "A Worshiper in the White House"; Marjorie Hyer and Marianne Bernhard, "Churches of the Presidents," *Sunday World Herald Magazine of the Midlands*, Apr. 26, 1981, 17.

32. Charles Fager, review of Aitken's *Nixon: A Life*, http://www.kimopress.com/nixon.html. See also Charles Cooper, *Whittier, Independent College in California: Founded by Quakers, 1887* (Los Angeles: Ward Ritchie Press, 1967), 159–61, 195–203.

33. Nixon, *Memoirs*, 16.

34. Richard Nixon, "What Can I Believe?" 32, 12, Nixon Family Collection, Whittier College, 1933–34, Nixon Presidential Library. Nixon had expected to abandon his childhood beliefs about "the divine creator and his plans for us" but he had found it "almost impossible" "to do so" (Nixon, "My Brother Arthur," Nixon Family Collection, Series V, folder 7).

35. Nixon, "I Believe," 11, 22–23; first quotation from 11, second and third from 22, fourth from 23.

36. Nixon, "I Believe," 23.

37. Richard Nixon, "Proclamation 3907—Announcing the Death of Dwight David Eisenhower," Mar. 28, 1969, http://www.presidency.ucsb.edu/ws/?pid=1985.

38. Richard Nixon, "Second Inaugural Address," Jan. 20, 1973, http://www.presidency.ucsb.edu/ws/?pid=4141.

39. Nixon, "I Believe," 32 (first and seventh quotations), 24 (second and third quotations), 25 (fourth, fifth, and sixth quotations), 26 (eighth quotation).

40. Richard Nixon, "Christmas Message to Hospitalized Veterans," Dec. 16, 1970, http://www.presidency.ucsb.edu/ws/index.php?pid=2852&st=&st1=#axzz1T70

GBUDt; Nixon, "Proclamation 4170—Thanksgiving Day, 1972," Nov. 17, 1972, http://www.presidency.ucsb.edu/ws/index.php?pid=72478&st=&st1=#axzz1T7 0GBUDt.

41. Nixon, "I Believe," 25.

42. Nixon, "Nation's Faith," 4.

43. RN to J. Edward Smith, Mar. 15, 1969, RM, Bibles 1/69–12/70, Box 3, public statement for the Pocket Testament League.

44. Richard Nixon, "Statement about National Bible Week," Oct. 22, 1969, http://www.presidency.ucsb.edu/ws/index.php?pid=2279&st=.

45. Nixon, "I Believe," 25, 27 (first and second quotations), 28 (third quotation), 29 (fourth quotation).

46. Nixon, "I Believe," 27, 30–32; first quotation from 27, second and third from 30.

47. "A Conversation with the President," Mar. 22, 1971, http://www.presidency.ucsb.edu/ws/index.php?pid=2945&st=.

48. RN to Paul Carlson, Apr. 24, 1972, RM, Religious Services in the White House, 1/1/72–12/31/72, Box 15 (hereinafter cited as RSWH). Cf. RN to Douglas Coe, June 14, 1972, RM, PPP, 1/1/71, Box 6.

49. RN to William Schladebeck, Dec. 24, 1969, RM, RM3-1, Catholic, 69/70, Box 18.

50. David Stewart to RN, Oct. 10, 1973; RN to Stewart, Oct. 17, 1973, White House Central Files, RM, 1/1/73–7/31/74, Box 3 (hereinafter cited as WHCF).

51. Asher Souder et al. to RN, Aug. 8, 1970, RM, 8/18/70–12/31/70, Box 1; Arlene Hudson to RN, July 21, 1972; Edna Allen to Nixon, July 6, 1972; all in WHCF, RM, 1-1-71–[12-72], Box 2; quotations in that order.

52. Warren Mendenhall to RN, Aug. 11, 1972, RM, 8/1/72–10/31/72, Box 2.

53. New Life Club to RN, Mar. 25, 1969, RM, PPP, 3/24/69–3/27/69, Box 4. Cf. Dr. and Mrs. Earl Dorrance to RN, Mar. 15, 1969, RM, PPP, 3/14/69–3/24/69, Box 2.

54. Rose Mary Woods to James Schaal, May 19, 1972, in RM, 11/1/72–12/72, Box 2.

55. Maurice Stans, "A Balance Sheet," in Kenneth W. Thompson, ed., *The Nixon Presidency: Twenty-two Intimate Perspectives of Richard M. Nixon* (Lanham, MD: University Press of America, 1987), 30; Ehrlichman interview in Anthony Summers with Robbyn Swan, *The Arrogance of Power: The Secret World of Richard Nixon* (New York: Viking, 2000), 12. E.g., John Dellenback to John Ehrlichman, Oct. 15, 1971, RM, PPP, 1/1/71, Box 6; Ronald Ziegler to James Breig of *The Evangelist*, July 21, 1971, RM, 7/1/71–12/31/71, Box 2; Ziegler to Trude Feldman of *The Mayflower*, Aug. 11, 1971, ibid.; Herbert Klein to William Willoughby of the Washington *Star*, Dec. 21, 1971, WHCF, RM, 1-1-71–[12-72], Box 2.

56. Quoted in Russ Busby, *Billy Graham, God's Ambassador: A Celebration of His Life and Ministry* (New York: HarperOne, 2007), 148.

57. Roland Elliott to Judith Howard, Mar. 14, 1974, RM, PPP, 1/1/73, Box 6. Cf. Noble Melencamp to Mrs. F. Ward, May 3, 1971, RM, 7/1/71–12/31/72, Box 2.

58. E.g., Noble Melencamp to Donald Cameron, Jan. 12, 1970, RM, 1/70–8/17/70, Box 1.

59. Jane Beeson to RN, July 9, 1969, quoting Flossie Bayne to Beeson, June 11, 1969, RM, 1/69–12/70, Box 1.

60. William Blommer to RN, May 2, 1972, RM, 1/1/72–7/31/72, Box 2.

61. Representative Nixon statements that he was praying for people include RN to Catholicos Khoren I, May 12, 1969, WHCF, RM, 1-69/12-70, Box 1; Nixon, "Telegram to the Mayor of Kellogg, Idaho, about the Sunshine Silver Mine Disaster," May 4, 1972, http://www.presidency.ucsb.edu/ws/?pid=3395.

62. Richard Nixon, "Remarks at the Presidential Prayer Breakfast," Oct. 22, 1969, http://www.presidency.ucsb.edu/ws/?pid=2278.

63. Richard Nixon, "Remarks at the National Prayer Breakfast," Jan. 31, 1974, http://www.presidency.ucsb.edu/ws/?pid=4329.

64. Ehrlichman interview, Summers, *Arrogance*, 12–13; Charles Colson, *Born Again* (Old Tappan, NJ: Revell, 1977), 179–80.

65. Billy Graham, *Just as I Am: The Autobiography of Billy Graham* (Grand Rapids, MI: Zondervan, 1997), 461.

66. Richard Nixon, "Address to the Nation on the War in Vietnam," Nov. 3, 1969, http://www.presidency.ucsb.edu/ws/?pid=2303.

67. Charles Hawbaker to RN, May 16, 1973, RM, PPP, 1/1/73, Box 6.

68. Richard Nixon, "Remarks at Dr. Billy Graham's East Tennessee Crusade," May 28, 1970, http://www.presidency.ucsb.edu/ws/?pid=2523.

69. RN to Charles Berger, Feb. 7, 1973, WHCF, RM, 1/1/73–7/31/74, Box 3. Cf. RN to Regis Barwig, June 24, 1970, RM, RM3-1, Catholic 69/70, Box 18.

70. RN to Harold Hughes, Oct. 3, 1973, RM, 4/16/73–10/15/73, Box 17. Cf. RN to Douglas Coe, Oct. 3, 1973, ibid.

71. Richard Nixon, "Proclamation 3919—National Day of Participation Honoring the Apollo 11 Mission," July 16, 1969, http://www.presidency.ucsb.edu/ws/?pid=2128.

72. Richard Nixon, "Remarks at a Special Church Service in Honolulu," Apr. 19, 1970, http://www.presidency.ucsb.edu/ws/index.php?pid=2473&st=&st1=#axzz1SkkKMDw9.

73. Richard Nixon, "National Moment of Prayer and Thanksgiving," Jan. 26, 1973, http://www.presidency.ucsb.edu/ws/index.php?pid=3874.

74. Dwight Chapin to Robert Gronewald, Jan. 25, 1969, RM3-3, 69/70, Box 20. It would have been difficult for Nixon to attend this meetinghouse because many of its members strongly opposed the Vietnam War.

75. E.g., staff memorandum, Feb. 20, 1974, RM3-3, 1/1/73, Box 20.

76. Robert Giles to RN, Jan. 12, 1969, RM1, 2/28/69, Box 1.

77. Richard Curtis, *Hubris and the Presidency: The Abuse of Power by Johnson and Nixon* (Danbury, CT: Rutledge Books, 2000), 196. See also Hugh Sidey, "The Mandate to Live Well," *Time*, Apr. 5, 1974, 17.

78. Hugh Sloan, memorandum for H. R. Haldeman, Jan. 29, 1970, RM, PPP, 1/69–12/70, 1 of 2, Box 3; Chapin, memorandum for Haldeman, Nov. 23, 1970, ibid.; draft of a letter to Senator Jordan and Congressman Quie, n.d., ibid.

79. Ronald Walker, memorandum for Dwight Chapin, Jan. 21, 1971, RM, PPP, 1/1/71, Box 6.

80. Memorandum for the President, Nov. 10, 1969; Mark Hatfield, memorandum for Nixon, Nov. 11, 1969; Bryce Harlow, memorandum for Henry Kissinger, Nov. 13, 1969 (quotation); Suggested Reply from the President to Senator Mark Hatfield, n.d., all in RM, PPP, 1/69–12/70, 1 of 2, Box 3.

81. Henderson, *Nixon Theology*, 6, 191; quotations in that order.

82. Richard Reeves, *President Nixon: Alone in the White House* (New York: Simon and Schuster, 2001), 13.

83. Richard Nixon, *Beyond Peace* (New York: Random House, 1994), 237.

84. Nixon, *Arena*, 300.

85. Nixon, "My Brother Arthur," folder 7.

86. RN to Lonzie Clark, June 13, 1973, RM, 1/1/73, Box 6 (quotations); RN to Fred Littlefield, June 20, 1973, RM, 1/1/73, Box 2; Nixon, "Messages of Sympathy on the Death of President Barrientos of Bolivia," Apr. 28, 1969, http://www.presidency.ucsb.edu/ws/?pid=2020.

87. Richard Nixon, "Eulogy Delivered at the Capitol during the State Funeral of General Eisenhower," Mar. 30, 1969, http://www.presidency.ucsb.edu/ws/?pid=1987. See also Nixon, "Statement on the Death of President Lyndon Baines Johnson," Jan. 22, 1973, http://www.presidency.ucsb.edu/ws/index.php?pid=4152&st=&st1=#axzz1T70GBUDt; Nixon, "Eulogy at Memorial Services for Senator Dirksen of Illinois," Sept. 9, 1969, http://www.presidency.ucsb.edu/ws/?pid=2229.

88. Richard Nixon, "Eulogy for J. Edgar Hoover," May 4, 1972, http://www.presidency.ucsb.edu/ws/index.php?pid=3397&st=. In "Eulogy Delivered at Burial Services for Whitney M. Young, Jr., in Lexington, Kentucky," Mar. 17, 1971, http://www.presidency.ucsb.edu/ws/?pid=2940, Nixon refers to Young's immortality.

89. Nixon, *Arena*, 89. He omitted other quotations from his essay that suggested the resurrection was merely a myth or an inspiring story.

90. "Remarks by Dr. Billy Graham."

91. Ambrose, *Nixon: Education*, 620–21; quotation from 621. E.g., Aitken, *Nixon*, 364–65.

92. Stans, "Balance Sheet," 31, 34; quotations in that order.

93. Iwan Morgan, *Nixon* (New York: Oxford University Press, 2002), 32; Summers, *Arrogance*, 33 (quotation), 127–28; Melvin Small, *The Presidency of Richard Nixon* (Lawrence: University Press of Kansas, 1999), 220; Nixon, *Memoirs*, 29.

94. Summers, *Arrogance*, 351; Aitken, "Nixon Character," 245.

95. Nixon, *Memoirs*, 14. Nixon told Garry Wills in the late 1960s that his Quaker background, with its emphasis on privacy and "not making a display of religion," combined with his introverted personality, explained "why I never use God's name in speeches or quote the Bible" (Garry Wills, *Nixon Agonistes: The Crisis of the Self-made Man* [Boston: Houghton Mifflin, 1970], 32). More accurate is Nixon's statement that on the few occasions when he tried to "inject my

personal religious faith into my speeches" it "was uncomfortable and unnatural" (*Arena*, 89).

96. Richard Nixon, "Remarks at a Campaign Reception for Southern Supporters in Atlanta," Oct. 12, 1972, http://www.presidency.ucsb.edu/ws/?pid=3627; John R. Brown III to Raymond Seelhorst, Feb. 27, 1969, RM, PPP, 2/11/69–3/13/69, Box 4 (last quotation). Many other speeches used similar language. E.g., Nixon, "Radio Address: 'One America,'" Oct. 28, 1972, http://www.presidency.ucsb.edu/ws/?pid=3664.

97. Quoted in "Carl F. H. Henry, 90," Dec. 10, 2003, http://articles.latimes.com/2003/dec/10/local/me-henry10.

98. RN to James Iakovos, Jan. 24, 1969, RM, 1/69–12/70, Box 1. Cf. RN to Frances Caswell, July 31, 1974, RM, Bibles, 1/69–12/70, Box 3.

99. Charles Smith to RN, Mar. 6, 1969, RM, 3/1/69–4/9/69, Box 1. Cf. David Seaver et al. to RN, Feb. 22, 1969; RM, Bibles, 1/69–12/70, Box 3 and the dozens of petitions in this file.

100. Richard Nixon, "Remarks to the 89th Annual International Meeting of the Knights of Columbus in New York City," Aug. 17, 1971, http://www.presidency.ucsb.edu/ws/?pid=3119.

101. Nixon, "Thanksgiving Day, 1972."

102. Richard Nixon, "Remarks at the Presidential Prayer Breakfast," Feb. 5, 1970, http://www.presidency.ucsb.edu/ws/?pid=2646.

103. Richard Nixon, "Remarks at the 17th Annual Presidential Prayer Breakfast," Jan. 30, 1969, http://www.presidency.ucsb.edu/ws/?pid=1986 (quotation); Nixon, "Presidential Prayer Breakfast," Oct. 22, 1969.

104. Ron Graybill, "Going to Church at the White House," *Liberty* 68 (May/June 1973), 3.

105. Lucy Winchester, as quoted in Graham, *Just as I Am*, 451.

106. Richard Nixon, "Introduction," in Ben Hibbs, ed., *White House Sermons* (New York: Harper and Row, 1972), vi–vii; first and second quotations from vi, third and fourth from vii.

107. Noble Melencamp to Ray Bressler, Jan. 19, 1970, RM, RSWH, 1/1/70–1/31/70, Box 13.

108. Nixon, *Arena*, 90. See also "Billy Graham Cites Integrity: Nixon Seen as Shunning Political Use of Religion," *WP*, Nov. 16, 1968; "Praying with the President in the White House," *NYT*, Aug. 8, 1971.

109. Charles Wilkinson to Dorothy Smith, Mar. 21, 1969, RM, RSWH, 3/20–3/31/69, Box 10. Nixon and his staff evaluated various issues including the order of the service, which clergy to invite to preach, and how often the services should be held. See Charles Wilkinson to Billy Graham, Jan. 24, 1969, RM, RSWH, beginning–3/31/71, Box 6.

110. On Haley, see Sarah Booth Conroy, "The Preacher Was a Roommate," April 1971, RM15, RSWH, 4/1/71–4/30/71.

111. The normal formula was: Executive Department—50, President's Guests—50; Press—25, Diplomats—25; Congress—50; White House staff—45 (Charles Wilkinson to Lucy Winchester, Jan. 29, 1969, RM1-69/12-70, Box 1).

112. H. R. Haldeman, memorandum for Bud Wilkinson, July 1, 1969, RM, RSWH, 6/11–7/14/69, Box 7.

113. RN, memorandum for Bob Haldeman, June 30, 1969, RM, RSWH, 6/11–7/14/69, Box 7; Haldeman to Wilkinson, July 1, 1969, ibid. See also Nixon, "Introduction," viii.

114. Clifford Hardin to Walter Kennedy, Feb. 17, 1970, RM2-1, RSWH, 2/1/70–2/28/70, Box 13.

115. E.g., Robert Dole to RN, June 19, 1969, RM, PPP, 6/17/69–9/30/69, Box 5; Philip Crane to RN, Apr. 9, 1970, ibid.; Gerald Kaplan to RN, Jan. 29, 1970, RM, RSWH, 1/1/70–1/31/70, Box 13; and many of letters in RM, RSWH, 2-5-69, Boxes 7 and 8.

116. Morris Hoffman to RN, Jan. 30, 1969, RM, RSWH, 2/11/69, Box 7.

117. Mark Hatfield to RN, Feb. 3, 1969, RM2-1, RSWH, Begin–3/31/69, Box 6.

118. Michael Stephens to RN, Jan, 28, 1969, RM, RSWH, 2/11/69, Box 7.

119. Johnie Crumpler to RN, Jan. 31, 1969, RM, RSWH, 2/11/69, Box 7. Cf. Gene Thompson to RN, Jan. 28, 1969, ibid.

120. James Stanford to RN, Jan. 28, 1969, RM, RSWH, 2/11/69, Box 7.

121. Richard Marcovitz to RN, Jan. 31, 1969, RM, RSWH, 2/11/69, Box 7.

122. Robert Dole to RN, Feb. 4, 1969, RM2-1, RSWH, Begin–3/31/69, Box 6.

123. D. Elton Trueblood, "Worship in the White House," *Quaker Life* 13 (Jan. 1972), 37.

124. Ernest Miller to RN, Jan. 29, 1969, RM, RSWH, 2/21/69, Box 8.

125. Graybill, "Going to Church," 3.

126. H. R. Haldeman, memorandum for Charles Colson, Nov. 13, 1970, Colson Papers, NL, Box 86; John Ehrlichman, memorandum for the President, June 16, 1969, RM, 6/11–7/14/69, Box 7; Henley, *Mystique*, 67.

127. E.g., David Parker, memorandum for H. R. Haldeman, Jan. 8, 1973, RM, RSWH, 1/1/73–2/8/73, Box 17.

128. RN to Herb Klein, June 16, 1969, RM, RSWH, 6/11–7/14/69, Box 7; RN, memorandum for Bob Haldeman, June 30, 1969, ibid.; Fisher, memorandum for the President, Aug. 15, 1969, RM, RSWH, 10/1/69–12/31/69, Box 7.

129. E.g., Bill Timmons, memorandum for Bryce Harlow, June 28, 1969, RM, RSWH, 6/11–7/14/69, Box 7, which lists anti- and pro-surtax attendees.

130. Robert Brown, memorandum, Apr. 20, 1972, RM, RSWH, 1/1/72–12/31/72, Box 15. Brown recommended four black ministers who supported Nixon. Colson later frankly admitted that "we used the prayer breakfasts and church services for political ends" (Colson to William Martin in Martin, *With God on Our Side: The Rise of the Religious Right in America* [New York: Broadway Books, 1996], 98).

131. H. R. Haldeman, memorandum for Charles Colson, Feb. 23, 1970, Box 12. See also Dwight Chapin, memorandum for Rose Woods, Feb. 19, 1969, WHCF, RM3-1 Catholic [69–70]. Nixon's staff also assessed the potential political benefits of Nixon attending various religious services and producing an Easter Message on peace highlighting the president's "Quaker beliefs and heritage" (Dwight Chapin, memorandum for H. R. Haldeman, Mar. 19, 1970, RM, 1/69–12/70, Box 1; Charles Colson, memorandum for Dwight Chapin, Mar. 31, 1971, RM, PPP, 1/1/71 [quotation], Box 6).

132. Henderson, *Nixon Theology*, 30.

133. Dean Francis Sayre, rector of the Washington National Cathedral, as reported in John Jamrich to RN, Feb. 7, 1972, RM, PPP, 1/1/71, Box 6; "White House Worship," *Lutheran Forum*, Mar. 1969, 15.

134. Unknown staffer to Mr. Bagnall, Mar. 27, 1969, RM, RSWH, 3/20–3/31/69, Box 10.

135. Waldo Zimmermann, "'Church' in the White House Protested," letter to the editor; neither the newspaper nor the date is specified in RM, RSWH, 2/21/69, Box 8.

136. Reinhold Niebuhr, "The King's Chapel and the King's Court," *Christianity and Crisis*, Aug. 4, 1969, 211–12; Max Mueller, "Prophets, Protests and Politicians: Exploring the Political Theologies of Reinhold Niebuhr and Billy Graham through an Analysis of *Christianity and Crisis and Christianity Today*," *Cult/ure: The Graduate Journal of Harvard Divinity School* 3 (2008), 58–59; all quotations from Niebuhr except the next to last one, which is from Mueller, 59.

137. See James Gutmann, "Dr. Niebuhr Upheld," *NYT*, Aug. 19, 1969; Mordecai Kaplan, "Mr. Nixon's Preachers," *NYT*, Aug. 13, 1969, 46; John Krumm, "White House 'Church'," *NYT*, Aug. 15, 1969; Edward B. Fiske, "Controversy over those White House Services, *NYT*, Aug 10, 1969, E7.

138. Richard Wightman Fox, *Reinhold Niebuhr: A Biography* (New York: Pantheon Books, 1985), 289.

139. O'Hair to RN, Jan. 31, 1969, RM, 2/28/69, Box 1.

140. E.g., letters to Nixon signed by many different individuals on Mar. 23, 1973, Apr. 10, 1973, and Apr. 12, 1973, all in RM, RSWH, 4/1/73–6/74, 1 of 2, Box 18.

141. Louis Finkelstein in *White House Sermons*, 64. Cf. Charles Malik in ibid., 86.

142. Peale in *White House Sermons*, 56; Finkelstein in ibid., 68. Niebuhr quoted Finkelstein's words as an example of "what a simple White House invitation will do to dull the critical faculties" ("The King's Chapel," 211).

143. RN to John Pollock, Dec. 30, 1986, Post-Pres. Correspondence, Special People, A–K, Graham Billy and Ruth, 1990, 2 of 2; RN, memorandum to Aitken, May 29, 1991, *Nixon*, 338.

144. Peale to RN, Feb. 26, 1973, RM, RSWH, 1/1/73–2/8-73, Box 17.

145. See Edward Fiske, "The Closest Thing to a White House Chaplain," *NYT Magazine*, June 8, 1969, http://www.nytimes.com/books/97/07/06/reviews/

graham-magazine.html; Streiker and Strober, *New Majority*, 25–85, 169–98; Marshall Frady, *Billy Graham: A Parable of American Righteousness* (Boston: Little, Brown and Company, 1979), 446–66, 473–87; John Pollock, *Billy Graham: Evangelist to the World* (New York: Harper & Row, 1979), 171–83; Nancy Gibbs and Michael Duffy, *The Preacher and the Presidents: Billy Graham in the White House* (New York: Center Street, 2007), 157–231.

146. Graham, *Just as I Am*, 441; Wesley Pippert, "Billy Graham: Prophet or Politician," *Christian Life*, May 1971, 54; Henderson, *Nixon Theology*, 105–6, 108–9.

147. Billy Graham memories, Post-Pres. Correspondence, Rev. Billy Graham, 1974–1990, 2 of 2. See also Flora Rheta Schriber, "Richard Nixon," *Good Housekeeping*, July 1968; RN to Pollock, Dec. 30, 1986.

148. Graham, *Just as I Am*, 449–50; David Aikman, *Billy Graham: His Life and Influence* (Nashville, TN: Thomas Nelson, 2007), 211.

149. RN to Graham, Jan. 22, 1973, RM, RSWH, 1/1/73–2/8/73, Box 17. See also Nixon, *Arena*, 90.

150. Graham, *Just as I Am*, 454.

151. Aikman, *Graham*, 212 (first quotation); William Martin, *A Prophet with Honor: The Billy Graham Story* (New York: W. Morrow, 1991), 355 (second and third quotations).

152. Graham, *Just as I Am*, 459.

153. Frady, *Graham*, 452. Gibbs and Duffy call him a "de facto member of the first-term Nixon White House" (*Preacher*, 193).

154. E.g., Graham to Rose Mary Wood, June 9, 1971, RM, 1/1/71–[12/72], Box 2; RN to Graham, Feb. 1, 1972, RM, RM3, 1/171–12/31-72, Box 18; RN to BG, Feb. 6, 1973, RM, PPP, 1/1/73, Box 6.

155. Gibbs and Duffy, *Preacher*, 178–79. See also Dwight Chapin, memorandum for H. R. Haldeman, Feb. 16, 1969, RM, 1/69–12-70, Box 1.

156. Alexander Butterfield, memorandum for the President, July 16, 1969, RM, Prot., 69/70, Box 20.

157. Graham to RN, Jan. 27, 1973. Graham wrote Nixon: "Your counsel, advice and friendship means more to me than you can possibly realize" (Post-Pres. Correspondence, 1974–1979, Graham, Billy 1976–1979, 1 of 2).

158. RN to Pollock, Dec. 30, 1986.

159. See Randall King, "When Worlds Collide: Politics, Religion, and Media at the 1970 East Tennessee Billy Graham Crusade," *Journal of Church and State* 39:2 (1997), 273–95.

160. Graham to RN, Jan. 27, 1973.

161. Graham to RN, Feb. 9, 1973, RM, PPP, 1/1/73, Box 6.

162. "Watergate," *CT* 17 (May 25, 1973), 46.

163. BG to RN, Dec. 26, 1973, RM, RSWH, 10/16/73–12/31/73, Box 17.

164. BG to RN, Aug 17, 1974, Post-Pres. Correspondence 1974–1979, Graham, Billy 1974–1975, 2 of 2.

165. RN to Ruth Graham, Mar. 10, 1975, Post.-Pres. Correspondence, Graham, 2 of 2. Nixon ended the letter with "May God bless all the Grahams," a phrase he rarely employed.

166. Graham to RN, Mar. 15, 1973, Post-Pres. Correspondence 1974–1990, 2 of 2.

167. RN to Pollock, Dec. 30, 1986. See also Billy Graham, "Watergate?" *Christianity Today*, Jan. 4, 1974, 385–86, 389, 392, 395.

168. Frady, *Graham*, 484. Colson later stated that Nixon recognized the "political benefits" of his friendship with Graham (quoted in Mary Bishop, *Billy Graham: The Man and His Ministry* [New York: Grosset and Dunlap, 1978], 59).

169. Graham, *Just as I Am*, 458 (first quotation), 456 (remainder of quotations).

170. Aikman, *Graham*, 297. See also Gibbs and Duffy, *Preacher*, 219–31.

171. Jeb Magruder, memorandum for Dwight Chapin, Jan. 11, 1971, RM, 1/1/71– [12/72], Box 2.

172. Memorandum for the President, Mar. 25, 1971, RM, 1/1/71– [12/72], Box 2.

173. McLaughlin interview with the *Evangelist*, Aug. 2, 1972. Nixon met with World Council of Churches leaders on March 20, 1969, to discuss the role of the church in alleviating poverty, combating problems in the Middle East, and promoting disarmament ("Meeting with Representatives of the World Council of Churches," WHCF, RM, 1-69/12-70, Box 1). He also met with a group of ecumenical leaders on May 13, 1971.

174. Henderson, *Nixon Theology*, 39; Thomas C. Reeves, "Stuck in the Sixties," http://www.touchstonemag.com/archives/article.php?id=09-03-015-f.

175. E.g., RN to Bishop Leo Maher, Oct. 1, 1969, RM, RM3-1, Catholic, 69/70, Box 18; RN to the Diocese of Springfield, MA, July 22, 1970, ibid.; RN to John Cardinal Carberry, June 29, 1971, RM, 1/1/71– [12/72], Box 2; RN to *Today's Catholic Teacher*, Aug. 21, 1972, ibid.

176. See George Lardner, Jr., and Michael Dobbs, "New Tapes Reveal Depth of Nixon's Anti-Semitism," *WP*, Oct. 6, 1999, A31.

177. Kenneth Cole, memorandum for the President, Oct. 9, 1969. See also RN to Synagogue Council of America, Dec. 6, 1969, both in RM19, 3-2, Jewish, 69/70; RN to the Union of Orthodox Jewish Congregations of America, Apr. 26, 1972, RM, 3-2, Jewish, 1/1/71–2/29/72, Box 19.

178. E.g., RN to Harold Saperstein, president, NY Board of Rabbis, Nov. 26, 1970, RM3-2, Jewish 1-1-73 [8/74], Box 19.

179. On the 1960 election, see Nixon, *Six Crises*, 307–8, 327–28, 364–68, 421; Gary Scott Smith, *Faith and the Presidency: From George Washington to George W. Bush* (New York: Oxford University Press, 2006), 266–71; Shaun Casey, *The Making of a Catholic President: Kennedy vs. Nixon 1960* (New York: Oxford University Press, 2009); W. J. Rorabaugh, *The Real Making of the President: Kennedy, Nixon, and the 1960 Election* (Lawrence: University of Kansas Press, 2009). On the role of religion in the 1968 election, see Gibbs and Duffy, *Preacher*, 160–72.

180. Williams, "Religious Right," 153, 152.

181. John Brown, memorandum for Harry Dent, Dec. 19, 1969, RM, RM3-1, Catholic, 69/70, Box 18; Williams, "Religious Right," 152–53.

182. Roy Morey, memorandum for Ken Cole, Dec. 10, 1971, RM, RM3-1, Catholic, 1/1/71–12/72, Box 19; Arthur Finkelstein to Robert Marik, Dec. 16, 1971, ibid.

183. E.g., Jacques Torczyner, memorandum, May 20, 1971, RM3-2, Jewish, 1/1/71, Box 20; Charles Colson, memorandum for Len Garment, May 25, 1971, RM3-2, 1/171–2/29/72, Box 19.

184. "Nixon Refuses to Woo Jewish Voters," *Jewish Chronicle*, Feb. 11, 1972, 5.

185. See George Bush, memorandum for the President, Oct. 28, 1973, RM3-2, Jewish, 1/1/73, Box 19.

186. Gibbs and Duffy, *Preacher*, 182, 195, 205–6.

187. Wallace Henley, *The White House Mystique* (Old Tappan, NJ: Fleming Revell, 1976), 64–66.

188. Harry Dent, Schedule Proposal, Aug. 30, 1972, RM, 1/1/71–[12/72], Box 2; "Sen. McGovern Backed by GR Priest Group," n.d., no source, RM, 1/1/72–12-72, Box 2; "Should an Evangelical Support George McGovern?" *Grand Rapids Press*, Oct. 28, 1972, 9-A. See also Thomas Houser, "The Case for Nixon," *CC* 89 (Nov. 1, 1972), 1092–96; James Armstrong, "The Case of McGovern," ibid., 1096–98.

189. James Schaal to Rose Mary Woods, Oct, 31, 1972, RM, 11/1/72–12/72, Box 2.

190. Jeffrey Jones, "The Protestant and Catholic Vote," June 8, 2004, http://www.gallup.com/poll/11911/protestant-catholic-vote.aspx. See also "The Gallup Report: Changing the Pattern," June 17, 1972, RM3-1 Catholic 1-1 [12-72], Box 19.

191. Williams, "Religious Right," 153; "72's History, 73's Issues," *Eternity*, January 1973, 7.

192. Nixon, *Beyond Peace*, 239.

193. Suggested Remarks for Armed Forces Prayer Breakfast, Dec. 9, 1971, RM, PPP, 1/1/71, Box 6.

194. E.g., Nixon comment on memorandum, Haldeman to Nixon, July 18, 1970, Papers of the Nixon White House, 6:A. See Dean Kotlowski, "Nixon's Southern Strategy Revisited," *Journal of Policy History* 10 (April 1998), 214–15.

195. Nixon, *Arena*, 300.

196. Herbert Parmet, *Richard Nixon and His America* (Boston: Little, Brown, 1990), 21; Curtis, *Hubris*, 474; quotations in that order.

197. Kotlowski, "Southern Strategy," 210, 208; quotations in that order.

198. John Anderson, *Vision and Betrayal in America* (Waco, TX: Word, 1975), 115.

199. On Nixon's efforts to reform the welfare system, see Vincent and Vee Burke, *Nixon's Good Deed: Welfare Reform* (New York: Columbia University Press, 1974). In his "Statement on Transmitting to the Congress Proposals to Establish New National Wilderness Areas," Apr. 28, 1971, http://www.presidency.ucsb.edu/

ws/?pid=2991, Nixon proclaimed that the Bible taught that the first man "was placed by his Creator in a huge natural garden and charged 'to dress it and to keep it.' In the ages since, men have worked energetically at dressing and improving God's good earth—but their efforts at keeping and preserving it have been scant." Nixon also called drug usage a "spiritual problem" and invited eighty prominent religious leaders to a White House conference on the topic in March 1971, repudiated the 1970 report of the Commission on Obscenity and Pornography, recommended restructuring welfare, and opposed abortion. Some argue that these positions were rooted in his religious commitments to biblical moral law and the Protestant work ethic. See, for example, Ralph Moellering, "Civil Religion, the Nixon Theology and the Watergate Scandal," *CC* 90 (Sept. 26, 1973), 947–48. See also Richard Nixon, "Statement about Policy on Abortions at Military Base Hospitals in the United States," Apr. 3, 1971, http://www.presidency.ucsb.edu/ws/index.php?pid=2963&st: "I cannot square my personal [religious] belief in the sanctity of life" with "unrestricted abortion policies" or "abortion on demand."

200. C. L. Sulzberger, "Nixon, in Interview, Says This Is Probably Last War," *NYT*, Mar. 10, 1971, 1.

201. Richard Nixon, "Inaugural Address," Jan. 20, 1969, http://www.presidency. ucsb.edu/ws/index.php?pid=1941&st=&st1=; see also "Nixon as Peacemaker," *CC* 86 (Feb. 5, 1969), 171.

202. Richard Nixon, "Radio Address on Foreign Policy," Nov. 4, 1972, http://www. presidency.ucsb.edu/ws/index.php?pid=3692&st=.

203. RN to Abraham Feldman, Dec. 22, 1971, RM6, PPP, 11/1/71.

204. Nixon, "Foreign Policy."

205. Richard Nixon, "First Annual Report to the Congress on United States Foreign Policy for the 1970's," Feb. 18, 1970, http://www.presidency.ucsb. edu/ws/?pid=2835. Nixon also presented "Building for Peace" (1971), "The Emerging Structure of Peace" (1972), and "Shaping a Durable Peace" (1973) to Congress.

206. Sulzberger, "Nixon," 1, 14. The Philadelphia (Friends) Yearly Meeting responded in an open letter that Nixon's position was not their "understanding of the Quaker peace testimony" ("Quakers Assail Nixon War Stand," *NYT*, Apr. 8, 1971).

207. Nixon, "President's Mother"; Sulzberger, "Nixon," 1, 14.

208. "Toasts . . . at a State Dinner in New Delhi," July 31, 1969, http://www.presidency.ucsb.edu/ws/index.php?pid=2165&st=.

209. RN to Charles Bennison, Apr. 22, 1974, RM3-3, Prot. 1/1/73, Box 20.

210. Nixon, "Armed Forces Prayer Breakfast."

211. Richard Nixon, "Radio Address on Defense Policy," Oct. 29, 1972, http://www. presidency.ucsb.edu/ws/?pid=3672.

212. Richard Nixon, "Remarks at the National Prayer Breakfast," Feb. 1, 1972, http://www.presidency.ucsb.edu/ws/?pid=3597.

213. Richard Nixon, "Remarks on Accepting the Presidential Nomination of the Republican National Convention," Aug. 23, 1972, http://www.presidency.ucsb.edu/ws/?pid=3537.

214. RN to A. Patricia Palmer, May 14, 1972, WHCF, Peace, 2 of 2, 1/71–12/72.

215. E.g., Richard Nixon, "Memorial Day Statement," May 28, 1972, http://www.presidency.ucsb.edu/ws/?pid=3435.

216. E.g., Nixon to Phil Regan, RM, PPP, 1/1/71, Box 6. Forty governors and a hundred mayors had urged their constituents to pray for Nixon's trip (Henley, *Mystique*, 71).

217. RN to Alan Rowley, Apr. 17, 1972, WHCF, Peace, 2 of 2, 1/71–12/72.

218. E.g., RN to Seymour Siegel, Feb. 15, 1972; RN to Mrs. Dean Ostrum, May 21, 1973, RM, RSWH, 4/16/73–10/15/73, Box 17.

219. E. Ezra Ellis to RN, Aug. 6, 1971, WHCF, Peace, 1/71–12/72, 1 of 2.

220. Trueblood to RN, Nov. 4, 1971, RM, RSWH, 10/1/71–12/31/72, Box 15.

221. Nixon, "First Annual Report."

222. Memorandum for the President's File, June 2, 1972, Congressional leadership meeting, POF, Box 88, as quoted in Reeves, *Nixon*, 497.

223. RN to Reeves Wetherill, July 19, 1971, RM3-3, 1/1/71, Box 20.

224. "Man of the Year: Nixon: Determined to Make a Difference," *Time*, Jan. 3, 1972, http://www.time.com/time/magazine/article/0,9171,879010,00.html. See also Nixon, *No More Vietnams* (New York: Arbor House, 1985), 236–37.

225. Nixon, "Foreign Policy"; Nixon, "Remarks at the National Prayer Breakfast," Feb. 1, 1973, http://www.presidency.ucsb.edu/ws/?pid=3941.

226. Nixon, "Decision to Resign."

227. Henry Kissinger, "Eulogy for Richard Nixon," http://www.speaking-tips.com/Eulogies/Nixon-Kissinger-Eulogy.aspx.

228. E.g., Franklin Littell, "Nixon and American Isolationism," *CC* 90 (Mar. 14, 1973), 310–11.

229. Moellering, "Civil Religion," 948.

230. Henderson, *Nixon Theology*, 169–73.

231. "Senator Sam Ervin Explains the Meaning and Consequences of Watergate" (1974), http://www.wwnorton.com/college/history/archive/resources/documents/ch35_04.htm.

232. Aitken, *Nixon*, 468 (first two quotations), 467 (third quotation).

233. Gergen, *Eyewitness*, 97.

234. Stanley Chambers to Alexander Haig, June 5, 1974, RM, PPP, 1/1/73, Box 6.

235. RN to the National Prayer and Fast Committee. This committee included six senators and fifty Congressmen. See various papers in RM, PPP, 1/1/73, Box 6.

236. Anderson, *Vision and Betrayal*, 77–78, 114.

237. "Watergate Wrangle," *CT* 17 (Apr. 13, 1973), 31 (first quotation); "Watergate," *CT*, 46 (second quotation).

238. "Fifteen Turbulent Years," *CT* 18 (Oct. 30, 1974), 24.

239. Wesley Pippert, "Journalism and the Forgotten Virtues," *Spectrum*, Winter 1977, 9. See also David Howard, "Nixon's Watergate—Man's Depravity," *CT* 21 (June 3, 1977), 980–82; Colson, *Born Again*, 11.

240. Mayer, "Disownment," 1001–3; first quotation from 1002, second from 1003, third, fourth, and fifth from 1001.

241. T. Eugene Coffin, "Richard Nixon and the Quaker Fellowship," *CC* 91 (Jan. 2, 1974), 5–6; first two quotations from 5, last two from 6. See also "Nixon and the Church," *CT* 18 (Feb. 1, 1974), 43–44: Coffin explained that by regularly communicating with the church and making financial contributions, Nixon maintained "his status as an active nonresident member" (43).

242. "Advice from Some Friends," *Newsweek*, Jan. 14, 1974, 84; "Richard Nixon and American Religion," *CC* 111 (May 11, 1994), 488. There were about 800 local Quaker meetings (congregations). Although disownment still existed in Friends' books of discipline, it had only been used a couple of times in the twentieth century, usually against those who had sexually abused children, so the call to disown Nixon was purely political (H. Larry Ingle, email to author, Aug. 12, 2011).

243. Baruch Korff, *The Personal Nixon: Staying on the Summit* (Washington, DC: Fairness, 1974), 46 (first quotation); Summers, *Arrogance*, 13.

244. Small, *Presidency*, 309. Small also lauds Nixon for ending the draft, giving 18-year-olds the right to vote, and establishing OSHA. On Nixon's role in broadening the Republican Party, see William Berman, *America's Right Turn: From Nixon to Bush* (Baltimore: Johns Hopkins University Press, 1994), 5–20; Mary Brennan, *Turning Right in the Sixties: The Conservative Capture of the GOP* (Chapel Hill: University of North Carolina Press, 1995), 120–37.

245. Aitken, *Nixon*, 458–59.

246. Kissinger, "Eulogy."

247. Gergen, *Eyewitness*, 57 (first quotation), 59, 61 (second quotation).

248. Aitken, *Nixon*, 425.

249. Melvin Small, "Evaluating Nixon's Presidency—Without Watergate," *New England Journal of History* 56 (Winter 1999–Spring 2000), 1.

250. Gergen, *Eyewitness*, 19.

251. Bundy, *Tangled Web*, 518.

252. Reeves, *Nixon*, 15.

253. Gergen, *Eyewitness*, 61, 102; quotations in that order.

254. Small, *Presidency*, 309.

255. Quoted in Curtis, *Hubris*, 623.

256. Small, "Nixon's Presidency," 12.

257. Larry Berman, *No Peace, No Honor: Nixon, Kissinger, and Betrayal in Vietnam* (New York: Free Press, 2001).

258. E.g., Jim Rice, "The Last Comeback of Richard Nixon," *Sojourners* 23 (July 1994), 10.

259. Price, *With Nixon*, 29; Nixon, 1972 "National Prayer Breakfast"; Moellering, "Civil Religion," 948 (first quotation), 950, 951 (second quotation).

260. Wicker, "Nixon," 141, 139.

261. Aitken, *Nixon*, 339.

262. Small, "Nixon's Presidency," 1–2.

263. Aitken, "Nixon Character," 243–44.

264. Quoted in James Reston, Jr., *The Conviction of Richard Nixon: The Untold Story of the Frost/Nixon Interviews* (New York: Harmony House, 2007), 9.

265. Henderson, *Nixon Theology*, 192–93, 28, 203, 207; first quotation from 192, second and third from 193, fourth from 28, fifth from 203, sixth from 207.

266. Quoted in "Nixon and American Religion," 488.

267. Niebuhr, "King's Chapel," 212.

268. Moellering, "Civil Religion," 947 (quotations). See Streiker and Strober, *New Majority*, 169–87.

269. Mark Hatfield, *Between a Rock and a Hard Place* (Waco, TX: Word Books, 1976), 4. See also Raymond Haberski, Jr., *God and War: American Civil Religion since 1945* (New Brunswick, NJ: Rutgers University Press, 2012), 100–102.

270. Henderson, *Nixon Theology*, xii.

271. RN, interview with Aitken, Mar. 14, 1992, *Nixon*, 576. See also Nixon, *Arena*, 369; H. Larry Ingle, *Nixon's First Cover-up: The Religious Life of a Quaker President* (Columbia: University of Missouri Press, 2014), "Introduction," 1; Aitken, "Nixon Character," 246; Safire, *Before the Fall*, 599–606, 702.

272. Aitken, "Nixon Character," 241–42.

273. Ingle, "Introduction." See also Milton Mayer, *The Nature of the Beast* (Amherst: University of Massachusetts Press, 1975), 310; Henderson, *Nixon Theology*, 44; "His Quaker Upbringing Shaped His Personality, Biographers Say, but Not Necessarily His Actions," Apr. 30, 1994, Religious News Service, http://articles.latimes.com/1994-04-30/local/me-52214_1_richard-nixon.

274. Quoted in Gergen, *Eyewitness*, 78.

CHAPTER 9

1. E.g., "Remarks and a Question-and-Answer Session with the Magazine Publishers of America," July 17, 1990, http://www.presidency.ucsb.edu/ws/?pid=18685.

2. Wade Clark Roof and William McKinney, *American Mainline Religion: Its Changing Shape and Future* (New Brunswick, NJ: Rutgers University Press, 1987), 109–13, 195–213. See also David Holmes, *A Brief History of the Episcopal Church* (Valley Forge, PA: Trinity Press International, 1993), 159–78; Richard Prichard, *A History of the Episcopal Church* (Harrisburg, PA: Morehouse Publishing, 1999), 277, 283–85, 294.

3. Doug Wead, "George Bush: Where Does He Stand?" *Christian Herald*, June 1986, 14 (first quotation), 15 (second and third quotations).

4. Roof and McKinney, *American Mainline Religion*, 26–39, 223 (quotation); Alasdair MacIntyre, *After Virtue: A Study in Moral Theory* (Notre Dame, IN: University of Notre Dame Press, 1984); James Davison Hunter, *Culture Wars: The Struggle to Define America* (New York: Basic Books, 1991); John Pollock et al., *The Connecticut Mutual Life Report on American Values in the 1980s: The Impact of Belief* (Hartford: Connecticut Mutual Life Insurance Co, 1981); Christopher Lasch, *The Culture of Narcissism* (New York: Norton, 1979); Richard Neuhaus, *The Naked Public Square: Religion and Democracy in America* (Grand Rapids, MI: Eerdmans, 1984); Richard Merelman, *Making Something of Ourselves: On Culture and Politics in the United States* (Berkeley: University of California Press, 1984); Daniel Yankelovich, *New Rule: Searching for Self-Fulfillment in a World Turned Upside Down* (New York: Random House, 1981); Robert Bellah et al., *Habits of the Heart* (Berkeley: University of California Press, 1985); Robert Wuthnow, *The Restructuring of American Religion: Society and Faith since World War II* (Princeton, NJ: Princeton University Press, 1988); Dean Hoge, Benton Johnson, and Donald Luidens, *Vanishing Boundaries: The Religion of Mainline Protestant Baby Boomers* (Louisville, KY: Westminster John Knox Press, 1994); Roger Finke and Rodney Stark, *The Churching of America, 1776–1990: Winners and Losers in Our Religious Economy* (New Brunswick, NJ: Rutgers University Press, 1992); C. Kirk Hadaway and David Roozen, eds., *Church and Denominational Growth* (Nashville, TN: Abingdon Press, 1993); Thomas Reeves, *The Empty Church: The Suicide of Liberal Christianity* (New York: Free Press, 1996); George Lindbeck, *The Nature of Doctrine: Religion and Theology in a Post Liberal Age* (Philadelphia: Westminster Press, 1984); Gary Dorrien, *The Making of American Liberal Theology: Crisis, Irony, and Postmodernity, 1950–2005* (Louisville, KY: Westminster John Knox Press, 2006).

5. The best sources are Kjell Lejon, "Religion and the Presidency of George H. W. Bush," in Gaston Espinoza, ed., *Religion and the American Presidency: George Washington to George W. Bush* (New York: Columbia University Press, 2009), 395–423; Kjell Lejon, *George H. W. Bush: Faith, Presidency, and Public Theology* (Frankfurt am Main, Germany: Peter Lang, 2014); David Holmes, *The Faiths of the Postwar Presidents: From Truman to Clinton* (Athens: University of Georgia Press, 2012), 194–214; and Richard Hutcheson, Jr., "Religion in the Bush White House," *CC* 106 (Jan. 18, 1989), 37–38.

6. E.g., George Bush, "Remarks at the Annual Convention of the National Religious Broadcasters," Jan. 29, 1990, http://www.presidency.ucsb.edu/ws/?pid=18087; Bush, "Remarks at the Annual Convention of the National Religious Broadcasters," Jan. 27, 1992, http://www.presidency.ucsb.edu/ws/?pid=20540.

7. Bush used the phrase "one nation under God" in fifty-three of his public statements and addresses in four years as president, considerably more than Reagan, Clinton, or George W. Bush did during their eight years in office.

8. George Bush, "Remarks at a Barbecue in Beeville, Texas," Dec. 27, 1989, http://www.presidency.ucsb.edu/ws/?pid=17981.

9. George Bush, "Remarks at the Annual National Prayer Breakfast," May 4, 1989, http://www.presidency.ucsb.edu/ws/?pid=16997.

10. George Bush, "Remarks at the National Prayer Breakfast," Jan. 30, 1992, http://www.presidency.ucsb.edu/ws/?pid=20552.

11. George Bush, "Proclamation 6243—For a National Day of Prayer, February 3, 1991," Feb. 1, 1991, http://www.presidency.ucsb.edu/ws/?pid=47257.

12. George Bush, "Remarks to the Community in Thomasville, North Carolina," Oct. 21, 1992, http://www.presidency.ucsb.edu/ws/?pid=21634.

13. Quoted in Wead, "Bush," 16.

14. "Bishops Visit Bush," Aug. 19, 1989, *WP*.

15. "Episcopalians of the Year," *The Anglican Digest*, 1991, 30.

16. Herbert Parmet, *George Bush: The Life of a Lone Star Yankee* (New York: Scribner, 1997), 18; Fitzhugh Green, *George Bush: An Intimate Portrait* (New York: Hippocrene Press, 1991), 19; David Aikman, *A Man of Faith: The Spiritual Journey of George W. Bush* (Nashville, TN: W. Publishing Group, 2004), 23; Doug Wead, *The Raising of a President: The Mothers and Fathers of Our Nation's Leaders* (New York: Atria Books, 2005), 269 ff.

17. Parmet, *Bush*, 31; Joe Hyams, *Flight of the Avenger: George Bush at War* (New York: Berkeley Books, 1992), 27.

18. George Bush with Victor Gold, *Looking Forward: An Autobiography* (New York: Bantam Books, 1988), 27; Nicholas King, *George Bush: A Biography* (New York: Dodd, Mead, 1980), 18.

19. Bush said this as part of a family testimonial to her in 1985; quoted in Aikman, *Bush*, 23.

20. Doro Bush Koch, *My Father, My President: A Personal Account of the Life of George H. W. Bush* (New York: Warner Books, 2006), 4.

21. M. W. Stackpole, "A School Church at an Academy," *Education* 10:6 (Dec. 1915), 584–88; Claude Moore Fuess, *An Old New England School: A History of Phillip Academy* (Boston: Houghton Mifflin, 1917), 428; George Bush, "Remarks at the Bicentennial Convocation of Phillips Academy," Nov. 5, 1989, http://www.presidency.ucsb.edu/ws/?pid=17753.

22. See Doug Wead, *George Bush: Man of Integrity* (Eugene, OR: Harvest House, 1988), 1–8; George H. W. Bush, *All the Best, George Bush: My Life in Letters* (New York: Simon and Schuster, 1999), 49–52; Parmet, *Bush*, 50 ff.; King, *Bush*, 30 ff.; Bush and Gold, *Looking Forward*, 38–40.

23. Wead, *President*, 284.

24. Parmet, *Bush*, 79; Myra Gutin, *Barbara Bush: Presidential Matriarch* (Lawrence: University Press of Kansas), 13.

25. Bush and Gold, *Looking Forward*, 67–69 (quotation from 69); Gutin, *Barbara Bush*, 13–15. See also GB to Mr. and Mrs. Charles Antone, Sept. 25, 1995, in Bush, *Best*, 592; Barbara Bush, *Barbara Bush: A Memoir* (New York: Scribner's Sons, 1994), 44.

26. Paul Harvey, "George Bush on Religion," *Gettysburg Times*, Feb. 16, 1989. See also Bush, *Barbara Bush*, 42; Pamela Kilian, *Barbara Bush* (New York: St. Martin's Press, 2002), 43.

27. George Bush, "Inaugural Address," Jan. 20, 1989, http://www.presidency.ucsb.edu/ws/?pid=16610.

28. George Bush, "Address Accepting the Presidential Nomination at the Republican National Convention," Aug. 18, 1988, http://www.presidency.ucsb.edu/ws/?pid=25955.

29. George Bush, "Remarks at the Annual Convention of the National Religious Broadcasters," Jan. 28 1991, http://www.presidency.ucsb.edu/ws/?pid=19250.

30. Bush, "Inaugural Address." Cf. Bush, "National Prayer Breakfast," May 4, 1989.

31. George Bush, "Message on the Observance of Christmas," Dec. 18, 1989, http://bushlibrary.tamu.edu/research/public_papers.php?id=1344&year=&month.

32. George Bush, "Proclamation 6253—National Doctors Day, 1991," Feb. 21, 1991, http://www.presidency.ucsb.edu/ws/?pid=47267; Bush, "Proclamation 6181—Religious Freedom Week, 1990," Sept. 20, 1990, http://www.presidency.ucsb.edu/ws/?pid=1888; Bush, "Proclamation 6147—Father's Day, 1990," June 14, 1990, http://www.presidency.ucsb.edu/ws/?pid=1859; Bush, "Remarks to the Polish National Assembly in Warsaw," July 10, 1989, http://www.presidency.ucsb.edu/ws/?pid=17264.

33. George Bush, "Remarks to Representatives of Public Administration Groups," Oct. 24, 1991, http://www.presidency.ucsb.edu/ws/?pid=20134.

34. George Bush, "Remarks at the Annual Southern Baptist Convention," June 6, 1991, http://www.presidency.ucsb.edu/ws/?pid=19664.

35. Bush, "National Prayer Breakfast," May 4, 1989.

36. Bush, "Public Administration Groups." Cf. Bush, "Proclamation 6380—Thanksgiving Day, 1991," Nov. 25, 1991, http://www.presidency.ucsb.edu/ws/?pid=72485.

37. George Bush, "Remarks at the National Affairs Briefing in Dallas," Aug. 22, 1992, http://www.presidency.ucsb.edu/ws/?pid=21358; Bush, 1992 "National Religious Broadcasters."

38. George Bush, "Remarks at the Liberty University Commencement Ceremony," May 12, 1990, http://www.presidency.ucsb.edu/ws/?pid=18479.

39. George Bush, "Proclamation 6508—Thanksgiving Day, 1992," Nov. 20, 1992, http://www.presidency.ucsb.edu/ws/?pid=72486.

40. George Bush, "Proclamation 6394—Year of Thanksgiving for the Blessings of Liberty, 1991," Dec. 16, 1991, http://www.presidency.ucsb.edu/ws/?pid=20353.

41. George Bush, "Proclamation 6104—National Day of Prayer, 1990," Mar. 6, 1990, http://www.presidency.ucsb.edu/ws/?pid=1820.

42. Bush, "National Affairs Briefing."

43. Bush, "National Affairs Briefing."

44. George Bush, "Address on Administration Goals before a Joint Session of Congress," Feb. 9, 1989, http://www.presidency.ucsb.edu/ws/?pid=16660.

45. George Bush, "Remarks at the Cheltenham High School Commencement Ceremony," June 19, 1989, http://www.presidency.ucsb.edu/ws/?pid=17171.

46. Bush, 1992 "National Religious Broadcasters."

47. GB to Shirley and Randy Forbes, Oct. 16, 1992, White House Office of Record Management 358104 (hereinafter cited as WHORM). Religious Matters 020 (hereinafter cited as RM).

48. Bush, "Proclamation 6100—International Year of Bible Reading, 1990," Feb. 22, 1990, http://www.presidency.ucsb.edu/ws/?pid=1816.

49. Bush, "Bible Reading."

50. Wead, "Bush," 14 (first quotation); Larry Witham, "Diverse Faiths Helped Mold Candidates for White House," *WT*, Apr. 14, 1992 (second quotation); David Aikman, "Interview with Billy Graham: Preachers, Politics, and Temptation," *Time*, May 28, 1990, 12 (third and fourth quotations).

51. Bush, "Southern Baptist Convention."

52. GB to Wilson, Feb. 14, 1992, WHORM 313924, RM020. Cf. GB to Susan Overbey, Nov. 30, 1992, WHORM, 366332, RM020.

53. Bush, *Barbara Bush*, 215.

54. Richard Abel to GB, Apr. 25, 1991, WHORM 250311, RM020.

55. David Troyer to GB, July 19, 1989, WHORM 60416, RM020.

56. George Delo to GB, Apr. 5, 1991, White House Office of Public Liaison, Metz, L. A. files, Churches, Black 07162–044 (hereinafter cited as WHOPL).

57. George Bush, "Remarks at a Prayer Breakfast in Houston," Aug. 20, 1992, http://www.presidency.ucsb.edu/ws/?pid=21350.

58. GB to A. Max Gore, Mar. 9, 1990, WHORM 124385, RM020.

59. George Bush, "Remarks at the Annual National Prayer Breakfast," Feb. 2, 1989, http://www.presidency.ucsb.edu/ws/?pid=16637.

60. Bush, "Southern Baptist Convention."

61. GB to Ezra Taft Benson, Jan. 31, 1989, WHORM 004163, RM020; Bush, "Prayer Breakfast in Houston."

62. Donnie Ratcliffe, "President Bush and the Power of Prayer," *WP*, Jan. 8, 1991; Bush, "Prayer Breakfast in Houston."

63. E.g., GB to Catherine Douglass, Mar. 6, 1989, WHORM 015002, RM020; GB to Jean Stevens, Mar. 26, 1991, WHORM 212157, RM020; GB to Richard Halverson, Mar. 22, 1989, WHORM 032539, RM020. See also George Bush, "Remarks to the National Association of Evangelicals in Chicago," Mar. 3, 1992, http://www.presidency.ucsb.edu/ws/?pid=20677.

64. Mark Nehrbas to GB, Mar. 1, 1991, WHORM 227089, RM020.

65. E.g., "Offering a Prayer for the Nation's Chief Executive," *Daily Journal*, Feb. 25, 1989.

66. George Bush, "Proclamation 5936—National Day of Prayer and Thanksgiving, 1989," Jan. 20, 1989, http://www.presidency.ucsb.edu/ws/?pid=20424.

67. Bush, "Southern Baptist Convention." As president, Bush referred to Lincoln turning to God in prayer because he had nowhere else to go at least thirteen times.

68. Bush, "National Day of Prayer, 1990."

69. George Bush, "Remarks to the Knights of Columbus Supreme Council Convention in New York City," Aug. 5, 1992, http://www.presidency.ucsb.edu/ws/?pid=21300.

70. Lejon, "Bush," 400–403; e.g., George Bush, "Statement on the American Hostages in Lebanon," Aug. 10, 1989, http://www.presidency.ucsb.edu/ws/?pid=17419.

71. Bush, "National Association of Evangelicals."

72. George Bush, "Remarks at the Annual **National Prayer Breakfast**," Feb. 2, 1989, http://www.presidency.ucsb.edu/ws/?pid=16637.

73. Bush, "National Prayer Breakfast," Jan. 30, 1992.

74. E.g., George Bush, "Christmas," 1989; Bush, "Message on the Observance of Christmas," Dec. 18, 1990, http://www.presidency.ucsb.edu/ws/?pid=19165.

75. George Bush, "Message on the Observance of Christmas," Dec. 11, 1991, http://www.presidency.ucsb.edu/ws/?pid=20329.

76. George Bush, "Message on the Observance of Christmas," Dec. 8, 1992, http://www.presidency.ucsb.edu/ws/?pid=21764.

77. Bush, "Christmas," 1990.

78. GB to the Sisters of the Resurrection," Jan. 3, 1991, WHORM 209008, Messages 002-01 (hereinafter cited as ME).

79. GB to the 70th General Convention of the Episcopal Church," July 10, 1991, WHORM 254058, RM034-04.

80. GB to Harry Robinson, National Conference of Christians and Jews, WHORM 012211, ME002-01.

81. George Bush, "Proclamation 6394—Year of Thanksgiving for the Blessings of Liberty, 1991," Dec. 16, 1991, http://www.presidency.ucsb.edu/ws/?pid=20353. Cf. Bush, "International Year of Bible Reading, 1990."

82. Bush, "National Prayer Breakfast," May 4, 1989.

83. George Bush, "Address . . . on the Cessation of the Persian Gulf Conflict," Mar. 6, 1991, http://www.presidency.ucsb.edu/ws/?pid=19364 (quotation); Bush, "Remarks and a Question-and-Answer Session at the B'nai B'rith International Convention," Sept. 8, 1992, http://www.presidency.ucsb.edu/ws/?pid=21429; Bush, "Remarks at the International Drug Enforcement Conference in Miami," Apr. 27, 1989, http://www.presidency.ucsb.edu/ws/?pid=16974.

84. Wead, "Bush," 17.

85. George Bush, "Remarks at the Memorial Service for Crewmembers of the U.S.S. Iowa in Norfolk," Apr. 24, 1989, http://www.presidency.ucsb.edu/ws/?pid=16961.

86. George Bush, "Proclamation 6257—For National Days of Thanksgiving, April 5–7, 1991," Mar. 7, 1991, http://www.presidency.ucsb.edu/ws/?pid=47271.

87. E.g., GB to Juanita Wayne, Apr. 7, 1989, WHORM 028329, ME001-03; GB to Charles Nash, Apr. 21, 1989, WHORM 029575, ME001-03; GB to Mr. and Mrs.

Alfred Ball, June 16, 1989, WHORM 052912, ME001-03; GB to Mr. and Mrs. Joseph Bogucki, June 15, 1989, WHORM 365818, ME001-03.

88. GB to Mr. and Mrs. Alvin Adams, Apr. 28, 1989, WHORM, 036416, ME001-03; GB to Mr. and Mrs. Douglas Barlow, Feb. 19, 1991; WHORM 221798, ME001-03; Bush diary entry, Mar. 29, 1991, in Bush, *Best*, 515, diary entry, Nov. 19, 1992, ibid., 577.

89. Bush, *Best*, 409.

90. Jeffrey Engel, ed., *The China Diary of George H. W. Bush: The Making of a Global President* (Princeton, NJ: Princeton University Press, 2008), 26–27, 51, 80, 91, 128, 156, 218, 226–27, 340; Parmet, *Bush*, 177.

91. "Exchange . . . Following the Release of American Hostage Edward Tracy," Aug. 11, 1991, http://www.presidency.ucsb.edu/ws/?pid=19892.

92. http://www.nationalcathedral.org/about/presidnetialInugural1989.shtml.

93. Bush, *Best*, 409.

94. GB to G. Bradford Hall, Mar. 5, 1990, WHORM 122034, RM020. Cf. GB to Robert Howes, May 1, 1988, in Bush, *Best*, 425.

95. George Bush, "Remarks at Chongmenwen Christian Church in Beijing, Feb. 26, 1989, http://www.presidency.ucsb.edu/ws/?pid=16695.

96. GB to C. Frederick Barbee, June 25, 1991, WHORM 246532, RM035.

97. Quoted in Kim Lawson, "Bush Affirms Role of Religion in Public Life," *CT*, Apr. 29, 1991, 39.

98. E.g., Leigh Ann Metzger to John Morrett, Apr. 7, 1991, WHORM 213406, RM020. See also Larry Witham, "Security Won't Bar Bushes' Regular Church Attendance," *WT*, Jan. 9, 1989. Bush testified that St. Ann's "has given me so much strength and inner peace" (GB to John Allin, Sr., Kennebunkport, ME, Aug. 28, 1992, WHORM 348543, RM020). As vice president, when in Washington, Bush worshipped primarily at the National Cathedral and 19th Street Baptist Church (Wead, "Bush," 17). Over the years, Bush sometimes worshipped with African Methodist Episcopal congregations. See also GB to AME Anniversary Dinner, Feb. 18, 1989, WHORM 006947, ME002-01.

99. "Episcopalians of the Year," 30.

100. Walter Hichens to GB, Feb. 27, 1991; Mary McClure to Walter Hichens, Mar. 18, 1991, WHORM 217593, RM020; Larry Witham, "Prayer Meetings Have a Way of Easing Politicians' Woes," *WT*, Aug. 6, 1990.

101. George Bush, "Remarks and a Question-and-Answer Session at a Luncheon Hosted by the Commonwealth Club in San Francisco," Feb. 7, 1990, http://www.presidency.ucsb.edu/ws/?pid=18128; Bush, "Remarks during a Thanksgiving Day Service on Board the U.S.S. Nassau in the Persian Gulf," Nov. 22, 1990, http://www.presidency.ucsb.edu/ws/?pid=19087; Bush, "Remarks Following an Audience with Pope John Paul II," May 27, 1989, http://www.presidency.ucsb.edu/ws/?pid=17066; Bush, "Remarks at the Commercial Appeal's Thanksgiving Celebration in Memphis," Nov. 22, 1989, http://www.presidency.

ucsb.edu/ws/?pid=17864; Bush, "Remarks to the Christian Coalition Road to Victory Conference"; Bush, "Remarks to the Bethesda-Chevy Chase Rescue Squad," Apr. 25, 1990, http://www.presidency.ucsb.edu/ws/?pid=18412; Bush, "Remarks to Firefighters and Law Enforcement Personnel in Los Angeles," May 8, 1992, http://www.presidency.ucsb.edu/ws/?pid=20939; Bush, "Remarks on Signing the Giant Sequoia in National Forests Proclamation," July 14, 1992, http://www.presidency.ucsb.edu/ws/?pid=21228; Bush, "Proclamation 6355—National Children's Day, 1991," Oct. 11, 1991, http://www.presidency.ucsb.edu/ws/?pid=20095. Bush cited or quoted the Golden Rule nine times and the story of the Good Samaritan fourteen times in his speeches.

102. George Bush, "Remarks to Religious and Ethnic Groups in Garfield, New Jersey," July 21, 1992, http://www.presidency.ucsb.edu/ws/?pid=21244.

103. Bill Phillips to Lee Atwater and Doug Wead, Mar. 10, 1986; Wead to GB, Apr. 3, 1986; Wead to Ron Kaufman, May 13, 1986; Wead to Fuller, Aug. 21, 1986; all in Bush, V.P. Records, Office of the Chief of Staff, Craig Fuller Files, Evangelicals—Doug Wead [14298].

104. Bob Schieffer and Gary Paul Gates, *The Acting President* (New York: Dutton, 1989), 357; Kenneth Wald and Allison Calhoun-Brown, *Religion and Politics in the United States* (Lanham, MD: Rowman and Littlefield, 2011), 211.

105. See "Bush Battles the 'Wimp Factor,'" *Newsweek*, Oct. 19, 1987, 28–33; George Plimpton, "Sportsman Born and Bred," *Sports Illustrated* 69 (Dec. 26, 1988), 140–48.

106. See David Broder, Bob Woodward, and Dan Quayle, *The Man Who Would Be President: Dan Quayle* (New York: Simon and Schuster, 1992), 186–88, and Dan Quayle, *Standing Firm: A Vice-Presidential Memoir* (New York: HarperCollins, 1994), 14, 44, 57–58, 73, 262–63.

107. E.g., Bush, "Thanksgiving Day, 1992."

108. Jon Murray to GB, Dec. 19, 1988, WHORM 003896, Public Relations 013–15.

109. Murray to GB, Dec. 19, 1988; Gray to Murray, Feb. 21, 1989, both in WHORM 041388, RM030.

110. Murray to Gray, May 4, 1989; Murray to GB, May 4, 1989, both in WHORM 037871, Speeches; Nelson Lund to Charles Cheves, June 1, 1989, WHORM 040407, RM030.

111. Murray to Congressmen, Feb. 21, 1990, WHORM 157715, RM030.

112. Larry Witham, "Church Backs Away from Dukakis Stand," *WT*, Nov. 2, 1988; George Cornell, "Presidential Nominees Claim Strong Religious Ties," *WP*, Oct. 1, 1988; Rowland Evans and Robert Novak, "A Question of Orthodoxy," *WP*, May 5, 1988; James George Jatras, "Candidate Dukakis and the Church: 'Flatly Untruthful,'" *WP*, June 4, 1988.

113. Garry Wills, "The Secularist Prejudice," *CC* 107 (Oct. 24, 1990), 973.

114. GB to William Buckley, Jr., Sept. 9, 1987, in Bush, *Best*, 384.

115. Marjorie Hyer, "Shifting Religious Alliances Forming Strange New Political Bedfellows," *WP*, Nov. 5, 1988.

116. Michael Beschloss, "George Bush, 1989–1993," in Robert Wilson, ed., *Character above All: The Presidents from FDR to George Bush* (New York: Simon and Schuster, 1995), 224 (quotation), 236; David Mervin, "An Evaluation of the Presidency of George Bush," in William Levantrosser and Rosanna Perotti, eds., *A Noble Calling: Character and the George H. W. Bush Presidency* (Westport, CT: Praeger, 2004), 103.

117. Daniel Williams, *God's Own Party: The Making of the Christian Right* (New York: Oxford University Press, 2010), 221.

118. Bush, *Barbara Bush*, 248; Bush diary entry, Nov. 7, 1988, in Bush, *Best*, 404.

119. Megan Rosenfeld, "The President's Preacher," *WP*, Jan. 18, 1991; Wead, *Integrity*, 44–45 (quotation from 44).

120. GB to A. Bartlett Giamatti, July 28, 1982, *Best*, 320; Bush, 1990 "National Religious Broadcasters."

121. GB to Halverson, Mar. 22, 1989, WHORM 032539, RM020. Also see GB to Halverson, Apr. 5, 1992, WHORM 323335, RM020. For examples of Halverson's messages to Bush, see 1 Tim. 2:1–2 (Mar. 27, 1989); Phil. 4:4–5 (May 22, 1989); Isa. 40:31 (Feb. 27, 1990); Phil. 4:6–7 (Dec. 4, 1990), and James 1:5 (Jan. 22, 1991), all in WHORM 323335, RM020.

122. E.g., "Question-and-Answer Session with Teachers at the Shiloh Child Development Center," May 9, 1989, http://www.presidency.ucsb.edu/ws/?pid=17012; Bush, 1990 "National Religious Broadcasters"; GB to the General Conference of the African Methodist Episcopal Zion Church, July 28, 1992, WHORM 336888, ME 002-01.

123. See Bush, "Liberty University."

124. Jim Pinkerton to Chris Winston, Nov. 20, 1989, WHORM 091244, RM020.

125. "Evangelicals Complain Bush Is Ignoring Them," *WP*, Aug. 5, 1989.

126. Ralph Reed, "Active Faith: How Christians Are Changing the Soul of American Politics," http://www.washingtonpost.com/wp-srv/style/longterm/books/chap1/active.htm. However, the meeting focused on issues that were important to evangelicals—education, abortion, child care, and voluntary school prayer (Curt Smith, Memorandum for the president, Nov. 19, 1989, WHORM 091244, RM020).

127. Dee Fink of Women's Aglow Fellowship, International to Kathy Rust, Sept. 18, 1990, WHOPL, Metzger, L. A. Files, Doug Wead Firing—Reactions, 04380. Aglow also urged its members to write a letter to Bush and provided several sample letters.

128. Ray Waddle, "Bush Invitation to Gays Angers Baptist Leader," *Nashville Tennessean*, May 5, 1990, 1A–2A; Jerry Vines, "Bush and the Baptists," *WP*, July 1, 1990; Frank Murray, "Bush Sending 'Mixed Signals' on Gays, Evangelical Leaders Say," *WT*, Apr. 22, 1992 (quotations).

129. E.g., John Foust to GB, Sept. 21, 1990, WHOPL, Metzger, L. A. Files, Doug Wead Firing—Reactions, 04380.

130. Chapman to GB, July 9, 1992; Land to GB, July 1, 1992; Cizik to GB, June 30, 1992; all in WHOPL, Metzger, L. A. Files, Doug Wead Firing—Reactions, 04380.

131. Waddle, "Bush Invitation," 2A; Ann Devroy, "Bush Faults Special Laws for Gays," *WP*, April 22, 1992.

132. Shirley Green to Lillie Bell, June 27, 1990, WHOPL, Metzger, L. A. Files, Doug Wead Firing—Reactions, 04380.

133. Ralph Hallow, "Gay-Rights Questions Hurt Bush among Evangelicals," *WT*, July 24, 1992.

134. George Cornell, "Churches Find Friend in Bush," *Chicago Tribune*, Feb. 2, 1990.

135. "Church Leaders Assail Bush's Veto of Rights Bill," *WP*, Nov. 3, 1990.

136. E.g., Maurice Benitez to GB, Jan. 23, 1989, WHORM 005541, RM035-04.

137. Paul Djupe and Christopher Gilbert, *The Prophetic Pulpit: Clergy, Churches, and Communities in American Politics* (Lanham, MD: Rowman and Littlefield 2003), 41; David Hein and Gardiner Shattuck, Jr., *The Episcopalians* (Westport, CT: Praeger, 2004), 144; Prichard, *History*, 286–91. See also Edmond Browning, *No Outcasts: The Public Witness of Edmond Browning, XXIVth Presiding Bishop of the Episcopal Church*, ed. Brian Grieves (Cincinnati: Forward Movement Publications, 1997), 82–85, 88–98; David Sumner, *The Episcopal Church's History, 1945–1985* (Wilton, CT: Morehouse-Barlow, 1987); John Booty, *The Episcopal Church in Crisis* (Cambridge, MA: Cowley Publications, 1988), 119–22, 131–35; Robert Hood, *Social Teachings in the Episcopal Church* (Harrisburg, PA: Morehouse, 1990), 144–59.

138. E.g., Bush, "Catholic University"; "The 'Education President' Meets with Catholic Educators," *America*, August 5, 1989, 52–53; Bush, "Catholic University." In November 1991, Bush met with various Catholic agencies involved with senior citizen issues (Bobbie Kilberg to Cece Kramer, Oct. 26, 1991, Leonard, Jane Files, Catholics, Nov. 14, 1991); Bush met with Pope John Paul II in May 1989 to discuss how to increase efforts to promote peace and justice, and he gave a briefing to the pope on the Middle East peace conference in November 1991.

139. E.g., Hickey to GB, Feb. 13, 1992, WHOPL, Leonard, Jane Files, Catholics 07786-009. Law visited Bush in both Kennebunkport and the White House.

140. Joe Feuerherd, "Bush Hobnobs with Cardinals to Woo Church," *National Catholic Register*, Dec. 29, 1989.

141. Melady to GB, July 5, 1991, WHORM 251954, RM031.

142. Hyer, "Shifting Religious Alliances."

143. Leigh Ann Metzger, memorandum for Sherrie Rollins, Mar. 23, 1992, WHOPL, Leonard, Jane Files, Catholics, 07786-008. The list included William Simon, William Bennett, Congressman Henry Hyde, Phyllis Schafly, Edwin Feulner, Alan Keyes, Thomas Monahan, and other politicians, editors, professors, activists, and attorneys.

144. Paul McNeill to Thomas Melady, WHOPL, Leonard, Jane Files, Catholic Outreach, 07786-009.

145. Mary Thomas Noble to GB, Apr. 7, 1991, WHORM 245629, RM020.

146. E.g., Catholic Daughters of the Americas to Barbara Bush, Apr. 2, 1992, WHOPL, Leonard, Jane Files, New Catholic Contacts, 07786-013.

147. GB to the Friends of Cardinal Cooke Guild, Oct. 9, 1992, WHORM 356944, ME002.

148. Timothy McNulty, "Candidates Have Faith Religion Garners Votes," *Chicago Tribune*, Sept. 6, 1992; Kevin Phillips, "Pulpit Bullies," *LAT*, Sept. 6, 1992.

149. Russell Chandler, "Robertson Moves to Fill Christian Right Vacuum," *LAT*, May 15, 1990.

150. Robertson to GB, Feb. 12, 1992, WHORM, Foreign Affairs, F00030-02, Mutual Security 308413.

151. Bush, "National Association of Evangelicals." See also Joe Maxwell, "Poll Shows Strong Support for Bush among Evangelicals," *WP*, Mar. 7, 1992.

152. E.g., Catholics for Bush, WHOPL, Leonard, Jane Files, Catholic; [1992 Campaigns], 07786-051; Bush, "Knights of Columbus"; Bush: "Remarks at the Presidential Open Forum on Educational Choice in Philadelphia," July 21, 1992, http://www.presidency.ucsb.edu/ws/?pid=21243.

153. Memorandum for the Chief of Staff, Sept. 16, 1992; Reception at Pat Robertson's Residence, memorandum, Sept. 10, 1992; Address Christian Coalition Road to Victory Conference memorandum, Sept. 10, 1992; Meeting with Pat Robertson memorandum, Dec. 2, 1992, all in WHOPL, Metzger, L. A. files, Dr. Pat Robertson; David Von Drehle and Michael Isikoff, "Bush Focuses on Economy in Talk to Fundamentalists," *WP*, Sept. 12, 1992.

154. Ari Goldman, "Prayers for Democrats," *NYT*, July 11, 1992.

155. E.g., Cal Thomas, "Democrats Discover Religion," *WT*, July 26, 1992; Larry Witham, "Clinton, Bush Seek 134 Votes of Evangelicals," *WT*, Oct. 30, 1992.

156. George Bush, "Remarks to the Christian Coalition Road to Victory Conference in Virginia Beach," Sept. 11, 1992, http://www.presidency.ucsb.edu/ws/?pid=21446.

157. E.g., George Bush, "Remarks at a Rally in St. Louis," Oct. 30, 1992, http://www.presidency.ucsb.edu/ws/?pid=21713.

158. Bush, "Prayer Breakfast in Houston."

159. Joan Campbell to GB, Aug. 28, 1992, People for the American Way to GB, Aug. 27, 1992, both in WHORM 348702, RM030.

160. Cal Thomas, "Keeping the Faith, a Little Bit," *WT*, Aug. 30, 1992.

161. Gustav Niebuhr, "God Does Not Endorse Candidates," *WP*, Oct. 30, 1992.

162. "Century Marks," *CC* 109 (Oct. 28 1992), 956.

163. Jack Nelson, "Democrats Meet Amid Rising Hopes," *LAT*, July 13, 1992.

164. Wald and Calhoun-Brown, *Religion and Politics*, 232; Mark Henrie, "Rethinking American Conservatism in the 1990s: The Struggle against Homogenization,"

Intercollegiate Review 28 (Spring 1993), 11; Timothy Naftali, *George H. W. Bush* (New York: Henry Holt, 2007), 2.

165. Betty Glad, "How George Bush Lost the Presidential Election," in Kenneth Thompson, ed., *The Bush Presidency: Ten Intimate Perspectives of George Bush* (Lanham, MD: University Press of America, 1998), 187–89.

166. E.g., Parmet, *Bush*, 501.

167. See James Guth and John Green, "God's Own Party: Evangelicals and Republicans in the '92 Elections," *CC* 110 (Feb. 17, 1993), 172–73; Williams, *God's Own Party*, 221.

168. Ann Devroy, "Bush Maneuvers to Ease Conservatives' Concerns," *WP*, Feb. 23, 1992; Ronald Smothers, "Bush Less than Loved among Religious Right," *NYT*, Mar. 10, 1992.

169. Laura Olson and Adam Warber, "Mainline Protestants and the American Presidency," in Gaston Espinoza, ed., *Religion, Race, and the American Presidency* (Lanham, MD: Rowman and Littlefield, 2008), 35.

170. David Shribman, "Catholic Voters, Core of the 'Reagan Democrats', Returning to Their Party Amid Economic Fears," *WSJ*, Sept. 14, 1992; Jeffrey Jones, "The Protestant and Catholic Vote," June 8, 2004, http://www.gallup.com/poll/11911/protestant-catholic-vote.aspx.

171. Abram to GB, May 13, 1992, WHORM 328397, RM033.

172. Larry Witham, "Jewish Support for Bush Wanes," *WT*, Feb. 26, 1992; Gary Lee, "Jewish Activists Unhappy with Bush," *WP*, Apr. 8, 1992; James Wall, "Furthering Mideast Talks," *CC* 109 (Oct. 28 1992), 955–56.

173. Gerald Seib, "Whether or Not Perot Wins Over Jewish Voters, His Presence Alone Increases Their Importance," *WSJ*, June 26, 1992.

174. "Jewish Voting Record, 1916–2012," http://www.jewishvirtuallibrary.org/jsource/US-Israel/jewvote.html.

175. Bush, "Knights of Columbus."

176. GB to the pupils of Ms. Stevens's Sunday school class, Apple Valley, CA, Aug. 28, 1992, WHORM 348428, RM020.

177. GB to A. Max Gore, Mar. 9, 1990, WHORM 124385, RM020. Cf. Bush, 1990 "National Religious Broadcasters."

178. Bush, "Knights of Columbus."

179. George Bush, "Remarks at the Antiochian Orthodox Christian Church Annual Convention in Arlington, Virginia," July 25, 1991, http://www.presidency.ucsb.edu/ws/?pid=19829.

180. Bush, 1992 "National Religious Broadcasters."

181. George Bush, "Remarks to the Ace Hardware Convention in Denver," Oct. 26, 1992, http://www.presidency.ucsb.edu/ws/?pid=21666.

182. George Bush, "Remarks at the Annual Republican Congressional Fundraising Dinner," June 14, 1989, http://www.presidency.ucsb.edu/ws/?pid=17152.

183. GB to Joseph Tkach, June 7, 1991, WHORM 232068, RM020.
184. GB to the convocation of the Churches of God in Christ, International, Sept. 29, 1992, WHORM 002-01, 337594 (cf. GB to Jeannie Gonzalez, Sept. 11, 1992, WHORM 351464, RM020); GB to Congressman Ron Machtley, Aug. 15, 1990, WHORM 2414350; Bush, "Catholic University."
185. GB to W. Stan Tyson, Feb. 8, 1989, WHORM 005160, ME002-01.
186. Bush, "National Prayer Breakfast," May 4, 1989.
187. Bush, "Southern Baptist Convention."
188. Bush, "National Association of Evangelicals."
189. George Bush, "Proclamation 6029—Religious Freedom Week, 1989," Sept. 27, 1989, http://www.presidency.ucsb.edu/ws/?pid=1748.
190. George Bush, "Remarks to Members of the Anti-Defamation League of B'nai B'rith," Mar. 14, 1989, http://www.presidency.ucsb.edu/ws/?pid=16784.
191. Bush, "Thanksgiving Day, 1992."
192. George Bush, "Remarks at the University of South Carolina Commencement," May 12, 1990, http://www.presidency.ucsb.edu/ws/?pid=18477; Bush, "Remarks at a Meeting with Amish and Mennonite Leaders in Lancaster, Pennsylvania," Mar. 22, 1989, http://www.presidency.ucsb.edu/ws/?pid=16824.
193. Wead, "Bush," 209. See also Bush, *Best*, 325.
194. GB to Schuller, Jan. 4, 1990, WHORM 108188, RM035; GB to E. Brandt Gustavson, Dec. 9, 1991, and Gustavson to GB, Nov. 7, 1991, both WHORM 288864, RM035.
195. Quoted in Bush, "Catholic University."
196. Bush, 1992 "National Religious Broadcasters."
197. Bush, "Religious and Ethnic Groups."
198. Bush, 1990 "National Religious Broadcasters."
199. Bush repeatedly argued that "every family should have the freedom to choose a school" for their children (e.g., Bush, "Southern Baptist Convention"). As president, Bush repeatedly stressed that he supported "the sanctity of life" and strongly promoted adoption (e.g., 1990 "National Religious Broadcasters"). He also supported a Constitutional amendment to prohibit abortions in all cases except rape, incest, or when a pregnant woman's life was in danger (e.g., Bush, "Remarks to Participants in the March for Life Rally," Jan. 23, 1989, http://www.presidency.ucsb.edu/ws/?pid=16617).
200. George Bush, "Proclamation 6085—Earth Day, 1990," Jan. 3, 1990, http://www.presidency.ucsb.edu/ws/?pid=1802. Despite these achievements, some scholars criticize Bush for not doing enough to improve the environment and especially for the disastrous ecological consequences of the Persian Gulf War and his opposition to the Convention on Biodiversity. See Bryon Daynes and Glen Sussman, "Comparing the Environmental Policies of President George H. W. Bush and George W. Bush," in Anthony Eksterowicz and Glenn Hastedt, eds., *The Presidencies of George Herbert Walker Bush and George Walker Bush: Like Father Like Son?* (New York: Nova Science Publishers, 2008), 58, 66.

201. Letter in an exhibit at the GHWB Library.

202. John Robert Greene, *The Presidency of George Bush* (Lawrence: University Press of Kansas, 2000), 75 (quotation), 77–78.

203. Bush, "Earth Day, 1990."

204. George Bush, "Remarks to Students at the Teton Science School in Grand Teton National Park," June 13, 1989, http://www.presidency.ucsb.edu/ws/?pid=17136.

205. GB to Pio Laghi, the Apostolic Nunciature, Washington, DC, Dec. 22, 1989, WHORM 106452, RM031; Lejon, "Religion and the Presidency," 408, called my attention to several sources in this section.

206. Bush, "Cheltenham High School."

207. George Bush, "Remarks at a Luncheon Hosted by the New York Partnership and the Association for a Better New York," June 22, 1989, http://www.presidency.ucsb.edu/ws/?pid=17198.

208. Bush, "Thanksgiving Celebration in Memphis."

209. George Bush, "Statement on Receiving the Report of the President's Advisory Committee on the Points of Light Initiative Foundation," Jan. 4, 1990, http://www.presidency.ucsb.edu/ws/?pid=18007.

210. "White House Fact Sheet on the Points of Light Initiative," June 22, 1989, http://bushlibrary.tamu.edu/research/public_papers.php?id=590&year=&month=.

211. George Bush, "Radio Address to the Nation on the Daily Points of Light Program," Sept. 28, 1991, http://www.presidency.ucsb.edu/ws/?pid=20036.

212. George Bush, "Remarks at a Celebration of the Points of Light," Jan. 14, 1993, http://www.presidency.ucsb.edu/ws/?pid=20458.

213. Bush, "Liberty University."

214. Bush, 1991 "National Religious Broadcasters."

215. Bush, "National Association of Evangelicals."

216. George Bush, "Remarks at the Southern Methodist University Commencement," May 16, 1992, http://www.presidency.ucsb.edu/ws/?pid=20978.

217. Bush, "Thanksgiving Day, 1992."

218. George Bush, "Remarks to the American Society of Association Executives," Mar. 6, 1990, http://www.presidency.ucsb.edu/ws/?pid=18224.

219. George Bush, "Remarks at the United States Military Academy Commencement," June 1, 1991, http://www.presidency.ucsb.edu/ws/?pid=19643.

220. Bush, "Catholic University."

221. Bush, "Observance of Christmas," 1991.

222. George Bush, "A Presidential Call," *Christian Herald*, September/October 1989, 7.

223. GB to religious congregations, April 1991; C. Gregg Petersmeyer, memorandum for Phillip Brady, Mar. 18, 1991, both in WHORM 222220, ME002-01.

224. Bush, "Liberty University."

225. Bush, "Celebration of the Points of Light."

226. Mervin, "An Evaluation," 299; Michael Duffy and Dan Goodgame, *Marching in Place: The Status Quo Presidency of George Bush* (New York: Simon and Schuster, 1992), 210–11; quotations in that order.

227. Melvin, "An Evaluation," 102 (quotation), 109; Charles, "Moral Leadership," 61.

228. Russell Chandler, "Persian Gulf Crisis Stirs Predictions of Final Conflict," *LAT*, Sept. 20, 1990.

229. David Briggs, "Head of Largest Black Church Body in Nation Criticizes Gulf Buildup," *Philadelphia Inquirer*, Sept. 5, 1990.

230. GB to the members of the Kentucky Annual Conference of the AME Zion Church, Oct. 2, 1990, WHOPL, Metzger, L. A. Files, Churches, Black, 07162-044.

231. Mahony to Baker, Nov. 7, 1990; Baker to Mahony, Nov. 30, 1990, WHOPL, Metzger, L. A. Files, Operation Desert Shield Religious Leaders, Negative 04380-030. Baker belonged to the same Episcopal Church in Houston that Bush did. As an example of Baker's faith, see James Baker, "Faith, Friendship and Collective Responsibility," *Decision*, May 1990, 10–12.

232. Daniel Pilarczyk, "Letter to President Bush: The Persian Gulf Crisis," *Origins* 20:25 (Nov. 29, 1990), 399; James Turner Johnson and Alan Geyer, "Just War Tradition and the War in the Gulf," *CC* 108 (Feb. 6, 1991), 134–35; http://www. scethics.org/book/export/html/2.

233. Ari Goldman, "Council of Churches Condemns U.S. Policy in Gulf," *NYT*, Nov. 16, 1990; Message and Resolution from the General Board of the National Council of Churches in the U.S.A., November 15, 1990, in James Turner Johnson and George Weigel, *Just War and the Gulf War* (Lanham, MD: University Press of America, 1991),105–11.

234. Oswald Johnson, "U.S. Bishops Call on Bush to Avoid War," *LAT*, Nov. 13, 1990.

235. Mary Ellen Lewis to GB, Oct. 15, 1990 (quotation); Jose Torres to GB, Jan. 12, 1991, both in WHOPL, Metzger, L. A. Files, Operation Desert Storm, Negative [3], 04380-033.

236. Mowahid Shah, "Perils of War: A Muslim View," *CSM*, Nov. 5, 1990.

237. Story to GB, Nov. 15, 1990, Metzger, Leigh Ann Files, Operation Desert Shield—Private Prayer Initiatives [OA/ID 04380-029] 194816.

238. Greg Fitch, memorandum for Speechwriters and Researchers, Nov. 16, 1990, WHOPL, Metzger, L. A. Files, Pro Desert Storm letters, 05398-001.

239. "The President's News Conference in Orlando," Nov. 1, 1990, http://www. presidency.ucsb.edu/ws/?pid=18984; Bush, "Remarks at a Republican Party Fundraising Luncheon in North Kingstown, Rhode Island," Aug. 20, 1990, http://www.presidency.ucsb.edu/ws/?pid=18776; Bush, "Radio Address to United States Armed Forces Stationed in the Persian Gulf Region," Aug. 29, 1990, http://www.presidency.ucsb.edu/ws/?pid=18789.

240. James Wall, "President Bush Ignores Arab Street Talk," *CC* 107 (Aug. 22, 1990), 755.

241. E.g., Thomas Friedman, "Mideast Tensions: U.S. Jobs at Stake in Gulf, Baker Says," *NYT*, Nov. 14, 1990. For Baker's assessment of the Gulf crisis, see James Baker, III and Thomas DeFrank, *The Politics of Diplomacy: Revolution, War, and Peace, 1989–1992* (New York. G. P. Putnam's Sons, 1995), 260–381.

242. Leigh Ann Metzger, memorandum for John Sununu, Dec. 6, 1990, WHOPL, Metzger, L. A. Files, Kuwait, 06887-026.

243. Bush, "U.S.S. Nassau."

244. John Dart, "Episcopalian Bush Opens Religious Counteroffensive for a "Just War,'" *LAT*, Feb. 2, 1991; Bush diary entry for Dec. 20, 1990, in George Bush and Brent Scowcroft, *A World Transformed* (New York: Knopf, 1998), 427–28; Sheryl Kujawa-Holbrook, *The Heart of a Pastor: A Life of Edmond Lee Browning* (Cincinnati: Forward Movement, 2010), 338–44, 346. Browning had previously objected to the Reagan administration's support of the Freedom Fighters in Nicaragua. See GB to Browning, Apr. 3, 1986, Bush, *Best*, 348; Kujawa-Holbrook, *Heart*, 231, 333–34. Browning declared that he and Bush had "different visions" of America's "responsibilities in this global village," but he appreciated Bush's openness to him and respected his faith and work (Kujawa-Holbrook, *Heart*, 233). See also Browning, "Statement on the Persian Gulf Crisis, October 5, 1990"; "Message to Episcopalians, January 17, 1991"; and "Remarks to US Delegates at VII Assembly of the World Council of Churches, Canberra, Australia, February 8, 1991," in Grieves, ed., *No Outcasts*, 163–71.

245. Dart, "Counteroffensive."

246. Chapman to GB, Jan. 4, 1991, WHOPL, Metzger, L. A. Files, Pro Desert Storm letters, 05398-001.

247. Clarence Pope, Jr. to GB, Jan. 7, 1991, Metzger, Leigh Ann Files Operation Desert Shield—Private Prayer Initiatives [OA/ID 04380-029] 203253.

248. LaHaye to GB, Jan. 9, 1991, Metzger, L. A. Files Operation Desert Shield—Private Prayer Initiatives [OA/ID 04380-027].

249. E.g., Lawrence Harper, pastor of the Thalia Lynn Baptist Church, Virginia Beach, to GB, Apr. 3, 1991, WHORM 2300328, ME002-01.

250. Intercessors for America Newsletter, Feb. 1991, 1.

251. George Weigel, "War, Peace, and the Christian Conscience," in Johnson and Weigel, *Just War*, 50–52; quotation from 52.

252. "War Is Not the Answer: A Message to the American People," in *Pressing for Peace: The Churches Act in the Gulf War Crisis* (New York: NCC-USA, 1991), 14–17.

253. "Church Leaders Return from Middle East Peace Pilgrimage Urging Peaceful Solution in the Gulf," Jan. 11, 1991, http://www/episcopalarchives.org/origin/EN S/EN Spress_releasepl?pr_number+91002.

254. Thom Fassett to GB, Dec. 21, 1990; Jose Torres to GB, Jan. 12, 1991, both in WHOPL, Metzger, L. A. Files, Operation Desert Storm, Negative [3], 04380-033.

255. "Delay Military Action, Give Peace a Chance: A Message to President Bush from American Church Leaders," in *Pressing for Peace*, 20–22.

256. See WHOPL, Metzger, L. A. Files, Operation Desert Storm, Negative [3], 04380-033.

257. Bush diary entry, Jan. 15, 1991, in Bush, *Best*, 504.

258. Bush and Scowcroft, *World Transformed*, 451.

259. Gibbs and Duffy, *Preacher*, 303; Bush and Scowcroft, *World Transformed*, 451.

260. GB to Law, Jan. 22, 1991, in Bush, *Best*, 505–7; Stephen Swecker, "Bush: No Ill Will Toward Religious Critics of War," *The United Methodist Reporter*, Apr. 5, 1991; "Bush Soul-searching Religion and Public Policy," Episcopal News Service, Apr. 29. 1991.

261. Bush, 1991 "National Religious Broadcasters."

262. Bush, 1991 "National Religious Broadcasters."

263. Bush, 1991 "National Religious Broadcasters."

264. Bush, "Arrival Ceremony."

265. "Interview with Middle Eastern Journalists," Mar. 8, 1991, http://www.presidency.ucsb.edu/ws/?pid=19375.

266. George Bush, "Address before the 45th Session of the United Nations General Assembly in New York," Oct. 1, 1990, http://www.presidency.ucsb.edu/ws/?pid=18883. See also Bush, "Remarks to the Federal Assembly in Prague," Nov. 17, 1990, http://www.presidency.ucsb.edu/ws/?pid=19064; Greg Fitch, Memorandum for Leigh Ann Metzger on New World Order, WHOPL, Metzger, L. A. Files, 07164-037. See also Meenekshi Bose and Rosanna Perotti, eds., *From Cold War to New World Order: The Foreign Policy of George H. W. Bush* (Westport, CT: Greenwood Press, 2002). On Bush's just war doctrine, see Andrew Rosenthal, "Bush Vows to Tackle Middle East Issues," *NYT*, Jan. 29, 1991, A13; Kenneth Walsh, "Bush's 'Just War' Doctrine," *U.S. News and World Report*, Feb. 4, 1991, 52–53; and Kenneth Woodward, "Ancient Theory and Modern War," *Newsweek*, Feb. 11, 1991, 47 See also Richard John Neuhaus, "Just War and This War," *Wall Street Journal*, Jan. 29, 1991, A18; John Howard Yoder, "Just War Tradition: Is It Credible? *CC* 108 (Mar. 13, 1991), 295–98; and Bryan Hehir, "The Moral Calculus of War," *Commonweal*, Feb. 22, 1991, 126.

267. Peter Steinfels, "Beliefs," *NYT*, Jan. 5, 1991; on Mormons, see George Cornell, "Mormons Stress Duty to God and Country in Times of Warfare," *LAT*, Mar. 9, 1991.

268. "Bohlmann Asks Support for President Bush," *Reporter*, Jan. 21, 1991, 1; Bevilacque to GB, Jan. 28, 1991, WHOPL, Metzger, L. A. Files, Operation Desert Shield, Religious Leaders, Positive, 04380-029.

269. Law to GB, Jan. 16, 1991; Law to GB, Jan. 25, 1991, both in WHOPL, Metzger, L. A. Files, Operation Desert Shield, Religious Leaders, Positive, 04380-029.

270. Robison to GB, Feb. 26, 1991, WHORM 223164, RM020.

271. Ogilvie to GB, Jan. 31, 1991; "Religious Leaders and Institutions Endorsing Desert Storm"; "A Pastoral Letter to Southern Baptists on the Persian Gulf War"; Rabbi Morris Sherer to GB, Feb. 4, 1991, all in WHOPL, Metzger, L. A. Files, Operation Desert Shield, Religious Leaders, Positive, 04380-029.

272. John-David Schofield to GB, Jan. 21, 1991, Metzger, Leigh Ann Files Operation Desert Shield—Private Prayer Initiative [OA/ID 04380-029] 208353. Cf. C. Brinkley Morton, Bishop of San Diego, to GB, Aug. 16, 1991, WHORM 263655, RM035-04.

273. Smith to GB, Jan. 28, 1991, WHOPL, Metzger, L. A. Files, Operation Desert Shield, Religious Leaders, Positive, 04380-029.

274. Peter Steinfels, "War in the Gulf: The Home Front; Church Leaders Reaffirm Opposition to War," *NYT*, Feb. 15, 1991.

275. James Turner Johnson, "The Just War Tradition and the American Military," in Johnson and Weigel, *Just War*, 30.

276. E.g., Larry Witham, "Many Area Faithful Answer President's Call for Prayer," *WT*, Feb. 4, 1991.

277. Bush, "National Day of Prayer."

278. Jean Bethke Elshtain, "Just War as Politics," in David DeCosse, ed., *But Was It Just? Reflections on the Morality of the Persian Gulf War* (New York: Doubleday, 1992), 49.

279. James Wall, "Crying Wolf over Saddam Hussein," *CC* 108 (Jan. 30, 1991), 99–100.

280. G. Stanford Bratton to GB, Feb. 13, 1991, WHOPL, Metzger, L. A. Files, Operation Desert Storm, Negative [2], 04380-32.

281. Peter Steinfels, "War in the Gulf"; "A Call to the Churches," in Turner and Weigel, *Just War*, 153–58.

282. National Emergency African American Leadership Summit on the Gulf War, "An Open Letter to President George Bush," WHOPL, Metzger, L. A. Files, Churches, Black, 07162-044.

283. George Bush, "Address to the Nation Announcing Allied Military Ground Action in the Persian Gulf," Feb. 23, 1991, http://www.presidency.ucsb.edu/ws/?pid=19331.

284. Bush and Scowcroft, *World Transformed*, 480.

285. Bush, "Cessation of the Persian Gulf Conflict"; Bush diary entry Feb. 24, 1991, in Bush, *Best*, 513–14.

286. GB to a gathering to honor Operation Desert Storm troops, June 3, 1991, WHORM 236661, ME002-01.

287. Leigh Ann Metzger to James Johnson, Mar. 20, 1991, WHORM 217958, RM020.

288. Bush, "National Days of Thanksgiving, April 5–7, 1991."

289. "The President's News Conference on the Persian Gulf Conflict," Mar. 1, 1991, http://www.presidency.ucsb.edu/ws/?pid=19352.

290. "Middle Eastern Journalists."

291. George Bush, "Message on the Observance of Passover," Mar. 29, 1991, http://www.presidency.ucsb.edu/ws/?pid=19431.

292. Lawson, "Bush Affirms," 39.

293. GB to Tkach.

294. Bush, "Southern Baptist Convention."

295. James Wall, "Another Failure in a Bankrupt Foreign Policy," *CC* 108 (Apr. 17, 1991), 419; Michael Walzer, "Justice and Injustice in the Gulf War," in DeCosse, ed., *But Was It Just?* 11; Stanley Hauerwas, "Whose Just War? Which Peace?" in ibid., 84, 88–90, 94.

296. George Weigel, "From Last Resort to Endgame: Morality, the Gulf War, and the Peace Process," in DeCosse, *But Was It Just?* 29; Elshtain, "Just War as Politics," 53.

297. George Bush, speech at John F. Kennedy School of Government, Harvard University, May 29, 1998 (first quotation); Bush, "Keynote Address," in Levantrosser and Perotti, eds., *Noble Calling*, 48 (second quotation); Bush, "Celebration of the Points of Light" (remainder of the quotations).

298. Mervin, "An Evaluation," 107–8; http://www.pointsoflight.org/who-we-are/our-impact.

299. See Dan Goodman, "In the Gulf: Bold Vision"; Michael Duffy, "At Home: No Vision," *Time*, Jan. 7, 1991, 20–30; and Charles-Philippe David, "Not Doing Too Badly for Guys Who Have No Vision Whatsoever," in Levantrosser and Perotti, eds., *Noble Calling*, 170 (quotation).

300. Bush diary entry, May 24, 1990, Office of George Bush, Houston.

301. Bush diary entry, July 7, 1991, in Bush, *Best*, 528; Naftali, *Bush*, 3, 176; quotations in that order.

302. Beschloss, "George Bush," 239; Michael Beschloss and Strobe Talbott, *At the Highest Levels: The Inside Story of the End of the Cold War* (Boston: Little, Brown, 1993), 469; Greene, *Presidency*, 186.

303. Thomas Friedman, "Bring Back Poppy," http://www.nytimes.com/2011/07/31/opinion/sunday/friedman-bring-back-poppy.html?nl.

304. E.g., Richard Rose, *The Postmodern Presidency: George Bush Meets the World* (Chatham, NJ: Chatham House, 1991), 48–49, 53, 307–8.

305. E.g., David, "Not Doing Too Badly," 171, 179; quotations in that order.

306. David Gergen, "America's Missed Opportunities," *Foreign Affairs* 70 (February 1991), 3. See also Strobe Talcott, "Post-Victory Blues," *Foreign Affairs* 71 (Feb. 1992), 53–69.

307. Michael Genovese, "George Bush and the Finitude of Presidential Power," in Levantrosser and Perotti, eds., *Noble Calling*, 84, 96; quotations in that order. See also Michael Genovese, *The Presidency in an Age of Limits* (Westport, CT: Greenwood, 1993).

308. Bryon Shafer, " 'We Are All Southern Democrats Now': The Shape of American Politics in the Very Late Twentieth Century," in Bryon Shafer, ed., *Present Discontents: American Politics in the Very Late Twentieth Century* (Chatham, NJ: Chatham House, 1997), 153–57; Duffy and Goodgame, *Marching*, 12 (second quotation); David Broder, "The Reactor President," *WPNWE*, Aug. 27–Sept. 2, 1990, 4; Charles Tiefer, *The Semi-Sovereign Presidency: The Bush Administration's Strategy for Governing Without Congress* (Boulder, CO: Westview Press, 1994); and Greene, *Presidency*, 183–85, who called my attention to these sources.

309. Greene, *Presidency*, 184 (quotation), 145. See David Mervin, *George Bush and the Guardianship Presidency* (New York: St. Martin's Press, 1996).

310. Genovese, "George Bush," 81 (first quotation), 82, 83; Bert Rockman, "The Leadership Style of George Bush," in Bert Rockman and Colin Campbell, eds., *The Bush Presidency: First Appraisals* (Chatham, NJ: Chatham House, 1991), 29 (second quotation).

311. Charles Kolb, *White House Daze: The Unmaking of Domestic Policy in the Bush Years* (New York: Free Press, 1994), 343 (first and fourth quotations), 346 (second quotations), 345 (third quotation), 3, 6 (fifth quotation).

312. Hugh Sidey, "Some Personal Reflections," in Kenneth Thompson, ed., *The Bush Presidency: Ten Intimate Perspectives of George Bush, Part Two* (Lanham, MD: University Press of America, 1998), 38.

313. Mark Rozell, "George Bush and the Public Presidency," in Thompson, ed., *Presidency, Part Two*, 118.

314. Kevin Phillips, *American Dynasty: Aristocracy, Fortune, and the Politics of Deceit in the House of Bush* (New York: Viking, 2004), ix (first two quotations), xi (third quotation); Duffy and Goodgame, *Marching*, 11; Tom Wicker, *George Herbert Walker Bush* (New York: Viking, 2004), 217; Stephen Graubard, *Mr. Bush's War: Adventures in the Politics of Illusion* (New York: Hill and Wang: 1992), ix.

315. Charles, "Moral Leadership," 55, 53, 54, 59, 71; quotations in that order; the first three quotations are phrases.

316. Bush diary entry, Nov. 4, 1992, in Bush, *Best*, 572; GB to John Bush, Nov. 30, 1992, ibid., 579; part of a speech Bush gave at his Greenwich Day reunion, recorded in ibid., May 29, 1997, 605.

317. Thomas Patrick Melady, "George Bush: Influence of the Family on His Values," in Levantrosser and Perotti, eds., *Noble Calling*, 6. Cf. James Baker, III, "Keynote Address," in ibid., 39.

CHAPTER 10

1. David Gergen, Matthew Cooper, and Donald Baer, "Bill Clinton's Hidden Life: An Interview with Bill Clinton," *US News & World Report*, July 20, 1992, http://www.usnews.com/news/national/articles/2008/05/16/bill-clintons-hidden-life.

2. Numerous scholars, journalists, and clergy have underscored the enigmatic nature of Clinton's faith. E.g., David Briggs, "Clinton's Faith an Enigma to Observers," *Baptist Standard*, Mar. 3, 1999, http://www.baptiststandard.com/1999/3_3/pages/clinton.html. The best analyses of Clinton's faith are James Penning, "The Religion of Bill Clinton," in Mark Rosell and Gleaves Whitney, eds., *Religion and the American Presidency* (New York: Palgrave Macmillan, 2007), 191–214; Gaston Espinosa, "Religion and the Presidency of William Jefferson Clinton," in Gaston Espinosa, ed., *Religion and the American Presidency: George Washington to George W. Bush* (New York: Columbia University Press, 2009), 431–75; and David Holmes, *The Faiths of the Postwar Presidents from Truman to Obama* (Athens: University of Georgia Press, 2012), 215–39.

3. Kenneth Woodward, "Sex, Sin and Salvation: To Understand Clinton the President, You Have to Meet Bill the Baptist, a Believer Whose Faith Leaves Plenty of License," *Newsweek*, Nov. 2, 1998, 37.

4. Stanley Renshon, *High Hopes: The Clinton Presidency and the Politics of Ambition* (New York: New York University Press, 1996), 7 (quotation), 117. Renshon argued that both of them had great ambition, "grew up in difficult economic and emotional circumstances in small rural towns," "had difficult fathers," "idealized their mothers," had "an explosive temper," and tended to vilify their opponents (117–18).

5. Bert Rockman, "Cutting with the Grain: Is There a Clinton Leadership Legacy?" in Colin Campbell and Bert Rockman, eds., *The Clinton Legacy* (New York: Chatham House Publishers, 2000), 284; "Historians Rank Presidential Leadership in New C-SPAN Survey," Feb. 21, 2000, http://www.americanpresidents.org/survey/amp022100.asp.

6. Tom Barrett, " 'My Lies' by Bill Clinton," June 29, 2004, http://www.aim.org/guest-column/my-lies-by-bill-clinton/; James Pfiffner, "Presidential Character: Multidimensional or Seamless?" in Mark Rozell and Clyde Wilcox, eds., *The Clinton Scandal and the Future of American Government* (Washington, DC: Georgetown University Press, 2000), 248 (quotation), 226.

7. E.g., Briggs, "Clinton's Faith."

8. See Bill Clinton, *My Life* (New York: Alfred Knopf, 2004), 429; David Maraniss, "Roots of Clinton's Faith Deep, Varied," *WP*, June 29, 1992, http://www.highbeam.com/doc/1P2-1012954.html.

9. Clinton attended Pentecostal summer camp meetings in Redfield, Arkansas, every year except one between 1977 and 1992. He also attended some Pentecostal Sunday worship services and had Pentecostal friends (*My Life*, 250–51). In addition, Clinton attended and spoke at many black churches during both of his presidential campaigns and as president. E.g., David Shribman, "Presidents and Prayer," *Boston Globe*, Dec. 11, 1994.

10. E. J. Dionne, Frontline 2004, http://www.pbs.org/wgbh/pages/frontline/shows/jesus/president/religion.html.

11. Maraniss, "Clinton's Faith."

12. Tony Campolo, "Errant Evangelical? A Presidential Counselor in the Line of Fire," *Brookings Review* 17 (Spring 1999), 32.

13. Quoted in Maraniss, "Clinton's Faith."

14. Michael Waldman, *POTUS Speaks: Finding the Words That Defined the Clinton Presidency* (New York: Simon and Schuster, 2000). Waldman, a Clinton speechwriter for seven years, explained that Clinton often revised drafts of major speeches (34, 36, 43, 109, 138, 152, 190, 197, 198, 232). See also Branch Taylor, *The Clinton Tapes: Wrestling History with the President* (New York: Simon and Schuster, 2009), 273, 420.

15. Holmes, *Presidents*, 217.

16. Quoted in Gergen, Cooper, and Baer, "Hidden Life," 30; John Gartner, interview with Patty Crider, July 18, 2006, *In Search of Bill Clinton: A Psychological Biography* (New York: St. Martin's Press, 2008), 103.

17. Clinton, *My Life*, 30; William Clinton, "Remarks at a Discussion at the Ministers' Leadership Conference in South Barrington, Illinois," Aug. 10, 2000, http://www.presidency.ucsb.edu/ws/?pid=1485; Maraniss, "Clinton's Faith"; quotations in that order.

18. Clinton, *My Life*, 23 (first quotation); Virginia Kelley, *Leading with My Heart* (New York: Simon and Schuster, 1994), 100–101, 70; quotation from 100; David Maraniss, *First in His Class: The Biography of Bill Clinton* (New York: Touchstone, 1996), 35.

19. William Clinton, "Remarks by the President at Prayer Breakfast," Feb. 4, 1993, http://www.presidency.ucsb.edu/ws/?pid=46711.

20. Clinton, *My Life*, 47, 40; quotations in that order.

21. Quoted in Jerome Levin, *The Clinton Syndrome* (Rocklin, CA: Prima, 1998), 26.

22. Clinton, *My Life*, 67.

23. Clinton, *My Life*, 294; Nigel Hamilton, *Bill Clinton: An American Journey* (New York: Random House, 2003), 132–33.

24. Clinton, *My Life*, 147–48.

25. Quoted in Priscilla Painton, "Clinton's Spiritual Journey," Apr. 5, 1993, http://www.time.com/time/printout/0,8816,978129,00.html.

26. Maraniss, *First*, 434; Maraniss, "Clinton's Faith." Some called Vaught Clinton's "spiritual mentor" ("Little Rock Church Draws Fire for Clinton Ties," *Dallas Morning News*, Feb. 27, 1994, 16A).

27. Clinton, *My Life*, 294.

28. See Paul Kengor, *God and Hillary Clinton: A Spiritual Life* (New York: Harper, 2007), 136–39; Sally Bedell Smith, *For Love of Politics: Bill and Hillary Clinton: The White House Years* (New York: Random House, 2007), 182–83; Maraniss, *First*, 433; Michael Kelly, "Saint Hillary," *NYT Magazine*, May 23, 1993; Hillary Rodham Clinton, *Living History* (New York: Simon and Schuster, 2003), 160, 167–68; Kenneth Woodward, "Soulful Matters," *Newsweek*, Oct. 31, 1994.

29. Maraniss, *First*, 432.

30. Smith, *Politics*, 49.

31. Clinton, 1993 "National Prayer Breakfast."

32. William Clinton, "Remarks at the Signing Ceremony for the Israeli–Palestinian West Bank Accord," Sept. 28, 1995, http://www.presidency.ucsb.edu/ws/?pid=50574.

33. William Clinton, "Remarks Celebrating the 160th Anniversary of the Metropolitan African Methodist Episcopal Church," Oct. 23, 1998, http://www.presidency.ucsb.edu/ws/?pid=55141; Clinton, "Message on the Observance of Christmas," Dec. 15, 1994, http://www.presidency.ucsb.edu/ws/?pid=49589 (first and second quotations); Clinton, "Message on the Observance of Christmas, 1999," Dec. 21, 1999, http://www.presidency.ucsb.edu/ws/?pid=57106 (third quotation).

34. William Clinton, "Prayer at Christmas II: Holy Eucharist Services," Jan. 2, 2000, http://www.presidency.ucsb.edu/ws/?pid=58105 (third quotation); Clinton, "Remarks to the Families of the Victims of the 1995 Bombing in Oklahoma City," Apr. 5, 1996, http://www.presidency.ucsb.edu/ws/?pid=52631 (first quotation); Clinton, **"Remarks at a Memorial Service for the Bombing Victims in Oklahoma City,"** Apr. 23, 1995, http://www.presidency.ucsb.edu/ws/?pid=51265 (second quotation).

35. William Clinton, "Message on the Observance of Easter, 1996," Apr. 4, 1996, http://www.presidency.ucsb.edu/ws/?pid=52627 (first and second quotations); Clinton, "Message on the Observance of Christmas, 1997," Dec. 22, 1997, http://www.presidency.ucsb.edu/ws/?pid=53733 (third and fourth quotations).

36. William Clinton, "Message on the Observance of Easter, 1999," Apr. 2, 1999, http://www.presidency.ucsb.edu/ws/?pid=57352; Clinton, "Remarks at the Metropolitan Baptist Church," Dec. 7, 1997, http://www.presidency.ucsb.edu/ws/?pid=53673; Clinton, "Message on the Observance of Easter, 2000," Apr. 21, 2000, http://www.presidency.ucsb.edu/ws/?pid=58399; Clinton, "President's Radio Address," Apr. 2, 1994, http://www.presidency.ucsb.edu/ws/?pid=49904; quotations in that order.

37. Clinton, "Prayer at Christmas," 2; Clinton, **"Address before a Joint Session of the Congress on the State of the Union,"** Jan. 24, 1995, http://www.presidency.ucsb.edu/ws/?pid=51634 (first quotation); Maraniss, "Clinton's Faith" (second quotation; Clinton's words); Clinton, "Remarks on the 40th Anniversary of the Desegregation of Central High School in Little Rock," Sept. 25, 1997, http://www.presidency.ucsb.edu/ws/?pid=54669 (third quotation); Clinton, "Remarks to Business Leaders in Stamford, Connecticut," Oct. 7, 1996, http://www.presidency.ucsb.edu/ws/?pid=52063 (fourth quotation); Clinton, "Remarks at a Breakfast with Religious Leaders," Sept. 28, 1999, http://www.presidency.ucsb.edu/ws/?pid=56598 (fifth quotation); Clinton, "Remarks at the National Prayer Breakfast," Feb. 6, 1997, http://www.presidency.ucsb.edu/ws/?pid=53402 (sixth quotation).

38. William Clinton, "Remarks at James Madison High School in Vienna, Virginia," July 12, 1995, http://www.presidency.ucsb.edu/ws/?pid=51608 (first and second quotations); "Interview with Religious Affairs Journalists," Feb. 2, 1995, http://www.presidency.ucsb.edu/ws/?pid=50687 (third quotation); Gergen, Cooper, and Baer, "Hidden Life."

39. Clinton, "Observance of Easter, 2000."

40. Quoted in Gergen, Cooper, and Baer, "Hidden Life."

41. William Clinton, "Remarks at the Full Gospel A.M.E. Zion Church in Temple Hills, Maryland," Aug. 14, 1994, http://www.presidency.ucsb.edu/ws/?pid=48979.

42. Clinton, "Leadership Conference."

43. Gartner, interview with Patty Criner; with Carol Willis, July 18, 2006; and with Paul Begala, Nov. 19, 2006, in *Search*, 105–6; quotation from 106.

44. Quoted in Philip Yancey, "The Riddle of Bill Clinton's Faith," *CT* 38 (Apr. 25, 1994), 27.

45. Clinton, "Zion Church."

46. William Clinton, "Remarks to Business Leaders in Belfast," Nov. 30, 1995, http://www.presidency.ucsb.edu/ws/?pid=50823.

47. E.g., William Clinton, "Remarks at Saint Paul's A.M.E. Church in Tampa," Nov. 3, 1996, http://www.presidency.ucsb.edu/ws/?pid=52205.

48. William Clinton, "Remarks to Business and Community Leaders in Athens," Nov. 20, 1999, http://www.presidency.ucsb.edu/ws/?pid=56969.

49. E.g., William Clinton, "**Remarks at the Dedication of Mount Zion A.M.E. Church in Greeleyville, South Carolina**," *June 12, 1996*, http://www.presidency.ucsb.edu/ws/?pid=52934; *Clinton, "***Remarks on Presenting Congressional Gold Medals to the Little Rock Nine**," *Nov. 9, 1999*, http://www.presidency.ucsb.edu/ws/?pid=56897.

50. "Religious Affairs Journalists."

51. Richard Agler, "All the President's Psalms," Speechwriters, Edmonds, Terry, Box 18, file 13, inspiration 10982, Feb. 24, 1995, William J. Clinton Presidential Library.

52. Yancey, "Clinton's Faith," 27.

53. Philip Wogaman, *From the Eye of the Storm: A Pastor to the President Speaks Out* (Louisville, KY: John Knox Press, 1998), 118; Wogaman interview with Paul Kengor, Oct. 13 and 24, 2005, in Kengor, *Hillary Clinton*, 173; Campolo interview with Kengor, Mar. 22, 2006, in ibid., 173; "Church Leaders Praise Bill Clinton's 'Spirituality,'" *Christian News* 38 (Nov. 13, 2000), 2; "Religious Affairs Journalists."

54. Gergen, Cooper, and Baer, "Hidden Life."

55. Clinton, "Zion Church."

56. William Clinton, "National Prayer Breakfast," Feb. 3, 1994, http://www.presidency.ucsb.edu/ws/?pid=49132.

57. Gergen, Cooper, and Baer, "Hidden Life."

58. Clinton, "Remarks at the National Prayer Breakfast," Feb. 5, 1998, http://www.presidency.ucsb.edu/ws/?pid=55104.

59. William Clinton, "Proclamation 7303—National Day of Prayer, 2000," May 4, 2000, http://clinton6.nara.gov/2000/05/2000-05-04-proclamation-on-national-day-of-prayer.html.

60. William Clinton, "**Remarks at a Celebration Commemorating the End of Ramadan**," *Jan. 10, 2000*, http://www.presidency.ucsb.edu/ws/?pid=58209; Clinton, "Remarks at the National Prayer Breakfast," Feb. 4, 1999, http://www.presidency.ucsb.edu/ws/?pid=56624.

61. E.g., Clinton, 1998 "National Prayer Breakfast."

62. Kelley, *My Heart*, 164; Maraniss, "Clinton's Faith"; William Clinton, "Remarks at the Funeral of Secretary of Commerce Ronald H. Brown," Apr. 10, 1996, http://www.presidency.ucsb.edu/ws/?pid=52624; Clinton, "Remarks at the Funeral Service for Admiral Jeremy M. Boorda," May 21, 1996, http://www.presidency.ucsb.edu/ws/?pid=52843; Clinton, "Remarks at a Memorial Service for Firefighters in Worcester, Massachusetts," Dec. 9, 1999, http://www.presidency.ucsb.edu/ws/?pid=57044; Clinton, **Memorial Service in Oklahoma City**"; quotations in that order.

63. Clinton, "Radio Address," Apr. 2, 1994; Clinton, "Remarks Announcing Guidelines on Religious Exercise and Religious Expression in the Federal Workplace," Aug. 14, 1997, http://www.presidency.ucsb.edu/ws/?pid=54535; quotations in that order.

64. On Horne, see Doug Smith, "Bearing the Presidential Cross: Rev. Rex Horne and Immanuel Baptist Face a Strange Challenge," *Arkansas Times*, Oct. 7, 1993, 13–14; Lynn Clayton, "So, What's It Like to Serve as the President's Pastor?" *Baptist Message*, Feb. 11, 1999, 1; "Little Rock Church," 16A. In 1996 Clinton listed his favorite preachers as Horne, Hybels, Campolo, Wogaman, Billy Graham, and Gardiner Taylor (Kenneth Woodward, "Heard Any Good Sermons Lately?" *Newsweek*, Mar. 3, 1996, http://www.thedailybeast.com/newsweek/1996/03/03/heard-any-good-sermons-lately.html).

65. Gustav Niebuhr, "Not All Presidential Advisors Talk Politics," *NYT*, Mar. 18, 1997, http://www.nytimes.com/1997/03/18/us/not-all-presidential-advisers-talk-politics.html?pagewanted=all&src=pm. See also WJC to Rex Horne, Feb. 10, 1993, Rex M. Horne Papers, Riley-Hickingbotham Library Archives and Special Collections, Ouachita Baptist University, Arkadelphia, Arkansas, 7.7 (hereinafter cited as R-HL); WJC to Horne, Sept. 7, 1993, R-HL 7.13.

66. Examples of their correspondence are WJC to Rex Horne, Apr. 14, 1993, R-HL 7.9; WJC to Horne, Oct. 13, 1993, R-HL 7.14; WJC to Horne, Oct. 18, 1993, R-HL 7.15; WJC to Horne, Dec. 2, 1994, R-HL 7.25; WJC to Horne, Jan. 9, 1995, R-HL, 7.27; WJC to Horne, Dec. 17, 1996, Horne 7.55. Horne suggested that Clinton meet with various individuals, including younger evangelical pastors (e.g., WJC to Horne, June 28, 1994, R-HL 7.21; Horne to WJC, Mar. 25, 1996, R-HL 4.20g). Clinton congratulated Horne on his reelection as president of the Arkansas Baptist Convention (WJC to Horne, Nov. 27, 1996, R-HL). After acknowledging his affair with Lewinsky, Clinton thanked Horne for "sticking with me in prayer and in person" (WJC to Horne, Sept. 11, 1998, R-HL 7.65). Clinton often praised Horne's ministry (e.g., WJC to Horne, Sept. 20, 1999, R-HL 7.73; WJC to Horne, Aug. 31, 2000, R-HL 7.77). Horne also wrote letters to encourage the president and discussed issues such as abortion and gays in the military (e.g., Horne to WJC, Oct, 1, 1993, R-HL 4.20b; "Personal and Confidential," June 11, 1993, R-HL 4.20c).

67. "Little Rock Church," 16A.

68. Lynn Clayton, "Arkansas Church Thriving Despite Clinton Controversy," *Baptist Standard*, Mar. 3, 1999, 12. See also Rex Horne, "Educating the President's Pastor: Politics and Immanuel's Pulpit," *Arkansas Times*, Nov. 18, 1994, 14, 16.

69. Greg Warner, "Rex Horne Likes the Challenge of Being the President's Pastor," *Baptist Standard*, Feb. 5, 1997, 12.

70. Yancey, "Clinton's Faith"; WJC to Rex Horne, Oct. 18, 1995, R-HL 7.38; "Little Rock Church," 16A.

71. WJC to Horne, Jan. 10, 2001, R-HL 7.82.

72. Paige Patterson to Rex Horne, Oct. 23, 1997, R-HL 4.20a.

73. WTC to Horne, July 27, 1999, R-HL 7.72.

74. Clinton, "Leadership Conference."

75. William Clinton, "Remarks at the Foundry United Methodist Church," Jan. 7, 2001, http://www.presidency.ucsb.edu/ws/?pid=73572. See also Clinton, *My Life*, 946.

76. Niebuhr, "Presidential Advisors." See also Campolo, "Errant Evangelical?" 33–35, and Ted Olsen, "Plus: Why Clinton Likes Him," *CT*, Jan. 2003, http://www.christianitytoday.com/ct/2003/january/4.37.html.

77. Laurie Goodstein, "Clinton Selects Clerics to Give Him Guidance," *NYT*, Sept. 15, 1998; Clinton, *My Life*, 810.

78. Niebuhr, "Presidential Advisors."

79. Clinton, "Leadership Conference."

80. WJC to Billy Graham, Mar. 15, 1995, White House Office of Record Management, ME001, 102163 (hereinafter cited as WHORM); WJC to Graham, Nov. 21, 1995, WHORM, ME001, 140548; GI001 186020 [OA/ID 23262]; WJC to Billy Graham, Dec. 2, 1996, WHORM, FG001-03, 197978. The Clinton library contains many other letters between Clinton to Graham.

81. Billy Graham to WJC, Apr. 26, 1995, WHORM, OA/ID 21799, DI 108775. See also WJC to Graham, Apr. 27, 1995, ibid.

82. Holmes, *Presidents*, 232–33. Graham, as quoted in Dan Balz and Ruth Marcus, "Activity Escalates, Focus Returns to Alleged Affair," *WP*, Mar. 8, 1998. See Cal Thomas, "Graham to Clinton: Go and Sin Some More," *Orlando Sentinel*, Mar. 10, 1998, http://articles.orlandosentinel.com/1998-03-10/news/9803100466_1_forgiveness-sin-graham. See also Nancy Gibbs and Michael Duffy, "Billy Graham: Hillary's Solace," *Time*, Aug. 8, 2007.

83. Larry Witham, "Churches Seek Clinton's Ear," *WT*, Dec. 7, 1992.

84. Clinton, *My Life*, 558. See also Steven Tipton, *Public Pulpits: Methodists and Mainline Churches in the Moral Argument of Public Life* (Chicago: University of Chicago Press), 253–59, 346–47.

85. E.g., William Clinton, "Remarks at a Reception for African-American Religious Leaders," Sept. 22, 1998, http://www.presidency.ucsb.edu/ws/?pid=54955; Clinton, "Remarks at a Reception for African-American Religious Leaders," Oct. 30, 2000, http://www.presidency.ucsb.edu/ws/?pid=1117.

86. William Clinton, **"Remarks to the Convocation of the Church of God in Christ in Memphis,"** *Nov. 13, 1993,* http://www.presidency.ucsb.edu/ws/?pid=46115.

87. "Clinton-Gore Stump Speech for African American Audiences," Speechwriters, Edmonds, T., Box 10, file 12, The Bible Gateway quotes, 10980 (first quotation); William Clinton, "Remarks at a Democratic National Committee Dinner," June 16, 1997, http://www.presidency.ucsb.edu/ws/?pid=54274 (second quotation).

88. Barry Hankins, *Uneasy in Babylon: Southern Baptist Conservatives and American Culture* (Tuscaloosa: University of Alabama Press, 2002), 57–58, 108, 115, 148, 163, 165–67.

89. H. Edwin Young, letter to fellow pastors, Nov. 15, 1993, R-HL 4.19g.

90. See Merrill Hawkins, Jr., "Attitudes toward the White House," *Baptist History and Heritage* 32 (Jan. 1997), 15–16.

91. Clayton, "Church Thriving," 12; Daniel Cattau, "Baptists Vote to Admonish President," *Dallas Morning News,* June 17, 1993, 31A, 35A; Steve Brunsman, "Clinton's Hometown Minister Denounces SBC 'Witch Hunt,'" *Houston Post,* A1, A24; "Motions Targeting Immanuel Church Ruled Out of Order," *Arkansas Baptist Magazine,* June 24, 1999, 5; Erica Werner, "Pastor Hopes Clinton Finds Forgiveness," *Arkansas Democrat-Gazette,* Sept. 14, 1998, 7A; Warner, "Challenge," 12.

92. Larry Witham, "Clinton Policies Could Swell Ranks," *WT,* Nov. 9, 1992.

93. Painton, "Spiritual Journey."

94. Yancey, "Clinton's Faith," 27; Clinton quoted in ibid.

95. E.g., Richard Land on Frontline 2004, 3.

96. Maraniss, *First,* 434–35.

97. Maraniss, "Clinton's Faith."

98. "Religious Affairs Journalists" (quotations); Yancey, "Clinton's Faith," 29.

99. Niebuhr, "Presidential Advisors"; Stephen Carter to WJC, May 21, 1997; WJC to Stephen Carter, May 23, 1997, both in Abortion Letters, Bruce Reed—DPC, Box 125, 102094 21208 102094-011.

100. Clinton, *My Life,* 239–40.

101. Yancey, "Clinton's Faith," 27.

102. Yancey, "Clinton's Faith," 27.

103. Goodstein, "Clerics." See Jeffrey Toobin, *A Vast Conspiracy: The Real Story of the Sex Scandal that Nearly Brought Down a President* (New York: Random House, 1999), 35–36.

104. "Little Rock Church," 16A.

105. Clinton, *My Life,* 76.

106. Larry Witham, "Catholic Bishops Face Values Shift in Clinton Regime," *WT,* Nov. 16, 1992.

107. William Clinton, **"Remarks Welcoming Pope John Paul II in Newark,"** Oct. 4, 1995, http://www.presidency.ucsb.edu/ws/?pid=50602.

108. Clinton, **"Church of God."**

109. Bishop John Ricard et al. to WJC, Nov. 10, 1993, DFC, Reed, Bruce, Churches, 21201, Box 105, folder 2; John Podesta, Memorandum for Mack McLarty et al., Dec. 14, 1993, ibid.

110. David Dalin and Alfred Kolatch, *The Presidents of the United States and the Jews* (Middle Village, NY: Jonathan David, 2000), 275, 278–82.

111. William Clinton, "Remarks to the Knesset in Jerusalem," Oct. 27, 1994, http://www.presidency.ucsb.edu/ws/?pid=49380.

112. William Clinton, "Message on the Observance of Yom Kippur, 1999," Sept. 17, 1999, http://www.presidency.ucsb.edu/ws/?pid=56530 (first quotation); Clinton, "Proclamation 7302—Jewish Heritage Week, 2000," May 2, 2000, http://www.presidency.ucsb.edu/ws/?pid=62290 (quotations).

113. See http://www.cnn.com/ALLPOLITICS/1996/elections/natl.exit.poll/index1.html.

114. Clinton, **"Address on the Observance of Id al-Fı́ tr,"** Jan. 19, 1999, http://www.presidency.ucsb.edu/ws/?pid=57522; Clinton, **"Message on the Observance of Eid Al-Fitr, 2000,"** Dec. 22, 2000, http://www.presidency.ucsb.edu/ws/?pid=1200; quotations in that order.

115. William Clinton, **"Message on the Observance of Ramadan,"** Jan. 10, 1997, http://www.presidency.ucsb.edu/ws/?pid=53950.

116. Clinton, **"End of Ramadan."**

117. Clinton, *My Life*, 560; Clinton, "Remarks at the New Psalmist Baptist Church in Baltimore," Nov. 1, 1998, http://www.presidency.ucsb.edu/ws/?pid=55210; quotations in that order.

118. Bill Clinton, "Remarks on Signing the Religious Freedom Restoration Act of 1993," Nov. 16, 1993, http://www.presidency.ucsb.edu/ws/?pid=46124.

119. Clinton, "James Madison High."

120. Quoted in Joseph Knippenberg, "Bill Clinton and the Bully Pulpit," Aug. 2004, http://www.ashbrook.org/publicat/guest/04/knippenberg/clinton.html. Although Clinton made this statement in 2004, it describes his perspective during his presidency.

121. Memorandum for Erskine Bowles, Feb. 7, 1995, from Don Baer, Bruce Reed, and Jeremy Ben-Ami, DPC, Reed, Bruce, New Covenant, OA 21207.

122. Clinton, "James Madison High" (first quotation); Clinton, "State of the Union," Jan. 24, 1995 (second and third quotations).

123. William Clinton, "The President's Radio Address," Mar. 11, 1995, http://www.presidency.ucsb.edu/ws/?pid=51091.

124. Clinton, 1995 "State of the Union."

125. **"Remarks and a Question-and-Answer Session with the American Society of Newspaper Editors in Dallas,"** Apr. 7, 1995, http://www.presidency.ucsb.edu/ws/?pid=51198 (first and second quotations); Clinton, "Remarks at Georgetown University," July 6, 1995, http://www.presidency.ucsb.edu/ws/?pid=51584 (third and fourth quotations); Clinton, "Remarks at a Democratic Leadership

Council Conference in San Jose," Apr. 3, 2000, http://www.presidency.ucsb.edu/ws/?pid=58321 (fifth quotation).

126. William Clinton, "Remarks at a Reception for Democratic Candidates in Des Moines," Nov. 3, 1994, http://www.presidency.ucsb.edu/ws/?pid=49427 (quotation); Clinton, "Remarks to the National Conference of Black Mayors," Apr. 28, 1994, http://www.presidency.ucsb.edu/ws/?pid=50060.

127. William Clinton, "Remarks in a Town Meeting in Charlotte," Apr. 5, 1994, http://www.presidency.ucsb.edu/ws/?pid=49912.

128. Clinton, 1995 "State of the Union," (first quotation); Clinton, "James Madison High"; Clinton, **"Address before a Joint Session of the Congress on the State of the Union,"** *Jan. 25, 1994,* http://www.presidency.ucsb.edu/ws/?pid=50409; "Religious Affairs Journalists" (second quotation).

129. "Religious Affairs Journalists."

130. William Clinton, "Remarks at the National Prayer Breakfast," Feb. 2, 1995, http://www.presidency.ucsb.edu/ws/?pid=50676 (first, third, and fourth quotations); Clinton, "Remarks at the National Prayer Breakfast," Feb. 1, 1996, http://www.presidency.ucsb.edu/ws/?pid=51934 (second quotation).

131. Renshon, *High Hopes,* 75 (quotation), 84.

132. Meredith Oakley, *On the Make: The Rise of Bill Clinton* (Washington, DC: Regnery, 1994), xiv; Elizabeth Drew, *On the Edge: The Clinton Presidency* (New York: Simon and Schuster, 1995), 241; John Brummett, *High Wire: From the Backwoods to the Beltway—The Education of Bill Clinton* (New York: Hyperion, 1994), 218; Joe Klein, *The Natural: The Misunderstood Presidency of Bill Clinton* (New York: Doubleday, 2002), 9; quotations in that order.

133. David Gergen, *Eyewitness to Power: The Essence of Leadership: Nixon to Clinton* (New York: Simon and Schuster, 2000), 341.

134. Clinton, "Religious Freedom Restoration Act"; Clinton, "Proclamation 6862—Religious Freedom Day, 1996," Jan. 12, 1996, http://clinton6.nara.gov/1996/01/1996-01-12-proclamation-of-religious-freedom-day.html; quotations in that order.

135. White House Press Release, Speechwriters, Edmonds, Terry, RFRA, Box 46, file 11, 16990 (first quotation); Clinton, "Remarks to the World Jewish Congress," Feb. 9, 1994, http://www.presidency.ucsb.edu/ws/?pid=49498 (remainder of quotations). In a 6–3 decision the Supreme Court struck down the RFRA in June 1997 as unconstitutional.

136. Clinton, "World Jewish Congress."

137. William Clinton, "Remarks to Native American and Native Alaskan Tribal Leaders," Apr. 29, 1994, http://www.presidency.ucsb.edu/ws/?pid=50070.

138. Clinton, "James Madison High."

139. William Clinton, "President's Radio Address," May 30, 1998, http://www.presidency.ucsb.edu/ws/?pid=56055; Clinton, "James Madison High," 1081; Clinton, "Town Meeting in Charlotte"; quotations in that order.

140. Clinton, "James Madison High."

141. William Clinton, "Memorandum on Religious Expression in Public Schools," July 12, 1995, http://www.presidency.ucsb.edu/ws/?pid=51609 (first quotation); Clinton, "James Madison High" (second and third quotations); Clinton, "Town Meeting in Charlotte" (fourth quotation).

142. Clinton, "James Madison High" (first and second quotation); Clinton, "Radio Address," May 30, 1998 (third and fourth quotation); Clinton, "Public Schools" (fifth quotation).

143. Clinton, "Federal Workplace."

144. Clinton, "Proclamation 7063—Religious Freedom Day, 1998," Jan. 16, 1998, http://clinton6.nara.gov/1998/01/1998-01-16-proclamation-on-religious-freedom-day.html (first and second quotations); Clinton, "Proclamation 6646—Religious Freedom Day, 1994," Jan. 14, 1994, http://www.presidency.ucsb.edu/ws/?pid=49910 (third quotation).

145. Clinton, "Radio Address," May 30, 1998; Clinton, "Religious Freedom Day, 1994"; Clinton, "**Federal Workplace**"; quotations in that order

146. Clinton, "Federal Workplace" (first quotation); Clinton, "James Madison High" (second and third quotations); Clinton, "Proclamation 7267—Religious Freedom Day, 2000," Jan. 14, 2000, http://clinton6.nara.gov/2000/01/2000-01-14-proclamation-on-religious-freedom-day.html (fourth quotation); Clinton, "Proclamation 7162—Religious Freedom Day, 1999," Jan. 14, 1999, http://clinton6.nara.gov/1999/01/1999-01-14-proclamation-on-religious-freedom-day.html (fifth quotation).

147. Clinton, "Religious Freedom Restoration Act" (first quotation); Clinton, "James Madison High" (second quotation); Clinton, "Remarks Following Discussions with Religious Leaders," June 18, 1998, http://www.presidency.ucsb.edu/ws/?pid=56158 (third and fourth quotations).

148. Clinton, "Religious Freedom Day, 1996" (first and second quotations); Clinton, "Federal Workplace" (third and fourth quotations); Clinton, "Religious Freedom Day, 1998" (fifth quotation); Clinton, "Religious Leaders," June 18, 1998 (sixth quotation).

149. Clinton, "Religious Leaders," June 18, 1998.

150. Yechiel Eckstein et al to WJC, June 15, 1998, NSC, Blinken, Anthony, Religious Freedom Event, June 18, 1998, 3380, Box 36.

151. "The President's News Conference with President Jiang Zemin of China in Beijing," June 27, 1998, http://www.presidency.ucsb.edu/ws/?pid=56229.

152. William Clinton, "Remarks and a Question-and-Answer Session with Students at Beijing University," June 29, 1998, http://www.presidency.ucsb.edu/ws/?pid=56236.

153. June Shih's draft for Clinton's remarks at Chongwenmen Church originally stated that everyone deserved "the freedom to pursue their beliefs without apprehension or fear" (NSC, Blinken, Anthony, China Trip, Church Remarks, Box 36, June 28, 1998). Clinton instead declared, "We rejoice to hear Reverend

Siu cite the numbers of churches and other places of worship where people are practicing their faith today" ("**Remarks at Chongwenmen Church in Beijing**," *June 28, 1998*, http://www.presidency.ucsb.edu/ws/?pid=56233).

154. William Clinton, "Statement on the International Day of Prayer for the Persecuted Church," Nov. 14, 1998, http://www.presidency.ucsb.edu/ws/?pid=55279 (first quotation); Clinton, "Message on the Observance of the International Day of Prayer for the Persecuted Church," Nov. 10, 1999, http://www.presidency.ucsb.edu/ws/?pid=56926 (second quotation); Clinton, "Religious Freedom Day, 1999" (third and fourth quotations); Clinton, "**Statement on Signing the International Religious Freedom Act of 1998**," Oct. 27, 1998, http://www.presidency.ucsb.edu/ws/?pid=55155 (fifth and sixth quotations); Clinton, "Religious Freedom Day, 2000" (remainder of quotations).

155. William Clinton, "President's Radio Address," July 8, 1995, http://www.presidency.ucsb.edu/ws/?pid=51593.

156. William Clinton, "**Remarks on Welfare Reform in Kansas City**," *June 14, 1994*, http://www.presidency.ucsb.edu/ws/?pid=50335 (first and second quotations); "**Newspaper Editors in Dallas**" (third quotation).

157. "Religious Affairs Journalists" (first, second, and third quotations); Clinton, "Radio Address," Mar. 11, 1995, (fourth quotation).

158. William Clinton, "Remarks at a Breakfast with Religious Leaders," Sept. 8, 1995, http://www.presidency.ucsb.edu/ws/?pid=51817.

159. Clinton, "**Newspaper Editors in Dallas**," *(first and second quotations)*; Clinton, "Radio Address," July 8, 1995, (third and fourth quotations).

160. "A Guide to Charitable Choice," http://www.cpjustice.org/files/CCGuide_0.pdf.

161. "Religious Affairs Journalists."

162. William Clinton, "Remarks at the Ecumenical Prayer Breakfast," Jan. 6, 1997, http://www.presidency.ucsb.edu/ws/?pid=53750.

163. "Clinton Asks Churches to Help Poor," *Baptist Messenger*, Jan. 16, 1997, 5.

164. Clinton, "Breakfast with Religious Leaders," Sept. 28, 1999.

165. Clinton, "New Psalmist Baptist Church"; Clinton, 1997 "National Prayer Breakfast"; Clinton, "Remarks on Lighting the National Christmas Tree," Dec. 7, 1994, http://www.presidency.ucsb.edu/ws/?pid=49562; quotations in that order.

166. Clinton, 1994 "National Prayer Breakfast."

167. E.g., William Clinton, "Remarks to the Progressive National Baptist Convention in Charlotte," Aug. 9, 1995, http://www.presidency.ucsb.edu/ws/?pid=51722.

168. Clinton, "Remarks to Business Leaders in Abuja," Aug. 27, 2000, http://www.presidency.ucsb.edu/ws/?pid=1418.

169. William Clinton, "Remarks at a Dinner Honoring Billy and Ruth Graham," May 2, 1996, http://www.presidency.ucsb.edu/ws/?pid=52761.

170. William Clinton, "President's Radio Address," Nov. 23, 1996, http://www.presidency.ucsb.edu/ws/?pid=52277.

171. http://clinton6.nara.gov/2000/08/2000-08-22-fact-sheet-on-welfare-reform. html; see also Clinton, "Statement on Welfare Reform," Aug. 22, 2000, http:// www.presidency.ucsb.edu/ws/?pid=1426.

172. Clinton, *My Life*, 721.

173. Clinton, "Remarks at a Breakfast with Religious Leaders," Sept. 14, 2000, http://www.presidency.ucsb.edu/ws/?pid=1366. See also Clinton, "Remarks Prior to a Meeting with Congressional and Religious Leaders and an Exchange with Reporters," Oct. 2, 2000, http://www.presidency.ucsb.edu/ ws/?pid=1432.

174. Betty Glad, "Bill Clinton: The Character Issue Revisited," in Todd Shields, Jeannie Whayne, and Donald Kelley, eds., *The Clinton Riddle: Perspectives on the Forty-second President* (Fayetteville: University of Arkansas Press, 2004), 10.

175. Paul Begala reported that Clinton repeatedly quoted this passage (Gartner, *In Search*, 107). Clinton had his Bible open to this passage when he swore his oath of office at his second inaugural, and he quoted it in several addresses.

176. Clinton, **"End of Ramadan."**

177. William Clinton, **"Remarks on Lighting the City Christmas Tree in Belfast,"** *Nov. 30, 1995*, http://www.presidency.ucsb.edu/ws/?pid=50829. He quoted the phrase "Blessed are the peacemakers" in eight additional addresses.

178. Clinton, "Remarks to the Knesset"; Clinton, **"Teleconference Remarks with B'nai B'rith,"** *Aug. 24, 1994*, http://www.presidency.ucsb.edu/ws/?pid=49014.

179. E.g., William Clinton, **"Remarks on the Observance of Eid al-Fitr,"** *Feb. 20, 1996*, http://www.presidency.ucsb.edu/ws/?pid= 52428.

180. William Clinton, **"Remarks to the Jordanian Parliament in Amman, Jordan,"** *Oct. 26, 1994*, http://www.presidency.ucsb.edu/ws/?pid=49373; Clinton, **"Eid Al-Fitr, 2000"**; quotations in that order.

181. Clinton, "Jordanian Parliament."

182. William Clinton, "Videotaped Remarks on Id al-Fítr," Jan. 29, 1998, http:// www.presidency.ucsb.edu/ws/?pid=54749.

183. William Clinton, "Remarks to the Clergy in Jamaica, New York," Oct. 30, 1998, http://www.presidency.ucsb.edu/ws/?pid=55192 (quotation); Pfiffner, "Presidential Character," 249.

184. William Clinton, **"Remarks to the Palestine National Council and Other Palestinian Organizations in Gaza City,"** *Dec. 14, 1998*, http://www.presidency. ucsb.edu/ws/?pid=55410.

185. Clinton, **"Palestine National Council."**

186. Clinton, "African Methodist Episcopal Church."

187. William Clinton, "Address to Arab Nations," Dec. 19, 1998, http://www.presi-dency.ucsb.edu/ws/?pid=55433.

188. Clinton, **"Television Address to the People of Pakistan from Islamabad, Pakistan,"** *Mar. 25, 2000*, http://www.presidency.ucsb.edu/ws/?pid=58295.

189. Gergen, Cooper, and Baer, "Hidden Life."

190. See Toobin, *Conspiracy*, 134–49; Melinda Henneberger, "Testing of a President: The Accuser," *NYT*, Mar. 12, 1998, A1; Michael Isikoff and Stuart Taylor, Jr., "The Paula Problem," *Newsweek*, Jan. 26, 1998, 24; and Neil Lewis, "Clinton Settles Jones Lawsuit with a Check of $850,000," *NYT*, Jan. 13, 1999, A14.

191. See Andrew Morton, *Monica's Story* (New York: St. Martin's Press, 1999), 64, 69–72, 77, 81, 86, 89, 90, 159, 249, 252.

192. William Clinton, "Remarks at a Breakfast with Religious Leaders," Sept. 11, 1998, http://www.presidency.ucsb.edu/ws/?pid=54886; Clinton, "Leadership Conference" (last quotation); Wogaman, *Storm*, 118, 40.

193. Smith, *Politics*, 352–53; *Time*, Sept. 21, 1998; *Newsweek*, Sept. 21, 1998 ("pornographic specificity"); *Philadelphia Inquirer*, Sept. 13, 1998 ("repeated, reckless deceits"); *USA Today*, Sept. 14, 1998; "Southern Baptist President Calls for Clinton's Resignation," as cited by Holmes, *Presidents*, 235; Chris Herlinger, "Clinton Tells Religious Leaders: 'I Have Sinned,' " Sept. 18, 1998, http://www. layman.org/news.aspx?article=9611.

194. E.g., *USA Today*, Sept. 14, 1998: 66 percent of Americans opposed impeachment, 62 percent opposed resignation, and 64 percent approved of Clinton's job performance; Wogaman, *Storm*, 74.

195. Werner, "Pastor Hopes Clinton Finds Forgiveness," 1A, 7A; the first quotation is Werner's words; the second is Horne's; both quotations from 1A.

196. Linda Caillouet, "2 Top Southern Baptist Leaders Turn Up Heat on Clinton's Pastor," *Arkansas Democrat-Gazette*, Sept. 12, 1998, 11A.

197. Quoted in Laurie Goodstein, "Washington Minister Joins Two Colleagues in Counseling Clinton," *NYT*, Sept. 18, 1998, http://partners.nytimes.com/library/politics/091898clinton-minister.html.

198. Cal Thomas, "Can Clinton's Religious Advisers Stop Him before He Sins Again?" http://articles.philly.com/1998-09-21/news/25759539_1_tony-campolo-religious-leaders-religion; Hanna Rosin, "Ministers to Give Clinton 'Pastoral Care,' " *WP*, Sept. 16, 1998, A31 (Campolo and Wogaman quotations); "Editorial: The President's Small Group: Turning Your Life around Is Not a Do-It-Yourself Project," *CT*, Oct. 26, 1998, http://www.ctlibrary.com/ct/1998/october26/8tco28.html.

199. Rex Horne's words as quoted in Woodward, "Sex, Sin and Salvation," 37. See also Erin Schulte, "Home Church Forgives Clinton," *Arkansas Democrat-Gazette*, Oct. 23, 1998, 1A, 14A.

200. Adelle Banks, *Arkansas Democrat-Gazette*, Nov. 6, 1998, 6B.

201. Gabriel Fackre, ed., *Judgment Day at the White House: A Critical Declaration Exploring Moral Issues and the Political Use and Abuse of Religion* (Grand Rapids, MI: William B. Eerdmans, 1999), 2. See also Alan Wolfe, "Judging the President: The Perplexing Role of Religion in Public Life," *Brookings Review*, June 1999, 28–31.

202. Campolo, "Errant Evangelical?" 35.

203. Harold Perkin, "The Tyranny of the Moral Majority: American Religion and Politics since the Pilgrim Fathers," *Cultural Values* 3 (Apr. 1999), 193.

204. "Interview with Dan Rather of CBS News," Mar. 31, 1999, http://www.presidency.ucsb.edu/ws/?pid=57340 (first and second quotations); Clinton, "Breakfast with Religious Leaders," Sept. 28, 1999 (third quotation); "Interview with Francine Kiefer and Skip Thurman of the *Christian Science Monitor* in Boston," Jan. 18, 2000, http://www.presidency.ucsb.edu/ws/?pid=58520 (fourth quotation).

205. Clinton, "Leadership Conference" (first three quotations); Clinton, *My Life*, 811 (fourth quotation), 846.

206. Clinton, *My Life*, 847; Renshon, *High Hopes*, 100.

207. E.g., Wogaman, *Storm*, 80, 136.

208. Gergen, *Eyewitness*, 339–40.

209. Lauren Berlant and Lisa Duggan, "Introduction," in Berlant and Duggan, eds., *Our Monica, Ourselves: The Clinton Affair and the National Interest* (New York: New York University Press, 2001), 3.

210. Gergen, *Eyewitness*, 340.

211. Rockman, "Grain," 286.

212. George Will, "Clinton's Mark," Jan. 12, 2001, http://www.jewishworldreview.com/cols/will011201.asp; William Bennett, *The Death of Outrage: Bill Clinton and the Assault on American Ideals* (New York: The Free Press, 1998), 5, 9, 10; quotations in that order; Barrett, "'My Lies' by Bill Clinton."

213. Glad, "Clinton," 2–5, 15–20; quotation from 20.

214. Pfiffner, "Presidential Character," 248.

215. Brummett, *High Wire*. 269; Todd Purdum, "Facets of Clinton," *New York Times Magazine* 19 (May 1996), 30; Renshon, *High Hopes*, 6–7; quotations in that order.

216. Pfiffner, "Presidential Character," 226–30, 235; quotation from 230.

217. Gartner, *Search*, 1–4, 114–15, first quotation from 4, second from 1–2, third from 2; Homes, *Presidents*, 236.

218. Gergen, *Eyewitness*, 328–29; quotation from 328; Don Van Natta, Jr., "Taking Second Chances: Par for Clinton's Course," *NYT*, Aug. 8, 1999, http://www.nytimes.com/1999/08/29/weekinreview/ideas-trends-presidential-mulligans-taking-second-chances-par-for-clinton-s.html. David Riesman advanced this explanation in *The Lonely Crowd: A Study of the Changing American Character* (New Haven, CT: Yale University Press, 1950).

219. Morris's assessment is reported in Gartner, *Search*, 114 (the longer quotation is Gartner's words); Maraniss, *First*, 451 (first two quotations); David Maraniss, *The Clinton Enigma* (New York: Simon and Schuster, 1998), 100 (third quotation).

220. Clinton, *My Life*, 58, 811; quotations in that order.

221. Thomas, "Sins Again."

CHAPTER 11

1. Stephen Mansfield, *The Faith of Barack Obama* (Nashville, TN: Thomas Nelson, 2011). See also David Holmes, *The Faiths of the Postwar Presidents: From Truman to Obama* (Athens: University of Georgia Press, 2012), 270–320; John Wilson, *Barack Obama: This Improbable Quest* (Boulder, CO: Paradigm Publishers, 2008), 131–41; and David Remnick, *The Bridge: The Life and Rise of Barack Obama* (New York: Alfred Knopf, 2010), 170–71, 174–75, 406–7, 421, 440–42, 449, 458, 468, 469, 543. The most comprehensive analysis of Obama's theological and biblical perspective and its influence on his policies is R. Ward Holder and Peter Josephson, *The Irony of Barack Obama: Barack Obama, Reinhold Niebuhr and the Problem of Christian Statescraft* (Burlington, VT: Ashgate, 2012). They argue that Obama's faith is genuine, informs his political philosophy and policies, and is strongly shaped by Niebuhr's Christian realism (see especially 6–7, 45–46, 70, 78).

2. Fea argues that "Obama's piety, use of the Bible, and references to Christian faith and theology put most other American presidents to shame." He stresses that Obama read the Bible regularly, claimed his faith motivated his work, was being spiritually mentored by evangelical pastors, and sought to aid "the least of these" (http://www.patheos.com/Resources/Additional-Resources/Vote-for-T his-Man-John-Fea-02-15-2012.html). In "America's Most Biblically-Hostile U.S. President," http://www.wallbuilders.com/LIBissuesArticles.asp?id=106938, David Barton accuses Obama of attacking "Biblical persons or organizations" and being hostile "toward Biblical faith," as evident in his assaults on scriptural values and "deference for Islam's activities and positions."

3. Mitchell Landsberg, "Obama Praised—and Pummeled—on Matters of Faith," http://articles.latimes.com/2012/apr/07/nation/la-na-obama-religion-20120408.

4. John Blake, "The Gospel according to Obama," http://religion.blogs.cnn. com/2012/10/21/to-some-obama-is-the-wrong-kind-of-christian/; David Gibson, "Obama's Faith-Based Presidency: 'Help the Needy, Walk With God,'" http:// www.politicsdaily.com/2011/02/03/obamas-faith-based-presidency-help-the-needy-walk-with-god/.

5. See Evan Thomas, *"A Long Time Coming": The Inspiring, Combative 2008 Campaign and the Historic Election of Barack Obama* (New York: Public Affairs, 2009); Dan Balz and Haynes Johnson, *The Battle for America 2008: The Story of an Extraordinary Election* (New York: Viking, 2009); Corwin Smidt et al., *The Disappearing God Gap? Religion in the 2008 Presidential Election* (New York: Oxford University Press, 2010); and Gaston Espinoza, ed., *Religion, Race, and Barack Obama's New Democratic Pluralism* (New York: Routledge, 2013).

6. E.g., Barack Obama, "Commencement Address for Joplin High School in Joplin, Missouri," May 21, 2012, http://www.presidency.ucsb.edu/ws/?pid=100921. Some evangelicals were perplexed by Obama's use of brother's keeper, "noting

that it comes from the mouth of Cain, history's most famous fratricide" (Daniel Burke, "Obama's Use of Scripture Has Elements of Lincoln, King," http:// sojo.net/blogs/2013/01/16/obama%E2%80%99s-use-scripture-has-elem ents-lincoln-king).

7. Lisa Miller, "Finding His Faith," http://www.thedailybeast.com/newsweek/2008/ 07/11/finding-his-faith.print.html.

8. Barack Obama, "A Politics of Conscience," June 23, 2007, http://www.ucc.org/ news/significant-speeches/a-politics-of-conscience.html.

9. Barack Obama, *Dreams from My Father* (New York: Three Rivers Press, 1995), 50.

10. Barack Obama, "Remarks by the President at National Prayer Breakfast," Feb. 3, 2011, http://www.whitehouse.gov/the-press-office/2011/02/03/remarks-president-national-prayer-breakfast. See also Edward Lee Pitts, "A President's Prayers: President Obama Shares Aspects of His Private Spiritual Life," http:// www.worldmag.com/webextra/17599.

11. Obama, *Dreams*, 37.

12. Mansfield, *Obama*, 15–16.

13. Barack Obama, *The Audacity of Hope* (New York: Three Rivers Press, 2006), 204. On Dunham, also see Janny Scott, *A Singular Woman: The Untold Story of Barack Obama's Mother* (New York: Riverhead Books, 2011).

14. Miller, "Faith."

15. Miller, "Faith."

16. Obama, *Audacity*, 206 (first two phrases); Obama, "Call to Renewal" (last phrase).

17. Obama, "Politics of Conscience," all quotations except the third one which is from Obama, *Audacity*, 208.

18. Mansfield, *Obama*, 26–52. On Wright, also see Clarence Earl Walker and Gregory Smithers, *The Preacher and the Politician* (Charlottesville: University of Virginia Press, 2009).

19. Barack Obama, "On My Faith and My Church," Mar. 14, 2008, http://www. realclearpolitics.com/articles/2008/03/on_my_faith_andmy_church.html; Mansfield, *Obama*, 65–69.

20. Obama, *Dreams*, 294.

21. Barack Obama, "Remarks by the President in a Backyard Discussion in Albuquerque," Sept. 28, 2010, http://www.whitehouse.gov/the-press-office/2010/09/28/ remarks-president-a-backyard-discussion-albuquerque-new-mexico (first three quotations); "Press Conference by President Obama," Sept. 10, 2010, http://www. whitehouse.gov/the-press-office/2010/09/10/press-conference-president-obama (fourth quotation) (cf. Obama, "Remarks at the National Prayer Breakfast," Feb. 3, 2011, http://www.presidency.ucsb.edu/ws/?pid=88960); Barack Obama, "The President's Weekly Address," Mar. 30, 2013, http://www.presidency.ucsb.edu/ ws/?pid=103429; (fifth and sixth quotation).

22. Barack Obama, "Remarks at the National Prayer Breakfast," Feb. 4, 2010, http:// www.presidency.ucsb.edu/ws/?pid=87473(first quotation); Obama, "Remarks at

a Church Service Honoring Martin Luther King, Jr.," Jan. 17, 2010, http://www.presidency.ucsb.edu/ws/?pid=87399 (second quotation); Obama, "Proclamation 8667—National Day of Prayer, 2011," Apr. 29, 2011, http://www.presidency.ucsb.edu/ws/?pid=90331 (third and fourth quotations); Obama, "Remarks at the Sandy Hook Interfaith Prayer Vigil in Newtown, Connecticut," Dec. 16, 2012, http://www.presidency.ucsb.edu/ws/?pid=102767 (fifth quotation); Obama, 2011 "National Prayer Breakfast" (sixth quotation).

23. Barack Obama, "Remarks at an Easter Prayer Breakfast," Apr. 5, 2013, http://www.presidency.ucsb.edu/ws/?pid=103445; "Q&A: Barack Obama," http://www.christianitytoday.com/ct/2008/januaryweb-only/104-32.0.html?paging=offObama; 2011 "National Prayer Breakfast"; Sarah Pulliam and Ted Olson, "Q&A: Barack Obama," Jan. 2008, http://www.christianitytoday.com/ct2008/januaryweb-only/104-32.0.html; http://blogs.suntimes.com/sweet/2010/04/obama_at_easter_prayer_breakfa.html. See also Steven Thomma, "As Muslim Claim Lingers, Obama Talks Up His Faith in Jesus," http://www.mcclatchydc.com/2010/09/28/101294/obama-talks-up-his-faith-in-jesus.html.

24. Barack Obama, "Remarks at an Easter Prayer Breakfast," Apr. 19, 2011, http://www.presidency.ucsb.edu/ws/?pid=90283.

25. Barack Obama, "The President's Weekly Address," Apr. 7, 2012, http://www.presidency.ucsb.edu/ws/?pid=100462. Cf. Obama, "Statement on the Observance of Easter," Mar. 29, 2013, http://www.presidency.ucsb.edu/ws/?pid=103397; Obama, "Remarks at an Easter Prayer Breakfast," Apr. 5, 2013, http://www.presidency.ucsb.edu/ws/?pid=103445.

26. Barack Obama, "Remarks at the National Prayer Breakfast," Feb. 7, 2013, http://www.presidency.ucsb.edu/ws/?pid=103241.

27. Obama, "Easter Prayer Breakfast," Apr. 5, 2013. Cf. Obama, "The President's Weekly Address," Dec. 25, 2013, http://www.presidency.ucsb.edu/ws/?pid=104513.

28. Barack Obama, "Remarks on the National Economy," Apr.14, 2009, http://www.presidency.ucsb.edu/ws/?pid=86000; Eamon Javers, "Obama Invokes Jesus More than Bush," June 9, 2009, http://dyn.politico.com/printstory.cfm?uuid=C27D4E5C-18FE-70B2-A8EA98A9D6C801E8.

29. Obama, "Remarks at the National Prayer Breakfast," Feb. 6, 2014, http://www.presidency.ucsb.edu/ws/index.php?pid=104675&st=&st1=.

30. Obama, "Discussion in Albuquerque" (first two words); Obama, "Remarks by the President at the Acceptance of the Nobel Peace Prize," Dec. 10, 2009, http://www.whitehouse.gov/the-press-office/remarks-president-acceptance-nobel-peace-prize (remainder of the quoted words).

31. Barack Obama, "Commencement Address at the University of Notre Dame," May 17, 2009, http://www.presidency.ucsb.edu/ws/?pid=86154.

32. Barack Obama, "Remarks at a Memorial Service for Victims of the Shootings in Tucson," Jan. 12, 2011, http://www.presidency.ucsb.edu/ws/?pid=88893. See

also Obama, "Remarks at the Holocaust Days of Remembrance Ceremony," Apr. 23, 2009, http://www.presidency.ucsb.edu/ws/?pid=86043; Obama, "The President's Weekly Address," Sept. 11, 2010, http://www.presidency.ucsb.edu/ws/?pid=88428.

33. Quoted in David Remnick, "Testing the Waters," *New Yorker*, Oct. 30, 2006, http://www.newyorker.com/061030 on_onlineonly04.
34. Quoted in Miller, "Faith."
35. Obama, 2011 "National Prayer Breakfast."
36. Barack Obama, "Interview with the First Lady and Barbara Walters," Nov. 23, 2010, http://www.presidency.ucsb.edu/ws/?pid=97100.
37. Barack Obama, "Remarks at the National Hispanic Prayer Breakfast," June 19, 2009, http://www.presidency.ucsb.edu/ws/?pid=86311 (first and second quotations); Obama, 2010 "National Prayer Breakfast" (third and fourth quotations); Obama, 2011 "National Prayer Breakfast" (fifth quotation).
38. Barack Obama, "Remarks at the National Prayer Breakfast," Feb. 2, 2012, http://www.presidency.ucsb.edu/ws/?pid=99207 (first three quotations); Obama, "Hispanic Prayer Breakfast" (fourth and fifth quotations); Obama, 2010 "National Prayer Breakfast"; Obama, 2011 "National Prayer Breakfast"; Barack Obama, "Remarks at a Church Service Honoring Martin Luther King, Jr.," Jan. 17, 2010, http://www.presidency.ucsb.edu/ws/?pid=87399 (final quotation). See also Lisa Miller and Richard Wolffe, "I Am a Big Believer in Not Just Words, But Deeds and Works," *Newsweek*, July 12, 2008, http://www.newsweek.com/2008/07/11/i-am-a-big-believer-in-not-just-words-but-deeds-and-works.html.
39. Barack Obama, "Remarks at the National Prayer Breakfast," Feb. 5, 2009, http://www.presidency.ucsb.edu/ws/?pid=85733; Obama, 2011 "National Prayer Breakfast."
40. Barack Obama, "Remarks Following a Roundtable Discussion at the Desmond Tutu HIV Foundation Youth Center in Cape Town, South Africa," June 30, 2013, http://www.presidency.ucsb.edu/ws/?pid=103885.
41. E.g., Barack Obama, "Statement on the 10th Anniversary of the Iraq War," Mar. 19, 2013, http://www.presidency.ucsb.edu/ws/?pid=103380; Obama, "Remarks Following a Meeting with African Leaders and an Exchange with Reporters," Mar. 28, 2013, http://www.presidency.ucsb.edu/ws/?pid=103442; Obama, "Remarks on the Terrorist Attack in Boston," Apr. 15, 2013, http://www.presidency.ucsb.edu/ws/?pid=103460; Obama, "Statement on the Explosion at the West Fertilizer Company Plant in West, Texas," Apr. 18, 2013, http://www.presidency.ucsb.edu/ws/?pid=103484; Obama, "Proclamation 8964—Workers Memorial Day, 2013," Apr. 26, 2013, http://www.presidency.ucsb.edu/ws/?pid=103524.
42. Barack Obama, "Remarks at a State Dinner Hosted by President Shimon Peres of Israel in Jerusalem," Mar. 21, 2013, http://www.presidency.ucsb.edu/ws/?pid=103388.
43. Obama, 2011 "National Prayer Breakfast"; Obama, 2013 "National Prayer Breakfast"; Obama, *Audacity*, 224 (quotations in that order); Judd Birdsall,

"Barack Obama: Evangelical-in-Chief?" http://www.christianitytoday.com/ct/2012/juneweb-only/barack-obama-evangelical-in-chief.html.

44. "Obama Contends Belief in Jesus Christ Not Necessary for Salvation," Mar. 27, 2008, http://www.onenewsnow.com/Election2008/Default.aspx?id=73553 (first and fourth quotations); "Obama Discusses His Christian Faith, Chides Republicans in Backyard Chat," http://www.washingtonpost.com/wp-dyn/content/article/2010/09/28/AR2010092803203.html (second quotation); Cathleen Falsani, "I Have Deep Faith," *Chicago Sun Times*, Apr. 5, 2005 (third quotation).

45. Falsani, "Deep Faith"; Barack Obama, "Eulogy at the Funeral Service for Senator Robert C. Byrd in Charleston, West Virginia," July 2, 2010, http://www.presidency.ucsb.edu/ws/?pid=88138; Obama, "Shootings in Tucson"; Obama, "Remarks in Aurora, Colorado," July 22, 2012, http://www.presidency.ucsb.edu/ws/?pid=101545; Obama, "Interfaith Prayer Vigil"; Obama, "Remarks at an Interfaith Prayer Service for the Victims of the Terrorist Attack in Boston," Apr. 18, 2013, http://www.presidency.ucsb.edu/ws/?pid=103500; Obama, "Statement on the Observance of Orthodox Easter," May 4, 2013, http://www.presidency.ucsb.edu/ws/?pid=103569; Obama, "Remarks at a Memorial Service for Victims of the Shootings at the Washington Navy Yard," Sept. 22, 2013, http://www.presidency.ucsb.edu/ws/?pid=104272.

46. "Did Andy Stanley Really Mean Obama Is 'Pastor in Chief'?" Interview by Mark Galli, http://www.christianitytoday.com/ct/2013/january-web-only/andy-stanley-obama-inauguration-pastor-in-chief.html?utm_source=ctweekly-.

47. Stephen Mansfield, "The Pastor and the President: A Tale of Faith," Mar. 5, 2012, http://www.huffingtonpost.com/stephen-mansfield/president-obama-pastors-joel-hunter_b_1311348.html.

48. Sarah Pulliam Bailey, "Has Obama Chosen a Church?" June 29, 2009; http://news.yahoo.com/obamas-attend-easter-worship-historic-dc-church-174737645--abc-news-politics.html; Sarah Pulliam Bailey, "The Obamas Attend a Church in D.C.," http://blog.christianitytoday.com/ctpolitics/2009/10/the_obamas_atte.html.

49. Alexis Garrett Stodghill, "President Obama and First Family Attend Services at Oldest Black Episcopal Church," http://thegrio.com/2013/01/20/president-obama-and-first-family-attend-services-at-oldest-black-episcopal-church/.

50. Jacqueline Salmon, "Obama Won't Choose One Church," *WP*, July 2, 2009; Eli Saslow and Hamil Harris, "Obamas Celebrate Easter in Southeast Washington," *WP*, Apr. 5, 2010; Hamil Harris and Peter Wallsten, "Marking Holiday at Metropolitan AME, Obamas Get New Invite," *WP*, Jan. 17, 2011; Jacqueline Salmon, "Navy Chaplain Carey Cash Takes Message from Iraq to Obama," http://www.washingtonpost.com/wp-dyn/content/article/2009/10/13/AR2009101303601.html; Amy Sullivan, "Why the Modern President Can't Belong to a Church," http://swampland.time.com/2011/12/16/why-the-modern-president-cant-belong-to-a-church/.

51. "Obamas Return to Camp David after 8 Month Absence," http://www. cbsnews.com/8301-503544_162-20070515-503544.html; "NYT White House Correspondent: Obama 'Hates' Camp David Because There's No Golf," http://news-busters.org/blogs/noel-sheppard/2012/05/27/nyt-white-house-correspondent-o bama-hates-camp-david-because-theres-n#ixzz2WCc6HY2O; "Obama: 'At Camp David, We Do Skeet Shooting All the Time,'" http://www.washingtonpost.com/ blogs/post-politics/wp/2013/01/28/obama-at-camp-david-we-do-skeet-shootin g-all-the-time/.

52. Ashley Parker, "As the Obamas Celebrate Christmas, Rituals of Faith Become Less Visible," *NYT*, http://www.nytimes.com/2013/12/29/us/ as-the-obamas-celebrate-christmas-rituals-of-faith-stay-on-the-sidelines.html; Teep Schlacter, "On Obama's Crackberry Jesus," Apr. 8, 2010, http://www. catholicvoteaction.org/americanpapist/index.php?p=6718; Lisa Fine, "Obama Criticized for Not Going to Church on Christmas," Politix, http://politix.topix. com/story/9576-obama-criticized-for-not-going-to-church-on-christmas.

53. Peter Wehner, "The Hazards of Questioning Obama's Faith," http://www.com-mentarymagazine.com/2011/04/25/the-hazards-of-questioning-obamas-faith/; Cal Thomas, "Why Do Christians Doubt Barack Obama's Faith?" http://www. squidoo.com/snobama; Sarah Pulliam Bailey, "Obama at Christmas Tree Lighting," Dec. 2, 2011, http://blog.christianitytoday.com/ctpolitics/2011/12/ obama_at_christ.html (Jones quotation). Graham later apologized for ques-tioning the genuineness of Obama's faith. See Adele Banks, "Franklin Graham Apologizes for Doubting Obama's Faith," *CC* 129 (Mar. 21, 2012), 19.

54. Tobin Grant, "White House Rebukes Franklin Graham for 'Preposterous Charges,'" Apr. 26, 2011, http://www.christianitytoday.com/ct/2011/aprilwe-bonly/whitehousefranklingraham.html (first quotation); Daniel Burke, "Obama Bares His Christian Soul," *CC* 127 (May 4, 2010), 14 (second quotation); Birdsall, "Obama" (third, fourth, and Hunter quotations).

55. Sarah Pulliam Bailey, "Poll: 24 percent Think Obama is a Muslim," Aug. 31, 2010.

56. "Growing Number of Americans Say Obama is a Muslim," http://www.pewfo-rum.org/2010/08/18/growing-number-of-americans-say-obama-is-a-muslim/ (moreover, 43 percent of respondents claimed they did not know what Obama's religion is); "Obama's Religion: A Hard Question for Americans," *CC* 127 (Sept. 21, 2010), 15. See also Kathryn Lopez, "Barack Obama's Religious-Identity Vacuum," Aug. 19, 2010, http://www.nationalreview.com/corner/244168/ barack-obamas-religious-identity-vacuum-kathryn-jean-lopez. In a *Time* maga-zine poll, 24 percent of respondents said Obama was a Muslim and 47 percent said he was a Christian (Alex Altman, "TIME Poll: Majority Oppose Mosque, Many Distrust Muslims," Aug. 19, 2010, http://www.time.com/time/nation/ article/0,8599,2011799,00.html#ixzz2WlePjnWj). See also "Evangelical Voters Strongly Support Romney Despite Religious Differences," http://publicreligion. org/research/2012/05/may-rns-2012-research/.

57. Adelle Banks, "As Polls Show Doubt, Obama Underscores Christian Identity," *CC* 128 (Jan. 11, 2011), 15.

58. Sarah Pulliam Bailey, "Franklin Graham: Obama Born a Muslim, a Christian Now," Aug. 20, 2010, http://blog.christianitytoday.com/ctpolitics/2010/08/franklin_graham_1.html; "Obama Speech Draws Strong Reactions," June 5, 2009, http://blog.christianitytoday.com/ctpolitics/2009/06/strong_reaction.html; "Obama's Religion," 15.

59. Amy Sullivan, "Barack Obama is Not a Muslim," http://swampland.time.com/2010/08/19/barack-obama-is-not-a-muslim/; John McCormack, "Pew: 18 Percent of Americans Think Obama's a Muslim: So What?," Aug 19, 2010, http://www.weeklystandard.com/blogs/obama-not-muslim; Ross Douthat, "Divided by God," http://www.nytimes.com/2012/04/08/opinion/sunday/douthat-in-2012-no-religious-center-is-holding.html?hpw.

60. Barack Obama, "Inaugural Address," Jan. 20, 2009, http://www.presidency.ucsb.edu/ws/?pid=44; Ken Blackwell, "The President's Confusing Messages on Religion," http://online.worldmag.com/2010/02/05/the-presidents-confusing-messages-on-religion/.

61. Barack Obama, "Remarks in Cairo," June 4, 2009, http://www.presidency.ucsb.edu/ws/?pid=86221. See also Dan Gilgoff, "Obama's Ramadan Speech Targets Muslims Abroad—and Non-Muslims at Home," *U.S. News and World Report*, Sept. 2, 2009; Brian Califano, Paul Djupe, and John Green, "Muslims and the 2008 Election," in Espinoza, ed., *Religion*, 128–48.

62. Barack Obama, "Remarks at the Iftar Dinner," July 25, 2013, http://www.presidency.ucsb.edu/ws/?pid=103937.

63. Blackwell, "Confusing Messages."

64. Barack Obama, "Remarks at the Iftar Dinner," Aug. 13, 2010, http://www.presidency.ucsb.edu/ws/?pid=88306; Obama, "Informal Remarks to Reporters in Panama City Beach, Florida," Aug. 14, 2010, http://www.presidency.ucsb.edu/ws/?pid=88353.

65. David Pryce-Jones, "Barack Obama, Apologist-in-Chief," Aug. 14, 2010, http://www.nationalreview.com/david-pryce-jones/243738/barack-obama-apologist-chief.

66. "Obama Fumbles Mosque Question," *National Review*, Aug. 16, 2010, http://www.nationalreview.com/articles/243756/obama-fumbles-mosque-question-editors.

67. Joe Carter, "Pledging Allegiance to Irreligion," Aug. 31, 2011, http://www.firstthings.com/onthesquare/2011/08/pledging-allegiance-to-irreligion/joe-carter; Tevi Troy, "The White House Seder and the Danger of Political Ritual," May 13, 2010, http://www.firstthings.com/onthesquare/2010/05/the-white-house-seder-and-the-danger-of-political-ritual.

68. Owen Strachan, "Why We Should Reexamine the Faith of Barack Obama," http://www.christianitytoday.com/ct/2012/juneweb-only/why-we-should-reexamine-the-faith-of-barack-obama.html.

69. John Chase and Liam Ford, "Senate Debate Gets Personal," *Chicago Tribune*, Oct. 22, 2004 (first and second quotations); Liam Ford and David Mendell, "Jesus Wouldn't Vote for Obama, Keyes Says," *Chicago Tribune*, Sept. 8, 2004 (third quotation); Obama, *Audacity*, 204.

70. "Transcript: Illinois Senate Candidate Barack Obama," http://www.washington-post.com/wp-dyn/articles/A19751-2004Jul27.html; see James Guth, "Religion in the 2008 Election," in Janet Box-Steffensmeier and Steven Schier, eds., *The American Elections of 2008* (Lanham, MD: Rowman and Littlefield, 2009), 117–36; Laura Olson and John Green, "The Religion Gap," *PS: Political Science and Politics* 39 (2006), 455–59.

71. Barack Obama, "'Call to Renewal' Keynote Address," June 28, 2006, http://www.sojo.net/index.cfm?NewsID=5454&action=news.display_article&mode=C. See also Bill Rocha and Jeffrey Morow, "Dancing on the Wall: An Analysis of Barack Obama's Call to Renewal Keynote Address," in David Weiss, ed., *What Democrats Talk About When They Talk About God: Religious Communication in Democratic Party Politics* (Lanham, MD: Lexington Books, 2010), 129–54.

72. E. J. Dionne, Jr., "Obama's Eloquent Faith," http://www.washingtonpost.com/wp-dyn/content/article/2006/06/29/AR2006062901778_pf.html. See also David Espo, "Obama: Democrats Must Court Evangelicals," http://www.washington-post.com/wp-dyn/content/article/2006/06/28/AR2006062800281_pf.html; Amy Sullivan, "In Good Faith: The Real Meaning of Barack Obama's Speech on Religion and Politics," July 3, 2006, http://www.slate.com/id/2144983/; Michelle Goldberg, "What's the Matter with Barack Obama?" June 30, 2006, http://www.huffingtonpost.com/michelle-goldberg/whats-the-matter-with-bar_b_24133.html?view; "God's Will in the Public Square: Democratic Senator Barack Obama Gets It Mostly Right," http://www.christianitytoday.com/ct/2006/september/4.28.html.

73. "Obama Works to Win Evangelicals Back for Democrats," July 14, 2006, http://www.npr.org/templates/story/story.php?storyId=5556961.

74. Obama's "Religious Biography," http://pewforum.org/religion08/candidates/barack-obama/.

75. John Kennedy, "Preach and Reach: Despite His Liberal Record, Barack Obama is Making a Lot of Evangelicals Think Twice," http://www.christianitytoday.com/ct/2008/october/18.26.html (all quotations); Sarah Pulliam, "Election Honeymoon," *CT* 52 (Dec. 2008), 15. On DuBois, see Mansfield, *Obama*, 119–25; Alex Altman, "Joshua DuBois: Obama's Pastor-in-Chief," *Time*, Feb. 6, 2009. See also Peter Boyer, "Can the Democrats Get a Foothold on the Religious Vote?" *New Yorker* 84 (Sept. 8, 2008), 24–31; Eve Conant and Richard Wolffe, "Obama's New Gospel," *Newsweek* 151 (May 12, 2008), 32–33.

76. James Guth, "Obama, Religious Politics, and the Culture Wars," in Steven Schier, ed., *Transforming America: Barack Obama in the White House* (Lanham, MD: Rowman and Littlefield, 2011), 80.

77. Obama, "Politics of Conscience."

78. Quoted in Jonathan Weisman, "Obama Addresses His Faith: Senator Describes Spiritual Journey," July 6, 2008, http://www.washingtonpost.com/wp-dyn/content/article/2008/07/05/AR2008070501854.html.

79. Obama, "Politics of Conscience." See also "The Candidates on Faith," Aug. 7, 2008, http://www.time.com/time/nation/article/0,8599,1830148-2,00.html.

80. Mark Tooley, "Post-Modern Prophet: Meet Donald Miller, the Evangelical Left's Poster-Boy," May 29, 2009, http://www.weeklystandard.com/Content/Public/Articles/000/000/016/557jmfcr.asp?nopager=1; Mark Rodgers and Loredana Vuoto, "Praying Politics: Abortion, the Religious, and the President," http://www.nationalreview.com/articles/226807/praying-politics/loredana-vuoto; Jim Wallis, "Healing the Wounds of Race," http://sojo.net/magazine/2008/05/healing-wounds-race; quotations in that order. See also Jim Wallis, "Obama's Faith-Based Plan," http://sojo.net/blogs/2008/07/01/obamas-faith-based-plan.

81. Kennedy, "Preach and Reach" (all material and quotations not from Obama); Obama, *Audacity*, 222.

82. Thomas, "Long Time Coming," 213.

83. Michael Powell, "Following Months of Criticism, Obama Quits His Church," http://www.nytimes.com/2008/06/01/us/politics/01obama.html?scp=5&sq=obama+church&st=nyt. See also Carl Grant and Shelby Grant, *The Moment: Barack Obama, Jeremiah Wright, and the Firestorm at Trinity United Church of Christ* (Lanham, MD: Rowman and Littlefield, 2013).

84. Obama's "Religious Biography."

85. Erin Gorski, "James Dobson Accuses Obama of 'Distorting' Bible," http://www.huffingtonpost.com/2008/06/24/james-dobson-accuses-obam_n_108851.html; http://www.wnd.com/files/Focusletter.pdf. See also Bob Pool and My-Thuan Tran, "Pastors Test IRS Ban on Politics," *LAT*, Sept. 29, 2008.

86. Gerald Beyer, "Yes You Can: Why Catholics Don't Have to Vote Republican," *Commonweal* 135 (June 20, 2008), 15–18; first quotation from 15, second, third, fourth, and fifth from 16, sixth from 18. For an alternative view, see David Carlin, "Two Cheers for John McCain," *Commonweal* 135 (May 9, 2008), 8–10.

87. 2004 American National Election Studies and the 2008 Henry Institute National Survey on Religion and Public Life as cited by Laura Olson, Adam Warber, and Kevin den Dulk, "Mainline Protestants and the 2008 Election," in Espinoza, ed., *Religion*, 41, 44–45.

88. Mansfield, *Obama*, xviii; Luiza Savage, "The Decline of the Religious Right," *Maclean's* 121 (July 7, 2008), 34–38.

89. Kenneth Wald, "Jews and the 2008 Election," in Espinoza, ed., *Religion*, 108–27; "Obama Meets with Jewish Leaders," *Jewish Daily Forward*, Feb. 28, 2008, http://www.forward.com/articles/12797/; Eric Fingerhut, "Rabbis for Obama Considered a First in American Politics," *Jewish Exponent*, Sept. 18, 2008, http://www.jewishexponent.com/article/17131/.

90. "Joel Hunter Leads Blessing for Obama," Interview by Sarah Pulliam, Jan. 23, 2009, http://www.nationalcathedral.org/pdfs/inaugural090121.pdf.

91. Bailey, "Has Obama Chosen a Church?"

92. Jaweed Kaleem, "President Obama's Faith Inspires Pastors' Defense of White House Religion Policies," http://www.huffingtonpost.com/2012/02/23/president-obama-faith-pastors_n_1297827.html.

93. "White House Releases Final Faith-Based Panel Names," *CC* 126 (May 5, 2009), 18; Amy Sullivan, "The Obamas Find a Church Home—Away from Home," June 30, 2009, http://www.time.com/time/magazine/article/0,9171,1908437-2,00.html; Laurie Goodstein, "Without a Pastor of His Own, Obama Turns to Five," *NYT*, http://www.nytimes.com/2009/03/15/us/politics/15pastor.html?_r=0; "Obama Picks New Round of Faith-Based Advisers," *CC* 128 (Mar. 8, 2011), 13. Obama also received spiritual counsel from Joshua DuBois, Muslim White House lawyer Rashad Hussain, and Baptist Navy chaplain Carey Cash. See Dan Burke, "Obama's 'Spiritual Cabinet' Offers Advice and Prayer," *CC* 127 (Apr. 6, 2010), 13–15.

94. Obama, "Discussion in Albuquerque."

95. Obama, "President's Weekly Address," Mar. 30, 2013. See also Obama, "Proclamation—Religious Freedom Day, 2014," Jan. 15, 2014, http://www.presidency.ucsb.edu/ws/?pid=104624; "The President's Weekly Address," Apr. 19, 2014, http://www.presidency.ucsb.edu/ws/index.php?pid=105124&st=&st1=.

96. Obama, 2009 "National Prayer Breakfast." See also Emily Belz, "Faith-based Function," Feb. 5, 2009, http://www.worldmag.com/webextra/14996.

97. Barack Obama, "The President's Weekly Address," Nov.28, 2013, http://www.presidency.ucsb.edu/ws/?pid=104451 (first and second quotations) (from 2009 to 2013, Obama used this phrase eighteen times); "Press Conference by President Obama," Sept. 10, 2010, http://www.whitehouse.gov/the-press-office/2010/09/10/press-conference-president-obama (third and fourth quotations);Obama, "The President's Weekly Address," Apr. 7, 2012, http://www.presidency.ucsb.edu/ws/?pid=100462 (fifth and sixth quotations); Bailey, "Breakfast Attendees."

98. E.g., Ed Powell, "President Obama Meets with Faith Leaders from Major Black Churches," Aug. 28, 2013, http://praisecleveland.com/1733743/president-barack-obama-meets-with-faith-leaders-from-major-black-churches/.

99. Don DiXon Williams, "Continue Mandela's Legacy," http://tcr-online.blogspot.com/2013/12/the-christian-recorder-online-english_3797.html; "NBCI . . . Demands President Obama to Order Attorney General Holder to File Civil Rights Charges Against George Zimmerman," July 22, 2013, http://www.nalt-blackchurch.com/pdf/uspresident-martinverdict.pdf.

100. Olson, Warber, and den Dulk, "Mainline Protestants," 47, 53.

101. "Mainline Churches Pledge Support for Obama," *CC* 125 (Dec. 2, 2008), 15–16.

102. Javers, "Obama Invokes Jesus."

103. "Obama Team Seeks Support of Progressives on Poverty," *CC* 126 (June 2, 2009), 17.

104. John Dart, "Obama Hears Concerns of NCC Leaders," *CC* 127 (Nov. 30, 2010), 15.

105. Jim Wallis, "President Obama Should Have Fought This One," http://sojo.net/blogs/2010/12/07/president-obama-should-have-fought-one.

106. Wallis, "President Obama"; Chris Herlinger, "Christian Left Foresees a Bolder Obama," *CC* 130 (Mar. 6, 2013), 14.

107. Landsberg, "Obama Praised."

108. Kaleem, "Obama's Faith."

109. Obama, 2012 "National Prayer Breakfast." See also Dan Gilgoff, "A New Role for Religion," *U.S. News & World Report* 146 (June 2009), 45–46; Adele Banks, "Faith-Based Reforms Get Mixed Reviews," *CC* 127 (Dec. 14, 2010), 14; and Guth, "Obama," 86–88.

110. Martin Morse Wooster, "The Hand of God in the Social Safety Net," May 24, 2010, http://www.weeklystandard.com/articles/faith-hope-and-%E2%80%89%E2%80%89%E2%80%89%E2%80%89.

111. Birdsall, "Obama."

112. Sarah Pulliam Bailey, "Obama, Evangelicals Meet on Religious Concerns," *CC* 128 (Nov. 15, 2011), 16; Robert Morrison, "NAE Meets the President—Abortion 'Did Not Come Up,'" http://townhall.com/columnists/robertmorrison/2011/10/27/nae_meets_the_president_%e2%80%93_abortion_did_not_come_up.

113. Melissa Steffan, "Obama Affirms 'Evangelical' Principles for Immigration Reform," http://blog.christianitytoday.com/ctliveblog/archives/2013/03/obama-affirms-evangelical-principles-for-immigration-reform.html. See also Morgan Lee, "Russell Moore, Jim Wallis and Other Christian Leaders Discuss Immigration Reform with President Obama," Nov. 14, 2013, http://sojo.net/press/russell-moore-jim-wallis-and-other-christian-leaders-discuss-immigration-reform-president-obam.

114. Mark Tooley, "A Further Perspective: Inaugural Prayer Controversies," *American Spectator*, Jan. 22, 2013. See also Eric Marrapodi, "Giglio Bows Out of Inauguration over Sermon on Gays," http://religion.blogs.cnn.com/2013/01/10/giglio-bows-out-of-inauguration-over-sermon-on-gays/. Evangelical pastor Andy Stanley did preach the sermon at a service at St. John's the morning of the inaugural. See also Adelle Banks, "Praying for Unity at National Cathedral Inaugural Service," *CC* 130 (Feb. 20, 2013), 15–16.

115. Obama, *Audacity*, 265; Joseph Loconte, "What Would Jesus Insure? The Religious Left Rallies for Obamacare," Sept. 4, 2009, http://www.weeklystandard.com/Content/Public/Articles/000/000/016/904buqdz.asp?nopager=1.

116. Jamie Dean, "Caps and Frowns," http://www.worldmag.com/webextra/15205; Dan Gilgoff, "Outrage Over Obama's Appearance at Notre Dame," http://www.usnews.com/news/blogs/god-and-country/2009/03/23/outrage-over-obamas-appearance-at-notre-dame-who-are-the-political-victims; all quotations from Dean's article except the ones pertaining the CNS petition. See also Joseph Bottum, "And the War Came," *First Things*, June/July 2009, 63–68.

117. "Obama & Notre Dame," *Commonweal* 136 (Apr. 10, 2009), 5.

118. Edward Lee Pitts, "Weakened Protections: The Obama Administration Strikes Elements of Conscience Protections for Pro-life Medical Providers," Feb. 21, 2011, http://www.worldmag.com/webextra/17672.

119. "Obama Ends Stem Cell Research Ban," http://www.cbsnews.com/2100-503767_162-4853385.html; "The Line on Stem Cells," *CC* 126 (May 19, 2009), 7.

120. Molly Fitzgerald, "Obama in Cairo," *Religion in the News*, Fall 2009, 8; Joseph Loconte, "Obama's Cairo Moment," June 2, 2009, http://www.weeklystandard.com/Content/Public/Articles/000/000/016/581picox.asp?nopager=1; "Strong Reactions."

121. Marvin Olasky, "Moment of Decision: Will Liberal Evangelicals Accept HHS Scheme Mandating that Insurance Plans Cover Abortion Drugs?" http://www.worldmag.com/articles/18478.

122. Sarah Pulliam Bailey, "Evangelicals Mounting Concerns over Obama Administration's Contraceptive Mandate," http://www.christianitytoday.com/ct/2012/februaryweb-only/contraceptive-mandate-concerns.html; "U.S. Bishops Vow to Fight HHS Edict," http://www.usccb.org/news/2012/12-012.cfm; Timothy George and Chuck Colson, "First They Came for the Catholics: Obama's Contraceptive Mandate," http://www.christianitytoday.com/ct/2012/februaryweb-only/catholics-contraceptive-mandate.html; Michael Gerson, "Violations of Religious Freedom," http://www.capitalcommentary.org/religious-freedom/violations-religious-freedom.

123. Helene Cooper and Laurie Goodstein, "Rule Shift on Birth Control Is Concession to Obama Allies," http://www.nytimes.com/2012/02/11/health/policy/obama-to-offer-accommodation-on-birth-control-rule-officials-say.html?hp. See also David Gibson, "Reactions Vary on Obama's Contraception Compromise," *CC* 129 (Mar. 7, 2012), 15–16.

124. Terence Jeffrey, "Notre Dame Faculty to Obama: 'This Is a Grave Violation of Religious Freedom and Cannot Stand,'" Feb. 12, 2012, http://cnsnews.com/news/article/notre-dame-faculty-obama-grave-violation-religious-freedom-and-cannot-stand; "Unacceptable," http://www.becketfund.org/wp-content/uploads/2012/02/Unacceptable2-14-7am.pdf; "The Freedom to Choose Birth Control," http://www.nytimes.com/2012/02/11/opinion/the-freedom-to-choose-birth-control.html?hp; "Senate Blocks Blunt's Repeal of Contraception Mandate," http://abcnews.go.com/blogs/politics/2012/03/contraception-mandate-goes-up-for-a-vote/; Gibson, "Reactions Vary on Obama's Contraception Compromise," 15–16.

125. David Gibson, "Stop Dividing 'Worship-Oriented' from 'Service-Oriented,' Nearly 150 Religious Leaders Tell HHS," http://blog.christianitytoday.com/ctliveblog/archives/2012/06/stop_dividing_w.html?utm_; Michael Gerson, "Catholics Won't Go Quietly," http://townhall.com/columnists/michaelgerson/2012/05/21/; Sarah Pulliam Bailey, "Wheaton College Joins Lawsuits

Fighting the Contraception Mandate," http://www.christianitytoday.com/ct/2012/julyweb-only/wheaton-joins-contraception-mandate-laws.html?utm_source=ctweekly-; "Obama Admin Loses 10, Wins 4 Contraception Mandate Lawsuits," http://www.christianpost.com/news/obama-admin-loses-10-wins-4-contraception-mandate-lawsuits-88299/#v1zfxIydlZPxoexO.99.

126. Margaret O'Brien, Steinfels, "A Losing Strategy," *Commonweal* 139 (May 4, 2012), 7.

127. Emily Belz, "Obama's Private Faith," http://online.worldmag.com/2010/02/22/obamas-private-faith/; Blackwell, "Confusing Messages"; George Neumayr, "Disinviting God to the Inauguration," http://spectator.org/archives/2013/01/16/disinviting-god-to-the-inauguration; Phyllis Schlafly, "Atheist Attacks on Christmas" http://townhall.com/columnists/phyllisschlafly/2012/12/11/atheist_attacks_on_christmas.

128. J. Peter Nixon, "Health Scare: Obamacare is Down but Not Out," *Commonweal* 140 (Dec. 20, 2013), 8–9; Jeff Madrick, "The Stakes," *Commonweal* 139 (Aug. 17, 2012), 19–21; "Now for the Hard Part," *Commonweal* 139 (Nov. 23, 2012), 5; "Catholics & Party Politics," *Commonweal* 139 (Sept. 14, 2012), 5.

129. Nathan Pippenger, "Common Ground? Closing the Immigration Divide," *Commonweal* 140 (Mar. 22, 2013), 11 (quotation) (cf. "Immigration Solutions?" *Commonweal* 139 [July 13, 2012], 5); Andrew Bacevich, "The War We Can't Win," *Commonweal* 136 (Aug. 14, 2009), 13–15; "Obama's Vietnam?" *Commonweal* 137 (Aug. 13, 2010), 5.

130. Wald, "Jews," 124. See also Lauren Markoe, "Jewish Voters Back Obama, Say Israel Not Top Issue," *CC* 129 (May 2, 2012), 16.

131. Mary Beth Cauley, "The Faith Factor: Religion's New Prominence in Campaign 2012," http://www.csmonitor.com/USA/Politics/2012/0401/The-faith-factor-Religion-s-new-prominence-in-campaign-2012.

132. See "Texas Governor Rick Perry," http://christiannews.christianet.com/1098362715.htm; Jeremy Peters, "Appealing to Evangelicals, Hopefuls Pack Religion Into Ads," http://www.nytimes.com/2011/12/28/us/politics/republican-hopefuls-pack-religion-into-ads-in-; "Q & A: Ron Paul," http://www.christianitytoday.com/ct/2011/octoberweb-only/ron-paul-church-abortion-narcotics-marriage.html; "Q & A: Michele Bachmann," http://www.christianitytoday.com/ct/2011/aprilweb-only/qamichele-bachmann.html; Ryan Lizza, "Leap of Faith," Aug. 15, 2011, http://www.newyorker.com/reporting/2011/08/15/110815fa_fact_lizza; Erik Eckholm and Jeff Zeleny, "Evangelicals, Seeking Unity, Back Santorum for Nomination," http://www.nytimes.com/2012/01/15/us/politics/conservative-religious-leaders-seeking-unity-vote-to-back-rick-santorum.html?; "Sen. Rick Santorum: I Draw No Line between My Faith and My Decisions," http://www.christianitytoday.com/ct/article_print.html?id=41847; Erik Eckholm, "Santorum Out, Evangelicals Edge Closer to Romney, but Warily,"

http://www.nytimes.com/2012/04/12/us/politics/evangelicals-move-to-support-romney.html?ref=evangelicalmovement; Jodi Kantor, "Romney's Faith, Silent but Deep," http://www.nytimes.com/2012/05/20/us/politics/how-the-mormon-church-shaped-mitt-romney.html?src=me&ref=general.

133. Tooley, "Further Perspective."
134. Nanette Byrnes, "Pulpit Freedom Sunday: Pastors Defy Tax Rules, Back Political Candidates," http://www.huffingtonpost.com/2012/10/08/pulpit-freedom-sunday-pastors-defy-tax-rules-back-political-candidates_n_1948284.html.
135. Peter Manseau, "Is Religious Freedom Really Primary?" http://campaign-stops.blogs.nytimes.com/2012/10/26/is-religious-freedom-really-primary/. As late as July 2012 only 51 percent of Americans knew that Romney was a Mormon and only 45 percent that Obama was a Christian (Tobin Grant, "Poll of Americans: Better a Mormon than a Muslim in White House," http://www.christianitytoday.com/ct/2012/julyweb-only/poll-americans-mormon-muslim-white-house.html?utm_source=ctweekly-).
136. Landsberg, "Obama Praised." See also Kasie Hunt, "Mitt Romney: Obama Administration Has 'Fought Against Religion,'" http://www.huffingtonpost.com/2012/02/21/mitt-romney-obama-administration-religion_n_1292473.html; "Rick Santorum Questions Obama's Christian Values," http://news.yahoo.com/rick-santorum-questions-obamas-christian-values-173855929.html.
137. Santorum's position as summarized by Pat Buchanan, "Is Obama's America God's Country?" http://townhall.com/columnists/patbuchanan/2012/02/21/creators_oped.
138. Matt Barber, "Christians Should Vote For Romney," http://townhall.com/columnists/mattbarber/2012/06/14/christians_should_vote_for_romney.
139. Bailey, "Christmas Tree." See also Tobin Grant, "Tony Perkins: Obama Is Hostile, Disdainful of Christianity," Nov. 14, 2011, http://blog.christianityto-day.com/ctpolitics/2011/11/tony_perkins_ob.html.
140. Jaweed Kaleem, "Religion and Politics Don't Mix, Major Religious Groups Tell Presidential Candidates," http://www.huffingtonpost.com/2012/02/21/religion-politics_n_1291624.html. See also Kaleem, "Obama's Faith."
141. "Better Witness," Feb. 22, 2012, http://betterwitness.wordpress.com/.
142. Melissa Steffan, "'Nastiness' Causes Rick Warren to Cancel Obama-Romney Forum," http://blog.christianitytoday.com/ctliveblog/archives/2012/08/rick-warren-cancels-obama-romney-saddleback-forum-over-nastiness.html?utm_source=ctweekly; David Brooks, "The Final Reckoning," http://www.nytimes.com/2012/11/02/opinion/brooks-the-final-reckoning.html?hp; e.g., Linda Chavez, "Why Mitt Romney Will Win," http://townhall.com/columnists/lindachavez/2012/11/02/why_mitt_romney_will_win/page/2; Douglas MacKinnon, "Obama Must End the Attacks on Mormons," http://townhall.com/columnists/douglasmackinnon/2012/05/14/obama_must_end_the_attacks_on_mormons; Tom Cohen, "Romney, Republicans

Increase Attacks on Obama," http://www.cnn.com/2012/09/14/politics/
campaign-wrap; Michael Scherer, "Interview: Obama on Partisanship
and Getting Things Done in Washington," http://swampland.time.
com/2012/08/30/what-he-knows-now-obama-on-popularity-partisanship-a
nd-getting-things-done-in-washington/.

143. Daniel Burke, "Obama, Romney Quizzed on Religious Perspectives," *CC* 129
(Sept. 19, 2012), 15.

144. Madrick, "The Stakes," 21; "Catholics & Party Politics," 5; Jim Arkedis,
"Reaching Catholics," http://campaignstops.blogs.nytimes.com/2012/05/18/
reaching-catholics/.

145. Ross Douthat, "Obama vs. Catholics, Catholics vs. Obama," http://cam-
paignstops.blogs.nytimes.com/2012/05/22/obama-vs-catholics-catholics-vs-
obama/?hp. See also Laurie Goodstein, "Obama Shift on Providing
Contraception Splits Critics," http://www.nytimes.com/2012/02/15/us/
obama-shift-on-contraception-splits-catholics.html?hp.

146. Michael Gerson, "Obama's Epic Screw-Up," http://townhall.com/columnists/
michaelgerson/2012/02/14/something.

147. Paul Moses, "Here To Stay," *Commonweal* 140 (Sept. 27, 2013), 10.

148. Tobin Grant, "President's Evolution Is Over: Obama Commits to Supporting
Same-Sex Marriage," http://www.christianitytoday.com/ct/2012/mayweb-only/
obama-commits-to-supporting-same-sex-marriage.html?utm_
source=ctweekly-(quotations); David Gibson, "Applying the Golden Rule to Gay
Marriage," *CC* 129 (June 13, 2012), 14–15.

149. Tobin Grant and Sarah Pulliam Bailey, "How Evangelicals Have Shifted
in Public Opinion on Same-Sex Marriage," http://www.christianitytoday.
com/ct/2012/mayweb-only/evangelicals-shift-same-sex-marriage.html (second quotation); Peter Baker and Rachel Swarns, "After Obama's Decision
on Marriage, a Call to Pastors," http://www.nytimes.com/2012/05/14/us/
politics/on-marriage-obama-tried-to-limit-risk.html?_r=1&ref=todayspaper
(first quotation); "Sojourners' Statement on President Obama's
Endorsement of Same-Sex Marriage," http://sojo.net/blogs/2012/05/10/
sojourners-statement-president-obamas-endorsement-same-sex-marriage.

150. Dennis Cauchon, "Black Churches Conflicted on Obama's Gay Marriage
Decision,"http://usatoday30.usatoday.com/news/religion/story/2012-05-
13/black-churches-gay-marriage-obama/54941862/1; "Pastor Says Black
Christians Should 'Withhold Support' from Obama over Same-Sex Marriage,"
http://www.theblaze.com/stories/2012/07/06/pastor-says-black-chri
stians-should-withhold-support-from-obama-over-same-sex-marriage/;
Paul Stanley, "Black Christians in an 'Adulterous' Relationship with
Obama, Says Evangelical Pastor," http://www.christianpost.com/news/
black-christians-in-an-adulterous-relationship-with-obama-says-evangelical-p
astor-75127/; "Black Pastor: Obama Better Get to Black Churches Soon to
Prevent Voter Apathy," http://www.realclearpolitics.com/video/2012/05/10/

black_pastor_obama_better_get_to_black_churches_soon_to_prevent_ voter_apathy.html; Peter Wallsten, "Black Church Leaders Try to Inspire Congregants to Vote for Obama," http://www.washingtonpost.com/politics/ black-church-leaders-try-to-inspire-congregants-to-vote-for-obama/2012/09/03/ 136b2da0-f3f0-11e1-892d-bc92fee603a7_story.html.

151. Wallsten, "Black Church Leaders"; final quotation by Clo Ewing.

152. Otis Moss II and Charles Jenkins, "The Black Church Must Stand Up for President Obama," http://elev8.com/606240/rev-otis-moss-ii-rev-charles-jenkins-standing-up-for-obama/2/Oct 5, 2012.

153. Susan Saulny, "With Less Time for Voting, Black Churches Redouble Their Efforts," http://www.nytimes.com/2012/10/29/us/politics/black-churches-in-florida-urge-congregations-to-vote.html?hp; e.g., Harry Jackson, Jr., "Black and Hispanic Christians Will Put Romney Ahead!," http://townhall. com/columnists/harryrjacksonjr/2012/10/30/black_and_hispanic_chris-tians_will_put_romney_ahead; "How the Faithful Voted: 2012 Preliminary Analysis," http://www.pewforum.org/2012/11/07/how-the-faithful-voted-2 012-preliminary-exit-poll-analysis/.

154. Rachel Zoll, "Democratic Faith See Waning Support for Obama," http://www. newsvine.com/_news/2012/06/03/12032536-democratic-faith-see-waning-support-for-obama.

155. Mark Silk and Daniel Burke, "Obama Campaign Taps Wear, 24, to Lead Religious Outreach," *CC* 129 (June 13, 2012), 17–18; Kevin Liptak, "'God' also Absent from Democrats' Platform," http://politicalticker.blogs.cnn.com/2012/09/04/ god-also-absent-from-democrats-platform/.

156. Daniel Burke and David Gibson, "Campaigns' Faith Outreach Has Centered on Economy," *CC* 129 (Oct. 31, 2012), 17.

157. Goodstein, "Christian Right."

158. Blake, "Gospel."

159. Mike Lux, "What Bible Is Santorum Reading?" http://www.huffingtonpost. com/mobileweb/mike-lux/what-bible-is-santorum-reading_b_1288094.html.

160. Michael Brown, "President Obama, More Religious Apostate than Religious Pioneer," http://townhall.com/columnists/michaelbrown/2012/10/22/presi-dent_obama_more_religious_prostate_than_religious_pioneer. See also Timothy Lee, "New Polls Suggest Assault on Religious Freedom a Political Loser," http://cfif.org/v/index.php/commentary/56-health-care/1350-new-poll s-suggest-assault-on-religious-freedom-a-political-loser.

161. E.g., Michael Youssef, "President Obama and the Bible," http://townhall.com/ columnists/michaelyoussef/2012/02/05/president_obama_and_the_bible; Floyd and Mary Beth Brown, "Marx, Jesus, or Obama, Who Are You Going to Believe?" http://townhall.com/columnists/floydandmarybeth-brown/2012/02/04/marx_jesus_or_obama_who_are_you_going_to_believe; Austin Hill, "Is Jesus on Board with Obama?" http://townhall.com/columnists/ austinhill/2012/02/04/is_jesus_on_board_with_obama.

162. Phyllis Schlafly, "Obama's War on Religious Liberty," http://townhall.com/columnists/phyllisschlafly/2012/02/20/phyllis_schlafly.

163. Molly Worthen, "Leaps of Faith," http://campaignstops.blogs.nytimes.com/2012/03/01/leaps-of-faith/?hp. Also see Jonathan Alter, *The Center Holds: Obama and His Enemies* (New York: Simon and Schuster, 2013), and Mark Halperin and John Heilemann, *Double Down: Game Change 2012* (New York: Penguin Press, 2013).

164. Steve Chapman, "Obama's Defense of Religion," http://townhall.com/columnists/stevechapman/2012/02/23/obamas_defense_of_religion; Judd Birdsall, "Obama's Religious Freedom Record," http://sojo.net/blogs/2014/01/22/obamas-religious-freedom-record; Barack Obama, "Proclamation—Religious Freedom Day, 2014," Jan. 15, 2014, http://www.presidency.ucsb.edu/ws/?pid=104624.

165. Rodgers and Vuoto, "Praying Politics."

166. Goodstein, "Christian Right"; Burke and Gibson, "Campaigns' Faith Outreach," 17.

167. See Jonathan Alter, *The Promise: President Obama, Year One* (New York: Simon and Schuster, 2010).

168. Goodstein, "Christian Right." See also Laurie Goldstein, "The Theological Differences behind Evangelical Unease with Romney," http://www.nytimes.com/2012/01/15/us/politics/evangelical-christians-unease-with-romney-is-theological.html?.

169. "How the Faithful Voted: 2012 Preliminary Analysis," http://www.pewforum.org/Politics-and-Elections/How-the-Faithful-Voted-2012-Preliminary-Exit-Poll-Analysis.aspx.

170. Laurie Goodstein, "Christian Right Failed to Sway Voters on Issues," http://www.nytimes.com/2012/11/10/us/politics/christian-conservatives-failed-to-sway-voters.html?hp.

171. Various email responders to Tobin Grant, "Post-Election Fight over the 'Evangelical' Brand," http://www.christianitytoday.com/ct/2012/november-web-only/post-election-fight-over-evangelical-brand.html?utm_source=booksandculture-.

172. Jim Wallis, "The New Evangelical Agenda," http://sojo.net/blogs/2012/11/15/new-evangelical-agenda.

173. Goodstein, "Christian Right."

174. Moses, "Here To Stay," 12.

175. Dorrien, *Obama Question*, 125; Mark Silk, "Barack Obama, Niebuhrian Progressive," http://www.religionnews.com/blogs/mark-silk/barack-obama-niebuhrian-progressive1; James Kloppenberg, *Reading Obama: Dreams, Hope, and the America Political Tradition* (Princeton, NJ: Princeton University Press, 2011), xi–xii, 63–64, 83 (quotation), 192–93, 221–22 (cf. Wilson, *Improbable Quest*, 124); Kloppenberg, *Reading Obama*, 119–21, 142–43; David Brooks, "Obama, Gospel and Verse," http://www.nytimes.

com/2007/04/26/opinion/26brooks.html?_r=0. See also Robert Westbrook, "The Liberal Agony," *CC* 128 (Sept. 20, 2011), 22–31; Casey Blake, "Obama and Niebuhr," *New Republic*, May 3, 2007, http://www.newrepublic.com/blog/open-university/obama-and-niebuhr; Roger Hodge, *The Mendacity of Hope: Barack Obama and the Betrayal of American Liberalism* (New York: HarperCollins, 2010), 176–95; Liam Julian, "Niebuhr and Obama," *Policy Review*, April–May, 2009, 19–33; Mark Tooley, "Niebuhr and Obama," *American Spectator*, Jan. 20, 2009; "Obama's Favorite Theologian? A Short Course on Reinhold Niebuhr," a conversation between Wilfrey McClay and E. J. Dionne, Jr., http://www.pewforum.org/2009/05/04/obamas-favorite-theologian-a-short-course-on-reinhold-niebuhr/; Joseph Loconte, "Obama Contra Niebuhr," Jan. 14, 2010, http://american.com/archive/2010/january/obama-contra-niebuhr; and John Blake, "How Obama's Favorite Theologian Shaped His First Year in Office," http://www.cnn.com/2010/POLITICS/02/05/Obama.theologian/index.html. Obama's Nobel Prize and Cairo speeches especially display Niebuhrian influences.

176. Holder and Josephson, *Irony*, 3, 7, 129 (quotation), 131.

177. "Negotiating the Presidency," *CC* 127 (Dec. 28, 2010), 7. See also R. Ward Holder, "The Postpartisan Partisan," *CC* 130 (Jan. 9, 2013), 12.

178. Kloppenberg, *Reading Obama*, 41–44; quotation from 41, 101–2, 219–21; Barack Obama, "Remarks at a Democratic Congressional Campaign Committee Dinner in Minneapolis," Oct. 23, 2010, http://www.presidency.ucsb.edu/ws/?pid=88629.

179. Barack Obama, "Remarks at the Town Hall Education Arts Recreation Campus," Dec. 4, 2013, http://www.presidency.ucsb.edu/ws/?pid=104522.

180. Obama, 2010 "National Prayer Breakfast."

181. Obama, 2012 "National Prayer Breakfast." Cf. Obama, 2011 "National Prayer Breakfast"; Obama, 2014, "National Prayer Breakfast." "Our faith," he declared, teaches that we must be Good Samaritans and combat suffering. Isaiah proclaims "Do right. Seek justice. Defend the oppressed." The Koran instructs us to "Stand out firmly for justice."

182. Obama, 2012 "National Prayer Breakfast."

183. Obama, 2011 "National Prayer Breakfast." Cf. "The President's News Conference with Prime Minister Matteo Renzi of Italy in Rome, Italy," Mar. 28, 2014, http://www.presidency.ucsb.edu/ws/index.php?pid=105074&st=&st1=.

184. Barack Obama, "Remarks at the Congressional Black Caucus Foundation," Sept. 24, 2011. http://www.presidency.ucsb.edu/ws/?pid=96802 (quotation); Obama, "The President's News Conference," Feb. 15, 2011, http://www.presidency.ucsb.edu/ws/?pid=88991; Barack Obama, "Inaugural Address," Jan. 21, 2013, http://www.presidency.ucsb.edu/ws/?pid=102827; Obama, "Remarks at 'Christmas in Washington,'" Dec. 15, 2013, http://www.presidency.ucsb.edu/ws/?pid=104520. See also Jim Wallis, "Courage for the

Common Good: Obama's Second Term," http://sojo.net/blogs/2013/01/21/ courage-common-good-obamas-second-term; David Gibson, "Obama Extols a Biblical Vision of Equality for All in Second Inaugural," http://sojo.net/ blogs/2013/01/21/obama-extols-biblical-vision-equality-all-second-inaugural.

185. All four are quoted in Javers, "Obama Invokes Jesus." See also Jonah Goldberg, "Spreading Christianism," June 9, 2009, http://www.nationalreview.com/ corner/182978/spreading-christianism/jonah-goldberg.

186. Barack Obama, "Remarks at a Town Hall Meeting and a Question-and-Answer Session in Green Bay, Wisconsin," June 11, 2009, http://www.presidency.ucsb. edu/ws/?pid=86271; Obama, "Remarks at . . . the White House Forum on Health Reform," Mar. 5, 2009, http://www.presidency.ucsb.edu/ws/?pid=85825; Obama, "Address before a Joint Session of the Congress on Health Care Reform," Sept. 9, 2009, http://www.presidency.ucsb.edu/ws/?pid=86592. See also Tim King, "Jim Wallis Responds to President Obama's Speech on Health Care Reform," *Sojourners*, Sept. 9, 2009, http://sojo.net/press/ jim-wallis-responds-president-obama%E2%80%99s-speech-health-care-reform.

187. Barack Obama, "Remarks at a Democratic National Committee Fundraiser in Austin," May 10, 2011, http://www.presidency.ucsb.edu/ws/?pid=90369; Obama, "Remarks at a Town Hall Meeting and a Question-and-Session in Grand Junction, Colorado," Aug. 15, 2009, http://www.presidency.ucsb.edu/ ws/?pid=86543 (first and second quotations); Barack Obama, "Statement on the 45th Anniversary of the 1965 Voting Rights March," Mar. 7, 2010, http:// www.presidency.ucsb.edu/ws/?pid=87616 (third quotation); Obama, "Remarks at the Families USA Health Action 2011 Conference," Jan. 28, 2011, http:// www.presidency.ucsb.edu/ws/?pid=88948 (fourth and fifth quotation); Obama, "Remarks on the United States Supreme Court Ruling on the Affordable Care Act," June 28, 2012, http://www.presidency.ucsb.edu/ws/?pid=101087 (sixth quotation). See also "In it Together," *CC* 126 (Oct. 6, 2009).

188. Kathleen Gilbert, "Obama: 'We Are God's Partners in Matters of Life and Death,'" http://www.lifesitenews.com/news/archive//ldn/2009/aug/09082014. See also Sarah Pulliam Bailey, "Obama Attempts to Debunk Rumors in Call to Faith Leaders," http://blog.christianitytoday.com/ctpolitics/2009/08/obama_attempts. html.

189. Alicia Cohn, "Obama Admin. Pulls Faith Leaders on Health Care Bill," http:// blog.christianitytoday.com/ctpolitics/2011/01/obama_admin_pul.html.

190. Gilbert, "God's Partners."

191. Arthur Jones, "A Doctor Makes Sense of the Health-Care Debate," http://sojo. net/blogs/2009/09/01/doctor-makes-sense-health-care-debate.

192. Gilbert, "God's Partners."

193. E.g., Rob Moll, "Will Section 1233 Hasten Patient Deaths?" http://blog.christi-anitytoday.com/ctliveblog/archives/2009/08/section_1233_ma.html.

194. Obama, 2012 "National Prayer Breakfast."

195. "Remarks by the President to the Clinton Global Initiative," http://www.whitehouse. gov/the-press-office/2012/09/25/remarks-president-clinton-global-initiative.

196. Barack Obama, "Remarks on the 'My Brother's Keeper' Initiative," Feb. 27, 2014, http://www.presidency.ucsb.edu/ws/index.php?pid=104799&st=initiati ve&st1=. See also Obama, "Remarks at an Easter Prayer Breakfast," Apr. 14, 2014, http://www.presidency.ucsb.edu/ws/index.php?pid=105112&st=&st1=; Obama, "Remarks Following a Meeting With the My Brother's Keeper Task Force," May 30, 2014, http://www.presidency.ucsb.edu/ws/index.php?pid=105 224&st=brother%5C%27s+keeper&st1=; Obama, "Remarks at a 'My Brother's Keeper' Initiative Town Hall Meeting," http://www.presidency.ucsb.edu/ws/ index.php?pid=105465&st=brother%5C%27s+keeper&st1=.

197. Miller, "Faith."

198. Stephen Mansfield, *The Faith of Barack Obama* (Nashville, TN: Thomas Nelson, 2008), 143 (first and second quotations), xxi (third and fourth quotations). All other references in this chapter are to Mansfield's updated 2011 version of this book.

199. Stephen Mansfield, "Obama's Faith Fits Our Times," http://usatoday30.usa-today.com/printedition/news/20090601/column01_st.art.htm. See also Scott Lamb, "Stephen Mansfield: Obama's Big-Tent Religion," http://online.world-mag.com/tag/pluralism/.

200. Mansfield, *Obama*, 157; Douthat, "Divided by God."

201. Barber, "Obama's Anti-Religious Implosion"; Corsi interview with Mansfield, *Obama*, 136.

202. George Neumayr, "Obama's Pulpit Politics," http://www.realclearreligion.org/ articles/2012/07/20/obamas_pulpit_politics_106532.html; Kate Hicks, "Got Religion? Obama Justifies Policies by Misapplying Christianity," http://town-hall.com/tipsheet/katehicks/2012/02/02/got_religion_obama_justifies_poli-cies_using_jesus; quotations in that order.

203. See David Neff, "The Ironies of Obama's National Prayer Breakfast Speech," http://www.christianitytoday.com/ct/2012/februaryweb-only/prayer-breakfast-irony.html; Barack Obama, "Remarks on Transportation Infrastructure Improvement and Job Growth Legislation," Nov. 2, 2011, http:// www.presidency.ucsb.edu/ws/?pid=96987; Hicks, "Got Religion?"

204. Kyle Drennen, "Newsweek's Evan Thomas: Obama Is 'Sort of God,'" http:// newsbusters.org/blogs/kyle-drennen/2009/06/05/newsweek-s-evan-thomas-o bama-sort-god; Michael Gerson, "Obama vs. the Deniers," http://www.wash-ingtonpost.com/wp-dyn/content/article/2009/06/09/AR2009060902594.html; Jonah Goldberg, "Closing Time," Aug. 25, 2009, http://www.nationalreview. com/liberal-fascism. See also "Obama Melds Social Gospel, Personal Salvation Theology," July 7, 2008, http://blog.beliefnet.com/godometer/2008/07/ obama-melds-social-gospel-pers.html.

205. Matthew Avery Sutton, "Why the Antichrist Matters in Politics," *NYT*, Sept. 27, 2011, http://www.nytimes.com/2011/09/26/opinion/ why-the-antichrist-matters-in-politics.html; Francis Martel, "Lawrence O'Donnell Investigates: 'Is Barack Obama the Anti-Christ?'" http://www.mediaite.com/tv/lawrence-odonnell-investigates-is-barack-obama-the-anti-christ/ (cf. Brent Bozell, "The Year of 'Our Savior' Obama," http://townhall.com/ columnists/brentbozell/2012/12/19/the-year-of-our-savior-obama-n1469888); Mark Edward Taylor, *Branding Obamamessiah: The Rise of an American Idol* (Grand Rapids, MI: Edenridge Press, 2011), 333.

206. Marvin Olasky, "Worthy Challenge: With *Radical-in-Chief*, Stanley Kurtz Shows the Right Way to Criticize President Obama," Jan. 15, 2011, http:// www.worldmag.com/articles/17463; Joseph Loconte, "Obama's Prayer Warriors: Can Religious Leaders Faithfully Serve the President and God at the Same Time?" Mar. 18, 2009, http://www.weeklystandard.com/Content/Public/ Articles/000/000/016/290farmg.asp?nopager=1; Dorrien, *Obama Question*, 9 (quotation), 10. See also Robert Westbrook, "The Liberal Agony," *CC* 128 (Sept. 20, 2011), 22–31; Chris Herlinger, "Christian Left Foresees a Bolder Obama," *CC* 130 (Mar. 6, 2013), 14–15.

207. Dorrien, *Obama Question*, 13 (first two quotations), 14 (third, fourth, and fifth quotations), 3 (sixth quotation); David Brooks, "Where Obama Shines," http://www.nytimes.com/2012/07/20/opinion/brooks-where-obama-shines. html?_r=1&src=me&ref=general.

208. Holder and Josephson, *Irony*, 12; R. Ward Holder and Peter Josephson, "Obama's Niebuhr Problem," *Church History* 82 (Sept. 2013), 686, 683, 679, 687.

209. John Harris and James Hohmann, "Accomplishments and Miscalculations in the Obama Presidency," in Schier, ed., *Transforming America*, 106.

210. Obama, "Call to Renewal."

211. Falsani, "Deep Faith."

CONCLUSION

1. William Inboden, *Religion and American Foreign Policy, 1945–1960: The Soul of Containment* (Cambridge: Cambridge University Press, 2008), 116.

2. Most of these men were academicians before entering politics. It is debatable how systematic Bryan's and Hatfield's political philosophy was. See Michael Kazin, *A Godly Hero: The Life of William Jennings Bryan* (New York: Random House, 2007); Mark Hatfield, *Between a Rock and a Hard Place* (Waco, TX: Word Books, 1976); John Anderson, *Vision and Betrayal in America* (Waco, TX: Word, 1975); Paul Henry, *Politics for Evangelicals* (Valley Forge, PA: Judson Press, 1974); Douglas Koopman, ed., *Serving the Claims of Justice: The Thoughts of Paul B. Henry* (Grand Rapids, MI: Paul B. Henry Institute, 2001). See also Charles

Colson, *God and Government: An Insider's View on the Boundaries between Faith & Politics* (Grand Rapids, MI: Zondervan, 2007).

3. See David Bebbington, *William Ewart Gladstone: Faith and Politics in Victorian Britain* (Grand Rapids, MI: Eerdmans, 1993); James Bratt, *Abraham Kuyper: Modern Calvinist, Christian Democrat* (Grand Rapids, MI: Eerdmans, 2013). Although Kuyper did not become prime minister until 1901, he actively participated in Dutch politics during the previous twenty-five years. Moreover, he gave his *Lectures on Calvinism* at Princeton Theological Seminary in 1898 in which he laid out a holistic biblical vision for politics.

4. On Niebuhr, see Harry Davis and Robert Good, *Reinhold Niebuhr on Politics* (New York: Scribner, 1960); D. B. Robertson, ed., *Love and Justice: Selections from the Shorter Writings of Reinhold Niebuhr* (Louisville, KY: Westminster/John Knox Press, 1992); and Richard Crouter, *Reinhold Niebuhr on Politics, Religion, and Christian Faith* (New York: Oxford University Press, 2010).

5. For Reformed analyses, see Paul Marshall, *Thine is the Kingdom: A Biblical Perspective on the Nature of Government and Politics Today* (Grand Rapids, MI: Eerdmans, 1986); Marshall, *God and the Constitution: Christianity and American Politics* (Lanham, MD: Rowman and Littlefield, 2002); James Skillen, *The Scattered Voice: Christians at Odds in the Public Square* (Grand Rapids, MI: Zondervan, 1990); and Skillen, *In Pursuit of Justice: Christian-Democratic Explorations* (Lanham, MD: Rowman and Littlefield, 2004). For evangelical appraisals, see Doug Bandow, *Beyond Good Intentions: A Biblical View of Politics* (Westchester, IL: Crossway Books, 1988); Stephen Charles Mott, *A Christian Perspective on Political Thought* (New York: Oxford University Press, 1993); J. Budziszewski, *Evangelicals in the Public Square: Four Formative Voices on Political Thought and Action* (Grand Rapids, MI: Baker Academic, 2006); Jim Wallis, *God's Politics: Why the Right Gets It Wrong and the Left Doesn't Get It* (San Francisco: HarperSanFrancisco, 2005); Wallis, *On God's Side: What Religion Forgets and Politics Hasn't Learned about Serving the Common Good* (Grand Rapids, MI: Brazos Press, 2013); P. C. Kemeny, ed., *Church, State, and Public Justice: Five Views* (Downers Grove, IL: IVP Academic, 2007); David Gushee, *The Future of Faith in American Politics: The Public Witness of the Evangelical Center* (Waco, TX: Baylor University Press, 2008); Stephen Monsma, *Healing for a Broken World: Christian Perspectives on Public Policy* (Wheaton, IL: Crossway, 2008); Michael Gerson and Peter Wehner, *City of Man: Religion and Politics in a New Era* (Chicago: Moody, 2010); Miroslav Volf, *A Public Faith: How Followers of Christ Should Serve the Public Good* (Grand Rapids, MI; Brazos, 2011); Ronald Sider, *Just Politics: A Guide for Christian Engagement* (Grand Rapids, MI: Brazos Press, 2012); and David Ryden, ed., *Is the Good Book Good Enough?: Evangelical Perspectives on Public Policy* (Lanham, MD: Rowman and Littlefield, 2011). For Catholic assessments, see Clarke Cochran and David Carroll Cochran,

Catholics, Politics, and Public Policy: Beyond Left and Right (Maryknoll, NY: Orbis Books, 2003) and numerous papal encyclicals on social issues issued since the 1890s. For an Anabaptist perspective, see John Howard Yoder, *The Politics of Jesus* (Grand Rapids, MI: Eerdmans, 1972).

6. http://www.pewforum.org/2012/07/26/section-2-religion-and-politics/.

7. See Ian Scott's review of my *Faith and the Presidency* in the *Journal of American Studies* 41 (2007), 699.

Index

baptism of, 51

and becoming a minister, 50

broad-ranging religious interests
of, 58–59

and Catholics, 63, 66, 70

character of, 50, 54, 85

church attendance of, 64

and Congress's appointment of
chaplains, 74, 76

and the Continental Congress,
49, 74, 75

correspondence of, 52, 54, 57, 58–59,
61, 64–65

on the creation of the universe, 59

criticism of Calvinism by, 57

criticisms of, 82, 85

death of, 86

debate over the religious views of,
51–58, 448n43

defense of federalism by, 50

as a Deist, 53, 56, 57, 58

education of at Princeton, 51, 66,
72, 445n18

as an Episcopalian, 51

evaluation of as president, 50, 456n239

as an evangelical, 53

faith of, 58–66, 86, 447n39, 447n42

on God's providence, 49, 60–61, 78

on the government's promotion of
the common good, 73

gratitude to God of, 61, 84

impact of the faith of on policies of,
70, 71, 78, 86

on the importance of religion to
promoting morality, 64, 65, 66

on the impossibility of creating an
earthly utopia, 62

influence of on the
Constitution, 49, 50

influence of the Enlightenment on,
57, 58, 73

and Jews, 66, 70

knowledge of theology and
philosophy of, 50, 58, 420

leading of devotions by, 52

and the limits of government, 109

little interest of in creeds and
dogma, 51

and mail delivery on Sunday, 74

marriage of, 52

as a member of the House of
Representatives, 69–70

and national days of prayer and
fasting, 74–75, 81–82

and the need for checks and balances
in government, 54, 62, 72–73

on the negative effects of established
churches, 67, 68–69

and never joining a church, 51

opposition of to the Alien and
Sedition Acts, 70

opposition of to granting
charters of incorporation to
churches, 76–77

opposition of to a national
university, 110

as an orthodox Christian, 53

participation of in the Virginia
Constitutional Convention, 50

personality of, 50, 85

as a philosopher king, 50

political philosophy of, 53, 54, 71–73

promotion of the First Amendment
by, 69–70, 77

relationship of with religious
groups, 65–66

on religious liberty, 9, 49–50, 54, 55,
59, 65, 66–71, 74, 84–85, 86

and all religious systems as
essentially equal, 59

reluctance of to discuss religious
convictions, 50–51, 53, 54–55, 65, 86